ANTIQUARIAN BOOKS

Biblia Latina, Mainz, J. Gutenberg, c.1454–55.
Copy on paper. Leaf with Erfurt style decoration. [Eton College Library]

Antiquarian Books
A Companion
for Booksellers, Librarians and Collectors

Compiled and edited by
Philippa Bernard with
Leo Bernard and Angus O'Neill

University of Pennsylvania Press
Philadelphia

© Philippa Bernard, Leo Bernard and Angus O'Neill, 1994

All rights reserved.

First published 1994 by Scolar Press.

First published in the United States 1994 by the University of Pennsylvania Press.

U.S. Library of Congress Cataloging-in-Publication Data

Bernard, Philippa, 1932–
    Antiquarian books: a companion for booksellers, librarians and collectors / compiled and edited by Philippa Bernard with Leo Bernard and Angus O'Neill.
      p.   cm.
    Includes bibliographical references and index.
    ISBN 0–8122–3268–2
    1. Antiquarian booksellers—Great Britain.   I. Bernard, Leo, 1925– . II. O'Neill, Angus, 1960– . III. Title.
Z326.B47   1994
381′.45002′0941—dc20   94-2436
                         CIP

Typeset in 11 point Bembo by Photoprint, Torquay, Devon and printed in Great Britain at the University Press, Cambridge.

CONTENTS

Preface	vii
Acknowledgements	viii
Specialist contributors	ix
Some notes for the reader	xiii
Abbreviations	xiv
Bookselling in a changing world Anthony Rota	1
Antiquarian Books	7
Author Bibliographies	413
Appendix I: Latin and other foreign place-names	440
Appendix II: Roman numerals	443
Appendix III: The spread of printing	444
Appendix IV: Book trade directories	447
Index	448

PREFACE

This Companion sets out to provide, in a single volume, much of the essential information required by those who sell antiquarian and secondhand books, and by those who buy them. It cannot claim to deal exhaustively with all the questions that arise in the course of these pursuits; such a project would call for a massive encyclopaedia rather than a useful Companion. However, many questions can be succinctly answered and many terms can be cogently defined. Where deeper study is needed the aim has been to provide all the necessary guidelines, and much care has been taken to refer the reader only to reference works of established reliability.

A number of major articles have been contributed by booksellers and other specialists with a formidable range of experience in the world of books. The editors are pleased that this weight of knowledge and expertise has not squeezed out the individuality (nor even eccentricity) which characterize the antiquarian book trade.

These extended studies are augmented by over 400 shorter entries summarizing essential information about the printing, illustration and binding of books, and explaining many of the terms used to describe them. Many bookselling and bibliographical terms are defined inadequately, if at all, in even the best dictionaries; and although there are other guides in this field (notably John Carter's admirable *ABC for Book Collectors*), changing trends and usages often call for new appraisal.

One of the main aims of the Companion is to help its readers to save time and trouble. Experience shows that apparently elusive facts may lurk in some surprising places; and often the most complicated questions have the simplest answers. There are a great many cookery books in existence, but few will tell you that the best way to chop onions without tears is to chew some bread. This Companion does not guarantee to take all the tears out of the reader's life, but it may help to prevent a few.

Dealers in antiquarian books are a varied community, in which the great metropolitan firms, the country bookshops, the book-fair exhibitors and the catalogue specialists all play their part; and their customers are no less diverse. This work has been compiled with particular attention to the needs of those who do not have ready access to all the necessary reference sources; but the editors would like to think that it will prove useful to a much wider readership. Their special hope is that it will play some part in maintaining the high standard of accuracy to which the antiquarian book trade aspires, and on which its customers depend.

P. B., L.B., A.O'N.
Chelsea, 1993

ACKNOWLEDGEMENTS

The Editors wish to express their thanks to all the friends and colleagues who have helped them in the compilation of this book.

Our principal debt is, of course, to the contributors of the Introduction and the specialist articles, whose knowledge and experience have added immeasurably to the authority of the Companion. We are no less grateful to Clifford Currie, formerly Librarian of William and Mary College, Williamsburg; Hans Fellner, consultant, Printed Books and Manuscripts, Christie's, London; and Professor J. E. Spence, Director of Studies, the Royal Institute of International Affairs. These three scholars each undertook the formidable task of reading through the entire typescript, and their comments and suggestions were of great value. We hasten to add that we alone are responsible for any errors and omissions which may be found in the editorial entries, and that the specialist contributors are responsible only for the articles which appear under their names.

We have benefited at every stage from the facilities of the British Library, the London Library and the Amsterdam University Library, and we greatly appreciate the help of their staff.

Finally, we owe very special thanks to Sue McNaughton and Ellen Keeling of Scolar Press, whose encouragement has been invaluable from first to last; to Giles Mandelbrote, whose wide-ranging contribution has greatly enhanced our work; and to Rachel Spence, whose practical help has been crucial to the whole project.

SPECIALIST CONTRIBUTORS

John Byrne – Private press books
John Byrne has dealt in private press books for Bertram Rota since 1967. He reviews occasionally for *The Book Collector, Crafts* and *The Times Literary Supplement*.

David Chambers – Book collecting
David Chambers was born in 1930. He was a non-marine underwriter at Lloyd's, but is now retired. He is the Hon. Publications Secretary and Chairman of the Council of the Private Libraries Association. He is a private printer and book collector.

Janet Clarke – Cookery books
Janet Clarke is an antiquarian bookseller, specializing in books and ephemera on gastronomy. An excellent cook herself, she enjoys entertaining family and friends at her home in Bath.

Robin de Beaumont – Victorian books
Robin de Beaumont qualified as an architect in 1953 following studies at Cambridge and with the Architectural Association. Always a book collector, he set up an antiquarian book department for stamp dealers Stanley Gibbons in 1978. Since 1982 he has been an independent bookseller, working from his home in Chelsea.

Sophie Dupré – Autographs and manuscripts
Sophie Dupré, an expert in autograph letters and manuscripts for over 16 years, has become well known internationally as a specialist in material relating to royalty. She lives with her family in Wiltshire and issues regular catalogues.

Clive Farahar – Travel books
Clive Farahar, an antiquarian bookseller of 23 years' experience, lives in Wiltshire with his family, and specializes in books and manuscripts on voyages and travels. He has appeared regularly on the BBC Antiques Roadshow and has written many articles on book collecting.

ANTIQUARIAN BOOKS

James Fergusson – Catalogues
James Fergusson was a full-time book dealer for nine years before, in 1986, becoming Obituaries Editor of *The Independent*. His monthly column reviewing book catalogues has appeared in *Antiquarian Book Monthly Review* since 1980.

Keith Fletcher – Incunabula
Keith Fletcher is a third-generation antiquarian bookseller. After an informal apprenticeship with Jack Joseph in Charing Cross Road and Fritz Neidhardt in Stuttgart, and a year at Yale, he joined his father in the family business of H. M. Fletcher. He is a past president of the ABA and currently Hon. Librarian of the Worshipful Company of Stationers.

Mirjam Foot – Fine bookbinding
Mirjam Foot is Director of Collections and Preservation at the British Library. She has published five books and numerous articles on the history of bookbinding, including *Studies in the History of Bookbinding*, Scolar Press, 1993.

Tony Gilbert – Military and naval books
Tony Gilbert is a specialist in books on military and naval history. Before establishing his own business six years ago he spent 14 years with two leading bookshops, Francis Edwards and Sotheran's.

Robin Greer – Illustrated books
After leaving Oxford, Robin Greer worked with the Civil Rights movement in Mississippi and wrote Concrete poetry; but he 'wandered into the book trade' in 1966 and is a prominent dealer in children's and illustrated books and related pictures.

Amanda Hall – English literature from 1500 to 1700
Amanda Hall was born in Hertfordshire in 1967 and educated at St Mary's Ascot and Trinity Hall, Cambridge. She currently deals in English literature for Pickering and Chatto.

Martin Hamlyn – English literature of the eighteenth century
Martin Hamlyn, a former president of the ABA, is the owner of Peter Murray Hill Rare Books, specializing in the English eighteenth century, and an occasional chronicler of book trade events and people.

Andrew Hunter – Science and medicine
Andrew Hunter, who entered the antiquarian bookselling trade in 1976, is a director of Bernard Quaritch Ltd, and head of the firm's science department.

John Kerr – Book auctions
Lord John Kerr gained some ten years' bookselling experience with E. P. Goldschmidt

SPECIALIST CONTRIBUTORS

and Co. and with Sanders of Oxford before joining Sotheby's in 1963. Since 1982 he has been chairman of Bloomsbury Book Auctions.

Brian Lake – English literature of the nineteenth century
Brian Lake is a partner in Jarndyce Antiquarian Booksellers, publishers of a wide range of author and thematic catalogues, but best known for nineteenth-century English literature and for all things Dickensian.

Melanie McGrath – Booksellers as publishers
Melanie McGrath is a freelance writer, researcher and publishing consultant.

Elizabeth Merry – Colour plate books
Trained at Bernard Quaritch, Elizabeth Merry then joined Christie's Book Department. Ten years of freelance work included assignments for Christie's in Amsterdam, for Sims, Reed and others. She now runs the Book Department at Phillips.

David Miles – Children's books
David Miles has specialized in children's books since 1972, when he issued his first catalogue. He exhibits regularly at book fairs in the UK and in America, and runs his own bookshop in Canterbury.

Peter Miller – Art and architecture
Peter Miller has been a full-time bookseller since 1968 at Spelman's Bookshop in York and specializes in books on art and architecture.

Brian North Lee – Bookplates and book labels
Brian North Lee, who was a schoolmaster, is president of The Bookplate Society and has written numerous articles and books on ex-libris, including *British Royal Bookplates*, Scolar Press, 1992. He is editor of *The Bookplate Journal*.

Charles Ross – Computers for booksellers
Charles Ross is an Honorary Fellow of the British Computer Society. He designed the CLUE programming language used by many antiquarian booksellers and by all Regional Crime Squads.

Anthony Rota – Bookselling in a changing world
Anthony Rota is managing director of Bertram Rota Ltd. He is a past president of the ABA, and immediate past president of ILAB.

Rob Shepherd – Restoration and repair
Rob Shepherd became interested in bookbinding and restoration while studying for a fine art degree in the early 1970s, and after graduating he took up bookbinding. A period as a self-employed binder led to the establishment of Shepherd's Bookbinders in 1988, where he headed a highly qualified team of book and paper conservation specialists.

ANTIQUARIAN BOOKS

Gillian Stone – Natural history books
Gillian Stone was born in Mauritius and educated in Jerusalem and Edinburgh. She runs Titles, the Oxford bookshop, with her husband, and has been involved in recent years in the building up of an important natural history collection.

Karen Thomson – Dictionaries
Karen Thomson worked for a number of antiquarian booksellers before establishing her own business. She has been dealing in books on language since 1987.

H.R. Woudhuysen – Bibliography
H. R. Woudhuysen is a lecturer in English at University College, London; he has written regularly about sales of books and manuscripts for *The Times Literary Supplement* since 1985.

SOME NOTES FOR THE READER

The arrangement of the Companion is largely self-explanatory, but two points should be noted: cross-references are indicated by means of SMALL CAPS in the unsigned entries, and all bibliographical sources are published in London unless otherwise stated.

Variations in publishers' schedules may mean that books are published slightly later, or earlier, than intended. Accordingly, a discrepancy of a single year between a date in a library catalogue and that printed in the book itself does not necessarily indicate the existence of a different title or edition.

ABBREVIATIONS

ABA	Antiquarian Booksellers' Association
ABAA	Antiquarian Booksellers' Association of America
a.e.g.	all edges gilt
a.f.	as found
BAR	Book Auction Records
DNB	Dictionary of National Biography
ESTC	Eighteenth-Century Short-Title Catalogue
f.e.p.	front endpaper
GKW	Gesamtkatalog der Wiegendrucke
ILAB	International League of Antiquarian Booksellers
NCBEL	New Cambridge Bibliography of English Literature
n.d.	no date
PBFA	Provincial Booksellers' Fairs Association
PMM	Printing and the Mind of Man
STC	Short-Title Catalogue
t.e.g.	top edge gilt
t.l.s.	typed letter, signed
w.a.f.	with all faults

BOOKSELLING IN A CHANGING WORLD

Anthony Rota

The popular conception of antiquarian bookselling is probably of a trade which has continued unchanged for generation after generation; but the truth is a very different matter. Indeed, in my time in the trade (I entered it in 1952), I have seen dramatic changes in the pattern of supply and demand and in the way in which dealers attempt to match the two. The changes in demand reflect both the kinds of books that are sought after and the nature and geographical location of those who seek them. The changes in supply tend, alas, to represent an accelerating drying-up of sources and lead inevitably to higher prices.

In London bookshops in the 1950s we used regularly to see many American visitors during the summer season, say from early June to late August, but by September they had all gone home. Gradually the season grew longer – until it extended from January right through to December. Now the visitors no longer come from North America alone; every week brings welcome visits from dealers in Europe, and periodically from colleagues in Japan and similarly Australasia. I myself probably visit as many bookshops in the United States and Europe in the course of any 12 months, as I do bookshops in my own country. This interchange and the awareness it brings of the books that are in demand, the books that can be supplied, and the prices at which demand and supply meet, make for something very close to the economist's dream of a perfect market.

That we live in a time of highly volatile exchange rates is beyond dispute. What may not be remembered is that this was not always the case. Changes in the relationship between the pound and the dollar, between the Deutschmark and the yen, did take place, of course, but they tended to be more gradual. Certainly the strength of the dollar throughout the 1950s and 1960s meant that the trade across the Atlantic was almost entirely from east to west, from Europe to the United States. By the 1980s things changed a little, and dealers from Great Britain and continental Europe were able to buy regularly and profitably in North America. Indeed, one highly successful bookseller in Washington DC has told me that sales to visiting British booksellers now form an important part of his turnover.

In the 1980s we also saw an increase in the flow of Western books from Europe and America into Japan, influenced no doubt by the relative strength of the yen against the dollar and the European currencies, particularly the pound. We must ask whether this will continue as the Japanese economy runs into squalls. Moreover, as Lord Rees-Mogg has succinctly put it, there is a limit to the number of Japanese libraries which need a first edition of *The Wealth of Nations*.

In addition to these stately flows of material following the long-term strengths of various currencies and economies, I have been amused to note smaller eddies and flurries. For example, if the pound fell five cents against the dollar, my firm could count on an early visit from a certain California bookseller. If the Swiss franc strengthened by ten per cent, a dealer from Geneva would arrive in London the next day. I little thought when I became a bookseller that I should have to pay such close attention to the financial pages of the newspapers!

Just as there have been changes in the geographical pattern of demand over the last several decades, so there have been switches in emphasis in the importance of particular categories of book buyer. The 1950s saw the beginnings of an upsurge in buying by university libraries, particularly in North America. This was partly as a result of what was known as 'the learning explosion', when every 18-year-old seemed determined to exercise what he saw as his right to a university education. In consequence, small universities became large ones. What had been teachers' training colleges became fully fledged universities. In both instances the institutions sought to demonstrate their new stature by building a library of rare books. This was a period of almost indiscriminate expansion and it came to its peak in the mid-1960s. By then the buying power of American universities was the despair of many private collectors, who felt they were being priced out of the market.

After that apogee, various factors began to combine to reverse the swing of the pendulum. First there was the demographic shift. The number of children reaching university age started to dwindle. This brought about a decrease in the capitation fees paid to universities from central government. Then there was the spirit of anti-élitism that was abroad in the land. Suddenly, spending tax dollars on rare books and manuscripts seemed a less worthy thing to do. Furthermore there was disenchantment after the unrest on many United States campuses. At the same time inflation added to universities' budget problems; rare books had always been regarded as the icing on the cake, and when there was not enough money to buy all the cake that was wanted, the icing had to go.

Happily, demand from the private sector has taken up much of the slack, and books that would once have been sold to institutional libraries are bought instead for private collections. For the bookseller this is a mixed blessing. We have largely lost our wholesale buyers, who might order 50 or 100 items from a catalogue, or buy author and subject collections *en bloc*, and have exchanged them for exacting private buyers, purchasing on a volume by volume basis. We therefore have to work much harder to produce the same results. On the other hand there is a hidden bonus; when a book is sold to a university library it has, save in the rarest circumstances, vanished from the market for all time. What a dealer sells to a private collector he has a reasonable hope of buying back again, either from the collector when he changes his interests, or possibly from the collector's heirs in the fullness of time.

The switch back to the predominance of the private collector has had the effect of polarizing the market in the first editions of modern English literature in which I happen to specialize. Where university libraries tended to build their holdings across a wide range of authors, private collectors nowadays seem to concentrate on a much narrower band, often following fashion to a degree which causes many worthy authors to be totally neglected. Similarly, while a library might be content with any copy of the original text that was in sound condition, today's collectors are far more inclined than their predecessors to insist on pristine state. Dust-wrappers, for long seen only as an adjunct of the book, are now regarded as *de rigueur*. It is good that their importance and significance should at least be recognized but there is now a huge dichotomy between, say, an early book by Seamus Heaney in a dust-wrapper which has not been price-clipped, and a merely sound copy of Arnold Bennett's *The Card*.

Over the last few decades both private collectors and librarians have been showing more interest in books which are landmarks in science and philosophy. The same is true of works which mark steps forward in the history of book production. Moreover, those who form author collections are more adventurous than were their fathers and grandfathers. Where their predecessors were content to collect only the first printing of each book by the authors in whom they were interested, the present generation builds in greater depth. In the case of English authors, for example, they seek not just the first edition published in England but the first American edition as well. They are anxious to have significant new editions too, and sometimes also translations into foreign languages. In short, their wholly admirable aim is to build collections which chart the entire publishing history of their chosen authors. This is a trend which we can only applaud.

Although book fairs have been with us since the Middle Ages, in their modern form they have a fairly short history. Their recent development can be said to have begun in London just 35 years ago. Now major fairs are held regularly, some of them with sales comfortably in excess of two and a half million pounds. Smaller fairs proliferate. I do not think there is a weekend when there is not at least one fair somewhere in Great Britain, for example; they take place in America with equal frequency. Whether fairs are a 'good thing' or a 'bad thing' is a subject in itself. I do not propose to discuss it at length now, but would merely point out that the small fairs (as opposed to the large and carefully regulated fairs sponsored by the International League of Antiquarian Booksellers and its member associations) give those seeking to enter the antiquarian book trade an effective and inexpensive way of doing so. What I regret is that these newcomers, welcome though they may be, do not necessarily serve an apprenticeship in an established firm and thus acquire the training and experience which I believe to be necessary if they are to serve the public in the best traditions of the trade.

Despite the phenomenon of the book fair, the bookseller's catalogue remains an important way – some would say the most important way – of selling books. It is true that there are booksellers who never issue catalogues at all, but these are a definite and small minority. I have made no statistical analysis of the number of catalogues that arrive on my desk every week, but I have a very clear impression that the quantity has grown markedly in recent years, and is still growing. Again I have undertaken no research to prove the point, but I am sure that the standard of scholarship in these catalogues has also risen and is continuing to rise. The new generation of dealers seems to make good use of the flood of bibliographies published in recent times. Indeed, if anything they make too much use of them, giving bibliographical citations for commonplace and straightforward books which present no bibliographical problems either to buyer or to seller.

It has always been said that booksellers' catalogues make good reading, whether or not one has any serious intention of buying the books that they list. That is particularly true where a specialist has gathered together an impressive assemblage of books in one particular field and presents them with scholarly footnotes which advance our knowledge in that area. I could give many examples but I will choose only one, the fine series of catalogues devoted to books about architecture, issued by Ben Weinreb. These are models of what such things ought to be.

There is a difference between catalogue footnotes which are genuinely informative and those which merely make gratuitous value-judgements. The former may perhaps cast new light on even the most familiar of books and can add to our knowledge. The latter simply give half-baked, home-spun philosophical reflections on books which need no help of this sort to sell them. I have in mind one dealer who catalogued *The Bible* with the footnote that 'although no believer' himself, he thought it 'a great work of literature'!

I am quite sure that typographical standards in catalogue production are improving dramatically. A number of dealers have employed the best professional typographers to design house styles for them. Others use computers, and the desk-top publishing programs that accompany them, to produce clear text at a reasonable price. The days of barely legible lists, run off in basements on aged and badly serviced duplicating machines, are surely past us now.

Although desk-top publishing programs help to keep costs down, printing is not cheap and postage costs are also a considerable factor in the economics of bookselling. These two considerations are bringing changes in the pattern of catalogue distribution. In earlier days, while booksellers eagerly sought new names to put *on to* their mailing list, they hardly ever gave attention to taking names *off* it. Private collectors might well remain on a list for life, even if they made scarcely a single purchase; institutional libraries were never removed from mailing lists at all. How all that has changed. Today I know of no dealer who does not regularly prune his mailing list, removing from it automatically those who have not ordered for a specified period of time, and this weeding-out process applies almost as rigorously to libraries as it does to private collectors.

One development which I personally do not welcome unreservedly is the growing prominence of the auction houses. Here I speak not so much of the firms which are part retail booksellers and part auctioneers, as is often the practice on the continent of Europe. Rather am I concerned with the multinational corporations whose growing power in the market seems to me to have dangerous implications for the long-term health of the bookseller's trade. The auction houses used to be primarily wholesalers. That is to say that they sold books in quite large lots, and most of their buyers were dealers who would divide these lots up and sell them to their own customers volume by volume.

Today the major auction houses – and I speak particularly of Sotheby's and Christie's – employ powerful publicity and public relations machines to woo and court the private buyer. Their publicity campaigns have been so successful that there is now an alarming tendency for *all* the best collections to go for auction when the time comes for them to be sold, and fewer and fewer private libraries are in consequence offered to the bookshops.

In their defence the auction houses tell us that they have created many new customers for the booksellers, and that they have moved prices upwards for everyone's advantage. That they have found new markets may be good, but my fear is that the new prices run the risk of making book collecting a hobby that only the rich can afford.

BOOKSELLING IN A CHANGING WORLD

Perhaps the trend which I most deplore is the marked diminution, in the Western world at least, in the number of traditional secondhand bookshops in town and city centres. In Europe and North America good, old-fashioned, general secondhand and antiquarian bookshops are becoming quite scarce. Do not misunderstand me: the number of dealers is not diminishing, indeed it is growing; it is the medium-sized firm with a 'walk-in' bookshop which is disappearing. The reason, of course, is the high cost of operating in prime shopping sites. It seems that only airline offices, supermarkets and boutiques can profitably do so today. As a result we have seen and are continuing to see two distinct and opposed movements in the pattern of antiquarian bookselling.

First there is the move towards one-man specialist firms. Such businesses usually operate from apartments in the residential quarter of the city, or from rooms in private houses in the country. The other and contrary trend is for more and more business to pass into the hands of fewer and fewer large and powerful firms. The one-man specialist firms provide a very useful service. Their expertise and the degree of personal attention they give represent a great boon to the book-buying community at large – but there is a drawback. A librarian or book collector visiting a distant city, perhaps in another country, could easily visit its bookselling district, its Charing Cross Road, its Fourth Avenue or its Kanda. A number of shops could be seen in the course of the day. It is much harder to make a tour of the one-man businesses, some of which are located at remote addresses. Moreover, the mere fact of having to telephone to make an appointment, and perhaps having to walk through a man's drawing-room to reach the bookcases where he has his stock, creates an artificial atmosphere between buyer and seller. There is not the same freedom to roam the shelves and to buy or not entirely as one pleases.

Does this really matter? The answer has to be yes. We are losing the base of the pyramid, the street-level, open-access shop, where both young dealers and tyro-collectors are trained. Moreover booksellers operating from offices or from home do not enjoy the same buying opportunities as those in conventional shops.

It can be argued that the world's stock of rare books is divided into two parts: those that the world knows about and those it hasn't discovered yet. The first kind sets us no problem, but the second kind is a cause for concern. Owners who are not themselves collectors of rare books, but who have perhaps inherited a small library, might well approach the bookseller in his familiar shop in their local High Street. Certainly most of us have bought many good books from just such a beginning. The seller I have in mind would be less likely to seek out a dealer in a remote cottage in rural England – or rural *New* England for that matter.

Because the general open-access bookshop is vanishing, the world of rare books is thus losing in three ways: the training ground for assistants; the place for young collectors to cut their teeth, as it were, on relatively inexpensive books; and a chance to buy unexpected rarities. If this volume was about ecology rather than bookselling, I should be writing about the danger to the species when the habitat, the feeding-ground, is in peril.

What about investment in rare books? This is not a new phenomenon, but of late it has certainly been on the increase. There are a number of reasons for this. One is that investment analysts and financial advisers noted the acceleration in the rate of increases in book prices. Another is that, in days of high inflation and uncertainty about money values, people have increasingly been seeking to put their savings into objects rather than share certificates, hoping that the objects would rise in price at least as fast as money fell in value.

Is this increase in investment in rare books wholly a good thing? Personally I have reservations. They arise from stories I heard at my father's knee about the crash in the 1930s. Of course the situation then was vastly different: books had been driven up in price far beyond the levels that were truly supported by their significance and their rarity. Nowadays I believe that prices, although high, are more soundly based, but even so they are at a level where purchasers need to think seriously about the potential re-sale value of the books they buy. My personal belief is that the best reason for buying a book is because one likes it: if it happens to go up in value then that is a bonus.

I suspect that investment buying will be with us for many years to come, but it is still only a small part of the whole antiquarian book trade and I for one hope that it will remain so.

These, then, are some of the changes and some of the trends in the antiquarian book trade today. Booksellers, like the collectors and librarians they serve, are conservative creatures. By their very nature they are resistant to change; yet they are caught up in the changes that beset us today, and if they do not welcome them they must at least learn to adapt to them if they are to flourish. The antiquarian book trade has managed to cope with changes over a number of centuries now, and I do not doubt for a moment that it will continue to do so.

A

Abbey, J. R. (1894–1969)
Major John Roland Abbey began collecting books after a distinguished military career in the First World War. The Abbeys, an old Brighton family, owned the Kemp Town Brewery, later taken over by Charringtons, and John succeeded his father as chairman during the Second World War. His great collections of private press books, fine bindings, colour plate books and illuminated manuscripts have had a lasting influence on collecting trends.

Abbey's first area of interest was the books of the English private presses, particularly in fine bindings. He owned a Kelmscott Chaucer bound at the Doves Bindery to a design after William Morris. He assembled complete sets of the works issued by the KELMSCOTT, ASHENDENE and GREGYNOG Presses and his interest in fine bindings led him to the work of the GUILD OF WOMEN BINDERS, ROGER POWELL, SYBIL PYE and KATHARINE ADAMS. As well as the finest contemporary English binders, he patronized the best French craftsmen, commissioning examples from Bonet, Martin, Michel, Crette and other masters of the Société de la Reliure Originale. The modern bindings, French and English, were the subject of an Arts Council Exhibition in 1949. It included items from all the major private presses, showing the work, among others, of Blair Hughes-Stanton, T. J. COBDEN-SANDERSON, DOUGLAS COCKERELL, and three books with bindings designed by Abbey himself and executed by Roger de Coverley.

Early books also claimed Abbey's attention; his collection included some 80 INCUNABULA in original bindings, the six-volume folio Aldine Aristotle, of 1495, in a Parisian binding of 1565 by Grolier's last binder, and a German Bible bound by the Saxony court binder, Jakob Krause, in 1575. He assembled, too, a complete set of the ROXBURGHE CLUB publications.

In 1946 the founder of the ASHENDENE PRESS, C. H. St John Hornby, sold his collection of illuminated manuscripts to Major Abbey for the sum of £40,000. He continued buying in this field, advised by Hornby himself and SYDNEY COCKERELL.

Abbey chose his mentors well; A. N. L. MUNBY, G. D. Hobson and many others all lent their skills, so that Abbey's collection, in addition to giving him pleasure, might also be of lasting value to scholars and collectors.

Major Abbey's fourth main area of collecting, and the one which has proved of most importance to later bookmen, was his comprehensive assembly of colour plate books. His three works (in four volumes) on aquatint and lithography from 1770 to 1860 – *Scenery of Great Britain and Ireland*, 1952; *Life in England*, 1953; and *Travel*, 1956–7 – remain the most important reference works of their kind. Forming a *catalogue raisonné* of Abbey's colour plate collection, they cover such a wide range of printed books in this field that the catalogue note 'Not in Abbey' carries considerable weight. The catalogues were edited by Michael Oliver and privately printed by the CURWEN PRESS; Oliver Simon was the typographer. The subjects covered by the four volumes are (1) the scenery and topography of the British Isles; (2) architecture, drawing books, art collections, magazines, the Navy and Army, panoramas; (3) the World, Europe and Africa; and (4) Asia, Oceania, Antarctica and America. There is also much useful information on printing processes and publishing procedures. The four volumes were reissued in 1972.

The colour plate collection was bought in its entirety by Paul Mellon and housed in a library specially built for the purpose at Yale University. The KELMSCOTT PRESS collection was bequeathed to Eton College, and some of the finest bindings to the BRITISH MUSEUM. The rest of the collection, one of the largest ever assembled, was dispersed in a series of 11 sales which started in Major Abbey's lifetime and continued after his death, the last six sales comprising his collection of medieval manuscripts.

Arts Council, *Catalogue of An Exhibition of Modern English and French Bindings from the Collection of Major J. R. Abbey*, 1949.
The Book Collector, Spring, 1961.
Hobson, G. D., *English Bindings in the Collection of J. R. Abbey*, 1961.
Sotheby's Sale Catalogues, 1965, 1966, 1967, 1970, 1974–5.

Ackermann, Rudolph (1764–1834)

Born in Saxony, the son of a coachbuilder, Rudolph Ackermann was apprenticed to his father. He worked in Paris for a while and then came to London where some of his designs were used for important state carriages. In 1795 he married an English woman and set up a factory in Chelsea. Here he put into production several of his early inventions including a movable carriage axle and a waterproofing system, illuminating the establishment by one of the first systems of gas lighting.

He soon moved to the Strand, first to No. 96 and later to No. 101, which he called The Repository of Arts and where he revitalized an existing drawing school and built up a prosperous business dealing in fancy goods, artists' materials and prints. The drawing school was later given up to expand the publishing side of the business. Many of the stream of émigrés from post-revolutionary France found work and shelter under Ackermann's roof and he raised funds for the relief of Prussian soldiers, refugees from Germany and exiles from Spain.

However, it is in the publishing field that Ackermann's name is best remembered. The first volume of his monthly magazine, also called *The Repository of Arts*, appeared in 1809. The print of the Repository itself shows a light spacious shop, the wall hung with framed prints with others in portfolio stands on the floor. Fashionable ladies examine lamps, firescreens, books and other articles at the counter, while in the background young girls are colouring prints at worktables. Above them, a domed lantern in the roof gives them light to work by, and around the cornice are notices of the goods for sale: Embossed White and Gold Ornaments, Colours and Requisites for Drawing, Pasteboard and Ornaments of all Descriptions, Medallions and Borders, Gold, Size and Cement, Variety of Large and Small Transparencies.

The large room at 101 Strand, formerly the drawing school's studio, was set up as a public library, specializing in the fine arts. It was from this address that the great outpouring of fine COLOUR PLATE BOOKS began to flow, starting in 1808 with the

Microcosm of London: or London in Miniature. Ackermann used the finest artists, not always well known, to execute the drawings from which the aquatints were engraved, and an army of colourists – many of them French refugees – to colour the prints by hand, after which the work was issued in parts. The *Microcosm*, as Ackermann explained in the Preface, brought together the architectural drawings of Augustus Pugin with his 'uncommon accuracy and elegant taste' and the figure sketches of Thomas Rowlandson 'with whose professional talents the public are already so well acquainted that it is not necessary to expatiate on them here'.

Ackermann continued to publish books illustrated with coloured aquatints on subjects such as architecture, travel, topography and social satire, as well as *The Repository of Arts, Literature, Commerce, Manufactures, Fashions and Politics*, which covered events of the day and matters of universal interest. Its editor, Frederick Shoberl, also edited the 42 small volumes of *The World in Miniature* published by Ackermann from 1821–27.

The invention of lithography by J. A. Senefelder in 1798 intrigued Ackermann. He used an illustration by Samuel Prout to introduce and explain lithography to the British public in the *Repository* in 1817 and published in 1819 a translation by A. Schlichtegroll of Senefelder's *A Complete Course of Lithography*. The only book Ackermann published to be fully illustrated with lithographs was his last, Edward Upham's *History and Doctrine of Buddhism*, 1829.

Rudolph Ackermann died in London after a stroke in 1834, but his name continued as a publisher and printseller until 1991.

Gentleman's Magazine, 1834.
Hardie, Martin, *English Coloured Books*, 1906.
Notes and Queries, 1869.
Ford, John A., *Ackermann, 1783–1983: The Business of Art*, 1983.

Adams, Katharine (1862–1952)
Katharine Adams studied bookbinding under SARAH PRIDEAUX and for a short time under DOUGLAS COCKERELL, before setting up her own bindery in Gloucestershire. Here her family were acquainted with William Morris from whom came her first commission. She worked for many of the great private presses and collectors of the day, including St John Hornby, T. J. COBDEN-SANDERSON and C. W. Dyson-Perrins.

Katharine Adams's designs, often on small books, have a simple delicacy. She made much use of fine pointillé circles with birds' heads, flowers and wreaths for decoration, and frequently lettered the upper cover of her books. Her signature was a tiny flower motif with the letters KA above. Adams designed her own tools which were specially cut for her and which are now in the BRITISH LIBRARY. There are examples of her work there and in the BODLEIAN. One of her most distinguished pieces, now in the British Library, is a leather casket containing six Shakespeare Head Press booklets, each bound to a different design and in a different colour.

Advance copy
Often confused with 'proof copy', this denotes a book supplied before publication to, for instance, a reviewer or publisher's representative. Normally the text will have been corrected, the index completed, etc., but the binding may differ from that of the first edition and the standard of production may well be inferior. Advance copies do

not command as great a premium as proof copies, which differ substantially from the book as published.

Advertisements
Printers and publishers have used their books as vehicles for advertising since the sixteenth century; at an even earlier date CAXTON's well-known advertisement for the Sarum Missal, pinned up in public though it did not appear in any of his books, drew the attention of his readers to a forthcoming publication, even adding *supplico stet cedula* (please leave this notice alone). Notices of other works by the same author, or from the same press, often occupied the final leaves of a book. Although these advertisements bore no relation to the text, and were often discarded by the binder, they were nevertheless an integral part of the printed book. Advertisement leaves of this kind are called for at the end, or occasionally at the beginning, of many English books up to the end of the eighteenth century, and copies which lack them must be considered technically incomplete. The fastidious collector of early English literature may covet a rare advertisement leaf much as others covet a twentieth-century DUST-WRAPPER, though it can be argued that both were expected to have a short life.

Towards the end of the eighteenth century, changing publishing practices led to the use of separately printed advertisements, in the form of publishers' lists or CATALOGUES. These were supplied to the binder for insertion in a particular title, or in a series of books from the same publisher. If the books were issued in BOARDS or in WRAPPERS the inserted advertisements were often discarded by a later binder; but with the advent of primary cloth bindings they might be expected to survive in any copy that was not rebound. However, the presence of a particular insert, or of any advertisements at all, in every copy of a book was by no means assured. Binders might on occasion run out of copies of a catalogue, and either proceed without it or use the remainder of an earlier issue. Later, provincial or export distributors might insert their own catalogues in copies bound up from 'remaindered' quires. These practices often make it difficult for bibliographers to reach any confident decision as to whether advertisements are essential to the completeness of a particular EDITION or issue, or to what extent they can be seen to determine priority of issue. Publishers' catalogues were often dated, and an insert with a later date than that of the book's first publication tells a clear story; but it does not follow that a catalogue of FIRST EDITION date authenticates a first edition copy. All in all, inserted advertisements have aided and baffled bibliographers in roughly equal measure.

A third form of advertisement remains to be considered. Nineteenth-century books issued in parts became a favoured advertising medium not only for other publications, but also for numerous products ranging from balsams to cork hats. These advertisements took various forms: inserts, slips, complete sheets, occasionally actual samples. The inclusion of a particular advertisement was, in part, dependent on the vagaries of a haphazard and often hasty make-up procedure, and the bibliographers of Dickens, Thackeray, Trollope and many other authors of books issued in this way can sometimes do little more than indicate the sequence of advertisements most frequently present.

Aldine Press
The printing press set up by Aldus Manutius

in Venice in 1490 was intended to express the printer's affection for all things Greek. He was a considerable scholar whose desire to extend the spread of classical literature and philosophy was met by the new invention of printing. Financed by the Mirandolas (his immediate patron was Alberto Pio of that princely family who, with his brother Lionello, had studied under Aldus), he was the first to print Greek texts, using his extensive scholarship to ensure that they were trustworthy. His love of the early Greek and Latin classics inspired his work, and Alan Thomas considered that 'no other publisher has ever made such a staggering contribution to the human spirit'.

The type used by Aldus in these early days of printing was inherited from Jenson, but it was the new roman type cut for him in 1495 by Francesco Griffo (Francesco da Bologna) that was to influence later roman faces. This was followed in 1501 by the entirely new sloping type that came to be known as italic.

The popularity of Aldus's printed books bore out his belief that the splendour of the classical writers deserved a wider readership. To fulfil this demand he printed Latin and Greek texts in a smaller format facilitated by the italic face, and these found a ready market. Although Venice had no university in Aldus's time, dependable Greek manuscripts were available, and his Press became a centre for visiting scholars, including Erasmus and Linacre, with Aldus himself *primus inter pares*. The Aldine editions and the house device of an anchor and dolphin – an ancient classical symbol – mark an unrivalled contribution to the spread of knowledge through the printed book.

Barker, Nicolas, *Aldus Manutius and the Development of Greek script and type in the Fifteenth Century*, Sandy Hook, Connecticut, 1985.

Lowry, Martin, *The World of Aldus Manutius – Business and Scholarship in Renaissance Venice*, Oxford, 1979.

Morison, Stanley, *Four Centuries of Fine Printing*, 1924 (reprinted and revised, 4th edn, 1960).

Renouard, A. A., *Annales de l'Imprimerie des Alde*, 3rd edn, Paris, 1834 (reprinted, 1953).

Allibone

A Critical Dictionary of English Literature and British and American authors living and deceased, by S. A. Allibone, was first published in five volumes in 1858 in Philadelphia with two supplementary volumes added in

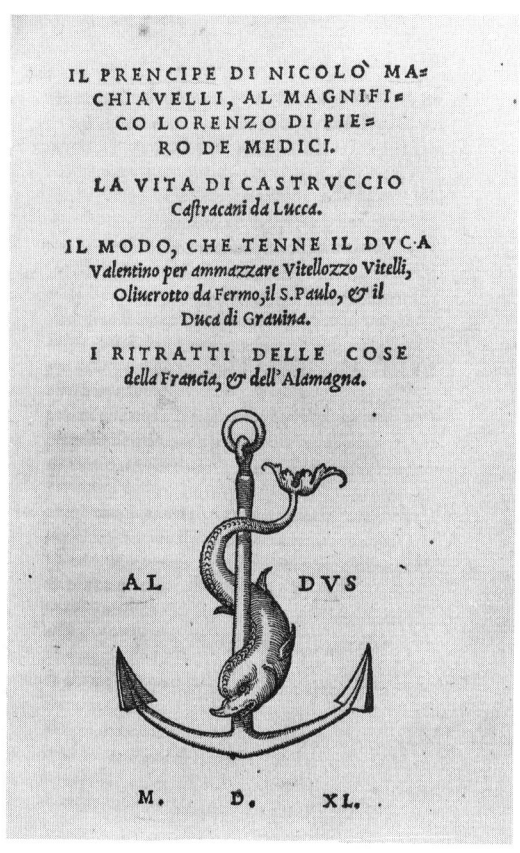

An Aldine title page

1891. It was reprinted several times, most recently in 1965. Although most of the material can be found elsewhere, its concise formulation can be very helpful. Entries carry a biographical note on the author, a list of works, with dates, and a brief critical comment. The compiler has included almost all authors writing in the English language and many of the entries probably represent the only source of information about minor figures. As the 1965 edition is simply a facsimile reprint, the work is much outdated, but 'Allibone' is one of those reference works that may gather dust on a bookseller's shelf for months or years – and then unexpectedly provide a much-needed piece of information.

All published

A term that indicates that a book, or series of books, for which a continuation was apparently projected, is in fact complete, no further volumes having been published. The term is also used of periodicals.

Almanacs

An almanac is a yearly list of astronomical information. It may in addition include dates of important events, details of prominent persons and places, and sometimes astrological prognostication. The two best-known publications are perhaps *Old Moore's Almanack*, named after Francis Moore, the original seventeenth-century compiler, and still published today; and *Whitaker's Almanack*, a comprehensive annual volume of information on such subjects as politics, law, sport, and national events.

Almanacs of the eighteenth and nineteenth centuries were frequently published in very small, 'bijou' format, for use in a pocket or purse. Many were attractively bound in tooled morocco with matching slipcases for protection. The *London Almanack* first appeared in 1690 and was published regularly until 1912. Most issues contained engravings, sometimes with folding plates of London views, and carried a calendar of events, details of the Royal household, government and City corporation, and information on tides, eclipses and phases of the moon. They measured about 2¼" × 1¼" and were published by the Stationers' Company.

During the nineteenth century several other series were published, one of the finest being *Schloss's Bijou Almanacs*. These were illustrated with portraits and topographical views and included poetry, essays

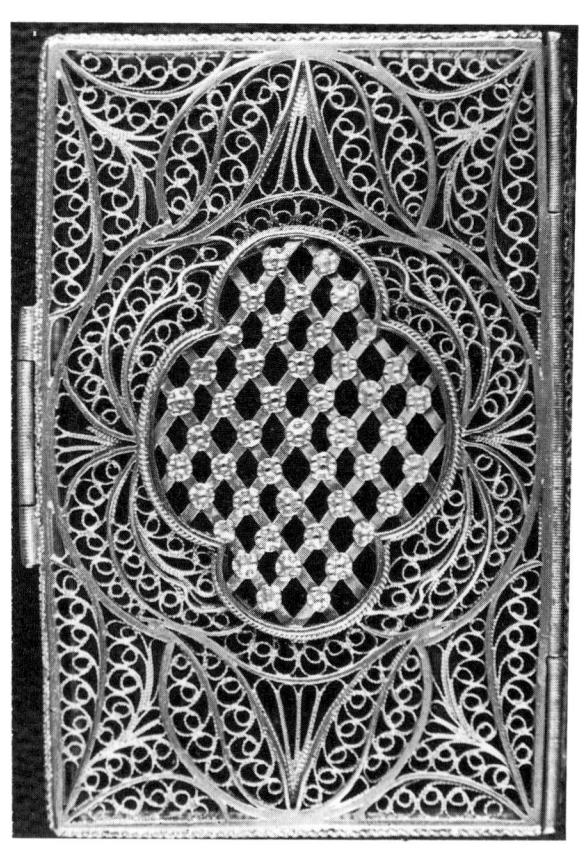

London almanac, 1880, 2½ × 1⅝ in.
[H. M. Fletcher]

and notes. They were very tiny – less than an inch square – but the engraving and printing was of remarkable clarity. Other series included the *Fashionable Remembrancer*, Tilt's *Miniature Almanack* and the *Royal Miniature Almanack*.

Almanacs were even more popular in France, where during the eighteenth century many hundreds of different titles were published. These are often found in very fine morocco or needlework bindings.

Bondy, Louis W., *Miniature Books*, 1981.
Grand-Carteret, John, *Les Almanachs Français, Bibliographie–Iconographie 1600–1895*, Paris, 1896, describing 3633 titles.

Alphabet books

Alphabet books present themselves most often to booksellers and collectors in the form of CHILDREN'S BOOKS. These tend, predictably, to be didactic in purpose; the first English alphabet in book form – Thomas Petyt's, printed in 1538 – is typical in combining the ABC with a rhymed version of the Ten Commandments; and while 'A' stands traditionally for Apple Pie, 'R' is often represented by Rod! Nevertheless, many fine illustrators have enlivened the alphabet with charm and wit: Harrison Weir, Kate Greenaway, Walter Crane, William Nicholson come to mind, together with unnamed earlier artists; and ABCs very properly represent an important division of any collection of children's books.

The alphabet in its broader significance is admirably described and illustrated in David Diringer's study, *The Alphabet, A Key to the History of Mankind*, two volumes, revised edition, 1968.

American Book Prices Current
See AUCTION RECORDS

American first editions

Most British publishers of the twentieth century have helped bibliographers and booksellers by making FIRST EDITIONS easy to identify, if only on negative evidence: if a commercially published British book does not say 'reprinted' or 'second impression/edition' on the verso of the title-page, then it is most probably a first edition. Exceptions, of course, are numerous, and have to be learnt with experience; but they are sufficiently uncommon, statistically, to be forgivable.

With American books, no such happy situation prevails. This is a legacy from the days of piracy, when US law offered scant copyright protection; in any event the problem has existed for a long time. Even in the 1920s Henry S. Boutell responded to the need for guidance by composing a book of publishers' own statements on the subject, which was revised three times and eventually formed the inspiration for the first book listed below; but, inevitably, those publishers who were most helpful to Boutell and his successors tended to be those who were scrupulous about identifying reprints of their publications. Some of the responses almost defy belief: 'Next time we reprint I will try to remember to put second edition in' is typical. The second of the books listed below is useful, as the relevant chapter was written, critically, by one who had experience of the problem as a bookseller; we recommend that, in the absence of a competent author bibliography, the two should be consulted together.

However, there follows an abbreviated guide to this treacherous terrain. The first step is straightforward: proceed as for British books by making sure that nowhere is there any clear indication that the book in question is *not* a first edition. This may be anywhere in the PRELIMS, or (and here the fun starts) on the DUST-WRAPPER; many Book Club editions are only differentiated by a few words, often on a corner of the flap. So, avoid price-clipped or incomplete dust-wrappers, and of course books without them, if they were published in the last 60 or so years; this is not as high-handed as it may seem, for (as with British first editions) only a handful of post-war books are of interest to collectors without their wrappers anyway.

The second step is to look at the 'copyright page', or COLOPHON, usually to be found on the VERSO of the TITLE-PAGE. If here you find a string of consecutive numbers or letters, or occasionally a single number or letter, make sure that the lowest of them is '1' or 'A' (unless the book is published by Duell, Sloane and Pearce or by Harper Brothers, in which case see below). These strings may run 12345... or 54321, or may be arranged symmetrically around the middle of the page, for instance 246897531; their function is to enable the printer to erase successive digits or letters each time the book is reprinted, and the last example enables this to be done without spoiling the look of the page. (This practice is not unknown in Britain; in particular, the first edition of Salman Rushdie's *The Satanic Verses* can only be identified in this way, as the publishers appear for some reason to be coy about stating openly how many times the book has been reprinted.)

The third step is to compare the date on the copyright page with the date on the title-page; this should be the same. (Occasionally the title-page date may correctly be a year later, but this should be checked in a bibliography.)

These three operations will enable booksellers to weed out the majority of REPRINTS with the minimum of trouble. But some publishers operate, or operated, more complex systems, or no systems at all, and a necessarily selective list of these, with an indication of how to determine first editions of their books, is given below.

D. Appleton (after 1933, D. Appleton-Century; after 1948, D. Appleton-Century-Crofts): either the numeral '1' appears at the foot of the last page of text, or the copyright page bears the words 'First edition'.

Bobbs-Merrill: a minefield, go straight to the bibliography – although a bow and arrow on the copyright page is a good sign.

Colt Press: blameless themselves, but New Directions (see below) published a reprint of Henry Miller's *The Colossus of Maroussi* which is identical to the 1941 Colt Press edition *in every detail including the imprint* except that it is shorter than the required 24 cm!

Columbia University Press: first editions have the date on the title-page.[1]

George H. Doran: either the words 'first printing' or the GHD 'colophon', or monogram, should appear on the copyright page.

Duell, Sloane and Pearce: either the words 'first edition' or 'first printing' or the Roman numeral 'I' should appear on the copyright page.

Farrar and Rinehart: with earlier books a small oval 'colophon', or monogram should appear on the copyright page; later books follow standard practice.

Grosset and Dunlap: no book from these publishers is ever a first edition.

Harper and Brothers: from 1912 these

---

[1] Composite or commissioned publication, within the United States or internationally, has become a large imprint activity of the university presses and results in a breach from time to time and without catalogue or colophon explanation, of familiar house styles.

publishers used a two-letter code system on the copyright page to date their books. The first letter denotes the month of printing and runs from A to M, omitting J; A is January, B February, and so on. The second letter indicates the year, and here a 25-letter alphabet, also omitting J, was used, but starting at M for 1912: so Z is 1925 or 1950, A 1926 or 1951, and so on. These dates should correspond with the copyright date as stated *en clair*. However, the good news is that after May, 1922, most first editions are clearly so stated.

King's Crown Press: first editions bear a date on the title-page.

New Directions: notoriously difficult. A bibliography is essential.

Charles Scribner's Sons: from 1929 until 1973, the letter 'A' must appear on the copyright page. They now use a string of numbers as described above, but this feature is omitted in New York-published Scribner books designed or printed in England.

The foregoing list does not claim to be definitive, or anywhere near it; at best it may save the bookseller going to time and trouble to check books which can be easily dismissed or authenticated using the above guidelines. Ultimately, no claim should be made for any American book without either a good bibliography or, of course, adequate experience.

Zempel, Edward N. and Verkler, Linda A., *First Editions: A Guide to Identification*, Peoria, Illinois, 1984.
Tannen, Jack, *How to Identify and Collect American First Editions: A Guide Book*, New York, 1976.

This also seems the best place to mention I. R. Brussel's invaluable *Anglo-American First Editions, 1826–1900: East to West*, 1935, describing first editions of English authors whose books were published in America before their publication in England; and the same author's *Anglo-American First Editions, 1786–1930: West to East*, 1936.

Ames, Joseph (1689–1759)

Bibliographer, cataloguer and publisher of portrait-engravings, and antiquary. His *Typographical Antiquities*, published in 1749, was one of the first systematic studies of the history of printing in England. Ames catalogued some thousands of early English books in a methodical and analytical manner, and his work provided the basis on which the SHORT TITLE CATALOGUE was founded. Much of his own substantial library was dispersed after his death, but the BRITISH LIBRARY holds a large manuscript collection and a collection of printed TITLE PAGES.

Annuals

Every bookseller who is asked about annuals knows that the word can describe a wide variety of books. From Rupert Bear back through such old favourites as Pip, Squeak and Wilfred to the boys' and girls' volumes of Edwardian times, books have been published once a year, usually in time for Christmas, to meet the demand by children for a regular anniversary appearance of their favourite characters.

However, the term annual is more generally applied to the yearly compilations first introduced by ACKERMANN and intended for the adult female reader, which enjoyed such names as *The Keepsake, The Gem, The Literary Souvenir, The Bijou* and *Friendship's Offering*. The bindings were of embroidered or ribbed silk, embossed LEATHER or textured paper.

It was the illustrations that particularly endeared these charming gift books to the lady readers of early Victorian England, and they sold in their thousands. These were the early years of engraving on steel, and the clear sharp images, capable of satisfactory reproduction in far greater numbers than their copperplate predecessors, have retained their attraction for later collectors. Some of the plates engraved for the LARGE-PAPER editions were printed off separately and sold in portfolios.

The destination of these literary annuals was the drawing-room of the intelligent, fastidious, patrician family, and many famous authors were only too pleased to contribute to them. They contained poems, essays, reviews and sometimes fashion and social gossip; and writers such as Wordsworth, Coleridge, the Brownings, Dickens, Thackeray and Tennyson were all represented. Distinguished artists, whose work was engraved for the purpose, also contributed, among them Turner, Stanfield, Stothard and Landseer.

These little books have now become hard to find in good condition. Often the bindings were fragile and many of the engravings, especially of unusual foreign views, have been extracted by printsellers. Nevertheless, the short duration of their popularity (most had disappeared by about 1870 and were never reprinted) and the light they throw on an important phase of social history, make them a desirable and relatively inexpensive field for collectors.

Faxon, Frederick W., *Literary Annuals and Gift Books. A Bibliography, 1823–1903* (reprinted with supplementary essays by Eleanore Jamieson and Iain Bain, Pinner, 1973).

Renier, Anne, *Friendship's Offering, an Essay on the Annuals and Gift Books of the Nineteenth Century*, 1964.

Antiquarian Book Monthly Review
Established in 1979, ABMR (as it is generally known) occupies the middle ground in British magazines for book collectors and dealers; less austere than *The Book Collector* and more scholarly than its rivals, it reaches probably the widest cross-section of readers. In 1993 the journal changed its name (and format) to become *Antiquarian Book Monthly*.

Antiquarian Booksellers' Association
The ABA, founded in December 1906, was the first organization of its kind to be established and is the oldest association of the bodies now affiliated to the INTERNATIONAL LEAGUE OF ANTIQUARIAN BOOKSELLERS. At the Association's inaugural meeting at the Criterion Restaurant in London, its aims were defined as 'the promotion of professional and honourable standards in the antiquarian book trade at national and international levels'. The Association's first president was Henry Stevens; he was followed in 1907 by Ben Maggs, and the familiar names of later presidents indicate that several leading antiquarian firms have been active members for more than 80 years.

Membership of the ABA is open only to booksellers with at least five years' full-time experience in the trade, and the integrity and expertise of applicants for membership is tested by a meticulous election procedure. Despite occasional charges of élitism, the Association's insistence on high standards of professionalism is widely respected, as is its commitment to scrupulous practice in the saleroom. The membership, initially just over a hundred, now stands at some four hundred.

In recent years the Association's annual London BOOK FAIR, first held (for 14 days!) at the National Book League's Albemarle

Street headquarters and later at other central London locations, has come to be regarded as the most important event in the international antiquarian bookselling calendar. This book fair, and others in Edinburgh, Bath and recently also in Chelsea, have tended to overshadow the ABA's other activities; but these too are of much importance to ABA members and to many others in the world of books. The ABA represents the trade on the National Book Committee, the Art Trade Liaison Committee and on other national bodies whose work is relevant to its aims. It maintains an effective 'stolen book chain', employing telephone and fax to inform members rapidly about thefts. Its library provides an important facility, especially for those members without easy access to bibliographical reference books; and its benevolent fund brings ready help to members or their dependants in times of hardship. A monthly newsletter and regular social events contribute to a collective spirit.

The antiquarian bookselling community has seen many changes since the ABA was founded, and its present leaders are the first to recognize that the Association must adapt itself to contemporary needs and interests. Nevertheless its strength is seen to lie in its patient insistence on the highest standards of professional skill and integrity.

The History of the ABA, 1906–1984, Newsletter of the International League of Antiquarian Booksellers, 1984.

Armorial binding

Armorial bindings are so described because they bear the owner's coat of arms, usually in gilt, though occasionally blind-stamped, on the upper cover. Identifying the arms is usually time-consuming, but Fairbairn's *Book of Crests* may be helpful.

It is, if possible, important to attempt to identify the armorial, particularly in older books, as it indicates provenance and may considerably add to the value. French armorials are much easier to find by using the very well-indexed reference work: Olivier, Eugène, *Manuel de l'amateur de reliures armoriées françaises*, Paris, 1924–38, in 30 volumes (available in most large libraries).

Art and Architecture
Peter Miller

Art and architectural books form a vast field and few outside major institutional libraries would make any attempt at a comprehensive coverage. This brief survey will be confined to European art and architecture, and will provide a few pointers to areas of specialization for the collector and to the effects of taste and fashion on collecting habits. Art books can best be dealt with in four main areas, with reference to some of the outstanding books.

Technical books

Of these perhaps the largest body of work was devoted to the study of perspective. Perspective was developed in Italy in the early fifteenth century and it made possible the accurate rendering of three-dimensional space in two dimensions. Alberti's *L'Architettura*, 1485, was the first printed book to deal with the re-awakening interest in classical forms of building and the new science of perspective; it was to have a profound influence on the subsequent development of the sister arts of architecture and painting and were printed in innumerable editions throughout Europe.

Perspective was seen as basic to the practice of painting for nearly four centuries and the many manuals for the artist form a large if rather dry collecting field in themselves. Particularly impressive is the baroque exposition by Andrea Pozzo, *Prospettiva de Pittori*, 1693–1700, and John Lodge Cowley's delightful *Theory of Perspective*, 1765, which, with the aid of drawn threads, forms three-dimensional models of the stiff card plates.

'Books of Secrets' hold much interest. They tend to be small chunky books with a charming diversity of practical information on gilding, japanning, mixing colours, dyeing, dressing leather, etc. They were designed primarily for the artisan and consequently have generally survived only in poor condition.

Of books on specific techniques, mention should be made of Abraham Bosse's *Traité des Manières de Graver*, 1645, which, surprisingly, was the first technical book devoted to the subject of engraving and which can still be used for reference with the aid of the detailed plates. John Baptist Jackson's *Engraving and Printing in Chiaroscuro*, 1754, offers a dramatic example of how prices for these often rare technical books have changed. A copy sold at auction in 1958 for £38; a complete copy would now fetch about £5000. This spectacular increase reflects the value placed on these technical treatises for the detailed evidence of artistic practice which they afford and for information useful for conservation.

Other technical treatises that interest collectors include manuals of anatomy, most famously Dürer's book on Geometry and Proportion, and lithography, with Senefelder's *A Complete Course of Lithography*, 1819, perhaps holding pride of place. The development of colour theory is dominated by Isaac Newton, Robert Boyle and Goethe. James Sowerby's *A New Elucidation of Colours*, 1809, with its brilliant colour plates, is a most attractive book in this area, and Chevreul's *De la Loi du Contraste Simultane des Couleurs*, 1839, was of importance to printers and textile manufacturers alike and had a profound

Andrea Pozzo, *Prospettiva de Pittori*, 1693–1700. Frontispiece to one of the most visually striking of all treatises on perspective, with magnificent *trompe l'oeil* plates [Ken Spelman]

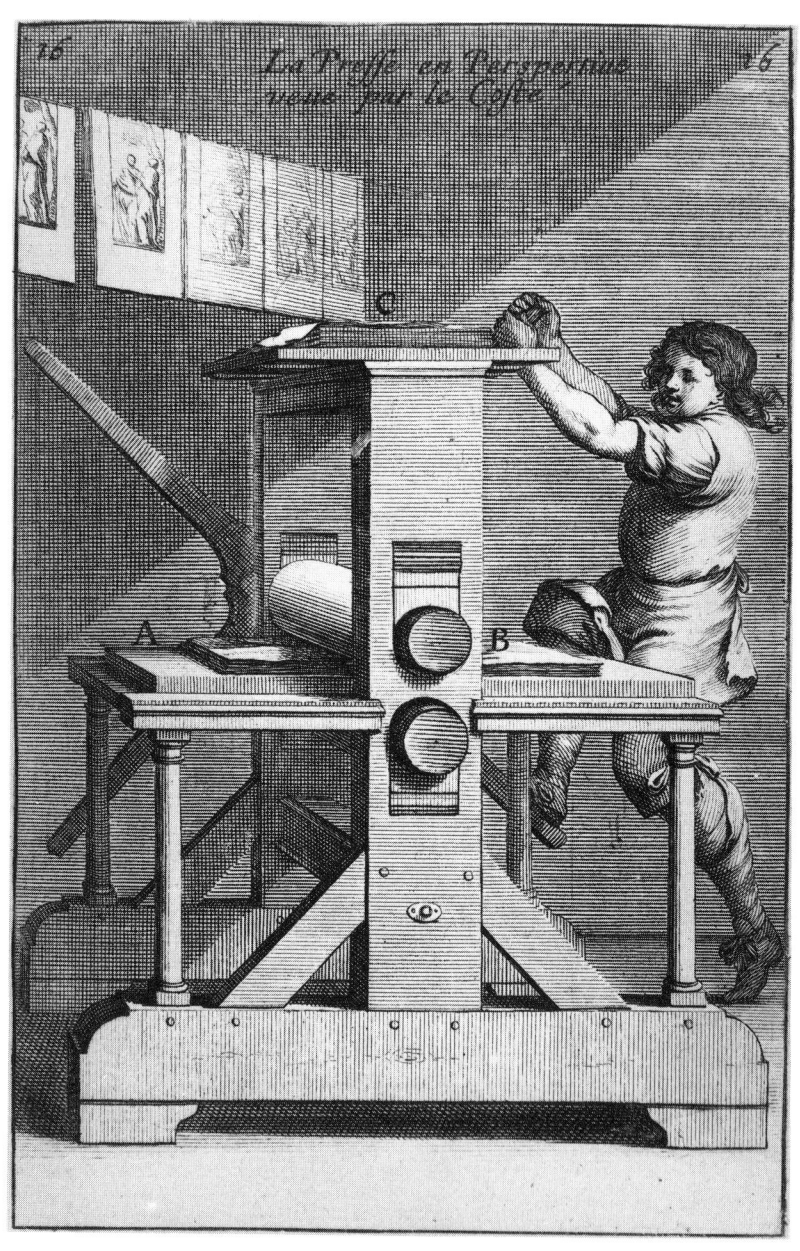

Abraham Bosse, *Traite des Manières de Graver en Taille Douce sur l'Airain*, 1645. The first technical treatise on engraving. [Ken Spelman]

ART AND ARCHITECTURE

influence on the French Impressionist painters. Of the more general early technical treatises a particular favourite is Alexander Browne's *Ars Pictoria . . .* , 1669, with its fine frontispiece portrait of the handsome author, illustrating why Pepys was jealous of his wife's teacher.

These technical treatises were originally aimed at the professional artist but by the late eighteenth century drawing and watercolour painting had become a polite accomplishment. Between 1790 and 1830 three hundred manuals were published in England for this amateur market. They are often illustrated with coloured aquatint plates and form a particularly attractive area for the collector. They range from David Cox's magnificent *Treatise on Landscape Painting*, 1813, which established the artistic reputation of the young drawing master, to John Laporte's relatively modest but delightful *Progress of a Watercolour Painting*, 1805. Laporte used aquatint in a series of 12 plates to illustrate the first application of washes through to the finished watercolour. Bicknell and Munro's catalogue *From Gilpin to Ruskin*, 1988, is a useful guide to these manuals.

Collectors and collecting

Private collecting and collections have always been the expression of surplus wealth. Until the late seventeenth century this was largely the province of kings and princes of church and state. Books that described these great private collections were originally no more than collections of prints; the prints were often issued separately and would be collected by the patrons and the artists themselves. Rembrandt put together a vast collection of prints not only for reference, but also as a reflection of his social position.

In the eighteenth century, as England emerged as the wealthiest country in the world, the base of patronage and collecting broadened. It became the mark of a gentleman to demonstrate his taste by collecting pictures, books and sculpture. Leaders of taste such as the Earl of Shaftesbury, Lord Burlington and Horace Walpole exercised enormous influence. Great collections were formed, like Sir Robert Walpole's at Houghton. Horace Walpole's catalogue of this collection, *Aedes Walpolianae*, 1752, was a gesture of family pride, but also one of the earliest catalogues of a private picture gallery in England. Books celebrating these collections and their dispersal are now increasingly collected as a mirror of taste. The catalogues of the celebrated sales of the eighteenth and nineteenth centuries were often elaborately printed, incorporating the prices realized, for the expanding collecting market.

With the upheaval of the Napoleonic Wars came great dispersals of painting and libraries. While many objects found their way from Italy to France, the collections of the French nobility, like the celebrated Orléans collection of pictures, largely found their way to England. William Buchanan's *Memoirs of Painting, with a Chronological History of the Importations of Pictures by the Great Masters into England since the French Revolution*, 1824, is a fascinating insider's account of this.

In 1838 Gustave Waagen, the first director of the Royal Picture Gallery in Berlin, published *Works of Art and Artists in England*, which revealed the great wealth of pictures and their locations in this country for the first time. This became a sort of shopping list for American dealers and collectors as the balance of wealth shifted to the New World in

David Cox, *A Treatise on Landscape Painting and Effect in Watercolours*, 1814. A beautiful book which established the young Cox's reputation. The 56 plates illustrate all the stages of a watercolour from pencil outline, through monochrome washes to the finished work. [Ken Spelman]

the late nineteenth and early twentieth centuries. We are still living in the shadow of that shift in wealth and subsequent dispersal. In the chronicling of collecting fashion it is the minor areas that are today most keenly sought by collectors and dealers. The major sale catalogues and descriptions of collections have been adequately described, but attention now focuses on the lesser, and particularly on the provincial, sale catalogues, which unlike those of the grand sales have never been reprinted.

The development of the art book

Before looking at the development of the art book it would be useful to examine particular problems in its production. William Ivins in his pioneering work *Prints and Visual Communication*, 1953, brilliantly examines the development of the print, which he defines as the 'exactly repeatable pictorial statement'. Before this was introduced it was not possible to distribute pictorial information accurately. It is no accident that it developed in Europe in the fifteenth century at about the same time as movable type, and the development of the art book is, in a sense, the history of the refinement of printing techniques. The woodcut, line engraving, aquatint, lithography and so on form particular areas of collecting in themselves, but share the problem of being only approximations to the original works of art depicted. As prints were often the only form in which the pictures were seen, severe restrictions were placed on the development of art scholarship.

Art books, the 'Museum without Walls' as André Malraux so memorably termed them, are a relatively recent phenomenon. Francis Haskell in *The Painful Birth of the Art Book*, 1987, places their birth in the early eighteenth century. The art book, as Haskell defines it, combines text with reproductions of the works of art and is published for public distribution. As such he dates it from the production of the *Cabinet de Crozat*, 1721–1742. This was originally conceived as a magnificent set of plates based on the collection of paintings of the King and the Duc d'Orléans. It was published in parts and sold on subscription. It developed into a description of the schools of European painting and was provided with a text by Jean-Baptiste Massé which broke new ground by concentrating on the technique rather than the subject matter. The *Cabinet de Crozat* gave rise to similar productions: the magnificent *Dresden Gallery*, 1753–1759, is acknowledged as one of the finest printed books of the eighteenth century. The art book as we know it, with text and relevant reproductions of paintings, had been born.

This is of course too narrow a definition of the art book for the collector. The great Festival and Funeral books in the seventeenth and eighteenth centuries form a collecting field in themselves: likewise, the magnificent celebrations of temporal power produced at the same time by royal presses in France and Germany. But these were largely for private distribution and even the resources of kings and princes would hardly support the magnificence of their production.

For the art historian the seminal work in the study of Italian painting and sculpture is Vasari's *Lives of the Painters*, 1550 (illustrated edition 1568). For the first time artists and their works were celebrated in a systematic manner and this book formed the basis of the subsequent study of Italian art. In view of its importance it is interesting that the first complete edition published in English was a translation by Mrs J. Foster in the Bohn

Library as late as 1850. The biographical treatment of artists became popular in other countries although predominantly in national groups. Horace Walpole's *Anecdotes of Painters in England*, 1762–1763, was the first similar celebration of English painting and Pilkington's *Dictionary of Painters and Engravers*, 1770, was the first English dictionary of European artists.

Illustrated monographs on individual artists are a surprisingly late development. The first illustrated *Life of Michelangelo Buonarroti* by Richard Duppa was published in London in 1806. The first on Raphael, by Friedrich Rehberg, appeared in Munich in 1824.

The development of photography has transformed art scholarship and the first book to use photographs for illustration was William Stirling-Maxwell's *Annals of the Artists in Spain*, 1848. But it was initially an expensive process; only 25 copies were printed and subsequent editions reverted to outline illustrations. Until the refinement of the photographic process the besetting problem for art books was the difficulty of producing good illustrations cheaply. This has made some of the nineteenth-century monuments of art historical scholarship unattractive to modern eyes and many are still undervalued.

The twentieth-century art book

The art books of the present century can be roughly differentiated as the book as object and the book as information. The book as object finds its finest expression in this country in the productions of the private press movement. Burne-Jones illustrated the Kelmscott *Chaucer*, 1896, still a benchmark for book values, and perhaps the finest twentieth-century English book is the Golden Cockerel Press *Four Gospels* illustrated by Eric Gill, 1934. But many more modest productions contain distinguished work. *High Street*, printed by the Curwen Press and illustrated with delicious coloured lithographs by Eric Ravilious in 1938, which now fetches several hundred pounds, was originally published by Country Life Books for 7/6d. The products of the Curwen Press are a fruitful collecting field in themselves. But the book as object reached its apogee in the 'livres d'artiste' published in Paris in the last hundred years. These are more properly seen as part of the art market, with beautiful lithographs and etchings by the major artists of the twentieth century interspersed with text. As such they have always been the province of the very wealthy.

With the great expansion of the art market and the development of art history as a separate academic discipline there has been a great proliferation of art books in the twentieth century. This development has been made possible by the parallel refinement of photographic reproduction. The modern catalogue of a major exhibition is now expected to reproduce all the exhibits in colour. In many cases the apprehension of art is through the reproduced image and accompanying information rather than through the pictures or objects themselves.

Art history in this country has been dominated by German scholarship in this century. The Warburg Institute, since its removal to London in the 1930s, helped to set new standards. The removal of the Phaidon Press to London from Vienna at about the same time was a great stimulus to the appreciation of art in this country, making good reproductions and reliable scholarship available at a remarkably low price. Anton Zwemmer's shop in the Charing Cross Road was a beacon of modernism in the thirties and forties. Nikolaus Pevsner, like Gustav Waagen before him, introduced the British to the riches of their own heritage. His *Buildings of England* and the *Pelican History of Art* (of which he was commissioning editor) are extraordinary achievements and in both cases the most ambitious British projects in their field.

As the value of art works has soared, the *catalogue raisonné* has become the most expensive modern informative art book. Short print runs have contributed to this but when pictures fetch millions of pounds the essential *catalogue raisonné* seems comparatively cheap at hundreds or even thousands. Book collecting in this field is overshadowed by the market in pictures and follows its fashions. For example, the mistrust of modernism of the 1980s resulted in a rise in interest in figurative art and the books and pictures of the early twentieth-century British school became increasingly sought after.

Reitlinger's book, *The Economics of Taste*, was the first to chart in detail the vagaries of the art market. It would be useful for the dealer and collector to have such a reference for the books about them. At present it is necessary to collate information from runs of *Book Auction Records* and specialist catalogues. It might be an instructive application of computer technology to tabulate this information to provide a historical record of the shifts in taste in art books.

Architectural books

The collecting of architectural books in this country has suffered from the relative paucity of bibliographical information. The publication of the bibliography of the *Fowler Architectural Collection* in 1961 certainly helped, but collecting was stimulated more than anything else by Ben Weinreb's architectural catalogues from the early 1960s through to the late 1980s. These set new standards in cataloguing and spawned and influenced a whole generation of dealers and collectors.

The practice of architecture in Europe was dominated by classical forms, particularly as reinterpreted by the architects of the Italian Renaissance, until the nineteenth century. Its influence can be gauged by the fact that 170 of the 448 items in the Fowler collection are editions of Vitruvius (40), Alberti (14), Serlio (33), Vignola (39), Palladio (32) and Scamozzi (12). These architects and their books formed the foundation of architectural appreciation and practice and were translated into all the main languages of Western Europe.

In the seventeenth century the centre of architectural practice moved increasingly from Italy to France. Magnificent books like Fréart's *Parallele de l'architecture antique et de la moderne*, Paris, 1650, and Perrault's *Treatise of the Five Orders*, 1683, underlined the position of France as the arbiter of architectural taste in Europe. By the eighteenth century England was in an economic position to challenge this dominance, and the early decades of the eighteenth century saw an explosion of books on architecture in this country. The Italian forms were assimilated with the publication of the first English editions of Alberti in 1726 and of Palladio in 1715–19, followed by Ware's more complete text in 1738 under the patronage of Lord Burlington. Inigo Jones, the seventeenth-century progenitor of the Italian style, was finally honoured in 1727 with the publication of two handsome folio

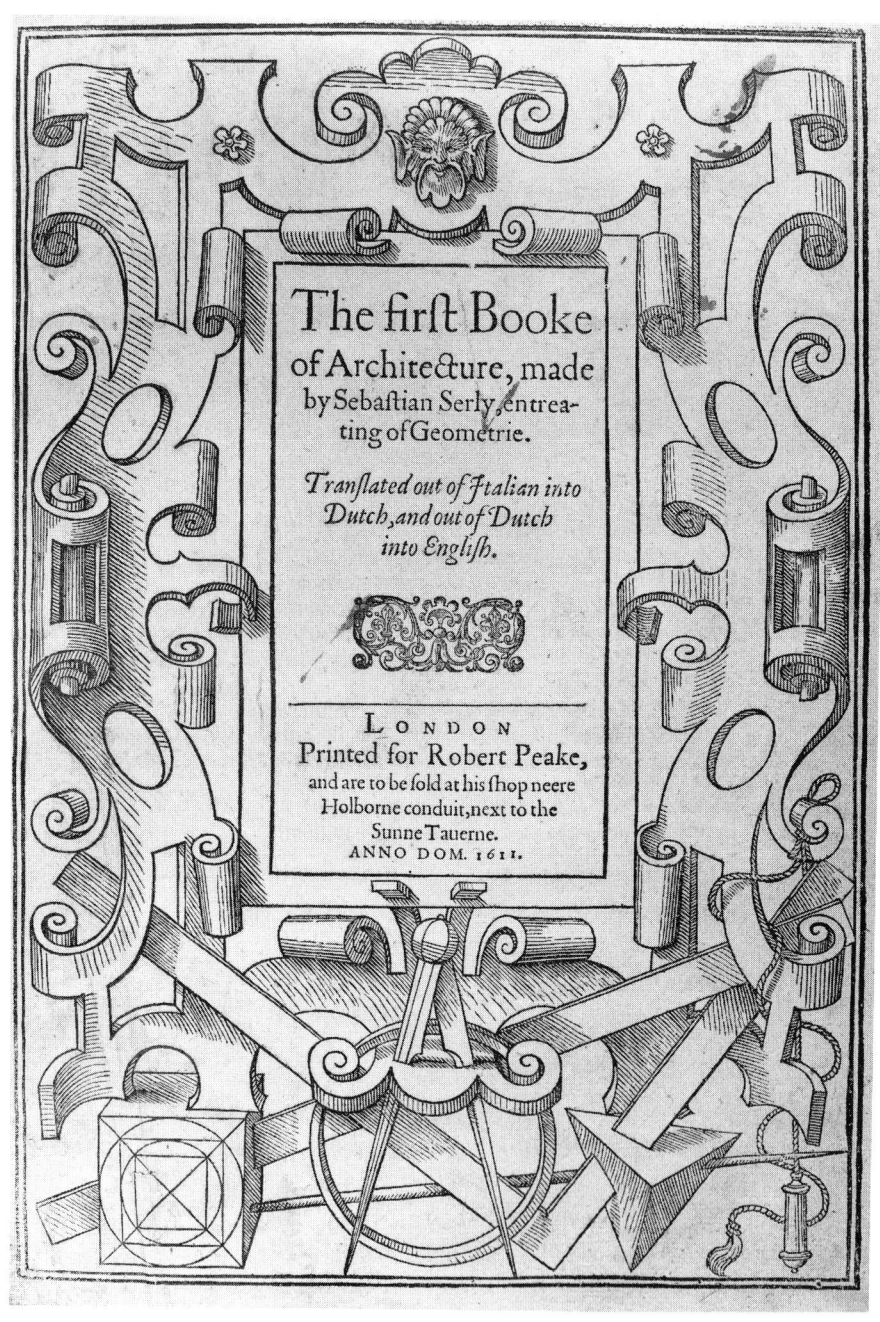

Sebastiano Serlio, *The First Booke of Architecture*, first English Edition, 1611. One of the earliest books in English devoted to architecture. [Ken Spelman]

volumes edited by William Kent, again under Burlington's patronage. Architectural practice was based on the classical Five Orders, and James Gibbs in his *Rules for Drawing the Five Orders*, 1732, was the first to make their measurement easily accessible to those who were 'but little skill'd in Arithmetic'. These skills were further popularized in Edward Hoppus's *Gentleman's and Builder's Repository*, 1737, and Batty Langley's *Builder's Compleat Assistant*, 1738. Batty Langley (1696–1751) was a crucial and heroic figure in this golden age of English building and gardening and his books cover the whole range of architecture, landscape, gardening and husbandry.

Pattern and design books followed to supply the mania for building, of which James Gibbs's *Book of Architecture*, 1728, was probably the most influential. These provide examples, often idealized and unbuilt, for architects and their patrons to choose from. Specialized manuals also made their appearance at this time. It is interesting that the first carpentry manuals in this country appeared as late as 1738, with James Smith's *Carpenter's Companion* and Francis Price's *Treatise on Carpentry*.

The exploration of architectural forms inspired the exact measurement of Greek building for the first time: Robert Wood's *Ruins of Palmyra*, 1753, and *Balbec*, 1757, and Stuart and Revett's *Antiquities of Athens*, 1755, were acclaimed throughout Europe. These splendid productions informed the taste of two generations of patrons and connoisseurs.

The parallel art of landscape gardening was developed in this country in the eighteenth century to become the most characteristic English contribution to European sensibility. Like architecture it initially depended on foreign books in translation. Works like Dezallier d'Argenville's *Theory and Practice of Gardening*, translated from the French in 1712, conceive of the garden as a formal enclosed construction. The English contribution was to remove the idea of enclosure and include the whole landscape, the 'tempting prospect'. Books by Stephen Switzer and Batty Langley and the practice of Charles Bridgeman at Stowe and William Kent at Rousham articulated a new climate of thought towards the relationship of nature and art. Switzer writes of his gardens being open to the whole view 'to the unbounded felicities of distant prospect, and the expansive volumes of nature herself' (*The Nobleman, Gentleman, and Gardener's Recreation*, 1715). In creating such 'natural' gardens the landscape gardeners and their patrons were following the examples of literature and art. They were recreating the Virgilian pastoral as interpreted by Claude Lorrain and Poussin in their paintings. These in turn contributed to the theory of the picturesque which was such a crucial influence on gardening, painting and architecture in the later eighteenth century and whose influence is still felt today.

If, in the eighteenth century, gardening and architecture were dominated by man in relation to nature, nineteenth-century architects had to address the increasing urbanization in Western Europe following the industrial revolution. Schinkel, the great German architect, on his travels in England in the early nineteenth century, visited the industrial centres rather than the picturesque sights. The many and beautiful villa books produced in the early nineteenth century in this country increasingly focused on the building of elegant homes and gardens on the edge of towns. J. C. Loudon's most popular books in the 1830s and 1840s were manuals for middle class suburban living. Architectural manuals were predominantly concerned with solutions to city living, be they models for housing the poor, civic commissions or competitions for clothing engineering advances in an acceptable style. With the breakdown of the classical hegemony there was the struggle between classical and gothic forms. The cacophony of styles, until a generation ago still disparagingly referred to as Victorianism, resulted. In the mass of books and manuals that reflect this, perhaps the most attractive to present taste are the design and pattern books and trade catalogues. Often elaborately produced with chromolithographic plates, they are a triumph of nineteenth-century colour printing and from being unconsidered are now among the most expensive items in this field. Perhaps the most neglected area today is that of the books on church and ecclesiastical architecture which would need a powerfully reforming hand to bring them back to their former esteem.

The triumph of modernism in the twentieth century replaced the nineteenth-century diversity of styles with a new dogma to rival the classical forms. Its unpopularity at present makes it a good area for collecting. The optimism for a brave new world in town planning and functional living now represents a rich collecting field for those who can fight off the nostalgic yearnings for earlier forms.

In this short introduction to collecting books on art and architecture it has only been possible to provide a few pointers, and most collectors or dealers will find themselves specializing. As the world is increasingly dominated by visual images this area will inevitably continue to grow in popularity with collectors. As tastes change so does the collecting of books. It is a fickle area and collectors do well to stick to their own enthusiasms rather than follow the latest change in fashion. The best collections are always those that reflect an honest and thorough-going enthusiasm.

Archer, John, *The Literature of British Domestic Architecture 1715–1842*, Cambridge, Massachusetts, 1985.

Bicknell, P. and Munro, J., *From Gilpin to Ruskin, Artist's Manuals*, Cambridge, 1988.

Bolten, Jacob, *Method and Practice: Dutch and Flemish Drawing Books 1600–1750*, Landau, Pfalz, 1985.

Colvin, Howard, *A Biographical Dictionary of British Architects 1600–1840*, 1954 (reprinted, 1978).

Fowler, L. H. and Baer, E., *The Fowler Architectural Collection of the Johns Hopkins University: Catalogue*, Baltimore, Maryland, 1961 (reprinted Woodbridge, Connecticut, 1982).

Harris, Eileen, *British Architectural Books and Writers 1556–1785*, Cambridge, 1990.

Haskell, Francis, *Patrons and Painters: a Study in the Relations between Italian Art and Society in the Age of the Baroque*, 1963 (2nd edn, 1980).

——— *The Painful Birth of the Art Book*, 1987.

Henrey, Blanche, *British Botanical and Horticultural Literature before 1800*, 1975.

Herrmann, Frank, *The English as Collectors*, 1972.

Ivins, W. M., Junior, *Prints and Visual Communication*, 1953.

Katalog der Ornamentstichsammlung der staatlichen Kunstbibliothek Berlin, Berlin, 1936–1939.

Levis, H. C., *A Descriptive Bibliography of the most Important Books in the English Language relating to the Art and History of Engraving and the Collecting of Prints, with Supplement and Index*, 1912–1913 (reprinted Folkestone, 1974).

Lloyd, C. and Ledger, T., *Art and its Images*, Oxford, 1975.

Pears, Iain, *The Discovery of Painting: the Growth of Interest in the Arts in England 1680–1768*, 1988.

Pevsner, Nikolaus, *Academies of Art Past and Present*, Cambridge, 1940 (reprinted New York, 1973).

Romaine, L. B., *A Guide to American Trade Catalogs 1744–1900*, New York, 1960.

Schmid, F., *The Practice of Painting*, 1948.

Strachan, W. J., *The Artist and the Book in France: the 20th Century Livre d'Artiste*, 1969.

Universal Catalogue of Books on Art, London, South Kensington, 1870–1877.
Weinreb, B., Architectural Catalogues issued by B. Weinreb Architectural Books Ltd.

As found
Abbreviated to a.f. in book catalogues (and easily confused with a shortened form of w.a.f.), the term signifies a total abdication of responsibility for a description (almost invariably by an auctioneer).

Ashendene Press
The private press of C. H. St John Hornby, founded at Ashendene in Hertfordshire in 1895. Only ten small books, now highly desirable, were printed there, and most of the Press's output dates from after Hornby's move to Chelsea in 1900.

Although Hornby's choice of texts was never particularly original, his taste, craftsmanship and enthusiasm for what he called 'a certain gaiety of treatment in the use of coloured initials and chapter-headings' have caused Ashendene Press books to be among the most highly regarded of the entire private press movement. Inspired by the DANIEL PRESS, Hornby favoured the Fell types, but later (with Emery Walker and SYDNEY COCKERELL) he designed the Subiaco type, with which the Press has been closely associated ever since. This type was based on one used by Sweynheim and Pannartz, formerly of Mainz, for their edition of Cicero's *De Oratore* printed at Subiaco in Italy in 1465. It was not an easy type to work with, but the Ashendene Press succeeded.

The Press operated for so long (until 1935) that no single publication stands out clearly above the others; Dante's *Tutte le Opere*, 1909, has always commanded high prices, but Hornby's own favourites were Spenser's *The Faerie Queene*, 1923, and

[Maggs Bros Ltd]

Malory's *The noble and joyous book entytled Le morte d'Arthur*, 1913. One of the few Ashendene titles to be remarkable for its illustration was Longus's *Les amours pastorales de Daphnis et Chloë*, 1933, with wood engravings by Gwendolen Raverat. Many of the Press's books appear in fine bindings: some of these were provided by KATHARINE ADAMS. Collectors need not be disconcerted by bindings signed 'W. H. Smith': Hornby was a director of the firm, and Ashendene titles bound by

Smith's bindery were executed by Douglas Cockerell.

Descriptive Bibliography of the Books Printed at the Ashendene Press, illus. G. Hewitt, Ashendene Press, 1935.

Franklin, Colin, *The Ashendene Press*, Dallas, Texas, 1986.

Association copy

A book distinguished from other copies by its PROVENANCE. The most desirable association copies are those whose previous owners were directly connected with the writing of the book or who used it extensively to produce an important book of their own. Books owned by families or friends of the author are also attractive to collectors. Booksellers are well advised not to let their imaginations run away with them; Ernest Hemingway's copy of a book on bull-fighting, for example, would be highly desirable, but a pencilled 'E. H.' in a book on flower-arranging would need corroborative evidence before it aroused much excitement.

Auction records

Auction records provide booksellers and collectors with an indispensable guide to the value of books, and are often a source of useful bibliographic information. Nevertheless they must be used with care and with patience. A single auction price can, for a host of reasons, be misleading; a succession of prices will always provide a more reliable guide. Descriptions of condition are necessarily brief.

Book Auction Records (common abbreviation, BAR) The first issue covered the year 1902; records appeared quarterly at first but this soon became too cumbersome and publication became annual, with a five-year cumulative index. The entries cover sales at principal auction houses in Britain, in several European countries and in the USA. Information about individual books (composite lots are excluded) covers author (and/or illustrator), title (or series), date, plates, usually a word on condition, and any other brief note essential for an adequate description of the book. Entries end with the price fetched, and in many cases the identity of trade buyers. Atlases have always been covered (though autograph material is not), but in recent years, with the growth of interest in cartography, individual maps have a section of their own at the end of each volume.

American Book Prices Current The title of this work does not do justice to its scope: it reports auction prices of autographs, manuscripts and books sold at auction in the USA and Britain, with selective coverage of Germany and the Netherlands and occasional sales in other countries. ABPC has been published annually since 1895; a two-volume index appears every four years. Its intelligent editorship, convenient format and competitive price have endeared it to many British as well as American book dealers.

Jahrbuch der Auktionspreise (yearbook of auction prices) The title of this useful work, comparable to BAR or ABPC, continues '. . . für Bücher, Handschriften und Autographen: Ergebnisse der Auktionen in Deutschland, den Niederländen, Österreich und der Schweiz' (for books, manuscripts and autographs: results of auctions in Germany, Holland, Austria and Switzerland). It has appeared annually since 1950.

French Auction Records These were published in three series: from 1944–56 as *Le*

Summer Ducks, from Audubon's *Birds of America*, 1827 (see page 32).

Guide du Bibliophile et du libraire; from 1966–72, *Catalogue Bibliographique des Ventes Publiques – La Cote Internationale des Livres*; and from 1982, *L'Argus du Livre Ancien et Moderne, Repertoire Bibliographique*, continued as *Catalogue Bibliographiques des Ventes Publiques*.

The earliest systematic book auction records, Gabriel Peignot's *Essai de Curiosités Bibliographiques*, appeared in Paris in 1804.

Audubon, John James (1785–1851)
Born in the West Indies and educated in Paris, Audubon spent the early years of the nineteenth century travelling around America, observing and painting the wild birds and animals that he found there. His observations were to find expression in what Alan Thomas, in *Great Books and Book Collectors*, 1975, called 'the most splendid book ever produced in relation to America, and certainly one of the finest ornithological works ever printed'.

This first work, *The Birds of America*, was issued in 87 parts, consisting of 1065 life-size illustrations, in four double ELEPHANT FOLIO volumes. The original work was priced at $1,000 (then about £180) and found ready subscribers. In 1989 a set of the first edition fetched $3,500,000 at auction. A contemporary reviewer wrote: 'No one can see these splendid drawings and compare them with the ordinary illustrations of natural history, in which animals appear as spiritless as if they had been sitting for their portraits, without admiring his taste and skill.'

The first 10 plates were engraved by Lizars, the rest by Robert Havell. The accompanying text to *The Birds of America* was published separately in 1831–9 in Edinburgh, and in 1839 Audubon brought out *A Synopsis of The Birds of America* – a catalogue of all known species of birds in the American continent north of Mexico.

In 1849 Audubon published (together with the Rev. John Bachman) *The Quadrupeds of North America*, containing 100 colour plates in two volumes. His sons Victor and John assisted in the work's production.

A facsimile reprint of *The Birds of America* was issued in double elephant folio in 1972–3 by Ariel Press in an edition of 1000, and there have been several octavo editions.

Anker, Jean, *Bird Books and Bird Art*, Copenhagen, 1938 (reprinted, New York, 1974).
Chancellor, John, *Audubon: A Biography*, 1978.
Fries, Waldeman H., *The Double Elephant Folio: the Story of Audubon's Birds of America*, Chicago, Illinois, 1974.

Autographs and Manuscripts

Sophie Dupré

Autograph collecting has a long history, but has been pursued with growing interest since the spread of literacy and general education in the mid-nineteenth century. Collections nowadays range from important scholarly and historical material to current television stars. Autograph collecting is a hobby which can appeal to anyone, in any walk

Signed photograph of Prince Edward, later Edward VIII and Prince George, later George VI, 1904.

of life, and collections have been formed by many eminent people. In 1834 the 15-year-old Princess Victoria received a letter from James Madison, the 83-year-old ex-President of the United States: 'It being intimated that an autographic specimen from me . . . would be acceptable for a collection which the Princess Victoria is making; these few lines with my signature . . . are offered for the occasion . . .' The Queen's collection, together with that of Prince Albert, is now preserved at Windsor Castle. By the middle of the nineteenth century autograph albums had become very popular, and in the compact social circles of the time some fascinating collections were assembled. Letters replying to requests for an autograph are probably only second in abundance to replies to dinner invitations!

There are many subject areas in which an autograph collection can be formed, and as with book collecting the choice will depend on individual interests; but a few popular fields can be indicated.

British royalty

A collection of the autographs of British monarchs going back to Henry VIII is still reasonably obtainable but the first two signatures would probably cost more than all the rest. Documents signed by Edward IV, Edward V, Richard III or Henry VII rarely come on to the market; Edward VI and Mary are also extremely rare. Henry VIII and Elizabeth I are regularly offered for sale but they are coveted and expensive. Over the past few years it has become increasingly difficult to find good examples of the Stuart monarchs at reasonable prices, while it is still relatively easy to buy signed documents dating from the Hanoverian kings to the present day; autograph letters of the current royal family are more difficult to find. Royal collections often extend to other members of the family. For example, a collector might seek autographs of all the descendants of Queen Victoria – a search that could extend all over Europe. Historical documents, for example those signed by the ministers to the monarchs, might be a further extension.

British prime ministers

Prime ministers have always been another popular field for collectors, though there is always discussion as to who was the first. Originally the principal minister of the government was the first Lord of the Treasury. Sidney Godolphin (1645–1712), Queen Anne's Lord High Treasurer, is regarded by some as the first Prime Minister, but an autograph collection dating back to him will be considerably harder to achieve than one ranging from the generally accepted first premier, Sir Robert Walpole (1676–1743) to the present day, even though the second Earl of Waldegrave, who held the position for only four days in 1757, may prove elusive.

Prime ministers' autographs are usually quite easy to find and generally inexpensive, and a collection would include some of the best known names in British history: William Pitt, the first Duke of Wellington, Sir Robert Peel, Disraeli, Gladstone, Chamberlain, Lloyd George and Churchill, as well as some of the less remembered names such as Lords Russell and Salisbury. The very early autographs can be more difficult to acquire; the 4th Duke of Devonshire (1720–1764) and John Stuart, 3rd Earl of Bute (1713–1792) are among

Letter from Robert Browning, 1883.

the rarest – but many others are plentiful. It should be emphasized that the more expensive are not necessarily the rarest; Winston Churchill and Disraeli both command high prices, but are in good supply.

Literary autographs

The collecting of autographs of famous writers has a diverse following. There are many book collectors who like to enhance their collections with original autograph material from the authors they favour, having perhaps already acquired all readily available printed material. On the other hand, there are autograph collectors who have no interest at all in books. The literary field is so wide-ranging that it is wise to select a particular period, or a single author, or a small group as a basis for a collection. The price range in this field is immense. A manuscript by Jane Austen or one of the Brontës would command a fortune, but letters by Robert Southey or a later Poet Laureate, John Masefield, can be bought for quite modest sums.

AUTOGRAPHS AND MANUSCRIPTS

Music

This is one of the most expensive, competitive and specialized fields of autograph collecting. Examples of the great names – Beethoven, Mozart, Bach – do occur but the prices are beyond the reach of all but institutions or the very rich. Even less prominent names can command quite impressive prices.

As well as autograph letters from composers, other types of autograph material are available. Musical scores are usually the most expensive, followed by musical quotations,

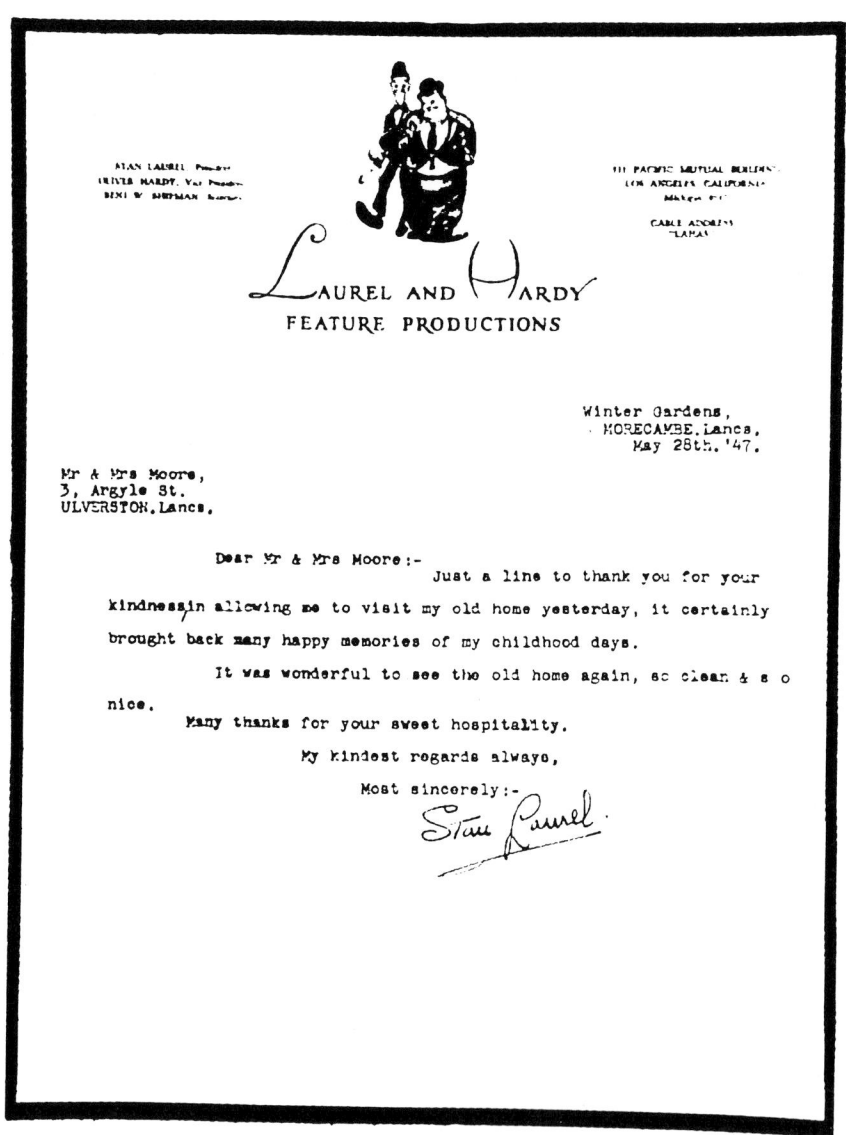

Letter from Stan Laurel (of Laurel and Hardy), 1947.

ideally from the composer's best-known works. A wide variety of ephemera can also be collected: signed photographs and programmes, tickets, menus and other memorabilia.

Art

The autograph letters of Victorian painters are a great deal cheaper than their pictures. A very modest investment can buy a fine letter of Lord Leighton, Sir Edward Poynter or Sir Frank Dicksee; all three were presidents of the Royal Academy and any one of their pictures would be very desirable. It is rather less easy to acquire letters of the artists who were also writers, or leading Pre-Raphaelites such as William Morris, Dante Gabriel Rossetti and Sir Edward Burne-Jones. An interesting collection can be assembled without too much difficulty, but as in all fields the legendary names are expensive to acquire.

The performing arts

This is another popular field. Collectors tend to specialize in one area – theatre, cinema, ballet or perhaps music hall, and often in a particular period. Collections are frequently made up entirely of signed photographs and some collectors look only for a certain type of photograph – 10″ × 8″ or postcard size. It is still possible to find good letters from such famous personalities as Charles Kean, Sarah Siddons, Sir Henry Irving or Dame Ellen Terry; these and others of similar fame can be surprisingly inexpensive. Collectors benefit from the readiness of actors to give out signed photographs. Delightful postcards of music hall stars are plentiful but the reference sources are sketchy and it is often impossible to identify the performer. Unlike film stars, who are immortalized on celluloid, many earlier entertainers have faded from memory and some of those who were once household names, like Marie Lloyd and Vesta Tilley, are little in demand.

Military and naval

Collectors in the military field often specialize in a particular conflict – the Crimean, Napoleonic, Boer, Peninsular or American Civil wars are all energetically searched for. Collectors of this kind will try to assemble letters from as many as possible of the prominent people involved, preferably from the right period and ideally with content relating to particular battles. Others may seek examples of all Napoleon's generals or Nelson's admirals. Those interested in twentieth-century material often concentrate on winners of the Victoria Cross, airmen from the Battle of Britain, or themes of this kind.

Science

Science is an increasingly popular subject area, and one in which there tends to be a discerning influence in significant content; fewer collectors in this field are seeking only the autographs of particular people. However, the major figures – Albert Einstein, Sigmund Freud, Charles Darwin, Marie Curie, Louis Pasteur and others of this eminence – are always keenly sought after. Fine letters from other major scientists, such as Michael

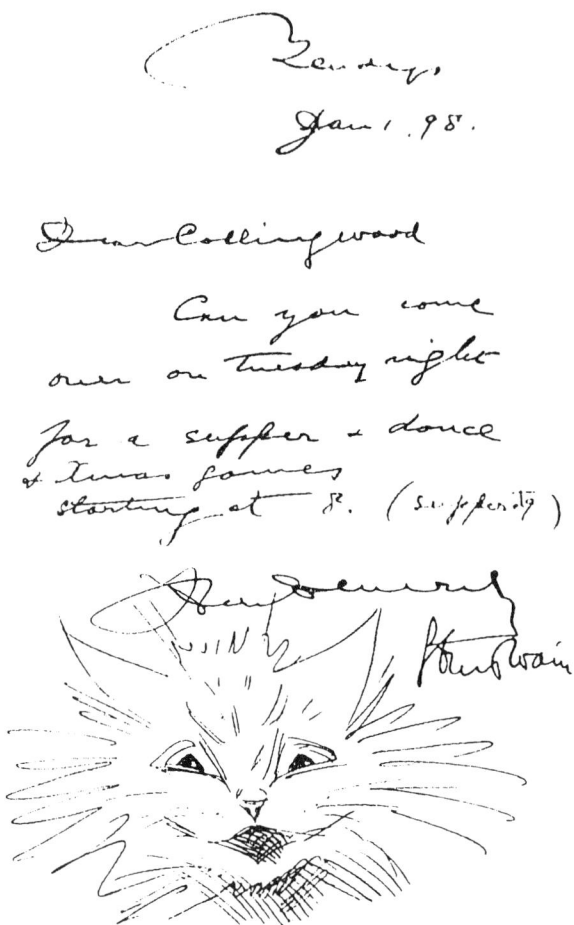

Note from Louis Wain (with sketch of cat), 1898.

Faraday, Sir Humphry Davy or Sir Joseph Hooker are comparatively inexpensive. Twentieth-century science and technology have stimulated new areas of collecting: aviators, Nobel prize winners and astronauts are examples of recent interest.

Exploration and travel

Letters from the great explorers such as Livingstone, Stanley, Baker, Scott, Shackleton and Nansen are keenly sought after, and are becoming increasingly hard to find. The letters that command the highest prices are those in which the conditions and achievements of important expeditions are discussed.

AUTOGRAPHS AND MANUSCRIPTS

Other subjects

A few favoured areas of interest have been mentioned, but the potentialities of autograph collecting are almost without limit. There is, for example, a flourishing market in American presidential material; religious subjects attract some collectors, as does sport, with cricket and golf especially prominent.

Consideration must now be given to some matters that concern all collectors.

Terminology

It may seem hardly necessary to list these terms, but on one occasion a collector of many years standing was heard to ask a dealer, rather sheepishly, 'What exactly is an als?' The standard abbreviations used in dealers' catalogues are as follows: A – Autograph; D – Document; L – Letter; MS (or MSS) – Manuscript; Mus – Musical; N – Note; PC – Postcard; Q – Quotation; S – Signed. Hence an ALS is an autograph letter signed, a TLS is a typed letter signed, and an AMusQS is an autograph musical quotation signed.

Values

As most pieces of autograph material are unique, the question of value is rather more complicated than in the case of antiquarian books. Desirability, rarity and content are the main factors which influence prices but the type of document, date and place all have to be taken into account. The most intriguing letter will be of little value unless the writer inspires interest in some quarter. In some fields, position alone will make a person collectable, though not necessarily valuable: prime ministers, presidents and royalty all fall into this category. In other areas, such as literature and the performing arts, fashion is crucial. At the beginning of the twentieth century Galsworthy was very desirable, but now he is scarcely collected; Nijinsky has suffered a similar fall from grace. Conversely, the popularity of Oscar Wilde and Byron has greatly increased. In topics like science, travel and exploration and sport, achievement is the key feature. The theories and discoveries of figures like Darwin, Curie or Pasteur ensure that they will always be sought after, as does the courage of Livingstone and Scott and, in a different way, of pioneers such as Orville and Wilbur Wright. A certain romanticism often creeps into the equation; for example Czar Nicholas II of Russia and his family are all greatly sought after, as is anything to do with passengers who perished in the Titanic. Given that a letter or document has been written by some interesting correspondent, its content is the next important factor. If a letter has a real historical value, actually adding to the sum of scholarly knowledge about the writer, or giving some new insight into a life, it is obviously going to be worth very much more than one which is simply an example of that person's handwriting. However, although the short 'note of reply' is the least valuable, there are many collectors who particularly want single-sided notes with pretty signatures to frame.

Rarity, needless to say, is extremely important. If a person dies very young, or papers are destroyed, then the few surviving documents acquire a much greater value. Many

AUTOGRAPHS AND MANUSCRIPTS

American collectors are looking for 'Signers' of the Declaration of Independence, and the rarest of these is Button Gwinnett. Outside the autograph field few people would know his name; yet in 1979 a document signed by Gwinnett sold for $100,000 and the price would now be considerably higher. He was killed in a duel in 1777, and a few years later there was an epidemic in Georgia, his home state. It was thought that disease might be carried in letters and thousands were burned, including most of those signed by Gwinnett. Another cause of rarity may be the collecting together of an individual's papers by a library or institution. Anything which then comes on to the market is likely to bring fierce competition among collectors in rivalry with the institution. The relative rarity of manuscript material of Lord Byron is a special case. During the Second World War, the owner of the Paris publishers A. & W. Galignani made an unscheduled visit to his clerk's office on a particularly cold day and found that despite the lack of any sort of fuel, the room was warmed by a blazing fire. On investigation, this was found to have been fed with original manuscripts and letters of Byron and other Galignani authors.

The form and date of a piece can also make a considerable difference to its value. Generally an ALS is the most desirable kind of autograph, but this can depend on the circumstances of the writer. Queen Victoria, for example, signed many thousands of documents during her 64-year reign; each one was genuinely signed (no stamps or autopens then), and they remain relatively easy to find. However, the Queen's autograph letters signed in full are quite scarce, and the price reflects this. It was required by law that the Queen should sign all documents in full, but she signed much of her personal correspondence with initials. Queen Victoria is no exception to the general rule that the more complete the signature the more desirable it is. However, during the first few days of her reign she had not realised that a full signature was required and so the first 12 'Royal Sign Manuals' take the form 'V.R.I.'; it would be difficult to suggest a valuation for one of these. Napoleon signed in many different ways: originally 'Buonaparte' (the earliest and rarest signature); at the age of 27 he dropped the 'u'; at 35 he became Emperor and began to sign 'Napoleon', variously shortened to 'Napole', 'Napol', 'Nap', or 'Np'. All other factors apart, the more letters in his signature, the more valuable the document. An important date or place will obviously increase value – a document signed by Nelson on the day of the Battle of Trafalgar will be more valuable than a similar one signed on another date.

Reference works

Biographical dictionaries are an essential aid for the dealer or collector. In the field of British autographs the most important reference work is the *Dictionary of National Biography*; this is, on the whole, an easy work to use but it lists people under family names and not under titles – Burghley as Cecil, Wellington as Wellesley, Palmerston as Temple. Chambers and Macmillan both publish biographical dictionaries with a world-wide range. Burke's *Landed Gentry* (last published in 1965) and *Debrett's Peerage* can both be useful but are often unexpectedly difficult to follow. The same can be said of Burke's *Royal Families of the World* series, but for royalty collectors or dealers these are nonetheless indispensable. *Who's Who* and *Who Was Who* are useful references for twentieth-century autographs.

Grove's *Dictionary of Music and Musicians* is the most comprehensive work in the music field, but Everyman's *Dictionary of Music* has a good selection of biographies in a convenient format.

Mention should also be made of books concerned specifically with autograph collecting. Ray Rawlins is the author of two works: *Four Hundred Years of British Autographs*, 1970, and *The Guinness Book of Autographs*, 1977. Although these are not infallible – some forgeries and misattributions have crept in – they should not be disregarded as they contain many facsimiles and brief biographies. The Manuscript Society of California's *Autographs and Manuscripts: A Collector's Manual* is an excellent guide, and several American dealers have produced books and pamphlets on the subject.

Facsimiles and forgeries

Inevitably a major concern of collectors and dealers alike is the authenticity of any piece of manuscript material. Genuine 'intending to deceive' forgeries are not the only hazard; there are also facsimiles, secretarial, stamped or printed signatures, and the infamous autopen. It is essential to remove a frame before examining a document as glass makes a facsimile much more difficult to detect.

Among facsimiles that are seen most frequently are those sent out by Winston Churchill. He could not possibly have replied personally to the great number of letters which he received on each birthday, at Christmas and after major parliamentary events. He therefore wrote a single letter and had it excellently reproduced. Although they are skilfully printed, these letters are not at all difficult to detect. The first indication of a facsimile is that it has no greeting but starts immediately with the text. The date is usually only month and year, and the content is always a general 'thank you' which will adequately answer many thousands of letters.

Excited telephone calls offering a valuable Byron letter are familiar to many dealers. The caller is usually (though not always) discouraged by the questions then asked – would it by any chance be a letter about 'The Vampire' to the editor of Galignani's *Messenger*? Is the date 27 April 1819 and the letter written from Venice? The response to these questions is usually an astonished 'How did you guess?' The facsimile of this four-page ALS was issued by the publishers Galignani in all editions of their *Works of Lord Byron*, including the *Suppressed Poems*, from the first edition in 1826. The watermark of the letter is 1823 in the first edition and later in subsequent ones.

There are several other indications that a letter is printed: (1) the ink does not have the shading caused in genuine writing by the strokes overlapping, or by the ink's uneven flow. A facsimile will have an absolutely even look, and sometimes very small white dots can be detected; (2) there is no track from the pen moving over the paper, which should show varying pressure in different places; (3) ink eradicator will not remove printer's ink, but this test should be used with extreme care so as to avoid damage; (4) a facsimile ALS will generally have a typed envelope.

Printed signatures on signed photographs are much easier to detect, as they are printed with the image and are usually quite obvious to the eye. Secretarial signatures are also quite common, especially on signed photographs of film stars. Letters requesting these arrive on the secretary's desk and are often dealt with without reference to the celebrity at all. This was especially prevalent during the golden days of Hollywood; genuine signatures of the major stars are quite rare and often valuable. Stamped signatures occur on both documents and photographs, but they are usually quite easy to recognize.

True forgeries range from the obvious, clumsy attempts of amateurs to the highly professional and almost undetectable deceptions which require the aid of forensic tests to show that they are indeed not genuine. The first indication of a forgery is often that it is 'too good to be true' – this is often because it is *not* true. Although it would be splendid to find a letter from Darwin commenting on the *Origin*, from Wilde on his homosexuality, or from Dickens regarding problems with the plot of *Great Expectations*, the letters usually found are simply declining dinner invitations. When the splendid ones occur they should be looked at with extreme caution.

Forgeries are sometimes betrayed by careless mistakes – a book is mentioned before it was actually written, a letter is dated after the death of the writer, the form of signature is from a later period of the writer's life. It should be noted, however, that heads of state have occasionally signed blank documents which were completed after their death.

Problems of attribution can arise where two people share the same names. There are several cases of famous fathers, such as Charles Dickens or Sir Robert Peel, with a son of the same name, or a grandson, as in the case of Winston Churchill. There are also people who happen to have the same name as a famous contemporary – William Pitt, Robert Walpole, Robert Scott. In the British Royal family the same names are used in generation after generation, and although there is seldom any confusion among the principals of the family, it can become extremely difficult to distinguish between minor members. Dates, addresses and occupations at different times can all provide clues to help ensure that the right person is identified.

Handwriting

Authentication of any document should start with comparison of the handwriting. Samples of correspondence from well-known people can be found in books in major libraries, and original manuscript material can be consulted in such institutions as the British Library and the Bodleian Library. Writing changes during the course of a lifetime, so it is important to find an example from the same period as the piece under study. Handwriting is an almost unconscious activity – the thought is in the composition. Hesitant or shaky writing may indicate that the writer was concentrating on copying a style. Another cause of suspicion may be indications that the pen has been lifted from the paper in an unnatural way, in the middle of words or letters, or that a word has been over-written. Although handwriting varies to some extent, there are always unchanging characteristics – the types of loops and crosses that are used, the flourishes on a signature, and other details of this kind.

Paper

In addition to examination of the handwriting, it is necessary to ensure that the paper is of the expected date and type. Laid paper can be recognized by the grid marks created by the wire frames used in its manufacture, and watermarks, which are common from about 1400, can be dated by means of reference books. Wove paper, which does not have a grid pattern, was used in Europe from the mid-eighteenth century and in America from about 1800. Wood pulp has been in use from the middle of the nineteenth century. Forgers often 'age' paper artificially with tea or coffee, but this produces an uneven result and does not achieve quite the same shade as natural ageing.

Ink

Early inks (prior to 1880) were made of iron gall and are acidic. They are completely permanent and so are not affected by water, but will often have eaten into the paper. Aniline ink was introduced at the end of the nineteenth century and is not permanent in water; but it does not attack the paper. If a small section of writing from a letter supposedly written before the introduction of aniline dyes is tested with a drop of water there will be no ill effect if the piece is genuine.

The autopen

The infamous autopen is a menace to collectors of modern autographs, especially those of American presidents. The original idea dates back a long time. Thomas Jefferson invented and used a mechanical writer which is now in the University of Virginia library. A French inventor, P. M. Durand, invented a machine called the Signo in 1916, which is the precursor of today's machines. The modern device has been in use since the 1960s. The person whose signature is to be reproduced signs a plastic matrix and the machine can then reproduce exactly the same signature any number of times using fountain pen, biro, felt tip or any other writing tool. Each characteristic stroke or pressure point will be identical on each letter or document. Indeed, this is the only way to detect the facsimile as no two genuine signatures are entirely identical. Thus if comparison can be made between two such examples and they are a perfect match, it is likely that the document is machine-signed. In the United States the machine is used widely by public officials. President Kennedy started to make use of an autopen in 1962, although the White House was not prepared to admit to its use for many years. In this country it is less popular, although Christmas cards from the Queen and Prince Philip dated after 1960, and many documents from politicians, are often autopen-signed.

The best safeguard a collector can have against finding himself the less than proud owner of a forgery or facsimile of any sort is to rely on a reputable dealer who will guarantee that the material is genuine. The Manuscript Society keeps a list of dealers who fall into this category.

Provenance

This can be crucially important in authenticating historical documents. In a case like the discredited 'Hitler Diaries', plausible explanations had to be invented for the sudden discovery of the books and for their existence having been previously unsuspected. However, if a letter or document has been in an important collection since it was written, this can be seen as a convincing provenance.

Conserving manuscripts

Preservation is an important consideration for all collectors. If autographs are framed they should be backed with acid-free paper and put into acid-free mounts. If they are modern there is a danger that the ink will fade, and it is wise to use a special glass which filters out most of the ultra-violet light that is the main cause of fading. However, it is more difficult to see the document clearly under screened glass. Like water-colour paintings, autographs should not be exposed to direct sunlight. The ideal way to store unframed autograph material is in acid-free perspex folders, out of the light. This can be a satisfactory way to display a collection if the folders are kept in albums, as the material can be easily viewed, but is protected both from light and from undue handling. However, many people prefer to frame their collections and with the precautions mentioned this presents no problem; but it should be realised that there is some danger of long-term deterioration and a careful eye should be kept on the pieces so that any problems can be dealt with at an early stage.

B

Backstrip
The relationship between the terms 'spine' and 'backstrip' is somewhat equivocal; they are sometimes used interchangeably to describe the back of a book, whether leather-bound, cloth-bound or wrappered; but the word 'backstrip' would seem to be more correctly descriptive of the back of a paper-bound book. There may, however, be some justification for the phrase 'original backstrip laid down' in the description of a leather-bound book that has been re-backed; it may simply serve to indicate that the strip that has been preserved is slightly narrower than the new spine below it.

Baedeker
These small red guides, compact enough to fit comfortably into a greatcoat pocket, have attained an important place in travel literature. Karl Baedeker, who was born into a bookselling family, published his first guide in 1832, reprinting in French a 'Rheinreise' published in 1828 by another firm whose business he had taken over. The first Guide to bear his own name came out in 1849.

Most of the guide books, though not all, were published in German, French and English, with new areas and destinations being added at frequent intervals. After Baedeker's death in 1859 the firm continued under the control of his three sons. By 1939 the series comprised 94 titles, but the war brought the house of Baedeker to an end and many records were lost.

However, the imprint was resuscitated in post-war Germany and, in collaboration with other firms, remains active to this day in the publishing of road books and touring guides.

The slightly humorous view of the earnest German traveller has stalked Baedeker from the beginning. He has even been blamed erroneously for 'I need a room – my postillion has been struck by lightning'. But he did suggest that: 'Oxford is on the whole a more attractive town than Cambridge to the ordinary visitor; and the traveller is therefore recommended to visit Cambridge first or to omit it altogether if he cannot visit both' (*Great Britain*, 1887).

Among the scarcest Baedekers in English are: *Palestine and Syria*, 1876, *Egypt*, 1885, *USA*, 1893, *Canada*, 1894, *Russia*, 1914 (even the reprint of 1971 is sought after), *Madeira*, 1939; and in German *Konstantinopel*, 1905, *Indien*, 1914 and *Dalmatien*, 1929.

The Baedeker guides are often discussed and collected in conjunction with Murray's Guides, a series published only in English. It has been said that the meticulous Baedekers are better to travel with, the more stylish Murrays better to read. The first syllable of 'Baedeker' is pronounced 'Bay' rather than 'By'.

Hinrichsen, Alex, *Baedeker's Reisehandbücher, 1832–1990*, (2nd edn, Bevern, 1991).
Shapero, Bernard, *Baedeker Catalogue*, 1989.

Bagguley, G. T.
Most of the bindings executed by Bagguley's workshop at Newcastle-under-Lyme

were designed by Leon Solon. The bindery perfected the technique of decorating VELLUM bindings with coloured toolings; these were commissioned by the Duchess of Sutherland and named after her. The Sutherland process was patented in 1896.

Bartlett, Roger (1633–1712)

Roger Bartlett worked in London until his bindery was devastated by the Great Fire of 1666. He then returned to his home county, setting up a workshop in Oxford. His many commissions from the University included the binding of a book presented to Cosimo de Medici on his visit to Oxford.

Bartlett's tools, many of leaves, flowers, sprays and wreaths, have been catalogued (see below); his work is much sought after.

Nixon, H. M., 'Roger Bartlett's bookbinding', in *The Library*, March, 1962.

Baskerville, John (1706–75)

Baskerville's standing as one of the greatest British typefounders is unchallenged, but his printing career began late in life, after he had been a letter carver in stone and writing master for some years and had grown prosperous from a successful japanning business established in his native Birmingham. Baskerville's love of lettering led him to set up a press for which he designed type in the style of his predecessor Caslon and which he employed with meticulous attention to layout and presswork. The printed page was immediately pressed between two hot copper plates giving a silky gloss to the paper and to the type. He attached particular importance to simplicity of design, eschewing all superfluous embellishment and allowing the clarity and elegance of the letters to make their own impact.

It was not only type design and layout that preoccupied Baskerville. He experimented with new types of wove paper, made for him at Whatman's mill, and manufactured his own ink. Contemporary printers disapproved of a fellow tradesman who had served no apprenticeship and whose perfectionism militated against financial success; and Baskerville's typography has not escaped some later criticism. But from his Virgil, 1759, onwards, his editions of English writers – Addison, Milton, Congreve – and of classical authors are among the most highly prized of any English press. These books, together with his fine editions of the Bible and of the Book of Common Prayer, represent eighteenth-century English taste at its best.

A large collection of books and ephemera printed by Baskerville is held in Birmingham Public Library.

Barlow, William P., Jnr, *A Baskerville Collection*, The Book Collector, Summer, 1989.
Benton, Josiah Henry, *John Baskerville: Type Founder and Printer, 1706–1775*, Boston, Massachusetts, 1914 (reprinted New York, 1968).
Gaskell, P., *John Baskerville, A Bibliography*, Cambridge, 1959 (corrected and reprinted, Newport Pagnell, 1973).
Pardoe, F., *John Baskerville of Birmingham*, 1975.
Straus, Ralph and Dent, Robert K., *John Baskerville: A Memoir*, Cambridge, 1907.

Baumgarten, John (fl. 1759–82)

John Baumgarten was one of the earliest of the German school of bookbinders who set themselves up in London. He worked with WALTHER and was in touch with other bookbinders of German extraction such as HERING, KALTHOEBER and CHARLES LEWIS. Baumgarten's designs were often in the rococo style though never over-elaborate. He is also believed to have introduced tree-marbling on calf into England. He signed his bindings only with initials, if at all.

Baxter, George (1804–67)

In 1835 Baxter patented a form of colour printing using a mixed method of intaglio and relief combined with the use of superior oil-based inks. He licensed his invention to other printers, but their work did not always achieve his own combination of delicacy and dramatic quality. Most Baxter prints bear the identification 'printed in oil colours by George Baxter, patentee'. Books illustrated with Baxter prints include his own *Pictorial Album*, 1837 and Nicolas's *History of the Order of Knighthood*, 1842; but the majority carry only a frontispiece and many are small pocketbooks and diaries. The separate prints, e.g. *Gems of the Exhibition*, 1854, are now much collected.

Etheridge, Ernest, *Baxter Prints: Guide to the Collection*, 1930.
Lewis, C. T. Courtney, *The Picture Printer of the Nineteenth Century: George Baxter, 1804–67*, 1911.
—— *The Baxter Book*, 1919.
—— *George Baxter, the Picture Printer*, 1924.
—— *The Story of Picture Printing in England During the Nineteenth Century*, 1928.
Mitzman, Max E., *George Baxter and the Baxter Prints*, 1978.

Bay Psalm Book

The first book printed in what is now the United States of America[1] was a metrical translation of the Psalms, issued in 1640, twenty years after the landing of the Pilgrim Fathers, in Cambridge, Massachusetts. Eleven copies are known to exist; only two are in private hands, and only three can be described as perfect. The case of the Yale *Bay Psalm Book* rocked the American antiquarian book world when Rosenbach of New York bought a copy of the book for Yale in 1947 for $151,000, then the highest price ever paid for a printed book at auction. Yale was unable to raise the full amount, so Rosenbach himself put up the outstanding sum, making it known that he expected 'no remuneration'. By this he meant 'no commission', but Yale assumed that he expected no repayment and the distinguished American bookseller found himself $50,000 out of pocket.

Haraszti, Zoltan, *The Enigma of the Bay Psalm Book*, Chicago, Illinois, 1956.

Bedford, Francis (1799–1883)

Francis Bedford was for some years apprentice, and then journeyman, to the distinguished London bookbinder Charles Lewis, assuming the management of the business on Lewis's death. He opened his own bindery in 1851.

Bedford's work was superbly executed, but most of his designs owed much to the style of earlier binders. He set great store by the preservation of tall copies, refusing to trim margins unnecessarily. His patron, the Duke of Portland, encouraged him to study the work of the great French binders of the day, and although he admired them he 'did not see why that which was done by ten fingers in France should not be as well done in England'.

The French influence greatly strengthened Bedford's reputation and he successfully copied the styles of Grolier, Maioli and others. He was highly skilled in the art of what would now be termed 'paper restoration'.

Bénézit

Emmanuel Bénézit's *Dictionnaire Critique et Documentaire des Peintres, Sculpteurs, Dessinateurs et Graveurs . . .* first appeared

---

[1] The first book to be printed on the American continent appeared in Mexico in c.1539.

between 1911 and 1923. It contains critical biographies of a wide variety of artists, as well as listing works in public collections, auction prices, and details of catalogues and other reference works. No English equivalent exists. The latest edition, in ten volumes, appeared in Paris in 1976.

Bentley, Richard (1794–1871)

An enterprising figure in the publishing world of Victorian England, Bentley secured Charles Dickens in 1837 as editor of his new magazine *Bentley's Miscellany*; the contract was to include Dickens's next two novels. *Oliver Twist* was duly published by Bentley in 1837–8, but the partnership ended and the next novel, *Barnaby Rudge*, was published by Chapman & Hall in 1841. The *Miscellany*, however, continued with William Harrison Ainsworth as editor.

Bentley's publication of the 127-volume series *Standard Novels* from 1831–54 proved as successful as the *Miscellany*. It introduced to an increasingly literate public a wide range of inexpensive books, attractively produced and easy to read.

Sadleir, Michael, *Bentley's Standard Novel Series. Its History and Achievements*, 1932.
Gettman, R. A., *A Victorian Publisher, A Study of the Bentley Papers*, Cambridge, 1960.

Besterman, Theodore (1904–1976)

Born in Poland, but brought up and educated in Britain, Besterman was for most of his life engaged in librarianship and bibliography. His involvement in international studies included work for UNESCO's Department for the Exchange of Information, the International Congress on the Enlightenment, and the Academies of Dijon, Lyons and Marseilles.

Besterman's massive bibliographical work (the full title is *A World Bibliography of Bibliographies and of Bibliographic Catalogues, Calendars, Abstracts, Digests, Indexes and the like*) first appeared in 1939. It was reprinted in 1947, 1955 and finally in 1965 in Lausanne, revised and greatly enlarged throughout.

The work is arranged alphabetically under subjects and authors. Country headings have subject divisions (Australia, for example, covers (1) bibliographies, (2) general, (3) cartography and topography, (4) law, (5) official publications, (6) South Australia and (7) Western Australia). The works within each category are listed chronologically with date and place of publication, number of entries and relevant notes. In his preface to the fourth edition, Besterman promises it will be the last. He adds that the work was 'undertaken entirely single-handed, without any kind of subsidy, in his own time and at his own risk'. He was always conscious of his enormous investment of time and resources in *A World Bibliography* . . . and dealt abrasively with the mildest suggestion for its improvement. It runs to five volumes and covers 117,000 works. It includes all works in western languages and covers bibliographies of manuscripts, letters, documents and deeds, though not catalogues of book sales, works of art or libraries. It would be unjust to deny the usefulness of this encyclopaedic and generally accurate work of reference; but it was always cumbersome and has inevitably become out-of-date.

The Library Association awards an annual Besterman Medal for the best bibliographical work of the year.

Bestiary

The medieval bestiary has its origins in the ancient Greek text of The Naturalist (*Physiologus*) which dates from the second century AD and links early tales and myths of birds and animals with Christian teachings. Early illustrated manuscripts in Latin and in the vernacular draw on versions from many lands, interpreting the legends in terms of their effect on ethical behaviour.

The printed texts of manuscript bestiaries were often enlarged with theological and scientific material. Modern bestiaries, while holding to the tradition of mythical beasts with moral undertones, use contemporary means of expression in art and literature. David Day's *A Tolkien Bestiary* (New York, 1979), is a case in point.

James, M. R., *The Bestiary*, Oxford, 1928.
McCulloch, Florence, *Medieval Latin and French Bestiaries*, Chapel Hill, North Carolina, 1960 (revised, 1962).
Clark, Willene B., McMunn, Meradith T. (eds), *Beasts and Birds of the Middle Ages*, Philadelphia, Pennsylvania, 1989 (contains a good bibliography of recent studies).

LE BESTIAIRE
OU CORTÈGE D'ORPHÉE
GUILLAUME APOLLINAIRE / RAOUL DUFY

A modern Bestiary illustrated by Dufy

Bewick, Thomas (1753–1828)
A native of Northumberland, Bewick was apprenticed to a Newcastle engraver, Ralph Beilby. Here he worked at first mainly on metal but later started to experiment with fine engraving on wood. In 1777 he became Beilby's partner and received commissions for cuts for chapbooks and children's stories. His use of the cross cut of a wooden block, instead of the flat grain, employing a graver rather than a knife, achieved an effect which brought him immediate popularity.

The woodcuts of the early years of printing had been crude black-and-white line engravings. Bewick developed in his work a softer shaded tone; he called it 'colour on the block'. Attempts had been made to achieve such variation of line on wood by cross-hatching but the effect was harsh. Bewick worked with a variety of tools on boxwood rather than pear, apple or beech; and his imaginative practice of including the whole block in his design (edges, corners and background) gave his work the delicacy and charm of a watercolour painting.

While still engaged in Beilby's workshop on children's books, cards, ballads and other ephemera, Bewick began to set aside drawings and ideas for more ambitious work. In 1779 he published an edition of Gay's *Fables*, and its success encouraged him to embark on his major works on animals and birds. *The General History of Quadrupeds* came out in 1790, followed seven years later by the *Land Birds* volume of *The History of British Birds* and in 1804 by the *Water Birds*. Bewick's love of nature and the countryside lends special distinction to his vignettes and to the background of his illustrations. He insisted on drawing from life whenever possible, greatly prolonging the production of the books but

achieving a charm and natural beauty seldom previously found in books of this kind. Many of the vignettes embody moral teaching for younger readers; others, with appealing candour, depict animals or children in postures not often illustrated in popular literature!

Other books illustrated by Bewick, alone or with his brother John, include poems by Goldsmith and Parnell, Bloomfield and Somerville; fables by Gay and Aesop, and many minor pieces. Bewick's birthplace, Cherryburn in Northumberland, is now a museum displaying examples of his work, and a Thomas Bewick Society has been established for study and research.

Bain, Iain, *Thomas Bewick: an Illustrated Record of his Life and Work*, Newcastle, 1979.
——— *The Watercolours and Drawings of Thomas Bewick and his Workshop Apprentices*, 1981.
Boyd, Julia, *Bewick Gleanings*, Newcastle, 1886.
Dobson, Austin (ed.), *A Memoir of Thomas Bewick Written by Himself*, 1887 (new edn, 1975, edited by Iain Bain).
Doncaster, Susan, *Some Notes on Bewick's Trade Blocks*, Newcastle, 1980.
Roscoe, S., *Thomas Bewick – A Bibliography Raisonné of Editions of the General History of Quadrupeds, the History of British Birds and the Fables of Aesop, issued in his lifetime*, 1953 (reprinted, 1973).

Stone, Reynolds, *Wood Engravings of Thomas Bewick*, 1953.
Thomson, D. C., *The Life and Works of Thomas Bewick*, 1953.

Bibles

The commanding place of the Bible in book history was established in the earliest days of printing, with more than 90 Latin and Greek editions ranking as incunables and with a succession of influential translations following in the first part of the sixteenth century. Much has been written about these early continental editions, but special mention may be made of the excellent account in Alan Thomas's chapter on the Bible in his *Great Books and Book Collectors*, 1975. Turning then to the English versions, he remarks, 'When we consider the fundamental place that the Bible has held in English life, the innumerable editions published, and the sincere study of the scriptures by so large a part of the people, it comes as a surprise to realize that the first edition in English was printed long after the vernacular translations in other countries'. There follow notable studies of the Tyndale Bible, Cologne and Worms, 1525, 1526; the Coverdale Bible, (probably) Marburg, 1535; 'Matthew's Bible', Antwerp, 1537; Henry VIII's Great Bible, 1539; the Geneva, or 'Breeches' Bible, 1560 (thought to have been read by Shakespeare and Bunyan); the Bishop's Bible, 1568; and the Authorised Version, 1611.

Alan Thomas was one of the relatively few antiquarian booksellers of recent times in whose catalogues early Bibles were always prominent, and several fine examples figured appropriately in the exhibition accompanying the memorial meeting at Lambeth Palace Library following his death in 1992. But if few booksellers nowadays encounter these historic versions, the

Bible has an assured place on various shelves. The later translations, not least the Revised Version, 1881–95, and the New English Bible, 1961, 1970, are, like their forerunners, an integral part of English literature. Baskett, BASKERVILLE, COBDEN-SANDERSON, BRUCE ROGERS and other fine printers have brought their skills to notable editions; the illustrators of the Testaments, and of their individual books, have included outstanding artists of each generation, from Cranach to Chagall, and the Bible has been bound by many excellent craftsmen. In most bookshops and catalogues, Bibles will accordingly be found in company with other books of similar period or distinction. Every bookseller with a general secondhand stock will hope, too, to have on hand sound octavo editions to meet the constant demand from those who wish to read the Bible or to give it to others to read, though the large and heavy 'family' volumes of the nineteenth century find little favour in modern homes. As to the multiplicity of versions, A. Edward Newton ends a graceful essay on the subject with the words of a young curate to his congregation: 'If the King James Version was good enough for St Paul, it is good enough for me.'

Cambridge History of the Bible, 1963–70.
Darlow, T. H. and Moule, H. F., *Historical Catalogue of the Printed Editions of Holy Scripture*, 4 vols, 1903–77.
Herbert, A. S., *Historical Catalogue of Printed Editions of the English Bible 1525–1961*, 1968 (a revised edition of the English part only of Darlow and Moule).

Bibliographical Society

The Society was founded in 1892 under the presidency of W. A. Copinger. It exists to promote bibliographical research through meetings, lectures and scholarly publications. Its quarterly journal, *The Library*, publishes new work on manuscripts and printed books and reviews books on similar subjects, including printing and publishing history. The Society was responsible for the spread of bibliography as a scholarly discipline, as it is understood today. Its major task has been the revision of the SHORT-TITLE CATALOGUE, but it has published many other works of bibliographical importance.

Its centenary in 1992 was marked by the launching of an appeal to fund further bibliographical research, and by a special exhibition at the ABA's June book fair.

Bibliography

H. R. Woudhuysen

I

Traditionally, bibliography is the study of books as material objects. While it has to a certain extent moved away from the study of manuscripts (particularly medieval manuscripts), yielding its place to codicology, it has become usual to accept that bibliography is concerned with any objects, such as maps, inscriptions or playing cards, which use systems of signs to convey meaning. If bibliography cannot be said to be an exact science, as some writers have claimed, it is at least a method, a way of looking at books. Although bibliographers, notoriously, fail to agree about what the subject is, they are more often inclined to agree about what they do. Essentially there are five branches of the subject which can be broadly distinguished. The first two are perhaps of most immediate importance to bookdealers and collectors, but it would be unfortunate for them to think that the last three are irrelevant to their interests.

For most people a bibliography is a list of books, journals or manuscripts. The list may be organized in several ways, for example by author, by subject matter, by date or by place of publication. This sort of bibliography, known as enumerative bibliography, although extremely useful in providing an outline map of knowledge, is essentially uncritical; it tells the user little about the recorded items themselves. For example, most enumerative bibliographies do not explain how and why individual copies of the same book might differ, or, in a case where two editions of a book were published in the same year, which came first, or how many pages or plates a book should contain.

A second sort of bibliography tries to come up with a way of describing printed books which allows all copies of a book to be compared against an ideal, as it were 'objective' copy, of it. Descriptive bibliography is concerned with this problem of, first, how to distinguish between different editions, impressions, issues, variants and states of a book and, second, how to describe each one so that the description can be applied to every copy of it.

Outside these two varieties of bibliographical practice (which are outlined in more detail below), some bibliographers, mostly academics, are concerned with three more types of project. The first is known as analytical bibliography and seeks to establish a book's physical history. It begins by considering the nature of the copy from which it was set, goes on to determine whether that copy was cast off, how many compositors were employed in setting the text, in what order the sheets were imposed and printed off, what if any proof correction there was, and so on. At its most detailed, it will consider the spelling practice and typographic habits of identified compositors, the history of individual pieces of type and, by examining the damage which they sustain while in use, chart their appearance in the book's printing and so help to reconstruct the history of its production.

Most academic bibliographers inhabit departments of literature in universities and are chiefly concerned with the study of the transmission of literary texts. The aim of their study is either to shed biographical or critical light on the development of a writer's mind through an examination of the transmission of his texts, or to edit one or more of those texts. Editors use bibliography to locate texts by an author and to establish which of them the author actually wrote. By examining the transcribing or the individual printing history of particular copies of a book and by collating one text against another, they try to establish the history of the work's textual transmission. Usually they draw up a stemma which is meant to show the genealogical descent of texts from the author's 'original'. They then determine which text they are going to print and may collate several copies to locate press variants in it. They will try to purge their copy-text of errors by simple corrections, detected by a knowledge of habitual printing house errors, by consulting other editions or by emendation. Bearing in mind their audience and the publisher's demands, editors have to decide how their edition is going to be treated in terms of whether it should be printed in old or modern spelling, how and where textual variants should be recorded and how and where it should be annotated.

There is a final and growing group of bibliographers, again mostly academics, who may be found in almost any university department. They are concerned with the book as a cultural artefact and with its influence on society. In their view a subject is made up of the books which deal with it and the books must be studied not just from the point of view of their contents but in terms of their printing and publishing histories, their reception, circulation, use and influence; history becomes book history. This sociological approach to bibliographical practice can be applied not just to the traditional fields of literature, history and the arts, but also to mathematics, the sciences and law. It attaches great importance to the context in which books are written and printed, to the methods by which they are published and distributed and to their readerships. Book history is concerned with the reproduction of texts in general by handwritten, mechanical or electronic means and has, perhaps, a tendency to find all books, however intellectually or imaginatively thin, of cultural significance.

In its present form, book history is a relatively new branch of bibliography, but it is inevitably connected with the older, historical study of books. Bibliographers had always concerned themselves with drawing up lists of books and with describing the historical circumstances under which some books were printed and published. Almost exclusively these early bibliographers worked on the study of incunabula, their intention being to produce a list of all books printed before 1501 and to establish who invented the art and how it spread throughout Europe. The motives for this sort of work were a mixture of the antiquarian, the nationalistic and the aesthetic; although early printed books, especially the first editions of the classics, had long been collected, their textual importance was not much considered. By their nature incunabula pose particular problems because they may have no statement of where they were printed, by whom or when. Assigning them places, printers and dates, where they had none, led scholars to the study of the distinctive types in which they were set.

Although written to a consistent formula, descriptions of incunabula, however, tended to be only of the copy or copies held by one owner; other copies elsewhere might differ in many different ways. Bibliographers turned their attention to this problem in order to establish a standard way of describing books. Descriptive bibliography has evolved from being a statement of a book's author, title, place of publication and date, with perhaps a mention of its size and the number of pages it contains, to a highly detailed and comprehensive statement of its physical make-up. The amount of information which a bibliographical description contains may vary from a few lines to several pages of detailed and precise notes covering a wide range of information. The essential requirement of a descriptive bibliography is that there should be consistency between entries – that each description should follow the format which has been established and that, where possible, the same kinds of information should appear in all entries.

For books produced during the hand-press period (that is, before about 1800), most descriptive bibliographies will include transcriptions and/or facsimiles of title-pages and, where they exist, of colophons or imprints, an indication of the book's format, a formula of collation, indicating how the sheets of which it is made up are folded and signed and an account of its pagination, especially if it is irregular. They will describe the order and contents of the book, paying particular attention to its preliminary and any blank pages, note the title which occurs at the beginning or head of the text, the running titles which occur on the top of the pages of each opening, with any variants, check the catchwords at the foot of pages against the text at the beginning of the next page, again noting any discrepancies, and list press figures, where these occur. Some bibliographers will identify the type or types in which a book is set, giving a standard measurement such as how many millimetres 20 lines fill, and note the occurrence of ornaments and plates. The paper on which the book has been printed may sometimes be recorded and any watermarks and countermarks described; work on the analysis of ink used in a book's printing is still at an early stage and rarely included in descriptive bibliographies.

Standards of bibliographical description vary a great deal. Many of the features of descriptions of books from the hand-press period will find their place in a modern bibliography, but formulas of collation tend to be omitted, running-titles and catchwords (where they exist) ignored and details of type often passed over. Far more attention is paid to the book's binding, any advertisements it may contain, and where these are available from printer's or publisher's records, details of the book's publication history, such as date of publication, price and so on. Bibliographers pay a great deal of attention to the book's binding, including in recent times its dust-wrapper and edges, specifying the colours used in them and the position of any words, numbers or ornaments they may contain. Both sorts of bibliographies sometimes contain lists of the copies which have been examined to produce the description and their location. Some may go beyond this and try to compile a census of all known extant copies as well as those listed in booksellers', auctioneers', private and public library catalogues; the information derived from presentation and association copies, or more generally from other records of ownership, especially contemporary bindings, may be particularly valuable.

These sorts of author bibliographies are usually arranged chronologically, placing the primary texts first, followed in varying order by translations, adaptations, contributions to other books and periodicals, musical versions and non-book forms such as gramophone records, films and so on. Not all of these items will be described to the same standard and if they include details of secondary materials (books and articles about the author), these may appear in a very abbreviated form. A few bibliographies will include details of manuscripts, proofs, and letters and provide accounts of books an author has owned. Bibliographies of this kind usually distinguish the items which they describe by a system of letters and numbers and may add references of a similar kind to other bibliographies in which the book is listed.

Most booksellers and collectors will use bibliographies mainly to identify the book which they own, to give it a shorthand reference and to check that it is complete or whether it varies in any way from the published description. To understand more about the part the book played in the work's textual transmission they may have to resort to analytical bibliography, or to consult published editions of the work, or to consider the part it plays in the history of the book more generally.

II

The foundations of modern bibliography can be traced to the work of Henry Bradshaw (1831–86) at Cambridge University Library, where he began the detailed study of type in incunabula. His work and methods were followed by Robert Proctor (1868–1903) at the British Museum who began to compile indexes of books printed before 1520 in the Museum and at Oxford, arranged according to countries, towns and presses. This work was the foundation of the British Museum's great catalogue of incunabula, which was begun under the direction of A. W. Pollard (1859–1944). Pollard was interested in early printed books, but he also had a special concern for Shakespearian bibliography and worked on the problems posed by the early quartos and the First Folio. In this research he was assisted by the most prominent bibliographer of the century, W. W. Greg (1875–1959). At Trinity College, Cambridge, in the 1890s Greg had discussed bibliographical problems with R. B. McKerrow (1872–1940) and in their subsequent work they paid particular attention to the writings of Shakespeare and his contemporaries.

McKerrow's first achievement was to produce, between 1904 and 1910, a fully annotated, five-volume, old-spelling edition of the writings of the Elizabethan pamphleteer Thomas Nashe, according to strict bibliographical and editorial principles. It set a high standard for future editors of literary texts and led him to compile the first manual of modern bibliographical practice, *An Introduction to Bibliography for Literary Students* (1927). The *New Introduction to Bibliography* by Philip Gaskell (1972) incorporates modern research into the subject and describes book production in the post hand-press period. Having mastered Elizabethan palaeography, Greg turned his formidable intelligence to the bibliographical and textual problems posed by early dramatic works, editing plays for the Malone Society and beginning to compile his four-volume *A Bibliography of the English Printed Drama to the Restoration* (1939–59). This work encouraged him to write important accounts of the nature of bibliography and the theory of editing, particularly as applied to the choice of a copy text, in addition to many articles dealing with analytical points arising out of his study of early dramatic texts.

These articles found a natural home in the journal *The Library*, which was taken over by the (London) Bibliographical Society in 1919. The Society had been founded in 1892 to promote bibliographical studies and its Honorary Secretary from 1893 to 1934 was A. W. Pollard, who was succeeded by McKerrow. It was Pollard who initiated the *Short-Title Catalogue of English Books 1475–1640*, which was published in 1926 (revised edition in three volumes 1976–91). Its publication initiated the succeeding volumes covering 1641–1700, begun by Donald G. Wing, and finally the eighteenth-century and nineteenth-century short-title catalogues. A Bibliographical Society had been founded at Edinburgh in 1890, and subsequently similar societies were established at Oxford in 1922 and Cambridge in 1949. These societies issued specialized publications and, with the foundation of *The Book Collector* in 1952, they all provided an outlet for bibliographical research. Commercial publishers issued detailed bibliographies of individual authors by such collectors and scholars as Sir Geoffrey Keynes (1887–1982). A series devoted to describing the works of particular authors, known as the Soho Bibliographies, was set up by Rupert Hart-Davis. Larger, enumerative projects, such as *The Cambridge Bibliography of English Literature*, edited by F. W. Bateson, appeared in four volumes from Cambridge University Press in 1940. (A supplementary volume was produced in 1957 and the whole work was revised as *The New Cambridge Bibliography of English Literature* in five volumes published between 1969 and 1977.)

In America bibliographical studies have been particularly associated with the work of Fredson T. Bowers (1905–91) who published his seminal work *Principles of Bibliographical Description* in 1949 and edited the important journal *Studies in Bibliography* from 1948–9. As well as being the leading theoretical writer on editing and bibliographical method, Bowers attracted many followers and was involved in the production of numerous scholarly editions. In addition to *Studies in Bibliography* the other most important bibliographical journal in the USA is *Papers of the Bibliographical Society of America*, founded in 1904.

Following the example of Bowers's work, much American scholarship has been concerned with analytical bibliography, the outstanding example being Charlton Hinman's two-volume *The Printing and Proof-reading of the First Folio of Shakespeare*, 1963. The prominence given to this sort of work has to a certain extent yielded to the growing interest in the history of the book. One of the most important works which promoted this field of study is Lucien Febvre and H.-J. Martin's *L'Apparition du Livre*, 1958, but more recent works such as Elizabeth L. Eisenstein's *The Printing Press as Agent of Change*, two volumes, 1979, have done much to turn bibliographers towards a larger study of the role of books in society. Some of the findings of analytical bibliography have also been challenged by comparing what bibliographers believe happened when books went through the press with what surviving records actually reveal about printing practices. The chief proponent of this approach is D. F. McKenzie (born 1931) who has made a detailed study of the early archives of Cambridge University Press and has put forward a theory relating to *Bibliography and the Sociology of Texts*, 1986, which attempts to link the traditional concerns of the subject with modern literary theory.

Although the history of the book has become a leading project for bibliographers, more traditional forms of bibliographical research have been given a new impetus by electronic publishing. Work on the Eighteenth Century and Incunabula Short-Title Catalogues (ESTC and ISTC) suggests that the traditional, enumerative interests of bibliographers have by no means disappeared.

Bibliomania

It would be hard to improve on JOHN CARTER's definition of a bibliomaniac as 'a book-collector with a slightly wild look in his eye'; but those who wish to explore the subject fully should turn to THOMAS FROGNALL DIBDIN's *Bibliomania*, 1809, or Holbrook Jackson's *The Anatomy of Bibliomania*, two volumes, 1930. The latter is a cheerful but scholarly book modelled on Burton's *Anatomy of Melancholy*. A few chapter headings will convey its flavour: 'Doting Without Reading', 'Bibliopegic Dandyism', 'Of Letter Ferrets and Book Sots', 'Bibliobacity With a Digression of Ecstasy', 'Reading at the Toilet', 'How the Bookworm Discovered America', 'Reading many Books at once', and 'Men who become Books: Biblianthropus Defined'. There is no known cure.

Bibliophobia

The fear of books has an unfortunate tendency, as many collectors will testify, to flourish in the same households as bibliomania; cynical commentators might suggest that the latter encourages the former. The best general introduction remains DIBDIN's *Bibliophobia: Remarks on the Present Languid and Depressed State of Literature and the Book Trade,* in a letter addressed to the author of *Bibliomania,* published in 1832 under the pseudonym of Mercurius Rusticus. This entertaining book was based on close observation of the market: Dibdin traces a single copy of Sweynheim and Pannartz's vellum *Livy,* 1469, through three auctions, the Edward sale of 1815 (£903), the Sykes sale of 1824 (£472.10s) and the Dent sale of 1827 (£262.10s). He blames the slump on the twin evils of cholera and the Reform Bill: contemporary parallels may be imagined.

The bookseller of today may be comforted by the topicality of many of Dibdin's remarks, which help to emphasize the cyclical nature of recession: and he cannot but applaud the principles of the collector John Rennie, as quoted by Dibdin – 'I am upon good terms with all the booksellers, and there is one thing for which they *ought* to like me – I never go to a *Sale* for any thing that I can get at a *shop*.'

Binders' tickets

Nineteenth-century trade edition binders' signatures, or binders' tickets came into use with the general acceptance of CLOTH as a binding material after about 1830. LEATHER bound books often carry the binder's name on the turn-down of the binding; on cloth books early signatures normally took the form of a printed or embossed stamp to the front END-PAPER but, after about 1840, the use of stamps in a variety of shapes and often self-adhesive, placed in the bottom left-hand corner of the rear pastedown, became common. Douglas Ball, in *Victorian Publishers' Bindings,* 1985, gives the most detailed listing so far. He identifies 104 firms in Great Britain, the majority in London, with stamps ranging from c.1829 to c.1890, the hey-day being the 1850–1870s. Many firms used tickets which varied in shape, colour and text at different periods and an attempt is made at classification based on the dated title pages of copies seen or reliably recorded by others. From this, some guide to the priority of different bindings on the same book with the same dated title page could be made, though many questions remain to be answered. For instance, why do some firms appear to use different tickets on the same book with the same date and binding? Was this because old sheets were bound up at a later date as demand grew? Why do only some copies of an apparently identical book with the original end-papers have tickets? What occasioned the change of design of the tickets if the name and address of the firm remain constant? Was it just whim or fashion? At present the Victoria and Albert Museum Library and the British Museum Prints and Drawings Department are recording the binders' tickets in two collections of books in original cloth of the period. With Douglas Ball's listing as a common base, and the copious notes he built up over the years, some sound conclusions can now perhaps be drawn. Certainly much research has yet to be done on these small clues to nineteenth-century trade practices. Booksellers who trouble to include the recording of the binders' tickets when cataloguing (even with only the name of the firm rather than the actual Ball variant number) will be performing a valuable service.

Birdsall and Son of Northampton
William Birdsall set up the family bindery in Northampton in 1792 (he was a freeman of the borough) and the firm was carried on by members of the family until 1961. Birdsall was among the first to offer a cheap method of binding books for libraries, and his 'Stronghold' patent was successfully used for mechanized binding.

The bindery employed a very large workforce and the family were always open to new ideas. Although they seldom produced bindings of the highest distinction, their work was always of excellent quality. When the firm was closed their large collection of tools went to the University of Toronto. After the death of Anthony Birdsall in 1982, books which had remained in the possession of the family were sold at Sotheby's.

A. & C. Black colour books
The distinctive decorative covers and attractive colour illustrations of the A. & C. Black colour books (Twenty Shilling Series) have secured for them a unique place in the affections of book collectors.

The first colour book in the series, *War Impressions*, was written and illustrated by Mortimer Menpes and published in 1901. It appeared in both trade and limited editions, and employed Carl Hentschel's three-colour process, an effective and inexpensive method of reproducing the subdued tones of water-colour painting. Adam Rimmer Black and W. W. Callender, the partners in the old Edinburgh publishing firm, whose founder, the first Adam, had been apprenticed to James Lackington in London at the end of the eighteenth century, were encouraged by the success of *War Impressions* to produce further books in the series. The next few titles, *Japan*, *World's Children*, *World Pictures* and *Durbar* all involved Menpes, often with his daughter Dorothy, but the list of artists soon expanded to include John Fulleylove, Helen Allingham, Warwick Goble, Sutton Palmer, Ella Du Cane, Rose Barton and many more. There are 92 volumes in the Twenty Shilling Series and many more with fewer illustrations were published at a lower price. In addition to travel and topography, the subjects include gardens, history, art, religion and costume. There are also separate series on 'Motor Routes', 'People', 'Beautiful Britain', and 'Watercolours'; and also books for children and a 'popular' series in plain blue cloth.

Many A. & C. Black titles were reprinted from time to time up to the Second World War. The standard of production was high, although the plates tend in time to loosen and become frayed. The value of fine copies has increased steadily as collectors have come to appreciate the merits of the series.

Inman, Colin, *The A. & C. Black Colour Books, A Collector's Guide and Bibliography, 1900–1930*, 1990.

Blackmer, Henry
The Blackmer collection of books on Greece, Turkey and the Levant included fine colour-plate travel and topography, books on costume, art and archaeology from the sixteenth to the nineteenth centuries, and a large number of maps, prints and original paintings.

Harry Blackmer was born and educated in America, but in 1963 he made his home in Athens where he could indulge his deep interest in the Ottoman Empire and the

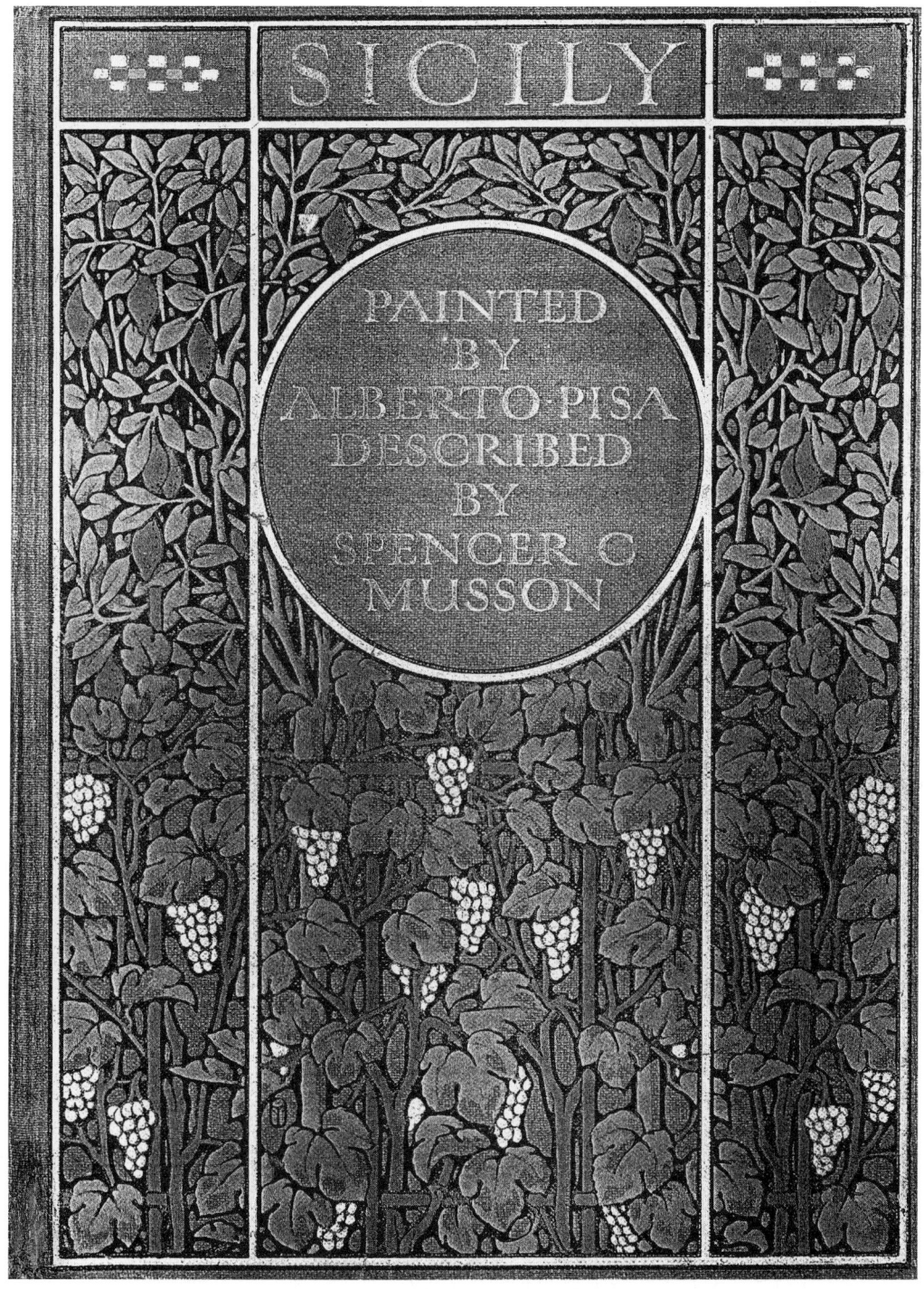

A typical A. & C. Black cover in the Twenty Shilling Series

changing face of the Levant. After his death in 1988 the collection was sold in London by Sotheby's, and Maggs Bros published the catalogue of the library in a limited edition of 300 copies. The Blackmer sale catalogue is now an important source of reference for books on the Levant.

Black Sun Press

Harry Crosby, nephew and godson of the American banker John Pierpont Morgan, began what later became the Black Sun Press with his wife (who wrote under the name Caresse Crosby) in Paris in 1925. The Press operated on a small scale, producing only the Crosbys' own work, until 1928, when it took its familiar name and expanded rapidly. After Harry Crosby's suicide in 1929, his widow continued the Press, and introduced a series of cheap paperback reprints of modern literature – the 'Crosby Continental Editions', much in the style of Tauchnitz. However, by 1932 the Press had run out of money, and no further books were issued from Paris, although Caresse Crosby published books elsewhere under the Black Sun imprint at irregular intervals between 1936 and the early 1950s.

Much the most prolific of the Parisian expatriate private presses, it is hard to single out highlights from the Press: authors published include Hart Crane, René Crevel, James Joyce and Ezra Pound. The press's colophons are notoriously unreliable; Minkoff's *Bibliography* should always be consulted.

Beach, Sylvia, *Shakespeare and Company*, New York, 1959.
Cunard, Nancy, *These Were the Hours*, 1969.
Ford, Hugh, *Published in Paris: American and British Writers, Printers and Publishers in Paris, 1920–1939*, New York, 1975.
McAlmon, Robert, *Being Geniuses Together*, 1938; revised, with supplementary chapters, by Kay Boyle, New York, 1968.
Minkoff, George R., *A Bibliography of the Black Sun Press*, Great Neck, New York, 1970.
Wolff, Geoffrey, *Black Sun*, New York, 1976.

Blades, William (1824–1890)

Printer and bibliographer. Blades's name is today chiefly associated with CAXTON scholarship. His pioneering study of Caxton's types lent importance to his principal work in this field, *The Life and Typography of William Caxton*, two volumes, 1861–63; this was of considerable value to later bibliographers. *The Enemies of Books*, 1880, deals wittily with hazards ranging from bookworms to book thieves, but appeals mainly to anthologists. Blades's own books are housed at the St Bride Printing Library.

Blind-stamped

A blank design impressed on a binding by a tool or stamp, without the use of ink or gold leaf, is said to have been blind-stamped or blind-tooled. Blind-stamped panels were frequently used by English binders in the fifteenth and sixteenth centuries, and are found on bibles and prayer books of later date. While panels were stamped on the binding by means of a press, individual tools were heated and pressed into the leather by hand.

Block books

These were the earliest form of printed book. They were printed from wooden blocks, usually on one side of the leaf only, and consisted mainly of pictures with some accompanying text; hand colouring was sometimes added. The earliest examples date from the mid-fifteenth century and were printed in Germany and the Low

Countries, though a method of copying from carved blocks had been known in China much earlier. The European books were intended for unsophisticated readers and were generally religious in nature; *Ars Moriendi*, *Apocalypse* and *Biblia Pauperum* are among the best known. The production of block books continued for some years after the invention of printing from movable metal type.

Hind, Arthur Mayger, *An Introduction to a History of Woodcut*, New York, 1963.

Astrological block book, 1478(?)

Boards

In the language of antiquarian bookselling, the term 'boards' has come to signify especially the original paper-backed board in which many books were cased from around 1740 to the third decade of the nineteenth century, when CLOTH started to supersede temporary covers. Books that survive from this period in original boards, fragile in themselves and intended only as a temporary protection, have a special appeal to the collector, and are often of much greater value than copies in contemporary leather bindings.

More widely defined, the term describes the sides of any book bound, or cased, in hard covers of material other than leather; this may be wood, paste-board, or any other hard base, whether covered or uncovered. The description may be elaborated in such terms as 'marbled boards' or 'cloth-backed boards'. The term 'original boards' should be used only in the special sense first mentioned.

Bodleian Library

The principal library of the University of Oxford, and one of the five copyright libraries of the United Kingdom. In 1598 Sir Thomas Bodley (1545–1613) – scholar, diplomat and pilchard magnate – wrote to the vice-chancellor of Oxford University. He offered to rescue the former university library, one of whose benefactors had been Duke Humfrey of Gloucester, from its then ruinous state. His enthusiasm attracted widespread and substantial support, and he obtained a promise from the Stationers' Company to donate a copy of every book registered at Stationers' Hall. Known familiarly to its users and friends as 'Bodley', the library is open to accredited scholars for research. Its holdings of manuscripts is especially strong, and it is the largest library in the UK after the BRITISH LIBRARY.

Birrell, Augustine, *In the Name of the Bodleian, and Other Essays*, 1906.
Macray, W. D., *Annals of the Bodleian Library, 1598–1867*, 1890.
Philip, Ian, *The Bodleian Library in the Seventeenth and Eighteenth Centuries*, Oxford, 1983.
Rogers, David, *The Bodleian Library and Its Treasures*, Henley-on-Thames, 1991.

Bodoni, Giambattista (1769–1813)
Italian printer and punch-cutter. Types cast from his original matrices were used by Mardersteig for the first books from the OFFICINA BODONI.

Brooks, H. C., *Compendiosa Bibliografia di Edizioni Bodoniane*, Florence, 1927.

Bohn, Henry George (1796–1884)
Bohn's education was paid for by George III, his father holding the warrant of Court bookseller. He entered the family business and travelled widely through Europe, but set up his own establishment when his father refused him a partnership: one of his earliest apprentices was the young Bernard Quaritch. Bohn published a series of cheap editions of European literature, drawing upon his own knowledge and linguistic ability. Among the Bohn editions are the *Standard Library*, the *Antiquarian Library*, the *Scientific Library* and the *Classical Library*, about 600 books in all. He reprinted WILLIAM LOWNDES's *Bibliographer's Manual* in 1835, after buying the copyright, and employed Lowndes himself as a cataloguer. He retired from the book trade in 1864 and devoted himself to his art collection and to the literary society of London. The Bohn titles were acquired by George Bell (of Deighton, Bell of Cambridge).

Book Auctions

Lord John Kerr

That Julius Caesar's boast, 'I came. I viewed. I conquered.' is the earliest record we have of auction sales in this country may be debatable; but the suggestion that Boudicca's use of scythes on her chariot wheels was her way of discouraging the activities of the Ring seems to verge on the ludicrous. It is not quite impossible, however, since auction sales were a feature of Roman commerce. The Emperors Caligula and Marcus Aurelius both organized sales of furniture and works of art to raise money to pay off debts, in the former case the debts being personal and the goods sold seized from Senators and other Roman citizens. Marcus Aurelius's sale was to satisfy State debts, and it is not recorded whose goods were sold. In AD 193 the Roman Empire itself was put up for sale by the Praetorian Guard. The hammer fell on a bid of 6,250 drachmas for each soldier, and the purchaser, Didius Julianus, survived to enjoy the trappings of Emperor for all of 66 days before being assassinated himself.

We have to look to the reign of Henry VII for indisputable evidence of the holding of auctions in England, and it is possibly worthy of note that at that time sales were a state monopoly. The business of selling by auction was confined to an officer called an Outroper, and all other persons were prohibited from selling goods or merchandise by public claim or outcry, the system still prevailing in France at this time. But that was only an interlude, and by the time it is heard of again the practice had become a more general tool of trade. In the last quarter of the seventeenth century booksellers took to using it as an alternative method of moving stock (sparsely, however – not more than about 30 sales seem to have been held annually in the first 100 years), but thereafter specialist auctioneers began to appear and took over this aspect of the business. In the late eighteenth century we see such names as Thomas Ballard, who sold the enormous library of the bibliophile antiquary, Thomas Rawlinson, in a series of 16 sessions spread over a period of thirteen years. More recently, the dispersal of the gigantic collection of manuscripts and printed books formed by Sir Thomas Phillipps (1792–1872) – 'I wish to have one copy of every book in the world' – has taken more than a hundred years; only a part of that however (albeit a substantial part: two sales a year from 1971 to 1978) being by auction.

Christopher Cock, who held some 38 sales of books but also successfully pioneered picture sales, was responsible for the sale of the great library of Edward Harley, Earl of Oxford, which had been bought *en bloc* by the bookseller, Thomas Osborne. It was perhaps not the first time (certainly not the last) that a bookseller had decided that a special or 'named' collection would be dispersed to best financial advantage by this means. It was certainly among the first instances of an auctioneer employing an outside expert to catalogue a collection. The fact is particularly remembered because the expert in question was the young Samuel Johnson.

Sam Johnson is not the only book auction cataloguer to have made his name later in a different, if related, world. In our time A. N. L. Munby and P. J. Croft, both one-time members of Sotheby's book department, followed each other as Librarian of King's College, Cambridge. More usually, however, cataloguers who leave the auction business do so to set up as booksellers on their own account or as members of a bookselling firm; and the auctioneer who has trained them can only wish them well through gritted teeth and comfort himself with the thought that there goes another potential buyer who at least will be familiar with auctions. I am told that it is even more frustrating when departure is followed by the setting up of a new auction house.

The eighteenth century also saw the arrival of an auctioneer who, with his successors, became one of the handful of firms which led the book auction world during that century and the succeeding one, and for a time was the dominant firm in this one. Samuel Baker set up as a bookseller in 1734 at the age of 22, issuing printed fixed price catalogues of his stock; but in 1744 he turned to auctioneering with the sale, on 11 March and ten succeeding nights, of the library of Sir John Stanley Bt. Thereafter his sales proliferated and Baker prospered mightily. In 1767 he took in the 25-year-old George Leigh as a partner. After Baker's death in 1778 Leigh was joined by John Sotheby, changing the name of the firm to Leigh and Sotheby, the first of three generations of that family who were in charge of the business until 1861. Since then there have been no Sothebys in the firm but the name has remained.

Sotheby's, however, did not hold total sway in the market, and indeed in 1812 the most

BOOK AUCTIONS

spectacular sale of the nineteenth century went to their rival, Robert Harding Evans, when he dispersed the library of John, 3rd Duke of Roxburghe; 9,353 lots, spread over 42 days, realized a total of £23,341. It was said at the time that the Duke had not spent more than £5,000 on the collection.

It may be thought that auction fever is a phenomenon of the twentieth century only. Not a bit of it. The *Morning Chronicle* for 24 May reported, 'At no time did the Bibliomania rage with more violence than at present. At the Duke of Roxburghe's sale Tuesday last a book on remarkable characters, chiefly of persons tried at the Old Bailey, sold for £94.10.0., the Boke of St Albans, printed 1480, £147., the Mirrour of the World, Caxton, 1480, £35.15.0.'; and the issue of *The Gentleman's Magazine* for June of the same year, reviewing Thomas Frognall Dibdin's *Bibliomania*, enthused, 'Even the sanguine spirit of Mr Dibdin could not have foreseen the *bella, horrida bella*, which a competition for the Roxburghe treasures has since occasioned'.

For the full flavour of the bubbling excitement of those days in the Spring of 1812 we must turn to Dibdin himself and his *Bibliographical Decameron*. His style is not to everyone's taste and he is not easily abridged, but he does have zest. 'For two and forty successive days – with the exception only of Sundays – was the voice and hammer of Mr Evans heard with equal efficacy in the dining room of the Duke – which had been appropriated to the vendition of the books: and within that same space (some 35 feet by 20) were such deeds of valour performed, and such feats of book-heroism achieved, as had never been previously beheld.' In fact the sale started fairly quietly; but the pressure was building up. 'The curiosity of the spectators was increased in proportion to the numbers which flocked into the room. Short men were smothered; and nothing but the standing on a contiguous bench saved the writer of *The Bibliographical Decameron* from suffocation.' The plum of the collection was a copy of the first edition of Boccaccio's *Decameron*, Venice, Valdarfer, 1481, then thought to be unique. 'The marked champions for the contest were pretty well-known beforehand to be the Earl of Spencer, the Marquis of Blandford and the Duke of Devonshire. The honour of firing the first shot was due to a gentleman of Shropshire, unused to this species of warfare, and who seemed to recoil from the reverberation of the report himself had made! – "One hundred guineas", he exclaimed. Again a pause ensued; but anon the biddings rose rapidly to 500 guineas. Hitherto, however, it was evident that the firing was but masked and desultory. At length all random shots ceased; and the champions before named stood gallantly up to each other resolving not to flinch from a trial of their respective strengths.

'"A thousand guineas" were bid by Earl Spencer – to which the Marquis added "ten". You might have heard a pin drop. All eyes were turned – all breathing well nigh stopped . . . every sword was put home within its scabbard – and not a piece of steel was seen to move or glitter save that which each of these champions brandished in his valorous hand. See, see! – they parry, they lunge, they hit; yet their strength is undiminished, and no thought of yielding is entertained by either . . . Two thousand pounds are offered by the Marquis. Then it was that Earl Spencer, as a prudent general, began to think of a useless effusion of blood and expenditure of ammunition – seeing that his adversary was as resolute and "fresh" as at the onset. For a quarter of a minute he paused; when my Lord Althorp advanced one step forward, as if to supply his father with another spear for the purpose of renewing the contest – his countenance was marked by a fixed determination to gain the prize – if prudence, in its most commanding form, and with a frown of unusual intensity of expression, had not bade him desist. The father and son for a few seconds converse apart, and the biddings are resumed. "Two thousand, two hundred and fifty pounds", said Lord Spencer. The spectators are now absolutely electrified. The Marquis quietly adds his usual "ten" . . . and there is an end of the contest. Mr Evans, ere his hammer fell, made a due pause – and indeed, as if by something praeternatural, the ebony instrument itself seemed to be charmed or suspended "in mid air". However at length down dropt the hammer . . . and the echo of the sound of that fallen hammer was heard in the libraries of Rome, of Milan, and of St Mark.'

Not all of an auctioneer's life is like that. Most of it is gritty day to day stuff. The life of an auction cataloguer has been compared to that of a battery hen, condemned to turn a flow of undigested properties, books of any age, on any subject, in any condition, pamphlets, periodicals, maps, ephemera, anything written or printed, into coherent, accurate, bibliographically correct lots, which will attract but not deceive potential buyers. That may be too harsh a view; individuals usually have one or more subjects which appeal to them more than others, and become more experienced in one field than another.

There can be fun in so arranging the lots in a sale as to make attendance easy or attractive to buyers whose interests do not embrace the whole arena. There is above all the pleasure, familiar to everyone in the book trade, of handling the most attractive of artefacts, or of discovering in an unpromising property, on top of a cupboard or in an outhouse perhaps (it does happen) a completely unexpected treasure.

A look at the business of auctioneering must not neglect another equally important aspect. I remember once being told by a financier, 'You auctioneers do not realize how lucky you are; you do not have to worry about stock'. In a sense that is true, but an auctioneer does have his stock, a living, active, easy-going, pernickety, friendly, grumpy, trusting, suspicious, diffident, arrogant stock: his clients, the people with books to sell. They want two things: the best prices, and to be paid on time, and sometimes the latter is the more important. For the first the auctioneer depends on his cataloguers, for the second on his administrators.

If each owner had only one lot to sell and it sold first time round, life would be bliss: one catalogue entry, one pre-sale advice, one cheque, but of course that rarely happens. A property may be divided between different sales, it may bear different rates of commission (prints, for example, or manuscripts), lots (say it in a whisper) may not sell at the first offering, the client may want one part of the proceeds to be paid in one way and another differently, or all these problems may converge; and the client rightly expects the auctioneer to be able to give him the exact state of play at any moment. Some buyers too, it has to be said, are less swift to pay for their purchases than others and some more aggressive when payment has to be squeezed from them. Catalogue subscribers need to be reminded when renewals fall due; some firms make a practice of letting non-subscribers know when books of interest to them are to appear in a sale. All these matters, and others, fall to the administrators, and if they lose touch the auctioneer loses his stock.

If it is all so gritty, why does the auctioneer do it? My colleague, Frank Herrmann, has written of the Rawlinson sale in 1756, 'This sale was spread over 50 sessions, so Baker's take at the end of each evening was £23.5.0., of which he would only keep, say, 10 per cent for himself as commission, so book auctioneering in general was not something that would lead to instant riches'. For my part I can give some sort of an answer by means, improbable for those who know me, of a sporting analogy.

Dibdin has described the atmosphere before a sale from the point of view of the spectator. The auctioneer's feelings are different, and I have a strong sense of sympathy for the batsman at a cricket match who has been sitting for a long time in the pavilion, padded up and waiting to go in. He has watched the wicket, seen what the ball is doing, analysed the form of the bowlers that day, but he knows that, until he gets into the middle, he cannot forecast what will happen – and the butterflies are fluttering in his stomach. The auctioneer too has watched and analysed in the weeks and days before the sale, but he too knows that nothing is certain, and he too has his butterflies, and the adrenalin begins to run. If he has done his job right, and good fortune is with him, the sale will take off, the runs or bids flow freely, and he may even experience that extraordinary and thrilling stillness and tension which comes into the room when a lot is achieving a spectacular result. That is one of the reasons why I love this life of the sale room, and why I shall probably have to be dragged kicking and screaming from the rostrum at the end of my last sale.

The following information may be helpful to those not familiar with auction sales, but it must be borne in mind that practices differ from one auction house to another.

Sellers
1. *Commission.* This covers all expenses after the property has been delivered to the auctioneer, with the exception of insurance, catalogue illustrations, and any special advertising. The amount charged varies widely, but is generally related to the value of the item. Special terms are usually offered to trade sellers.
2. *Insurance.* A premium is charged unless the seller prefers to make his own arrangements; in which case he should inform the auctioneer when delivering the property and should bear in mind that the auctioneer will not then be liable for any loss.
3. *Illustrations and special advertising.* If the auctioneer considers that a consignment will benefit from illustration in the catalogue or from special advertising, he may ask the seller to contribute to the cost. He will do so only when he considers that the cost will be justified by the extra bidding that it will attract to the consignment.
4. *Reserves.* The seller may place a reserve on any lot, that is, a sum below which the lot will not be sold. This figure remains confidential between the seller and auctioneer; and the reserve will normally be given effect by the auctioneer, bidding on behalf of the seller. The seller is prohibited by law from bidding himself on any lot on which he has placed a reserve: and, in the remote eventuality of this happening, the auctioneer will disregard the reserve. It may sometimes happen that a bookseller, having placed a reserve on a lot, may receive a commission to buy it for a client. In that case he should inform the auctioneer before the sale; otherwise he may find that it has been sold without reserve. Unsold lots may often be re-offered in a subsequent sale with a lower reserve.
5. *Pre-sale advice.* The seller receives an advance copy of the relevant catalogue, with a note of the lot numbers and a list of suggested or agreed reserves.

6. *Payment*. Payment of the net proceeds is made within a stated period after the sale. In exceptional cases, payment may be withheld by the auctioneer until it has been received from the buyer.

7. *Cataloguing*. It usually takes between two and three months for a consignment to appear in a sale. This may seem an unduly long delay, but it is accounted for by the need to allow adequate time for the printing and world-wide circulation of the catalogue; this is essential if the maximum possible competition is to be achieved. It may sometimes be advisable to hold lots back for a specialized sale.

Buyers

1. *Viewing*. Viewing is usually scheduled for at least two full days before a sale and is often possible on the morning of a sale.

2. *Bidding steps*. The amount of advance at any stage is at the auctioneer's absolute discretion; nevertheless he will normally accept rises of £5 up to £100, £10 between £100 and £200, £20 between £200 and £500, £50 between £500 and £1,000, £100 between £1,000 and £2,000, and so on.

3. *Commission bids*. If a buyer cannot or does not wish to attend a sale, the auctioneer will execute bids on his behalf. There is no charge for this service, and lots will be bought as cheaply as allowed by other bids and by any reserve that may have been fixed.

4. *Payment*. Payment of the total amount (that is, hammer price, buyer's premium, and VAT on the premium) is due immediately after the conclusion of the sale unless credit arrangements have been made; this will minimize any problems which may otherwise arise over the clearance of purchases.

5. *Export licences*. A licence from the Department of Trade and Industry is required before manuscript material over 50 years old may be removed from the country. Certain other items also require Export Licences.

6. *Estimates*. All auctioneers are prepared to advise owners of the sort of price an item is likely to realise, and most publish those estimates in their catalogue. They are based on prices paid for other copies or similar items, or, sometimes, on the auctioneer's instinct developed by long immersion in the market.

Sellers and buyers

1. *Premium*. A separate premium representing a percentage of the price at which the hammer falls is usually paid to the auctioneer by the buyer.

2. *Imperfect books*. If any named item proves to be defective in text or illustration, and the defect is not mentioned in the catalogue, the lot may be returned within a stated period and the sale rescinded. There are some exceptions to this practice, such as periodicals, manuscript material, music, atlases and prints. This is a long-established aspect of book auctions, a paragraph to this effect being included in the earliest recorded 'Conditions of Sale' in the seventeenth century.

Cooper, Jeremy, *Under the Hammer – The Auctions and Auctioneers of London*, 1977.
Herrmann, Frank, *Sotheby's – Portrait of an Auction House*, 1980.
Lawler, John, *Book Auctions in England in the Seventeenth Century*, 1898.
Munby, A. N. L. (ed.), *Sale Catalogues of Libraries of Eminent Persons*, 12 vols, 1971–5.

Book Collecting

David Chambers

Bibliomania is the essence of the matter. Were we free of this irresistible urge to fill more and more shelves with books of every sort and size – and the rarer the better – there would be no need for the dealers who strive so eagerly to gratify our needs. This they know, and treat our lusts for possession with all the skills of a Pandarus trained in the best schools of American psychiatry. But though there would be no dealers if there were no collectors, it is just as true that the relationship is one of mutual self-interest: we must have more books or our world falls apart – they must find them for us or *their* world will fall, and even more quickly.

A dealer needs to understand the temperament of his collectors (the masculine pronoun is a convenience only) to know how far they can be guided and how far he should simply search for the books on their 'wants' lists, appreciate the quality of the books that they will buy, know how much can reasonably be asked, and how much more can be had if the book is rare enough and badly enough needed. Added to which he must have the skills to find the books that his customers will buy. I write, I must add, as a collector, having rarely sold any of the books I have bought, and having usually had to replace these at a later date (and, plainly, a higher price).

Many of us start collecting at school, these days, no doubt, buying paperbacks, though the Nelson Classics with which I started looked much nicer on the mantelpiece. Then the secondhand shops start to lure, and this is when the business really begins, for if the dealers – so much older, so much more learned in bookish matters – if they are friendly, if they offer new temptations, then back one goes, again and again, for more books and for more advice.

The quality and style of a bookshop plainly depend on the character of its owner, but there are other things apart from the size of its stock that will attract customers. Decent lighting and reliable ladders are essential, and some degree of order on the shelves is a great help. Of nearly as much importance, however, is the provision of comfortable seating for the wives or husbands who have been drawn in by their partners for just the ten minutes that will be needed to see whether there is anything new in the shop. A loo is something else that would often be appreciated.

Book Fairs and the specialist dealers are for later, when one has enough knowledge to withstand the pressure to buy *The Lord of the Rings*, or whatever is currently in fashion, for far more than its relative value set against *Urne Buriall*. There are those who complain of the effect of book fairs on prices and fashions, and it is certainly infuriating that dealers should move round a fair before it has opened snapping up whatever seems modestly priced. From a collector's point of view, the general levelling of prices upwards is just as provoking, so that there are no longer great differences to be found as one travels the country. To set against such grievances, there is the enormous advantage of being able to visit 30 or 40 dealers under one roof, talk with them, persuade them to search for what is wanted, and look at an enormous range of material brought together from all over the country – sometimes buying, sometimes (too rarely) not.

Specialist dealers are another matter. For a young collector they can be very intimidating, though one can understand a certain aloofness from someone who is accustomed to selling books worth hundreds or thousands of pounds when confronted with beginners in the field. Yet here I have found that too many of the top dealers have so overawed me in the past that I have been unwilling to visit them at a later date, when I could better afford to buy some of their books. Those who have eventually become friends have, of course, proved masters in the joint endeavour to buy finer, rarer material, but it must be said that such a relationship has not always been easy to achieve.

Catalogues have always been one means of access to the more expensive dealers, for here the stock can be looked over at leisure, without the embarrassment of walking away uneasily if nothing affordable can be found. For a dealer working from private premises, catalogues are vital, and here his problem is to ensure that his catalogues reach those collectors interested in the books that are listed; for the collector the problem is easily solved by reference to one of the several guides which index dealers by their specialities. General catalogues should be clearly subdivided so as to make them more easily scanned by collectors, whether specialist or otherwise, who ought perhaps to be rushing to work rather than working slowly through a long and confusing list. The layout, too, needs to ensure quick understanding: bold, perhaps, for the author, titles in upper and lower case, publisher/printer and date at the end, notes in italic below the entry, not too many catch phrases, which only confuse the eye, an index, which can be invaluable. Catalogues are among the great pleasures of collecting, to be studied at length after the rush to buy has passed, but booksellers should remember that they need to be read very quickly when first received.

'Wants' lists are another great source of pleasure, especially now that one can prepare them on word-processors, with purchases easily deleted, if only to be replaced by twice as many titles from the latest enthusiasm. Some say that such lists are best kept strictly to oneself and a few chosen dealers, but if what one is seeking has really become difficult to find, then it seems to me to be best to pass lists on to anyone who is likely to be able to help – provided only that it is made clear that the books are not to be advertised for, so as to avoid over-publicity.

One difficulty with wants lists is that old versions need updating; new lists have to be issued at regular intervals; and even then one cannot be certain that the list will be consulted; I have on several occasions found books listed in catalogues from dealers who hold my lists, and though I have usually been in time to secure the books, the value of the lists has been called into question.

Buying at auction is enjoyable, and sometimes productive, but Sotheby's and Christie's now sell all but the higher priced books in bundles aimed at trade buyers – though at Bloomsbury Book Auctions there are still many smaller lots, which make life much easier for the private collector. In general it is usually much more convenient to rely on a bookseller to search the catalogues, and view the books; an enormous amount of time can be spent in the weekly search through auction catalogues, and in any case many of the books offered are concealed under the phrase 'and ten others'.

Fashions in collecting have always been subject to change, and though one is likely to start off on the common course, buying poetry and prose for reading, moving on to first editions, illustrated books, contemporary private press books, topography and so on, there is much to be said for following less popular paths as soon as one gains enough experience. In Dibdin's day the wealthy collectors bought incunabula and manuscripts, as they still do, but in the short term values fell against them as enthusiasms waned. 'Run of the mill' books are even less stable currency, moving more with popular taste, which is in turn influenced by what books are available. To move into more specialized fields will make collecting a good deal less easy, but often much more fun. Whatever books one collects, they must plainly be those which are liked for themselves, whether for their texts or illustrations, their provenance or binding. Buying simply for investment is like dealing in shares, and often as dangerous; the idea has merit only as a last defence against the more prudent, less bookish members of the family. Buying within the current craze, for a particular author or illustrator that everyone else is seeking, is a particularly expensive way of collecting, and it should be possible to make much finer collections of less fashionable books.

So much for generalities. From a young collector's point of view, where should he turn to find a narrow field of interest that has not already been made popular by earlier collectors, one of whom has perhaps written up the subject and raised prices in the process? Much depends on how much money is available, but even if funds are very limited some degree of specialization will be well worthwhile. Suggestions publicly made may be invidious, for part of the excitement is to be hunting for things that the rest of the world passes by; but a few general ideas are worth offering. One of the notable series of books that have been published over the years might be considered, such as Everyman's Library in this century, or the various literary and technical series published during the last – there are many different groups of books which look splendid if bought in good condition. Or there are the first editions of some of the less collected minor authors of the eighteenth and nineteenth centuries, though again, the texts must seem, if only to the individual collector, to justify the effort involved. Alternatively, to offer generalities within which much narrower fields can be selected, there are all the inventions which might be pursued; on a historical or archaeological basis there is almost unlimited scope for detailed specialization. The range of subjects is as wide as any one collector's interests may extend, but concentration in a narrow field will prove most effective.

It is after all in this area of the generally unfamiliar that the collector can display his skills in research, for when he has a large part of what is available (though not before), he may write it all up, and publish *the* guide to the subject: a nice achievement – even if one has to admit that the subject is only worth one such account. Moreover, the collection will probably rise in value when the book is published, though by the time any beneficiaries get their chance to sell, it will have doubtless fallen back again. Despite such a cynical view, it must be said that collectors have often led the way in bibliographical research, starting, as they do, with the advantage of having the books concerned in the shelves behind their desks.

My own particular enthusiasm has been for books printed in private houses during the eighteenth and nineteenth centuries, and for many years I kept very quiet about this, buying in a field with few competitors. As the years have drawn on it has seemed wiser to pursue the books more openly: those for which I am still searching are of the rarer sort, the more restricted editions from Strawberry Hill, Lee Priory, Middle Hill and Daniel, and the books which are scarcer still from the presses that hardly anyone has heard of. Nowadays dealers will sometimes offer books before they have been catalogued, and though there is the likelihood that I may drive the market up against myself, it is easy enough to decline the more absurdly priced offerings. In a few years time I hope to publish a detailed account of such presses, with a bibliography that will include all that has been listed by Martin, Lowndes and Dobell, and add whatever else I have been able to trace, whether in my own collection, at the British Library, or elsewhere.

The books on collecting in the library of the Bishopsgate Institute were those which first guided me when I left school. They were mostly from the turn of the century, and full of references to books that were quite out of reach so far as my pocket was concerned; but I still learned of tall Elzevirs, *Le Pastissier François*, of Aldines and Gutenberg, of manuscripts and incunabula. Then for my 21st birthday I was given a copy of Holbrook Jackson's *Anatomy of Bibliomania*, which analyses so completely the moods of the collector. There have been many such books published over the past hundred years – guides for new collectors and bibliographies of particular subjects to lead them on to greater extravagances. There have also been a great many periodicals that served at the time to keep enthusiasm at fever pitch, and which now make most pleasant reading at the end of the day. There are indeed journals and societies catering for the needs of collectors in many countries, including many devoted to particular authors or subjects. However necessary it may be to smuggle books secretly into the house, or to keep them for a while in the office, societies such as these, and the flurry of book fairs throughout the country, have made it easier to meet kindred spirits whose lives are similarly governed by that overriding need for a room, for several rooms, or a house or two, filled to overflowing with carefully chosen books.

We have a skull looking down from the top of a bookcase with a portrait of Sir Thomas Phillipps hanging on one side, and given a straight face it is sometimes possible to persuade visitors that it is his – a better *memento mori* of that irascible collector than are the rows of his Middle Hill Press books that stand behind my desk. I can too easily sympathize with the vello-mania that brought some sixty thousand manuscripts into his house, and with his need to have a copy of everything ever printed that brought in nearly as many more books to his collection. His private press is another enthusiasm that I can understand, for the idea of printing the texts of the manuscripts that he had collected was to give a good reason for their possession. Yet his spirit lies uneasily within our house, for my wife always fears that she will be driven, as was Lady Phillipps, into half a room, with space for only a dressing-table – and I find his collection, marvellous though it was, too haphazard, and his printing too inaccurate to be valued as much more than a curiosity. Book collecting, serious collecting, needs a narrower field, deeply researched, with scope eventually for essays or for a book. And much in awe as I am of Sir Thomas, it is specialized collectors such as Sir Geoffrey Keynes, A. N. L. Munby, and Douglas Cleverdon whom I would follow.

We have, in any case, no room for a hundred thousand books.

The Book Collector

The Winter 1990 number of *The Book Collector* reproduced with a new caption a nineteenth-century *Punch* drawing of Father Christmas distributing gifts: Poor Little Waif – 'Please Sir, I ain't got no Christmas dinner.' Father Christmas – 'Never mind, my little man, here's a copy of *The Book Collector* to cheer you up.' The Christmas Catalogue that followed the drawing contained the usual collection of authentic booksellers' blunders, including, on this occasion, the offer for £12 of the first edition of Aldous Huxley's *Eyeglass in Gaza*.

If *The Book Collector* has not always cheered its readers up, this is because its highly articulate scholarship, deployed over a broad range of bibliographic and bibliophilic subjects, must often have induced among them a sense of inadequacy, if not despair. Since 1952, when it first appeared as the successor to *The Book Handbook*, *The Book Collector*'s authoritative editorial boards have called upon contributors of great distinction in their various fields: important collectors and unfamiliar collections, bindings, presses, notable books, bookselling history, bibliographic projects – these and numerous other aspects of book collecting have been carefully described. 'Bibliographical Notes and Queries' have provided a forum for many issues of specialized importance; by Winter 1992, Notes had numbered more than 500 and Queries some 400. The quarterly 'News and Comment' feature has cast a magisterial but humane eye across the world of collectors, libraries and dealers, and the book reviews have maintained the scrupulous standards of the main contributions. The annual indexes provide cumulative access to articles and notes which often represent the only source of authoritative information on their subject matter. It should be added that *The Book Collector* has never relaxed the fine standard of production set by its first printer, the Shenval Press.

Book fairs

If a bookseller from the 1930s were miraculously to return to his calling, there are many aspects of the antiquarian book trade in Britain which would be immediately familiar to him. Some of the leading dealers of that time are still in business; auctions continue, much as before; and, although technological advances and rising prices might cause a raised eyebrow or two, he would find most catalogues and their publishers still recognizably in his own tradition. However, if he were to drop into a Bloomsbury hotel for a Sunday lunchtime drink, he might be faced with something quite alien: several hundred yards of books on folding wooden shelves, well over one hundred stallholders, and at least as many non-exhibiting dealers, to say nothing of collectors, librarians or simply curious members of the general public.

This is a book fair. The monthly two-day PBFA London fair is the most regular of the major British fairs; the three-day ABA event each June is the country's grandest; but, from these and other prestigious fairs such as those at Bath, Chelsea, Edinburgh and Oxford, down to modest (and traditional) one-day events on trestle tables in village halls organized under the auspices of no one, scarcely a day seems to pass without a book fair taking place somewhere. Indeed, at times (most notably in June, when a plethora of more or less efficient fairs benefit from the momentum of the ABA and PBFA events), the phenomenon seems to be out of control, and there have been signs that serious private and institutional customers are beginning to tire.

Nevertheless, many regular exhibitors make a good living from book fairs; they offer an excellent opportunity to part-time dealers, or those just starting in business; and there are few booksellers who do not derive benefit from exhibiting at least at one or two of the principal annual fairs.

However, the prevalence of fairs may well have made its own contribution to the undoubted decline of the provincial bookshop. Few experiences are more frustrating than a long drive to a remote shop, full of rather tired stock, only to be refused access to the dozen potentially interesting books behind the counter on the grounds that they are being 'held back for the next Book Fair' – when, in all probability, they will change hands at least once between exhibitors even before the fair opens. Still, book fairs work very well for a number of dealers, and many enjoy the camaraderie which attaches to them (for which a taste for traditional British coffee, and a strong head for beer, is often desirable).

Exhibitors at fairs organized by the ABA and PBFA must be members of the respective organizations; but many other organizers exist. Details may be found in book trade periodicals.

Bookmark advertising the works of P. G. Wodehouse (see page 74).

Book labels

Book labels are simpler and smaller than BOOKPLATES, usually giving only the owner's name, and both are recorded together below. Booksellers (Shakespeare and Co. of Paris is a notable example) and binders are sometimes identified in the same way, usually in a corner of the front ENDPAPERS.

Bookmarks

Booksellers, book buyers and, indeed, all those who read books are constantly reminded of their predecessors' methods of marking their progress through a book. Perhaps the most common, and certainly one of the most objectionable devices, is the turned-down upper corner of the page, none too easily located when reading is resumed but leaving a conspicuous crease. The pressed flower or fern might run the creased corner close as a hazard, but disastrous as its traces might be, it will often have been inserted by an amateur naturalist rather than a reader. Among the more innocuous bookmarks are bus tickets, silver paper, income tax demands and (as a few booksellers can confirm) splendid old white five-pound notes. A comprehensive study of the EPHEMERA found in books, whether as purposeful place-markers or as sentimental deposits, would bring to light a whole world of eccentricity.

Nevertheless the bookmark has a dignified history: embroidered silk, 'Stevengraphs' (52 designs are recorded), thick Florentine leather (usually too thick), Scottish Widows' Insurance advertisements – every bookseller could add to the list; if something is just about thin enough to be inserted in a book without totally distorting the shape, it will in time be found between the pages.

This minor but by no means uninteresting aspect of book history, seen at its most conventional form in the binder's silk marker, was the subject of an exhibition at the Antiquarian Booksellers' Association's 28th Annual Book Fair in 1987. Some 200 exhibits collected by Hilary Sturt ranged from the illuminated vellum page-corners favoured in the eighteenth century to the first silk marker, commemorating the avoidance of everything from 'careless talk', through waste, to venereal disease.

Bookplates and Book Labels

Brian North Lee

Years of experience have shown that booksellers have very varying attitudes towards ex-libris (the alternative name for bookplates and book labels), but the situation is improving. Whatever the degree of artistry displayed by these marks of ownership, there is renewed awareness of their bibliographical, genealogical and sometimes heraldic importance. Collectively, they are our fullest nominal record of the history of book collecting and donation. It is good, therefore, that catalogue comments such as 'Bookplate, condition otherwise good' are now rare. Ex-libris belong in books, and ideally should never be removed from them.

It is fully understandable that many booksellers feel somewhat out of their depth when detailed descriptions of bookplates are needed. There are countless thousands of British

Twentieth century pictorial bookplates

examples, and a surprisingly sizeable but often elusive literature about them. The largest catalogue is that of the Franks Collection,[1] but its some 34,000 items are inadequately recorded; there is little use in listing, say 'Smith, John, Armorial' followed by 'Smith, John, Armorial (another plate)', without indicating the difference between them. Whether it is essential for booksellers to build up a little library of bookplate literature depends upon the size of the business. Such works are worth keeping if they turn up, and the particular usefulness of some is indicated in the list of reference works below. However, The Bookplate Society is always glad to answer queries, and libraries, including St Bride's, have much relevant literature. It seemed therefore best to address this short article principally to booksellers who, while acknowledging the importance of bookplates, are too busy to do much research into them.

Bookplates have been used in Britain since 1574, when Sir Nicholas Bacon's gift of some 70 books to Cambridge University Library was marked by a hand-coloured woodcut armorial plate.[2] A few printed labels were made earlier in that century; and for decades afterwards they remained the most familiar form of ex-libris, many of them marking donations. The present writer's *Early Printed Book Labels* describes and illustrates dated examples to 1760 chronologically, showing the developments of style and ornament. Often printed in very small quantities, some were probably unique. Since the eighteenth century the engraved label has been a popular alternative, and both forms, in sizeable print runs, have continued in use since. When describing them it is helpful to give their full wording (they are often dated) and to indicate the manner of their execution. There are four main possibilities: printed, with or without border or ornament; similarly engraved; printed within an engraved frame (probably part of the printer's stock); and, in the twentieth century, engraved in calligraphic style on wood or reproduced from drawings with the same effect. Except where the engraver is identifiable (Eric Gill, Reynolds Stone and Leo Wyatt were most notable practitioners), examples of the last category are best described as 'calligraphic book label of . . .'.

Another category likely to be of especial interest to book collectors and occurring since the late 1800s, indicates that the volume is 'From the library of . . .' a well-known and most often literary figure. It should be understood, however, that these were often placed in books after the owner's death (the Augustus Hare label is explicit on this), usually when the library was dispersed. A notable exception is the little series of labels in Kelmscott 'Golden Type', of which only Morris's[3] was posthumous; but later admirers used reproduced rather than type-set versions, so some caution over attribution is advised.

---

[1] See the list of reference works. Franks's foreign plates are still uncatalogued, and some are just in envelopes. George Heath Viner gave the British Museum bookplates 'not in Franks'. Likewise uncatalogued, some bound into comparable albums, but those arranged by artist are still in boxes.

[2] See the writer's *British Bookplates*, p. 19 or, for a fuller account, 'The origin of Sir Nicholas Bacon's bookplate' (*Transactions of the Cambridge Bibliographical Society*, Vol. II, Part V, 1958).

[3] It was printed at the Kelmscott Press on 25 February 1898, at the same time as labels for Edward Burne-Jones, Charles Fairfax Murray, May Morris, Laurence W. Hodson, H. C. Marillier, John and Margaret Mackail, and Emery Walker (with the III Hammersmith Terrace address). Walker's later label for No. VII was probably printed by line-block. The William Morris label should not be confused with a similarly-worded one in Lining Jensen Oldstyle No. 2.

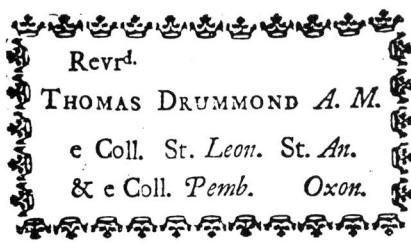

FROM THE LIBRARY
OF EMERY WALKER
NO. III THE TERRACE
HAMMERSMITH

Most bookplates, as distinct from labels, fall generally into three categories: armorials, pictorials, or a mixture of the two. In respect of the last, the terms 'pictorial-armorial' or 'armorial-pictorial' should place the predominant feature first. Ex-libris collectors now seem to find pictorials, or largely pictorial compositions, more interesting than armorials. This is understandable. Until the 1860s most bookplate makers were trade engravers. Since then, noted book illustrators and graphic artists have made a memorable contribution to ex-libris design. In earlier days several pictorial subjects predominated. The first to appear, from about the same time, were 'allegoricals' and bookpiles. 'Allegorical' implies that the depiction includes gods, goddesses, cherubs and the like. These became modestly popular subjects from the early eighteenth century, some early ones being by engravers settled here from the Continent. One of the finest was William Hogarth's ex-libris, in two states, for John Holland, a herald painter. Its armorial and figures are depicted in a room, and similar interior compositions naturally showed a preference for libraries.

Books also naturally featured on ex-libris, sometimes littered about in extraordinary fashion. 'Bookpile', by contrast, signifies an orderly arrangement of books, most often in three tiers, with a central compartment occupied by an armorial or on occasion an inscription.[4] This style was devised by Samuel Pepys in 1698, and it remained a minority option for more than 200 years. Pepys did not, however, use the style himself, and the best-known of his own ex-libris are the portrait plates in two sizes; but elsewhere portraits as a subject for bookplates found scant favour, perhaps because they savour of self-importance.

The 'landscape' pictorial, which has flourished in a variety of manifestations since c.1750, saw perhaps its apogee in the ex-libris output from Thomas Bewick's workshop, in the medium of wood engraving. The Ann Hill bookplate by Richard T. Austin is in the same mould. So diverse, however, have been the expressions of this style that aficionados would readily cite more recent exponents, including the J. and E. Bumpus engravers (c.1896–1928),[5] E. H. New, Rex Whistler,[6] Joan Hassall,[7] and many contemporary wood engravers – for fine ex-libris are still made. 'Urn' plates were a fashion mostly in the later eighteenth century, possibly under the impact of such works as Gray's 'Elegy', when thoughts of mortality were acceptable. There were also 'trophy' ex-libris, incorporating flags, cannon, guns, etc., generally as adjuncts to an armorial. Such simple but effective indications of military or naval profession were never numerous, but there are also a few trophies of other kinds: a bibliophile artist, for instance, could opt for palette and brushes, if the fancy took him.

Every type of pictorial subject has sometimes accompanied armorials, but, whatever the form, it will be desirable to ascertain the approximate date. There are three principal aids to this. The first is the paper: is it laid or wove? Until about 1790 it would have been

---

[4] A study of Bookpile Bookplates by the writer was published by The Bookplate Society as the 1992 free book for its members.

[5] Listed in Horace Jones, *Bookplates signed 'W. P. B.' 1896–1928*, Berkhamsted, James Wilson and The Bookplate Society, 1978.

[6] See the writer's *The Bookplate Designs of Rex Whistler*, Pinner, Private Libraries Association for The Bookplate Society, 1973.

[7] See David Chambers, *Joan Hassall Engravings & Drawings*, Pinner, 1985.

(John Holland)

the former, but in any event, booksellers develop an 'eye' for the age of printed materials. This will help, too, when later reprints of old bookplates are encountered. There was probably no dishonest intention in their making. Sons were often named after fathers, or others of the family, and an old copperplate at hand could still serve. The abolitionist, William Wilberforce, for instance, used a Chippendale armorial probably engraved for his grandfather in the eighteenth century; and his son, 'Soapy Sam', sometime Bishop of Oxford, used his father's plate amended in manuscript.[8] In earlier times, sons would cut off inscriptions, the armorial itself remaining apposite. Reprints of early plates were also taken in the late nineteenth century to provide images for collectors, again with no desire to defraud.

The second aid to dating is the evidence of the heraldry itself. Here we may be least at ease, for heraldry seems like a foreign language until it is mastered; but then it proves beguiling, and by no means as complicated as may have been imagined. Burke's often reprinted *The General Armory*, 1884, has a usefully simple heraldic introduction and glossary, and numerous other basic heraldic guides are available.

The third guide to dating is invaluable in all but the matter of reprints: the ornamentation of the arms. While there are exceptions to the rule, armorial decoration has, since Tudor times, undergone changes which reflect fashion. They are easy to discern, even if their 'bookplate' terminology, derived from Warren's *Guide*,[9] may seem idiosyncratic. The few plates made before c.1635 are styled 'Tudoresque', and the Bacon armorial shows its characteristics: a squarish shield and restrained mantling, which tends to have tassels at base. In the decades around the mid-century a style – if such a term is appropriate to so few examples – designated 'Carolian' is typified by incorporation of a wreath around the arms. Then, from the 1660s, though not to become widespread for almost four decades, the so-called Early Armorial made its appearance. Only about 200 bookplates were made before 1700, 20 of which are shown in the writer's *British Bookplates*. Most are rarely encountered, but when they are it is worth seeking documentation from The Bookplate Society.

Armorials made since 1700 are commonly encountered, and most of them are not individually of great note. In outlining their styles and comparative date, one caveat should be observed: the London engravers were more attuned to fashion than their provincial counterparts, and there is thus some overlapping of styles. The first two were in any case for a time concurrent, and are termed 'Early Armorial' and 'Jacobean' (so called, oddly, because of its similarity to ecclesiastical woodwork, mouldings and ornament in the later seventeenth century). Both styles, and popular usage of bookplates, owe a great debt to William Jackson, who clearly employed several engravers in his workshop near the Inns of Court in London, and created over 600 ex-libris between 1695 and 1715.[10] The Early

---

[8] There are in fact two different coppers, both of which were used by the emancipator, so the earlier was either lost or copied when the original showed wear.

[9] See the list of reference works. This book was so ahead of its time that hardly any copies sold for years; and by the time they did, its author had turned against bookplates, for he would have preferred to have made his mark as a poet.

[10] Jackson undertook ex-libris for many of the Oxford and Cambridge colleges. For interesting insights about his work see Anthony Pincott's article, 'Oxford bookplates by William Jackson', *The Bookplate Society Newsletter*, June, 1974.

Carolian

Early Armorial

Jacobean

Armorial Lechmere plate and the Jacobean Mary Savage were from his workshop and the Jacobean Micklethwaite plate was the work of Simon Gribelin.[11] Jackson also made a feature of Early Armorials in large and small size, for books of varying dimensions – a good idea, for wealthy clients, but one that never caught on significantly.

Illustration here of examples of style makes verbal detailing unnecessary. Early Armorials and Jacobeans were both symmetrical, and the latter's ornament could include scallop-shells, brackets, and fish-scale, diaper or lattice patterns round the arms; they proved lovely complements to ladies' lozenge armorials. The former style was unfashionable by about 1730, though coppers were still adapted, but the latter were approved for 20 more years. Their successors, represented by the Emmet armorial, were 'Chippendale' or rococo plates, which appeared before 1740 and dominated the next four decades. Their true essence was a light fancifulness, the scallop becoming the very framework, frilly and intricate. In time, however, it became overburdened with pictorial ornament, such as shepherdesses, sheep, cherubs, dragons, trees and baskets of flowers. No other bookplate form would be so used until the so-called 'die-sinker' armorial (a misnomer) held sway through the 1800s, when anybody who thought himself someone had at least one made.

Between 1775 and 1800 there was an understandable reaction against late Chippendale extravagance. The result was another symmetrical style, its spade-shaped shields ornamented with festoons or wreaths and ribbons such as Richard Brinsley Sheridan favoured: the ideal accompaniment to books of the period. As with earlier armorials, a trophy or scene could be incorporated. It is worthy of note, however, that latterly not only was their decoration pared but that of existent coppers was simplified, unostentation being the order of the day. The early 1800s saw an increase of elaborate detail at the hands of engravers on steel. Two ex-libris of the Duke of Sussex, Queen Victoria's uncle, are unusual in declaring that they are made from 'Perkins and Heath Patent Hardened Steel Plate'.[12]

Although bibliography calls for full documentation, collectors of bookplates are not enamoured of such armorials unless they belonged to well-known figures. It would be idle to hope that important bibliophiles or 'personalities' always commissioned significant marks of ownership for their books. Indeed, the reverse is often seen to have been the case. However, booksellers often wish to cater for special interests, and citing previous owners is worthwhile; for names unfamiliar to us may be important to others. Most nineteenth century armorials are like very dull dinner companions: quite proper and correctly attired but boring to spend long with. Since 1860 there has been a renaissance of superb copper-engraved armorials, mostly the work of Charles William Sherborn and his followers; but fewer and fewer are now made, partly because of the greatly increased costs of engraving and printing, but also because copper engraving is now little taught.[13]

---

[11] There is an article on Gribelin's ex-libris in *The Bookplate Journal*, Vol. 6, No. 1, March 1988.
[12] See *British Royal Bookplates*, Nos. 23–24, pp. 40–41.
[13] See C. D. Sherborn, *A Sketch of the Life and Work of Charles William Sherborn*, London, Ellis, 1912; G. H. Viner, *A Descriptive Catalogue of Bookplates . . . by G. W. Eve*, Kansas City, The American Bookplate Society, 1916; and the writer's *J. A. C. Harrison. Artist & Engraver*, Frederikshavn, Denmark, The Bookplate Society and Førlaget Exlibristen, 1983, for monographs on fine copper practitioners.

Chippendale

Spade shield wreath and ribbon

Spade shield trophy

(Duke of Sussex)

In respect of the contribution to bookplate history which has been made by book illustrators and graphic artists, the bookseller who is also a connoisseur has the advantage. Many such ex-libris are either not signed or merely bear initials, and ours is the task of identifying them. It is pleasing that monographs on artists now often include such modest – and privately commissioned – creations, and an increasing number of studies are devoted to the bookplate output of notable practitioners. Since, however, the field is unusually wide and the endeavour slower than could be wished, perhaps collectors and booksellers can assist each other to advantage.

However admired artists may be, examples of their work may be rare. Some bookplate owners known to the writer could scarcely be bothered to use them; conversely, when others die or dispose of their books the market may be surfeited. The bookseller David Low, for instance,[14] when he sold Herbert Charles Pollitt's library, acquired a pile of unused prints of Aubrey Beardsley's 'MR. POLLITT'S BOOKPLATE',[15] which he let collectors have cheaply; but Beardsley's ex-libris for Olive Custance is scarcely ever seen. Only a very few bookplates add significantly to a volume's worth. Those artists most admired include Jessie M. King,[16] who designed the Begg plate, and Stephen Gooden,[17] whose works include the magnificent ex-libris for the Royal Library, Windsor. Few people would recognize the Watt plate as an etching by Martin Hardie, but compositions by Lucien and Esther Pissarro, Rex Whistler or Joan Hassall are more easily identified.

Collectors of bookplates respect their place in books, but prefer to acquire loose prints, which are not hard to come by. Many of them surfaced at the disposal of artists' studios, or of libraries (like Pollitt's), or came from books in the heady days of collecting, 1891–1910. The last was not always as wicked as may appear, for many were from boards of volumes destined for pulping. That a number of these ex-libris were notably early and rare suggests that some of the books they adorned might, later on, have had a kindlier fate. Noted old bookplates *per se* had then a greater draw than now, partly because today's collectors have different horizons. If a print of the Bacon gift plate, Pepys's ex-libris or the like turn up, excitement might mount in buyers' and sellers' breasts; but rarity and choiceness have, for scholars, much wider parameters. A majority of contemporary devotees have little inkling of the importance of many old bookplates, but any such setting of sights is the individual's prerogative. The essence of worthwhile collecting is that it be personally absorbing and thus fulfilling. The sharing of insights and dissemination of knowledge follow naturally.

Booksellers, bibliophiles and bookplate collectors should collaborate to common advantage. Should booksellers be tempted to view collectors a little askance, ex-libris being mostly modest artefacts, they should bear in mind the documentation they have made available, not least in the last 20 years. Bookselling is, historically, an important business, but in going somewhat beyond what is strictly required there may be much

---

[14] See David Low, *With All Faults*, Tehran, The Amate Press, 1973, pp. 101–2.
[15] There is a brief article on this in *The Bookplate Society Newsletter* for March, 1977, p. 56.
[16] An inadequate article – information being wanting – on the bookplates of Jessie M. King is in *The Bookplate Society Newsletter* for September, 1977, pp. 74–76.
[17] Campbell Dodgson's *An Iconography of the Engravings of Stephen Gooden*, Elkin Mathews, 1944, is the only text detailing his work, but an updating is in hand.

advantage. The writer has at hand both catalogues and dealers' letters he would not be parted from. The surest test of catalogues is whether the question, 'Will this assist future scholars and bibliographers?', is simply answerable in the affirmative. Such opportunities for lasting usefulness should not be lightly thrown away.

Arellanes, Audrey Spencer, *Bookplates, A Selective Annotated Bibliography of the Periodical Literature*, Detroit, 1971. Includes an index to *Journal of the Ex Libris Society*, 1891–1908.

Castle, Egerton, *English Book-Plates*, 1892, new and enlarged edition, 1893. A helpful general and stylistic survey, also detailing later nineteenth-century bookplate makers.

De Tabley, see Warren.

Ex Libris Society, Journal of, 1891–1908, ed. W. H. K. Wright. Reprinted 1970, Westport, See also Arellanes.

Fincham, Henry W., *Artists and Engravers of British and American Book Plates*, 1897. Signed ex-libris arranged by engraver/artist. Most useful, though inaccurate in detail.

Hamilton, Walter, *Dated Book-plates*, 1895. British and Continental plates arranged chronologically; but consult the index and addenda pp. 215ff.

Hardy, W. J., *Book-plates*, 1893, 2nd edn, 1897. A sound introduction, with chapters on American, French and German ex-libris, etc.

Howe, E. R. J. Gambier, *Catalogue of British and American Book Plates* bequeathed to the Trustees of *the British Museum by Sir Augustus Wollaston Franks*, 3 vols, 1903–1904. See the comments on p. 1.

——— *Catalogue of the . . . Collection of Book-plates of the late Julian Marshall*, 1906. Helpful indication of scarcity and rarity of bookplates.

Labouchère, Norna, *Ladies' Book-plates*, 1895. Brief cataloguing, but including dated and undated plates, bibliophiles and artists, heraldry and foreign ex-libris.

Lee, Brian North, *British Bookplates, A Pictorial History*, Newton Abbot, 1979. Includes a section on book labels.

——— *British Royal Bookplates and ex-libris of related families*, Aldershot, 1992. Includes immediate descendants and relations, illegitimate offspring, and lists dubitable ex-libris.

——— *Early Printed Book Labels, A catalogue of dated personal labels and gift labels printed in Britain to the year 1760*, Private Libraries Association, 1976. Includes short appendices on early American labels, printers' gifts and book stamps.

Marshall, see Howe.

Vaughan, Herbert M., *The Welsh Book-plates in the Collection of Sir Evan Davies Jones, Bart*, 1920. *Welsh Book-plates (Sir Evan Davies Jones' Collection) Supplement*, Carmarthen, 1928. Alphabetical with brief biographical details.

Warren, The Hon. J. Leicester, *A Guide to the Study of Book-plates*, 1880 (2nd edition as Lord de Tabley, but published posthumously), Manchester, 1900. The pioneer work on the subject, it includes Continental ex-libris and their makers. F. J. Thairlwall's index to it was reprinted from the *Journal of the Ex Libris Society*, Vol. IV.

George W. Fuller's *A Bibliography of Bookplate Literature*, Washington, 1926 (republished in Detroit, 1973), is now of course sadly out of date, and there is urgent need for a new bibliography of bookplate literature in the English language. Its lack is doubtless due to its being so sizeable an undertaking. The Bookplate Society alone has published in the last 20 years about as much in books and articles as appeared during the years of the Ex Libris Society.

Booksellers as Publishers

Melanie McGrath

Whatever happened to the arcadian days of the eighteenth century when booksellers kept little presses in the back room for running off the odd pindarick? Big business, that's what happened. Most publishing houses are now multinational conglomerates with huge distribution networks and marketing budgets far beyond the pocket of the average bookseller. This should not daunt the bookseller with a good idea. In fact the very size of most publishing firms leaves booksellers with more opportunities than ever to publish selectively and with success in specialized areas. Many are publishing on a semi-regular basis today. The kinds of books they issue range from facsimile reprints of local maps to lavish colour plate books with hand-coloured title pages. The cardinal rules are simple – watch your costs with religious fervour, don't be over ambitious and know your market as if your life depended on it.

Identifying markets

Never publish a book unless you understand what kind of people might want to buy it and you are convinced that it will offer them something not currently available by way of new information or new ideas. Of course, major publishing houses occasionally issue books more speculatively, but they can afford to take the risk of the book not finding a market.

Does your bookshop specialize in a period or subject area? If so, always publish to your strengths. If you have a data base of customers, use it. You could send out questionnaires to them for initial market research or even ask them to subscribe to your projected publication before you commit yourself to any investment. Remember that rare books librarians will not by and large be involved in selecting new books and that for American libraries decisions to buy books retailing at more than about $500 are usually taken by committee, which takes time.

Are most of your customers local? If so, local interest books may work for you. If not, think about your customer profile and gear your publications accordingly. Don't expect your Japanese customers to be interested in books on the Norfolk Broads in the sixteenth century. If you deal regularly with other booksellers, books about books may do well. Don't try to widen your nets: keep the market you have in mind specialized, limited and easy to reach. Publishing in the same area in which you specialize may find you new customers for your old books and add to the prestige of your operation. A dealer in incunabula who publishes a Marilyn Monroe picture book is in big trouble.

What type of book is saleable?

The simple answer is that any type of book can be saleable if there is a market for it. As a rule books fall into two categories – those which convey useful or essential information a group of people really must have, and those it would be nice for someone to buy.

Dictionaries fall into the first category, novels into the second. The more essential your book to your market the better it will sell and the higher you can price it. However, the market for 'essential' books is competitive so you will do best if you can find an unplugged gap. It is always good to bear in mind that facsimiles will be cheaper to produce than reset books, black and white print cheaper than colour, paperback cheaper than hardcover. High price, low volume, essential information books will make a good return. Low price, high volume, general books may be more fun to publish but they imply a much greater risk. Some books are more sensitive to the state of the economy than others. Libraries often cut facsimile budgets first but will be loath to drop the purchase of seminal reference books and annuals.

Presentation

Once you are sure of your market, consider how to present the book. If it is a reference work for libraries, it should have a good solid cover and it will be a false economy to publish it in paperback. If it is a plate book it should be printed on acid-free paper to preserve the colour balance, and so on.

Copyright, libel and contracts

The copyright law is extremely complex and it is a wise precaution to read a potted version of the Copyrights and Patents Act, 1988. Generally, a book is in copyright for 50 years after its first publication or 50 years after the death of the author, whichever is later, after which it enters the public domain. However, the typographical arrangement of public domain texts can also be under copyright to a publisher. A straightforward facsimile reproduction of a Penguin Classic may well be an infringement of copyright. If your book is written by someone other than yourself draw up a contract specifying the terms and conditions. A recent judicial ruling advised that spoken promises constitute a contract, so always make notes of anything you might agree over the table or the telephone. Since libel awards soared into the stratosphere, most publishers cover themselves by issuing contracts containing an indemnity clause protecting the publisher from responsibility for libel suits, but if there is any danger that the book you intend to publish contains any material of a libellous nature it is wise to let a libel lawyer read it. *Always* get agreements in writing. At all costs avoid the law courts.

The process of publishing

1. *Costing the book.* Always cost a book before making a final decision whether or not to publish. Cost in editorial fees (try to avoid royalties since they are cumbersome to administer – pay the author a fee instead), the cost of photographing the original text if your book is to be a facsimile, the cost of typesetting if not. Next add in the cost of printing and binding the book, allowing for paper costs, head and tail bands, spine blocking and so on. Remember that printers' terms are *always* negotiable. Finally make a provision for marketing the book (the publishers' rule varies but is generally 7–15 per cent

of the revenue the book is expected to bring in any one year). If you are keeping the book on your own premises, there may be an extra provision for insurance; if the book is housed elsewhere (printers will often store books for a fee), cost in the storage fee. Lastly, if you are using outside distributors to invoice and send out the books, cost in their fee. In general try to keep the process as simple as possible. House your own books, invoice and process orders yourself.

New books should be priced at about five times their unit cost in order to give you a healthy margin. However, you should always price to your market and try to reduce costs rather than attempt to sell your book at an unrealistic price. The more specialized and 'essential' your book, the higher the price the market will bear. If you can't make the figures work don't even contemplate publishing the book. Keep print runs low, even though this increases the unit cost of each book a little. The cost of keeping stock is high and even the most worthy of books dates fairly quickly.

2. *Producing the book*. The easiest book to produce is the facsimile. So long as the quality of the original text is sound, the pages are not tightly bound, the paper not badly foxed or holed and the book complete, it is a simple process to have the book photographed and film made up for the printer. Many printers specialize in facsimile book production and can take on the work through to finished book. One way to cut the cost of producing a book without its looking too amateur is to facsimile the text from a laser-printed paper copy of the manuscript.

If the book needs to be typeset, this can be done most cheaply from computer disk. It is always wise to check that the typesetter can handle your word-processing software and does not require that special codes be put into the text. Desk-top publishing is an art in itself, and requires a fairly large investment in expensive computer software, so it is best left to those who publish regularly. Books can also be set straight from a typewritten paper ('hard') copy, of course but typesetters cannot be expected to interpret hard copy covered in scrawl and tippex.

It is cheaper and wiser, if possible, to have the book typeset straight into page proofs, but if the setting is complex or there will be revisions to be made at a late stage then the typesetter will set into galley proofs and make up pages at a later stage. It goes without saying that the fewer the stages, the cheaper the process will be. Once the proofs have been checked and corrections made the camera-ready copy can be sent to the printer. The printing process is quite complex and you are referred to the bibliography below for references. Allow about six months for the process of converting manuscript into a finished book; three months for facsimiles.

3. *Timing*. Publishing is a cyclical business. Forty per cent of all books are sold in the run up to Christmas and there is generally a blip at the beginning of the summer as readers buy books for the beaches. Timing itself is less crucial for specialist books but your book will always get more press attention, and probably sell better, if you can publish it to mark an anniversary or cover a news story. That said, missing an anniversary or event is the very worst thing you can do. One prestigious publisher recently brought out the 'authoritative' account of communism in Eastern Europe. It appeared in November 1989.

4. *Marketing, selling and distributing the book*. Booksellers have a big head start in their ability to sell the books they have published: their customers. If you have selected your

book wisely your customers will want it. Make quite sure that you present your book accurately. Many people will assume that a book published by a bookseller will be a facsimile. If yours is not you will have to work hard to make that clear.

There are agents who will hawk your book round bookshops but they take a large cut and if you have been wise enough to choose to publish a specialized book you should be able to reach your core market quite easily, preferably by mail. If your book might have a good American sale, try to persuade a friendly bookseller in America to publicize and distribute it for a fee or a percentage of the takings.

Do not rely wholly on new bookshops, unless your book is of local interest or there exists a bookshop selling new books in your specialized field. New bookshops often expect discounts of 35–40 per cent, with payment terms of 60–90 days and almost everything is sold on a sale or return basis.

Publishers in the UK are sometimes snobbish about selling new books to customers on the telephone, but many people, particularly librarians, are very responsive to telephone selling if it is managed well.

If after a few weeks the market proves singularly underwhelmed by your offerings there are ways of retrieving the situation and remaining cautious friends with your bank manager. There are many free publicity outlets for your book, from local stores, clubs and societies to the highly suggestible world of the media. Send press releases and review copies to the book pages of newspapers and magazines and follow them up with phone calls. If you can construct a story around the publication of your book then even better; literary and features editors often respond positively to a ready-made story line. Wheel your author out, if you have one, and make him/her talk at the Rotary Club. A word of caution: one publisher recently organized a media circus for a famous novelist only to discover that he spoke with a severe stammer when nervous, thus rendering him almost totally incomprehensible on the radio and TV. Inevitably, the publicity tour had to be cancelled with much loss of face on the publisher's part. Continue to send leaflets or information sheets to your core market; people often need more than one exposure to a piece of publicity material before they take it in. Exploit any forthcoming anniversaries or related events by sending out a press release on your book to local bookshops and the media.

Publishing a book provides the great satisfaction of having made something solid and lasting, something people want and need and which may, in its modest way, change a few minds and turn a heart or two. It is hard work bringing it off, and likely only to pull in a modest profit. But then, when did the prospect of hard graft for humble returns ever deter a bookseller?

Baverstock, A., *How to market books*, 1993.
Cassell's Directory of Publishing, 1991.
Clark, Charles, *Publishing Agreements*, 3rd edn, 1988.
Godber and Webb, *Marketing for Small Publishers*, 1992.
Peacock, J., *Book Production*, 1989.
Turner, Barry (ed.), *The Writer's Handbook*, 1993.
Writers' and Artists' Yearbook, published annually.

Bookselling in England – a Brief History

Philippa Bernard

Until William Caxton set up the first printing press in London in 1476, the history of the distribution and sale of books in England revolved largely around the Church and the universities. The great monastic houses certainly exchanged scholarship, offering their manuscripts to others of their order and despatching their scribes and copyists to help their brothers; and accounts exist of the purchases made by important libraries, such as those at York, St Albans, Jarrow and Exeter. The distribution of the work of Bede, Alcuin, Lanfranc and other medieval scholars depended upon the speed and accuracy of the young novices who wrote down the text, usually from dictation, and upon their ability to produce multiple copies in the shortest possible time.

The two English universities of Oxford and Cambridge enjoyed a highly developed trade in books. They licensed the *stationarii* who were granted the privilege of selling books, censored texts for heretical opinion and had some regard for the welfare of their licensees. There were also wealthy private collectors and patrons, though not a great deal is known of them or their libraries. One such was Richard de Bury, Bishop of Durham, who travelled widely and wrote the *Philobiblon*, 1345, a tribute to the collecting of books, advising his readers to turn to books: 'You will not find them asleep; if you err, no scoldings on their part; if you are ignorant, no mocking laughter'.

The stationers of London (remaining in one 'station' instead of peddling their wares from town to town) came together in 1403 to form the Stationers' Company and established themselves as a recognized guild with official sanction to buy and sell books.

England's first contribution to the spread of learning by means of the printed word was closely directed towards popular taste. The early continental printers were preoccupied with religious literature and classical texts, but in England Caxton – though himself a considerable scholar – was more concerned with romance, legend and fable, bringing his enterprise immediate success among those who could read his books. Continental printers had taken a considerable share in the restricted market for scholarly works and the early English printers found alternative – and profitable – outlets for their new technology. Caxton's use of the vernacular, and the home-spun flavour of books such as Chaucer's *Canterbury Tales* and Aesop's *Fables*, gave the early English book trade an immediate commercial advantage over imported material. Legal textbooks, too, formed an important part of the output of English printers, especially of Richard Pynson, the first Printer to the King. The influence of the early continental printers on English trade gave rise to considerable anxiety. Foreign workers were forbidden to participate in the new craft of printing and many who had been employed here for some years found themselves ostracized, though their skills remained unmatched by native printers for some time.

In 1557 the Stationers' Company was granted a royal charter, under which it was empowered to control and censor all printed works, with suitable punishment meted out to any who contravened its powers by printing, selling or even possessing banned literature. Two years later the Company was ordered to license any book offered for sale;

and its powers diminished further in 1577 when Queen Elizabeth offered the prerogative of printing and selling certain types of books (grammars, music, and prayer books among them) to some of her favourites as privileges of the Court. The booksellers appealed against the ruling with some success; several of them had in any case already declared that they would print whatever they liked (an early manifestation of the independence, not to say obstinacy, that has always characterized the trade).

A similar confrontation with the Queen occurred when the booksellers learned of her interest in the King of Sweden as a possible suitor, and printed portraits of the two side by side. They were duly reprimanded and their material was confiscated.

By Shakespeare's day London booksellers were well established as a licensed trade with the majority of dealers settled around the area of St Paul's Churchyard. The old Gothic cathedral, with the longest nave in Europe, was surrounded by small alleyways and narrow closes such as Paternoster Row and Ave Maria Lane. Most traders lived above the shop or maintained small stalls in the lee of the Cathedral, many acting as printer and publisher of their own publications and as retailer for those of others. However, the reputation of the English trade in the second half of the sixteenth century was sadly inferior to that of most of the great cities of Europe. The quality of English printing was hardly comparable to the great achievements of Venice, Leyden or Antwerp. Techniques and equipment were often outdated and workmen insufficiently skilled. Markets continued to exist for the romantic literature that Caxton had popularized, but demand for the scholarly works that would have brought English craftsmen into contact with their continental colleagues was answered by the foreign printing presses. London booksellers were commercial rather than academic in their outlook, and their standing suffered accordingly.

The distinction which was later taken for granted between printer, publisher and bookseller, was less clearly drawn in the sixteenth century; but printers and publishers were already beginning to go their separate ways. A printer was essentially a craftsman occupied with work requiring technical skill, investment in plant and equipment and an aesthetic appreciation of the appearance of the printed page. The bookseller/publisher took on the work of handling the book both before and after it reached printing stage. He dealt with the author, as does a modern publisher, commissioning work or reading proffered manuscripts, negotiating fees, cooperating with other booksellers in joint ventures, seeing his investment through the press and finally, when the work was complete and the sheets delivered, undertaking the whole sales operation: binding, sub-contracting a part of the printed edition, warehousing and advertising. Few booksellers' catalogues or publishers' advertisements have survived from this period but sometimes extra copies of the title-pages were printed to be hung up to public view as advertisements; the proximity of one bookshop to another must have ensured that information about new books travelled fast.

Outside London in the sixteenth century there was a thriving provincial book trade. There were of course both printers and booksellers in the university towns, but the number of printers was strictly controlled and bookselling was mainly confined in the early years to cathedral towns such as York, Chester and Exeter; however, by the middle of the sixteenth century there were bookshops in most country towns and chapmen and itinerant traders were to be found in fairs and markets.

The booksellers of seventeenth-century England suffered like other merchants from the political and domestic events that affected the whole nation. The Puritan obsession with fundamentalist Biblical teaching linked to political power led to proscription and censorship and inevitably to clandestine printing shops. Those who sold forbidden literature were more vulnerable even than those who printed it; but the book trade flourished well enough during the period of the Civil Wars and the Commonwealth. Some of England's greatest literary works appeared at this time, reflecting the intellectual forces at work in the country: the first authorised edition of Thomas Browne's *Religio Medici*, 1642, Milton's *Eikonoklastes*, 1649, Thomas Hobbes' *Leviathan*, 1651, and in a lighter vein Izaak Walton's *The Compleat Angler*, 1653.

The devastation of the Plague caused havoc among Londoners of every calling. The court withdrew in 1665 from London to Oxford, depriving the bookselling trade of a large and important part of its market; and it also had to contend with the belief that the handling of books was one of the causes of infection. The widespread hardship caused by the great fire in 1666 was felt especially by the London book trade. The flames brought almost total destruction in the area around St Paul's, devastating the shops, warehouses and homes of the booksellers in the neighbourhood. They had stored much of their stock in the small crypt church of St Faith's under the cathedral. Evelyn's description of the scene is even more graphic than Pepys's: 'It was astonishing to see what immense stones the heat had in a manner calcined, so that all the ornaments, columns, friezes, capitals and projectures of massy Portland stone, flew off, even to the very roof, where a sheet of lead covering a great space (no less than six acres by measurement), was totally melted. The ruins of the vaulted roof falling, broke into St Faith's which being filled with the magazines of books belonging to the Stationers, and carried thither for safety, they were all consumed, burning for a week following.' Evelyn estimated that the value of the material lost amounted to about £200,000. As the first edition of *The Compleat Angler* was priced at 18 pence, it is clear that the extent of the losses was immense.

The booksellers of the sixteenth and seventeenth centuries are shadowy figures. Their names appear on title-pages, in the records of the Stationers' Company, on contemporary legal documents. John Day, the printer, was imprisoned during Mary's reign to reappear in Elizabeth's. He printed Foxe's *Book of Martyrs* in 1563 (the author called weekly to read his proofs), and kept a printing shop in the old city Ald Gate. He became master of the Stationers' Company and is better known as a printer than as a bookseller. Such names as William Jaggard, Thomas Thorpe and Edward Blount will always be associated with Shakespeare and the names of most of the better known early booksellers are linked to the authors they represented.

Little is known about their shops. The area around St Paul's was limited and, although the shops were small, space was much sought after. It made good sense to have a fashionable showroom where authors and customers could be entertained while taking advantage of a cheaper location for a workshop or printing house, as had Queen Elizabeth's printer Christopher Barker. Marjorie Plant, in *The English Book Trade*, 1939 (revised 1965), mentions 94 dealers in books in the city of London in 1600. By 1624 there were perhaps too many; George Wither complained about them in *The Scholler's Purgatory*: 'How many dung-boats full of fruitless works do they yearly foist on His Majesty's subjects'. In 1663, Plant mentions, the French traveller Samuel de Sorbière, in *A Journey*

Contemporary print of James Lackington, Bookseller, of 'The Temple of the Muses', Finsbury Square, 1795.

to England, noticed 'the vast number of booksellers' shops . . . twice as many as in the Rue Saint Jacque in Paris'.

Examination of early records does bring to light a little information about the shops themselves. They opened early, closed at about dusk, and had by law to close on Sundays and feast days. The Stationers (not all booksellers were members of the Company) controlled trade practices, refusing permission to trade in books to pedlars and itinerants, and to booksellers to trade with other merchants. However, booksellers themselves could conduct their business, provided they did so honestly, in whatever way they wished. Some offered books for reading without the necessity to buy; a small subscription allowed the visitor the facilities of a library, though he could not take the books away. John Ogilby, the cartographer, advertised book lotteries, with the purchase of a ticket offering the chance of winning a book as a prize.

Licensing of new books had been covered by an Act of Parliament which lapsed in 1695. In 1710 a new bill offered to an author some degree of protection in the printing and sale of his work, but the Act extended control only for 14 years, and that only in Britain: this brief freedom from piracy and unauthorized reprinting did not extend to the pirated editions which appeared in Ireland or the Netherlands, causing many difficulties for English authors (and later for dealers and collectors). Samuel Johnson's relationship with his booksellers is well documented. As the son of a bookseller himself, he saw both sides of each issue. No system of royalties existed, so financial arrangements relied on the sale of copyright. The risks taken by a bookseller in the purchase of unknown work might be reflected in a miserly fee to the author, who could not recoup if the book later proved successful. Some astute booksellers, sure that they were on to a good thing, allowed the author to name his own terms. Thus, Johnson asked 200 guineas for his *Lives of the Poets*, negotiated for 300 and might have received a thousand if he had persisted.

Tonson, with Bernard Lintot, Robert Dodsley, John Dunton, Edmund Curll and others, are known mostly for the works they published. Literary biographies and correspondence of the period mention meetings with booksellers and visits to bookshops, but it was not until James Lackington published *Memoirs of the First Forty-five Years of His Life* in 1791 that the business practices of one bookseller at least were publicized in sufficiently detailed form to shed considerable light on the way such a business operated. Lackington's preoccupation with Methodism and his self-opinionated style do not prevent his readers from gaining much information about the way he ran his shop. His name appears at the foot of many title-pages, so it is clear that he was widely involved in publishing ventures; the British Library holds documentary evidence of some of his dealing, and he makes it clear in the memoirs that he was in business to make money (in which he certainly succeeded). He allowed no credit to anyone, kept his profit margins low to undercut his competitors and bought up remainders (usually sold off very cheaply or destroyed) to resell at full price. He travelled widely throughout Britain in search of stock and regularly produced by his own efforts catalogues of some 12,000 items. It is probable that he was thoroughly disliked throughout the trade (not least because he made a great deal of money), but the enormous bookshop that he built in Finsbury Square was an important attraction for visitors to London. After his death his successors at 'The Temple of the Muses' were approached by Shelley in an attempt to find a publisher for his wife's new novel, and *Frankenstein* eventually appeared under the imprint of Lackington, Allen and Co. of Finsbury Square.

Apart from their involvement in publishing, booksellers had much else to occupy them. Trade sales by auction were an important source of antiquarian and secondhand stock, with the auction houses centred round the Covent Garden area. Samuel Paterson, who continued his bookselling activities throughout his life as an auctioneer, was known for the scholarly quality of his catalogues. These were available from sources other than the auctioneer, and it was not unusual to find one bookseller offering another's catalogues for sale. Paterson's catalogues were arranged in order of format: folios, then quartos, followed by octavo and duodecimo. The auction sales were often held on several successive evenings, with excellent dinners provided. The bidding usually rose by sixpence until it reached five shillings, though Hutchins, another Covent Garden auctioneer, allowed the bidding to advance by threepence; Mrs Hutchins sat in the chimney corner to supervise operations and to make sure all was fair and above-board (or, if not, that any bias favoured the auctioneer). The auctioneer George Leigh always brought his snuffbox to the auction. 'When a high priced book is balancing between £15 and £20', said Dibdin, 'It is a fearful signal of it reaching an additional sum if Mr. Leigh should lay down his hammer and delve into this said crumple-horn snuffbox.'

It was usual for booksellers to take on articled apprentices. An advertisement of 1801 seeks a young man of liberal education: 'He will receive every attention and have the

Dr Syntax and Bookseller, from William Combe's *The Tours of Dr. Syntax*, 1812–22, illustrated by Thomas Rowlandson.

fullest opportunity of acquiring a knowledge of the old as well as the new book trade. A premium will be required'. Adam Black was apprenticed to Lackington before returning to Edinburgh to found with his brother Charles the firm of A. & C. Black.

Frank Mumby, in *The Romance of Bookselling*, 1967, calls the eighteenth century 'The Golden Age of Bookselling'. Nostalgia has its place, but the changes that overtook the trade in the following century were by no means all unhappy. Many of the close links between bookseller and publisher were ending – the divisions in the trade were more between dealers in old and in new books. Some of today's great antiquarian bookshops were founded: Sotherans in 1812, Bernard Quaritch in 1847, Maggs in 1855, Francis Edwards in 1855, Charles Sawyer in 1894. In many ways it was the books that were changing, not the booksellers. Colour printing, steel engraving, cheap editions, cloth bindings – all these were pushing the Victorian booksellers out of their comfortable armchairs into a more complex world. The Great Exhibition made the nation aware of its industrial inheritance. Empire, railways, the penny post; bookdealers had to come to terms with new technology and with new classes and countries where they might find their customers. Some took up the challenge, forming close links with wealthy collectors in America, compiling scholarly catalogues taking full advantage of new bibliographical research and cooperating closely with other dealers at home and abroad. Others preferred to remain quite independent, perhaps even reclusive, choosing the company of their books rather than their customers.

By the outbreak of the 1914–18 War the world of antiquarian books was acquiring an identity of its own. The booksellers' *quartier* in London was by now Charing Cross Road. No. 84 did not achieve its unforeseen fame until 1969 but Ben Marks had set up shop there as early as 1904. The Bloomsbury area around the British Museum was another favoured setting in the years between the wars, and was to see a revival in the 1970s. Cecil Court's prominence dates from the 1960s, though several booksellers took up residence much earlier, H. M. Fletcher and Harold Storey among them.

The twentieth century saw the emergence of a relatively new figure. Until then the bookbuyer was represented first and foremost by the gentleman of ample means and leisure, who assembled a handsomely bound library, acquired from deferential bookshops in a prosperous part of town. Or he might be a scholar, to whom condition was not greatly important and whose own pencil notes could be added to those of previous owners. And there was the snapper-up of popular literature, eager for the new cheap editions and with a healthy appetite for new fiction, adventure or romantic poetry. The new phenomenon was the book *collector*, knowledgeable in his own field, scrupulous as to condition, building up a relationship with his bookseller in a special field of interest. The modern first edition market, in particular, nurtured this robust infant.

The modern interest in antiques of all kinds, stimulated especially by American participation, had its parallel in the world of books. Most of the older provincial towns had at least one antiquarian book shop; York, Bath, Cheltenham, Edinburgh, Oxford and Cambridge were all important centres. The rapid growth of the Provincial Booksellers' Fairs Association reflected the greatly increased role of booksellers without shops. And the broadening of the bookselling community was also seen in the growing participation of women; the A.B.A. has had four women presidents in recent years.

[1]

To Book Collectors & Lovers of Books.

THE attention of Book-Buyers generally, at home and abroad, is especially directed to the unrivalled Stock of

H. SOTHERAN & Co.,

136, STRAND, LONDON.

(Established upwards of Fifty Years.)

*** Their Stock, consisting of upwards of 200,000 Volumes, includes not only Standard Works and New Books in all classes of Literature and the Fine Arts, but a most interesting Collection of **RARE & CURIOUS BOOKS** of every description. The extensive purchases they are constantly making at Auctions, and of Private Libraries, enable them to offer Books in fine Second-hand condition, at prices much lower than is usually charged.

The well-known character and experience of the Advertisers are sufficient guarantees to Book-Buyers in distant parts that all Orders entrusted to them will be executed with intelligence, care, and promptitude.

Their **PRICE-CURRENT of LITERATURE**, containing 1000 articles, ever-varying, is published monthly and forwarded for 3/- per annum " post-free."

JUST PUBLISHED (for 1870-71), price 6d, post free, or to the Colonies, 1/-, OUR CATALOGUE OF BOOKS FOR THE LIBRARY; comprising a selection of the best Library Edition of Standard Works by the best English Authors, mostly in calf, Russia, or Morocco Bindings, on sale at very moderate prices, by H. SOTHERAN & CO. (late Willis & Sotheran, New and Second-hand Booksellers, 136, Stand (next Waterloo Bridge), London.

To EXECUTORS & SELLERS of LIBRARIES.—H. SOTHERAN & CO., who have for many years been widely known as the most extensive purchasers and sellers of Books of every class in London, beg to inform executors or gentlemen having for sale Libraries of Books, either large or small, that they are ready at all times to give the HIGHEST PRICE for them, or to EXCHANGE the same for others. They also value Libraries for probate either in town or country,

Advertisement for Sotheran & Co., c.1870.

Bolleter's Bookshop, 94 Charing Cross Road, c.1912. The figure in the doorway is young Robert Fletcher. [H. M. Fletcher Ltd.]

Two world wars, women's emancipation, computerization and many other changes have affected bookselling as they have other trades. In particular high overheads have forced many booksellers out of their shops. When the history of twentieth-century bookselling is told it will surely take note of the trade with Japan, English catalogues priced in dollars, fax machines and portable telephones, rising auction premiums and CD-ROM bibliography. Will there be a bookseller left to write the history of the twenty-first?

Curwen, Henry, *A History of Booksellers*, 1873.
Growoll, A., Eames, Wilberforce, *Three Centuries of English Booktrade Bibliography*, 1903 (reprinted in facsimile 1964).
Isaac, Peter (ed.), *Six Centuries of the Provincial Book Trade in Britain*, Winchester, 1990.
Knight, Charles, *Shadows of the Old Booksellers*, 1865 (reprinted 1927).
Marston, Edward, *Sketches of Booksellers of Other Days*, 1901.
Mumby, Frank A., *Publishing and Bookselling*, 5th edn, 1974.
Myers, Robin, *The British Book Trade From Caxton to the Present Day*, 1973.
Plant, Marjorie, *The English Book Trade – An Economic History*, 1939 (revised 1965).
Roberts, William, *The Earlier History of English Bookselling*, 1892.
Studies in the Book Trade: in honour of Graham Pollard, Oxford, 1975.

Booksellling Practice

Leo Bernard

The purpose of these notes is to outline, primarily for newcomers to the antiquarian book trade, some of the basic procedures of bookselling; to explain, that is, how books are bought and sold. Young men and women who are fortunate enough to find a place in a well-established bookselling firm can gain this knowledge by daily experience; but such opportunities are few, and in any event many newcomers to bookselling come to the trade from other occupations: from the teaching profession, from the civil service, from industry, from careers which may have run parallel to an informed interest in books and bookselling. As the pages of this Companion testify, efficient and successful bookselling calls for a wide range of knowledge and a variety of skills; the antiquarian book trade is not hospitable to those who hope to prosper without serious application and effort. Clearly an 'apprenticeship' of some kind is a desirable starting-point; but no bookseller would question the important role of later entrants, many of whom bring valuable specialist knowledge into the trade. It is significant that in recent decades presidents of the Antiquarian Booksellers' Association, the trade's oldest and most authoritative body, have included members whose 'first careers' were in teaching, in accountancy and in the theatre.

This outline of bookselling practice is concerned only with those aspects of the trade which are, by and large, peculiar to it, rather than with the general commercial considerations which govern the success of all trading ventures. It will be convenient, and logical, to consider first the buying of books.

Booksellers acquire their stock in three ways: by private purchase, by buying at auction, and by buying within the trade. The part which each of these activities plays in a bookselling business varies widely according to individual needs and circumstances; many specialist dealers acquire their books almost exclusively in the salerooms and within the trade, whilst those with a more general stock, and with shops that provide convenient points of contact, may rely heavily on the private vendor.

Advertising can play an important part in obtaining offers of the kind of books a dealer wishes to buy. The book trade press – weekly, monthly and quarterly – provides a means of making known both specific and general 'wants', and private vendors can be reached through a wide variety of local and national media. However, press advertising is costly and must be used patiently; it does not, as a rule, bring quick results, and inevitably a high proportion of 'call outs' end with disappointment. Many dealers prefer to rely on personal contacts, with professional advisers such as solicitors often proving helpful; and antique dealers will sometimes pass on useful contacts to bookselling friends. But as in so many aspects of business life, a reputation for fair and considerate dealing is in the end the most important factor. Private sellers who feel that they have been given 'a square deal' will often mention a bookseller to their friends, sometimes many years later.

The buying of books from a private source always calls for care as to the vendor's right to sell. In many cases this will not be in doubt, but many booksellers adopt certain routine precautions when buying from sellers not previously known to them. A simple form can be used to record details of the purchase and this will help to indicate that the bookseller has exercised the reasonable caution legally required of him. Every bookseller will have his own means of judging the honesty of those who offer books for purchase; and those who are members of one of the major trade associations will have the benefit of regular information about books stolen from other dealers, from institutions or from private owners.

Appropriate payment for books bought from private sellers must be largely a matter of sound judgement, and no standard formula can apply to all purchases (though it is said that one well-known firm used to value run-of-the-mill books by laying them out on the counter and employing a tape measure). In one important aspect private buying differs from other transactions: in the saleroom, the bookseller pays the price he chooses to bid; when he buys from a fellow dealer, he is entitled to expect a price to be asked – if only as a basis for discussion; but when books are offered to him privately he is usually expected to take the initiative by making an offer. If that offer is rejected, he may have an opportunity to improve on it if he wishes to do so; if it is accepted, he should feel that his judgement has been sound and bravely dismiss the thought that a lower offer might have been successful.

It need hardly be added that buying from private sources demands proper appraisal of what is offered, as well as fair policies and sound judgement. No experienced bookseller will pay for a book of any consequence without first examining it carefully. The extent of that examination may vary from meticulous collation (especially important in the case of books illustrated with plates) to a brisk look under the dust-wrapper and through the pages of a modern first edition; but care is always needed. The advice given here comes from one who remembers buying 'across the counter' an important two-volume reference work in immaculate dust-wrappers, only to find some weeks later that the volume-two wrapper concealed a second copy of volume one.

A word may be said here about the practice of selling books 'on consignment' for private owners or trade colleagues. This is often a convenient alternative to outright purchase, with the dealer avoiding an investment about which he may have reservations, and the owner receiving a better price when the book is sold. Arrangements of this kind have always had a place in bookselling practice, and often play an important (if invisible) part in the filling of shop and book fair shelves; but they call for some caution. On the practical level there should always be a clear understanding as to the terms of the arrangement and responsibility for any loss or damage; and a dealer who accepts books on consignment must be prepared to 'grin and bear it' if, on occasion, a 'borrowed' book is preferred to one of his own that he would dearly have liked to sell.

Buying advantageously at auction also calls for care and patience, and the dealer new to the trade may be well advised to sit silently through a few sales with eyes and ears alert to every aspect of procedure and tactics. Not that auction procedure is particularly complicated; generally speaking it differs only in minor aspects from one saleroom to another, and even a beginner may feel that if he has viewed carefully and marked up his catalogue wisely, it remains only to raise his hand at the right moment. So it may be – but how should bids be decided upon? How do they relate to estimates, and how do estimates relate to reserves? And when should a hand be raised – at £100, more in hope than expectation, or at £250, as the estimate drops out of sight? These questions, and others of this kind, find ready answers as experience grows; but the newest bookseller can take encouragement from the fact that even though the formidable Mr A may have his habitual seat and the pretty Miss B her expected smile from the rostrum, all are equal when bidding starts. The bookseller who has only yesterday 'put up his sign' can (and sometimes will) outbid the veterans of the trade.

Buying within the trade can take three forms: books can be ordered from catalogues, at a colleague's premises, or from a book fair stand. In the case of personal transactions, a trade discount, normally 10 per cent in the United Kingdom, can be expected; catalogue prices, however, are often 'net', or subject to trade discount only after a stated interval.

Booksellers are in any event well advised to visit other dealers, both individually and at book fairs, as often as their own commitments allow. Such contacts are valuable in several ways: they encourage colleagues to set aside books that are likely to interest those who visit them regularly; they prompt reciprocal visits; and, perhaps most importantly, they enable a bookdealer to keep closely in touch with general trends in the trade as a whole: prices, fashions, priorities. A bookseller who spends all his time among his own shelves is likely to become as narrow in his outlook as a restaurateur who eats only at his own table. Some booksellers have been known to admit to hesitation about visiting colleagues who trade by appointment from their home, on the grounds that in those circumstances courtesy seems always to demand a purchase or two; but such inhibitions are usually dispelled by a tactful host and a friendly glass.

The more formal aspects of transactions within the trade – discounts, credit terms, 'on approval' arrangements – generally follow accepted practices in the business world as a whole; but it should be mentioned that as a rule credit cards are not acceptable as a means of payment for trade purchases.

So much for buying. (Not that more than an introductory word has been said; private acquisitions, especially, take the buyer into a great variety of human situations, and one bookseller will long remember the general's widow who asked for an evening's respite so that she might consult her late husband about an offer for his books. Happily, it was accepted from on high.) Selling is in some respects a more difficult subject to condense usefully, as the factors upon which success depends vary widely according to trading methods: shop, book fairs, catalogues, combinations of these; and the factors which apply in all these situations are those about which it is easy to labour the obvious. Such basic considerations as accuracy and clarity in the description of books, whether in a few words pencilled on an endpaper or in a full catalogue description, and good sense in their pricing, whether in tens, hundreds, or thousands of pounds – these are clearly skills upon which good bookselling must always depend. Pricing, especially, demands a subtle blend of knowledge and instinct, restraint and self-confidence. For the newcomer to the trade (and not for him alone), there are useful guides – auction records and annual compilations of catalogue prices; but these must always be tempered by individual judgement. Auction prices are instructive when a consistent pattern can be seen over a number of years; a single price, with condition only briefly described, can often mislead. Catalogue prices can give valuable guidance, but here too, some care is needed; it is useful to know something of the pricing habits of the dealers whose figures are quoted, and it is well to remember that while auction records do at least record an actual sale, catalogue prices may or may not have achieved that result.

Book fairs and booksellers' catalogues receive well-merited attention elsewhere in this Companion; but, despite the impact of escalating costs, bookshops remain at the centre of the antiquarian bookselling scene. They are as varied in size, scope and 'personality' as might be expected in a famously individualistic trade, and no doubt their variety pleases the buyers of books. Some collectors are quite at ease, and full of high hopes, in a small room or two full of half-sorted books, some on shelves, some in piles, some still in boxes; others may prefer the well-organized bookroom, efficiently furnished and carefully arranged. It would be sad indeed if these contrasts were to give way to some neatly shelved sameness of plan, but they should not distract attention from a few important considerations that affect all bookshops, large or small, dignified or modest.

Security must rank high among these general concerns. Theft from bookshops is a daily occurrence, and some dealers who feel especially vulnerable are now adopting the electronic security systems that have been in use for some years in other fields. However, a small shop can achieve a good measure of security by taking quite simple precautions – good lines of sight from bookseller to shelves, locked bookcases for stock of significant value, courteous but firm insistence on bags being set aside when necessary. It is well to remember, too, that books are not always a thief's priority; a handbag or wallet will often yield quicker rewards. Serious book thefts should always be reported to the ABA and PBFA – both organizations have highly efficient communications systems which quickly advise a large part of the trade of stolen books; and every bookseller should consider using a discreetly placed pencilled code-mark to assist the identification of his stock.

One quite different form of security calls for mention. However austerely a bookshop may be arranged, it should provide adequate surfaces for the inspection of the books that need particularly gentle handling. It is highly distressing to see the lower cover of a book hanging down helplessly as it is inspected and damage will be avoided if there is always somewhere to put a book down. Perhaps a more controversial question is whether there should be somewhere to put a customer down. Perhaps a chair or two – but on this policies will differ widely. There can be no doubt that chairs attract the more deadly species of bookshop bore as jam jars attract wasps; but no doubt, too, that a good customer will enjoy perusing a book in some comfort.

A review of bookselling practice, however limited, should take into account two aspects of a dealer's work which are not always directly related to buying or selling books. The first of these is essentially the province of the binder; but few booksellers escape – or wish to escape – the task of giving advice on the restoration of books. Most will have a mutually advantageous relationship with one or more binders, to whom they can pass on work of this kind or to whom (if they wish to remain uninvolved) they can refer enquiries. Virtually all booksellers require such contacts, if only to ensure efficient attention to their own needs; but some may hesitate to become widely involved in repair and restoration work. The cost of this work has increased dramatically in recent years, and the addition of an adequate 'handling charge' may sometimes prove difficult. Some booksellers prefer to handle repair work only for their more important customers; but all should be familiar with the main types of repair and rebinding, and with the results that can be achieved by the best modern restoration techniques.

The second peripheral aspect of antiquarian bookselling which requires mention is the provision of valuations. These are required for various purposes, of which probate and insurance are perhaps the most common. Insurance valuations normally assess the cost of replacement, while probate valuations are expected to indicate current market values. A word of advice on the value of a single item, or of a few, may sometimes be given without charge, but valuations of substantial collections of books often require quite extensive research and paperwork; in these circumstances a pre-arranged fee or a percentage charge is appropriate. However, valuations may sometimes be followed by an opportunity to purchase books, and it may then be thought fair to cancel any charge. Every bookseller will know – or will quickly learn! – that there is often a reverse situation, in which the offer of books for sale is made simply as a painless means of obtaining a valuation; but this must be regarded stoically as one of the hazards of the trade. A charity box is sometimes a useful means of exacting some small reward.

It has been said that antiquarian bookselling is one of the pleasantest ways to make very little money; and though the saying is called into question by the existence of some booksellers who are morose and others who are rich (and, indeed, some who are both), it does tell a certain truth. The trade is one that offers exciting prospects, in buying no less than in selling, and much stimulating companionship; but the very uncertainties that make it an endlessly interesting business do perhaps preclude some of the high-powered techniques of money-making. Nevertheless, it should be practised with all the efficiency that such an important amenity deserves.

Bowers, Fredson (1905–1991)

Following in the footsteps of W. W. GREG, the American bibliographer Fredson Bowers sought to improve on the standards of contemporary textual criticism by insisting on meticulous accuracy and attention to detail. His *Principles of Bibliographical Description*, Princeton, New Jersey, 1949, has remained unsurpassed for its close pursuit of precision in bibliographical analysis. He worked, like Greg, on the editing of Shakespearean texts as well as on other literary subjects, and was editor for many years of the periodical *Studies in Bibliography* (based in Charlottesville, at the University of Virginia). He will be remembered as one of the leading figures in the evolution of modern BIBLIOGRAPHY.

Breaker

A term applied to a book which is valued only for its plates. Most print dealers, and booksellers who also deal in prints, will with a clear conscience make use of the illustrations in a book already damaged or incomplete. Copper or steel engravings, hand-coloured illustrations of natural history subjects and of course maps from early atlases are all suitable for use as individual prints. Breaking up dilapidated books has the merit of rescuing what remains intact; but it must be admitted that some dealers are prepared to exploit any book in which the sum of the parts offers more profit than the whole.

Bremer Presse

Founded in 1911 in Bremen by Willy Wiegand, this important German private press is included here because it produced a number of English texts, finely and austerely printed, often enhanced by the superb decorative initials of Edward Johnston's pupil, Anna Simons. The Press continued until 1964.

Lehnacker, Josef, *Die Bremer Presse: Königin der Deutsche Privatpressen*, Munich, 1964.

Britain in Pictures

The first book in this inexpensive and still popular series, David Cecil's *The English Poets*, appeared in 1941. Series I was entitled *The British People in Pictures*; Series II, *The British Commonwealth in Pictures*; and Series III, *The English Poets*. In all, 126 titles were published from 1941 to 1950 (the figure is sometimes given as 127, one book – *English Pottery and China* – having been re-issued with a variant title). The subjects form an extensive review of British life and achievements, and the books, even during wartime, were attractively produced with many colour plates. Among the titles most keenly collected are *The English People*, a George Orwell 'first'; Graham Greene's *English Dramatists*; and Cecil Beaton's *British Photographers*. Several omnibus volumes, bringing together related titles, were issued later. Although the series is collected, the individual books are only of any value if they are in fine condition with dust-wrappers.

Eads, Peter, Britain in Pictures, *The Private Library*, Autumn, 1986.
Wickham, D. E., A Further Look at Britain in Pictures, *The Private Library*, Autumn, 1987.

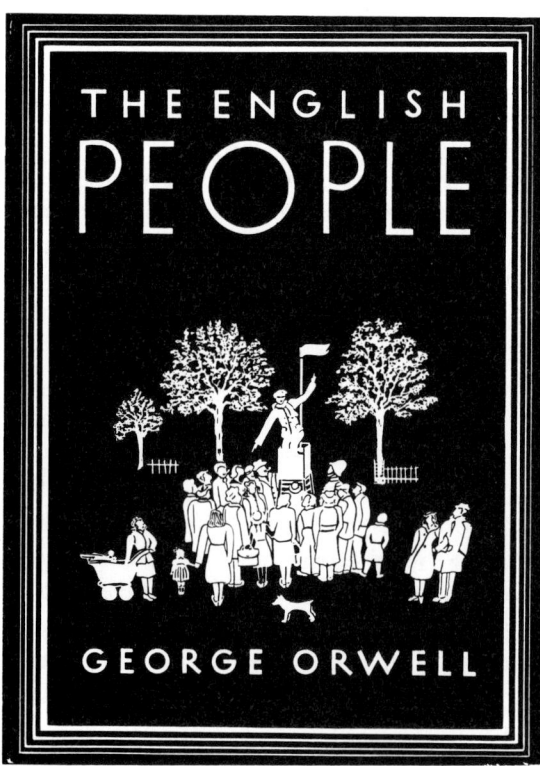

The British Library

The first annual report of the Board of the British Library after its establishment in 1973, expressed its objective as 'a great modern library at the hub of the nation's library system, setting the pace in meeting the multiple needs of today's users and satisfying new needs by creating new services'. It is good to know that present and future users of the Library's unique services are to be well taken care of; this service will continue a noble tradition and it is to the past history of the British Library, formerly the library of the British Museum, that we must first turn to enable us to consider more recent developments.

The Museum was established by Act of Parliament in 1753, after Sir Hans Sloane had offered to the nation his vast collection of books, manuscripts, coins, medals, fossils and curios of all kinds, including, according to Horace Walpole, one of the original trustees, 'a shark with one ear'. The King himself refused the collection for the named price of £20,000, but the government accepted it, along with the two other British Museum foundation collections, those of Robert Harley, the Earl of Oxford, and of Sir Robert Cotton, built up in earlier centuries and bequeathed to the nation by his descendants.

The concept of a nationally owned collection of books and manuscripts available for consultation by anyone of an enquiring mind was entirely new, and one of the earliest public libraries in the world was established in old Montagu House in Bloomsbury, where the first three important collections were housed. A year or two later George II presented to the Museum a large part of the Royal Library, a fine collection of illuminated manuscripts, early printed books and important medieval documents, and the library, already outgrowing the space allocated to it, opened for business.

In spite of the pleasantly rural surroundings of Bloomsbury in the mid-eighteenth century, all was not idyllic within Montagu House. Thomas Gray, who spent much time there, taking lodgings in Southampton Row to be near the new Museum, was much aware of the internal problems of the new institution. Money was short and the keepers were quarrelsome. Gray noted that the Principal Librarian (the title given to the overall head of the Museum) had blocked up the passage to the privy used by his colleagues because they had to pass the windows of his house on the way. New acquisitions depended upon gifts and legacies as there were no endowments or investment policy for the purchasing of books, but in 1823 George IV presented to the library much of the valuable collection assembled by his father.

Space was now very short; the rest of the Museum, too, was extending its collections and a new building was clearly essential if the Museum was to survive. Sir Robert Smirke's building, with its pillars and colonnades, reminiscent of a Greek temple, was completed in 1852 with the Library housed in the East Wing. In 1973 the library was separated from the Museum and became The British Library, a self-regulating organization.

The Reading Room The famous Round Reading Room was opened in 1857 under the direction of Sir Anthony Panizzi, Keeper of Printed Books and then Principal Librarian. It was the Museum's seventh Reading Room. The earlier ones, reminiscent of comfortable London clubs where gentlemen – and ladies – could relax in easy chairs before a cheerful coal fire, were inadequate. The new Reading Room could accommodate 500 readers, and has changed little since its early days. The rows of readers' seats radiate out from a central desk where applications for books are dealt with. This desk is circled by book stacks containing the catalogues. On arriving in the Reading Room a reader must establish himself at one of the numbered desks. A comfortable leather chair, padded writing table and good reading lamp await him, though the brass rail under the desk is no longer filled with hot water to warm his feet, as it was in Panizzi's day. Around the walls of the Reading Room are certain categories of reference works including dictionaries and encyclopaedias in many languages, topography and county histories, some state papers, genealogy and history. Books on these open access shelves may be taken to readers' desks without

THE BRITISH LIBRARY

preliminary notification and returned after use.

Most books in the British Library are on closed access. Order slips are available beside the catalogues and must be completed and handed in, with the number of the reader's desk noted on them. The books are delivered to that desk, usually within two hours, and they may be reserved in the Reading Room overnight.

There is another Reading Room in the North Library, added just before the First World War, where early printed books may be consulted. Here special lighting, the use of pencil only, and the delivery of requested books to a central collection point, ensure particular care in the use of these often fragile books. Similar precautions extend to the use of the Map Library, the Department of Manuscripts and the Oriental Collections. Conservation is a vital concern of the Library.

The collections The foundation collections of Sloane, the Harley family, Cotton and George II included some of the greatest works now in the British Library. They are mostly housed – some on display – in the old East Wing, built for the purpose in 1828, and have been augmented by other benefactions, such as the New Royal Library of George III, Thomas Grenville's collection of early printed books, Rev. C. M. Cracherode's library bequeathed in 1799, the natural history collection of Sir Joseph Banks and more recently the Huth and Ashley Libraries, and books from the BROXBOURNE LIBRARY and from that owned by John Evelyn, dispersed in 1977.

Among the Library's treasures are the world's earliest dated book, the Diamond Sutra, printed in AD 868, many books from the presses of the fifteenth and sixteenth centuries, fine bindings from Samuel Mearne to COBDEN-SANDERSON, the autograph manuscript of *Alice's Adventures Under Ground* illustrated by the author, and unique works from many countries.

Copyright deposit The Copyright Act of 1709 provided that one copy of every book registered at Stationers' Hall should be presented to the Royal Library. After the establishment of the British Museum, the right to receive a copy of every book published was extended to that institution and strictly enforced by Panizzi as a way of extending the collections in spite of the government's parsimony. Today publishers of all new works must lodge a copy with the British Library and thus the allocation of finance to the library can be devoted to special purchases and to foreign books.

Specialist collections It is not only in the field of printed books and manuscripts that the British Library excels. It also holds extensive collections in the Map Library, the Newspaper Library (at Colindale in North London), the Science Reference Information Service, the former India Office Library, the Oriental Collection, and the National Sound Archive (in Kensington), all of which offer a comparable service. There are also specialist collections of music, official publications, state papers and postage stamps. The National Art Library is at the Victoria and Albert Museum.

The catalogues The catalogue shelves in the centre of the Round Reading Room hold 2,008 green folio loose-leaf volumes, listing some fifteen million printed books. Books published up to 1955 are catalogued here in columns with space alongside to add acquisitions from 1956 to 1970. From 1971 to 1975 pages of new entries are added at the end of the relevant volume and books received after 1975 are on microfiche in the Reading Room as well as on computer: the microfiche cataloguing lags slightly behind the computer entries.

Panizzi's old cataloguing system has long been outmoded. Always difficult to follow, it was at least an improvement on the original hand-written catalogue, the only one available until 1841. But the publication of the Anglo-American Cataloguing Rules in 1967 as an internationally accepted code made it essential to update the old cumbersome system. The process of modernizing such a vast catalogue will inevitably take time. Meanwhile the old catalogues still offer a wealth of well-organized information to the librarian, bibliographer and bookseller.

Although books are listed by author, with a comprehensive subject catalogue, useful additional information can be gained by the cross-referencing of joint authorship, editing, illustration, revision, translation and also of material concerning the main author such as bibliography, biography, memoirs, criticism, etc. It is thus possible to discover what additional material is in existence and where it may be found. Under the author's name are listed collected editions, letters by, single works, selections and works about. Information about the book sought is limited; the catalogue does not claim to be a bibliography. The date of publication, format and number of pages are given, but not usually the number of plates or anything concerning the contents of the book.

Most public libraries keep sets of British Library catalogues, often on microfiche, and in 1967 the *General Catalogue of Printed Books to 1955* was reprinted in a Compact Edition of 27 volumes (with later supplements).

Using the library Access to the Reading Room and thus to the Library is by reader's pass only, and no books may be removed from it at any time. Applications for a reader's pass must be made in person; passes are normally issued only to applicants who need 'to use material not readily available elsewhere', who are over 21 and are not studying for a first degree. Proof of identity is required, together with a note of the research being undertaken, countersigned by a college or university tutor, or employer. No charge is made for a reader's pass but a photograph of the applicant (taken in the Issuing Office) is attached to it. A separate pass is needed for the Department of Manuscripts.

Ancillary services There are facilities in the British Library for the use of typewriters, which may not be used in the reading rooms (though personal computers are permitted), sound-proof cubicles for dictating machines or for helping the blind, and computerized searches. A photocopying service is available, or readers may make their own copies. This service is not usually available for books printed before 1850, nor for those in poor condition. The Photographic Service can provide colour or black-and-white photographs or transparencies on request.

The new Library Plans to expand the facilities of the British Library culminated in the decision to develop an extensive site beside St Pancras Station. Here the Library will eventually house all the London collections, except the Newspaper Library and the Sound Archive; these will remain at their present locations. Included in the new buildings will be restaurants, conference rooms, exhibition halls and an open air piazza. New technology will improve cataloguing, retrieval and conservation, and there will be a two-tier system of passes for readers in the much larger Reading Room and to the other collections.

Such an important project has inevitably brought considerable problems. The plan to move was not universally popular. The abandonment of the Round Reading Room in particular invoked much dismay and letters to the press flowed freely. Delays over funding and withdrawal of finance for certain art and design features have slowed down progress. (Plans for a large mural by R. B. Kitaj illustrating T. S. Eliot's *The Waste Land* have been held back.) A major setback arose over the mobile shelving which refused to run smoothly and led to a delay in moving the books from Bloomsbury. However, the Director of the new project, according to a recent bulletin, is optimistic that by 1996 the whole occupation will have been completed, and London, already the location of one of the greatest libraries in the world in terms of its collections and services, will enjoy the same distinction in terms of amenity and centralization of resources.

Barker, Nicolas, *Treasures of the British Library*, 1988.

Harris, P. R. (ed.), *The Library of the British Museum: Retrospective Essays on the Department of Printed Books*, 1991.

Broadsheet

The term broadsheet, or broadside, is most commonly used to describe a proclamation, notice, ballad or other text printed on one side only of a single sheet of paper without folds, though it is also a correct description of any item printed on a whole unfolded sheet, whether on one or both sides. The designation 1° is sometimes used to indicate an unfolded sheet.

Broadside

See BROADSHEET

The Broxbourne Library

The most important section of the Broxbourne Library, formed by Albert Ehrman (1890–1969), was the collection of fifteenth- and sixteenth-century books assembled to illustrate the spread of printing in Europe. The collection comprised some 300 incunabula and about 500 books printed in the sixteenth century. Some of the rarest volumes were presented by Ehrman, and later by his son, to the British Library, the Bodleian, Cambridge University Library and the John Rylands Library, now of Manchester University.

The remaining books were sold at Sotheby's in November 1977. The two-volume catalogue describes books printed in more than 120 towns; it is arranged alphabetically (Abbeville–Lyons; Madrid–Zwolle) and its comprehensive indexes of authors, titles, printers, etc. give it considerable reference value. The Bodleian received the collection of fine bindings, and also the early book catalogues used by Graham Pollard in *The Distribution of Books by Catalogue From the Invention of Printing to AD 1800*. The type specimens and books on typography went to Cambridge.

Ehrman, Albert, The Broxbourne Library, *The Book Collector*, 1954.

Fern, A. M., Type specimens of the Broxbourne Library, *The Book Collector*, 1956.

Nixon, Howard, *Broxbourne Library: Styles and Designs of Bookbindings from the Twelfth to the Twentieth Century*, 1956.

Pollard, Graham, *The Distribution of Books by Catalogue from the Invention of Printing to AD 1800, based on Material in the Broxbourne Library*, Cambridge, 1965.

Brunet

Jacques-Charles Brunet's monumental *Manuel du Libraire et de l'Amateur de Livres* first appeared in Paris in 1810. Its most useful edition is that of 1860–80, which consists of eight volumes in seven with two supplements. The best modern reprint was published by Rosenkilde and Bagger of Copenhagen in 1966. Brunet provides a wealth of information on the books of some 400 years, and not just those of French interest; his terse and often critical comments are informed by considerable experience and taste.

The author entries – more than 30,000 – are arranged alphabetically and are supplemented by an extensive 'Table Méthodique' with main subject headings and numerous sub-divisions. There is no English translation.

Buckram

See CLOTH

C

Calf
See LEATHER

Cancel
Usually this means a single leaf attached to the stub of a leaf which was removed after the book was bound. Possible reasons for this excision include passages disputed in legal actions or (in the case of cancel title-leaves) a 'co-edition' or the sale of copies to another publisher. Another type of cancel title results from the publishers making a change in the title, or selling unsold copies to another publisher (*Paradise Lost* is the best-known example). However, the meaning of the term may be extended to refer to anything from a few letters to several pages. In *Saturday Book No. 4*, for instance, an entire essay by George Orwell was removed from most copies by the publishers, who feared prosecution for obscene libel, and a short story by another author was substituted. In this case, as in many others, the uncancelled version of the book would be highly valued by collectors; it would be described as the first state, if the cancellation was carried out before publication, or as the first issue if it followed publication. In seventeenth- and eighteenth-century books, a leaf intended for cancellation was often partly slit by the printer as a guide to the binder.

The more technical terminology of the subject, in which a distinction is made between the cancelland, or original leaf, and the cancellans, its replacement, is found only in more scholarly descriptions.

Chapman, R. W., *Cancels*, Bibliographia Series 3, 1930.

Care of books
See RESTORATION AND REPAIR

Carter, John (1906–1975)
John Carter's achievements as a bibliographer have had a lasting influence among book collectors and antiquarian booksellers. His analytical and investigative skills are perhaps best represented by his excellent 1947 Sandars Lectures, given at Cambridge University where he was Sandars Reader in Bibliography, and published in the following year as *Taste and Technique in Book Collecting* (reprinted 1970); and by his celebrated collaboration with Graham Pollard, *An Enquiry into the Nature of Certain Nineteenth Century Pamphlets*, 1934. Wise's forgeries were only one of many bibliographical and literary themes that interested Carter: binding variants, the history of publishers' cloth, the highways and byways of Victorian fiction, Thomas Browne's prose and Housman's poetry all feature in his work. His influence is strongest, however, in two works of reference: PRINTING AND THE MIND OF MAN, which he edited with Percy Muir, and *ABC For Book Collectors* (1952, last reprinted 1993), his succinct and witty guide to book-collecting terminology. His definitions of some 500

descriptive words and phrases range from a few lines to a few pages; their clarity and elegance set an exacting standard for all later work in Carter's field, as the editors of this Companion acknowledge only too readily. It was typical of Carter's good-humoured approach to his subject that he reviewed his own book anonymously for *The Book Collector*, giving a highly critical verdict.

Catalogue Bibliographique des Ventes Publiques
See AUCTION RECORDS

Catalogue raisonné
A publication which describes in full detail the entire corpus of a particular artist or school. An essential tool for art dealers, any authoritative *catalogue raisonné* is likely to command a much higher price once it goes out of print than a superficially similar 'coffee table' book.

Catalogues

James Fergusson

Book catalogues come in as many forms as booksellers. Where booksellers may have graduated to their trade from the merchant marine, strawberry-wholesaling, prep-schoolmastering or Christie, Manson and Woods, or (like many schoolmasters) may never have graduated from anywhere at all, having taken up dealing where a childhood collecting habit left off; where the premises these days are less likely to be a medieval shopfront in a cathedral close (though they might be) than the back parlour of a private house or at best a stall on the Portobello Road or a cubbyhole (only open alternate Wednesdays) off the Grassmarket; and many booksellers seem to have no premises at all, but operate out of old wine-cartons lugged in and out of strange hotels booked by the Provincial Booksellers' Fairs Association: so, catalogues come in all shapes and sizes, numbered, unnumbered, on regular, art or recycled paper, described as lists, bulletins or 'More from the Ragbag', pointless catalogues, catalogues bristling with 'points', fat catalogues, impossibly slight catalogues, catalogues that fall apart in the hand, multi-volume hardbound encyclopaedias of catalogues upstanding enough for the bookshelf itself, specialist catalogues, extra-specialist catalogues, catalogues so specialist that, surely, they can be for three customers only, old-fashioned catalogues laid out in columns and divided into a thousand different subjects, designer catalogues with natty covers and startling modernistic typography, austere catalogues printed by a friend on discreet hot metal, friendly catalogues tumbled off a third-hand school duplicator which stretches the skins and squeezes the characters (and the middles of the Os have all dropped out), invisible catalogues taken off a photocopier with no toner from a computer-printer with no ribbon, handwritten catalogues, catalogues with drawings by the bookseller's daughter, great lush luxurious catalogues with a million pounds' worth of stock, most of it illustrated in full colour printed from countless separations in Milan with a cover of matt-laminate that makes London auction-house catalogues look vulgar – all these will have passed through the letter-box, and most of them into the bin, of every bookdealer and collector. What every catalogue has in common – and has had since secondhand booksellers first started issuing catalogues – is that customers or would-be customers everywhere will, whatever its quality, settle on it as though their lives depended on it. For book-buyers are curious folk, curious for knowledge or for a bargain or for that desideratum that has always eluded them, or – just curious. The short-term job of the catalogue-maker is plain: to sell his or her books. The middle-term aim is not to have them sent back again; or to leave their buyers feeling resentful or robbed. A longer-term aim is to lure new customers, make friends with them, flirt with them down the years: so that of all their morning mail it is to your catalogue that they first turn, and then they won't put it down until they have finished. And the ultimate accolade is that when they have finished they don't throw the catalogue away, but put it in a quiet place to re-read occasionally, even use for reference; and once in a while, months, maybe years later, you receive an apologetic telephone-call or postcard inquiring whether, by any remote chance, item 144 is still available. What follows is an 'A to V' of practical if occasionally imperious hints as to the construction, presentation and despatch of the book-catalogue. *How* to catalogue a book is beyond the scope of this study. It is one of those large questions like what a book is worth: only time tells. Very few booksellers these days receive formal tuition – there are few large firms left to teach them and there were never many auction-houses; most people teach themselves, learning by trial, error and imitation. Aside from those two definitive standbys, Ronald B. McKerrow, *An Introduction to Bibliography*, and Philip Gaskell, *A New Introduction to Bibliography*, the best background reading by far remains John Carter's *ABC for Book-Collectors*, an evergreen and elegant work of scholarship carelessly worn.

Abbreviations Beware of needless abbreviations. Customers are not code-breakers. The bookseller has a duty of evangelism – of explanation and persuasion. A catalogue should be like an open shop; you should be able to wander freely among the stacks, finding your way instinctively and without resort to the map. Bibliojargon is a language that takes a little learning, but reduced excessively to abbreviations ('sl w in v sl w dw ow g+−' etc.) it is just cultish.

Addenda These are always read first by the *cognoscenti*, on the principle that they might be newly acquired stock at bargain prices. This is not always the case; they are just as likely to be very old, substandard stock used to plug a gap. Addenda sections are properly for filling a page or a gathering and should never be allowed to outstay their welcome.

Addresses Booksellers have a blind spot about their own addresses. Always check your address, character by character, wherever it is quoted. The consequences if it is incorrectly printed can be unfortunate.

CATALOGUES

Advance copies There is no harm in sending out a few advance copies of your catalogue, provided it is only a few. They should be marked 'Advance Copy', or enclose a personal letter, and they should be reserved for favourite customers or those to whom you misguidedly once offered first bite at some particularly tasty cherry. Librarians will be especially grateful as they may need special authorization for expenditure.

Advertising Of the many places a bookseller can advertise, the best noticeboards for book catalogues remain *The Times Literary Supplement* (weekly) and *Antiquarian Book Monthly*, though the former has lost impact since moving its 'Books and Prints' off the back page. *ABM* further offers a free listing to subscribers. The trouble with advertised catalogues is that respondents assume theirs have arrived last and may not devote the attention to them that they might to their regular post.

Alphabetical order No excuse suffices for failure to alphabetize. A higgledy-piggledy catalogue is an unreadable catalogue. Catalogues in reverse or mischievous order on alphabetist or other grounds should be eschewed too, as tiring to the general reader. One modern first dealer began a catalogue at Z giving as his reason that he was sick to death of opening with J. R. Ackerley's *My Dog Tulip*; he would however have had a much better chance of selling *My Dog Tulip* if he had left it where it was. (It is notable that a high proportion of modern collected authors' names begin with A or B; women novelists particularly favour B.) Some dealers will issue author catalogues entitled 'A–K'. This is a mistake: it alienates perhaps half their customers and the chances are that they will never get round to 'L–Z'. 'St', incidentally, should be alphabetized as though it were 'Saint' and 'Mc . . .' as though it were 'Mac . . .': useful conventions, rarely observed.

Answering machines All booksellers at the close of the twentieth century should have telephone answering machines. If you have a shop, you must remember that, hungry though your customers will be to read your catalogue, not all of them enjoy the ability to do so in opening hours; some indeed may prefer to read it in the evening, in the peace of their armchair. It is vital to catch these armchairpersons' covetousness on the wing; if you don't have an answering machine, their urge to order will pass as sure as Exodus follows Genesis. To have a fax machine is not enough; it assumes of your customers that they have access to faxing when fax machines are not yet prevalent.

Approval, ordering on Although ordering books on approval tends to be frowned on (the sort of person who does it almost invariably returns them) most booksellers subscribe to the convention that if you don't like a book for any reason, then you may send it back; provided only that it is done promptly and that the book returns in the **Condition** in which it went out.

Bank accounts Some booksellers are fond of including banking details in their **Rubric**; some find that if money is remitted straight into their account they can never find out where it came from. The Japanese prefer paying direct to a National Girobank.

Bibliographies These are a bookseller's best friend. The art of bibliography is an obscure one, the practitioners of which are a strange sect of page-counters and arcane jigsaw-puzzlers. The best of them open new areas of book-collecting and – therefore – opportunities for virtuosity in the book-cataloguer. The worst of them, especially those whose mechanical and undescriptive checklists masquerade as bibliographies, are completely useless. There are two schools of thought about bibliographical **References** in catalogue-descriptions: one promotes them, the other, particularly in the case of modern or what might be regarded as 'inconsiderable' books, deplores them, on the grounds that scholarship should be discreet or that tradespeople aren't scholars. The rule for the doubtful bookseller, in this as in all aspects of book-cataloguing, should be: Be Consistent. If you give a reference for one book by an author, then give references for all books by that author; and if you have given references for one author, then try – if there are respectable bibliographies available – to give references for other authors, too. And if you give a reference, make sure that you have checked the book against the bibliography; a reference should never be a mere decoration.

Capitals Beware of capital letters. THEY ARE EXTREMELY DIFFICULT TO READ OVER A LONG DISTANCE.

Codewords ('The codeword VIRGO will be taken to mean "Please send from catalogue 1 the following item (s)"') are an innocent diversion even if largely redundant with the demise of the telegram, but they should aim to be efficient rather than jocular. See **Jokes**.

Computers Computers made everything possible for the back-parlour bookseller. An only moderately sophisticated computer (and there are now many competing programmes tailored to cataloguing) can produce camera-ready copy to a very high standard. Where once the back-parlour drudge perforce toiled over duplicator skins and intoxicating solvents, now all is cunning screenwork and disks and printouts. With new possibilities, however, come new hazards. **Design** becomes a need rather than a luxury. Computers make catalogue production much easier and catalogues may become repetitive (see **Recycling**). Worst of all, many booksellers offering multiple titles by the same author will, instead of obeying the old practice of using an em-dash or two, repeat the author's name on each item. This makes a catalogue boring to read and hard to use.

Condition It is an elementary rule of mail-order dealing that goods should be properly described. The extent to which a cataloguer needs to go in explaining the condition of a book will, however, vary depending on the customer's expectations. A rough division exists in the trade between 'secondhand' books (i.e. used books, books bought to read) and 'antiquarian' books (i.e. old or rare books, not necessarily antiquarian, often bought as objects). In the case of the former, there is an average 'reasonable secondhand condition' which admits of few variations, and few customers would require them. In the case of the latter, the 'collectables' category, a much clearer account is demanded. The bookseller's duty is to be prompt in listing defects and economical in description. An honest admission of defects is more helpful by far than any number of 'selling' adjectives ('OTHERWISE *a fine bright copy*' etc.). The most condition-sensitive area of bookdealing is the modern first edition market (a quality which persuades old-guard dealers of its meretriciousness). The complicated gradations conventionally used here are famously euphemistic: Mint (i.e. fine), Fine (i.e. not mint), Very good (i.e. not very good), Good (i.e. not good at all), etc. Correspondents in the *Bookdealer* have for years proposed the standardization of these terms. Because they are so relative and book-cataloguers so hopeful, they never will be standardized. It is, rather, up to each bookdealer to establish a relationship of **Trust** with his or her customers: then, which is the point of it all, they will know exactly what to expect.

Courage of your convictions, having the Once you have your catalogue ready for publication, publish it. There are very few times of the year – Christmas perhaps – when it is inappropriate to issue a catalogue. One dealer, on finding that he could sell a fair proportion of his catalogue by sending out a dozen **Advance copies** to his favoured customers, could not face dispatching the balance; this will have irritated several hundred of his old reliables. The same dealer was once reduced to issuing a catalogue entitled *A Selection from Our Forthcoming Catalogue*. This is not generally on.

Covers The cover of your catalogue gives you your first and best opportunity to attract the wayward attention of your customer. Even if you choose to have no **Illustrations** inside, you should give some thought to a flourish on the front. The most commercially straightforward solution is to feature a star item from your catalogue stock. Many booksellers, to be economical, commission or invent a cover which can be reused (varying cover colour, say) from catalogue to catalogue. See **Design**.

Credit cards In any other mail-order business these are a *sine qua non*. The book-trade is still quite reluctant to use them, given the low average value of any single transaction and the high and in some cases almost extortionate fees charged.

Crossheads Can be helpful in breaking up text, but should be used sparingly and avoid trivial sensationalism; you are not competing with the tabloid press. 'ABRAHAM LINCOLN'S COPY', yes. 'PERHAPS THE MOST DISGUSTING COPY IN THE WORLD!!?!!', no.

Customer is always right, the Very few booksellers subscribe even verbally to this old dictum. They don't like customers having books on **Approval**, they don't like being taught to suck bibliographical eggs by them (although collectors often know more about their small chosen subject than anyone else living), and they certainly don't like having books returned on the grounds of **Condition**.

Dates For the benefit of any who may find or refer to your catalogue in the future it is charitable to date it, even if discreetly and only by year. Dating it by month may be a mistake if your printer's binding machine breaks down or your staff (or wife or husband) catches measles and publication is delayed; it is also the equivalent of posting a 'sell-by date', which may deter the laggardly.

CATALOGUES

Design   The traditional book-catalogue was a plain and unattractive pamphlet, a thing of service rather than of beauty. With the facilities available to the modern catalogue-maker (see **Computers**), a handsome, well-designed catalogue, easy on the eye and efficient to use, is within the reach of all. An ugly catalogue is an inefficient catalogue.

Dollar dealers   For UK dealers to price catalogues in US dollars is an intolerable (not to say unpatriotic) affectation. If they are uneasy about sterling, they should price in *ecus*.

Fax   A fax facility is still a luxury for the secondhand book trade, though probably not for long. See **Answering machines**.

Foreign currency   Full payment details for overseas customers should be included in your **Rubric**. Do you accept **Credit cards**? Do you hold US or National Giro **Bank accounts**? Do you accept personal dollar checks? If so, do you make a conversion charge? (Ask your bank, and you may be surprised how much they charge for converting a single foreign cheque.) If you decide you will only accept sterling cheques or drafts, then you must say so, or you will become embroiled in terrifying aerogrammatic squabbles.

Forewords   If your catalogue represents something special – an individual's library, an author-collection, an anniversary celebration – or if you are trying to make a particular point with it, then a statement of intent or introduction by way of foreword (by yourself or by an outside authority) may be useful or interesting (see **Subjects**). If you make a feature of a foreword for its own sake, do not test your customers' indulgence too far (see **Personal touch**).

Illustrations   Although they may be hard to organize and sometimes expensive to execute, illustrations relieve a catalogue (see **Design**) and may make a sale. Too few booksellers use them.

Jokes   Some cataloguers cannot resist a joke; they think it shows their human side (see **Personal touch**). Jokes are very risky; a large proportion of customers read catalogues at breakfast.

Mailing list   Mailing lists are slow to build (unless borrowed or stolen) and unwieldy to handle. The arrival of **Computers** has allowed the electronically literate to contrive ways of coping with the sprawling mailing list, but they are often extreme and impersonal. There is something insulting about being told by a catalogue over your fried egg that if your 'mailing-label' has (say) 'NBG' in the right-hand corner, then this is the last catalogue you will ever receive unless you send a begging letter with a cheque for £10. It tends to erode your **Trust**.

Master-copy   When you publish your catalogue, talk to, write in, look after, feed and water your master-copy of it; record in it who orders anything, regardless of whether they are successful, or whether the orders are in writing or by telephone. The master-copy of an old catalogue is your infallible guide to your customers' interests.

Net prices It is common to read among the **Terms** the notice 'All prices are net(t)'. This old-fashioned expression is probably carried over from the period of the book-price wars at the turn of the century, before the Net Book Agreement for new books arrived. It means that no **Trade discount** is offered and that those impertinent enough to haggle over individual prices (see **Customer is always right**) will have their wrists slapped.

Notes The description of a book should identify it by author, title, place of publication and date; it should give an indication of **Condition** and possibly make reference to **Bibliographies**. But the creative catalogue will also, when helpful, add notes; it should give one a reason for buying the book if one needs one, it should place the book in a larger context if one hasn't heard of it. The best catalogues – and the best booksellers – are the ones who make a book or a market, by intuition or scholarship or taste; the best notes are worth reading for themselves even after the catalogue has passed its sold-by date.

Otherwise John Carter defined the 'else fine' school as 'the never-say-die type of cataloguer'. 'Otherwise' is a weasel word of special pleading, and should be used in catalogue descriptions with caution (see **Condition**). The language of book catalogues should approximate as far as possible to that of ordinary life; but be franker.

Personal touch, the The relationship between the mail-order bookseller and the customer depends by its nature on **Trust**. Booksellers are, besides, often peculiar creatures: one-person bands, dropouts from the professions, academics or writers reformed or *manqué(e)s*. They must apply every eccentricity in their personal armoury to the difficult task of wooing new customers and exploiting the old. The variety of the secondhand book trade is its strength, and sometimes, its joy. One North British bookseller produces a list so thoroughly interspersed with diary entries and weather reports that it is less a book catalogue than a family newsletter. It makes only the mildest genuflexion to orthodox principles of cataloguing and none at all to **Alphabetical order**. This is taking the personal touch to its logical conclusion.

PO Boxes Although it may look odd, or even suspect, to adopt a PO Box, it has its uses, first if you are anxious to protect private premises against book-collectors ringing your doorbell whenever it rains, second if you are away and need your post to be held. (You cannot obtain a PO Box without a fixed address.) There is a charge for the service, which increases if you require delivery. NB: the inquisitive can seek you out if they must by researching your postcode in their local library, or asking the Post Office!

Postage and packing Your **Rubric** must make clear what your practice is for postage and packing; every bookseller approaches this mundane but tricky subject differently. Do you include them in the price advertised (very rare, this)? Do you add them secretly into the last item billed (an odd practice)? Do you charge a fixed price per volume? Do you

CATALOGUES

send orders worth over a certain sum free? Or do you charge, as most do, *pro rata*? What do you do, if applicable, about the tax element (see **VAT**)? How do you send parcels overseas – by surface, by air, by ASM, by another carrier? All this must be specified.

Pricing How you price your books is your business, but it is prudent to calculate at the outset the face value of your catalogue and evaluate its economics. A fair number of catalogues published look as though they would never make any money for the dealer even if every item sold. If 60 people order one item and most of them are in the trade you may assume that you have underpriced it. Put this down to experience; don't pretend you have lost the book and then re-catalogue it at a higher price.

Printing As opposed to duplication, photocopying, etc., printing is now the best way of presenting most catalogues. With the prevalence of **Computers**, and a little concentration on **Design**, camera-ready copy or disks for typesetting can be prepared in shop or parlour; and in recent years printing prices have become more and more competitive. Several printers (all usually advertise in the trade journals) print book catalogues almost exclusively. Most booksellers print too many copies of a catalogue; prepare your **Mailing list** carefully each time.

Pro forma invoicing It is common practice in the book trade to stipulate that new customers must expect to pay *pro forma*; in practice it hardly happens. Some bold (militantly anti-**Approval**) booksellers require *pro forma* payment from all, but they are unusual.

Recycling There is nothing wrong with recycling stock unsold from past catalogues, provided that it is done tactfully and not too frequently. Unsold stock is to the secondhand or antiquarian bookseller what remainders are to a publisher. Before recycling, booksellers should ask themselves 'Why did this book not sell?' Was it the time, or the price, or the catalogue description, or, most simply, what it was catalogued under? If you have confidence in the book, often a tweak to the original catalogue description is what is needed to sell it.

References These are functional and should never simply be decorations (see **Bibliographies**). Will a cluster of bibliographical numbers around a cheap book really help sell it? References to the *DNB* or the *Encyclopaedia Britannica* should generally be omitted; they indicate a mean reference library.

Rubric What may be called the rubric (not that it need be printed in red, of course, but it should be laid out to attract notice) should include all the business-matter of the catalogue: **Addresses**, **Telephones**, **Answering machines**, **Fax**; **Terms**, ordering on **Approval**, **Foreign currency** arrangements, **Bank** details, arrangements for **Postage and packing**, rates of **VAT** (if applicable); a list of Contents (if applicable), general conditions (e.g. 'All books are published in London unless otherwise stated'), and perhaps

Abbreviations (particularly if obscure). The rubric need not be long, rather it should be economical, but it should be comprehensive and obvious in order to save tears later.

Sold   Marking a book 'Sold' in a catalogue is unpardonable. If the book is sold while the catalogue is in the press, it should either be removed from the catalogue or the entry should be left as it is. To argue that the few people who might order the book will be disappointed to find that it has sold is specious. By marking the book 'Sold' you will have disappointed every one of your customers.

Subjects   Catalogues devoted to special (unusual, unusually specific) subjects are especially welcome to your public. They attract attention, they often have a shelf-life, above all they are creative – which is what all booksellers should aim to be, for their own sake as much as for their customers.

Telegraphic addresses   (BOOKS LONDON etc.) are, in a post-telegraphic age, otiose. They have a certain antique air about them – but as if one still engraved one's railway station at the top of one's writing paper. See **Codewords**.

Telephones   If you advertise a telephone, it should work and be manned during business hours unless you announce in your **Rubric** to the contrary. Out of hours you switch on your **Answering machine**.

Terms   Your trading terms should be advertised prominently in your **Rubric**. You should make it clear whether **Postage and packing** are included, what your position is on **Trade discount** and **Net prices** and how long you offer people to pay. Most booksellers specify payment on receipt, which does mean on receipt for the trade (a courtesy) and perhaps 30 days for others, but allow longer for libraries and institutions.

Trade discount   The courtesy of offering a 10 per cent discount to fellow members of the trade is only observed spasmodically by catalogue dealers. They normally declare in the **Rubric** that no discount is offered to the trade, either for a certain period (usually a month) or at all, then offer it selectively to their friends or to colleagues who return it. There is no rhyme or reason to this except that up to 10 per cent of the cover price of the book may already be accounted for by catalogue costs – and that there is something rather irritating about receiving an order for a book from a bookseller who takes discount, then five orders (which can't be filled) from real customers who don't. Once upon a time catalogues were not sent out to the trade – if at all – until a fortnight or four weeks after everybody else. See **Net prices**.

Trust   Trust is the state of friendship and ease that exists between a good bookseller and a happy customer. The bookseller will communicate mainly by catalogue, the customer by ordering from it. They will understand each other, the bookseller being in control of his or her **Mailing list**, the customer having faith in his or her descriptions of **Condition**, glorying in his or her **Notes**. The **Personal touch** will be gentle, less evident perhaps in the catalogue than in cunning reaction to the customer's ordering pattern – for one of the benefits of a good catalogue is that you will discover by trial and error and chance the nature and range of your customer's interests; and you may even extend them. By deft **Recycling** and skilful variation of **Subjects** you will sell your customers books they didn't yet know they wanted. Thus you will replicate by mail what happens over the counter; statistics reveal a cheering oddity about the book trade – that most customers leave bookshops with books they had never intended to buy and indeed had never heard of. So it should be with book catalogues.

VAT   This is a curse. It applies to manuscripts, unless, oddly, they are bound in the form of books; and it applies to the service of **Postage and packing**. If you are registered for VAT and are in any doubt as what to do, you should consult a professional adviser. VAT does not, at the time of writing, apply to books. Thank God.

Catchwords

The practice of anticipating the first word of a page at the foot of the preceding page had its origin in medieval times when scribes used this device to assist the binder in gathering up the leaves of a manuscript. Its use in early printed books was intended to serve a similar purpose, but was to some extent merely imitative, as signatures, also printed at the bottom of the page, generally sufficed to guide the binder in folding and collating the finished sheets correctly. Catchwords may also have been seen as an aid to continuity in the reading of the text, especially when they appeared at the foot of each half of a double-column page; but they were little used after the end of the eighteenth century. Their importance lies in their clear (though not infallible) indication of completeness.

Cathedral bindings

Architectural motifs were much used in the decoration of bindings in the first half of the nineteenth century, and their characteristic details – columns, pediments, windows, arches – and their Gothic quality led to their being called 'Cathedral' bindings. English binders of this school usually employed a range of tools; French binders favoured a single block.

Caxton, William (?1422–1491)

Caxton was born in the Weald of Kent and apprenticed to Robert Large, a mercer, who became Lord Mayor of London in 1439. The trade between London and Flanders led to Caxton leaving for Bruges, to return to London from time to time when his apprenticeship was complete. He lived in Bruges as part of the English merchant community and occupied the semi-diplomatic post of 'Governor of the English Nation'. His command of French was excellent and he employed it to translate the *Recuyell of the Histories of Troy* from the version of Raoul Lefèvre; this was to become the first book printed in the English language.

Caxton's governorship ended about 1470 and he entered the service of Margaret of York, sister of Edward IV. He spent some time in Cologne, where he continued his literary studies and completed the translation of the *Recuyell* before returning to Bruges. His version of the ancient narrative was much in demand, and this led to a crucial decision. 'I have promised to diverse gentlemen and to my friends to address to them as hastily as I might this said book,' Caxton wrote in his preface, 'Therefore I have practised and learned at my great charge and dispense to ordain this said book in print after the manner and form as ye may here see.'

Following Gutenberg's initiative some two decades earlier, several German towns by now had a printing press, as did some in the Low Countries and in Italy. Caxton probably learned to print while he was in Cologne, and set up his own press in Bruges in 1474. Here the *Recuyell* was printed in an edition of about 500 copies.

Caxton's second book (his own translation from the French) was *The Game and Playe of Chesse*, an allegorical work symbolizing in chess terms the dependence of each stratum of society upon the one above and below it, from royalty through civil administration to the humble labour force. Caxton himself was still much involved in the diplomatic activity of Margaret's court, and it is likely that Wynkyn de Worde took much of the responsibility for supervising the press. Four more books (all in French) were printed in Bruges before Caxton left for England in 1476 to re-establish his press in the shadow of Westminster Abbey.

In the years following his return to England, Caxton printed *The History of Jason*, *The Dictes and Sayings of the Philosophers*, *The Canterbury Tales* (his first printing of a major English work), *Morte d'Arthur*, and Boethius' *Consolationes*. By

Reynard the Fox, Westminster: W. Caxton, 1481. Last leaf with colophon. [Eton College Library]

1479 he had moved into the Almonry, at the Sign of the Red Pale, and here printed many short pieces as well as the *Chronicles of England*, the *Polychronicon*, *Aesop's Fables*, *The Golden Legend* and *Mirror of the World*. He gained much patronage from his friends at court, and worked on many official records, statutes and royal documents. He died in 1491 having printed about 100 books, and Wynken de Worde took over his premises and his press.

Caxton would today be regarded primarily as a publisher and bookseller, financing and supervising the production and distribution of books. Though he introduced printing to England, the composing of his type and the operation of his press was almost certainly the work of de Worde and other trained assistants whom he brought from Bruges to Westminster. Nevertheless, he is justly regarded as the father of the printed book in England.

Aurner, Nellie S., *Caxton: A Study of the Literature of the First English Press*, 1926.
Blades, William, *The Biography and Typography of William Caxton*, 2 vols, 1877 (reprinted, 1971).
Crotch, W. J. B., *Caxton's Prologues and Epilogues*, 1928 (reprinted New York, 1971).
de Ricci, S., *A Census of Caxtons*, 1909.
Duff, Edward G., *Fifteenth Century English Books*, 1918.
Painter, George D., *William Caxton: A Quincentenary Biography of England's First Printer*, 1976.
Plomer, Henry R., *William Caxton*, 1925.

Chain lines

Laid (as distinct from wove) PAPER exhibits evenly spaced vertical lines made by the chains at the bottom of the mould used in the manufacturing process. These chain lines, and the closer-set horizontal wire (or laid) lines can be seen when the paper is held up to the light, and as the spacing (usually between one and two inches) varies in different papers, the chain lines can provide a useful indication as to whether a suspect leaf in a book is genuine. Machine-made papers are sometimes given imitation chain lines.

Chained libraries

The problems of security which trouble booksellers and librarians today were no less a concern of their medieval predecessors. Books in religious institutions were usually locked up in strong oak chests or available for reading in stalls and chained to the wall.

The English chained library dates from the fourteenth century, the bookcases (or presses) set before writing tables, with catalogue frames within reach. There are now only three chained libraries in Britain, though many early foundations have a few books with surviving chains and many more own volumes with traces of chains, hinges, clips or clasps still visible. Hereford Cathedral library dates from the mid-thirteenth century. It had fallen into disrepair by the time of Queen Elizabeth I when it was removed to the Lady Chapel; in the nineteenth century it was returned to the old muniments room where it had originally been established. Hereford has 1,444 chained books and manuscripts, some dating from the tenth and eleventh centuries.

Less well-known than the Cathedral library is the smaller collection of chained books in the Church of All Saints in Hereford. It was bequeathed to the Church by a parishioner in 1715 in the form of a collection of some 300 chained books well-preserved in their original shelving. A London bookseller actually bought the library in 1858 to ship to America but was stopped by the Bishop whose permission had not been sought. The library can be seen by appointment.

Wimborne Minster's chained library contains some 200 books with chains. It is housed in a tiny chamber but is carefully maintained; the system shows some similarities to the Laurenziana in Florence.

Winchester Cathedral appears to have had a chained library before the depredations it suffered during the Civil War. After the Restoration the Cathedral's library was greatly enlarged by the bequest of Bishop Morley's books, and it now has an important collection; only four books have chains.

Blades, William, *Books in Chains*, 1890 (reprinted Detroit, Michigan, 1968).
Ker, Neil R., *Medieval Libraries of Great Britain* (2nd edn, 1964).
Streeter, Burnett Hillman, *The Chained Library*, 1931 (reprinted New York, 1970).

Chapbooks

Chapbooks derive their name from the chapmen, or pedlars, who sold unsophisticated pamphlets from their trays or from market stalls in English towns and villages. The eighteenth century was the great age of the chapbook, with the distribution of a mass of popular culture in the form of ballads, chronicles, juvenile tales and other small printed pieces, usually illustrated with woodcuts. The pedlar's booklets now have an important place in the history of juvenile and popular literature. They were usually folded to give 8, 12 or occasionally 24 pages, and though the text and woodcuts were often crudely printed, THOMAS BEWICK and other important illustrators were sometimes employed. Banbury, Newcastle, Northampton and other provincial towns were the principal centres of chapbook distribution.

Despite their fragility, many chapbooks have survived and collections can still be attempted; but those in good condition now command high prices.

Ashton, John, *Chap-Books of the Eighteenth Century*, 1882 (reprinted 1992).
Neuburg, V. E., *The Penny Histories: a Study of Chapbooks for Young Readers over Two Centuries*, 1968.
—— *Chapbooks: A Guide to Reference Material*, 2nd edn, 1972.
Spufford, Margaret, *Small Books and Pleasant Histories: Popular Fiction and its Readership in Seventeenth-century England*, 1981.

Chemise

In binding terminology, a chemise is a loose leather covering fitted over the boards of a book, usually with pockets into which the boards were inserted. Many of these loose covers were later given permanence by means of bosses which riveted them to the boards, or by the pasting down of the turn-ins after the pockets had been cut away.

Nowadays the term is often used more broadly to describe any additional loose covering protecting a book within a box or slip case.

Children's Books

David Miles

To walk into a specialist children's bookshop, or the children's section of one of the big chains, is to witness the sheer wealth of newly published material available to our children. The colour printing may pale when compared to the sumptuousness of late nineteenth-century chromolithography, or the technical mastery of wood-block illustration shown in the books printed by Edmund Evans, but the compensations afforded by the massive choice, particularly for younger children in the picture-book category, and the almost complete relaxation of subject and language taboos – most evident in the work of the late Roald Dahl – are overwhelming. Simply put, the child of the 1990s is spoilt for choice. And hurrah for that! Or, as John Newbery, the originator of the 'children's book', would have said, 'Trade and Plumcake for ever, Huzza!' For Newbery was not only a publisher who obviously delighted in children and childish things, he was also a man who cherished the rewards of commerce.

The same richness of material, however, is sadly not always evident when the stock of the average antiquarian and secondhand bookshop is viewed. Though there are some

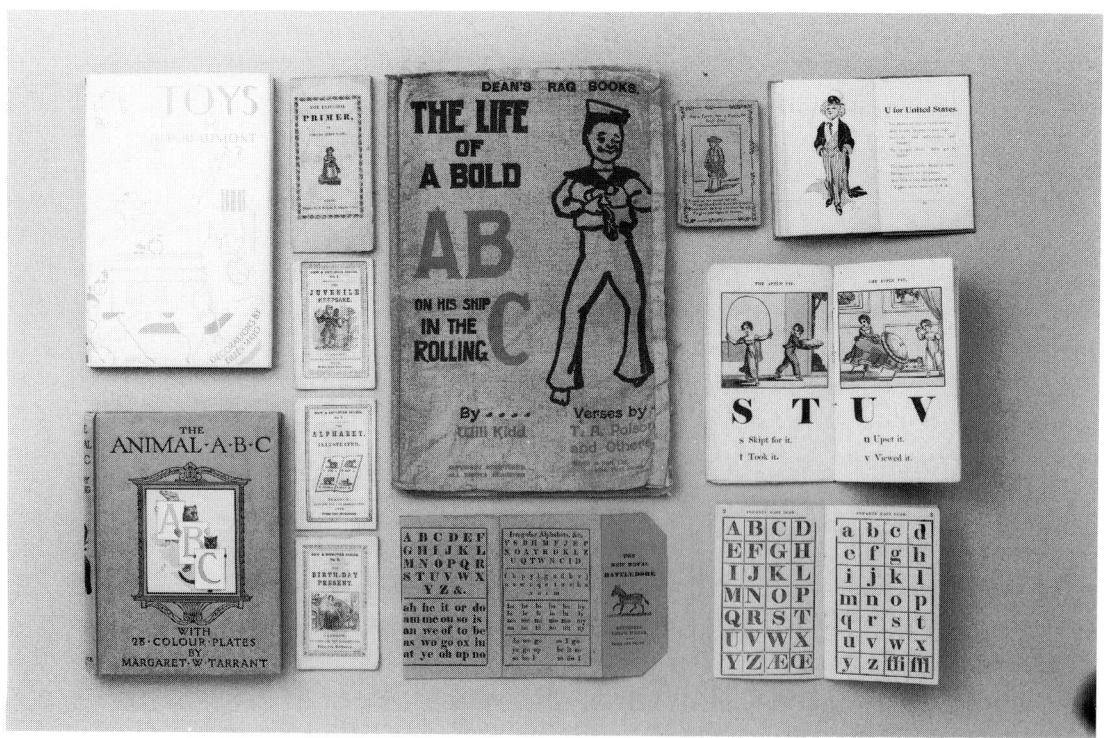

ABCs and Chapbooks.

notable exceptions, an examination of the shelves quite often reveals a rather sad collection of failures. The only books in reasonable condition may well be Victorian Sunday School prizes; their contents dull and dulling; their still shiny bindings testimony to the fact that while children are quite happy to accept the proffered sweet, they won't swallow any old humbug, no matter how stylish the stripes.

The primary reason for this all too frequent lack of attractive stock is quite simply that demand exceeds supply. Since the 1960s the popularity of this area of collecting has soared; and to cater for what amounts to an almost insatiable appetite, a veritable army of specialist dealers has assembled, many of whom work from home, issuing catalogues, and exhibiting at book fairs. Free from the constraints of shop premises, they are at liberty to scour the country in search of plums, with a thoroughness that makes it difficult for the general dealer to maintain anything approaching a satisfactory stock.

However, one of the great advantages of specialist dealers is that they produce, in the main, excellent catalogues which are a mine of information not only for the collector, but also for the general dealer who takes the trouble to study them rather than consign them to the wastebin. For there still lingers in the antiquarian book trade a view that somehow, with a few obvious and 'valuable' exceptions, children's books are not really important – that they don't count. How often one is met with a mildly disdainful, 'We don't really stock children's books'. Or, demonstrating another widely held misunderstanding, 'We have some Rackhams in the glass case'. Not many children between 1906 and now have been either fortunate, strong, or trusted enough to have learnt the story of Peter Pan while balancing Arthur Rackham's huge quarto on their little knees. It is much more likely that they developed their affection aided by the illustrations of Alice B. Woodward, Francis D. Bedford, or Mabel Lucie Attwell. The efforts of these illustrators may not have been presented with quite the elegance lavished on the gift books of Arthur Rackham, but they are worthy of just as much respect.

A great many collectors, whether limited by funds or disciplined choice, or both, restrict their interest to specific authors, illustrators, subjects, or categories of children's books. Some search only for those few memorable books cherished from childhood, and are completely uninterested in all others. These requests, highbrow or lowbrow, Narnia or Noddy, are rarely easy to satisfy. One longs for the customer who enters the shop and asks, 'I would like a copy of Philippa Pearse's *Tom's Midnight Garden*. I believe it won the Carnegie Medal in 1958.' The request would probably be met with initial failure, but the simplicity of the exchange would be refreshing. Much more familiar is the caller who, though retaining all the joy the revered book engendered, remembers nothing but a few isolated details: no title, no author, no date. 'I had it as a child,' is often the unsurprising opening remark. 'It had a blue cover, I think, and was about a girl called Anne and a pair of blue slippers.'

These customers often become very disturbed when the dealer not only cannot identify the half-remembered book, but also fails to pluck it immediately from the nearest shelf. The matter of price can also come as a great shock. A chair close at hand is a good idea, not simply for the suddenly unsteady, but also for the serious pilgrim who, having failed to discover the title from you, can be sat down with a copy of Margery Fisher's *Who's Who In Children's Books*, and left to conduct their own search. It is surprising how often this works the trick; a glimpse of Ameliaranne Stiggins and her chubby-faced siblings opens the floodgates of memory and the discovery of that long-lost title, *Ameliaranne And The Jumble Sale*, one of a highly popular series begun in 1920 which, despite a variety of authors, were all illustrated by Susan Beatrice Pearse, an artist whose cherubic children also graced many a cover of *The Playbox Annual*.

The interests of the true collector may prove as varied as they are finite. Among others, alphabets, from the wood-engraved primers and readers of the eighteenth century, to the lavishly illustrated picture-books of today, are a great favourite. Cats, especially those depicted in the books of Louis Wain, are always keenly pursued; but dogs, as if admitting to their inferiority, lag somewhat behind, and even the canine efforts of Wain struggle to find a home. Signed copies and, when available, limited editions of modern children's books, including those by Michael Hague, Jane Hissey, Maurice Sendak, Chris van Allsburg, and the marvellously inventive Ahlbergs (Janet and Allen), are laid down in quantity, like cases of wine, by those with an eye for the 'futures market' – an investment certain to mature if well selected and carefully kept. But unlike wine, it is doubtful if the books will ever be consumed by those they were created for, which for many would sour the project. The exploits of the following three disparate characters are all eagerly searched for: Biggles, W. E. Johns's tireless defender of the skies; Billy Bunter, Frank Richards's 'stuffed Owl of the Remove'; and William Brown, Richmal Crompton's endearing outlaw from Metroland. Equally, the enthusiasm for the school stories of Dorita Fairlie-Bruce, Angela Brazil, Elinor Brent-Dyer, and Elsie J. Oxenham, shows no sign of diminishing. Fairy tales are as popular as ever, particularly those of George MacDonald and the coloured compilations of Andrew Lang, beginning with *The Blue Fairy Book* in 1889 and ending with *The Lilac Fairy Book* in 1910. Of the numerous 'bears', Rupert – much preferred as drawn by Alfred Bestall rather than by his creator Mary Tourtel – still reigns supreme, with Pooh in close attendance, and Paddington some way behind. Much sought after by collectors from the United States are books with a black theme or interest. Obvious favourites are the Golliwogg books of the Uptons (Florence and Bertha), all versions of the nursery rhyme *Ten Little Niggers*, and the much prized highlight, despite its obvious Indian origin (a fact missed by many) Helen Bannerman's *The Story of Little Black Sambo*, first published as the fourth title in the Dumpy Books Series in 1899.

The individual collector will inevitably find some of his own favourites missing from any list, for the choices and demands of collectors are often as surprising as they are varied – a constant challenge to the dealer. However, nobody could be forgiven for omitting the tales of Beatrix Potter. Her little books, despite the uproar occasioned by their complete redesign in 1988, are still best sellers, and copies of first editions have doubled many times over since the early 1970s when they were being resisted at the exorbitant price of five pounds each!

But not even Peter Rabbit can challenge the collector's true heart's darling, Lewis Carroll's great classic, *Alice's Adventures In Wonderland*. From her first brief appearance in 1865 until the beginning of 1898, when Charles Dodgson died, 86,000 copies of the standard red edition and 70,000 of the 'People's Edition' had been issued by the publishers Macmillan in the United Kingdom and colonies alone. When the copyright finally lapsed in 1907, rival publishing houses were so desperate to break into the market that within the year nine new editions had been released, each with a completely fresh set of illustrations to rival John Tenniel's originals.

As is the case with Heinrich Hoffmann's great 'horror' classic of the nursery, *Struwwelpeter*, 1848, the demand for Alice in whatever form of parody, imitation, or guise she chooses to appear is relentless, and is not so much flattery as a mark of true respect for what remains a revolutionary work of children's literature.

To build an historically representative collection of children's books is a vastly different matter from compiling a simple thematic one. As well as demanding a substantial bank balance, it requires a great deal of luck and a certain measure of knowledge.

Excepting primers, catechisms, courtesy books, religious guides, and school texts, all of which are sought after by collectors, only a few books were specifically designed for children in the seventeenth century, and these are now mostly known in only one or two copies. Mention should also be made of a 'best seller' – Comenius' *Orbis Pictus*, illustrated and translated in many European languages. However, books written with some understanding of a child's mind, and expressly created to give children pleasure, were unknown until the middle of the eighteenth century; nor was this juvenile market recognized as an important and lucrative area of business. Prior to this, though John Locke's *Some Thoughts Concerning Education*, published in 1693, had emphasized the importance of illustration, and the creation of 'stories apt to delight and entertain a child', books passed on to children to be read for entertainment were no different from those read by their parents. There was no attempt to understand the concepts of 'play' and 'pleasure', or to use them as a way of building character and for developing educational skills. The prevailing attitude was that children were no more than grown-ups in waiting, and that they should, as expediently and efficiently as possible, be hastened to accept the responsibilities and standards of the adult world.

The literary diet of the parents and, therefore, that of their children was one comprised mainly of fables and romances. *Reynard The Fox* and *Aesop*, together with De Worde's text of the *Gesta Romanorum*, formed the foundation of the fable element. Printed mainly in chapbook form and sold by itinerant pedlars (chapmen), romances were primarily a legacy of the Middle Ages. They recalled the chivalrous exploits of St George, Bevis of Southampton, Robin Hood, and Jack the Giant-Killer. Myths and legends, many pure folklore, some, like the story of Jack, bordering on the realm of pure fairytale, amounted to a long, lingering look back to the Golden Age of Arthur and beyond. But in the first 40 years of the eighteenth century this regular diet was to undergo a radical revision with the addition of some totally new staples.

The least exciting of these, though by no means the least significant, was, paradoxically, the only work especially created for children – and therein lies its chief importance. This was Isaac Watts's *Divine Songs Attempted in Easy Language for the Use of Children*, 1715. This is a real prize for the collector, for its publication was an isolated indicator of changing attitudes; its influence was extensive, and copies of the first edition, with or without the engraved portrait frontispiece, are extremely rare.

More exciting, and certainly less puritanical, if only by contrast, was the printing, between 1705 and 1708, of the *Arabian Nights*. It is impossible to imagine the impact this fantastic work must have produced on the subjects of Queen Anne. We know that it enjoyed an unrivalled success. Discounting the chapbook editions, it had already reached its eighth edition by 1736, and attracted a clutch of imitations along the way. It would be difficult to imagine the children's library without Aladdin, Ali Baba, Sinbad, and the nightly trauma of Scheherezade.

The radical influence occasioned by the translation from the French of Madame D'Aulnoy's *Contes Des Fées*, 1707, and Charles Perrault's *Histories, or Tales of Past Times, Told by Mother Goose*, 1729, was to permeate the domestic library even more. The fairy tale, prior to the publication of these two collections, had remained almost exclusively the province of oral tradition. There were isolated excursions into print – Tom Thumb, perhaps, being the most commonly reprinted tale. But in the main fairy tales belonged, as the famous frontispiece to Perrault's work shows, to the shadowy world of the fireplace: winter's tales passed on from old to young. Spenser, Chaucer and Shakespeare had shown the bright side of the fairy realm, but predominantly it was a dark world, a place of sprites, hobgoblins, changelings, and bogeymen, of witches, nightmares, and curses. And while children had for centuries been held spellbound by these tales – scared witless as often as delighted – the established church and, particularly, the puritans had opposed what they saw as superstition or heresy, and had actively discouraged its printing.

Even in the early nineteenth century the prejudice against Mother Goose was still being voiced by such as Mrs Trimmer, and it was not until the subject had been made respectable under the banner of 'folklore' by the Brothers Grimm and Samuel Croker that this legacy of guilt and distrust was finally abandoned and the way made clear for George MacDonald to place his masterpiece, *At The Back Of The North Wind*, 1871, before the public.

The final new addition to the diet – by now a veritable feast – was made by the emergence of the new literary form, the novel. Though neither was intended for children, two classics, cornerstones of the juvenile library, Daniel Defoe's *Robinson Crusoe*, 1719, and Jonathan Swift's *Gulliver's Travels*, 1726, were immediately hijacked by them and gulped down as greedily as any sweets.

These new literary forms, appearing as they did in such a short period of time, reflect a society in the midst of social change. There is a new spirit of freedom in the air. The world appears a bigger, brighter place, full of new possibilities. Books tell of strange lands, inhabited by fantastic creatures and noble and ignoble savages; of wishes come true, rags to riches, and romance. The burgeoning middle classes, full of ambition for their children, as well as for themselves, appear ready to take the stage.

Enter one John Newbery, a farmer's son from Berkshire, born in 1713; a young man who by 1740 had married his master's widow and become a partner in the printing firm in Reading. By 1743 he had moved to London and opened for business at The Bible and Crown near Temple Bar, moving again in 1745 to nearby St Paul's Churchyard, where the business remained until well after his death in 1767. In this relatively short space of time he was to establish himself as a leading publisher and bookseller, issuing the works of such notable literary figures as Oliver Goldsmith and Dr Johnson.

However, in the field of children's books, Newbery neither wrote nor published a true masterpiece. Not even *Goody Two-Shoes*, 1765, his most successful children's book by far and the first sustained piece of fiction for children, could be called that. His genius lay in recognizing and understanding the gaping void in the market, and in finding opportunities to fill it with a clever mixture of the old and the new. His books not only pleased the child because they were light-hearted and amusing as well as being pleasurable objects to look at and handle; they pleased the parents too. For Newbery, a father himself, never lost sight of the parent's fundamental desire to instruct and educate.

His first 'true' children's book, *A Little Pretty Pocket Book*, 1744, which has a frontispiece entitled 'Delectando monemus. Instruction With Delight', was actually sold with either a ball or a pincushion for 'Little Master Tommy and Pretty Miss Polly'. This combination of education and enjoyment reveals a precise understanding, not only of the market, but of the new educational theory. John Newbery's books at their best lead children, via amusement and play, to the path of learning in the true spirit of John Locke. At last, after centuries, children and the world of childhood were to be recognized as having value *per se*. Suddenly it is adults who must adapt to children and not vice versa. This is the revolution from which all 'modern' children's books are born.

But Newbery should not get all the credit for this breakthrough, for there were precedents of which he would certainly have been aware. Thomas Boreman had published his wonderful series of *Gigantick Histories* between 1740 and 1743. These, despite their tongue-in-cheek title, were miniature in size, the text was good-humoured and illustrated

Some modern children's books

CHILDREN'S BOOKS

with commissioned woodcuts, and all 12 titles were bound, as was to become the norm, in glittering Dutch floral boards.

In deference to the wish to offer harmless pleasure without didactic intent, the publisher Mary Cooper issued the first-ever collection of children's rhymes in 1744, the year in which Newbery's *Little Pretty Pocket Book* appeared. It was called *Tommy Thumb's Pretty Song Book*, and was issued in two volumes, illustrated throughout with spirited wood-engravings. It is a tremendously important and charming little book, again bound in Dutch paper, and rivals anything that Newbery ever published. It is known by a single rebound copy of volume two held by the British Library.

Sadly, as far as we know, neither Boreman nor Cooper contributed anything more of any real significance. Both would have been a threat to Newbery's pre-eminence if they had persevered.

The history of eighteenth- and early nineteenth-century children's books, once John Newbery had established a base, continues to be dominated by publishers rather than authors, and this is reflected in the collecting of books from this time. Newbery's, Marshall's and Harris's books are favoured, as opposed to the great classics. In the children's literature of this time the latter simply didn't exist. If there were classics, then they were either borrowed from adult fiction, like *Robinson Crusoe*, and imitated again and again; or, as in the case of *Goody Two-Shoes*, they were simply the best of a rather unimaginative lot.

John Marshall, a publisher who relied heavily on imitations of Newbery, and produced at least three rivals to *Goody Two-shoes*, specialized exclusively in books for children. He built up a stable of authors, predominantly women, as was to become the norm, and issued some notable titles. But as much as we remember Dorothy and Mary Kilner, and Lady Eleanor Fenn, we remember more, and long to own, one of his superbly conceived and gloriously tactile miniature boxed libraries, beautifully crafted creations that straddle the line between toy and book. Similarly, in the case of John Harris, successor to Elizabeth Newbery, no significant piece of prose stands out to distinguish its author. Instead, it is the quality of the printing and the excellence of the colouring employed for his 'Cabinet' and such charming little books as his *Visit To The Bazaar*, 1818, that we recall. Of William Darton's publications, there are ten collectors vying for a chance to buy his *Dame Trot* titles for every one choosing the sobriety of Mary Elliott.

The children's literature of this time is too often wanting in imaginative power. Only in the attention given to the physical presentation of the product itself does it begin to soar. In truth, once Newbery has set the standard, there is little progression in terms of significant range until Catherine Sinclair's *Holiday House*, 1839, which signals the start of an avalanche. The first masterpiece, Edward Lear's *Book Of Nonsense*, is published in 1846, and then it is but a brief sleep before *Alice*, 1865, and the awakening of the imagination in Victorian England.

The books our children read today – the tales of Nesbit and Narnia; of Mole and Ratty, and Roald Dahl; of 'Wild Things' and the Ahlbergs – owe much to Newbery's sound judgement of what was wanted by the young readers of his day; but in a broader context they can be seen as the outcome of a process, with its origins in the seventeenth century, prompted by our primary desire, especially in childhood, for free play of the imagination.

Darton, Harvey, *Children's Books in England*, 2nd edn, 1970.
Hürlimann, Bettina, *Three Centuries of Children's Books in Europe* (translated by Brian W. Alderson), 1967.
Muir, Percy, *English Children's Books, 1600–1900*, 1954 (reprinted, 1979).
The Osborne Collection of Early Children's Books, 1566–1910, A Catalogue, Toronto, 1966 (reprinted, 1975).

Chivers, Cedric (1853–1929)
Chivers of Bath is credited with several innovations in the binding of books. He introduced a reasonably priced library binding service, patenting a method of neat, firm stitching for this purpose. He is perhaps best known for his 'vellucent' bindings; Chivers achieved a similar effect to Edwards of Halifax by a different method, painting a picture on the front boards which was then covered with transparent VELLUM. The first book produced with such a binding was a 1903 edition of the *Rubaiyat of Omar Khayyam*.

Christmas books

Allen Lane The Christmas books published in limited edition by Allen Lane, the founder of PENGUIN BOOKS, between 1928 and 1965, were intended as gift books for presentation to friends. Gray's *Elegy* came out in 1928, followed by *A Very Victorian Christmas* and *The Dog* in 1929 and 1930. There was then an interval of 15 years, punctuated by Lane's first Penguin paperback, and by the Second World War. In 1945 the series resumed with *The Ancient Mariner*, illustrated by Duncan Grant. This was followed by a succession of attractive books illustrated by Lynton Lamb, David Gentleman, Ronald Searle and other artists of note. *The Trial of Lady Chatterley*, together with *The House of Lords Debate*, 1963, deserves special mention.

Gili, Jonathan, Allen Lane's Christmas Books, *The Private Library*, Autumn, 1984.

Cambridge University Press In 1930, Walter Lewis, printer to the University of Cambridge, brought out the first of the 'Christmas Books' printed 'for friends in printing and publishing' and distributed as gifts. The project had originally been the idea of STANLEY MORISON, and the first title was John Dunton's *Sketches of the Printers, Stationers, Binders and Engravers of the City of London*. It was followed in 1931 by John Trusler's *The Art of Carving* and subsequently by Morison's own *Edward Topham . . . a Gentleman of fashion and public character*. Other titles varied from short dissertations on aspects of printing to a book about trains, a particular enthusiasm of Morison. One of unusual interest was Desmond Flowers's edition, 1954, of Voltaire's *Essay on Milton*, printed with Baskerville types on wove paper specially made by Balston of Maidstone, successor to Whatman.

After a gap during the war years the Christmas books resumed with a selection of engravings by Reynolds Stone and continued until 1973 with only two omissions – in 1959 when a printers' strike held up all the Press's work, and 1963 when it moved to new premises. The usual limitation was about 500 copies and the meticulous standards of design and production were such that even the most distinguished recipients must have been delighted with them. Many of the volumes are concerned with private presses, typography or engraving, some with the university and town of Cambridge, and others with the personal interests of those who designed them.

Crutchley, Brooke, *The Cambridge Christmas Books*, Brighton, 1976.
—— *To Be A Printer*, 1980.

Chromolithography

Basil Gray, in *The English Print*, 1937, describes chromolithography as 'a medium which has been much maligned, misunderstood and disregarded'. There is some truth in this assessment; chromolithography is often undervalued in comparison with hand-coloured illustration, and its appearance in the history of book illustration was comparatively brief. In 1836 Godefrey Englemann worked out a method for one-colour stone plates to be assembled in a single lithographic process. Each stone might carry more than one tone and each colour or tone required perfect registration. Twenty or more stones were often used in one printed illustration. The sheer mechanical ingenuity needed for perfect reproduction often militated against the spontaneity and freshness of the artist's work, but once the process had been perfected a very high standard of printing could be achieved. Martin Hardie in *English Coloured Books*, 1906, gives a clear account of the process.

The bright, dense colours obtainable by chromolithography were exploited by such artists as Noel Humphreys, Owen Jones and Henry Shaw. Their work was often inspired by medieval illuminated manuscripts and is most successful where colour is a vital and functional aspect of the book, as in Jones' *The Grammar of Ornament*, 1856.

Chronogram

An occasional conceit of printers and publishers in which the title-page inscription contains (usually in the author's name or the book's title) a date in the form of numerical letters. The relevant letters were usually identified openly, by being either underlined or supplied from a different fount. Owing to the small likelihood of the letters occurring in the right order to satisfy the Roman system of numeration, the rule of subtraction does not apply, and the letter-values are simply added together: for instance, ECho In MeDICINa (printed in Helmstedt) is dated 1703.

Hilton, James, *Chronograms*, 3 vols, 1882–1895.

Clandestine printing

The clandestine production of books – that is, under conditions of anonymity or secrecy, for fear of reprisals from church, state or the military – is a phenomenon almost as old as books themselves. However, some areas are better documented than others, and offer interesting opportunities for dealers and collectors.

There are four main categories of clandestinely produced books: the politically subversive, the heretical or heterodox, the pornographic or bawdy, and the straightforwardly piratical. The first of these is typified by the seditious literature suppressed by the French authorities during the eighteenth century; much of it originated in Holland and Switzerland, and printers used a variety of false imprints. Some of these were real place-names chosen to suit the subject matter, such as Freetown or Villefranche; others were more extravagant, for instance Bagatelle, Merdianopolis and Regiopolis.

The second category is equally extensive: bodies such as the Roman Catholic church (whose *Index Librorum Prohibitorum* was finally discarded as recently as 1966) have invariably seen the printed word as an important weapon. Writers in this area, such as Edmund Campion, worked under the peculiar difficulty of having to produce books wholly without misprints, as these would have been seized upon as evidence of falsehood.

The third category, the pornographic, sometimes overlaps with the previous ones; but the rise of libertinism, from the mid-seventeenth century onwards, encouraged a wide variety of straightforwardly obscene and bawdy publications both in Britain and on the Continent, many of them issued under false imprints.

Finally, many books have been published clandestinely not out of any real fear of reprisal but merely out of disregard for the civil rights of a copyright holder.

The twentieth century has not been without its share of clandestine publications: during the Second World War, the German occupation of the Netherlands failed to dampen the enthusiasm of many accomplished printers, of whom the most noteworthy was Hendrik Nicolas Werkman, shot dead three days before the liberation of Groningen in 1945; while the work of French printers in the same period was recorded by no less a photographer than Robert Doisneau.

Brunet, Gustave, *Fantaisies Bibliographiques*, Paris, 1864.
——— *Imprimeurs Imaginaires et Libraires Supposés*, Paris, 1866.
Craig, Alec, *The Banned Books of England*, 2nd edn, 1962.
Darnton, Robert, *The Literary Underground of the Old Regime*, 1982.
——— et al., *The Widening Circle: Essays on the Circulation of Literature in Eighteenth-century Europe*, Pennsylvania, 1976.
De Jong, Dirk, *Het Vrije Boek in Onvrije Tijd: Bibliografie van Illegale en Clandestiene Bellettrie*, Leiden, 1958.
Foxon, David, *Libertine Literature in England, 1660–1745*, New York, 1965.
Imprimeries Clandestines (anon.), Le Point, Souillac, 1945.
Mendes, Peter, *Clandestine Erotic Fiction in English, 1800–1930*, Aldershot, 1993.
Myers, Robin and Harris, Michael, *Censorship and the Control of Print in England and France, 1600–1910*, 1992.
Simoni, Anna, *Publish and Be Free: A Catalogue of Clandestine Books Printed in the Netherlands 1940–1945, in the British Library*, 1975.
Thompson, Roger, *Unfit for Modest Ears*, 1979.

Cloth

Cloth has been used as the binding material for the vast majority of cased (as distinct from paper-backed) books published in the English-speaking world since 1825, when it was first employed by Archibald Leighton. Considerable attention has been given, notably by Michael Sadleir and John Carter, to the description of the many varieties of fabric and grain which are found in the early years of cloth binding, and alternative systems of classification have been adopted by American scholars. These studies are of much importance in facilitating precise bibliographic description, especially where variant bindings may determine priority of publication; but the cataloguers, and collectors, of modern books are usually content with a brief indication ('All books are in original cloth bindings unless otherwise described . . .') that all is as it should be. Colour, texture and other features are seldom specified unless they are bibliographically significant.

Publisher's cloth, however, must be distinguished from binder's cloth – a term applied only to the binding of an individual copy. Cloth has been frequently used in the binding of books, journals and pamphlets preserved only for occasional reference or thought undeserving of leather binding; and John Carter points out that from the collector's point of view these 'cloth rebinds' fall 'with something of a thud' between the two stools of original state and handsome renewal. Where both durability and distinctive appearance have been desired, buckram has often provided the right qualities. The fabric – usually cotton or linen – is stiffened with size or paste, and looks and feels congenial.

Sadleir, Michael, *Evolution of Publishers' Binding Styles, 1770–1900*, 1930.
Carter, John, *Binding Variants in English Publishing, 1820–1900*, 1932.

Cobden-Sanderson, Thomas James
(1840–1922)

It was at the suggestion of William Morris's wife that T. J. Cobden-Sanderson gave up his career at the bar in order to learn bookbinding. He apprenticed himself to Roger de Coverley in London in 1882 and began his life-long commitment to the design and production of fine English books.

Cobden-Sanderson worked on 52 books under De Coverley's guidance. His own first binding was George Sand's *La Mare Au Diable*; the finishing was not his but he soon learned gold-tooling and describes elatedly in his journal how 'the gold stuck when I swept the gold rag over it, and the problems of the future appeared to be solved'. He set up his own bindery in Covent Garden and began to design and execute the fine bindings associated with his name. In 1887 he beat into second place the master binder of ZAEHNSDORF's in a competition organized by the Society of Arts; his entries were *The Germ* and Ruskin's *Unto This Last*.

Cobden-Sanderson was associated both socially and professionally with the Arts and Crafts movement and with William Morris in particular. Like Morris, he wanted to preserve the hand skills of the Middle Ages, and he used only the very best materials. Although his designs include flowers and leaves, wreaths and garlands, he used only gold-tooling, never embellishing his work with coloured onlays or dyes.

In 1893 Cobden-Sanderson founded the Doves Bindery in Hammersmith, near William Morris's KELMSCOTT PRESS; though not in good health, he was able to design the bindings, organize the work and do most of the finishing himself. The bindery handled most of the Kelmscott work, especially the binding of the recently printed Chaucer; but Cobden-Sanderson was not entirely happy with Morris's work as a printer, and was anxious to start a press of his own.

Emery Walker, the typographer who advised Morris on printing, joined Cobden-Sanderson in setting up the DOVES PRESS in 1900. The partnership was a difficult one and in 1905, seeking to bring his son in as a partner, Cobden-Sanderson quarrelled with Walker. The partnership was dissolved in 1908, but the two men were in bitter dispute over who owned the type. The well-documented story of the demise of the press tells how Cobden-Sanderson in 1913 spent many evenings carrying armfuls of type to the Thames and throwing them into the water from Hammersmith Bridge.

In attributing bindings to Cobden-Sanderson's hand, care must be taken to

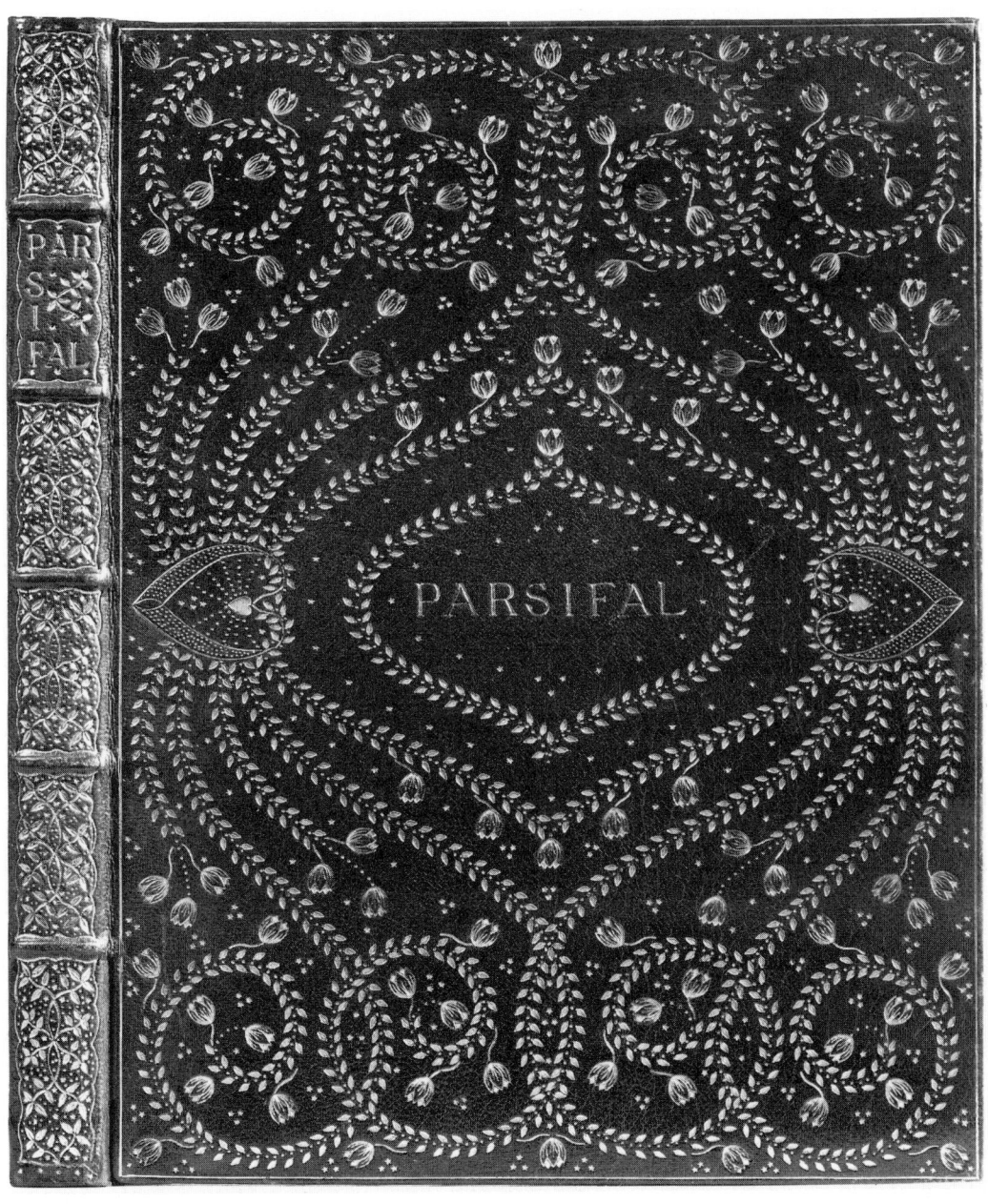

Wagner's *Parsifal* bound by Cobden-Sanderson, 1889 [Maggs Bros. Ltd.]

distinguish between the form of signature which indicates his own work, and the very similar signature used on books bound under his supervision at the Doves Bindery. It should also be noted that these signatures have on occasion been simulated on other books. This matter is fully dealt with in the last book noted below.

Baine, J. S., *A Bookseller Looks Back*, 1940.
Foot, Mirjam M., *Studies in the History of Bookbinding*, 1993.
Nixon, H. M., *Five Centuries of English Bookbinding*, 1978.
Tidcombe, Marianne, *The Bookbindings of T. J. Cobden-Sanderson*, 1984.
———, *The Doves Bindery*, 1991.

Cockerell, Douglas (1870–1945)

Cockerell worked with COBDEN-SANDERSON at the Doves Bindery for some years before setting up his own bindery, where he employed for a time both Francis Sangorski and George Sutcliffe. He taught bookbinding for the London County Council and became director of the binding department of W. H. Smith.

Cockerell was one of a small but distinguished group of 'amateur' binders whose influence on the trade was considerable. He insisted on raised cords for sewing, introduced zigzag endpapers and always used materials of the highest quality. He fought against slovenly practices used by some trade binders, and his own immaculate forwarding and handsome designs brought him considerable acclaim. He was chosen to rebind the British Museum's *Codex Sinaiticus* in 1935 (his choice of pigskin for the binding was rejected on religious grounds and he settled for tawed goatskin instead). His own book on the craft, *Bookbinding and the Care of Books* (1901, reprinted 1978), has greatly influenced those who followed him.

Cockerell, Sir Sydney (1867–1962)

As a young man Cockerell was employed in the family firm of coal merchants. He worked in his spare time for Octavia Hill and through her became friendly with John Ruskin who introduced him to the attractions of art, literature and European travel. He met William Morris and his family and his close friendship with Morris, Emery Walker and the Burne-Joneses lasted for many years. He became a good friend, too, of Wilfrid Scawen Blunt, the orientalist, for whom he acted as secretary. He was also invited to assist Dr M. R. James in cataloguing books and manuscripts of the collection of Henry Yates Thompson who had bought a large part of the Ashburnham library in 1898.

Sydney's younger brother, Douglas, was already launched on a successful career as a bookbinder, and after toying with the idea of joining Quaritch and entering the field of antiquarian bookselling, Sydney joined Emery Walker to found a firm of process engravers. Through his work and his friends, he became associated with the KELMSCOTT, DOVES and ASHENDENE presses (St John Hornby was an old friend of the Morris family).

Sydney Cockerell was appointed Director of the Fitzwilliam Museum in Cambridge in succession to his old collaborator, M. R. James, an unusual appointment for a man with no academic background. He was elected to the ROXBURGHE CLUB and complained vigorously about its declining standards of scholarship and taste.

Much of Cockerell's long life was spent in promoting the cause of fine book production. He became a friend of Thomas Hardy, Shaw and other literary figures of his day. In 1934 he received a knighthood and later published two volumes of letters from his friends; he wrote many letters for publication, edited those of Freya Stark, and retained his interest in medieval manuscripts and fine books. He is perhaps best remembered in the bookselling world for his involvement in the private press movement.

Blunt, Wilfrid, *Cockerell*, 1964.

Collation
In the most general sense, collation means examination and comparison. In bookselling, the word denotes an attempt to retrace the work of the binder in putting the book together, and to determine the book's completeness or otherwise; in practice this usually means the comparison of a printed book with, ideally, an accurate bibliographical description or, failing that, another copy. It may, more loosely used, mean only that the presence of illustrations, maps, etc. has been checked against the contents leaf; and in the absence of other indicators, collation may simply involve making sure that there are no obvious gaps. The golden rule, given that collation is based on counting sheets rather than pages, is to take no notice whatever of page numbers, concentrating instead on signatures, with the help, in books produced before 1800, of CATCHWORDS.

The word may also refer to the full bibliographical description of a book's FORMAT, and to the formula used to express it. Given a clear head, and a copy of GASKELL's *A New Introduction to Bibliography*, these formulas are by no means as impenetrable as they may appear.

Colophon
A bibliographical note, usually at the end of a book, though occasionally (as with some modern limited editions) among the prelims; a verso of title-page colophonic information is becoming regular in North American publishing. It may identify the book's title, author, illustrator, designer, typographer, printer, type-face, place of printing, size of edition, paper, binding and date. (A few go even further: see the Cranach Presse *Hamlet*, for instance.) The word is sometimes wrongly taken to mean 'device'.

Colour Plate Books

Elizabeth Merry

In 1951 J. R. Abbey, collector and compiler of the fundamental bibliography for British books using aquatint and lithography between 1770 and 1860, wrote concerning the extensive research involved in its compilation, 'I have found it a fascinating subject in a field in which there seem to have been few serious collectors'. Some forty years later the first part of the description still holds true; the study of these books exemplifying the art of the hand-coloured plate and by extension the whole field of colour plate books, continues to generate considerable interest. The latter part of Abbey's comment, however, could hardly be less appropriate today. There are a growing number of collectors, and

COLOUR PLATE BOOKS

colour plate books in general account for a significant proportion of antiquarian book sales in this country.

The very act of delineating and describing any field of activity focuses interest upon it. Before Abbey had completed his four-volume bibliography, the most lavish and splendid books with fine hand-coloured plates attracted steady prices and a degree of interest tempered only slightly by fashion. If we turn to the auction records for the 1890s, for example, the best titles by Ackermann and Daniell feature much at the level one would expect (although at a fraction of the price they cost subscribers). There is a steady, but slow, increase in prices through the decades, with the predictable exception of the years of war and economic depression; but it is generally accepted that the turning point came in the 1950s. With a marked increase of commercial activity, conditions were ripe for the publication, first, of Abbey's four volumes (1952–57) and in 1954 the re-issue in a significantly enlarged edition of Tooley's *English Books with Coloured Plates 1790 to 1860* (first published in 1935). Both bibliographies were received with enthusiasm and have

From Rudolph Ackermann's *Microcosm of London*, 1808–10. [Phillips, Son & Neale]

Herald's College, from Ackermann's *Microcosm of London*, 1808–1810 [Christie's]

since determined the status of most books within their field. Although both are valued, it is Abbey's meticulous listing – including as it does much information about the precise details of publication and the variations between, for example, large paper, subscriber's and standard copies – that is held in higher esteem.

However, the current definition of colour plate books extends beyond both Abbey and Tooley, especially since both bibliographies chose to adopt significant limitations. Abbey refers, in his Preface, to the catalogue of the Schwerdt collection of hunting, hawking and shooting books, published in 1928–37, which he had decided not to duplicate in any way. He chose to refrain from listing any natural history books and he was not entirely comprehensive on caricature and costume books either, though very nearly so within his chosen field. Tooley similarly excluded both botany and ornithology from his bibliography. (Many of the titles now most prominent in any list of colour plate books would be precisely within the area of natural history; but since this field of study is covered separately in these pages it will not be considered here.) The definition of colour plate books is often by implication based upon quality, with attention focused on proportions and high values of production; but it extends right through to books employing some degree of colour-printing, and further again to those which, like Owen Jones' spectacular *The Grammar of Ornament*, 1856, are entirely chromolithographed.

COLOUR PLATE BOOKS

Any enumeration of major colour plate titles is inevitably incomplete, although guidelines are provided in such works as David Bland's *History of Book Illustration*, 1958, and Alan Thomas's *Great Books and Book Collectors*, 1975. For brevity, since it was published as an article in a periodical, it is hard to better Gordon Ray's *One Hundred Outstanding Illustrated Books Published in England between 1790 and 1914*; though here too the omissions are revealing. Apart from Lear's *Parrots*, 1830–32, there are no natural history titles, the list having been compiled in the 1960s before this subject gained its full status and popularity. Ray lists several of Ackermann's publications, including his *Microcosm of London*, 1808–10 and *The History of the University of Oxford*, 1814 and Combe's *Tours of Doctor Syntax*, 1812–21, illustrated by Rowlandson. His list continues with Malton's *Views of Dublin*, 1794–95 and the same author's *Tour through the Cities of London and the West*, 1792; Havell's *A Series of Picturesque Views of Noblemen's and Gentlemen's Seats*, 1814–23; Daniell and Ayrton's *Voyage round Great Britain*, 1814–25; Pyne's *Royal Residences*, 1819; Roberts's *Holy Land*, 1842–49; Shotter Boys's *Picturesque Architecture in London*, 1839 and *Original Views in London*, 1842; Alken, Surtees and Prout are mentioned, and the list ends with Wyatt's *Industrial Arts*, 1851–53 and the previously mentioned *Grammar of Ornament*, a roll-call that gives us many of the most important titles, hints at the breadth of the field and subordinates all other considerations to the essential factor of colour quality.

Appropriately, Gordon Ray's list gives prominence to Rudolph Ackermann (1764–1834). It was Ackermann's publication of fine colour plate books that set both the

From John Papworth's *Select Views of London*, 1816. [Phillips, Son & Neale]

COLOUR PLATE BOOKS

Windsor Castle, from Pyne's *History of the Royal Residences*, 1819 [Christie's]

standards and the fashion in the early nineteenth century. In the words of the *Dictionary of National Biography* 'the establishment of lithography as a fine art is due to him'. Pressure in the shape of the demands of an increasing family had led Ackermann to open his print shop, the Repository of Arts, in the Strand in 1795. A man blessed with enormous energy and flair, he was then ideally placed to coordinate the work of artists, engravers, colourists and authors. The books he published in the early years of this career are a fitting tribute to the varied talents he was able to draw together. Apart from the *Microcosm* and *The History of the University of Oxford* mentioned above, the years that followed brought *The History of the University of Cambridge*, 1815; *The History of the Colleges*, 1816 and *The Repository of Arts* in 40 volumes, 1809–28; this last series had no less than 3,000 subscribers by the end of the first year. It was Ackermann who was able to bring together the skills of Rowlandson as illustrator, and the poetry of Combe, in the famous Doctor Syntax series; and he also published several fine books exemplifying the vogue for the depiction of magnificent buildings; Papworth's *Select Views of London*, 1816, is a well-known example.

It was the desire for colour, to reproduce the beauties of nature and art in order to please the eyes and loosen the purses of an increasingly wealthy clientele, that spurred the

COLOUR PLATE BOOKS

development of the two printing processes, aquatint and lithography, at the end of the eighteenth century. Both in their different ways were ideally suited to reproducing the watercolour and the crayon sketch, and the unique cultural position occupied by English watercolours underlies the rise to prominence of the colour plate in this country. A growing interest in colour reproduction provided the necessary impetus for experimentation with the two processes, both of which had first been developed on the continent. It was fortunate that at this time Britain was blessed with a group of talented artists, engravers and etchers whose skills were the basis of the new techniques. Aquatint was in a mechanical sense the most natural development, in that it is a variety of etching, an extension of an existing and well-established process. However, the aquatint technique was able to provide a uniquely broad range of tonal values, and when this was combined with the hand-colouring that was at the time always employed with aquatint, the effect produced was, at its best, extraordinarily fine. The origins of aquatint are said to go back to the experiments of Jean Baptiste Le Prince with granulated resin around 1768. The gradations of tone were produced on the plate by the progressive etching-through and stopping-out of a porous ground, usually made by allowing a solution of resin in spirit to dry out and craze in the surface of the plate. Each plate was then individually hand-coloured, and the subtlety of tone variation produced an effect that is often considered to be more delicate than that achieved by lithography.

Lithography began some 30 years later with the work of Senefelder in 1798. Etching was then no longer needed. The design was drawn in the greasy coating and when the stone was wetted and inked with a roller the ink adhered only to the design. Senefelder's discovery led the way to the development of lithography which has provided, with the exception of later photographic means, one of the most faithful means of reproduction. In addition, unlike metal plates, the stones used in lithography are subject to virtually no wear. The process therefore permitted an almost unlimited number of copies, and being relatively cheap was ideally suited to the increasing demands of nineteenth-century book production; Philip Gaskell suggests in his *New Introduction to Bibliography*, 1972, that colour printing was used in conjunction with lithography as early as around 1818. This was done initially by using a tint stone, usually pale buff, which was then printed over a part or whole of the design. In the late 1830s Engelmann, in France, and Hullmandel, in England, developed the processes of chromolithography, in which plates in full colour were printed from suites of stones. The way was then open for the creation of a market for high-quality colour plate books in the 1840s; but until that time publishers relied almost entirely on the individual hand-colouring of each aquatint or lithographed plate. The end result was thus largely dependent on the skill of the colourist as well as on the quality of the plate itself. Meticulously applied watercolour could bring figures in the foreground into perspective, for example, and lend depth to an entire plate. It was particularly suitable for British scenery, with the prevalence of water, cloud and mist and the effects of weather; and ideal, too, for celebrating the elegance of buildings and the military and naval exploits of the country. Turner, Girtin and Sell Cotman were among the many famous artists who began as colourists. Specimens of colouring were made either by the artists themselves or by the master colourists, and given to the general colourists to copy. It was obvious that (with the possible exception of Ackermann's publications) this procedure could lead to considerable variation in the quality of the colouring of any given title; and it is important here to note the distinction between colouring done around the time of publication, known as contemporary colouring, and colouring added at a later date. In addition to significant variation in the quality of contemporary colouring, many important books were issued in two states: in a standard edition, and with a limited number of large paper copies with the plates either printed directly on to card, or mounted.

It was Major Abbey who undertook much of the necessary research into the precise details of these variant editions. The assumption is generally made that the large paper copies of any work show the best colouring. Works like Daniell and Ayrton's *Voyage round Great Britain*, 1810–1825, bear this out. Possibly as few as 25 copies (though Abbey suggests more) were produced with the plates mounted on card. A large paper copy at the time cost the considerable sum of 90 guineas, with £66 as the price of the standard issue. That the work was so expensive (compare the original cost with the price of the same work at auction, £10, in 1898!) was an indication of the lavish scale on which it was produced. These special copies apart, it is still necessary for the collector to assess the relative merit of the colouring of individual copies of the same book. It is seldom possible now to place one copy beside another for comparison, as many of these books are scarce; the quality of colouring has to be assessed on grounds of personal judgement tempered with taste, and by means of such comparison as can be made by memory of other copies. Generally speaking, the variation in standards of contemporary colouring is relatively slight in comparison to the range seen in later attempts, some of which are very poor.

The incidence of later colouring, especially of lithographed plates, increased sharply with the growth of an independent print market. In the 1960s the numbers of dealers in decorative prints increased dramatically, and it is an indication that prints now represented a serious sector of the market that the major auction houses first set up separate print departments at that time. The interest in decorative prints was a response to a specific cultural trend, with an emphasis on interior design, and on the importance of colour. Fashion came into play in an increasingly important way; all those colour plate books whose purpose was the display of the grand interiors of palaces or stately homes, or even the country house, were increasingly sought after. At the same time came the substantial rise in prices for the most striking exemplars of the art of colour, the fine bird and flower books published from the 1840s onwards, and the growth of an international market. It is now the case that any international crisis, as well as the cycles of economic recession and recovery, can bear upon the demand for key books. The widely varying prices achieved by Roberts' *Holy Land* (published in six volumes between 1842–49) in its two major states, fully hand-coloured and tinted, over the last 30 years, are symptomatic of the periods of economic growth and confidence alternating with those of uncertainty and crisis. They are also an indication of the fashion for any one category of subject matter. It is true to say, however, that most colour plate books have now been reappraised not simply in terms of the quality of the work that was devoted to them, but also as highly desirable books which it is still possible to buy. The great publications may be out of reach, but many of the lesser travel and topographical items are still available in good sound copies. To return to Major Abbey, these books 'were after all mass-produced copies

Completism

A completist is a type of collector, much loved by booksellers, whose devotion to a single author (or, occasionally, subject) provokes a desire to own every item in the canon, no matter how slight or tangential. An extreme example would be an M. R. James collector who insisted on possessing the complete *Dictionary of National Biography* on the grounds that Dr James contributed a few entries to it.

Computers for Booksellers
Charles Ross

The majority of booksellers buy a computer to help them produce their catalogues, write their letters, produce their invoices, keep notes of their customers' wants, and generally keep track of their business.

Many booksellers have excellent memories, but everyone's memory is fallible. The memory of a computer is different. Once you have entered some information into a computer it will never forget whatever you have keyboarded. If you ask the computer to search its files it will always draw your attention to every item with any reference to the particular information you have requested. If you enter all your stock, then you can select all books by a particular author, on a particular subject, published between two dates, over a certain cost, and indeed meeting any other criteria you can conceive. Furthermore you can select any combination of these criteria: if you enter all your customers, including all their interests and wants, you can list every customer who wants a certain book in a few seconds – absolutely accurately every time!

Most booksellers claim to have paid for the cost of their whole computer installation from the direct savings they have made in producing their catalogues. For instance a complete system – computer, laser printer and software – costs about £2,000. Written off over five years that is £400 p.a.; this sum can be set against tax, so the net cost is about £300 p.a. How much does a printer charge to typeset one catalogue?

Anyone not using a computer to prepare their catalogue may therefore be wasting not only money, but also time and effort. The traditional way of typing out items, or sending filing cards to a typesetter, means that all the information has to be keyboarded a second time and all the proofreading may thus have to be done in a panic just before going to press. With a computer, items are keyboarded as they are acquired so proofreading can be done as each item is entered to the system. Once in the computer the information need never be keyboarded again. If a book is sold and another copy acquired, the original text can be reinstated and just edited.

Catalogues can be produced directly on a laser printer in fully made-up pages of proportionally spaced type ready for publication; alternatively a disk can be sent to the typesetter containing all the text ready to be set automatically. Laser printers can now produce very good quality typesetting at about four A4 pages a minute. They can print all the European accented characters, the Greek alphabet and many shapes and symbols in many different typefaces from eight point up to 36 point (½ inch high). Good software makes it possible for the text to be set out in roman, *italic*, and **bold** type, and for the spaces between lines to be adjusted to an accuracy of 1/72nd of an inch vertically (a printer's 'point'), and the spaces between letters to 1/300th of an inch horizontally.

The advantage of using properly designed cataloguing software is that data can be entered to the computer so that the program knows which information is the author, the title, the description, and so forth. This means that all the power of the computer can be used to print, or display, different combinations of the information in different formats quite automatically. For instance, some accounting information, such as the cost of an item, and from whom it was bought, can be printed on the accounting schedules. However, sensitive information of this sort would not appear in catalogues, or when a customer might be able to see the screen. Similarly a catalogue could be printed with all the information available, including scholarly notes, whereas a short list might show only basic information. Most software provides a number of pre-set catalogue layouts, and these can usually be quite easily re-designed and amended to suit changing needs.

Another major advantage of software designed especially for booksellers is that all the little details – like the special way in which pen names are dealt with – are catered for. Similarly the stock file can contain all items of stock, but any required can be printed in a catalogue. Sold items can be left in the file, but flagged so that they are not processed. If the book is sent on approval this can be logged as a reminder of its whereabouts. If two or more customers order the same item from a catalogue a note can be made so that when another copy is bought it can immediately be offered. The computer makes it easy to send quotation letters to customers offering one, two or a small number of items, and personalized short lists of this kind are nowadays an important sales technique.

Keeping track of customers' wants and addresses is an important task, and a computer can be used to file all names, addresses and purchases, with general interests and specific wants. Just as books can be selected in accordance with various criteria, customers in a particular district can be pinpointed so that they can be invited to a book fair. It is possible to select every customer interested in a particular author, or those who have asked specifically for a particular edition of a particular title. Lists, or sets of labels can be printed, and a letter can be composed and individually addressed to a selection of customers; this process is called *mailmerge*.

If all customer and stock information is filed in the computer, all the data is present to produce invoices and labels for parcels automatically. *Accounting software* will process these invoices, produce statements, and print lists of debtors, sales ledgers and bank reconciliation lists. If other income and items of expenditure are entered, all the other accounting schedules right up to the profit and loss account can be produced.

Many owners now use a computer as a bigger and better typewriter to produce all their letters, reports, theses and even books. Very few publishers now receive a manuscript; they expect a typed draft and a 'floppy disk' that they can hand to their printer. The joy of using a computer for all these purposes is that even the inexpert typist can produce a perfect result. It is easy to correct mistakes, change the grammar of a sentence, move paragraphs around and generally manipulate text so that the element of drudgery is removed.

A few people are still intimidated by the thought of getting to grips with an 'electronic brain', but almost all the design effort of the last ten years has been devoted to making systems easy to understand. In particular the information on the screen now always tells the user what to do next. The average number of queries from people starting to use the leading 'Booksellers' software is as little as two or three calls, even from people who have never used a computer before. One well-known bookseller produced a catalogue three weeks after her first computer was delivered. Nevertheless, those new to computing are best advised to choose one application and master that before moving on to the next task.

Computers are surrounded by a great deal of jargon and mythology; but the decision to buy one is actually no different from the decision to buy a typewriter, a fax, or a car. All cars will go from A to B, but some are modest and economic, others fast and flash. Similarly with computers: they come in all sorts of configurations but, as well as buying the actual computer and printer (the hardware), the new user also needs the programs that make the computer useful to booksellers rather than bankers or beekeepers (the software). Poor software may limit the benefits of even the best new hardware; cheap hardware may not release the benefits of sophisticated software. Many people find the problem of choosing a hardware/software combination quite intimidating, but there are a number of basic rules which will lead towards the best solution:

1. First of all decide clearly what you want the computer to do for you.
2. Never buy a computer (hardware and software) without 'driving it' yourself. Insist on actually trying out the exact system you are being offered, preferably with a piece of your own work – *you* hit the keys.
3. Ask as many colleagues as possible about their experience in using the various systems on offer and about the help and support they receive from their supplier.
4. Time and effort spent on reconnaissance is rarely wasted.

How to choose hardware

Broadly speaking, all computers of similar specification are very similar under the covers. Many are made in the same factories. A new generation of processors (the processor is the engine) came on the market recently: the brochures list them as 20286, 20386 or 20486 processor *chips*. Salesmen make great play with the speed of these processors, quoting 12, 20, 25 and higher *megahertz* (the 'miles per hour' of computing), and will wax lyrical about the means of transferring information around inside the processor. To a bookseller, all this is largely irrelevant; in a cataloguing application there is relatively little processing – what matters is the capacity and speed of the memory units (the filing cabinets).

It is entirely practical to catalogue on a computer using conventional *twin interchangeable floppy disk drives*: one for the program, one for the data. Each disk can hold 1,400,000 characters (about 200 pages of catalogue). Nowadays they are considered slow; each time the software uses a drive the motor has to start spinning the disk, so average access time is about two seconds. It is a bit like using a Mini on a motorway.

An *internal hard disk* spins continuously and holds some 40 million characters. Average access time is about 1/25th of a second. These are definitely the better buy. The one disadvantage is that to duplicate, or *back-up*, all the data as a security measure, the contents of the hard disk have to be copied from time to time onto a library of floppy disks. As this is a bit tedious, users tend to put off the chore, but they do so at their peril. Computers, like everything else, can develop faults, and common sense demands that essential data should be safeguarded.

The most suitable computer on the market for most booksellers has *twin interchangeable hard disks* called *datapacs*. They are fast, and hold from 40 to 200 million characters each. One instruction duplicates all the information from one datapac to another in a minute or two. This is so easy and convenient that it can be done every day. A complete duplicate of several years' work can be easily updated for storage in another location as an insurance against fire or theft.

A system that is likely to be popular is the very small *notebook* computer. These machines can easily be carried around and used anywhere: in a sale room, at a book fair or on a train. In the office the computer is plugged into a *docking station* which has a conventional screen and keyboard; this makes concentrated working easier, while automatically recharging the notebook.

Screens are of two sorts. Mono screens can be black on white, green on green, or orange on orange. Alternatively, colour screens provide a complete palette of colours, and tend to reduce eye strain. They are more costly, but can be a good investment if a computer is to be used fairly continuously.

In printing out information, users tend to get what they pay for. *Dot matrix printers* are the cheapest but quality is not very good. The expensive versions can work at two speeds: in the fast mode they are good for printing invoices and listings, in the slower 'near letter quality' mode the results look much better. *Ink jet printers* are at the top end of the dot matrix market. The quality of the individual characters is very good but they are not as versatile as laser printers. All dot matrix and ink jet machines print line by line, while laser printers print a whole page at a time – virtually providing a typesetter on the desk. A range of typefaces with typesizes from 8 point to 36 point can be called upon. Catalogues, correspondence, even invoices have style and quality, giving a very professional image to the business. Laser printers can print text in double, or even treble columns; the latest print to an accuracy of 600 dots to the inch, almost equivalent to typesetting.

How to choose software

Most computer suppliers offer a *free* 'word processor' software package. It is entirely possible to produce a catalogue with one of these products, just as though it were one long letter; but the practical limitations soon become apparent and, when additional software packages have to be made to interface together, the cost soon mounts up.

Most booksellers use cataloguing software packages specially designed for their needs. Some 400 systems of a popular package were installed in the ten years from 1981. This system combines a word processor that can carry out all the intricacies of typesetting, a database that allows any amount of information to be entered in any record, and a language that makes it easy to adjust the system to the individual user's requirements. Once the information about stock has been entered, just four keys will produce a complete camera-ready catalogue. Because it has been developed over the years by booksellers for booksellers, the system is very flexible. It can be used with one file of all stock, both current and sold; or one file for each catalogue, plus an archive; or any combination of these. It is easy to separate items out of one file to merge files and to sort files to a new sequence.

Software of this kind is designed for booksellers with differing temperaments. There are four alternative ways of entering and editing information, plus a learning mode. Some users like to enter author, title, description, etc. methodically, while others prefer to dart about entering information as it comes to mind. Each system can be tailored to suit individual needs. The designers will do this tailoring, or provide a manual for those who enjoy the intellectual challenge of doing it themselves. The product is supplied with both book and address databases and a word processor for correspondence, and can be used on the minimum configuration of any IBM compatible micro computer, using twin floppy disks, hard disk, or twin interchangeable hard disks called datapacs. The software drives all Hewlett-Packard compatible laser printers, and a range of typefaces is available which includes all the European accented characters. An optional extra is a catalogue design pack with an additional manual and examples of catalogue layouts, and instructions for printing indexes to catalogues and other more sophisticated features. Most users need only one day's training to produce their first catalogue.

Multi-user systems

Traditionally, microcomputers have been used by one person at a time. The software can be changed over to do cataloguing in the morning and invoices in the afternoon, and to play computer games in the evening; but with one processor, one keyboard and screen and one printer, only one person can use the system at any one time.

Ordinary microcomputers are now some fifty times faster and can store a thousand times as much information as the systems of ten years ago. This enormous increase in power means that software can be more sophisticated and provide more help to the operator, but also it means that more than one person can use a system at the same time. Two, three or more keyboards and screens can be linked to one computer, so that cataloguing, invoicing and letter writing can all be going on at the same time, all using the same files. If a customer telephones, or pays a visit, all the information can be on a screen in a second or two, while other people carry on with other jobs.

The computer world calls this 'networking', or 'multi-user', but there is a significant difference between the two. Networking connects together a number of microcomputers, each with its own program, to a central filing computer, which itself has another program. Multi-user is more like the big mainframe computers: there is one central computer with one program and all the files. Each user has a terminal, which can be just a screen and a keyboard. To a casual viewer both systems may appear very similar in operation, but the multi-user solution is both more robust and cheaper.

Future developments

Colour   It is possible to store colour images of books with the other information in a computer to display it in colour on the screen and to print it out on a colour laser printer. An experimental system was demonstrated at the ABA June book fair in 1990.

Character recognition   It is now possible to 'scan' typeset text and convert it to computer-readable text. A commercial service already scans many auctioneers' catalogues and reports items coming up for sale of specific interest to each of their customers.

Speech recognition   The Radar Research laboratory at Malvern has developed an accurate speech recognition system. It currently works on a limited range of sentences used by airline pilots; but one day we shall talk to our computers.

Grammar   British Telecom's research teams have developed a system that can analyse sentences into their grammatical structure. This is a first step to effective language translation.

Interrogation   Bristol University is working on 'natural language' systems to allow anyone to ask computer systems questions, as if interrogating Yellow Pages. Similar research by various other institutions is being funded through the 'Esprit' programme from Brussels.

The Oxford English Dictionary and the British Library   The entire OED is available on one CD ROM (Compact Disc Read-Only-Memory). Soon the *Dictionary of National Biography* will be published in similar form. The complete contents of the British Library catalogues are also available on CD ROM. A CD ROM driver currently costs about £400, plus software to access the huge amount of data that can be stored on one disc; but this cost is likely to drop dramatically as the technology becomes popular.

Other developments   The entire works of many major authors will in the near future be available on CD ROMs. Various suppliers are working on different products; one is offering the works of Jane Austen in text, voice and video.

Conclusion

The best way to start gaining efficiency and saving money by using a computer is to choose a tried and tested system, and become familiar with doing just one job – entering the stock and producing catalogues, for example. When that is mastered, move on to the next job. Those who say they have experienced problems have usually invented their own systems, or tried to do everything at once – usually on the first day! But as everyone's systems, or tried to do everything at once – usually on the first day! But as everyone's working becomes steadily more complex and as the cost of employing staff gets ever higher, the computer points the way to getting more work properly done in less time. People who have used a good computer system for any length of time will insist that they could not now get all their work done without one.

The computing world is changing with breathtaking speed, and some booksellers may be inclined to wait until the next system is available; but like 'tomorrow' the 'next' system never comes. The wise start modestly with a clear, simple target, and as new developments become available they are able to evaluate them in the context of their experience. In computing the tortoise always beats the hare!

Conjugate

'The leaves which "belong to one another", i.e. those that if traced into and out of the back of the book, are found to form a *single* sheet of paper, are said to be "conjugate"' (McKerrow). The term is often used in discussion of the problems of PRELIMS, blanks, ADVERTISEMENTS, CANCELS, etc. Non-conjugate leaves are known as SINGLETONS.

Connolly, Cyril
See 'THE MODERN MOVEMENT'

Contact Editions

The private press in Paris of Robert McAlmon, an American expatriate married to Winifred Ellerman, who is better known under her pseudonym 'Bryher'. Her father, the shipping magnate Sir John Ellerman, financed the enterprise, which began publishing in 1923 and ceased upon McAlmon's departure from France in 1929. The press, which worked in close liaison with William Bird's THREE MOUNTAINS PRESS, published a number of important expatriate writers; its most sought-after title is Ernest Hemingway's first book, *Three Stories and Ten Poems*, published in an edition of 300 copies in 1923.

Cookery Books

Janet Clarke

To live – even to survive – man must eat and drink, and from the moment he discovered that cooking with fire and hot stones made raw produce more palatable and that the preservation of foods by air-drying and smoking prolonged the edibility of scarce comestibles, he has been searching for ever more sophisticated methods of producing food and drink for the table. Cooking methods advanced with the introduction of pottery and bronze and iron cauldrons, with the advent of salt mining and, more importantly, the spread of agriculture. Food and eating loomed large in the ancient world, as we can read in Herodotus; Homer was considered to be an authority on the ordering of a banquet; Horace wrote several odes on the subject of wine; and in AD 43 the Romans brought to this country such innovations as new cereals and grains and querns and domed bread ovens for the baking of fine loaves made from the soft white wheat they preferred. Domestic fowl became plentiful, pigeons were housed in columbaria, exotic birds such as pheasant, peacock and guinea-fowl were intensively reared in special enclosures; and the Romans also brought with them their own methods of livestock management, constructing game parks where wild animals were preserved.

Although milk, butter and soft cheeses had played a part in the diet of this country from the neolithic period, it was the Romans who introduced the manufacture of hard cheeses, that is, those made with the use of rennet, which could be left to mature and be stored for lengthy periods. Honey and spices for flavour and preservation were not unknown, but here too the Romans brought with them sophisticated methods and a huge variety of spices; these included the all-important pepper, as well as saffron, ginger, cassia, sumach and spikenard. The cultivation of fruits and vegetables became an economic necessity and those that could not be grown here were dried in their country of origin and imported.

Wines were made not only with grapes but also with a variety of fruits and flowers, though beer continued to be the most readily available drink for rich and poor alike. Along with all this Graeco-Roman cuisine the Romans brought with them the great works of Celsus and Galen, with their emphasis on the four humours, hot and cold, dry and moist, which have featured over the centuries in one form of diet or another; and most famous of all, Apicius, the celebrated gourmand of the time of Augustus and Tiberius, whose work has often been faithfully resurrected, discussed and debated. It seems incredible that all this sophistication should have disappeared when the Romans left after the barbarian invasions. The Anglo-Saxons virtually started all over again and were greatly dependent on game – wild beasts, birds and water fowl – to supplement their poor diet. The Norman conquest brought new ways of farming, but these were times of war and famine, plenty with scarcity, king's peace with baronial anarchy, and it was not until the introduction of printing and the spread of the Renaissance to these shores in the 1500s that new and wondrous ingredients were available with instructions as to what to do with them.

Many of the early books were concerned with diet as distinct from the pleasures of food and eating; etiquette, too, received much attention, as did the presentation of the food and wine. Fast days as ordained by the Church meant that almost half the year was meatless, but of course there was advice on what could or could not be served. Perhaps the most important work of this period was Baptista Platina's *De honesta voluptate et valitudine*, widely acknowledged to be the earliest printed book on cookery. Four editions of this work appeared in the fifteenth century, Vicaire dating the first as 1474. The work deals with the most beneficial diet for the human body, discussing at length the varieties of meat, fish, vegetable, fruits, etc., giving methods of their preparation and their correct sauces, and containing in all about three hundred recipes.

In France, Taillevent (c.1312–1395) was considered to be the forerunner of professional chefs, and his work, *Le Viandier*, published in 1490, almost 100 years after his death, shows that his cookery was basically sound as well as being decorative and colourful. After this, printed works abound in Latin, French, German, Dutch and English on the diet of the king and the nobleman, the drunkard and the vegetarian, on wines, on beer and on milk. Works of this period include The School of Salerno, *Regimen Sanitatis Salernitatum*, 1541, on the importance of hygiene and diet; Rabelais, *La Plaisante et Joyeuse histoyre du grand Géant Gargantua*, 1532; Messisbugo, *Banchetti compositioni di vivande et apparecchio generale*, 1549, with its marvellous woodcut of a kitchen scene of cooks and scullions preparing an enormous feast of fish, fowl, vegetables and fruit with a great pole balanced over all from which hang geese and little birds, a turtle and a huge basket overflowing with vegetables.

In 1570 Bartolomeo Scappi's *Opera, Cuoco Secreto di Papa Pio V*, with its 26 full-page woodcuts, illustrated the full 'batterie de cuisine' in all its glory, much of which remained unchanged until the present century. In 1508 the first book entirely concerned with the table appeared on the scene: *The Boke of Kervynge*, by Wynkyn de Worde. The carver was an important member of the Court or noble household and was expected to be an expert at his job. The list of instructions sound romantic – 'alaye that fesande, wynge that partryche, dysfygure that pecocke, unlace that cony, tayme that crabbe, barbe that lobster' – but correctly performed meant that whatever was presented on the trencher appeared in an elegant manner with the minimum of waste. Forks not yet being in use, food was carried to the mouth by a pointed knife or, if wet, by a spoon.

Manners were all important and various works list advice, much of which still applies today: 'Eate softly and drink manerly, beware ye do not quaffe. Scratch not thy head or finger when thou art at meate; Keepe still foot and hand, at meat time begin ye no stryfe; Do not drink too much'. There is advice for children too: 'Touch nothing until you are fully served; Don't wipe your knife on the cloth and don't wipe your nose at table'. (Hollywood and television producers, please note.) These early books on manners, *The Boke of Curtasye*, c.1430, the *Boke of Nature*, 1577, and others, including *Two Fifteenth-Century Cookery Books*, edited by Thomas Austin, were later to be reprinted by the Early English Text Society in the late nineteenth century.

Thomas Tusser appears on the scene in the sixteenth century with his gentle *Five Hundred Points of Good Husbandry*. For December, after all the hard winter work of housing and feeding the animals, checking the stables and corn lofts, the gardens and the bees is done, he exhorts 'Good Husband and Huswife, now chiefly be glad, things handsome to have, as they ought to be had. They both do provide, against Christmas do come, to welcome their neighbours, good chere to have some. Good Bread and good drinke, a good fire in the hall, brawne, pudding, and souses, and good mustard with al. Biefe, mutton, and Porke, and good Pies of the best, pig, veale, goose and capon, and turkey wel drest, Chese apples and nuttes, good Caroles to heare, as then, in the countrey is counted good chere.' It was deserved; life on the land was arduous and must surely at times have reaped little reward. Tusser's work first appeared in 1557 and was reprinted many times through the centuries. Perhaps one of the most charming editions is the 1931 facsimile of the 1571 edition, collated and edited by Dorothy Hartley.

La Varenne is widely considered to be the founder of French classic cookery. His book, *Le Cuisinier François* was first published in 1651 and ran to 30 editions over the following 75 years. It was translated into English under the title *The French Cook*, 1653. La Varenne brought order and knowledge to the kitchen and many of his recipes could well be used today. Massialot's *Le Cuisinier Roial et Bourgeois*, 1691, published in various editions until 1750, was the work of another of the great French cooks of the period, and was followed by Menon whose works include *Nouveau Traité de la Cuisine*, 1739, *La Nouvelle Cuisine*, 1742, *Les Soupers de la Cour*, 1755 and *La Science du Maître d'Hôtel, Confiseur*, 1750 with its wonderful designs for desserts set out in the manner of parterre gardens.

The early seventeenth century brought many books to English noble households, many of them directed for the first time to the housewife: Plat's *Delightes for Ladies*, 1600, and *A Closet for Ladies and Gentlewomen*, 1608; *The English Hus-Wife* by Gervase Markham, 1615; John Murrell's *A New Book of Cookerie*, 1617, gives directions to furnish an extraordinary, or ordinary, feast, either in Summer or Winter together with Bills of Fare for Fish-Dayes, Fasting Dayes, Emberweekes, or Lent. Murrell later brought out *A Delightfull Daily Excercise for Ladies and Gentlewomen*, 1621; his *Two Bookes of Cookerie and Carving* was published in 1631. *The Queen's Closet Opened*, 1655, comprised three volumes bound in one, being *The Pearle of Practice*, *The Queens Delight* and *The Compleat Cook*. *The Pearle of Practice* was concerned only with medical receipts, with the two other books devoted to cookery. Closets abounded, and perhaps the most noted of all were *The Closet of the Eminently Learned Sir Kenelme Digby, Kt., Opened*, 1669, and *The Queen-Like Closet*, by Hannah Wolley, 1670. Kenelme Digby was a charismatic character of aristocratic birth who managed to be a favourite of several monarchs (a rare feat at that time) and travelled widely. Many of his recipes are of continental origin and he was an expert on the various methods of making mead, metheglin, hydromel and many other such drinks as well as wines and ales.

Robert May, on the other hand, was a professional cook whose career spanned four reigns and the Interregnum; his book, *The Accomplisht Cook, or the Art and Mystery of Cookery*, first appeared in 1660 after 50 years of experience and industry. He was the son of a cook and had at one time been sent to France, which may account for the number of recipes for frogs and snails in his book; but more interesting are the many recipes for grand sallets, a whole chapter devoted to the cookery of eggs, as well as fish cookery, elaborate pies and tarts, illustrated with charming woodcuts. It is the preface to this book which contains the famous description of the Triumphs and Trophies to be used at Festival times, with ships, guns, cannons, carriages made of pastry, false pigs filled with frogs and birds and a pastry stag filled with wine – when the arrow is pulled from the stag's side the 'blood' flows out, the trails of powder to the ships and cannons are set alight, the ladies throw eggshells full of sweet waters to sweeten the stink of powder, the lids are removed from the pies 'allowing the frogs to leap out and the birds to fly – thus making the ladies to skip and shreek'. After all this jollity the banquet is brought in.

Travel of course brought to light exotic new ingredients. From the Americas came chocolate, vanilla, fruits such as pineapples, tomatoes, pimentos, avocados (known as alligator pears), vegetables including maize, yams, several types of bean such as the kidney, runner and lima beans, and the most important of all vegetables, the potato. From the East came sugar from Syria; citrus fruits spreading through from China and India made their way to Europe; almonds, peaches, apricots, aubergines, pepper, nutmeg, cloves, cinnamon and all manner of valuable spices, coffee from Arabia – the list is

Item 1

Moulds for Custards, from Robert May's *The Accomplisht Cook*, 1685.

seemingly endless, but all these ingredients eventually found their way into the dishes of wealthy Europeans and finally on to the pages of their cookery books.

By the eighteenth century most of these ingredients were easily available and at a considerably reduced cost. Household account books are invaluable sources of information as to what was in everyday use. From the household book of the Currer family in Yorkshire in 1711 we learn that they were able to buy 2 oz sinnamon (sic) 9d, 1 oz cloves 10d, ½ lb black pepper 8d, ¼ lb Jamaica pepper 9d as well as carraway, nutmeg, mace, saffron, cumin, currants, raisins, rosewater, and two different types of ginger, six oranges and six lemons 2s 6d, 6 lb sugar 3s, ½ lb green tea 2s 6d, 2 lb chocolet 7s 6d, to the carrier of a litle parsel (sic) to York, a distance of some 25 miles, 4d.

Printed works on chocolate and coffee appeared in the seventeenth century, the most notable being Du Four's *Commentaires . . . sur le Thé, le Caphé, le Chocolate*, Paris, 1671. By the middle of the eighteenth century professional female cooks had started to produce cookery books of note: E. Smith, *The Compleat Housewife*, 1727; Mrs Sarah Harrison, *The House-Keeper's Pocket-Book*, 1733; Elizabeth Moxon, *English Housewifery*, 1749; Anne Battan, *A Collection of Scarce and Valuable Receipts*, 1749; Mrs Fisher, *The Prudent Housewife*, c.1750; Mary Johnson, *The Young Woman's Companion*, 1753; Arabella Fairfax, *The Family's Best Friend*, 1753; Elizabeth Cleland, *A New and Easy Method of Cookery*, 1759; Catherine Brooks, *The Complete English Cook*, 1762; Mrs Anne Barker, *The Complete Servant Maid*, 1762; Elizabeth Raffald, *The Experienced English Housekeeper*, 1769. Mrs Raffald, a redoubtable woman of enormous energy, kept a confectioner's shop and three inns, bore her husband 16 daughters in 18 years and brought out a Manchester directory.

But by far the most influential book of the period is *The Art of Cookery Made Plain and Easy by a Lady*, 1747. The lady, Mrs Hannah Glasse, borrowed recipes from other works as did most authors, but on the whole her own recipes are written in a concise manner with ingredients accessible to most people rather than only the rich. However, it may well be that it was not so much the content that made the work so fashionable as the fact that the first edition was a slim, elegant folio and not the usual dumpy octavo. The work – corrected, enlarged, revised and pirated – remained in print for over 75 years.

At the end of the eighteenth century two revolutions radically changed the eating habits of both the French and the British. For Britain the industrial revolution brought a huge reversal of the population in town and country. Until that time over 90 per cent of the population worked on the land; but then came the migration to the industrial cities where huge fortunes were made by some; but for others the change brought slave labour, slum housing and little food (most of which had been adulterated) or even worse, starvation. We know that spirits were cheap and available: 'drunk for a penny – dead drunk for tuppence'. Printed matter poured out of the presses for the newly rich; they needed to learn the ways of housekeeping and how to cope with unskilled, illiterate, slovenly servants – and there were many willing to instruct them through the printed page. *Domestic Management, or the Art of Conducting a Family with Instructions to Servants in General*, 1800, *The New Practice of Cookery*, 1804, *The Family Director*, 1807; *A New System of Domestic Cookery Formed upon the Principles of Economy* (this by Maria Elizabeth Rundle rivalled Mrs Glasse in popularity, remaining in print in one form or another from 1808 until 1893); *The Female Economist*, 1810; *The British Housewife*, 1810; *The Young Woman's Companion*,

A New System of Domestic Cookery, by a Lady (Maria Rundle), 1819.

1811; *The Female Instructor*, 1815; *The Housekeeper's Accompt-book (Improved by Red Lines across the Pages)*, 1820; *The Footman's Directory*, 1823; *The Complete Servant*, 1825; *Domestic Duties*, 1825; *Kidd's Practical Hints for the Use of Young Carvers*, 1830 – the list is seemingly endless.

In 1845 Eliza Acton published *Modern Cookery in All its Branches*. Here we have an author who really did understand her subject to the very last degree; every recipe was painstakingly tested in her own kitchen, and she even noted the difference the weather made to the various fruits for jams and jellies. In the recipe for Raspberry Jam, for example, she notes '(The fruit) which grows in the shade has less flavour than the fruit which received the full warmth of the sun'. For each recipe she notes the amount of each ingredient and the cooking time. Often there is an added observation: 'Obs. A more refined preserve is made by pressing the fruit through a sieve after it is boiled tender; but the jam is excellent without'. Her recipes are as bright today as they were when first published and she has seen a great revival in popularity. Sadly, 16 years later Eliza Acton was eclipsed by Isabella Beeton with her *Book of Household Management*. First published in one volume by her husband Sam in 1861, the book was an immediate best-seller, for it incorporated all that the emergent middle-class housewife needed to know in order to run a home efficiently. After Isabella's early death at the age of 29, Sam Beeton ran into financial difficulties and sold the copyright to Ward, Lock; they are still printing an up-to-date version, and it is an impressive memorial for her name to be selling books nearly 130 years after her death.

These books and many others – the charitable cookery for the poor and the working classes, for vegetarians, the temperance books, the wonderful books with an Indian flavour, *The Khwan Niamut or Nawab's Domestic Cookery*, Calcutta, 1839, *Indian Domestic Economy*, Bombay, 1849; *The Curry Cook's Assistant*, by Daniel Santiagoe with charming afternotes: 'N.B. must use a wooden spoon to all Curries . . . better than a plate one'; *The Madras Cookery Book for the People, by an Old Lady-Resident, Anglo-Indian Cookery at Home, Indian Cookery* by Richard Terry, Chef-de-Cuisine at the Oriental Club, London, 1861. Flora Annie Steel and Grace Gardiner, *The Complete Indian Housekeeper*, and of course *Culinary Jottings for Madras* by Col. A. H. Kenny Herbert, together with the high-class cookery for the rich by professional chefs employed by royalty and the aristocracy such as Frederic Nutt's *The Imperial and Royal Cook*, 1809, G. A. Jarring's *The Italian Confectioner*, 1830, William Kitchener's *The Cook's Oracle*, 1817, Thomas Masters' *The Ice Book*, 1844, *A Complete System of Cookery*, by John Simpson, cook to the Most Noble the Marquis of Buckingham, 1806, *Practical Gastronomy and Recherché Cookery* by C. H. Senn (founder of the Food and Cookery Association), the works by Alexis Soyer, that exuberant anglophile who rushed off to the Crimea and saved more lives by feeding the troops than ever Florence Nightingale did; the translations from the French of Carême, Gouffé, Dubois and others – all these continue the pattern laid down in earlier centuries that the Englishman's castle is his home and there he will stay to eat, whatever his financial status.

However, across the Channel things were moving in a totally different direction. The selling of food was rigidly controlled by *traiteurs*, those who had licence to sell cooked meats and sauces, *charcutiers*, those who cured meat and made terrines and pâtés (but were not allowed to kill the pigs themselves), and cafés, where *pâtisseries* and ices were sold. In the late 1760s in Paris, Boulenger, who sold soups, added to his list a dish of sheep's feet in a creamy sauce and put out a sign stating 'Venite ad me, omnes qui stomacho laboritis et ego restaurabo vos'. The furious *traiteurs* brought a lawsuit against him but they lost, Parliament having decreed that sheep's feet in a cream sauce was not a *ragoût*. And so the restaurant was born. In 1782 Beauvilliers opened the first high-class restaurant, where diners could choose individual dishes from a menu and were served at individual tables. More restaurateurs followed suit, so that by 1789 there were some 100 or so restaurants in Paris. Marie-Antoinette told the masses to eat cake; the masses retaliated by cutting off the heads of the royal family and every possible aristocrat they could lay hands on, thereby creating massive unemployment among the chefs, pastry-cooks and confectioners previously employed within these vast households. There was nothing they could do except flee the country, and many came to other parts of Europe, including the British Isles, where the political climate was less unsettled. Others migrated to the cities and set up their own establishments serving not princes or peers but the public at large.

Menu of some 400 dishes of Beauvilliers Restaurant, Paris, c.1808.

By 1804 there were some 500 restaurants, and so began the French practice of habitually eating high-class food in public establishments and buying professionally prepared *charcuterie*, *pâtisserie* and confectionery to be eaten at home.

Some of these restaurateurs, bakers, confectioners and others, including Beauvilliers, produced cookery books. Grimod de la Reynière brought out the first *Almanach des Gourmands*, 1803, containing a calendar of foods, and itinerary of a gourmet in Paris, including a guide to the best and most interesting restaurants and recipes. This is a series of eight volumes, each illustrated with a gastronomic frontispiece. Throughout the rest of the century thousands of books were published on every gastronomic subject, from the art and history of the table to vinegar. By far the most famous chef of the period, whose standing is as high today as it was then, is Marie-Antoine Carême; his brilliant career started in a *pâtisserie* in Paris, continuing as chef to kings, emperors and the Tsar of all the Russias, to Talleyrand, Prince Esterhazy and to Baron Rothschild. He cooked for the Prince Regent for a short while but not surprisingly left, longing to be back in Paris where his heart was. His books *Le Pâtissier Pittoresque*, 1854, *Le Maître d'Hôtel*, 1822, *Le Cuisinier Parisien*, 1828, and *L'Art de la Cuisine Française*, 1833, were painstakingly written and illustrated with intricate drawings of an architectural nature of his most elaborate dishes. These works were a legacy to all gastronomes and are generally thought of as the cornerstones of a serious collection.

Carême's successors were legion in number. Dubois, Lacam, Josef Favre, Salles and Montagné are a few among them. Brillat-Savarin, not a chef but a philosopher and scholar, wrote *La Physiologie du Goût* in 1826. Still in print today, it is a book known by most but (I would dare to add) read in full by only a few. In 1902, *Le Guide Culinaire* by August Escoffier in collaboration with Philéas Gilbert and Emile Fétu took the culinary world by storm. Written by chefs for chefs, it brought order to the repertoire where before there had been none. So popular was this book, so respected and so much used as a kitchen bible, that it is rare to find it in good condition. Escoffier and his followers had brought professional cooks into the twentieth century and although recent trends have been for a lighter and less formal style his knowledge and methods are still respected today.

Édouard Nignon also had followers, a small but passionate band of chefs, writers and gourmets who preferred his less rigid way of thinking to that of Escoffier. Nignon cooked for the Tsar and then for the Emperor of Austria before becoming chef and later maître d'hôtel at the famous Larue restaurant in the rue Royale in Paris. He wrote three books, *Les Plaisirs de la Table*, *Eloges de la Cuisine* and the fabled *L'Heptaméron des Gourmets*, published in 1919 in an edition of only 150 copies and dedicated to his son who died in 1914 on the Somme. It is said that Nignon was the spiritual ancestor of the modern lighter approach to cookery.

Collectors of books on food, cookery and wine seem a breed apart. For most of them the motivation is, of course, food: the fascination of it, the chemistry and the mystery of the individual ingredients which might in themselves be quite ordinary but which when put together produce a sublime dish. Chefs, food writers, journalists and cooks, forever seeking something new, may happen upon a secondhand book of interest, and from that moment the search is on and the passionate hunger for knowledge of the history of food has begun. For others it may be the other way round, with historians gradually realizing

SOYER'S SULTANA'S SAUCE, Analysed by Dr. Hassall.

I have examined with much care several samples of M. Soyer's New Eastern or Sultana Sauce, and I am of opinion that it is an excellent preparation. While it is a good stomachic, its flavour is delicious; moreover the ingredients of which it is composed are of the purest and most wholesome description.

ARTHUR WILLIAM HASSALL, M.D.,
Author of "Food and its Adulterations," "Adulterations Detected," &c. &c.

8, Bennett Street, St. James's Street,
14th August, 1857.

SOLE AGENTS—MESSRS. CROSSE AND BLACKWELL.

Advertisement for M. Soyer's Sultana Sauce.

the enormous part food has played in political and social evolution. Collectors in this field are, as a rule, well versed in their subject and expect the same of their booksellers. Customers can demand patience; every spring when the violets bloom in my garden I remember the many hours spent on behalf of one who was trying to trace the origin of Hilda Leyel's Violet Salad. We never managed it – but I always serve violet salad once a year and think of a customer who became, as many do, a good friend.

Books on wine

It is inevitable that the majority of important works on oenology belong to France. The earliest, usually in Latin, were on the properties of wine and came, in the main, from France, Italy and Germany. As with books on food many were Roman and Greek in origin, such as Apicius, Cato, Columella, Hippocrates and Platina. From the seventeenth century to the present day the French have produced thousands of books on wine of every type and from every region, many illustrated with woodcuts, copper plates, hand-coloured plates and chromolithographs. Dejean, *Traité Raisonné de la Distillation*, 1753; Chaptal, *L'Art de Faire le Vin*, 1807; Jullien, *Topographie de tous les Vignobles*, 1813; Louis Pasteur, *L'Étude sur le Vin*, 1866; Bertall, *La Vigne*, 1878: these are a few notable studies. The most sumptuous of all wine books must surely be the seven volume *Ampélographie, Traité Général de Viticulture* by Viala and Vermorel, 1901–1910, with 500 colour plates; it is rare in its complete form.

The first book in English devoted entirely to the subject of wine is William Turner's *A new boke of the natures and properties of all wines that are commonly used here in England*, 1568, a work of great rarity. Other early books in English are, not surprisingly, on the distillation of spirits, the brewing of ale and beer, and the manufacture of cider and perry, as well as the use and abuse of wine, such as Thomas Whitaker's *The Tree of humane life, or, the blood of the grape, proving the possibilitie of maintaining humane life from infancy to extreme old age without any sicknesse by the use of wine*, 1638, and Samuel Ward's *Warning piece to all Drunkards*, 1682. The most famous eighteenth-century work of this kind was Sir Edward Barry's *Observations Historical, Critical and Medical on the Wines of the Ancients and the analogy between them and modern wines*, 1775.

This vein continued into the nineteenth century with Henderson's *History of Ancient and Modern Wines*, 1824, and Samuel Morewood's *A Philosophical and Statistical History of the Inventions and Customs of Ancient and Modern Nations in the Manufacture of Inebriating Liquors*, Dublin, 1824.

Various factors established port as 'the Englishman's wine', and there were many books, treatises and pamphlets on the subject. The most important were John Croft's *Treatise on the Wines of Portugal*, 1788, James Warre's *The Past, Present and Probably the Future State of the Wine Trade*, 1823, many works by Joseph James Forrester, said to be 'the most remarkable man the Port trade has produced', Vizetelly's *Facts about Port and Madeira* and Charles Sellers' *Oporto Old and New, being a Record of the Port Wine Trade*, 1899. Vizetelly also wrote on sherry, as did Ermitano, *A Shillingsworth of Sherry*, 1874, and Cozens, *Sherryana*, 1887.

The eighteenth century brought advice on the planting and growth of vines, as in *The*

Vineyard, an anonymous work published in 1727, J. Locke's *Observations on the Growth and Culture of Vines*, 1766, Vespre's *Dissertation on growth of vines in England*, 1786, and William Speechly's *A Treatise on the Culture of the Vine*, York, 1790. The nineteenth century was awash with books on wine and wine-making in all its branches; British wines and cordials, the management of foreign wines in England and of the vineyards and wines of America, South Africa, and Australasia.

The most influential author of the twentieth century in this country was without a doubt André Simon. Born in 1877, he came to England in 1902 as agent to Pommery, the champagne house. In 1905 his first book, *The History of the Champagne Trade in England*, was published, and from then until his death in 1970 at the age of 93 he wrote over a hundred books and pamphlets on wine and food. He was a founder member of the Wine Trade Club and co-founded the Saintsbury Club; but his major contribution to gastronomy on this side of the Channel was the founding in 1933 of the Wine and Food Society. The Society enjoyed immediate success, holding wine tastings and dinners around the country and publishing a Quarterly Review edited by Simon with contributions from such leading writers as H. Warner Allen, Dr Maynard Amerine, Hilaire Belloc, Edward Barnard, Ian Campbell, Marcel Boulestin the first television cook, Ambrose Heath, James Laver, George Rainbird, and Cyril Connolly. Elizabeth David, another contributor, became in turn an enormous influence on food, cookery and their commentators of today, with her vast knowledge of the regional cuisine of France and the foods of the Mediterranean and the Levant. Simon continued to edit the review until 1964 and it should be on every collector's table; the articles cover all aspects of gastronomy, historical and contemporary, and take us from the elegant pre-war period through war-time austerity and on to the new generation of wine and food lovers.

Cookery and food
Bitting, Katherine, *Gastronomic Bibliography*, San Francisco, 1939 (reprinted London, 1981).
Driver, Elizabeth, *A Bibliography of Cookery Books Published in Britain, 1875–1914*, 1989.
Hazlitt, William Carew, *Old Cookery Books and Ancient Cuisine*, 2nd edn 1902.
Kansas State University, *America's Charitable Cooks*, Library Catalogue.
Lincoln, Waldo, *Culinary Americana, American Cookery Books 1742–1860*, enlarged by Eleanor Lowenstein, Massachusetts, 1929 (reprinted, 1954).
MacLean, Virginia, *A Catalogue of Household and Cookery Books in the English Tongue 1701–1800*, 1981.
Maggs Bros. Ltd, *Food and Drink through the Ages*, Catalogue, 1937.
Oxford, A. W., *English Cookery Books to the Year 1850*, 1913 (reprinted, 1979).
——— *Notes from a Collector's Catalogues*, 1909.
Pennell, Elizabeth, *My Cookery Books*, New York, 1903.
Simon, André, *Bibliotheca Gastronomica*, 1953 (reprinted, 1978).
Vicaire, Georges, *Bibliographie Gastronomique*, Paris, 1890 (reprinted London, 1978).
Westbury, Lord, *Handlist of Italian Cookery Books*, Florence, 1963.

Wine
Amerine, Maynard, *A Check List of Books and Pamphlets on Grapes and Wine, 1938–1948*, California, 1971.
Gabler, James M., *Wine into Words*, Baltimore, Maryland, 1985.

Noling, A. W., *Beverage Literature*, New Jersey, 1971.
Oberlé, Gérard, *Une Bibliothèque Bachique* (sale catalogue of the library of Kilian Fritsch, 1993.
Simon, André, *Bibliotheca Bacchica*, 1927–32 (reprinted, 1972).
——— *Bibliotheca Vinaria*, 1913.
——— *Wine and Gastronomy* (all three *Bibliothecas* in one volume, indexed by Gail Unzelman).

Copperplate
See TECHNIQUES OF ILLUSTRATION

Copyright
The legal right to publish. It applies not only to texts and illustrations; typographical arrangements, critical editions and so on are protected as well. Both the history of copyright and the present application of the law (which varies substantially from country to country) are of great complexity; the former is well recounted in *The Oxford Companion to English Literature* and the latter is summarized in each edition of *The Artists' and Writers' Yearbook*.

Booksellers sometimes derive a useful subsidiary income from reprinting unavailable books of interest to their customers such as works on local history or by local authors; before committing themselves to such projects they should take legal advice as to whether copyright restrictions apply.

Corvinus Press
One of the most truly private of private presses, the Corvinus Press (named for Matthias Corvinus, the bibliophile king of Hungary) was founded in 1936 by Viscount Carlow. Carlow, a friend of T. E. Lawrence, produced around 50 books, many in very small editions for his friends; he died in a plane crash in 1944, and in the following year the plant was sold to Lord Kemsley for his Dropmore Press. Underrated for many years, this remarkable press is finally beginning to receive the attention it deserves.

Flavell, A. J. and Nash, Paul, *The Corvinus Press: a History and Bibliography*, Aldershot, 1994.

Cosway bindings
'Cosway' bindings have one or more miniature watercolour paintings set into the upper cover of the book. Sotheran's, the London booksellers, first commissioned bindings with this feature from RIVIERE, who bound the books in elaborately tooled morocco, setting the miniature into the boards, protected by glass. Occasionally miniatures were set in both covers.

Miss C. B. Currie, who also executed FORE-EDGE paintings for Sotheran's, painted the portraits in the style of the miniaturist Richard Cosway. Some were executed on vellum and a few on ivory. Miss Currie painted some 900 miniatures for Sotheran's. Most were bound by Rivière but SANGORSKI AND SUTCLIFFE did execute some, usually with the miniature set in the inside of the upper cover.

The subject of the painting was usually related to the book; a portrait of the author, for example, or the hero or heroine of the story.

Cottage binding
During the second half of the seventeenth century, English binders sometimes employed a design in which the top of a rectangular panel was reshaped with slop-

ing lines in a style reminiscent of a cottage gable. Some examples of this popular design came from Samuel Mearne's bindery. It remained in use during the eighteenth century, but was by then largely confined to prayer books and pocket almanacs.

Cranach Presse
Founded in Weimar in 1913 by Count Kessler, this important German private press followed closely in the COBDEN-SANDERSON tradition; two of the Cranach Presse employees, J. H. Mason and H. Gage-Cole, had previously worked at the DOVES PRESS. Edward Johnston also participated in the work of the Press, whose finest achievements include Virgil's *Eclogues*, 1926 and 1927, with woodcuts by Aristide Maillol, and Shakespeare's *Hamlet* with woodcuts by Edward Gordon Graig, 1930; other illustrators included Eric Gill. Connoisseurs of the colophon would be well advised to study some of Kessler's, which successfully convey the atmosphere of dedication and thoroughness surrounding the work of the Cranach Presse.

Müller-Krumbach, Renate, *Harry Graf Kessler und die Cranach-Presse in Weimar*, Hamburg, 1969.

Cropped
Cataloguers use a number of terms to describe the cutting down of a book's margins in the course of binding. 'Cropped' is perhaps the most ominous of these, suggesting a drastic incursion; 'shaved' has a slighter implication (JOHN CARTER, in the guise of a bibliographical Conan Doyle, describes a shaved page as one which has 'grazed the text and drawn blood'); 'tall copy' indicates better fortune. Whatever term is used, any loss of printed matter – page numbers, headlines, shoulder notes, catchwords – should always be specifically noted.

Cuala Press
The poet W. B. Yeats's sisters Elizabeth and Lily founded the Dun Emer Press in Dundrum, Co. Dublin, in 1903, together with Evelyn Gleeson, as part of an enterprise that also produced weaving and embroidery. Its first publication was Yeats's *In the Seven Woods*, done in a limited edition of 325 copies. In 1908 the Press moved, with its associated companies, to another address in Dundrum, and was renamed the Cuala Press.

Stylistically the productions of the two presses are indistinguishable. As well as publishing the work of Yeats and his friends, usually in editions limited to between two and five hundred copies, the Cuala Press also produced (between 1908 and 1915) attractive 'Broadsides', poem pamphlets illustrated by W. B. Yeats's brother, Jack. This series was briefly revived in 1935.

Although it remained in existence, producing prints and greeting cards, the Cuala Press produced no books between 1946 and 1970, when it was reorganized and revived.

The Cuala Press 1903–1973: an Exhibition Arranged by the National Book League . . . Dublin and London, 1973.
Maxwell, William, *The Dun Emer Press and the Cuala Press*, 1932.

Cuir-Ciselé
An uncommon form of binding decoration, little used since medieval times, in which the design is cut or scratched into the leather. The technique originally flourished in Germany, Austria and Spain, but its brief revival in France in the nineteenth century accounts for the name it bears.

Curwen Press
Founded in Plaistow, East London, in 1863 by the Rev. John Curwen, the firm of J. Curwen and Sons became an important music printer and publisher. As such it would have attracted scant attention from bibliophiles; but, in 1908, the firm was invigorated by the arrival of Harold Spedding Curwen, grandson of the founder, who had trained under Oscar Brandstetter in Leipzig. The death of John Spencer Curwen in 1916 left Harold with a free hand to develop the Press in the unexpected direction of fine printing and illustration, and 1920, the most momentous year in the history of the Press, saw the arrival of Albert Rutherston's nephew Oliver Simon as a trainee on a year's trial.

Simon immediately embarked on an ambitious and dazzlingly successful programme; employing artists such as Edward Bawden, E. McKnight Kauffer, Paul Nash and Eric Ravilous, he changed the course of British book illustration and design. In 1921 he and STANLEY MORISON founded THE FLEURON; in 1924 he and others instigated the DOUBLE CROWN CLUB; and, using the POCHOIR process introduced by Harold Curwen in 1926, he produced the famous edition of Sir Thomas Browne's *Urne Buriall* and *The Garden of Cyrus*, with Paul Nash's illustrations, 1922, a book which is perhaps the finest ever produced by a modern commercial printer in Britain. Indeed, a large number of what are often thought of as 'private press' books, for instance many of the publications of the NONESUCH PRESS, turn out on close examination to have been printed at the Curwen Press.

As well as books, the Curwen Press produced an impressive range of other printed wares, from patterned paper to full-size posters, of which those produced for the London Passenger Transport Board are perhaps the best known.

The Curwen Press separated from its parent company in 1933 and continued until recent years to produce commercial printing of a high standard.

Simon, Oliver, *Printer and Playground: An Autobiography*, 1956.
[Harley, Basil], *The Curwen Press: A Short History* [1970].

Cuts
An all-embracing and now outdated term for wood or metal engravings in the text. It is most frequently found on the title pages of children's books (especially CHAPBOOKS), and other popular literature, in the statement 'illustrated with cuts'.

D

Daniel Press
The Daniel Press is generally considered to be the immediate forerunner of the modern English private press movement. Its origins date back to 1845, when Henry Daniel, the nine-year-old son of the vicar of Frome in Somerset, began printing 'by the use of types and thumb and inking'; even his earliest work shows considerable similarities in taste and style to his mature productions, down to such details as the blue paper wrappers characteristic of his later books. His first book, *A New Sermon of the Newest Fashion*, was printed at Oxford in 1874, and made use of the Fell types which had been lying unused at the Clarendon Press for 150 years.

Many of the texts chosen by Daniel were concerned with the history of Oxford; he was appointed Provost of Worcester College in 1903 and remained in the post until his death in 1919. He also printed many of the poems of the future Poet Laureate, Robert Bridges, whose current neglect may help to account for the relative obscurity of the Daniel Press today. Many of Daniel's other productions were designed to raise funds for charitable causes.

Daniel was assisted by his daughters, and his wife, a capable binder who had been taught by KATHARINE ADAMS. Many Daniel Press books were attractively bound, as the usual form in which they were issued (blue paper wrappers which extended slightly over the edge of the text pages) was an impractical one.

The most sought-after book from the Press is *The Garland of Rachel, by divers kindly hands*, published in 1881 at a price of four guineas. Intended as a first birthday present for one of Daniel's daughters, the distinguished list of contributors included Lewis Carroll. An attractive book, with ornaments and illumination by Mrs Daniel, it was set in Fell type, printed on van Gelder hand-made paper and bound in vellum. Thirty-six copies were issued.

Madan, Falconer, *The Daniel Press: Memorials of C. H. O. Daniel with a Bibliography of the Press, 1845–1919*, Oxford, 1921 (reprinted, with addenda and corrigenda, Folkestone, 1974).

Dating
The great majority of books carry a publication date on the TITLE-PAGE, on the verso of the TITLE-PAGE or, in some early printed books, in the concluding colophon. Books that do not carry this information may nevertheless be reliably dated in bibliographies and other reference works, their publishing history being clearly known.

There remains a small but troublesome minority of books which cannot be precisely dated either from internal evidence or from wider reference. These are often books whose precise date of publication is of no major importance, and here an intelligent guess ('c.1880') is acceptable. Familiarity with changing fashions in typography and book production will often suffice, but advertisements (even if themselves undated) and other textual indications can be helpful, as can inscriptions.

When cataloguing a book whose date is not present but can be determined from other sources, it is usual to note the date in brackets.

Deckle edges

The edges of books intended for individual binding by the bookseller or by the first owner were usually left untrimmed, and are known as deckle edges, on account of the part played by the deckle, or frame, in the papermaking process. Where the rough edges have survived, they indicate with certainty that the leaves are untrimmed, and this evidence has a strong appeal to collectors of books printed before the advent of edition binding; but it was intended that the edges *should* be cut by the binder.

More recently deckle edges have been a feature of some private press books and other limited editions; they tend to attract dust.

Dedication copy

Often misused as a synonym for 'presentation copy', a dedication copy is one inscribed by the author to the person (or any of the persons) named on the printed dedication page of the book. For example, the dedication copy of T. S. Eliot's *The Waste Land* would be inscribed to Ezra Pound. These are by general consent the most desirable of PRESENTATION COPIES.

Dentelle

Any lacy decoration on the edges of a binding can correctly be described as 'dentelle', but the term now tends to be used more specifically to describe the decoration of the inside edges. Dentelle is properly an adjective, but 'inside dentelles' has passed into common usage.

Derôme, Jacques-Antoine (1696–1760)

Perhaps the greatest of French binders, Derôme made much use of coloured onlays and lavish rococo decoration with birds, flowers and ornate curved ornaments. His son, Nicolas-Denis (Derôme le Jeune), employed much of his father's flourish and embellishment: his use of such motifs as a bird looking backward was said to exemplify the feminine influence at the French court.

De Sauty, Alfred

A member of the Hampstead Bindery, Alfred de Sauty was an engineer by profession. He joined RIVIERE to learn bookbinding and then set up his own bindery, working mainly in the tradition of the Arts and Crafts Movement. He emigrated to the USA where he continued to work as a binder in Chicago.

Device

An identifying symbol or design used by printers and (later) publishers as a trademark; examples range from ALDUS's famous fifteenth-century dolphin entwined with an anchor to today's familiar PENGUIN. The first known printer's device was Fust and Schoeffer's linked shields which appeared in their Bible of 1462.

McKerrow, R. B., *Printers' and Publishers' Devices in England and Scotland, 1485–1640*, 1913.
Davies, H. W., *Devices of the Early Printers 1457–1560*, 1935.
McMurtrie, Douglas C., *Printers' Marks and their Significance*, Chicago, 1930.

Dibdin, Thomas Frognall (1776–1847)

The Rev. Thomas Dibdin was steered towards his long career as an insatiable book collector by the second Earl Spencer, whose library he catalogued. The library at Althorp, still one of the finest private collections in the country, expanded in scope under Dibdin's supervision. He had caught the attention of George Spencer (later one of the founders of the ROXBURGHE CLUB) with the publication of his *Introduction to the Knowledge of Rare and Valuable Editions of the Greek and Latin Classics*, 1802. His reward for the preparation of the seven volumes of the Althorp catalogue was four pints of the best Tokay.

However, the Earl did infect the young clergyman with his own enthusiasm for books, sending him on foraging expeditions for early texts both at home and abroad. So extensive was the library that Dibdin suggested a small pony might be kept to ferry the more delicate visitors around the shelves.

Dibdin's main works – *Bibliomania*, 1809, *The Bibliographical Decameron*, 1817, and *A Bibliographic Antiquarian and a Picturesque Tour of France and Germany*, 1821 – are witty and colourful accounts of Georgian book collecting, and influenced the taste and technique of contemporary and later collectors. His accounts of the great book sales of his day (he describes the huge price paid for the Roxburghe Decameron: '. . . when the Hammer came down Boccaccio turned in his grave') give a fascinating glimpse of the Georgian bibliophile at work. It is unwise to rely too much on Dibdin's scholarship but his books have had an assured place in the affection of several generations of collectors.

O'Dwyer, E. J., *Thomas Frognall Dibdin*, 1967.
Jackson, William A., *An Annotated List of the Publications of the Rev. Thomas F. Dibdin*, Cambridge, Mass., 1965.

Diced leather

See LEATHER

Dictionaries

Karen Thomson

'Dictionary, s. (*dictionarium*, Lat.) – a book containing the words of any language in their alphabetical order, with explanations of their meaning, or definitions: how little those books which go by this name in the English language may deserve it, may easily be perceived by considering that none claim any merit but scraping together as many synonimes as they can, and leaving the reader to pick out the meaning from the rubbish that is collected.'

This rather damning view of dictionaries is expressed by William Rider in his *New Universal English Dictionary*, a little-known folio volume published in 1759, four years after the appearance of Dr Johnson's *magnum opus*. Rider was certainly acquainted with Johnson's work, and frequently refers to it but clearly did not think it the triumph of lexicographical achievement that it is generally held to be today. Although there is no doubt that, as James Murray declared, Johnson's great work 'raised English lexicography altogether to a new level', it is worth remembering that English lexicography *did* indeed already exist and that Johnson's work belongs in an historical context. In the past there has been a tendency for his dictionary to be coveted because of its fame rather than its intrinsic interest and its place in a tradition. Johnson had a long line of more or less distinguished predecessors, on whose work he built, and they deserve to be remembered and studied, as do his many successors.

No doubt Johnson is the grandest and most colourful of our *littérateurs*. We often know little about those other 'harmless drudges' (as Johnson called them) outside their dictionaries, but they are not generally self-effacing and strong personalities emerge. Their reasons for taking up lexicography are many and various. The anonymous author of the *Gazophylacium anglicanum*, 1689, explains frankly that 'the chief reason why I busied myself herein, was to save my time from being worse employed'. For Noah Webster, the great nineteenth-century American lexicographer, the drudgery seems less innocent: 'While engaged in composing my Dictionary, I was often so much excited by the discoveries I made, that my pulse, whose ordinary action is scarcely 60 beats to the minute, was accelerated to 80 or 85 . . .' John Baret, in the charming preface to his English–Latin Dictionary, first published in 1574, explains why he turned his hand to lexicography, and in what manner: 'About eighteene yeeres agone, hauing pupils at Cambridge studious of the Latine tongue, I used them often to write Epistles and Theames together, and dailie to translate some peece of English into Latine . . . And after we had a little begun, perceiving what great trouble it was to come running to me for euerie worde they missed (knowing then of no other Dictionarie to helpe us, but Sir Thomas Eliot's Librarie, which was come out a little before:) I appointed them certaine leaues of the same booke euerie daie to write the english before the Latin . . . Thus within a yeere, or two, they had gathered together a great volume, which (for the apt similitude betweene the good Scholers and diligent Bees in gathering their ware and honie into their Hive) I called then their Aluearie . . .' Baret's *Alvearie*, of which a second edition appeared in 1580, has a most attractive title-page with a wood-cut of a beehive. Rather surprisingly, the eminent Methodist John Wesley produced an English dictionary, whose title-page reads *The Complete English Dictionary, explaining most of those hard words, which are found in the best English Writers. By a Lover of good English and Common sense. N.B. The Author assures you, he thinks this is the best English Dictionary in the World*. At least this outrageous piece of self-congratulation does predate Johnson's dictionary by a couple of years.

In the past language books have been neglected by collectors and somewhat undervalued. It is true that they are seldom pretty; reference books are hard to find in good condition, as a result of the kind of handling to which they are subjected: consulting the Dictionary, unlike that other large book on most people's shelf, is not a reverential act; and perhaps familiarity has tended to breed contempt. Dictionaries of slang, jargon and local dialect vocabularies have a more immediate appeal. There is a healthy market for seventeenth- and eighteenth-century roguery, and early accounts of 'low-life' skulduggery have become much sought-after; they are often expensive because their popular and ephemeral nature means that they were seldom preserved and are now rare. Some include lists of slang phrases of the time, thieves' cant and the like, and can be very

DICTIONARIES

entertaining. 'Rum squeeze at the spell: A kind of harvest for pick-pockets. When the king goes to the play, and there is an overflow of the house; the Spell is cant for the theatre . . . Lully prigging: stealing wet linen off the hedges . . . Blue pigeon flying: fellows who steal lead off houses, or cut pipes away. They will out chif sometimes, that is, their knife, and cut a hundred weight of lead, which they wrap round their bodies next to the skin, this they call a bible, and what they steal and put in their pockets, they call a testament . . .' (from George Parker's *Life's Painter of variegated Characters in public and private life . . . To which is added, a Dictionary of modern Flash, or Cant Language*, [1798?]). Elisha Coles, who published his English dictionary in 1676, was the first English lexicographer to include these cant words, and he excuses himself on practical grounds: "Tis no disparagement to understand the Canting Terms. It may chance to save your throat from being cut, or (at least) your Pocket from being pickt'. Edward Cocker, in his dictionary (1704) regards this as patently absurd, and leaves them out: '. . . as if these Miscreants would be kinder to any one for speaking or understanding of their Gibberish'. The earliest English dictionaries were dictionaries of 'hard words' and it was over a century before the idea that a dictionary should include *all* the words in the language was contemplated; even Murray in the first edition of the *Oxford English Dictionary* felt that he had to exclude taboo words. Johnson's similar delicacy is delightfully reflected in an anecdote reported by Henry Digby Beste: 'Mrs Digby told me that when she lived in London with her sister Mrs Brooke, they were, every now and then, honoured by the visits of Dr. Samuel Johnson. He called on them one day, soon after the publication of his immortal dictionary. The two ladies paid him due compliments on the occasion. Among other topics of praise, they very much commended the omission of all naughty words. "What! my dears! then you have been looking for them?" said the moralist. The ladies, confused at being caught, dropped the subject of the dictionary'.

Early language books can be hard to find but fortunately for the collector there are plenty of twentieth-century word books that are still available and moderately priced. Our best-loved archaeologist of words, Eric Partridge, was a prolific compiler of word books on a wide range of fascinating subjects. Known for his slang dictionaries – *Slang Today and Yesterday*, 1933; *A Dictionary of Slang and Unconventional English*, 1937; and *A Dictionary of the Underworld, British and American*, 1949 – he also studied names, clichés, official jargon (in a book pseudonymously published as *Chamber of Horrors*) and catch-phrases. These books are accessible treasure-troves. (There is a useful checklist of Partridge's publications appended to *Eric Partridge in his own Words*, edited by David Crystal, Deutsch, 1980.)

Dictionaries reflect the culture of their age and of the society that calls them into being. Specialist dictionaries such as *Chamber of Horrors*, published in 1952, can capture the spirit of a decade before it evaporates: 'subminiaturization: Gobbledegook, originally scientific, for "the technique of making even smaller devices, such as radio valves, that are already small".' A now very scarce dictionary brought out in purple paperback in 1972 wonderfully entitled *The Queen's Vernacular*, most of which I would not dare to quote, depicts the gay underworld of the sixties and seventies: '**mad** (*cf* hipster sl **crazy** of the '50s) 1. unrestrained, avant garde "Who *was* that mad masked thing who rode away with that Indian?" 2. ostentatious "That diamond she had on her *pinky* was absolutely *mad* – I don't know how she managed to lift her hand" 3. exciting, refreshing 4. tickling the gay's funnybone; a corker, humdinger "This sun-tan lotion is *mad*; it really works – on my left armpit".'

Foreign and polyglot dictionaries reveal different linguistic preoccupations: French dictionaries had a large number of words for the play of light on water well before Monet's *Giverny*; Eskimo dictionaries have an extensive array of words for snow; the Greek of the tragedians has a range of words for gift signifying different degrees of required reciprocity and reflecting an important aspect of the way in which that primitive society organized itself. Old dictionaries reflect the concerns of an earlier age. In the sixteenth century many general language dictionaries included a section on falconry and hunting terms. At the beginning of the eighteenth century, with the popularization of science, a growing interest in scientific and technical vocabulary led to the publication in 1704 of John Harris's *Lexicon Technicum* (a second volume followed in 1710). Francis Grose's late eighteenth-century understanding of Bostonian behaviour differed considerably from the later perception of Henry James: '*Gouge*, to squeeze out a man's eye with the thumb, a cruel practice used by the Bostonians in America' (*Classical Dictionary of the Vulgar Tongue*, 1785). Collectors of early books, whatever their subject, find their collection enhanced by the possession of vocabularies of the time.

Where definitions are accurate, dictionaries are useful and interesting books, and where the imagination has been allowed licence they can provide much entertainment. Early attempts at etymologizing are a good source of the latter. John Minsheu's *Ductor in linguas*, a folio polyglot dictionary published in 1617 (incidentally the first book published by subscription) is full of charming examples of guesswork and folk mythology. Here is his unlikely explanation of the origin of the word *Cockney*: 'A COCKNEY or COCKNY, applied only to one borne within the sound of Bow-bell, that is, within the city of London, which tearme came first out of this tale: that a cittizens sonne riding with his father out of London into the country, and being a novice and meerely ignorant how corne or cattell increased, asked when he heard a horse neigh, what the horse did; his father answered, the horse doth neigh; riding farther he heard a cocke crow, and said doth the cocke neigh too? and therefore *Cockney* or *cocknie* . . .' The anonymous author of the *Gazophylacium anglicanum* mentioned above kept himself out of trouble with such speculation as 'Hassock, from the Teut. Hase, a hare, and Socks; because hair-skins are sometimes worn instead of socks, to keep the feet warm in winter.' Even as recently as 1834 wild surmise was an admissible indulgence. 'TO DINE WITH DUKE HUMPHREY; in the meaning of, to go without eating, without the usual meal; to be dinnerless. *Toe dijn wijst d'huich onvreê*; i.e. with you the swallow indicates an uneasy state; your throat seems to want greasing; you look as if you wanted something to eat . . .' John Bellenden Ker's *Essay on the Archaeology of Popular English Phrases*, which attempts to derive English sayings from Low German and Dutch, was first published in a slim octavo in 1834 and was popular enough to appear in a two-volume second edition in 1837. He hoped that his researches might 'lead to a better handling of the etymology of our language, and rescue that science from the obloquy it too justly labours under in regard to the English'.

Although dictionaries and books on language have been given little attention by most booksellers, some useful and comprehensive reference works have been compiled. In 1927 a professor of English at Stanford University, Arthur Kennedy, produced *A Bibliography*

DICTIONARIES

of Writings on the English Language from the Beginning of Printing to the End of 1922. It is a remarkably complete listing of almost every work on the English language. It usually gives pagination (but not details of illustration), and is reasonably well-indexed. It was reprinted in 1961. Robin Alston's *Bibliography of the English Language 1500–1800* is monumental; 22 volumes are planned, 12 have so far been published. The first ten volumes were reprinted with additions and corrections in 1974. An essential reference work for the eighteenth century and earlier, it gives library locations (gathered single-handedly by Dr Alston driving an old Volkswagen around Europe and America) and usually collations, although often neglecting illustrations. Volume V covers the English dictionary.

These two works are essential tools for finding out about English language books. I hope that in addition the following check-list of bibliographical and historical works on language books in general will be found helpful, and will encourage the pursuit of these interesting and appealing volumes.

Alston, Robin, C., *A Bibliography of the English Language from the Invention of Printing to the Year 1800. A Corrected Reprint of Volumes I–X*, Ilkley, 1974.
Baugh, Albert, *A History of the English Language*, London, 1951 (4th edn, 1993).
Bonser, Wilfrid, Stephens, T.A., *Proverb Literature: A Bibliography of Works relating to Proverbs*, 1930.
Burchfield, Robert, *The English Language*, Oxford, 1985.
Burke, W. J., *The Literature of Slang*, New York, 1939 (reprinted 1965).
Burkett, Eva Mae, *American Dictionaries of the English Language before 1861*, Metuchen, New Jersey, 1979.
Collison, Robert, *Dictionaries of English and Foreign Languages*, New York, 1988.
Cordell O'Neill, Robert K., *English-Language Dictionaries, 1604–1900*, New York, 1988.
Craig, Hardin, *A Bibliography of Encyclopaedias and Dictionaries dealing with Naval and Maritime Affairs 1577–1971*, 4th edn, Houston, Texas, 1972.
Hayashi, Tetsuro, *The Theory of English Lexicography 1530–1791*, Amsterdam, 1978.
Hulbert, James Root, *Dictionaries: British and American*, London, 1955 (revised, 1968).
Kennedy, Arthur G., *A Bibliography of Writings on the English Language*, Cambridge and New Haven, 1928 (reprinted 1961).
Landau, Sidney I., *Dictionaries. The Art and Craft of Lexicography*, New York, 1984.
Maggs Bros. Ltd, *Dictionaries and Grammars*, Catalogue 891, 1964.
Mathews, M. M., *A Survey of English Dictionaries*, Oxford, 1933.
Michael, Ian, *English Grammatical Categories and the Tradition to 1800*, Cambridge, 1970.
Osselton, Noel, *The Dumb Linguists: A Study of the Earliest English and Dutch Dictionaries*, Leiden, 1973.
Skeat, Walter W., *A Bibliographical List of the Works that have been Published . . . Illustrative of the Various Dialects of English*, London, 1873–77.
Starnes, De Witt T., *Renaissance Dictionaries: English–Latin and Latin–English*, Austin, Texas, 1954.
——— *Robert Estienne's Influence on Lexicography*, Austin, Texas, 1963.
——— Noyes, Gertrude, *The English Dictionary from Cawdrey to Johnson*, Chapel Hill, North Carolina, 1946 (reprinted 1961).
Steiner, Roger J., *Two Centuries of Spanish and English Bilingual Lexicography 1590–1800*, The Hague, 1970.
Wells, Ronald A., *Dictionaries and the Authoritarian Tradition: A Study in English Usage and Lexicography*, The Hague, 1973.

Dictionary of National Biography

One of the original editors of the DNB, Sir Sidney Lee, described its function as '(providing) full, accurate and concise biographies of all noteworthy inhabitants of the British Isles and the Colonies (exclusive of living persons) from the earliest historical period to the present time'. The Dictionary was founded in 1882 by George Smith, a partner in the house of Smith, Elder and Co. which originally published the work. Sir Leslie Stephen was co-editor with Lee. Initially the nineteenth-century DNB comprised 63 volumes which appeared quarterly from 1885 until 1901. A three-volume supplement covered those subjects who had died during the production of the work (thus making them eligible for inclusion) and those who had been omitted inadvertently.

1908–9 saw the first reprint of the DNB, with the use of a thinner paper reducing its size to 22 volumes. In 1903 Sidney Lee had produced an *Index and Epitome* which was later known as *The Concise DNB to 1900*. This was followed in 1912 by the first of the decennial volumes, covering the first decade of the twentieth century.

In 1917 ownership of the DNB was transferred to Oxford University Press at the request of the Smith family, and OUP have continued to publish the Dictionary up to the present day. A Compact Edition of the DNB appeared in two volumes in 1975; the text is unabridged but much reduced in size; and a magnifying glass is provided for the use of all those with less than perfect sight. Now out of print, this edition fetches high prices at auction.

The original Dictionary remains in print in 22 volumes (1992), as do the twentieth-century decennial volumes to 1980, and a 1981–85 volume. A reprint of the Compact Edition is under consideration. In 1992 Oxford issued *The Concise DNB* in three volumes, containing over 36,500 entries; a new work, *The Dictionary of National Biography – Missing Persons* appeared in 1993, and an entirely new DNB is now in preparation.

Disbound

A book or pamphlet is correctly described as disbound only if it has at some time been contained in a binding. The term is most commonly applied to books or pamphlets, complete in themselves, which have been removed from composite volumes.

Ditchling Press

See S. DOMINIC'S PRESS

Divinity calf

Many of the numerous theological and devotional works published in the nineteenth century were bound in an austere style in smooth calf of dark tone, often with bevelled boards and red edges, distinctively divided into rectangles by what are known as 'Oxford rules'. Divinity calf has come to denote serviceable, rather than elegant, bindings.

Dodsley, Robert (1703–1764)

Dodsley is best known for having suggested the idea of the Dictionary to Samuel Johnson, but he had a varied and valuable rôle in eighteenth-century literary life. Before becoming a bookseller he had been in domestic service, writing poetry while employed as a footman. *The Footman's Friendly Advice to his Brethren of the Trade* is a reissue of his earlier poem *Servitude*, and is valued as an 'etiquette' book.

Dodsley set up as a bookseller in London in 1735, having previously published two successful plays. His new career benefited from earlier contacts: he knew Pope and

Defoe and his own literary gifts brought him the respect and friendship of a wide circle. He never tried to hide his modest background; Walpole referred to him as 'decent, humble, inoffensive' and Johnson called him 'Doddy'.

Dodsley's shop, at Tully's Head, Pall Mall, was a fashionable literary meeting-place. He bought Johnson's first poem, *London*, for ten guineas and collaborated with other booksellers to publish and sell the Dictionary, his name heading the list. He also published Thomas Gray, through the good offices of Horace Walpole.

Nearing retirement, Dodsley made the mistake of turning down *Tristram Shandy*, for which Sterne was asking £50. The author published it himself as 'a lean edition' but Dodsley, now in partnership with his brother James, stepped in promptly to take over the publication and to pay a full fee for a valuable property.

Dodsley was always regarded with esteem in London's literary society. He published Shenstone, Swift, Burke, Young and Goldsmith, introduced the *Annual Register*, wrote further plays and poetry and maintained a relationship with his authors and customers that many publishers today might envy.

Straus, Ralph, *Robert Dodsley, Poet, Publisher and Playwright*, 1910.
Mumby, Frank A., *Publishing and Bookselling*, 5th edn, 1974.
Tierney, J. (ed.), *The Correspondence of Robert Dodsley*, Cambridge, 1988.

Dog
Antiquarian booksellers have been known to describe as a 'dog' a book that they have found, or would expect to find, hard to sell. The origin of the expression, as of much of the argot of the trade, is obscure; a glance at Eric Partridge's *Dictionary of Slang and Unconventional English* suggests several possible derivations that are best forgotten.

Dos-à-dos
Despite their French name, 'back-to-back' bindings are usually of English origin; the style was known in the sixteenth century, and flourished briefly in the early 1600s. Two books are bound with a single lower board, with their FORE-EDGES facing in opposite directions. The twin volumes might be a New Testament and a Prayer Book, and the dos-à-dos arrangement ensured that the book, however picked up, would open at a title-page. Embroidery was often used to embellish these bindings.

Double Crown Club
Many of the most distinguished printers, publishers, typographers and book designers of the past 40 years have been members, or dinner guests, of the Double Crown Club, at whose gatherings papers have been read on a wide variety of topics in the field of book production. The Club was founded in 1924, with Holbrook Jackson as the first chairman. The original members included Oliver Simon and Hubert Foss, who founded the Club, DOUGLAS COCKERELL, Harold Curwen, Robert Gibbings, Geoffrey Keynes, Francis Meynell, Paul Nash, and some 30 others. Eric Gill, Sir William Rothenstein, Roger Fry, Osbert Sitwell and Walter de la Mare were among the early guests of the Club. Oliver Simon, in his autobiography, recalls that Eric Gill's address to the Club was 'provocative to a degree' and led to pandemonium; but he does not say why.

The Club's menus are valued for their distinctive typography accompanied, in

Dos-à-dos binding in embroidered silks and silver wire, c.1619 [Maggs Bros. Ltd.]

Doublure

The practice of using leather, vellum, or occasionally silk as the inside lining of a leather-bound book, in place of a paper paste-down, was much favoured by French binders. As a result the French word 'doublure' is generally used to describe such a lining.

Douce, Francis (1757-1834)

Douce began collecting books and antiquities as a young man, against the wishes of his father and later of his wife. Comfortably placed, though not a rich man, he was appointed to the Department of Manuscripts at the British Museum and shortly afterwards to the post of Keeper. However, it was not until he inherited a handsome legacy in the will of the sculptor, Joseph Nollekens, that he was able to indulge his interest in early books, manuscripts, coins and ivory. On his death the books were left to the Bodleian Library. They were the subject of a special exhibition – The Douce Legacy – in 1984, the 150th anniversary of the bequest.

The collection included no less than 90 editions of Aesop's Fables, ranging from a fragment from Caxton's edition of 1484 to the 1818 edition illustrated by Thomas Bewick. Douce left seven complete Caxtons to the Library, and his collection of printed books included works on music, folly and mirth, *The Dance of Death*, ballads and ephemera.

The Douce Legacy, Bodleian Library Catalogue, Oxford, 1984.
Munby, A. N. L., *Connoisseurs and Medieval Miniatures, 1750–1850*, Oxford, 1972.
Rogers, D. M., 'Francis Douce's manuscripts: some hitherto unrecognised provenances', in *Studies in the Book Trade in honour of Graham Pollard*, Oxford Bibliographical Society Publications, NS XVIII, 1975.

Doves Press

'The Doves Press pages are the most devastating criticism ever made of the KELMSCOTT PRESS'. Ruari McLean's judgement (in his preface to *Cobden-Sanderson and the Doves Press*, 1964) would not be shared by all devotees of these presses, and seems unjust to Emery Walker, who was both William Morris's close associate and later T. J. COBDEN-SANDERSON's partner for nine years. Nevertheless the classic simplicity of the Doves books does contrast sharply with the more elaborate, medievally inspired Kelmscott style, and Emery Walker's Doves type, based on Nicholaus Jenson's fifteenth-century design, makes the books truly a pleasure to read. If a critical word is called for to balance Ruari McLean, let it be Sir Francis Meynell's remark (quoted by Colin Franklin) that there was 'something of the literary Tiller girls' in the unchanging style and format of the Doves Press books.

Cobden-Sanderson and Emery (later Sir Emery) Walker founded the Doves Press at Hammersmith in 1900. It was essentially a printer's press, with the aesthetic emphasis always on refined but basically functional typography and immaculate presswork; decoration was limited to the initial letters admirably drawn by Graily Hewitt and Edward Johnston and to the sparing but always well-judged use of red on the black and white page. The choice of texts was on the whole conventional, with English literature predominating: Shakespeare, Milton, Wordsworth, Keats, Shelley,

Browning, Ruskin, Carlyle, all feature in the list, together with Tacitus, St. Francis of Assisi, Goethe, and several of Cobden-Sanderson's own thoughtful but somewhat opaque writings. However, many collectors would point to *The English Bible*, 5 vols, 1903–1905, as the magnum opus of the Press; the memorable opening to Genesis, with Edward Johnston's red, page-long initial letter, is deservedly celebrated.

The Doves Press books were issued in the way favoured by most presses of its kind: generally between two and three hundred copies on paper, with a further five to 25 on VELLUM. The most common binding was limp vellum, but a few books were issued in boards, and many of the Press's publications were, of course, finely bound in morocco in Cobden-Sanderson's own Doves Bindery, under his supervision or by his own hand. Collectors must be on their guard against skilful imitations of

PARADISE LOST
THE AUTHOR
JOHN MILTON

OF MANS FIRST DISOBEDIENCE,
AND THE FRUIT
OF THAT FORBIDDEN TREE,
WHOSE MORTAL TAST
BROUGHT DEATH INTO THE
WORLD, AND ALL OUR WOE,
With loss of Eden, till one greater Man
Restore us, and regain the blissful Seat,
Sing Heav'nly Muse, that on the secret top
Of Oreb, or of Sinai, didst inspire
That Shepherd, who first taught the chosen Seed,
In the Beginning how the Heav'ns and Earth
Rose out of Chaos: Or if Sion Hill
Delight thee more, and Siloa's Brook that flow'd
Fast by the Oracle of God; I thence
Invoke thy aid to my adventrous Song,
That with no middle flight intends to soar
Above th' Aonian Mount, while it pursues
Things unattempted yet in Prose or Rhime.
And chiefly Thou O Spirit, that dost prefer
Before all Temples th' upright heart and pure,
16

Doves Press, 1902

Doves Bindery work, and of Cobden-Sanderson's own bindings.

The Doves Press remained active until 1916, when Cobden-Sanderson drowned the types in the Thames. Its special achievement was the influence that it exerted on book typography in later years. The Kelmscott books, for all their grandeur, hardly pointed a way ahead; the splendid ASHENDENE books were a model only for the affluent; but the Doves Press provided guidelines for some of the best book design of the twentieth century.

Catalogue Raisonné of Books Printed and Published at the Doves Press, 1900–1916, Doves Press, 1916.

McLean, Ruari, *Cobden-Sanderson and the Doves Press*, Wormerveer, Netherlands, 1964.

Dropmore Press

The private press of Lord Kemsley, who bought the plant of the Corvinus Press in 1945. The output of the Dropmore Press suffers by comparison with its forerunner: its books betray little of Lord Carlow's taste and none of his charm. One or two Dropmore Press titles fetch modest prices on the merits of their authors or illustrators.

Dropped initial

A dropped (or drop) initial is a typographic device in which the first letter of the first word of a chapter is aligned with the rest of the text at its top but allowed to descend to a depth of several lines. It was often used in the design of private press books. A striking example is the initial I of 'In the beginning . . .' in the Doves Press Bible, which descends to the last line of the page.

Dun Emer Press

The predecessor of the CUALA PRESS.

Dust-wrapper

The paper cover around nearly all modern books, whose original purpose was to protect cloth-covered or paper boards from damage on the way from publisher to buyer, and which has now become both an important marketing tool and a significant feature of the book's design. Though scorned by many a traditionalist collector and dealer (even, oddly, those who prefer early publisher's boards to the most splendid contemporary binding), their presence is now for commercial purposes mandatory on all but a tiny handful of post-1939 first editions, and highly desirable on anything earlier. Though of much less importance outside the world of literary first editions, the presence of a wrapper is always an advantage.

Dust-wrappers certainly existed during the nineteenth century, though few have survived. Little is known about them though research is continuing.

The debate over whether 'dust-wrapper' or 'dust-jacket' is a preferable term has been rumbling on for some decades. Carter recommends 'jacket', because it avoids confusion with 'wrappers', but this laudable attempt (like most prescriptive lexicography) seems to have foundered.

Tanselle, Thomas, 'Book-jackets, blurbs and bibliographers', *The Library*, June, 1971.

E

Editio princeps
Latin for first edition. Formerly a synonym for first edition, this usage would now be considered pretentious, and the phrase is only used to describe the first printed edition of a work which was widely circulated in manuscript before the invention of movable type.

Edition de tête
Most French, and occasionally a few English, limited editions are issued in more than one form; some may be on more luxurious paper or on vellum, others may contain extra suites of illustrations. The most desirable issue – usually, but not necessarily, that of which fewest copies were printed; and usually, but not necessarily, that bearing the lowest numbers or letters in the series – is known as the 'édition de tête'.

Editions

Editions and impressions That part of the *Oxford English Dictionary*'s definition of *edition* which most directly concerns the bookseller runs: '. . . The whole number of copies printed from the same set of types and issued at the same time'. The last few words are not usually taken very literally, and might perhaps be amended to 'at the same time, or at intervals until the type is reset or distributed', and 'set of types' is now taken to include printing from plates, monotype rolls and so on; but the basic definition is a good one. An *impression* comprises all the copies produced from that setting-up at any one time; the crucial distinction is that the type, or plates, etc., are not removed from the press.

Until the end of the eighteenth century, *edition* and *impression* were effectively synonymous; labour was cheap, equipment expensive, and so the printer would normally distribute type as soon as possible after printing. But technical advances during and after the Industrial Revolution (such as the advent of stereotyping and electrotyping during the nineteenth century) gradually led to today's situation, in which type or plates are kept standing ready for possible reprints; accordingly, *editions* may consist of several *impressions*, a new *edition* only appearing when the type has to be reset, or significant textual or editorial changes made.

Happily, however, the bookseller has less to worry about here than the bibliographer, for by common convention 'first edition' means 'first impression of the first edition', and any bookseller who attempts to disregard this will soon lose the respect of his customers and colleagues. Although in a very few cases the rarity of the first impression may lend some significant value to later ones, the pencilled note 'First Edition (fourth impression)' is almost always an indication of amateurishness.

Issues, states, variants, etc. The distinction between editions and impressions is fine enough; but issues and states, points and variants, secondary and remainder bindings, have posed untold problems for bibliographers and booksellers. Many of the differences between these terms can be understood much more easily by concrete example than by elaborate definition; accordingly, there follows an attempt to provide the printing history of an imaginary book.

The author of *My Life and Hard Times in the Rare Book Trade*, wishing to pass on in some way the knowledge gained from his years of experience, had at first considered compiling some sort of general reference work, which would contain a fund of factual information within its covers; but, being a wise man, he recoiled from the labour he realized this would involve and decided instead to write his memoirs. Having found a publisher, he completed his typescript and delivered it to his editor, who after various consultations ordered it to be set up in type.

The author's first sight of his words in print came in the form of *galleys*, or galley-proofs, long sheets of text not yet divided into pages. After correcting and returning these, he received *page proofs* (now divided into numbered pages) and from these, after checking his corrections and discovering several fresh errors, he was able to produce an index. Eventually the printers circulated a few *proof copies*, which for the first time approximately resembled the printed book, save that they were bound in wrappers; these enabled the author and publisher to check that there were no obvious howlers, such as the author's name being mis-spelt on the title-page. Finally the presses went into full operation.

The book was produced at one of those periods when paper was comparatively cheap and binding expensive; so the publishers ordered more sheets than they intended to have immediately bound up – as it happened, enough for 2,000 copies of the book. After about half had been printed, an assistant noticed a minor misprint that had evaded the eyes of proof-readers until then; but the head of the printing works decided that the misprint ('here' for 'her') was not serious enough to demand a cancel, let alone a reprint of the relevant sheets, and so the error was silently corrected and the presses restarted. He made no attempt to separate the incorrect sheets from the correct ones, and by the time they had been folded, trimmed and moved around the building, they were nicely mixed together; the result was that, when the publisher asked for some ADVANCE COPIES to distribute among representatives and reviewers (similar to proof copies, advance copies were bound in wrappers but with the paper and printing for the first time identical to that of the finished book), some of them carried the misprint and others did not. Accordingly, even though priority of manufacture could be established, at least for the sheets concerned, it would have been impossible to prove priority of *publication*; the book therefore existed in two *states*.

The publisher had meanwhile agreed to sell 750 sets of sheets to an American colleague, for publication in New York, so further sheets were printed with the latter's imprint on the title-page. Although these variants went on sale on the same day as their English counterparts, they are known not as a 'state' but as the 'American *issue*'; this dispensation, however, applies only to title-pages.

Eight hundred sets of sheets for the English edition were sent to the binder. But he had some difficulty in obtaining the precise shade of purple specified by the publisher, and he had to turn to two different suppliers, who provided him with subtly different colours of cloth. As no priority existed, these two bindings are known as *variants*. One of the bibliographical problems affecting modern books in particular is the precise description of colours. Most authorities recommend *The United States National Bureau of Standards' ISCC-NBS method of designating colors* and the related *Centroid color charts*, which are discussed by Gaskell. But this useful tool, costing a few dollars, has fallen out of print, to be superseded by one costing several hundred pounds; a replacement is badly needed.

Possibly because of its colourful descriptions of one or two unconventional colleagues, the book proved an unexpected success, and so the publisher ordered another 500 copies to be bound up; but he forgot to specify the colour, and as the binder had recently bought a quantity of pale green cloth very cheaply, he used that, thus creating a *secondary binding*.

However, a year after publication day, the author and his publishers received letters from solicitors representing a bookseller mentioned in the book. This man had been thought to be missing in the Amazonian jungle, but he had reappeared, and taken exception to some of the more personal remarks printed about him. He realized that there was little prospect of obtaining a large sum in damages, but the lawyers of both sides agreed that the offending passages should be removed, and a *cancel* leaf, bearing a more anodyne text, substituted. Because this change took place after publication, and a clear priority can be established, these copies now constitute the second *issue*.

Sales gradually declined, and eventually the publisher decided that the remaining 700-odd sheets of *My Life and Hard Times* were taking up too much warehouse space; rather than pulp them, he offered them to a wholesaler who specialized in *remainders*, publisher's unsold stock reissued at a fraction of its original price. This man made a low offer, as he had to take into account the cost of binding the sheets, however cheaply. But he envisaged a modest market for the book, the more so as the litigious colleague had recently died in mysterious and much-publicized circumstances in Central America. This would ensure some media attention for the reissue (as well as saving him the expense of further cancel leaves, or a reprint of the offending sheets); and so the book eventually reappeared as a third issue in a *remainder binding*.

Of course, not all books are as unfortunate as this one. But the complexities are as nothing compared to those of, say, the early novels of D. H. Lawrence; and nineteenth-century books tend to be even more difficult to disentangle. And if anyone can explain why the first edition of Jean Rhys's *After Leaving Mr. Mackenzie* always seems to have a cancel half-title, the editors would be delighted to hear from them.

Edwards of Halifax
The bindery was started by William Edwards in Halifax in 1755. William's four sons were all involved in the business which included bookselling and the sale of patent medicines as well as bookbinding. In 1785 the family patented a method of rendering vellum transparent so that a picture could be painted on the underside before the book was bound. The Edwards method, which was brought to London by James, John and Richard when they opened their own establishments there, differed from that used by Cedric Chivers whose

EIGHTEENTH-CENTURY STC

pictures were painted on board covered by transparent vellum.

The Edwards bindery also specialized in FORE-EDGE paintings (sometimes signed J. E.) and in Etruscan calf bindings.

Hanson, T. W., Edwards of Halifax, Bookbinders, *Book Handbook*, No. 6, 1948.

Eighteenth-century Short Title Catalogue (ESTC)

The ESTC, edited by R. C. Alston, comprises some 300,000 entries. They give details of all books published in England (and books in English published elsewhere) from 1701 to 1800. Pamphlets, catalogues and broadsheets are included. The work was published in 1982 and is on the British Library's computer database; a second microfiche edition, 1990, is now on-line and CD ROM. The work will be augmented by additional material as bibliographical knowledge extends. It is a particularly useful tool for booksellers as it gives copy locations, mainly in Britain and

The Book of Common Prayer, 1762, bound by Edwards of Halifax [Maggs Bros. Ltd.]

America, but gradually extending to include other countries. The computerized version can be searched for several different options, such as publishers, dates, etc. and information is included on pagination and illustration, not always easy to find.

Elephant folio
This term, occasionally outmatched by 'double elephant', was at one time a formal description of the largest books in folio format, with a page size of approximately 2′ × 1′2″. It is now sometimes used less precisely to describe any unusually large folio volume.

Elzevir
Louis Elzevir, the founder of the Dutch family of printer/publishers, set up in business in Leyden, then the second largest city in Holland, in about 1580. He was appointed bookseller to the university there, and expanded his activities into the printing and publishing of scholarly works with the encouragement of the university authorities. The business was continued by Louis's sons, flourishing greatly in the enlightened culture of the Netherlands in the seventeenth century. The Elzevirs' commercial and intellectual links with the rest of Europe were somewhat circumscribed by the Thirty Years War, but Dutch political independence and the development there of new theological doctrines gave much scope for the publishing enterprise.

The *Officina Elzeviriana* expanded rapidly, taking over the printing house of Erpenius, who held oriental type, and embarking in 1629 on the long series of classical texts (once described rather unkindly by STANLEY MORISON as 'dull duodecimos') for which the house perhaps remains best known.

Louis's grandsons continued in the family tradition, publishing works of theological significance, classics and general literature in several languages. Another office opened in Amsterdam, while the Leyden branch, managed by the widow of one of the grandsons, retained the university contract. By the end of the seventeenth century the standard of work and the quality of management at Leyden had deteriorated and the business and assets were sold.

In Amsterdam, too, the house of Elzevir was now faltering. Links had been established with Italy, Germany, France, Denmark and England (where Elzevir typography was considered as fine as any). A network of offices or branch printing-houses had been set up across Europe, but with the death of Daniel Elzevir in 1680 no

Title-page from Caesar's *Gallic Wars*

member of the family could cope with the management of a printing and publishing house of international proportions.

The name of Elzevir remains in high regard for typographical excellence and particularly for the small pocket-sized classical texts, an innovation at the time when quartos and folios were the norm. The Elzevir device was first an eagle grasping a quiver of arrows, and later a hermit under a tree. Three other marks appear on later publications: a palm tree and the motto *Assurgo Pressa* for the oriental printing; Minerva with her owl, olive tree and breastplate; and finally the sphere rotating on its axis.

Davies, David W., *The World of the Elzevirs, 1580–1712*, The Hague, 1954.
Putnam, George H., *Books and their Makers During the Middle Ages*, 1896–97 (reprinted, New York, 1962).
Willems, Alphonse, *Les Elzevier*, Brussels, 1880 (reprinted, Nieuwkoop, 1962).

Emblem books

The use of symbolism to convey meaning and moral is much older than the printed word, but emblem books, in which woodcuts or engravings are used to illustrate the human predicament, date mainly from the sixteenth and seventeenth centuries. They first appeared in England in the reign of Queen Elizabeth, flourishing in an atmosphere of courtly wit. Allegory, symbolism and a devotion to lyric poetry stimulated the emblem writers, and the contemporary association of literature with art found expression in this specialized form of creative writing.

Emblem books are essentially books of illustrated verse or prose, with some of the wording in motto form or as appended aphorisms or proverbs. The illustration is frequently crude and may leave its interpretation equivocal. After the secular, intellectual atmosphere of the Elizabethan court, emblem books in the next century became more religious and moralistic in tone and the tradition more or less ended with the comparable work of John Bunyan.

The best-known English writer of emblem books was probably Francis Quarles, but those by Henry Peacham, Geoffrey Whitney, Christopher Harvey and George Wither are also much valued.

Freeman, Rosemary, *English Emblem Books*, 1970.
Moseley, Charles, *A Century of Emblems – An Introductory Anthology*, Aldershot, 1989.

Embroidered bindings

Embroidered (or needlework) bindings, found most frequently on prayer books and psalters, were much favoured in England in Tudor and Stuart times, and the quality of surviving examples rivals anything achieved on the continent. Canvas was often used in the sixteenth century, but velvet and satin, embroidered with gold, silver and silken threads, later became more common. The quality of the materials used and the excellence of the needlework is indicated by the good condition in which some of these bindings have survived, despite their apparent fragility. This type of binding was a particular feature of the work carried out in the mid-seventeenth century by Nicholas Ferrar's community at Little Gidding.

Embroidered bindings tend to have contrasting origins: many are the work of devoted amateurs, whether princesses or schoolgirls; others were produced by trade binders, often for royal patrons. The craft underwent a revival at the end of the nineteenth century, with ambitious productions appearing from the Royal School of Needlework.

Nixon, Howard M., Foot, Mirjam M., *The History of Decorated Bookbinding in England*, Oxford, 1992.

Middleton, Bernard, *A History of English Craft Bookbinding Technique*, 2nd edn, 1978.

Encyclopaedia Britannica

The Encyclopaedia was first published in Edinburgh in 1771 in three volumes, with 160 copperplate engravings by Andrew Bell. The editor, William Smellie, received £200 for his work on this new dictionary of the arts and sciences; '. . . there are fifteen capital sciences which you will undertake for', he was told, 'and write up the subdivisions and detached parts of these, and likewise prepare the whole work for the press.'

The second edition, extended to ten volumes, was issued in 181 parts between 1779 and 1784. In book form the ten volumes are paginated consecutively, but there are many errors: page 7099, for instance, is followed by page 8000. The scheme of the second edition changed considerably to include historical and biographical entries, botanical tables, maps (placed together after Geography) and individual indexes to some of the longer articles.

The third edition, completed in 1797, contained more scholarly articles written by academic specialists; the print run of 13,000 copies sold out rapidly. Expansion continued in the fourth and fifth editions (1809, 1817), and the copyright was secured by Archibald Constable. He brought out a supplement of six volumes in 1824, but during the compilation of this, in 1823, the sixth edition of the main encyclopaedia appeared in 20 half-volume parts.

There was no further edition of the work for 20 years. The firm of A. and C. Black bought the copyright and in 1842 published a completely new edition, reset, with updated articles, text illustrations and dissertations by many distinguished men of science and the arts. The eighth edition came out in 1860 (21 volumes and index), the ninth in 1889 (24 volumes and index) and the tenth in 1902 (35 volumes, atlas and index). By this time American scholarship was much in evidence and an American publisher, Horace Hooper, contracted with A. and C. Black and with *The Times* (who were responsible for the retailing). When work began in 1903 on the celebrated 11th edition the Americans had taken over the ownership of the Encyclopaedia and Cambridge University Press were their publishers. This new edition was arranged on 'the dictionary plan' with articles printed in alphabetical order rather than as single treatises; all volumes were published together so that the work could be continuously updated during preparation and form an integrated whole. Bibliographical references appeared at the end of each entry and a classified table of contents was included with the index.

Thereafter the Encyclopaedia became essentially American, though it retained a London editor, with both the American and British offices producing year-books. The last completely new edition in the original format was the 14th in 1929; in recent years the work has followed a different plan.

The pace of scientific and technical change in the post-war years has had its effect on the value of earlier editions of Britannica and of other encyclopaedias; but the skilfully engraved plates of the eighteenth-century editions are highly regarded, especially where they depict the industrial machinery of the time. The 11th edition may carry a special prestige on account of a particularly distinguished group of contributors. It was also the first to use the dictionary arrangement, but the esteem in which it is held is possibly exaggerated.

Endpapers

Endpapers are the double leaves supplied by the binder at the front and back of a book. The leaves pasted to the covers are known as front and back paste-downs; the inner leaves as free endpapers. Books bound without endpapers were not uncommon in the sixteenth and seventeenth centuries, and in a few cheaply produced books of later date the first and last blank leaves are employed as endpapers; wartime austerity prompted some economies of this kind.

Endpapers often have a decorative element, in colour, tint, pattern or texture; and in modern books they are sometimes used to display maps, genealogical trees or other material illustrative of the text.

New endpapers usually indicate that a book has been either extensively repaired or simply recased; scrupulous dealers should always indicate when this has been done, as it is not always immediately noticeable.

English Catalogue of Books

This first appeared in 1914. It was the successor of many works in this field, some published annually, others at irregular intervals, such as the *Publishers' Circular*, the *Monthly Literary Advertiser* and the *London Catalogue of Books*. The first volume of the ECB covered the years 1801–36. It was a voluminous collection of material, covering 'in one alphabet under author, title and subject, the size, price, month and year of publication, and the publisher'.

The editors of the first edition confessed to finding some difficulties in establishing the true titles of the books included – Mansel's *Treatise in the Law of Demurrer* appeared as Mansel's *History of Demarara* (a very difficult book to find!).

The Catalogue appeared regularly until 1947 when it was taken over and reissued as Whitaker's *Cumulative Book List*, as it remains today. It contains a great deal of useful information about books published after 1800, but it is very cumbersome to use and contains little that cannot be found elsewhere. However, knowledge of the original published price of a book sometimes helps to establish whether a dustwrapper belongs to the first, rather than a subsequent or remainder, issue.

English Literature, 1500–1700

Amanda Hall

The early decades of the twentieth century saw a dramatic escalation in the demand for Elizabethan literature and early English books and the subsequent formation at dazzling speed of some of the world's greatest libraries. Legendary American collectors such as Henry E. Huntington, Henry Clay Folger and J. Pierpont Morgan, aided by great booksellers such as Dr Rosenbach, represent just a few of those who transformed the book market, taking it from the province of the gentleman antiquarian to the forum of public scholarship and the cut and thrust of international finance. The sixteenth and seventeenth centuries cover some of the richest literature in the English language, giving us Shakespeare's quartos and the four folios, the English Bible of 1611, Bunyan, Milton, the Metaphysical poets, as well as the great wealth of Elizabethan literature, and Jacobean and Restoration drama. The drive to bring together the greatest literature in the finest copies of works, often immensely scarce, created splendid libraries representative of a great era. Folger, for example, created his library in Washington DC as a great memorial to Shakespeare and his time; 'What was most vital in the Elizabethan age', it was said, 'relived through his tremendous absorption in the life of its greatest figure.'

The permanent disappearance of books from the market that resulted from this process has meant that unfavourable views of bookselling in this period are commonplace. So many of the books have been absorbed into institutions that the widely held conviction that 'it is all over bar the shouting' is hard to ignore. As Robert Nikirk suggested, 'Bookcollecting as some of us learned of it in Wolf and Fleming's *Rosenbach*, is no more'. Certainly, such heady days are past and such comprehensive wealth of material will not return. 'Early books of the type sold by Dr. R. and eagerly bought through nearly half a century by his customers are simply not around in sufficient quantity. The Houghton sales at Christie's in 1979–80 saw the last purely Rosenbachian collection dispersed, and when a leading bookseller can sell incomplete copies of early English poetry found in a basement to eager customers, we *know* an age has ended' (Robert Nikirk in *Rare Books 1983–4*, New York, 1984). That the range of books available to Rosenbach was infinitely richer than in today's market is impossible to refute, but the comparison is not a helpful one.

Admittedly, the market, once abounding in great books, is getting thinner by the year. It is now a very different scene, and nostalgia – tempting though it may be, leading us to an era breathtaking for its achievements and discoveries – is not entirely helpful to the business of the day. So where does this leave the bookseller? Scarcity is certainly now the crucial word, acting both as a limitation and a strength. To an extent, the present shifts in the market are prescribed rather than chosen. While a dealer specializing in modern literature may 'spot' the decline in Kipling or Masefield and speculate on Gissing or the poetry of Geoffrey Hill, the fluctuation of literary taste in the early period moves much more slowly. With certain strictures now firmly in place, taste gingerly finds its way around them.

There is still, however, a wealth of sixteenth- and seventeenth-century literature to be found. The high-spots, when they appear, are, it is true, very expensive, but there is still a quantity of desirable affordable material available to those with more modest budgets. In what other area of collecting in the arts can significant material of this age be purchased with relative ease? It is still easy to buy a seventeenth-century book for under £100, and though it may not be by Milton or Donne, or fall into the narrowest definition of English literature, it will still be a living example of English culture and history. To limit literature to the iconic is to overlook the climate in which these books were published.

The proliferation of printed sermons, for example, often dismissed as irrelevant or dull or simply 'oh no, not theology', reflects a real movement within society. The sermon was an expression of social concern and of the thinking of an age, just as more 'accessible'

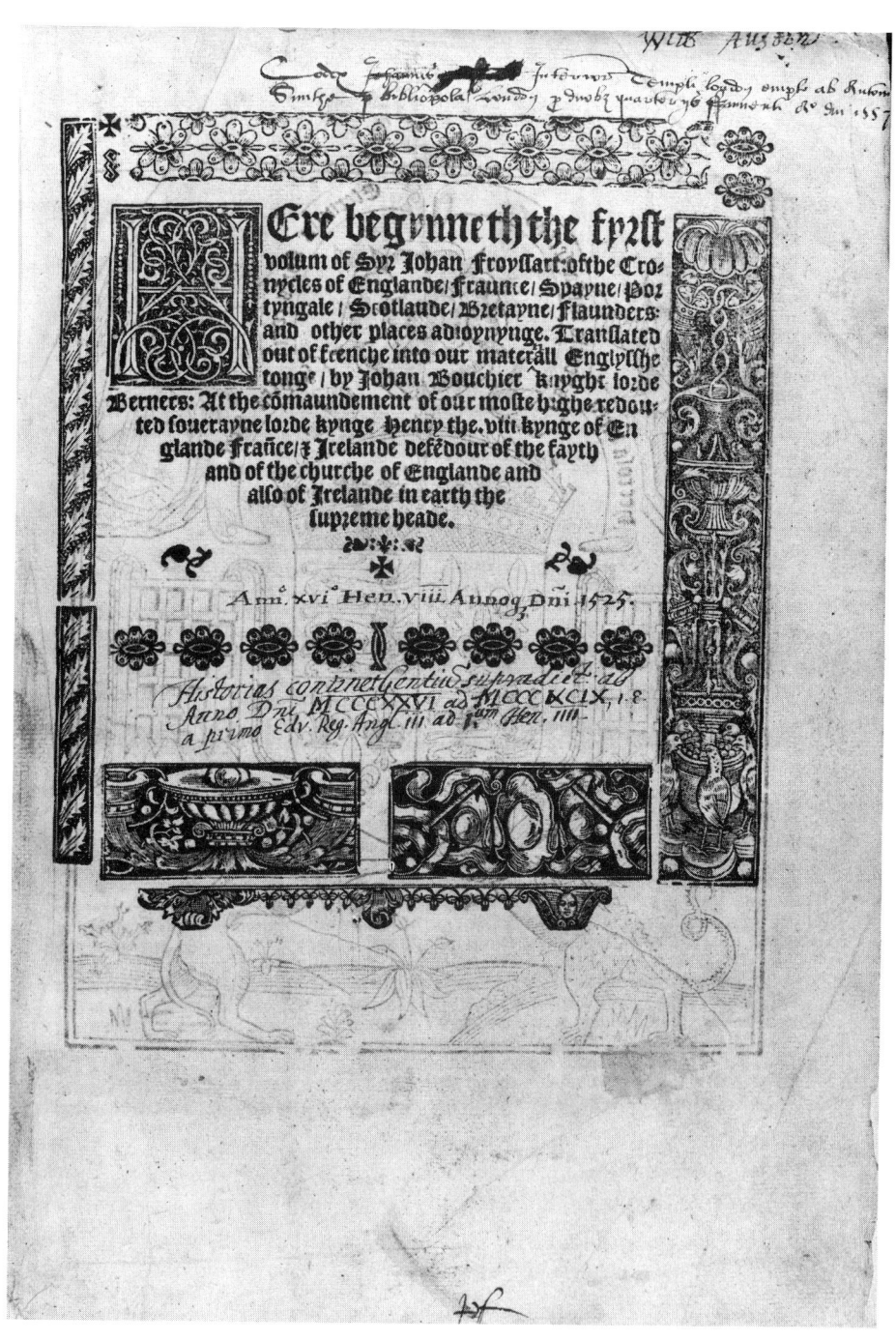

Second edition in English of Froissart's *Chronicles*, Part I, London, 1525. [Pickering & Chatto Ltd.]

Engraved title-page of Richard Lovelace's *Lucasta*, 1649. [Pickering & Chatto Ltd.]

forms such as newspapers were in later times. A sermon may be a vehicle for vigorous debate in any number of political, theological or philosophical spheres, and often as useful a guide to past ways of thought as the more readily approachable works. If we are to limit Literature to the most standardized forms and texts, we not only do the word an injustice, but we may well convince ourselves that the 'age' of this period of bookselling has indeed ended. While Shakespeare has become prohibitively expensive, however, classics such as Spenser's *Faerie Queene* (published in two parts, 1590–1596) can still be acquired without too large an investment. It remains possible to buy volumes of seventeenth-century poetry for very modest sums, while the great prose works, such as North's *Plutarch*, 1579, and Hooker's *Of the Lawes of Ecclesiasticall Politie*, 1593–97, command significantly lower prices than equally influential works in more fashionable genres.

For the bookseller the major reference work for the period before the Civil War is still 'STC'. Compiled by A. W. Pollard and G. R. Redgrave and now used in the revised second edition, the full title is *A Short-Title Catalogue of Books Printed in England, Scotland, & Ireland and of English Books Printed Abroad 1475–1640*. This lists a selection of locations for each book (not by any means comprehensive or intended to be so) and usually elucidates in brief the issue points. A glance down any page of STC shows how many books from this period are scarce in themselves and not just in the present market. As one bookseller who recently bought Latimer's *Sermons* remarked, 'Yes, my copy is incomplete, but then, so is Harvard's'.

Following on from STC is Wing's *Short-Title Catalogue of Books printed in England, Scotland, Ireland, Wales, and British America and of English Books Printed in Other Countries 1641–1700*. Donald Wing's major scholarly achievement continues under revision by a team of scholars, based at the Wing Revision Office at Yale University.

Outside STC and Wing there is a wealth of literary material still open to the bookseller who spreads the net wide enough. Lateral thinking in bookselling opens up areas of non-English printed works directly related to English literature. The essential reference source for these works in the STC period is M. A. Shaaber's *Check-list of Works of British Authors printed abroad, in Languages other than English, to 1641*, published by the Bibliographical Society of America in 1975. This not only covers such works as More's *Utopia*, Louvain, 1516, in the first edition, but also subsequent Latin or foreign language editions of major English works published on the continent. The transmission of early English literature through Europe, whether by translation or direct literary influence, is one of a number of growing scholarly concerns.

In addition to the mainstream literature, there is always an interest in works 'once removed', which are of significance for their relationship to the canonical texts. This peripheral material comes under increasing demand as collections near completion. Into this category in addition, fall continental and English sources of seminal works. Though now priced very highly and often approaching the prohibitive level of the works themselves, this is still a field in which good buying is possible with luck, timing and the right specialized knowledge.

Periods and authors do fall from grace, though, as in any area of bookselling. The Restoration period has largely ceased to be fashionable and therefore provides a lot of scope for collectors and for the dealer who wants to offer a selection of important literature

Thomas More, *Utopia*, 4th edn, Basel, 1580. [Pickering & Chatto Ltd.]

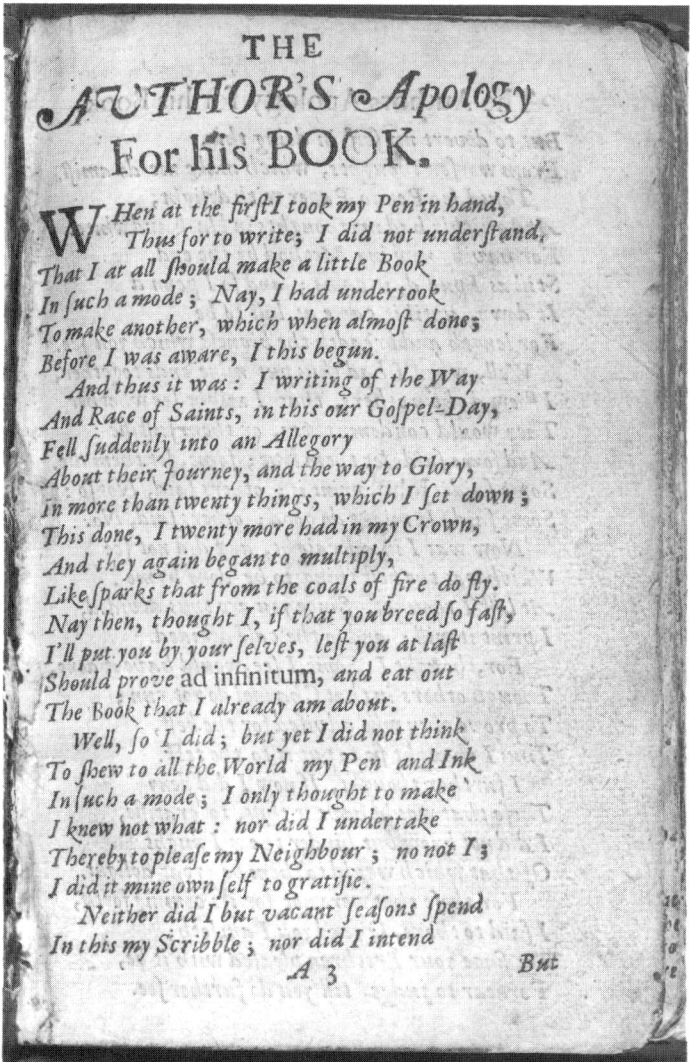

From the first edition of John Bunyan's *Pilgrim's Progress*, 1678. [Pickering & Chatto Ltd.]

at reasonable prices. Major names such as Dryden, Shadwell, Wycherley and Tate are all comparatively affordable and easy to obtain.

Outlets for early literature vary from one bookseller to another, but it seems fair to say that there is a familiar combination of the private collector and the librarian. Institutional budgets, it is true, have been shrinking in real terms over recent years, but university and national libraries are still a major force in the market. For a bookseller, the obvious advantage of institutional customers is in their breadth of interests, and although many libraries do not collect with quite the same catholicity as in the past, yet the same principle is there where resources allow. Funds may be less ample than in the past, but surprisingly often there is a benefactor with the money for the right book.

Two particular aspects of institutional buying patterns might be mentioned here. Awareness of other libraries and holdings within the same State is on the increase in North America and a book may become 'geographically undesirable' to a library if there is a copy in a nearby town. The first photo-facsimile of an STC book was published in 1864 (the 1600 quarto of *Much Ado about Nothing*), and since then the production of facsimiles has increased dramatically. There is now a huge mass of facsimile and machine readable material, microfiche, microfilm, CD ROM, etc., which is readily available to the librarian. This is a major factor in the consideration of a particular purchase.

In buying early English literature, well-established guidelines apply. Scarcity is an important factor for saleability but is not a guarantee. Condition is important, careful collation vital. Issue points carry as much weight in this period as any, and price differentials can be enormous. The first edition of *Paradise Lost*, 1667, for example, which was reissued with a succession of new title pages, varies greatly in price. Even though this is still a subject of debate, what is thought to be the true first edition commands prices much in excess of those for the later issues. Additionally, provenance – that alluring word – is a vital route to the heart of the demand for early English books. For book collectors, there is no better representation of an earlier era than a great book, perfect in itself, in a contemporary binding and with a fine provenance. Books from great libraries do still come on the market, and they remain the most potent expressions of the adventure of bookselling.

Case, Arthur E., *A Bibliography of English Poetical Miscellanies 1521–1750*, Oxford, 1935.
Greg, W. W., *A Bibliography of the English Printed Drama to the Restoration*, 1939–59.
Grolier Club, *Catalogue of Original and Early Editions of some of the Poetical and Prose Works of English Writers from Langland to Wither . . . & from Wither to Prior*, New York, 1893–1905 (reprinted New York, 1963).
Hayward, John, *English Poetry. An Illustrated Catalogue of First and Early Editions Exhibited in 1947 at 7 Albemarle Street London*, Cambridge, 1950.
Hinman, Charlton, *The Printing and Proof-Reading of the First Folio of Shakespeare*, Oxford, 1963.
Parkes, Cadman S. and Slade, William Adams, *et al.*, *Henry C. Folger*, New Haven, Connecticut, 1931.
Pollard, A. W. and G. R. Redgrave, *A Short-Title Catalogue of Books Printed in England, Scotland, & Ireland and of English Books Printed Abroad 1475–1640*, 2nd edn, revised and enlarged, 1976–91.
Schreyer, Alice D. (ed.), *Rare Books 1983–84; Trends, Collections, Sources*, New York and London, 1984.
Shaaber, M. A., *Check-list of Works of British Authors Printed Abroad, in Languages other than English, to 1641*, New York, 1975.
Wing, Donald, *Short-Title Catalogue of Books Printed in England, Scotland, Ireland, Wales, and British America and of English Books Printed in other Countries, 1641–1700*, 2nd edn, revised and enlarged, New York, 1972–88.

English Literature of the Eighteenth Century

Martin Hamlyn

At some time in the 1970s a visitor strode into our bookshop. 'What's an eighteenth-century book worth?' he asked somewhat truculently. I failed to counter with 'How long is a piece of string?', instead floundering somewhat into a considered explanation of the 'it all depends' variety. He soon lost interest and left, no doubt to hold forth on the ignorance, incompetence and unhelpfulness of booksellers.

Such matters are, of course, less simple than they seem. Historians properly remind us that history does not divide neatly into centuries (though eras may conveniently be dated as of 1660, 1789, 1914, and so on.) Still, centuries have their own flavours. The eighteenth may be seen as the Age of Enlightenment, of the Augustans, of the spread of Empire; population and industry expanded, towards the end dramatically, though in which order is endlessly disputed. There was wider literacy; newspapers proliferated and circulating libraries were invented. There was at least a veneer of elegance and 'civilization'; politico-religious strife, though bitter, was no longer likely to end in wholesale decapitation of the losing side. There was also, undoubtedly, poverty, squalor, and brutality beneath the comfortably complacent ease of the better-off – and a surge of organized philanthropy. The Hanoverian establishment had a nasty scare involving the last pitched battle on British soil, and negligently, but perhaps inevitably, lost a vast empire.

Almost any age can be presented as one of great change. The nineteenth and twentieth centuries were far more teemingly diverse, and their literary production incomparably vaster. Possibly that is one attraction of the eighteenth century; it is on a rather smaller and more manageable scale, and argues in a voice nearer to our own than that of the somehow darker and more urgent preceding ages.

All this really signifies is that it is useful to have some ideas about the period one chooses to deal in. The 'C18' is not an easy option in that, unlike the complaints which doctors describe, there is no longer 'a lot of it about'. Most of the all-time 'greats' will probably continue to be about, at a price; the *Gullivers, Crusoes, Vicars, Boswell's Johnson, the Dictionary, Blackstone*, latterly the socio-economic high-spots (*Wealth of Nations, State of the Poor*) – these are world books rather than eighteenth-century titles and will duly appear at auction or go to the emperors of the trade. Of course anyone would be glad of them, but they are not worth losing sleep over; they lock up expensive capital and are obtainable only at prices yielding some prestige but little profit. The dealer's maxim long ago quoted by Gordon Ray – 'the true profit of a shop comes from selling the first of *Gulliver* four times a year' – would not be a wise one to follow today. Unhappily, the once great wealth of background material – books, pamphlets, newspapers, broadsides – is now only the palest shadow of its former self. It would be hard now to start as an eighteenth-century specialist, and those drawn to the period would probably see it as a part only of their activities – though it would be a useful and rewarding part to be able to handle well.

Traditionally, of course, one learns by seeing and handling a great many books. Indeed the over-simplified image of the old-time trade is of people who scorned the insides of books and distrusted highbrow academics, but whose vast experience and photographic memory told them all they needed to know about half-titles or suppressed plates and enabled them to price any book unerringly to the nearest sixpence. But in those days one could walk into a bookshop or saleroom and be confronted with a wall (or several walls) of calf. True, there are still shops resplendent with magnificent sets in full leather gilt – but probably mostly of the nineteenth and twentieth centuries; the traditional wall of simple but pleasing eighteenth-century calf was something different. Even in recent years there has been the occasional splendid revelation of, say, a Colquhoun of Luss library – but too occasional, and probably too unrepeatable, to be much use for the gaining of experience. There is little of that quantity of calf to be bought or even seen. It is probably 30 or 40 years since the occasion when an old bookselling hand returned disgruntled from a saleroom with the report: 'Old calf's gone mad!' Like so much else, it has gone on getting madder, and has ended by hardly being there at all. More recently, an American visitor asked accusingly 'Where are your shelves of Johnsoniana?' We probably had at most half a dozen items (modern editions and criticism apart); the missing shelves were largely (with our active help) in his own country!

Prophets of doom are of course usually unpopular and often wrong; like most booksellers, I have been hearing all my life that the trade in old books is finished. In fact the date lines of what is possible keep moving forward. It seems that the eighteenth century is now approaching the situation of the seventeenth; the available books tend to be those of unconscionable dullness and to float around in the trade, seldom escaping into the outside world. One could probably do a careful survey of the proportion of eighteenth-century calf to more recent cloth at today's proliferating book fairs, and might well find the proportion fairly constant – and also the books; for older hands there is all too much *déjà vu* about titles, and sometimes copies.

All this means, of course, is that in this field things are, though not impossible, difficult. The eighteenth century in England has never been very popular. The great books, it is true, will always be wanted, and lesser books are regularly discovered to have some importance. But for many people a kind of mental time limit exists whereby anything beyond a century or so does not specially appeal and is indeed faintly worrying. The nostalgia effect works back two or three generations; before that, everything is just 'very old' and undistinguishable. (Thus a caller once displayed to me two books of 1710–20 at which I was clearly expected to show amazement. I gently indicated the whole bookcase full of pre-1700 material which we then could boast; he inspected this with clear disbelief for a few moments and then said 'Ah, but mine are originals'. An untypical case of course, but it illustrates in extreme form the sort of incomprehension one can be up against.)

Thus eighteenth-century collectors – and book-collecting is a minority interest to start with – are likely to be themselves a minority with a special feel for the period and a historical sense which is surprisingly uncommon even among well-informed people. Of course there is great scholarly interest and research pursued into immense and sophisticated detail, covering all aspects of eighteenth-century life and literature, with journals reflecting these studies (the *Scriblerian*, for Pope–Swiftian investigation and criticism, is only one

THE
RAPE of the *LOCK*.
AN
HEROI-COMICAL
POEM.
In FIVE CANTO'S.

Written by Mr. POPE.

—— *A tonso est hoc nomen adepta capillo.*
OVID.

LONDON:
Printed for BERNARD LINTOTT, at the
Cross-Keys in Fleetstreet. 1714.

Alexander Pope's *The Rape of the Lock*, 1714. [Pickering & Chatto Ltd.]

example), and at one time this activity was fuelled by massive institutional buying. Now, however, it seems that scholars use material already in libraries or available in reprint, and library buying has for many years been a trickle of the former flood. We have often been told that collection formation and marketing is the 'efficient' way for a bookseller to operate, a thesis I find hard to credit given the interest rates of recent decades and remembering that the rule-of-thumb, that ten per cent doubles every seven years, applies to costs incurred as well as to stock-in-hand. Probably only those with lucky access to idle capital can embark on such projects; and where is the material? A twentieth-century specialist recently offered some dozen author (or press) collections for sale, an abundance hard to envisage in the eighteenth century. And again, the libraries are far less active; this great fact, of little relevance in the world of book fairs which has been the growth area of recent times, must be accepted by anyone contemplating the marketing of eighteenth-century material. In the swinging sixties, a distinguished bookman told me he saw no reason to fear libraries would stop buying – the libraries were in place, their organizations up and running; it was in the whole establishment's interest to go on expanding and developing. It is never wise to take anything for granted.

However, despite what may seem the gloom of previous paragraphs, there remains some institutional buying, there are private collectors (though it seems to me, relatively few in Great Britain) and there are still opportunities and pleasant surprises. The latter can be relatively insignificant financially but still gratifying – finding the second edition of a weak poem known (but not too generally known) to have been revised by Johnson; working exhaustively at a collection of pamphlets bought for £500 and being able finally to produce £8000 from them; almost stumbling on a late eighteenth-century translation being used with other books to show off a pair of book-ends at an antiques fair, securing it for £28, confirming its sensational rarity and filling a 30-year-old second order for it at several hundred pounds; all these are standard book trade gossip, thoroughly enjoyable, statistically unimportant because they only marginally affect total profitability (they are not the sort of discoveries one could retire on) and they take no account of the years of expensive experience without which they could never have been exploited. Nevertheless, they show that even today the pleasantly unexpected can happen, with eighteenth-century books as with any others.

To return to the day-to-day level; the relative lack of supply *and* demand for eighteenth-century books may perhaps be piquantly highlighted as follows. Auction records for 1985 show some dozen or so copies of Ian Fleming's *Casino Royale* (allegedly 'rare'); in some cases two or three copies in a row appeared in the same sale. Apart from an inscribed copy, they made about £150 to £500 or so each depending on the state of the dust-wrapper. Of Swift's *Compleat Collection of Genteel . . . Conversation*, 1738, never considered particularly rare but still a celebrated and entertaining tour-de-force by one of the English-speaking world's greatest satirists, only two auction records appeared from 1985 to 1991; and for that same period of some six years my firm had a superb copy on the shelves and in two catalogues at £300, unsold until very recently; and we have been widely known as eighteenth-century specialists for about 40 years. In sale reports, too, English eighteenth-century books make no great showing.

Perhaps one great exception to the general indifference, or lack of comprehension,

THE COMPLAINT:

OR,

𝕹𝖎𝖌𝖍𝖙=𝕿𝖍𝖔𝖚𝖌𝖍𝖙𝖘

ON

LIFE, DEATH, & IMMORTALITY.

Sunt lacrymæ rerum, & mentem mortalia tangunt. VIRG.

H. Gravelot delin.   C. Mosley sculp.

LONDON:
Printed for R. DODSLEY, at TULLY's Head in *Pall-mall*;
And sold by M. COOPER, in *Pater-noster-Row*. 1743.
[Price One Shilling and Sixpence.]

Night Thoughts, by Edward Young, 1742–44. [Pickering & Chatto Ltd.]

appears in the towering figure of Johnson. Swift is admired, even occasionally referred to on satire shows; Pope has been heard of if not wholly understood; a few of the great novels have been televised; but Johnson is a universal figure, and to this day at least one notable firm fairly regularly issues catalogues devoted exclusively to Johnson and Johnsoniana (admittedly with a good proportion of non-eighteenth-century critical and biographical material). Indeed, Johnson and Boswell tend to dominate the second half of the century and thus overshadow much else that was going on. But even as one writes, one doubts the value of pointing in other directions. Where, after all, are the more beguiling by-ways to be followed: the minor novels, the minor verse, the lesser figures of the great Scottish-led movement in philosophy? (For years now, almost too much cataloguing resource has been devoted to frantic attempts to wrest some 'philosophical' content from formidably 'theological' material.) Where can one find early feminism (and surprisingly early some of it was), educational theory, books to illustrate the mini-explosion of industry, technology, and commerce? Travel has always been a field of its own (Cook appears rarely and at vast price). Not only the pioneering Americana of the beginning of the century, but the floods of publications reflecting the traumatic Anglo-American upheaval at the end seem to have almost dried up; even the once run-of-the-mill pamphlets on the Sacheverell hysteria of 1710, the 'Bubble' mania of 1720 (so uncannily comparable with the predictable – but largely unpredicted – booms and busts of 1929–31 and 1987), the 'Excise' row of the 1730s, and the Jacobite scare of 1745 – these were once the staple, indeed almost the background wallpaper, of eighteenth-century bookselling. Now they appear in twos and threes.

Indeed, the bricks of the walls of calf lamented earlier were often bound volumes of pamphlets. Few things could afford more wicked satisfaction than vandalistically dismembering such solidly bound volumes in search of exciting rarities. Many purists were horrified – provenance and association, it was claimed were being lost – and 'disbinding' was a dirty word. Yet there was no parallel with the 'breakers' of plate books; the pamphlets were all separately written, published, and marketed works, often only accidentally brought together at the whim of a country gentleman's bookseller or binder. And no purist would ever, and a librarian or collector hardly ever, consider acquiring such a volume of pamphlets 'as is', for its own sake; on the contrary, they would let it be known that when we came to split up the volumes, they would dearly like the first refusal of such-and-such items. Our own basement was piled high and wide with the Haddington pamphlet volumes bought in 1956 for a then rather sensational £1500. They sold in catalogues like hot cakes, and must have enriched many a library with material appropriate to its holdings. In such collections, still occasionally procurable at least into the 1970s, sermons rubbed shoulders with squibs, poetry with polemic, booklists with bawdry (then still quaintly listed as 'curiosa'); and a good deal of fun was to be had by all.

Now pamphlets (except those of the end of the century, usually on Catholic emancipation), newspapers (our firm produced whole catalogues of mainly eighteenth-century newspapers and periodicals) and broadsides (often giving a very vivid and 'actual' picture of the time) are hardly to be found. Or so it seems, to those of a certain age. But newcomers arrive, and see new possibilities. There may well be no new discoveries; as Percy Muir said ages ago, 'ideas from the past that strike you as important will already have occurred to someone else'; and the eighteenth century has its own regular rediscoveries, at which old hands smile indulgently. But the rediscoverers will be matched (despite the relative lack of collectors) by new customers, and at a new price level. Our own adventures into eighteenth-century pamphlets caused some head-shaking among the older generation who 'knew' that such hitherto little-regarded old stuff could not be worth anything much. Luckily, perhaps, no one ever 'knows' everything.

As for the equipment (besides money and luck) desirable for a dealer in eighteenth-century English books, the ESTC in some form must now be pre-eminent. No more expensive in real terms than the old BM Catalogue (condensed, with magnifying glass, and still immensely helpful) it charts titles of which hitherto all but a few were undocumented. FOXON's *English Verse 1700–1750* is a magnificent one-man effort thus comparable to, though quite different from, Wing, executed with immense care, industry, and enthusiasm. It might here be worth stressing how largely verse bulks in the whole century. Eighteenth-century man rushed into verse – pastoral, heroic (and more particularly mock-heroic), satirical, political, scurrilous, and nonsensical – at the drop of a hat, a fact to reckon with; one, or several, good quotation-books should be at a bookseller's elbow. Foxon, like NUC, ESTC, and others, now makes location-quoting easy. This can be overdone. It became absurd in the case of the seventeenth century with Wing (self-proclaimed not to be a census of copies but frequently so abused); Foxon, heroically enough, located up to five copies each in Britain and overseas and then stopped; but with ESTC we can now agonize as to whether 19, 24, 31, or whatever number of copies is 'rare' for the item in question. Number-crunching, I suggest, can get out of hand.

The standard (and often now elderly) author bibliographies – Griffith for Pope, Teerink-Scouten for Swift, Cross for Fielding and Sterne, Courtenay for Johnson, Hazen for Horace Walpole, etc. – are desirable (in case one should ever see the actual books again!), supplemented by as careful checking as is feasible of more recent research in journals, and by such superb author-biographies as Maynard Mack's masterly *Pope*. We have mentioned the *Scriblerian*; the recent annual *Shandean* (from 1989) is another valuable, and entertaining, aid. Where no bibliographies exist, a background of author-biographies is helpful though hard to assemble quickly. One never knows when a piece of knowledge may be useful, and may improve a description. The late Peter Opie thought our catalogues were too detailed, saying everything and leaving nothing that the buyer could with advantage discover for himself. If bookselling like litigation is an adversarial game, there may be something in this view; but I tend to discount it, believing that catalogues should be as interesting as possible (and heaven knows, a good many are less than riveting). To spread knowledge, and whenever possible entertainment, is not only a virtuous eighteenth-century precept, but makes bookselling somewhat more meaningful and a lot more fun. (The fun element should not of course be at the expense of accuracy; even the best bibliographically-equipped dealer will sometimes find himself on his own with eighteenth-century titles and must collate inferentially as well as he possibly can, even – in my submission – for the humblest pamphlet.)

Most people will of course expect to have NCBEL, DNB, and perhaps Lowndes (still sometimes useful); an eighteenth-century peerage can be invaluable for chasing provenances, patronages, dedications, and so on; and a twentieth-century *Oxford*

ELEGY
WRITTEN IN A
COUNTRY CHURCH YARD.

 THE Curfew tolls the knell of parting day,
The lowing herd wind flowly o'er the lea,
The plowman homeward plods his weary way,
And leaves the world to darkneſs and to me.

                                                             Now

Elegy in a Country Churchyard by Thomas Gray, 1st Dodsley edition, 1751. [Pickering & Chatto Ltd.]

Companion to English Literature, unbeatable for dates, brief lives, plots, trends, and movements. Most of us will have little Latin and no Greek at all; as the eighteenth-century, even down to coarse political satire, is soaked in classical allusion, a good classical and mythological dictionary is advisable. If I seem to have concentrated on literature, it is the only area I know anything about; but of course general bibliographies like Kress for economics, and Sabin for Americana, will cover the eighteenth among other centuries.

These rather rambling comments have emphasized how hard it is to acquire eighteenth-century books, without which all discussion of tactics is academic. Friends often say to me 'I suppose your job is getting hold of things customers want'. I probably mumble 'yes'. In fact of course I have to try to make people want the things I can still get. And what is wrong with that? In the absence of Caxtons, as Tim Munby said half a century ago, people will collect something else. Booksellers, librarians, and dealers alike must cultivate what is available. As the eighteenth-century song has it,

> 'What's gone, 'tis but vain
> To wish for back again.'

A dearth of material means that one must make more of what is still to be found. My own recommendation (unevenly pursued) is to read as widely as possible. No bibliographies can give you the 'feel' of the century. An old-timer once told me, 'I read all the time. *Book Auction Records* is my Bible – I take it to bed with me'. This was perhaps a bit too specialized. But as we have suggested, the old-timers were seeing, and learning from, thousands more books than we can. We may think ourselves more sophisticated, but we have to be. Like widespread scientific research, wide reading in and around the century will, occasionally, throw up something useful. It will also bring to life not just the 'literature' but the society, manner, humour, controversy and daily life of the past, and link it with the present. Booksellers, it is often said with some envy, have more chance than many people to enjoy their work. More involvement frequently adds to enjoyment; and there is always another century to choose.

Courtenay, William, *A Bibliography of Samuel Johnson*, Oxford, 1915 (revised by David Nichol Smith and reissued, 1925).

Cross, Wilbur L., *A Descriptive Bibliography of Sterne's Manuscripts and Published Works*, New York, 1909 (reprinted, 1929).

——— Bibliography in *The History of Henry Fielding*, New York, 1918.

Griffith, Reginald Harvey, *Alexander Pope, A Bibliography*, Austin, 1922–27 (reprinted, 1968).

Mack, Maynard, *Alexander Pope, A Life*, 1985.

Teerink, Herman, *A Bibliography of the Writings of Jonathan Swift*, revised and corrected by Arthur H. Scouten, Philadelphia, Pennsylvania, 1963.

English Literature of the Nineteenth Century

Brian Lake

When Jarndyce started bookselling in the late 1960s from a garret room in Oxford and a market stall in York, Pickering and Chatto under the guidance of Dudley Massey were the specialist dealers in nineteenth-century literature, and for Charles Dickens the collector would go to Walter T. Spencer, Sawyers or Sotherans; but we still thought that we could make a success of a small catalogue business. If we failed, there was not much to lose.

Our first catalogue in June 1970 was a miscellany recognizably Jarndycian: seventeenth to nineteenth-century books with the emphasis on the nineteenth – though some defective items (Lilly's *Christian Astrology*, 1647, with four leaves in facsimile at £18) and some in less than tip-top condition (*Johnson's Works*, 14 volumes, 1787–8, 'with quite a few boards detached') might not find shelf space now. The Dickens prices look quite reasonable (£10 was our maximum buying price for most first editions) with a *Master Humphrey's Clock*, original cloth 'in exceptional condition' at £20, *Little Dorrit* in parts at £52 and *Great Expectations* in half calf at £45. A first edition in cloth, recased, of George Eliot's *Scenes from Clerical Life*, at £40, compares interestingly with a 1992 buying price of £1300, while *Middlemarch* in 'original binders' cloth' (sic) was nevertheless still buyable at £17.10.0d. Minor literature did not sell well: Poole's *Little Pedlington and the Pedlingtonians*, two volumes, 1839 (Sadleir 1970) at £5, and Frank E. Smedley's *Harry Coverdale's Courtship*, 1864, at £2 failed to find buyers for many years.

Some 25 years later, we are moving towards our 100th catalogue. Prices have increased steadily – and, in some cases, dramatically. There has been a widening of interest in all aspects of Victorian life and letters, and collecting interests that could have been indulged with modest outlay and with little competition in the early seventies – juveniles and photography, for instance – now require serious investment. Specialist author collectors are matched by specialist author booksellers. Minor nineteenth-century poets that sat dusty and undisturbed on a 1970 shelf, however low the price, are now hard to find. Three-decker novels by obscure women writers are snapped up; in 1970 they were almost unsaleable except in the finest of fine 'Sadleir' condition. The increase in value of nineteenth-century books is due at least partially to the diminishing availability of books from an earlier period. But the main promoters of the nineteenth century were the 'Biblioboys' – Michael Sadleir, John Carter, Percy Muir, and latterly Dudley Massey, who combined bibliography, collecting and bookselling achievements in varying proportions. The publication in 1951 of the catalogue of Sadleir's *XIX Century Fiction* collection was a landmark; it is still used and quoted today, although overtaken in sheer quantity of items by the Robert L. Wolff Collection. Sadleir laid down the ground rules for collecting: always the best possible condition, preferably with a presentation inscription, and definitely in original binding.

Nineteenth-century English works in original boards. [Jarndyce]

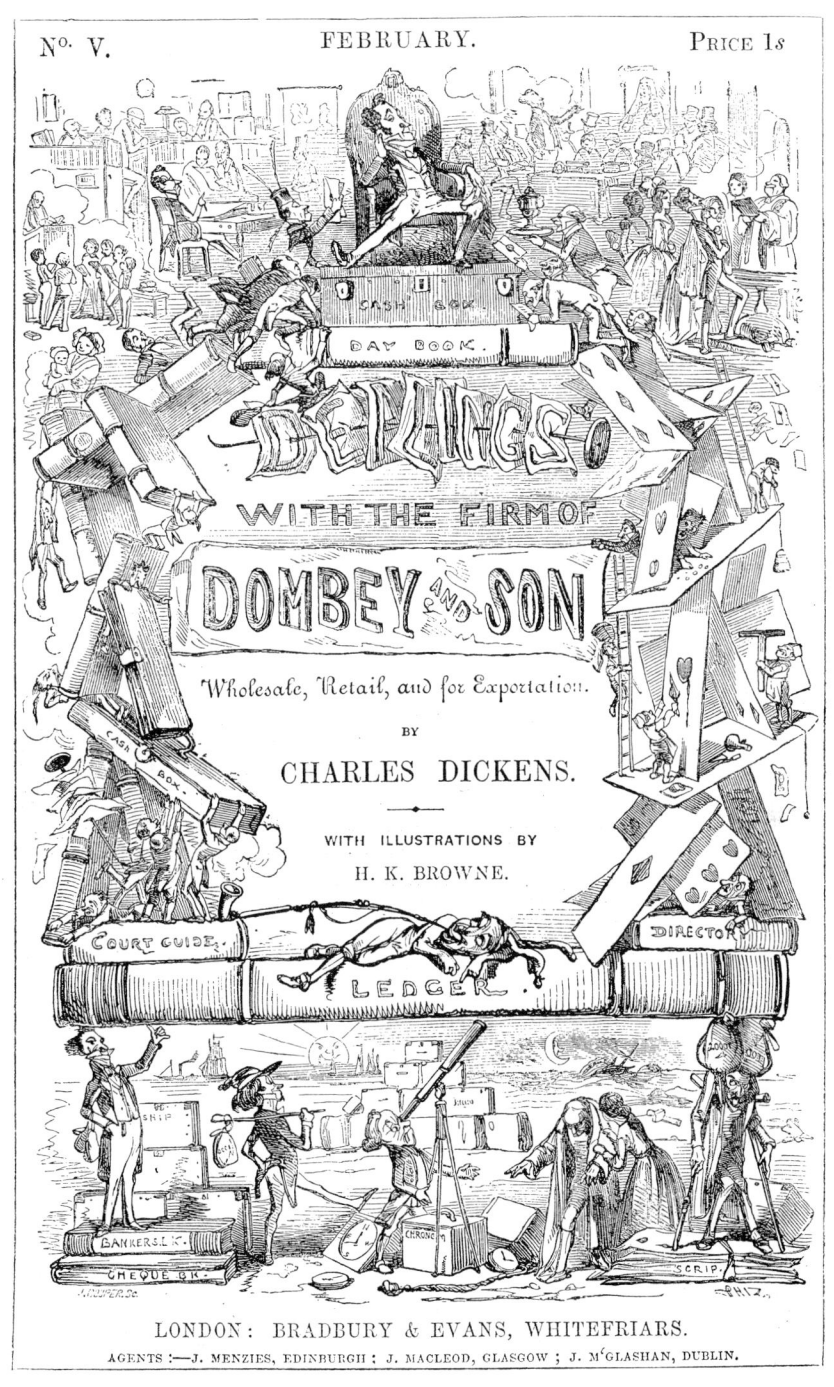

Dombey & Son by Charles Dickens, Part V. [Jarndyce]

Sadleir's rules have proved their worth in financial terms. For many years, the differential in price between, say, a finely bound first edition of *Bleak House* and a fine copy in original cloth was not significant. In fact, the fine binding would probably have been more expensive – even though Sadleir correctly pointed out the rarity of 'good-plus' copies of Dickens in cloth. There has since emerged a much greater appreciation of the importance of fine, original condition – particularly with an increasing proportion of poor copies on the market. The differential between a fairly good copy of *Middlemarch*, for example, in a contemporary binding, and a very good–fine copy in original cloth, would be at least tenfold (£200–£2,000) and this can be applied across a whole range of mainstream nineteenth-century literature. It even applies to an obscure three-decker of the 1880s by an unknown author: £30 in fair half calf; £300 in fine original cloth.

Sadleir and Wolff did not restrict themselves to 'big names' or 'high spots', and the market for nineteenth-century literature is a wide one. This is partially the result of the constant efforts to rediscover forgotten writers; and when publishers bring out inexpensive reprints of some of, say, Wilkie Collins' novels, leaving readers with whetted appetites, antiquarian bookshops are raided for first editions while not-so-good copies also rise in price.

That said, a carefully assembled collection of 'high spot' literature, in very good to fine condition in original bindings, would have proved the best investment in simple financial terms over the last twenty years. To build such a collection now would require tens of thousands of pounds per annum and a comparable rate of appreciation would by no means be guaranteed. Some booksellers, particularly in the USA, have done very well indeed by selling to collectors who have been persuaded that their status demands cabinets full of impressive books as well as a swimming pool. But how many of these collections will come back on to the market in difficult times? Will prices drop substantially as they did after the 1929 crash? The present recession has proved the basic principle of stocking 'both the best and the rest' to be a good one; selling a first-issue *Christmas Carol* for several thousand pounds is encouraging, good business, but it is just as important to have in stock a fourth edition at £300, or a recent reprint at £20. And by the same token, why should a collector be less happy with a fine second than with a shabby first edition?

Once again, it was Sadleir who pointed the way for the collector of lesser means. Half of his 1951 catalogue consisted of volumes in the numerous 'Library' series of cheap reprints issued throughout the nineteenth century, including a large section of 'yellowbacks' – novels issued in the second half of the century in brightly coloured pictorial boards. In 1990, a Jarndyce catalogue with prices between £25 and £150 was almost completely sold out. Sadleir also built a collection of nineteenth-century books on London, with emphasis on the city's low-life, and this was sold to the Lilly Library of the University of Indiana. In recent years, material of this kind has become increasingly hard to find, and prices have increased proportionately. The same can be said of books and pamphlets on nineteenth-century education, and on the English language: with seventeenth and eighteenth-century material elusive and expensive, interest inevitably moves forward in time.

The market for nineteenth-century books has altered quite dramatically over the past 20 years. The 1960s were dominated by United States libraries with the financial strength

Nineteenth-century Novels in original pictorial covers. [Jarndyce]

to buy whatever individual items or collections they wanted. Libraries continued to lead demand into the 1970s, but their dominance receded as more private collectors came on the scene. In the 1980s, Japanese booksellers, acting for the most part on behalf of government-funded universities, made a heavy impact in particular areas, especially nineteenth-century economics and, more recently, social history and literature. Japanese purchases were often in the form of thematic collections sold *en bloc*. More recently, with oriental library funds as limited as those in the occident, British private collectors have come into prominence.

What will be collected, and who will the collectors be, over the next ten years? Really fine copies of mainstream literature will continue to increase in price, but because of the difficulty in finding many titles the differential between average and fine will narrow. The greatest increase in demand will be for a wide range of nineteenth-century women writers, mainly of the second rank, such as Mrs Oliphant and Mrs Braddon; demand for the first rank, the Brontës and Jane Austen, is already greater than that for nearly all male novelists. Other areas which will be in demand include social history – poverty, crime, lunacy, housing, industry, shopping, health, fashion – with a resurgence of interest in economic history by private collectors, rather than by Japanese universities. Inexpensive books that are interesting and likely to increase in value include nineteenth-century education (including well-preserved school books), late nineteenth-century and early twentieth-century fiction, pre-1900 reprints of major authors, and original nineteenth-century bindings in paper, cloth or boards.

The mainstay of the British bookseller will remain the British collector. American, and to some extent British, libraries will continue to find funds for items and collections they really want – often by courtesy of 'The Friends of the Library'; and the private Japanese market will expand, while the library market remains relatively quiet. The big opportunity is for British dealers to develop direct working relationships with Japanese universities. It remains to be seen whether the Korean universities will take as keen an interest in Western cultural history as their Japanese neighbours have done. The recent affiliation of the Korean booksellers to the International League of Antiquarian Booksellers is an encouraging sign.

And what of Dickens? In 20 years prices for most of the commoner first editions have risen steadily from about £20 to £200, but for scarcer items prices have gone 'through the roof'. I mentioned a bound copy of *Great Expectations* at £45 in our first catalogue. In those early days we also bought a really fine and bright copy in original purple cloth at about £300 at auction, underbid by a sceptical colleague. His scepticism was borne out by two other booksellers who dismissed it as a wrong 'un. Not quite knowing what to do (the auctioneers having refused to take it back) I held on to it. Recently I took part in an investigation into the early impressions of *Great Expectations*, and the wrong 'un turns out to be right. Price: £20,000.

Ephemera

A useful general term which covers in the bookselling world most printed matter other than books. Few booksellers specialize in ephemera but most will have some in their stock and those who buy frequently from private sources will be unable to avoid it. Advertising material, printed cards (from valentines to *cartes-de-visite*), trade cards, menus, admission tickets and much else of social, trade or professional interest comes under this heading. The Ephemera Society exists to cater for those particularly attracted by the subject and frequent fairs are held under its auspices.

Lewis, John, *Collecting Printed Ephemera*, 1976.

Eragny Press

The private press of the painter and engraver Lucien Pissarro (son of Camille Pissarro), and his wife Esther. Founded in Epping in 1894, the Press moved to Bedford Park, West London, in 1897, and to Hammersmith in 1900.

A friend of Charles Ricketts and Charles Shannon, Pissarro worked on their periodical *The Dial* before publishing his first Eragny book, a translation of the French children's story *The Queen of the Fishes*. The text of this title was a photographic reproduction of Pissarro's handwriting, but the next 15 books from the Press were all set in Ricketts and Shannon's Vale type, and produced by the VALE PRESS under Pissarro's supervision. In 1903 Pissarro designed his own Brook type, however, which replaced the Vale type in Eragny Press productions.

Although the Press's books are minor pieces compared with those from the great private presses, they are highly regarded today. Pissarro's use of colour in wood engraving, and the twin influences of Normandy and Japan constantly evident in his work, appeal greatly to collectors, as does the link with the French impressionists through Pissarro's father. The Eragny Press ceased publication in 1914, an early casualty of the First World War.

Meadmore, W. S., *Lucien Pissarro*, 1962.
Moore, T. Sturge, *A Brief Account of the Origin of the Eragny Press*, 1903.
Pissarro, Lucien, *Notes on the Eragny Press, and a Letter to J. B. Manson*, Cambridge, Christmas, 1957 (with a preface by Brooke Crutchley and a supplement by Alan Fern).

Women's Social and Political Union.
4, CLEMENTS INN

VOTES FOR WOMEN

A SUFFRAGETTE DEPUTATION

WILL LEAVE

CAXTON HALL

FOR

THE HOUSE OF COMMONS

At 7.30,

On WEDNESDAY Evening, February 24

Read "VOTES FOR WOMEN," Weekly, One Penny, from all Newsagents and Bookstalls.

Printed by St. Clements Press, Ltd., Newspaper Buildings, Portugal Street, W.C.

Handbill for the Women's Suffrage movement (*see* EPHEMERA)

Errata

Errata, or corrigenda, are errors discovered after the printing of a book has been completed. In the earliest days of book printing, misprints or omissions were sometimes corrected by hand, but the usual form of correction is an errata list. Errors that came to light before the preliminary pages were printed were sometimes listed there, but the most common method of correction is an errata slip, tipped in in the course of binding; the same procedure may be used to note addenda – brief additions to the text.

Errata slips are often found in some but not all copies of a book, indicating either that the errors were not discovered until some copies had been issued, or that the slip was inadvertently omitted or torn out. It is thus difficult in many cases to judge whether a book is incomplete without a slip, or conversely of later issue if the slip is present; but it is generally thought that an errata slip *is* called for if one is present in a large majority of cases.

Errata slips have sometimes been amended themselves, when further errors have come to light after first publication. The existence of variant slips is occasionally helpful in determining priority of issue; but as errors are frequently corrected in the reprinting of the text, and errata slips sometimes left unamended, the bibliographer may be faced with unanswerable questions. Cataloguers may therefore think it best to treat errata slips cautiously unless there is convincing evidence of their status.

Essex House Press

C. R. Ashbee (1863–1942), a Socialist and pioneer of the Arts and Crafts movement, founded the Guild of Handicraft in East London in 1886. He started the Essex House Press, an adjunct to the Guild, at Essex House in the Mile End Road in 1898, having bought William Morris's two Albion presses (but none of the KELMSCOTT type or blocks). When the Guild moved to Chipping Campden in Gloucestershire in 1902, the Press moved with it.

Ashbee initially used Caslon type (not, in those days, so depressingly widespread as it has become), but also designed two types of his own, Prayer Book and (a smaller version) Endeavour. The most popular of the Press's books today are the 14 titles in the 'Great Poets' series, printed on vellum with frontispieces and decorations coloured by hand; they were printed in, for vellum, unusually large editions of around 150. The Guild of Handicraft operated a capable bindery.

Ashbee, C. R., *The Private Press, a Study in Idealism; to which is added a bibliography of the Essex House Press*, Chipping Campden, 1909.
Crawford, Alan, *C. R. Ashbee: Architect, Designer and Romantic Socialist*, 1985.
MacCarthy, Fiona, *The Simple Life: C. R. Ashbee in the Cotswolds*, 1981.

Etching
See TECHNIQUES OF ILLUSTRATION

Etruscan
See LEATHER

Everyman's Library

One of the earliest and most successful 'popular' editions of classic literature, J. M. Dent's Everyman's Library started publication in 1906; each volume bore the quotation: 'Everyman, I will go with thee and be thy guide; in thy most need to go by thy side.' The series was divided into subjects: travel, science, fiction, theology and philosophy, history, classical, for young people, essays, biography and romance; reference works were added later. Ernest Rhys edited the series from the beginning until his death in 1946.

The early volumes – the first was Boswell's *Life of Johnson* – had elaborately gilt *art nouveau* spines and cost one shilling. Many appeared in two bindings, cloth with flat back and coloured top edge, and leather with rounded corners and gilt top. With the growth of paperback publishing Dent issued the series in both soft and hard covers; but in 1988 the hardback rights were sold to David Campbell and Dent, now part of Weidenfeld and Nicolson, continued to issue the Library in paperback.

Collectors have been known to aspire to a complete set of the Everyman Library – more than 1,000 volumes – and an Indian maharajah in search of an 'instant library' is said to have ordered some 800 volumes from Dent in the 1930s; but most readers prize them simply as well-printed and reliably edited editions of good books.

Ex-library

A book is described as 'ex-library' when it has been in use, and bears the scars of, a lending or reference library. It is always a term of disparagement, especially where lending libraries (Boots, Smith's, etc.) are concerned, because of the general shabbiness of the books; but the extent to which the book is down-graded depends on category as well as condition. Important reference books which have fallen out of print are, if modestly discounted, still readily saleable, whereas only a tiny minority of twentieth-century first editions, even with the most discreet stamps, will retain any value at all.

Any bookseller who buys books from a library would be well advised to insist that the librarian supplies the books with a 'cancelled' or 'withdrawn' stamp, preferably bearing the name of the institution. Everyone who neglects this basic precaution will find that answering endless questions (which vary in tone from well-meaning concern to open suspicion) rapidly becomes irksome.

Ex-libris

See BOOKPLATES

Explicit

The 'explicit' can best be described as the forerunner of the colophon. Used at the end of a medieval manuscript, or an early printed book, the word, deriving from *explicitus est liber* – the book (or scroll) is unrolled – was usually followed by the title of the work and sometimes by the author's name. The colophon, with its more consistent formula, replaced the earlier device during the fifteenth century.

Export licence

A specific export licence is required to send abroad printed material more than 50 years old and amounting in value to more than £35,000 (in the case of photographs the figure is £6,000). Under the terms of the Open General Export Licence (Antiques) Act (1992), material of lesser value may be exported freely. Manuscripts, archives, documents and other hand-written material (including annotated books) are not covered by the OGEL Act.

Although further guidance is available from the Department of Trade and Industry, the complexity of the law in this area is such that members of the major trade organizations can benefit greatly from their advice. Moreover, forthcoming European Community legislation is likely to have some effect on UK practice in this field.

Extra-illustrated

A book is described as extra-illustrated when plates or other material not present in its original form have been added to it. A few additional illustrations may be tipped-in, but extensive extra-illustration involves rebinding, and often necessitates the expansion of a book into additional volumes.

The usual form of extra-illustration is the insertion of portraits, views and historical prints relevant to the text; original letters or documents may also be used. Books that have been extra-illustrated with discrimination are usually well regarded by collectors; for example, an early work on the theatre may be greatly enhanced by the addition of portraits of players and views of theatres, and such works as Pepys' *Diary* offer much scope for imaginative enlargement; but effective extra-illustration demands considerable skill. The additional leaves will often vary in size, and require careful mounting to achieve uniformity. It must also be noted that extra-illustration can easily become over-illustration, as when views and portraits are lavishly introduced to illustrate minor aspects of the text; Dibdin described a ten-volume *Decameron* as being 'ornamented to suffocation with embellishments'.

The practice of extra-illustration was encouraged by James Granger (1723–76), a publisher who provided blank leaves for the insertion of portraits, etc. in historical works. Extra-illustrated books are still sometimes described as 'Grangerized'.

F

Fable
A fable can be distinguished from a pictorial parable or EMBLEM by the fact that it tells a story; both conventions seek to employ animal characteristics and behaviour – in verse or prose – to illustrate human conduct or morality. Aesop the Phrygian, the earliest known fabulist, may have been a slave living in Greece about the sixth century BC; his fables, using wit to illustrate wisdom, have provided a pattern for many later writers in this field. CAXTON printed the first English translation of Aesop in 1484 and the fables have since been rewritten, translated and illustrated in hundreds, if not thousands of different forms; they occupy over 60 pages of the NATIONAL UNION CATALOG. Versions for children became popular at an early stage, both with the children as a form of recreation and with their elders as a useful instructional work. Early translators into English were John Ogilby, 1651, Francis Barlow (with the assistance of Aphra Behn), 1687, and Roger L'Estrange, 1692, who included additional myths and legends. In 1722 Samuel Croxall published *Select Fables of Aesop and Others*, a translation used by THOMAS BEWICK for his *Select Fables* of 1822, and in 1764 JOHN BASKERVILLE printed a handsome edition published by ROBERT DODSLEY.

The development of the fable received considerable impetus with the first publication of Jean de La Fontaine's *Fables Choisies*, Paris, 1668. La Fontaine, while using Aesop as his basis, expanded the stories to create a more sophisticated, satirical view of contemporary life. A vein of bitterness is allowed to creep into his verse; the cruel caricatures in Grandville's illustrations to the 1839 edition are particularly suited to La Fontaine's style.

Another English version of the Fables, again derived from Aesop but contemporary in style, is that of John Gay, 1727 and 1738 (two volumes). The poet uses political and social satire to portray the manners of the age, but the morality remains unequivocal and the meaning clear. The 1793 edition has 12 plates engraved by William Blake.

Aesop has remained a favourite for both children and adult readers throughout the ages and many distinguished artists have illustrated the book, including in more recent times, Charles Bennett, 1858, Randolph Caldecott, 1883, Charles Robinson, 1895, E. J. Detmold, 1909, Arthur Rackham, 1912, Agnes Miller Parker, 1931, Stephen Gooden, 1936, and Elizabeth Frink, 1968.

Although the greatest fabulists have taken their inspiration from Aesop, retaining his concise and recognizable structure, there have been other versions of the moral fable. Rudyard Kipling, for example, in his *Just So Stories*, can lay claim to the creation of a fable of a different kind. His animals have reason, emotions and morality. Beloved by younger readers, his tales, like Aesop's, are instructional as well as entertaining.

From La Fontaine's *Fables*, 1762 [Christie's]

Blackham, H. J., *The Fable as Literature*, 1985.
Briggs, Katherine M., *A Dictionary of British Folk Tales*, 1970.
Handford, S. A., *Fables of Aesop*, Harmondsworth, 1954.
Hodnett, Edward, *Aesop in England: the Transmission of Motifs in Seventeenth-Century Illustration of Aesop's Fables*, Charlottesville, Virginia, 1979.
Jacobs, Joseph, *History of Aesopic Fable*, 2 vols, 1889.

Facsimile

Facsimiles – exact copies of printed or hand-written matter – have a useful and creditable place in the world of books, both as a primary form of illustration and as a means of supplying missing text, plates or maps. As a means of illustration their most common use is in reproducing letters, documents or signatures; most booksellers have on occasion had to explain gently to a hopeful owner that they do not have a letter in Byron's own hand bound into their edition of his poems, or Charles Dickens' own inimitable signature at the foot of a frontispiece portrait. Facsimiles of this kind are not intended to deceive and rarely cause any serious misapprehension.

Nor is deception necessarily intended when a missing TITLE-PAGE, for example, is replaced by careful pen or type facsimile, or with a modern photo-lithographic copy. Many collectors and librarians accept this practice quite readily as a means of easing the pains of imperfection, while they perhaps continue their search for a perfect copy of the book in question. Early printed books which have lost their title-pages or index leaves (the first and last pages being most vulnerable) are often catalogued as having these supplied in facsimile, and pen facsimiles were at one time often attributed by name to an expert practitioner of the art.

Nevertheless this useful practice has its discreditable side, for as John Carter warns: 'an exact copy is a menacing thing to those who pursue originals'. Not that danger arises only when deception is intended; a careful facsimile, if it is not clearly identified as such, can deceive even an experienced eye, and acknowledgement of its presence may have been discarded by a binder or lost by the rubbing out of a pencilled note. But facsimiles are sometimes made with intention to deceive, as when the second edition of a book is supplied with a first edition title-page; and (to quote Carter again) 'it is better to be over-sceptical than over-trusting when a leaf or leaves in a book have a fishy look or feel'. Almost all facsimile leaves, or sections of text, can be detected by careful inspection of paper, type and ink; though the perpetrator of a deliberate fraud may rely on innocent trust.

It may, however, be somewhat misleading to describe such attempts as facsimiles, even though the term may be literally accurate. In everyday usage the word carries a certain implication of honest intent, as distinct from the purposes of fakers and forgers. Indeed, in some areas of scholarship, facsimile reproduction is an important aid to textual and graphic study, e.g. in architectural history.

False imprint

An imprint wilfully mis-stated by the printer or publisher, either to mislead (or to amuse or impress) the reader, or to confuse the authorities. Some are straightforward alterations of place or date; others are more fanciful, such as 'Cosmopolis', which regularly appeared on eighteenth-century books published in Paris. False imprints are virtually as old as books themselves, dating back even to Peter Schoeffer.

Hellinga, Lotte, 'Less than the whole truth': false statements in fifteenth-century colophons, in *Fakes and Frauds*, edited by Robin Myers and Michael Harris, Winchester, 1989.

Treadwell, Michael, On false and misleading imprints in the London book trade, 1660–1750, in *Fakes and Frauds*.

See also CLANDESTINE PRINTING.

Fanfrolico Press

The Fanfrolico Press, which evolved from the private press founded by John T. Kirtley in Sydney in 1923, moved to London in 1926. Its co-founder Jack Lindsay, son of the successful painter Norman Lindsay, produced a number of pleasing books, concentrating on reprints of the classics and on his own work, often illustrated by his father; some were printed by commercial printers such as the CURWEN PRESS, others (especially latterly, when Lindsay was joined by his brother Philip) by hand. The Fanfrolico Press's productions are variable in quality, from the frankly unhappy (Nietzsche's *Antichrist* set throughout in 16-point capitals) to the charming, if somewhat louche, erotic titles.

Perhaps the most enduring of the Fanfrolico Press books is *Loving Mad Tom: Bedlamite Verses of the XVI and XVII Centuries*, published in 1927 in an edition of 375 numbered copies, with a foreword by Robert Graves, musical transcriptions by 'Peter Warlock' (Philip Heseltine) and illustrations by Norman Lindsay.

Chaplin, Harry F., *The Fanfrolico Press: A Survey*, Sydney, 1976.
Lindsay, Jack, *Fanfrolico and After*, 1962.

Fascicule

A single part of a work published in instalments is sometimes known as a fascicule. The term generally describes the parts of a scholarly publication, and is little used nowadays.

Festschrift

A German word which has passed into English to describe a collection of articles or essays by various hands, published in honour of an individual, generally a scholar, and usually on the occasion of a birthday, anniversary or retirement.

Fillet

When used to describe the decoration of a leather binding the term fillet indicates a fine gilt line in the tooled design. It also describes the wheeled tool used to impress the line, which is usually gilded on bindings executed after 1700.

Fine Bookbinding

Mirjam Foot

The earliest surviving decorated leather bindings were made by Coptic craftsmen. Examples dating from the fifth to the tenth centuries are known and display blind lines, dots, roundels and a variety of decorative tools. Cut-out compartments, vellum strips and leather or vellum tracery are also found. The earliest-known European decorated binding comes from Northumbria and may date from the end of the seventh century. It covers the Stonyhurst Gospel MS (end-seventh century) and is made of red-brown goatskin with incised lines and an embossed floral design on the upper cover, while an incised step design decorates the lower cover. Three eighth-century decorated leather bindings, two Anglo-Saxon and one Continental, exist and are now at Fulda.

Medieval treasure bindings, made of ivory or precious metals, sometimes enamelled, often engraved or decorated in relief, with or without jewels, are usually found on liturgical books. During the twelfth and thirteenth centuries blind-tooled tanned leather bindings were produced mainly in monasteries in France, England, Germany and Austria. The frequently pictorial tools, reminiscent of Romanesque sculpture, are usually arranged in circles, in rows, or in concentric panels.

From the end of the fourteenth until the beginning of the sixteenth century we find, mainly in German-speaking countries, bindings decorated with cut-leather work (*Lederschnitt*), a technique whereby the design is either cut into the leather or where the leather has been cut away, leaving the design in relief. Blind tooling, which had all but disappeared in Europe, was revived during the fifteenth century. Interlacing strapwork with small rope or knot tools was popular in Italy and Spain; small tools depicting animals, birds, monsters, stylized flowers, and fleurons abound and were arranged in vertical rows (in France, but also in Oxford and London) or in diamond-shaped or triangular compartments formed by blind lines (in the Low Countries, Germany and England). Towards the end of the fifteenth century rolls (engraved brass wheels) were introduced, while panels (engraved or, more probably, cast blocks) came into frequent use during the late fifteenth and early sixteenth centuries, especially in the Netherlands (where they occurred as early as the second half of the thirteenth century) and England, but also in Germany and France. At this period most binders are known by nicknames, often derived from tools they used or patrons they worked for. Many binders are known by name, but can only rarely be linked with their products.

The technique of impressing heated brass tools through gold leaf into the leather is of Islamic origin. We find gold-tooled bindings in Morocco from the thirteenth century and by the second half of the fourteenth century the practice was well established in the Mamluk empire and Iran. Gold-tooling reached Italy early in the fifteenth century; it then came to Spain, Hungary, France, and from there to England, where the earliest example dates from 1519. Gold-tooling was also practised in the Netherlands and in Poland. German binders continued to use their tools in blind – very effectively on white-tawed

Guido Panciroli, *Notitia dignitatum*, 1608, bound in Cambridge by Daniel Boyse, possibly for presentation to Charles I, c.1627, in blue velvet, tooled in gold and silver [The British Library Board]

pigskin – although later in the sixteenth century gold (often of low quality) impressed with rolls and panels as well as with small hand tools, was also used.

Very fine gold-tooled bindings, usually in tanned or dyed goatskin, were produced in Italy throughout the sixteenth century, frequently modelled on Islamic, but also on classical sources. Splendid gold-tooled bindings were made in Paris, largely in calf, but also in goatskin. Especially, those made for François I, Henri II, François II, and Charles IX by their successive royal binders, and for such well-known collectors as Jean Grolier and Thomas Mahieu, are among the finest produced in Europe. During the last decades of the reign of Henry VIII and during the reigns of Edward VI and Mary I, gold-tooled binding in England showed distinct Italian or French influence. French influence remained strong during the reign of Queen Elizabeth when designs of interlacing ribbons combined with solid and hatched tools, as well as designs showing large corner and centre-pieces, prevailed. The latter continued during the reign of James I. Most fine binding was in calf, although goatskin was also occasionally used. Embroidered canvas, silk, satin, or velvet, frequently found on religious books, were popular in England during the reigns of the Tudors and the Stuarts. Embroidered bindings were less common in France, Holland, Spain and Italy.

In France during the second half of the sixteenth century, interlace designs developed into the fanfare style, employing a tooled ribbon with a single outline on one side and a double outline on the other to divide the covers into compartments. During the seventeenth century, this style developed further into mosaic designs. Compartments were frequently made of onlaid or inlaid pieces of leather of a contrasting colour and filled with small tools. At the same time, designs that covered the whole of the boards with a semis of small tools, sometimes as the background for a coat of arms, or with fleurons and drawer-handle tools, were popular in France and Holland, and a sprinkling of small tools remained fashionable in England during the reign of Charles I. During the first half of the seventeenth century Cambridge binders developed two distinct styles, showing either circles or concentric panels, effected with small tools. Interlacing ribbons, with or without coloured paint, were still popular in Germany in the eighteenth century, while we find echoes of the fanfare style in Holland, Italy and England in the seventeenth and eighteenth centuries. Corner and centre designs, now formed by whole or quarter fans, were current in Italy in the 1640s, in Spain in the seventeenth century and in Holland and Scotland in the eighteenth century. In France in the 1630s and 1640s we find tools with a dotted or pointillé outline. Such tools were much used in Holland during the seventeenth and still in the eighteenth centuries and in Italy in the later half of the seventeenth century. They first appeared in Cambridge in the 1640s and 1650s, soon to become one of the characteristics of English Restoration binding. Polychrome leather onlays and the cottage-roof design, also typical features of the Restoration, remained in use until the early eighteenth century. Most fine bindings of this period were made of goatskin. By now we can identify more binders by name, among whom Stephen and Thomas Lewis, Samuel and Charles Mearne, Robert Steel, Richard Balley, Alexander Cleeve (all in London), John Houlden (in Cambridge), Roger Bartlett and Richard Sedgley (in Oxford) are best known. Nicknames continue and the Queens' binders, the Naval binder, and the Centre-Rectangle binder, to mention but a few, are still awaiting identification.

The Book of Common Prayer, 1662, bound by Samuel Mearne in red goatskin, tooled in gold and decorated with black paint. [University Library, Durham.]

During the first decade of the eighteenth century the Geometrical Compartment binder introduced new designs; the binder who worked for Elkanah Settle in the first quarter of the century also showed some rather crude originality, but the next typical English design was developed for the Harleian Library by Thomas Elliott and Christopher Chapman. This library was the first in England to use goatskin imported from Morocco. Roll-tooled borders and large centre diamonds built up of small tools persisted well into the 1760s in London and Cambridge, while Neo-classical bindings were designed by James ('Athenian') Stuart and Robert Adam in the first half of the 1760s. Emblematic tools were found on bindings for Thomas Hollis and Jonas Hanway, as well as on Masonic bindings of the second half of the eighteenth century. During this period numerous German binders emigrated to England. Andreas Linde, John Ernst Baumgarten, Christian Samuel KALTHOEBER, Henry WALTHER, Staggemeier and Welcher, and Charles HERING produced fine bindings in London. During the later part of the century Roger Payne, an outstanding finisher, used finely engraved tools for comparatively simple designs, while the firm of Edwards of Halifax produced their 'Etruscan' bindings in calf as well as transparent vellum bindings with paintings on the under surface. They were also well known for their habit of painting scenes beneath the gold on the edges of the leaves. Vellum bindings painted on the upper surface were made in Italy, and painted and gold-tooled vellum bindings occurred in Germany, the Netherlands, Scandinavia, Austria and Hungary. Very fine bindings with characteristic white onlays (made of paper, vellum or leather) and floral or fan tooling were produced in Dublin in the eighteenth century, while in Scotland at that time we find both wheel and herring-bone designs as well as, later in the century, the rococo designs of Scott of Edinburgh. In Paris in the eighteenth century, binders' families such as Derome, Monnier, and Padeloup, worked mainly in two styles: the 'dentelle' style, showing wide, lace-like borders made with finely engraved small tools, and the mosaic style, effected with inlays and onlays of variously coloured leathers, often in bold, floral or pictorial designs.

During the seventeenth and eighteenth centuries we find again bindings made of engraved, chased or filigree metal work, of tortoiseshell, and of onlaid straw. Decorated paper bindings, already produced in Germany and Italy in the sixteenth century, became more popular during the eighteenth, especially for pamphlets and music, and survived well into the nineteenth century. Painted and lacquered wooden bindings were made in Persia from the sixteenth to the nineteenth centuries, gradually deteriorating in quality as time went on. Embroidered bindings still occur in Italy and Germany in the eighteenth century and we find printed and painted silk bindings in France, Italy and the Netherlands in the nineteenth century, especially on almanacs.

The first half of the nineteenth century witnessed a range of designs. Neo-classical bindings, simple panel designs, sometimes combined with elaborately tooled doublures, and more complex decoration effected with small tools, occurred side by side with bindings of thick, sometimes double, boards blocked and tooled in gold and blind. In the late 1820s embossing was introduced in France and Germany, and soon thereafter in England, where cathedrals as well as floral and chinoiserie motifs were depicted, embossed mainly on calf. Painted vellum was still current and we now also find black *papier mâché* moulded on a metal frame, often in Gothic designs. The second half of the century

The Works of Virgil, translated by John Ogilby, 1668, bound by Roger Bartlett in gold-tooled black goatskin. [Maggs Bros. Ltd.]

J. A. Symonds, *Walt Whitman*, 1893, bound by Sarah T. Prideaux, in gold-tooled dark green goatskin, 1902. [The British Library Board]

John Bunyan's *Pilgrim's Progress*, 1859, bound by Miss Edwards of the Guild of Women Binders, c.1903 in brown goatskin, onlaid in citron, green, red and fawn and tooled in gold. [The British Library Board]

favoured pastiches of earlier periods. At the end of the century, Marius Michel in France and COBDEN-SANDERSON in England broke away from imitations of the past and developed new and individual styles. Art Nouveau bindings were produced in France and also later in Holland and Germany, while in England the floral tools and simple but effective designs of Cobden-Sanderson exercised their influence well into the twentieth century. The amateur school of English binding, also influential in the United States, opened the field for women; besides the Guild of Women Binders, we find, among others, Sarah Prideaux, Katharine Adams and Sybil Pye. Throughout the twentieth century, but especially since the Second World War, binding design has reached remarkable standards in France and England, but interesting work is also produced in Germany, the Netherlands, the United States and Japan. A great many materials, such as metal, stone, perspex and plastics take the place of or are combined with leather, vellum, paper or textiles. The 'bookworks' of the late twentieth century are more akin to sculpture than to binding, but the tradition of well-designed and meticulously produced fine hand-binding still flourishes.

Finishing
See FORWARDING

First edition
Although an edition is not the same as an impression, the term 'First Edition' should only be applied to a first impression of the first edition, as this is what collectors want. From the commercial point of view, a miss is as good as a mile, so the description 'First Edition (second impression)' is self-contradictory as well as unprofessional and may well deter serious collectors from looking further. The term 'First English Edition' is used to describe the first edition published in England of a book previously published in another country.

First Edition Club
A. J. A. Symons and Max Judge founded the First Edition Club in 1922. Its aim was to provide a meeting place for book collectors, to promote high standards of book production and to publish works of an uncommon nature which might not be readily accepted by mainstream publishing houses. Appropriate exhibitions were mounted and bibliographical scholarship encouraged.

Many of the publications of the First Edition Club were printed by the CURWEN PRESS. *Letters from Aubrey Beardsley to Leonard Smithers*, 1937, *The Songs of Meleager Made into English*, with designs by Frederick, Baron Corvo, 1937, and Rudolf Koch's *The Book of Signs*, 1930, are typical of the list.

Stone Trough Books, *A. J. A. Symons, An Anniversary Catalogue*, York, 1991.

First edition thus
Not a first edition. This is a term to be avoided; if a particular edition of a work is in any way remarkable, the cataloguer is being careless (and unpersuasive) in not explaining why. 'First Edition with Russell Flint's illustrations', or 'First Edition with the introduction by T. E. Lawrence', are acceptable because interesting; but if the only alternative to 'First Edition thus' is 'first edition from this undistinguished reprint house', or 'first edition without the delightful illustrations which established this book as a children's classic', it is better to keep silent.

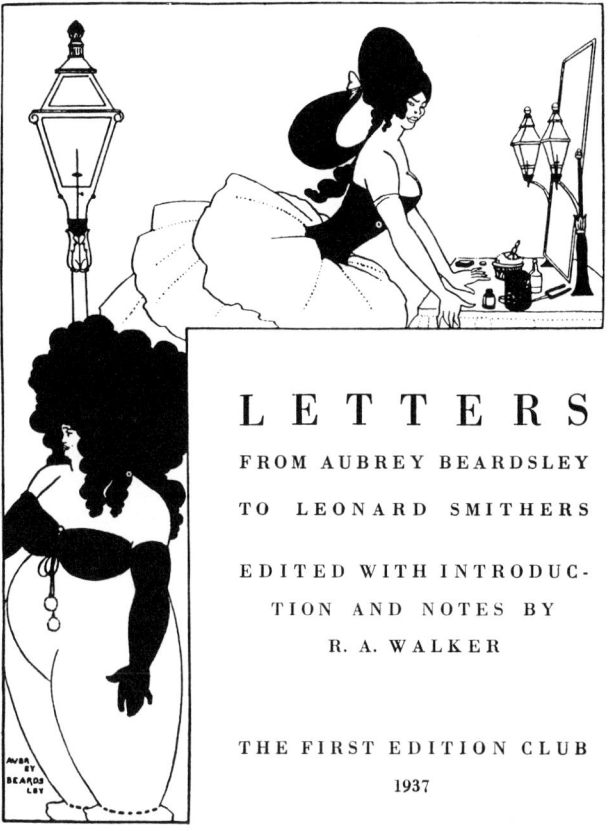

The Fleuron

An important typographical journal which came into being in 1923 as a result of the disbanding of the Fleuron Society after only one meeting. Oliver Simon, STANLEY MORISON, Harold Curwen, Bernard Newdigate, Holbrook Jackson and Francis Meynell had formed the Society to preserve high standards of printing, but could not agree upon the aims they wished to achieve. *The Fleuron* sought to embody the best principles of typography in articles from distinguished practitioners in many parts of the world. It included well-illustrated articles on printing history and on many aspects of book production, together with reviews of books and of typographical work.

Seven issues of *The Fleuron* were published, the last in 1930. Contributors included, as well as the original members of the Society, D. B. Updike, Frank Sidgwick, W. A. Dwiggins, Roger Ingpen and other distinguished European and American designers.

Shipcott, R. J. Grant, *Typographical Periodicals Between the Wars*, Oxford, 1980.
Simon, Herbert, *Song and Words – A History of the Curwen Press*, 1973.
Simon, Oliver, *Printer and Playground*, 1956.

Fly-leaf

The term fly-leaf should correctly be confined to the first or last integral blank page of a book, but it is now most often used to describe the front free endpaper.

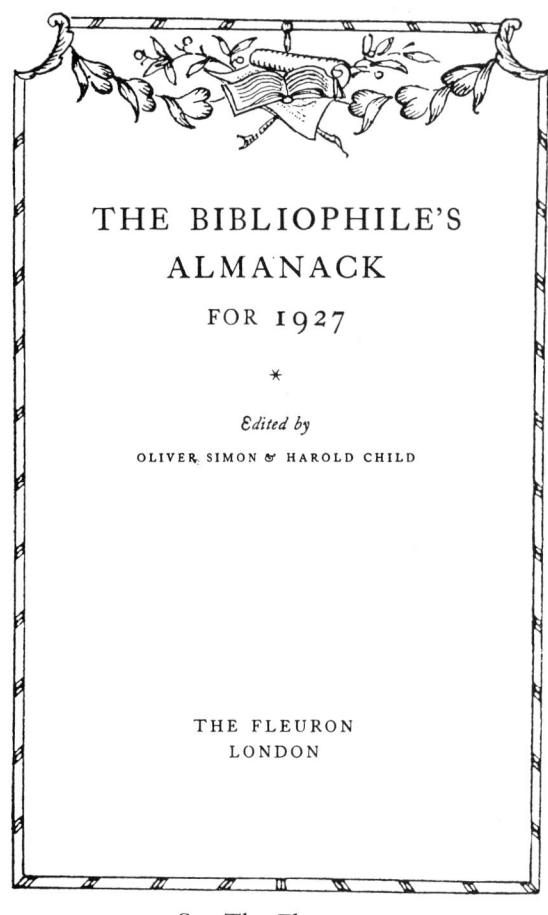

See The Fleuron

Fly-title
This term is used specifically to describe a second HALF-TITLE placed before the opening page of a book's text; or more generally to describe a title leaf (usually of half-title brevity) found at the beginning of a distinct section of a book, such as one of several essays or plays. In the second sense it has much the same connotation as 'divisional title'.

Folger Library
Henry Clay Folger's devotion to Shakespeare was formed during his student days at Amherst College, Massachusetts. When he graduated in 1879 he went into the oil business, becoming President of Standard Oil 32 years later. He and his wife Emily assembled over a period of some 40 years the extensive collection of Shakespeare-related material that was later to become the Folger Library. When Henry Folger died in 1930, his collection included 79 First Folios, 58 Second Folios, 24 Third Folios and 36 Fourth Folios. In addition to this unrivalled assembly of Shakespeare texts the collection included much additional material of importance to the study of Tudor and Stuart England and of Renaissance Europe.

Amherst College was named as Trustee of the collection and a generous endowment has enabled it to add greatly to its holdings, now housed in a purpose-built library near the Library of Congress in Washington. In 1938 the Trustees acquired the collection of Sir Leicester Harmsworth, doubling the holdings of early printed books. The Folger Library is still expanding, and supports scholarly endeavours of all kinds.

King, Stanley, *Recollections of the Folger Shakespeare Library*, Cornell University, 1950 (reprinted, 1959).
Wright, Louis B., *The Folger Library – Two Decades of Growth; 1948–1967*; Charlottesville, Virginia, 1968.

Folio
A book of folio format is one in which each printed sheet is folded once to make two leaves (four pages). The designation 2° is less commonly used than the related abbreviations 4to, 8vo, 12mo, and so on. The secondary terms 'folio in sixes' or 'folio in eights' indicate that sewing has been simplified by the use of gatherings of six or eight leaves.

The word folio is also used to describe a single leaf of a book or manuscript in which the leaves, rather than the pages, are numbered; and also to describe the numeral itself.

Folio Society
Founded in 1947 at a time when new ventures in publishing were constrained by paper rationing and other post-war difficulties, the Folio Society set out to produce well-designed and carefully printed editions of classic works of literature, history and travel. These were originally introduced to readers through bookshops, but problems arising from trade resistance to innovation prompted the Society to offer its books direct to a receptive public. The books were well calculated to appeal to readers wearied by years of austerity. They included distinguished authors (some in translation), many of the best of contemporary illustrators, and a high standard of design which extended from careful *mise en page* to imaginative pictorial or decorative cloth bindings. Some of the Society's early books are now keenly sought after: boxed sets of Jane Austen and the Brontës and of Gibbon's *Decline and Fall* provide welcome alternatives to scarcer or more lavish sets; Shakespeare's plays were illustrated by such leading stage designers as Oliver Messel and Roger Furze. By reprinting classic works in several fields, the Society has assembled a handsome library of fiction and non-fiction; and its use of well-made SLIPCASES has ensured that the great majority of its books remain clean and firm. The publication, well under way, of a complete edition of Trollope's novels, is indicative of the Folio Society's continuing enterprise. It operates on book club lines, but its publications are also available at its Gallery, now located in a central London bookshop.

The best of the Folio Society's books can be said to convey something of the spirit of a private press, at comparatively low cost.

Folio Forty, a Checklist of the Publications of the Folio Society, 1947–1987, with an Introduction by Nicolas Barker, 1987.

Font
See FOUNT

Front cover of The Folio Society's *Diary of a Nobody* by George and Weedon Grossmith, 1969.

Fore-edge painting

The practice of applying tooled or painted embellishments to the fore-edge of a book dates from the fifteenth century, and the fore-edge was also used on occasion to display the title of a book laid flat on the shelf. It was perhaps from these practices that fore-edge paintings evolved. They were originally unconcealed, but the term is now used to describe watercolour paintings executed on the spread fore-edge, which was then gilded so as to conceal the image until the edges are again fanned out. The painting is actually on the extreme edge of the upper surface of each leaf, and the technique involves clamping the book open.

The technique was largely confined to England, commencing in the middle of the seventeenth century, when several books bound in SAMUEL MEARNE's workshop for royal use bore a painting of the royal coat of arms under the fore-edge gilding. Such painting reached its highest accomplishment in the eighteenth-century work commissioned by the binder EDWARDS OF HALIFAX. Many of Edwards's fore-edge paintings reflected the contemporary interest in nature and romanticism: landscapes, country houses, river and seascapes, ruins and hunting scenes were favourite subjects, together with a few portraits or religious scenes where the contents of the book demanded them.

Little is known about the earlier artists who painted these pictures. A few are signed with initials which cannot be identified with certainty, (though J.E. may well be James Edwards), and the binder THOMAS GOSDEN signed a painting of Hadham Church on the fore-edge of Church's *Life of Alexander Nowell*; but apart from a few amateurs who decorated some of their own books, few such artists are known by name. One exception was Miss C. B. Currie who produced – and signed – many fore-edge paintings, mainly for Sotheran's, in the 1920s, though the books she decorated were usually printed some hundred or so years earlier.

Fore-edge paintings have appealed strongly to collectors, especially in the United States. This has led to many English books carrying paintings of American scenery; and some American artists have taken up the technique with enthusiasm. One of the most important collections of paintings (some 230) to have been dispersed in recent years was that belonging to Estelle Doheny, sold by Christie's in 1989. A comparable collection, including some double fore-edges, was bequeathed in 1985 by Ralph Wark to the College of William and Mary in Virginia at Williamsburg, and may be seen in the university library.

The value of fore-edge paintings depends largely on the delicacy of the painting, but its relationship to the book, and the quality and condition of the binding, are important factors. Double fore-edge paintings, which reveal different subjects when the edges are fanned in one direction or the other, are highly prized.

Books with fore-edge paintings cannot easily be rebound or recased, as the evenness of the fore-edge may be disturbed. In recent years display stands have been developed, but these involve clamping the fanned-out fore-edge and should be used briefly and cautiously, if at all.

Weber, Carl J., *A Thousand and One Fore-edge Paintings*, Waterville, Maine, 1949.
—— *Fore-Edge Painting*, Irvington-on-Hudson, New York, 1966.

Forgery and deception

The first problem in writing in general terms on this subject is that only the failures are documented: we are, inevitably, unaware of the successes. But even the failures fascinate, and some of the stories of their detection are, for booksellers, as intriguing as any thriller.

Forgery of printed material is mercifully rare. Perhaps this is because printed books are, in general, less valuable objects than banknotes or Picasso lithographs; a forger with the expertise required to deceive a bookseller or a librarian, even briefly, is more likely to turn his attentions towards such high-value items. Perhaps, too, it is because printed texts are, by their very nature, carefully scrutinized. But the most likely explanation is that a slavish copy of an existing piece of printing will always be detectable, while the invention of a plausible new text requires considerable literary skill.

THOMAS J. WISE, perhaps the most successful of literary forgers, solved this last problem by printing genuine texts under false imprints: his skill enabled him to deceive a wide public for decades. Similar tactics were employed more recently by Frederic Prokosch. When a promising young writer, he befriended some of the leading writers of the thirties and forties, including Auden, Eliot and Yeats, sending them copies of extracts from their own work, elaborately produced by Prokosch in tiny editions; he kept a few copies for himself, selling them gradually over the years as his royalties dwindled. As the supply ran out, he had the idea of producing further pamphlets, mis-stating the imprints in order to claim bibliographical status: these were sold at Sotheby's between 1968 and 1972. The last of these sales contained by far the greatest number, and similarities were noticed between pamphlets ostensibly produced some years and many thousands of miles apart. The story is told by Nicolas Barker, echoing Carter and Pollard, in *The Butterfly Books, an Enquiry into the Nature of Certain Twentieth Century Pamphlets*, 1987. Prokosch, unlike Wise, admitted responsibility, and even contributed an Epilogue to Barker's book. 'In looking back on it all', he wrote, 'I think that these little pamphlets . . . were primarily an obeisance to poetry . . . a childlike yearning for enshrinement.' Wise could hardly have made such a claim.

Another contemporary forger of printed material, Mark Hofmann, counterfeited Mormon records and the *Freeman's Oath* of 1639, no copy of which is known to survive. Hofmann, apart from his very considerable skill, is chiefly memorable for having raised the stakes by instigating a bombing campaign in which he murdered an associate and an innocent woman, and nearly killed himself.

More common than forgery of printed material is the forgery of bindings. French booksellers in particular were known to remove handsome bindings from inferior books and find grander occupants for them. Recent years have seen the identification of a number of spurious Doves Press bindings.

Forgeries of autograph or manuscript material are harder to identify categorically. Counterfeit inscriptions occasionally trouble booksellers, but they seldom stand up to comparison with authentic examples or careful investigation of provenance. Any sign of hesitation or lack of fluency in a signature or inscription may well indicate that it has been copied or even traced.

Deceptions exist in various forms. Some, such as the supply of missing leaves in facsimile, are innocent as long as they are carefully recorded; but such records do not always survive. Comparison of stains, wormholes and the like often help in determining whether a leaf has always lived between its neighbours.

These remarks have concerned themselves entirely with those forgeries and deception which are aimed directly at the antiquarian bookseller and collector. Essentially literary forgeries, such as Macpherson's 'Ossian' poems, are outside the scope of this book. Measures taken to deceive the authorities are discussed under FALSE IMPRINTS and CLANDESTINE PRINTING.

The extent to which forgeries fascinate collectors is indicated by the decision of many of the buyers of Prokosch's forgeries not to return their purchases for a refund. But, despite this fascination, forgers are the enemy of bibliographers and booksellers alike; when any campaign of forgery succeeds, even briefly, the reputation of the antiquarian book trade as a whole inevitably suffers.

Myers, Robin and Harris, Michael (eds.), *Fakes and Frauds: Varieties of Deception in Print and Manuscript*, Winchester, 1989.

Collins, John, *The Two Forgers: A Biography of Harry Buxton Forman and Thomas James Wise*, Aldershot, 1992.

Format

Those who mistakenly believe format to be essentially a matter of size and shape may feel that they are sanctioned by decades of usage in the book trade, but they are gently reproved in Ronald B. McKerrow's *An Introduction to Bibliography* (1927 and later editions): 'The terms folio, quarto, octavo, &c., are often taken to refer to the *size* of books, but this is hardly the correct way to regard them . . . Apart from the tendency to call any squarish book a quarto, and any rather small book a 12mo, some have described and even defined a quarto as one in which four leaves form a gathering. Among bibliographers at least the practice is now, however, quite fixed, and the terms in question are used solely with reference to the number of times the original sheet has been folded to form the leaves of the book.' McKerrow goes on to explain this deceptively simple sounding definition in much detail, with the aid of imposition diagrams. His patient exposition well deserves JOHN CARTER's tribute: 'To understand format, read McKerrow'. If Carter had been writing after 1972, he would most probably have added 'and read Gaskell', for PHILIP GASKELL, in *A New Introduction to Bibliography*, deals with the subject in what must seem to the layman to be almost relentless detail. This exhaustive analysis is necessary, however, for the simple definition of format as an indication of the number of times a printed sheet has been folded leaves much still to be said. Variations in folding methods, and in the way in which the folded sheets are gathered and sewn by the binder, may make the identification of format difficult; and recourse may be needed to the study of chain lines and other evidence to establish the correct designation.

For the bibliographer and the student of book production, McKerrow, FREDSON BOWERS, Gaskell and other authorities provide detailed information of a kind seldom needed by the bookseller or collector. Most catalogue descriptions confine the definition of format to the essential designations: folio, quarto, octavo, duodecimo, (or 12mo), and occasionally 16mo, 24mo, and 32mo. Sub-categories, such as large folio or small quarto, are sometimes used; but they are imprecise and actual dimensions may serve the reader better. The essential format descriptions do, however, need elaboration when the binder's GATHERINGS are not straightforward, consisting of two or more sheets, or of half sheets. A qualified description, such as quarto in 8's, or folio in 4's, is then adopted.

Forwarding and finishing

The work executed in a bindery on a book before it reaches the finishing stage, i.e. folding, beating and pressing, sewing, headbanding, glueing, trimming, edge gilding and endpapering. It may include such integral processes as the making of raised bands and preparation of boards or leather. The remaining processes – decoration, gilding, fitting, etc – are known as 'finishing'.

Foulis Press

The bookseller may expect to encounter books from two different Foulis Presses, which are quite distinct from one another. The first, in operation between 1740 and 1806, was founded in Glasgow by Robert and (in 1742) Andrew Foulis, who in their capacity as printers to the University of Glasgow produced many finely printed editions of classical and other literature.

The earlier Foulis Press should not be confused with the Edinburgh publishing firm of T. and N. Foulis, who around the turn of the century produced some imaginative illustrated books. Those featuring the work of Jessie M. King are often good examples of the Scottish interpretation of the Jugendstil or Art Nouveau movement, and are sought after.

Gaskell, Philip, *The Foulis Press*, 1964 (2nd edn, Winchester, 1986).

Fount (pronounced 'font'; the American spelling is 'font')

A complete set of type characters in a single face, including upper and lower case, numerals, punctuation marks, etc. A collection of founts of one design, comprising (for instance) roman, italic, bold, sanserif, etc., is known as a 'type family'.

Foxing

The brownish spots of discolouration which sometimes occur as a result of chemical reaction when paper becomes damp are known as foxing. The origin of the term, which dates from the nineteenth century, is obscure, but foxing is all too familiar to booksellers and their customers. Foxed plates can often be successfully cleaned by immersion, but cleaning preparations which claim to remove foxing 'in situ' should be viewed with reserve; the cure may be worse than the disease.

Iiams, Thomas M., Beckwith, T. D., *Notes on the Causes and Prevention of Foxing in Books*, 1937.

Foxon

David Foxon's *English Verse 1701–1750*, Cambridge, 1975, is an indispensable work of reference in the study of eighteenth-century literature. The first of the two volumes is a catalogue of some 10,000 separately printed poems, with notes on contemporary collected editions. The second volume provides indexes of subjects and first lines, together with a chronological index and other appendices.

Frontispiece

An illustration facing a book's title-page is known as the frontispiece. It may take the form of a portrait of the author or subject of the book, or fall within a series of similar plates. Descriptions of illustrated books should make clear whether the frontispiece is included in the enumeration of the plates.

G

Garrison-Morton
The principal bibliography of books on medicine, first issued as *A Medical Library. A Check-list of Texts Illustrating the History of the Medical Sciences*, by Fielding Hudson Garrison . . . revised by Leslie T. Morton, 1943; reprinted as Garrison and Morton's *Medical Bibliography*, 1954 and as Morton's *Medical Bibliography*, edited by Jeremy Norman, Aldershot, 1991.

Gaskell, Philip (1926–)
Just as a reference to 'McKerrow' is sufficient to identify R. B. McKerrow's classic *Introduction to Bibliography*, Oxford, 1927, so 'Gaskell' readily denotes Philip Gaskell's *A New Introduction to Bibliography*, Oxford, 1972 (reprinted, 1974, 1979). The later work was successor to, rather than a revision of, McKerrow. Like its predecessor, it set out 'to elucidate the transmission of texts by explaining the processes of book production'; but Philip Gaskell was able to take advantage of some 40 years of extensive bibliographical research, and gave attention for the first time to the printing practices and textual problems of the present century. Gaskell is also the author of the standard bibliographies of John Baskerville and of The Foulis Press.

Gathering
The terms gathering, section and quire are generally taken to be synonymous descriptions of the group of leaves formed after a printed sheet has been folded to the required size but before it has been combined with other sheets for binding. (Quire is perhaps best avoided, as it has other meanings in printing terminology.) John Carter explains cogently: 'The Sheet is the printer's unit, the Leaf the bibliographer's: the Gathering is the binder's.' Sheets for octavo books are normally folded three times and gathered singly; in quartos or folios the gatherings may consist of two or more sheets, and in small formats a gathering may comprise half a sheet. For bibliographical purposes, gatherings are described in terms of the number of leaves they comprise, so that a book made up of gatherings of four leaves is described as a folio (quarto, or octavo) 'in fours'. In the early days of printing, folios were often gathered 'in sixes' or 'in tens'.

Gatherings are usually indicated by a signature in the lower margin of the first leaf, and at their centre the binder's sewing thread will usually be visible.

Gauffered edges
The edges of a book are described as gauffered when a repeating pattern has been impressed on them with heated tools, usually before gilding. This form of decoration was much in favour during the sixteenth and seventeenth centuries, and enjoyed something of a revival among nineteenth-century binders. The *OED* gives gauffered, goffered and even gophered as alternative spellings.

Gesamtkatalog der Wiegendrucke

This comprehensive catalogue of incunabula commenced publication in Leipzig in 1925, after several years of work by the German editors and their collaborators in other countries. The project advanced slowly and had reached only the letter G when it was halted by the outbreak of the Second World War. Work resumed in 1970, and Volume 10, Part I, published in 1992, has reached 'Gregorius'.

GKW (the abbreviation is usual) is arranged alphabetically by author, and lists every book printed before 1501; locations are given for all known copies when fewer than ten are recorded. The passage of some 80 years since the catalogue was embarked upon inevitably puts the early volumes at a disadvantage, and less cumbersome works of reference are sometimes adequate for scholarly needs; but it remains a project of great distinction and value.

Gift books

See ANNUALS

Glassine

A highly transparent paper made from very high-quality pulp. However, the word (sometimes spelt 'glassene') seems to have passed into booksellers' vocabulary to describe a type of cellophane, or polythene, used for DUST-WRAPPERS from the 1950s onwards, often to protect the covers of more expensive books from abrasion against their SLIP-CASES. Sometimes it bears a printed design, and then its presence is highly desirable, the more so because of its fragility. More often it is plain, in which case it seems unwise to set a premium on its presence, as it is so easily substituted.

Goff, Frederick (1900–1982)

Goff, continuing the work began by Margaret Stillwell, was editor of *Incunabula in American Libraries: a Third Census of Fifteenth-Century Books Recorded in North American Collections*, published in 1964. His work has greatly enlarged the information available in the compilation of world listings of early printed books. He produced a supplement in 1972 and the whole work was reprinted in 1973.

Golden Cockerel Press

Although the Golden Cockerel Press was founded in 1920, its early publications were not particularly distinguished, and its important years began in 1925 after the Press was taken over by Robert Gibbings.

Close relationships with artists, perhaps most notably Eric Gill, led to the production of some of the finest British press books such as Gill's *Four Gospels* of 1931, and *Twelfth Night*, illustrated by Eric Ravilious, 1932. In 1934 the Press was sold to Christopher Sandford, who moved the headquarters from Waltham St Lawrence to London and transformed the Press's role from that of printer to commercial publisher. Sandford continued until 1961 to issue attractive books, often illustrated with original graphics, but (particularly after 1950) the Golden Cockerel Press lost much of its former creative impetus; however, almost all the books from the Press are of some interest to collectors.

Chanticleer: A Bibliography of the Golden Cockerel Press, April, 1921–August, 1936, 1936.
Pertelote: Being a Bibliography of the Golden Cockerel Press, October, 1936–April, 1943, 1943.
Cockalorum: Being a Bibliography of the Golden Cockerel Press, June, 1943–December, 1948, 1949. (All three reprinted in one volume, Folkestone, 1975.)
Cock-a-Hoop . . . being a Bibliography of the Golden Cockerel Press, September 1949–December 1961, Pinner, 1976.

Gosden, Thomas (1780–1840)

Thomas Gosden was a man of many talents and interests. He is known particularly for the sporting books that he bound, decorated with hounds and huntsmen. A devoted angler, he used fish and hook symbols in the binding of many of the great English angling books. He edited an edition of Walton's *Compleat Angler*, many copies of which he bound with appropriate designs. He is also known to have executed sporting paintings on the FORE-EDGE of some of these books. He wrote poetry and painted in watercolour. Gosden was a dealer in books and prints as well as a binder.

Grangerize

See EXTRA-ILLUSTRATED

Greg, Sir Walter W. (1875–1959)

Walter Greg, with R. B. McKerrow and A. W. POLLARD, belonged to the small group of Cambridge scholars who brought new analytical standards to the discipline of bibliography. He described it as the science of the transmission of literary documents, whose overriding responsibility must be to determine a text in its most accurate form. Greg's work on bibliographical convention – the description of a book in terms which may in principle apply to any printed work and which any reader may follow once he has learnt the 'code' – influenced many scholars, including particularly FREDSON BOWERS. The latter's *Principles of Bibliographical Description* is based to a large extent on Greg's work.

A Bibliography of the English Printed Drama to the Restoration, four volumes, 1939–1959, is Greg's principal work and is invaluable to any student of English dramatic literature. PHILIP GASKELL, in *A New Introduction to Bibliography*, 1972, comments: 'The scope and authority of Greg's great work of bibliographical analysis remain unparalleled'.

Other works by Greg on bibliographical and editorial analysis include investigations into the editing of Shakespeare, early English handwriting and autographs, punctuation and typographical convention, and other matters relating to early editions of English literature. Many of these essays can be found in his *Collected Papers* (ed. J. C. Maxwell), Oxford, 1966.

Gregynog Press

Two sisters, Gwendoline and Margaret Davies, began the Gregynog (pronounced, more or less, 'Greg*un*nog') Press in Montgomeryshire, Wales, in 1923. Unusually, the Press's books were set by hand but machine printed. Although the Press employed a variety of different staff (including, in 1931–33, Blair Hughes-Stanton and his wife Gertrude Hermes) its output remained consistent in style and high in quality until its closure in 1940. The equally distinguished bindery continued in operation, although on a reduced scale, until 1945.

As might be expected, Welsh literature in the vernacular figured prominently among Gregynog publications but classic English texts were also favoured, as were such later writers as Christina Rossetti, W. H. Davies and Bernard Shaw. Each collector might name a different favourite but *Four Poems by Milton* and *The Lamentations of Jeremiah*, 1933, both with wood engravings by Blair Hughes-Stanton, would be frequent choices, and among the Welsh texts *Llyfr y pregeth-wr*, 1927, is distinguished by David Jones's engravings. Many of the 235 items of ephemera – Christmas cards, concert programmes, orders of service – printed by the Press are desirable collectors' pieces.

Harrop, Dorothy A., *A History of the Gregynog Press*, Pinner, 1980.

The Grolier Club

Named after Jean Grolier (1479–1565), the renowned French collector of fine books and bindings, the Grolier Club was established by Robert Hoe in New York in 1884 for 'the literary study and promotion of the arts pertaining to the production of books'. Membership is by invitation only; the Club's meetings take the form of lectures, dinners, informal assemblies and scholarly exhibitions, and its publications include examples of the work of distinguished

typographers, designers and printers, as well as bibliographical monographs and other material concerned with collectors, librarians and booksellers. Grolier Club publications are much valued for their authority and elegance.

Grolier 75, A Biographical Retrospective to Celebrate the Seventy Fifth Anniversary of the Grolier Club in New York, New York, 1959.
The Grolier Club 1884–1984: Its Library, Exhibitions and Publications, New York, 1984.
Winterich, John T., *The Grolier Club, 1884–1967 – An Informal History*, New York, 1967.

Guild of Women Binders

The Guild was established by Frank Karslake in 1898, at a time when women were not accepted at most art and design colleges, nor as apprentices in the binding trade. However, the development of the private presses and with it the reintroduction of neglected book crafts encouraged women to enter a trade which utilized both their creative talents and their manual skills, and in which much of the work could be done at home.

Karslake, a bookseller and dealer in art materials who had been instrumental in establishing the ANTIQUARIAN BOOKSELLERS' ASSOCIATION, offered the newly founded Guild the use of his premises at 61 Charing Cross Road, and provided facilities for training. Individual members who wished to join could continue with the work they were already engaged in, but the Guild also invited the affiliation of Arts and Crafts associations.

It was possible to become an apprentice for one year for the sum of 50 guineas. Guild members offered a wide range of binding styles and materials: embossed calf, niger morocco, inlaid levant, embroidered bindings in silk, satin and velvet. They also bound presentation volumes, repaired books, made boxes and SLIPCASES, and designed BOOKPLATES. Their work never fell below a high professional standard, and their original designs (no design was ever repeated unless the owner requested it) won much critical acclaim. Queen Victoria admired the Guild's work and bought several of their books.

The Guild cooperated with the Hampstead Bindery (a similar men's association) to exhibit at the Paris Exhibition of 1900 where they won a silver medal.

Among the most distinguished Guild binders were Karslake's sister Constance, Edith and Florence de Rheims and Lilian Overton. Books bound by the Guild were seldom individually signed but it is sometimes possible to identify the binder by her initials or by the tools used.

The Guild of Women Binders continued for only six years, the final sale of their work being held at Sotheby's in 1904. Commercially the venture cannot have been very profitable; the members used only the finest quality materials and the average price of the books was about £3. Many of the women were of independent means and used the facilities of the Guild merely for the exchange of information and ideas or as an outlet for the sale of their work. However, their bindings were judged on their own merits, rather than as the work of women binders. As female emancipation advanced during the early years of the twentieth century, it became more usual for women to play an equal part in the creation of applied art and the Guild of Women Binders ceased to have any significant role to play.

Gutenberg, Johannes (1398–1468)

Although Gutenberg is traditionally credited with the invention of printing by movable metal type, the first book so printed, the 42-line Bible, appeared in 1455 while his press was under the control of Johann Fust and Peter Schoeffer. Fust had been Gutenberg's financial backer, but the two quarrelled when the debt could not be repaid. Fust's son-in-law, Schoeffer, designed the type Gutenberg proposed to use and the volume which is usually referred to as the Gutenberg Bible appeared with no TITLE-PAGE or COLOPHON to carry his name. Alan Thomas in *Great Books and Book Collectors*, refers to the first printed book as '. . . one of the most beautiful. The double columns

Johannes Gutenberg, 1398–1468

of splendid gothic type embody centuries of development by generations of scribes and express the very core of the German medieval spirit. It is almost incredible that the first essay achieved such breath-taking perfection.'

Gutenberg had invented a form of multiple reproduction from metal type in Strasbourg in about 1439, and he is known to have been engaged there in other scientific pursuits such as lens and mirror-making and stone-polishing. It was his move to Mainz and the need for capital that led to his involvement with Fust. The Bible took about five years to complete; it was the first book to be printed with movable cast metal type using large sheets in easily worked hand presses (earlier work had employed wooden blocks).

After Fust assumed the ownership of this first printing press, Gutenberg set up another where he printed indulgences, grammars, and particularly the *Catholicon*. But though an imaginative craftsman, he had little ambition or commercial flair; his invention was taken up by others with a shrewder view of the potentialities of the printing press.

Little is known of Gutenberg's life or character, but he will always be honoured as a craftsman whose inventive impulse altered human society.

Pollard, A. W., *Gutenberg, Fust, Schoeffer and the Invention of Printing*, The Library, NS, Vol. 8, 1907.

Todd, William B., *The Gutenberg Bible – New Evidence of the Original Printing*, 1982.
Winship, George Parker, *Gutenberg to Plantin: An Outline of the Early History of Printing*, Cambridge, Mass., 1926.

Gutta-percha

Few booksellers can think kindly of the gutta-percha method of book-binding, first employed in the 1840s, in which a flexible rubber adhesive replaced sewing as a means of holding together the leaves of a book. It was a promising invention, as sewing is the most laborious part of the traditional binding process; but while sewn gatherings remain firm if a book is handled gently, nearly all the gutta-percha bindings of the nineteenth century are now defective, the rubber having perished and many leaves having become loose.

Recent technology has overcome some of the limitations of this type of binding; but the modern thermo-plastic, or 'perfect' bindings, extensively used in the production of paperback books, are still fragile and in the long term unsatisfactory.

Gutter

This rather inelegant term is needed only when reference must be made to the single space formed by the inner margins of facing pages of a book.

H

Hafod Press
Thomas Johnes's press at Hafod House, near Aberystwyth, established in 1803, has no very eminent place in the history of fine printing; but his publications – mainly his own scholarly translations of early French romances – interest collectors as the products of one of the earliest of truly private, home-based presses.

Hain, Ludwig (1781–1836)
Hain's list of incunabula held at the Bavarian State Library in Munich the *Repertorium Bibliographicum ad annum 1500*, comprised more than 16,000 volumes and was published from 1826 to 1838. It was subsequently amended with additions by W. A. Copinger in 1895–1902 and indexed by Konrad Burger in 1891. Dietrich Reichling made further additions in a series of appendices, 1905–14 and the work was reprinted in Milan in 1948. Hain remains one of the most important bibliographies for the study of incunabula.

Hakluyt Society
The Society was founded in 1846 in honour of the early writer on travel, Richard Hakluyt the Younger (1552–1616). It undertakes the printing of rare and unpublished accounts of voyages and explorations of English travellers, making many of these accessible for the first time to modern readers. Hakluyt himself assembled all his documentary collections into three main series: *Divers Voyages*, 1552; *Principall Navigations*, 1589; and *Principall Navigations*, 1598–1600. These were reprinted by the Society in 12 volumes, 1903–5. A facsimile edition appeared in 1965.

The Hakluyt Society – the name is usually pronounced Hakl't – has reprinted many of its earlier publications; it is now housed at the British Library.

Parks, G. P., *Richard Hakluyt and the English Voyages*, 1928, reprinted, 1961.
Quinn, D. B., *The Hakluyt Handbook*, 2 vols, 1974.

Half-title
The leaf preceding a book's TITLE-PAGE (or frontispiece) and giving on its recto the title, is known as the half-title. The title, if lengthy, may be abbreviated, and though a volume number or series title may sometimes appear, the author's name is rarely given. The verso of the half-title may carry the printer's imprint (though this is more commonly placed on the verso of the title-page), or a list of other works by the same author or in the same series.

Half-titles are first found in books of the later seventeenth century, when they took the place of the protective blank leaf that often preceded the title-page in earlier times; but they were not invariably used, and even when initially present they were often discarded by binders. When a half-title is absent, and a collation cannot be consulted, it can be difficult to determine whether one is called for; but it can at least be assumed that if the first GATHERING lacks its first leaf, the missing leaf was either a half-title or a preliminary blank. The collector's desire for a half-title where one is known to have been issued reflects the fact that for all its brevity it is the first printed page of the book.

Halkett and Laing
The Dictionary of Anonymous and Pseudonymous English Literature, by Samuel Halkett and John Laing, evolved as a result of correspondence that had appeared first in *The Gentleman's Magazine* and later in *Notes and Queries*. The work was started in the 1850s and when Halkett, Keeper of the Advocates' Library in Edinburgh, died in 1871, was continued by the Rev. Laing and his daughter. The first edition in four volumes appeared from 1882, and was very soon out of print. The Rev. James Kennedy, who had been collecting additional material for some time, secured the backing of the Carnegie Trust for a new edition. This appeared in six volumes over several years from 1926, after Dr Kennedy's death, edited by members of the staff of the British Museum. Later, Volume VII was published as an Index and First Supplement, Volume VIII as a further Supplement in 1956, covering the years from 1900 to 1950, and Volume IX as Addenda in 1962.

The entries in Halkett and Laing are arranged alphabetically by title, ignoring the prefixes A and THE but taking into account preliminary prepositions such as ON and OF. Indexes give cross-references for pseudonyms and initials, true names, and book titles.

A proposed reprint of Halkett and Laing, to be published by Oliver and Boyd, was turned down in favour of a newly edited and completely revised work. The main difference was that the work would be reorganized in chronological order, the first volume to cover 1475–1640 (STC), the second 1641–1700 (Wing), the subsequent volumes 1701–1800 and so on. The Oliver and Boyd imprint was taken over by Longmans and John Hordern undertook the editorship, with the work organized jointly at the Bodleian and at North Texas State University, Denton. The first volume appeared in 1980, under the amended title *A Dictionary of Anonymous and Pseudonymous Publications in the English Language 1475–1640*, but went out of print in September 1991. No further volumes are planned, though some of the new material is incorporated in the new STC and Wing.

Hayday, James (1796–1872)
Hayday ran a large bindery in Lincoln's Inn Fields, catering for the fashionable society of mid-Victorian England. His work tended to the over-elaborate, with coloured onlays and much use of gold tooling, employing geometric and fan devices; but he was a meticulous craftsman and his name commanded respect. He was particularly concerned that the books he bound should open freely and lie flat, and he developed techniques to achieve this aim. Although at first he seemed to prosper, Hayday was a slow worker and eventually his bindery failed.

Headband
In the fifteenth and sixteenth centuries, binders attached headbands to the leaves (and sometimes also to the boards) at the top of a book's spine for practical as well as decorative reasons. The bands (often at top and bottom) provided useful reinforcement, and the silk or cotton, worked over a leather or cord base, could be a colourful feature of the binding. In the seventeenth century changes in binding methods made the headband technically obsolete; but it has survived as a decorative feature of

HERBALS

leather-bound books and of some cased books. In the latter it may often prove to be a simple insert of striped fabric rather than a hand-sewn band, and liable to fall out.

Herbals
See NATURAL HISTORY BOOKS

Hering, Charles (fl. 1794–1815)
One of a family of bookbinders of German origin, working in St Martin's Street in London, Charles Hering was the eldest of the family and the first to learn the trade. He was employed by many contemporary collectors and was considered one of the most skilful and elegant binders of the day, until – according to DIBDIN – he was superseded by 'the star of CHARLES LEWIS'.

Hinge
It might be thought that the pivotal points of a book were sufficiently important to its structure to have acquired precise description – one for the inner and one for the outer junction; but some uncertainty prevails. The term *hinge*, which seems best suited to the inside of a book, is generally used in that sense; but *joint* tends to be used interchangeably. However, confusion is easily avoided by the use of the prefixes *inner* or *outer*.

Historiated initial
The practice of decorating initial letters or borders with human or animal figures, usually with a narrative significance, is associated mainly with manuscripts; but 'historiated' initials, decorated by hand, are also found in early printed books.

Alexander, J. J. G., *The Decorated Letter*, 1978.

Hogarth Press
In addition to their separate careers as writers, Virginia and Leonard Woolf shared an interest in printing; this led them in 1917 to start a private press, initially as a diversion for Virginia, who was already beginning to show signs of mental instability. The Press took its name from their home, Hogarth House in Richmond, in whose dining room the equipment was set up.

The Woolfs' first publication was *Two Stories*, one by each of them; it appeared in July 1917, bound in wallpaper wrappers, in an edition of 150 copies. It proved a modest commercial success, and the Press gradually expanded to the point where, in 1919, it had to start employing outside printers. Although the Woolfs continued to set and print books themselves until as late as 1932, this became increasingly sporadic, and by the mid-twenties the firm was simply a useful source of income; it moved to London in 1924. Virginia Woolf (who died in 1941) withdrew from partnership in 1938, to be replaced by John Lehmann; in 1947 the Press became part of Chatto and Windus, after which its interest to collectors (at any rate as a Press) declines.

The importance of the Hogarth Press to British cultural life between the wars is hard to overestimate. The Woolfs' broad literary, artistic and political interests led them to publish, in addition to their own work, a wide variety of authors including T. S. Eliot, E. M. Forster, Robert Graves, Christopher Isherwood, J. M. Keynes and Katherine Mansfield; they would have liked to publish *Ulysses* but were unable to find a printer who would handle it. In its capacity as publisher to the International Psycho-Analytical Institute, the Press also became responsible for issuing the English translations of the works of Freud.

Although the breadth of the Woolfs' interests did not imply a comparable tolerance for the opinions of others (causing, among other criticisms, Samuel Beckett to dismiss the Press as the 'Hogarth Private Lunatic Asylum') most of the notable English (and, in translation, several important Continental) writers of the time came into their orbit at some time or another. The books themselves were often visually interesting as well, with their eye-catching DUST-WRAPPERS by (among others) Virginia's sister Vanessa Bell; many of the publications contained original graphics by members of the 'Bloomsbury group'. The continuing success of the whole Bloomsbury industry has helped sustain interest in the Press's publications, and prices are correspondingly high for the scarcer and more desirable items.

Woolmer, J. Howard, *A Checklist of the Hogarth Press 1917–1938*, 1976 (revised and expanded, 1986).
Woolf, Leonard, *Beginning Again*, 1964.
——— *Downhill All the Way*, 1967.

Holograph

A literary manuscript is described as holograph when it is wholly in the author's handwriting. The description is not applied to autograph letters or to inscriptions in books.

Honeyman

Robert B. Honeyman started to form his collection of scientific books and manuscripts in the 1930s. He was trained as an engineer but his interests covered a wide range of scientific endeavour. His books on science were sold by Sotheby's in a series of seven sales in 1978–80, and the catalogues are now an important source of reference. Honeyman also formed a large literary collection, which he donated to Lehigh University, Bethlehem, Pennsylvania, and to the University of California at Berkeley.

Horn-book

Early instructional books for children often took the form of 'horn-books' – a single sheet of paper pasted to a thin wooden board and protected by a transparent cover of horn. The page usually consisted of an alphabet, a religious text – perhaps the Lord's Prayer – or an instructional verse. A handle was usually incorporated in the design or attached later. Shakespeare refers to a horn-book in *Love's Labour's Lost*, and Thomas Bewick designed an alphabet for one, illustrated in Percy Muir's *English Children's Books*, 1954. A similar device for teaching children to read was the 'battledore', an illustrated card, folded and varnished.

Tuer, Andrew W., *The History of the Horn-Book*, 1896 (reprinted, Amsterdam, 1971).

Folmsbee, Beulah, *A Little History of the Horn-Book*, Boston, Massachusetts, 1965.

Hours Press

The French private press of Nancy Cunard. She bought William Bird's printing equipment (see THREE MOUNTAINS PRESS) and, with the help of Louis Aragon, established it in her farmhouse at Réanville near Paris in 1928.

The first book scheduled to appear from the Press, a revised edition of George Moore's *Peronnik the Fool*, was an immediate commercial success; by chance it was actually preceded by a reprint of a somewhat drier title, Norman Douglas's *Report on the Pumice-Stone Industry of the Lipari Islands*. The list rapidly expanded to encompass perhaps a wider variety of literary styles than other French expatriate private presses, from Arthur Symons to Ezra Pound. In 1930 the Press moved to Paris, where it issued Samuel Beckett's first separately published work, *Whoroscope*, 1930. Other highlights of the Press included Pound's *A Draft of XXX Cantos* and a book of piano pieces by Nancy Cunard's companion, the black musician Henry Crowder, *Henry-Music*, both 1930. The latter inspired her to begin collecting material for her celebrated anthology *Negro*, which eventually appeared in 1934; this work had gradually replaced the Hours Press as the focus of Nancy Cunard's interest, and the last book from the Press appeared in 1931.

Cunard, Nancy, *These Were The Hours: Memories of my Hours Press, Réanville and Paris, 1928–1931*, edited and with a foreword by Hugh Ford, Carbondale and Edwardsville, Illinois, 1969.

Howard-Hill, T. H.

Author of the *Bibliography of British Literary Bibliographies*, published in 1969 by Oxford University Press. It lists general bibliographies of English literature, regional bibliographies and works on private presses, printing, anthologies, maps, diaries, sermons, etc. There is also a wide-ranging list – from accounting to witchcraft – of subject bibliographies. Perhaps the most useful aspect of the work is that it covers not only material published in book form, but also contributions to journals and periodicals in Britain and America.

Although the work was planned for six volumes, volume III was never published. The volumes are as follows:

I – *Bibliography of British Literary Bibliographies*, 1969 (reprinted 1987).
II – *Shakespearean Bibliography and Textual Criticism*, 1971.
III – Not published.
IV – *British Bibliography and Textual Criticism*, 1979.
V – *British Literary Bibliography and Textual Criticism*, 1979.
VI – *Index*, 1980.

Humanism

A word with many meanings, but as far as booksellers are concerned the most important refers to the Renaissance enthusiasm for the study of classical antiquity, and the books relating to this.

Huntington Library

The Huntington family wealth derived from American railroads; and Henry Edwards Huntington (1850–1927) inherited a large fortune from his uncle and increased the inheritance by his own shrewd investments. His real estate purchases included land in San Marino, outside Los Angeles, where he built the splendid mansion that was to become the Huntington library and museum.

Huntington purchased early printed books, manuscripts and paintings from America and Europe, assembling in particular a fine collection of English and American literature. His wife Arabella extended and developed the gardens and they attract today almost as many visitors as does the library. Huntington gave the mansion and its contents to the nation and endowed them sufficiently for the collections to continue to grow.

The reputation of Huntington as a book-collector was made at the Hoe sale in New York in 1911. Every important antiquarian dealer was present: Maggs and Quaritch from London, Rosenbach and Walter Hill from America and several equally distinguished dealers from Europe. Their clients included Rockefeller, Pierpont Morgan, Henry Folger, Harry Widener and many others whose names were shrouded in secrecy. Huntington, however, spent nearly half the total realized, some half a million dollars. His purchases included a Gutenberg Bible on vellum.

He extended the collections by purchasing complete libraries from fellow bibliophiles and by successfully offering auctioneers large sums for the entire contents of sales. The purchases made for Huntington in England, usually by Dr Rosenbach, caused some dismay among the dealers and collectors, who were competing with a seemingly bottomless purse.

The prize possessions of the Huntington library remain the incunabula and early English literature, together with some 5,400 manuscripts. The collection of Shakespeariana is one of the finest in the world. There are also many modern editions – Kelmscott, Officina Bodoni, Cranach – of the great works of English literature.

Schad, Robert O., *Henry Edwards Huntington: the Founder and the Library*, San Marino, 1948.

Thorpe, James, Wark, Robert R., Billington, Ray Allen, *The Founding of the Henry E. Huntington Library and Art Gallery*, 1969

I

Illumination
The decoration of manuscripts in colour or with gold and silver leaf, is known as illumination. The term may also be applied to early printed books especially in the context of initial letters, but always indicates decoration by hand.

Illustrated Books 1850–1920

Robin Greer

Although generally considered together, children's and illustrated books are essentially two different fields of collecting. Children's books are books produced for the entertainment or education of young people, but not necessarily with illustrations, whereas it is these that are the essential characteristic of the illustrated book. Many books can be classified either way, and the overlap is such that most dealers and many collectors will have a mixture of both.

Illustrated books are, perhaps, better called 'imaginatively illustrated books' – a definition that excludes the many handsome illustrated books on natural history, or views of familiar or distant places, and enables us to concentrate on books whose illustrations are purely fanciful, depicting scenes and themes of the imagination. Many of these books are traditional fairy tales by the masters like Hans Andersen or the Brothers Grimm, or original fairy stories by such writers as Marion St John Webb, Rose Fyleman or, from an earlier period, E. H. Knatchbull-Hugessen. Equally intriguing are illustrated editions of Edgar Allan Poe's *Tales of Mystery and Imagination*, stories by Lord Dunsany, such as *The King of Elfland's Daughter*, or Vernon Hill's *Ballads Weird and Wonderful*. These clearly fall outside the field of children's books, but come from, and continue to inspire, the imagination.

The range of topics that are collected within these fields is wider than in most areas of collecting and leaves much scope for individual taste and personal whim. Some people collect first editions of great children's classics, others just one or two authors. Yet others collect children's books relating to a specific theme such as Cats, Alice [in Wonderland], Mountaineering or 'Robinsonnades' (the name given to stories derived from Robinson Crusoe). Some collectors are consumed by a passion to own each and every item illustrated by artists such as Arthur Rackham, Edmund Dulac, Kay Nielsen or the Brock brothers, while others only seek the high spots, concentrating on highly acclaimed titles. As in all

ILLUSTRATED BOOKS

book collecting, there is no 'right way' to collect other than for your own pleasure and the remarkable point about illustrated books is that there is still so much to discover. Even an illustrator such as Arthur Rackham, whose work has inspired three or four bibliographies, offers great scope for discovering unrecorded items. The eager collectors of Alice and Beatrix Potter material have not yet exhausted all the possibilities. A cursory examination of a recent bibliography of 'Robinsonnades' shows that there is still a great deal to be recorded. Thus every time a collector or dealer embarks on book hunting, he can hope to discover not only books he has been longing to find but even items which he did not know existed.

Perhaps this explains why there are so few bibliographies of the major illustrators. No matter how much work he may have done, how many collectors and libraries he may have consulted, the bibliographer knows that his work is incomplete. Nevertheless the publication of any bibliography is a great spur to the searching out of unrecorded titles. For dealers, a new bibliography gives the opportunity of trumpeting a previously unknown book as 'Not in White' or 'Not in Beare'. The increased chances of selling such unusual items provide a great incentive to hunt them out.

Often fortuitously, there have been imaginative illustrations as long as there have been books. However, as with children's books, it is a comparatively modern idea to produce books for sheer entertainment. It was the earlier part of the nineteenth century which saw the beginning of influences which flowered later. There can be no doubt of the debt that all illustrators owe to William Blake. It was he who first tried to marry text and illustration more intimately than had been attempted before, and introduced the free, swirling forms that became so popular later. His successors, the Pre-Raphaelites, introduced dramatic images from medieval themes such as *Le Morte D'Arthur*, which spoke of worlds beyond the all-dominant religiosity of the time. Arthur Rackham acknowledged the influence on him of Boyd Houghton's *Arabian Nights*, 1863, and the influence of Rossetti, Burne-Jones and Sandys on later illustrators is undeniable.

The imaginatively illustrated book came alive with the work of artists such as Richard Doyle and Eleanor Vere Boyle. The combination of the highly skilled colour printing of Edmund Evans and the quirky comic fairy drawings of Richard Doyle produced the glorious *In Fairyland*, 1870, and its derivative *The Princess Nobody*, 1884. There were two editions of *In Fairyland*, 1870 and 1875; apart from the date on the title-page there is nothing to distinguish between the two. The gutta-percha binding often causes damage to the edges, so that many copies are far from perfect. It was a unique achievement to take details from the larger plates of *In Fairyland* and adapt them suitably to illustrate Andrew Lang's story *The Princess Nobody*. It is hard to believe that nothing has been added, but comparing the two volumes side by side, and page by page, shows that everything in *The Princess Nobody* is taken from *In Fairyland*. Other Doyle books are pleasing but do not have quite the same appeal as these two.

It is difficult to quantify the appeal of the illustrations of the Hon. Eleanor Vere Boyle, or EVB as she usually called herself. Her first book was *Child's Play*, printed by lithography at the Appel's Anastatic Press in 1852. A few copies are found with the title-page coloured; it appears that this colouring is original and not by (as is sometimes assumed) some enthusiastic amateur. After this charming start her major works, which include a coloured

The School for Scandal, 1911, illustrated by Hugh Thomson.

version of *Child's Play*, 1865, its sequel *New Child's Play*, 1879, *Beauty and the Beast*, 1875, *Hans Andersen*, 1878 and the commonest title *Story Without An End*, 1868, are all vividly colour printed. The mixture of waif-like children, Pre-Raphaelite influence and bold colour makes for illustrations which break out of the Victorian mould and become more pleasing as time goes by. The bibliography of EVB is still far from complete: new items are being discovered, and the evidence suggests that there are further books to be found.

The colour printer, Edmund Evans, was intimately involved with three other important late nineteenth-century illustrators, Walter Crane, Kate Greenaway and Randolph Caldecott. The high quality of Evans's printing, which played such a major part in Doyle's *In Fairyland*, seems to have been instrumental in enhancing the success of all his artists. Crane produced many books; indeed he was a prolific artist, having fingers in many pies. Though many of his illustrations are rather uninspiring, his *Flora's Feast*, 1889, *The Flower Wedding*, 1905, and a few other books, are attractive and well worth including in any collection of illustrated books. Kate Greenaway, whose career was specifically promoted by Edmund Evans, has many devoted admirers; her neat, well-ordered little girls charm many people, but to those whose memories of childhood are still strong, or to children themselves, these images of a very controlled, inhibited existence are artificial and not very inspiring. Caldecott, on the other hand, has a light abandon in his style that grows more attractive the longer one looks. His books were a great success in his day and were published in large numbers, first by George Routledge and then by Frederick Warne. His people inhabit a rural world which is as unreal as any depiction of Fairyland. Although this ethos seemed old-fashioned when the revival of interest in Art Nouveau in the 1960s turned collectors' attention back to illustrated books, his gentle comic line has become more respected as the years go by. His direct successors, Hugh Thomson and the Brock brothers, are also appealing more and more to present-day collectors.

The end of the century saw the flowering of the Art Nouveau book, among whose leading illustrators were Charles Ricketts, Aubrey Beardsley, Laurence Housman and Jessie M. King. The work of this period was mainly in black and white, and it may be claimed that some of these illustrations have never been bettered. Devotees of the nineties view all later periods as a sad fall from grace. For the first time since William Blake, artists took control of all aspects of their books, not by producing limited editions on private presses, but working with commercial printers. The importance of Charles Ricketts is that he was able to produce books which, in their quiet way, are the equal of the Kelmscott Press and lead the way for beautiful books to be commercially produced. His own excellent illustrations are thus elegantly enhanced. For a perfect union of binding, form and illustrations it is hard to better Laurence Housman's edition of Christina Rossetti's *Goblin Market*, 1893. While the large paper edition may cost more, it loses the distinctive form of the trade edition, and hence its appeal. It can be said that this is an exemplary illustrated book and that any other edition of this text will always seem inferior.

Much the same can be said of Charles Robinson's version of Robert Louis Stevenson's *A Child's Garden of Verses*, 1895. Although the binding is not particularly noteworthy, the marriage of poems, decorations and illustrations is so felicitous that it is hard not to believe that they all sprang together from a single imagination. Indeed, the first edition of *A Child's Garden of Verses* seems a sad production in comparison, and even Charles

Cinderella, 1894, illustrated by Robert Anning Bell.

Robinson's own later edition of 1908, in larger format with added colour plates, does not satisfy quite as much as the earlier version.

Jessie M. King is Scotland's major contributor to the annals of British book illustration, although her first offering, in a National Art competition, was adjudged to be conventional and worth only a silver medal even though no gold medal was awarded that year. Just four years later, in 1903, *The High History of the Holy Graal*, with her illustrations, was published, followed the next year by William Morris's *The Defence of Guinevere*, 1904. These are the quintessential Jessie King books which have a special quality, inspiring fervent devotion among collectors and causing the art world, which normally sniffs at illustrators, to accord her a place as a fine artist. Although she illustrated many books, most of them were poorly printed, doing little justice to the original art work. The rare exception was The Studio special supplement *Seven Happy Days* which was published on 15 December 1913 with seven colour plates exquisitely heightened with silver and gold and eight smaller illustrations. These colour plates were so well printed that they are almost as good as original watercolours. Some of the greetings cards that Jessie King illustrated are of a similar quality, blending delicate colouring with willowy, appealing scenes.

Undoubtedly the key figure of the Nineties was Aubrey Beardsley. Although he died very young and illustrated only a small number of books, his influence was crucial. His daring translation of the Japanese technique of using negative space revolutionized book illustration. His illustrations to Oscar Wilde's *Salome*, 1894, *Lysistrata*, 1896, and Malory's *Le Morte D'Arthur*, 1893, rank high in the canon of classic illustration and were adapted and copied long after both in Britain and abroad. He was a true innovator. Beardsley's liberating technique was soon to be allied to the greater authenticity achieved by advances in colour printing. Carl Hentschel so improved the technique of photographic colour printing that the colour plates he produced were extremely faithful to the colours and tones of the original watercolours. The first major books published using Hentschel's process were Arthur Rackham's *Rip Van Winkle*, 1905, and *Peter Pan in Kensington Gardens*, 1906, followed the next year by Edmund Dulac's *Stories from the Arabian Nights*. The full richness of these colour plates, allied with sumptuous presentation, must have been an exciting revelation. The next decade saw a great outpouring of handsomely produced and richly illustrated volumes which mark the golden era of British book illustration. The books were expensive, generally costing 21 shillings, but fortunately there was an adequate market for them and they proved very successful. The delicacy and precision allowed to the illustrator was remarkable. Surviving colour proofs show that the artist was allowed to control the printing of the colour plates. Annotations by Dulac asking for a small area of blue to be heightened, and similar notes by W. Heath Robinson on proofs for *Bill the Minder*, 1912 and Hugh Thomson on proofs for *She Stoops to Conquer*, 1912, show how each colour plate was separately printed and indicate the extent of the artist's influence. In view of this it can be argued that the colour plates in the first printings of these books are original works of art, the preceding watercolour being but a stage in the process. The importance of first printings is certainly evident, because in later editions the colours tend to change and the precision is often lost.

There can be few people who have not heard of Arthur Rackham. His books were

From J. M. Barrie's *Peter Pan*, illustrated by Arthur Rackham, 1906 (the figure on the left is probably a self-portrait)

printed in great numbers and posters and postcards have been published using his illustrations. Rackham may have suffered from familiarity, but he was one of the greatest of all illustrators, and while both earlier and later in his career some of the work he produced was rather pedestrian, his major books are well worth a place in a collection almost regardless of parameters. His were the essentially English illustrations capturing a nostalgic whimsical tone with his gnarled trees and his 'light fantastic register'. *Peter Pan in Kensington Gardens*, 1906, was the first separate publication of a Peter Pan story, having originally been but a couple of chapters in a rather strange book called *The Little White Bird*, 1902. Most children have dreams of flying, and it would seem that Rackham was the first artist to depict this deep-seated desire. The colour plates are rich and exciting giving the impression that they are on old weathered vellum.

Of similar importance are Rackham's illustrations for *Grimm's Fairy Tales*, 1909, a lavish production with 40 mounted colour plates and 62 other pictures; Shakespeare's *Midsummer Night's Dream*, 1908, which has 40 mounted colour plates and 34 other drawings; the two Wagner volumes, 1910 and 1911, with their complement of 60 colour plates and the lavishly illustrated *Arthur Rackham Book of Pictures*, 1913. The complete *oeuvre* of Rackham is vast, but his appeal is so great that many collectors are happy to collect the most minor of his published works. Although there are several bibliographies and books about Rackham it is still possible to find unrecorded illustrations in the most unlikely of places.

The reputation of book production in Britain during the Edwardian era was high enough to attract illustrators from abroad. Edmund Dulac, originally Edmond, came from France, Kay Nielsen from Denmark via Paris, and Willy Pogany spent a decade or so working in Britain en route from his native Hungary to the United States. These foreign artists added greatly to the variety and quality of book illustration in England. Edmund Dulac's illustrations for *Stories from the Arabian Nights*, 1907, *Princess Badoura*, 1913, and *Sinbad the Sailor*, 1914, which provided a total of 83 colour plates depicting tales from *The Thousand and One Nights*, were so definitive that Rackham was never commissioned to illustrate any book of Arabian interest. Dulac achieved the same authority with his *Rubaiyat of Omar Khayyam*, 1909. The other distinguished publication of the *Rubaiyat* during this period was by René Bull and it is clear that Bull could not break away from Dulac's hold over the subject. As the major commissions dwindled, after the First World War, Dulac turned his hand to many other things, designing stamps, and the interiors which were used in the Canadian Pacific Liner, *Empress of Britain*. He was an artist whose style changed as the years progressed; an exponent of Art Nouveau in the frontispiece to his *Arabian Nights* but becoming, in his later work, closer to Art Deco. He was clearly an interesting and complex man, as his published work indicates.

Dulac's footsteps were followed by the young Kay Nielsen who left Denmark for Paris in 1903 when he was only 17. There he studied at the Academie Julien, where Dulac had been a student a few years earlier. It is interesting to note the strong oriental influence in the work of both men. In 1911 Nielsen came to England where an exhibition at the Dowdeswell Galleries in Bond Street launched his career. In 1913 he illustrated his first book, Sir Arthur Quiller-Couch's *In Powder and Crinoline*, which has some impressive plates. However, it was his next book, an edition of *East of the Sun and West of the Moon*, 1916, which was his masterpiece. This is possibly the most important of any of the

The Ugly Duckling from *Tales from Hans Andersen*, 1896, illustrated by Helen Stratton.

illustrated books published during this golden era; with the text handsomely printed with good wide margins, all the colour plates mounted over gold borders present original, striking images. Two further quarto volumes were published in Britain after Nielsen left in 1917 for New York, *Hans Andersen's Fairy Tales*, 1923, and *Hansel and Gretel*, 1925. The latter was only published in a limited edition in Britain, but there is a very acceptable American trade edition published by Doran. Neither of these two books quite captures the boldness of Nielsen's first works. His last two books were *Red Magic*, 1930, and *Eventyret*, published in Copenhagen in 1949 with just three black and white plates in an edition of 350 copies.

The short stay in Britain of Willy Pogany witnessed the publication of his most important book illustrations. His total canon runs to some one hundred titles, but most of them are not particularly exciting. However, the Wagner Trilogy – *Tannhäuser*, 1911, *Parsifal*, 1912 and *Lohengrin*, 1913 – together with his version of *The Rime of the Ancient Mariner*, 1910, stand out from the rest. These are comprehensively illustrated books, with Pogany providing colour plates, the lithograph illustrations, the binding and even the lettering. His style changed greatly after he moved to the USA, and most of his books became rather mundane, although his *Mother Goose*, 1927, and his *Alice*, 1929, are worthy of attention. It is curious to note Pogany's name as designer amongst the credits to the Busby Berkeley movies.

Among the other major illustrators of the Golden Age are the Robinson brothers, Charles and William Heath. Charles was the first to come to the fore in the 1890s. His sensual, swirling illustrations to his first book, *Aesop's Fables*, 1895, followed by the excellent series published by John Lane, *A Child's Garden of Verses*, 1895, *Make Believe*, 1896, *The Child World*, 1896, and *Lullaby Land*, 1897, set a high standard which he maintained throughout his career. He produced several excellent quarto colour plate volumes such as Oscar Wilde's *The Happy Prince*, 1913, *The Songs and Sonnets of Shakespeare*, 1915, and the profusely illustrated *The Big Book of Nursery Rhymes*, 1903, *The Big Book of Fairy Tales*, 1911, and *The Big Book of Fables*, 1912. Notable also is *The Secret Garden*, 1911, a wonderful children's classic by Frances Hodgson Burnett which was illustrated by Charles Robinson in its first edition. Blackie published a fascinating series of small oblong titles such as *The Mad Motor*, *The Awful Airship*, *The Silly Submarine* and *Peculiar Piggies* (all published in 1906), all of great interest graphically. William Heath Robinson, Charles's younger brother, has become a household name for his humorous cartoons featuring ingenious inventions. However, he was an excellent and sensitive illustrator as well: his illustrations for Poe's *Poems*, 1900, are probably the finest ever made. He went on to produce delicate editions of *A Midsummer Night's Dream*, 1914, *Hans Andersen's Fairy Tales*, 1913 and many other charming volumes. Most memorable, however, are the two books he wrote and illustrated himself, *The Adventures of Uncle Lubin*, 1902, and *Bill the Minder*, 1912. *Uncle Lubin*, which is mainly in black and white, is a comic masterpiece, well printed by Grant Richards. The colour plates for *Bill the Minder* rank among the finest produced in Britain during this period. There is a quality to Heath Robinson's work which marks him as an inimitably English illustrator, and his work seems to inspire increasing devotion as the years go by.

Even in this short survey mention must be made of a few of the other excellent illustrators working during the period. Ireland's Harry Clarke produced the definitive edition of Poe's *Tales*, 1919, and other outstanding volumes such as *Hans Andersen's Fairy Tales*, 1916. Warwick Goble's illustrated *Water Babies* is the most satisfying version of that children's classic. John Austen will always be remembered for his excellent Beardsleyesque illustrations for *Hamlet*, 1922. Other highly desirable volumes include Ronald Balfour's luxuriously printed edition of *The Rubaiyat*, 1920, and William Timlin's sumptuous masterpiece *The Ship that sailed to Mars*, 1920, a great classic of illustration and fantasy. Illustrators such as Hugh Thomson, Honor C. Appleton, Anne Anderson, Florence Mary Anderson, Cecily Mary Barker, Charles J. Folkard, F. D. Bedford, Frank C. Papé, Mabel Lucie Attwell, Alice B. Woodward, Willebeek Le Mair, Harry Rountree, Alastair, the Detmold brothers, Margaret Tarrant, and several others are all worthy of more attention than a fleeting mention may suggest.

The period between the two world wars saw Britain decline from its previous prosperity, and as a consequence the overall quality of books also declined. Many interesting illustrated books were published but in general without the care and expense of the earlier period. The inter-war style was generally more humorous, with a tendency towards the cute. It is arguable that the heyday of British book illustration was brought to a close with the emergence of cartoons in the cinema. It is certainly interesting to note that, according to Hamilton, family tradition has it that Rackham was invited to California by Walt Disney to work with him on *Snow White*, and that Nielsen and other illustrators certainly played a part in the production of Disney's *Fantasia*.

While attention has been focused on British book illustrators, this is not to suggest that there were no first-rate illustrators working elsewhere, in continental Europe and in the United States. The handsome productions by Munk in Vienna of illustrators such as Lefler, Urban and even Pogany are a great delight. Sweden's Gustaf Tenggren and John Bauer were illustrators of the highest rank. In the USA, besides the great names of Howard Pyle, Maxfield Parrish, N. C. Wyeth and Jessie Willcox Smith, many of whose books warranted English editions, there were many excellent, unsung illustrators.

Beare, Geoffrey, *The Illustrations of W. Heath Robinson*, 1983.
Hamilton, James, *Arthur Rackham: A Life with Illustration*, 1990.
Peppin, Brigid and Micklethwait, L., *Dictionary of British Book Illustrators: the Twentieth Century*, 1983.
Taylor, John Russell, *The Art Nouveau Book in Britain*, 1966.
White, Colin, *The Enchanted World of Jessie M. King*, Edinburgh, 1989.

Imprimatur

The Latin term 'let it be printed' denotes the permission granted by a religious or secular authority for a book to be printed. The granting of this permission was often printed at the beginning of sixteenth- and seventeenth-century books; a page devoted to it is known as a licence leaf.

Imprint

The name of the printer or publisher, the place of printing and the date, given in a printed book.

The first imprints were those of printers rather than publishers, and appeared at the back of the book; they are generally known as COLOPHONS. However, as TITLE-PAGES grew in importance, the imprint moved there; and gradually the publisher's imprint came to be combined with the printer's imprint, ultimately sending the latter back to the end of the book whence it came.

Throughout the history of printing, and especially in times of strife, the imprint was intended as much for the benefit of the authorities as it was for the reader. Indeed, since 1799 English law has required the name and abode of the printer to be given on all printed matter, intended for public distribution; Scottish law has a similar requirement.

The cataloguer should always use some caution in relying upon imprints for bibliographical information; sometimes they are straightforwardly false, more often merely inaccurate, as when publication is delayed until a year following the printing of the sheets, when correction might have been costly, or even a year after the distribution of the book, by which time it would have become virtually impossible. An extreme (though innocent) example of this is the Officina Bodoni edition of *The Poems of W. B. Yeats*, 1949; the sharp-eyed reader of catalogues might find it strange that a signed, limited edition appeared ten years after the poet's death, and nurse all kinds of suspicions of both publisher and bookseller. However, the explanation is a rational one; the sheets were printed, and signed by Yeats, shortly before his death in 1939, but publication was delayed by the Second World War.

Incunabula

Keith Fletcher

The word *incunabula* (plural, the singular is *incunabulum*) derives from the Latin *cunae*, a cradle, and is said to have been coined by the Parisian bibliographer, Philippe Labbe (1607–67) to describe the early art of printing. It was not until the late eighteenth century that it began to be used in its modern sense to mean the books themselves, and now, having achieved the status (and precision) of a technical term, it is used specifically to describe those books produced with movable type in the period from the invention of printing to the end of the year 1500. (In recent times it has sometimes been appropriated for use, in modified form, in other bibliographic fields, for example 'photographic incunabula' to denote the earliest books on that subject).

Page from *Biblia Sacra*, printed by Johannes Gutenberg c. 1454. [Maggs Bros Ltd]

    The story of the invention of printing, of Gutenberg and Fust and Schoeffer, has been told and retold, augmented and argued, many times; but it is surprising, as Alan Thomas has pointed out, that an event so influential and important in the development of mankind, and one in which all the participants must, of necessity, have been literate, should have no eyewitness account and so little contemporary documentation. The fact is that most of what we know has been pieced together from very fragmentary evidence, deduced from legal records, entries in parish or guild registers, and above all from careful and prolonged examination of the books themselves. From this evidence it is now generally accepted that printing with movable type was developed in Mainz by Johannes Gutenberg in the early 1450s (few people today still press the claim of Laurens Janszoon Coster of Haarlem to have printed with movable type in the early fifteenth century); and while there are various versions of the subsequent history of the invention – of what became of Gutenberg, and just how ruthless Johann Fust was in depriving him of the fruits of his genius – its success was immediate and understandable.

Printing was an early form of mass production, comparable with the best efforts of the Industrial Revolution 300 years later, and as with all good inventions, it arrived to fill a specific need – that of the growing mass of literate people spawned by the Renaissance and the Reformation. And again like its industrial counterparts, being a commercial product, the key to its success was 'distribution'. Though theology in all its branches was the most common subject-matter of printing, and the Church the source of educated book-buyers, it is no accident that the city-state of Venice, with its enormous mercantile empire, had in its few square miles more printers and printed more books during the fifteenth century than any other country in Europe. The fifteenth-century printers had much more in common with Henry Ford than they are given credit for. We tend to view the best of their products as objects of fine craftsmanship with an individuality quite incompatible with mass-production. Yet, however beautiful the design, exquisite the execution and full of character the finished product, Henry Ford should not be entirely forgotten. The study of incunabula often requires an insight into the printer's mind and methods, and the puzzle as to why a printer produced his book in a particular way may suddenly be resolved when one realizes that it was perhaps a commercial decision, rather than an artistic one.

People outside the world of antiquarian books often express surprise that books from the fifteenth century still exist; and are still more astonished that they can actually be bought, sometimes for relatively modest sums. Of course the supply is not what it was; even in the early years of this century, Jacques Rosenthal in Munich, Leo Olschki in Florence or Baer in Frankfurt could still issue catalogues with up to 3500 incunables in each; but neither are they yet as impossibly rare as many people believe. Most common are still the Venetian imprints. Produced in large quantities for distribution through the Serenissima's trading network, they begin, well before most other countries' books, to show definite signs of mass-production. The paper is no longer strong and white, but often grey with impurities and lacking in body; and the typography becomes less careful and more cramped for reasons of speed and economy. It should not be thought, however, that these were the only books to come from the early Venetian presses. Nicolaus Jenson, whose elegant roman type influences type design to this day, produced his masterpieces in Venice, as did Aldus Manutius, perhaps the greatest scholar-publisher of his age. A further area of influence that Venice exerted on early book production was in the field of illustration. The 'Venetian school' was vigorous and prolific, producing such masterpieces as the Malermi Bible, the *Hypnerotomachia Poliphili*, Dante and Terence, together with countless others illustrated in the so-called 'popular style'.

Following Venice in the current league-table of rarity come Italy and Germany, where, although original production figures may have been comparable with France, the latter's survival rate seems to be slightly lower. Despite the fact that the Low Countries produced incunabula in substantial numbers, they could not be described as plentiful on the market

A fifteenth century printed Bible, with Italian hand-illumination.

these days; and indeed, when they do come up at auction, they are competed for with unusual zeal by Dutch and Belgian dealers. Spain and Portugal's combined production must have been similar to that of the Low Countries but today their appearance on the market is even less frequent. It is not clear whether this is attributable to a low survival rate, or is the result of a lack of bibliographical research and of interest in the native heritage which has left a multitude of old libraries throughout Iberia lying neglected for centuries. Perhaps with the entry of Spain into the European Community and the late twentieth century all may be revealed; there is certainly much study still to be done on the subject. In Scandinavia and much of Eastern Europe printing arrived only in the last years of the fifteenth century, and though examples from these places do appear from time to time they are of almost legendary rarity (with prices to match!). And so to English incunabula, of which it may be said: all of them are rare and all of them, in almost any condition, are valuable. The single most striking feature of English incunabula is the very high percentage among them of vernacular texts. In addition to the usual bible stories, moral teachings and rules for the conduct of life, there are romances, myths and legends all designed for popular consumption by the lay public. Therefore, by their very nature, few copies were destined to lead sheltered lives in some scholarly library; they were literally read to destruction. And with the ever-increasing use of the English language in our modern world it is small wonder that the demand greatly exceeds the supply. Hence the fact that while a 'Jenson' lacking one leaf may be no longer acceptable, a 'Caxton' lacking most of its leaves can be still highly desirable.

This brief evaluation of the relative rarity and desirability of incunabula grouped geographically is necessarily highly simplified, and anyone dealing in today's market will soon find that his own experience will flesh out the bare bones given here. Before leaving the subject of desirability, three other factors should be mentioned that have a bearing on the matter: subject, language, and illustration. The traditional treatment of incunabula was to arrange them according to printer and location and to assess their worth from their place in a chronological list. Recently much more attention has been paid to the text, especially in booksellers' catalogues. Secular subjects are generally found more exciting than theological ones, and of these perhaps literature and science rank highest. With the decline of Latin as a universal language and the increase of interest in the text, it follows that in the main vernacular texts are the more desirable. Finally, whoever first maintained that one picture is worth a thousand words must have been an incunabulist – any illustrated book, from the glories of the Italian and German masters down to the meanest of woodcuts, is eagerly sought and hotly contested, and the occurrence of illustrations in even the dullest of texts often makes all the difference to a book's saleability.

The earliest evidence of the study of incunabula is a list published by J. Saubertus in Nuremberg in 1643 to celebrate the 200th anniversary of the invention. This was followed ten years later by Philippe Labbe's work, mentioned above, and then in 1719 by that seminal work, Maittaire's *Annales Typographici*, the first to arrange the books in the chronological order of publication. From these beginnings the literature on the subject has grown enormously and today would fill a good-sized library. The aim of the present essay is to provide those unacquainted with the subject with some practical hints on how to identify and research a fifteenth-century book, together with some signposts as to where in this vast literature they may be able to find the answers to their questions.

INCUNABULA

Most incunabula that come on to the market today have already been more or less accurately described by a previous expert and will come with some form of documentation. This, although it should always (no matter how illustrious the previous expert) be checked and verified, will at least provide a starting point for research. On those rare and exciting occasions when the research must start from scratch, the following observations may be helpful. Author, title and date are the traditional elements used to distinguish books, with the addition, in the case of incunabula, of the place of printing and the name of the printer. Title-pages, where it is usual to find this information in modern books, are rare in the fifteenth century; and where they do exist they are much more akin to the modern half-title, carrying a short title and perhaps mentioning the author, but very rarely the printer, the place or the date. All (or some) of this information, however, will be found in the colophon at the back of the book. The colophon may also give the author and title, but if not, these can usually be found in the heading on the first page of text. I have said that the colophon is at the back of the book; more specifically it is at the end of the text. Beware! That is not necessarily the end of the 'book' – various things can come after it – a register, indexes, addenda, for example – even misbound leaves! One useful aid to locating it can be the printer's device (if he uses one), for the colophon is usually to be found just above it. As soon as you have some elements of the book's identity you may proceed to the reference books for help. Start with Goff. Not only is it the most comprehensive short-title list available, it also gives full references to all the specialized bibliographies as well as very useful indexes and cross-references to variant forms of both authors and titles.

Once identified (even tentatively) the book should be collated. Various bibliographies give collations. My preference is for BMC whenever possible, but there are others that are equally good; for example GKW (though restricted to A–G), IGI (which only gives collations for exceptional rarities), Polain and Pellechet. Occasionally it may be necessary, *faute de mieux*, to resort to Hain, Copinger *et al.* to confirm a simple leaf count; but this should never be considered as satisfactory as a gathering-by-gathering collation. It is also possible that the book, particularly if it is Italian and printed in the latter part of the century, will carry its own collation in the form of a 'register' of signatures, usually on the colophon leaf. This is either (1) a simple list of signatures (for example, aa, bb, A, B, C, etc.) with the number of *bifolii* contained (for example, 'in quaternum' = eight leaves), or (2) a list of the first word of text of each *bifolium*. On these occasions remember that the Latin word 'alba' means white and signifies a blank page (or leaf) which may not always be present.

Reference to the printed signatures is the usual method of collating books, but their use was by no means universal in fifteenth-century printing shops. Indeed they are not found at all before 1472 (when Johann Koelhoff in Cologne was the first to use them) and many printers continued to use manuscript signatures at all times. These were usually placed right at the lower outer corner of the leaf so that they would be automatically trimmed off by the binder's knife. Their survival is therefore usually coupled with broad margins and a contemporary binding, and worth a catalogue note(!) (And if manuscript signatures are found, look also for manuscript catch-words at the bottom right of the verso of the last leaf of each gathering.)

For books without printed signatures it will be noted that bibliographies still give an alphabetical collation. For example [a4, b6, A–D8, E4, F–G6, H–X8]; the square brackets indicate that the lettering is arbitrary on the part of the bibliographer and not to be found in the book. Whether it is possible to check the copy in hand against this type of collation will depend very much upon the binding of the volume. The only way of ascertaining that each gathering has the correct number of leaves is by locating the centre of the gathering, as indicated by the stitching (and, by good fortune, by thin strips of vellum from an old manuscript used as sewing guards) and extrapolating from there. For instance, to check a volume against the collation given above count two leaves and look for stitching; count two + three leaves and locate the centre of signature 'b', and so on. If, however, the volume is so tightly sewn that the stitches are not visible then a simple leaf count must be relied on; though even here it is often possible to use a textual collation such as is given by Hain, Polain or GKW as further corroboration.

Once the book has been identified and its salient features and collation verified, this information should be recorded in a catalogue description. The old-style cataloguer usually arranged his information with the emphasis on printer, place and date, whereas modern practice favours the author and subject approach. The choice of style will probably depend on the book, or books, in question, as well as personal taste. There is no shortage of different models available both in booksellers' catalogues and those of the leading auction houses. A study of some of these will soon suggest a style suited to individual needs.

As will have been evident from frequent references to them, bibliographies are indispensable to the study of incunabula. I have used the conventional abbreviations (Goff, Hain, BMC, IGI, etc.) that are found in all catalogue descriptions, but a full identification of all these as well as several hundred others is given in Goff, Frederick R., *Incunabula in American Libraries. Third Census.* Kraus Reprint Co., New York, 1973. This list is fairly comprehensive and will be found most useful when reading catalogue descriptions. For those occasions when a specialized bibliography is needed the answer should be found in Theodore Besterman's *Early Printed Books to the end of the Sixteenth Century – A Bibliography of Bibliographies*, 2nd edition, New York, 1969, which is arranged, cross-referenced and indexed according to author, subject, printer, printing-places etc. Broadly speaking, these reference works fall into four main categories. Firstly, there are the 'listings', giving details of all known editions, the prime example of which is Hain, together with the supplements and appendices of Copinger, Reichling and Burger. First published in 1826, it remains to this day the foundation stone upon which all study of the subject rests. Secondly come the 'censuses' which may be either international such as GKW (*Gesamtkatalog der Wiegendrucke* – started in 1925, it has just reached volume ten and the letter 'G'), or they may be national such as Goff (cited above), Polain (for Belgium), IDL (for Holland), IGI (for Italy), and Pellechet (for France). Thirdly there are the catalogues of individual collections, from the monumental BMC (now the British Library) to private collectors such as Fairfax Murray or Lessing Rosenwald. Lastly, there are the 'specialized' reference tools: Davies on *Printer's Devices*, Hind's *History of the Woodcut*, Margaret Stillwell on *The Awakening Interest in Science*, and E. Ph. Goldschmidt on *Gothic Bookbindings* will serve to demonstrate the rich variety in this category, as well as the endless fascination of the study of incunabula.

Buhler, Curt F., *The Fifteenth Century Book. The Scribes; The Printers; The Decorators*, Philadelphia, 1960.

BMC: *Catalogue of Books Printed in the XVth Century now in the British Museum*, 1963–71.

Davies, H. W., *Devices of the Early Printers 1457–1560*, 1935.

Goff, Frederick R., *Incunabula in American Libraries. Third Census*, New York, 1964 (reprinted 1973).

Goldschmidt, E. P., *Gothic and Renaissance Bookbindings*, 1928 (reprinted, 1967).

Haebler, Konrad, *The Study of Incunabula*, New York, 1933 (reprinted, 1967).

Hain, Ludwig, *Repertorium bibliographicum, in quo libri omnes ab arte typographica inventa usque ad annum MD . . .*, Stuttgart and Paris, 1826–38.

IDL: *Incunabula in Dutch Libraries. A Census of Fifteenth-century Books in Dutch Libraries*, edited by Gerard van Thienen, Nieuwkoop, 1983.

IGI: *Indice Generale degli incunaboli delle biblioteche d'Italia*, Rome, 1943.

Labbe, Philippe, *Nova bibliotheca mss. librorum . . .*, Paris, 1653.

Maittaire, Michel, *Annales Typographici*, Vol. I, 'ab artis inventae origine ad annum MD', The Hague, 1719.

Pellechet, M., *Catalogue générale des incunables des bibliothèques publiques de France*, Paris, 1897–1909.

Polain, M.-L., *Catalogue des livres imprimés au 15. siècle des bibliothèques de Belgique*, Bruxelles, 1932.

Reichling, Dietrich, *Appendices ad Hainii-Coperingeri Repertorium bibliographicum. Additiones*, Munich, 1905–11.

Rosenwald, Lessing, *The Lessing Rosenwald Collection. A Catalog of the Gifts of Lessing J. Rosenwald to the Library of Congress, 1943–1975*, Washington DC, 1977.

Saubert, Johann, *Historia Bibliothecae Reip. Noribergensis . . . Accessit. Catalogus librorum proximis ab inventione annis usq: ad A. C. 1500 editorum*, Nuremberg, 1643.

Stillwell, Margaret, *The Awakening Interest in Science During the First Century of Printing, 1450–1550*, New York, 1970.

Thomas, Alan, *Great Books and Book Collectors*, 1975.

India paper

This paper, which is exceptionally thin and strong, enables publishers to offer a large number of pages in a compact format. Such editions can thus achieve gracefully the compression that once required the use of very small type and double column pages; Tolkien's *Lord of the Rings* trilogy in a single, quite slim volume is a typical recent example. India paper was originally made for the Oxford University Press and first employed in a bible issued in 1875; it is still much used for bibles and prayer books.

The term India proof paper describes thin paper originally imported from China in the eighteenth century for use in the proofing of engravings.

Inscription

Anything written by hand in a book, except perhaps for the details on a COLOPHON or limitation statement, is an inscription. Apart from presentation or association copies, virtually all inscriptions reduce a book's value, although the ownership signature of, say, a distinguished contemporary journalist, even if all attempts to turn the book into an association copy fail, does no harm. Otherwise, neat ownership signatures on the fly-leaf matter little, except in the case of very recent first editions, which are almost all so common that the slightest blemish renders them valueless to collectors. Ownership inscriptions in earlier books are viewed more tolerantly, and may sometimes hold some interest on their own account. Childish inscriptions on all but the most important children's books matter perhaps less than one might think, as many find them charming, but anything unsightly or embarrassing is bad news indeed. Colourful felt-tip pen inscriptions are particularly offensive, as are sums worked out in or on books; one of the present editors claims to have tested every such sum he has encountered, and never yet to have found one correct, which somehow makes it even worse.

In auction records the abbreviation 'inscr.' invariably (save for the odd error) refers to presentation inscriptions.

Inscriptions in foreign languages can be tantalizing; those in the roman alphabet can usually be guessed at with the help of the appropriate dictionary, but (for instance) Cyrillic handwritten letter-forms vary considerably from printed ones. A certain amount of initiative is necessary; a colleague admits to having worried for some days about a Chinese inscription before it occurred to him that his shop was across the road from a Chinese restaurant.

International League of Antiquarian Booksellers

The League was formed at a Congress held in Copenhagen in 1948 with a founding membership of six nations: Great Britain, France, Denmark, the Netherlands, Sweden and Switzerland. The aim of the League was to coordinate the work of the national associations in the spirit of friendship and mutual assistance expressed by its motto: *Amor Librorum Nos Unit.*

Membership of the League grew steadily (18 national associations are now affiliated to it); its Code of Usages and Customs has been adopted by each, though the League does not concern itself with the internal affairs of its members. It conducts its own affairs in English and French. A Congress is held every two years, and the League issues a directory of booksellers who are members of constituent associations.

ILAB has for some time sponsored a Triennial Bibliographical Prize for the best scholarly work in that field, and also produces a dictionary, due to be reissued, of terms relating to the antiquarian book trade in several languages, now including Japanese.

The League's newsletter keeps member nations in touch with one another and serves as a reminder of the world-wide nature of the trade.

The League comprises at present the national associations of the following countries: Australia, Austria, Belgium, Brazil, Canada, Denmark, Finland, France, Germany, Great Britain, Italy, Japan, Korea, Netherlands, Norway, Sweden, Switzerland and the United States of America.

Booksellers in the former Warsaw Pact countries are currently being encouraged to form associations and affiliate themselves to the League.

J

Jahrbuch der Auktionspreise
See AUCTION RECORDS

Japon
The terms japon and Japanese vellum (or Jap vellum) are often used almost interchangeably to describe the vellum-like hand-made paper much favoured by publishers of 'de luxe' editions. Japon is, however, a European imitation of the Japanese paper, which is in turn not to be confused with real vellum. These papers are stiffer and smoother than other hand-made varieties; their surface is easily disturbed by frequent handling.

K

Kalthoeber, Christian Samuel (fl. 1780–1816)
One of the German school of bookbinders working in London during the latter half of the eighteenth century, Christian Kalthoeber worked for a time with BAUMGARTEN and took over the business when Baumgarten died in 1781. He was considered one of the finest binders in the world at the height of his career, and his work was admired by George III and the Czarina of Russia.

His tools were frequently of classical designs, fillets, Greek-key, and wreaths with single motifs of anchors, mermaids and eagles.

Kelmscott Press
The first and greatest of the modern private presses, founded by William Morris in Hammersmith, West London, in 1891. Morris, a pioneer of the Arts and Crafts movement, had been interested in book design for some time, but towards the end of the 1880s he thought of using photographic enlargement to study the earliest movable types in minute detail. With characteristic thoroughness he set about analysing every feature of the first printed books; he persuaded the firm of Batchelors to provide suitable paper, but ink had to be imported from Germany. The first book to appear from the Kelmscott Press in 1891 was Morris's own prose romance, *The Story of the Glittering Plain*.

The first type designed by Morris for the Press was the Golden type, based on designs used by Nicolaus Jenson in 1476 and Jacobus Rubeus in the same year. But a Gothic type seemed more appropriate to some of the texts chosen by Morris, and so he designed the Troy type (influenced by Schoeffer, among others) and, later, a smaller version known as Chaucer, after the title for which it was created.

Although Kelmscott Press books have never met with universal affection, usually because of their density of ornament, their place in the history of printing has effectively placed them beyond the reach of criticism. The greatest book from the Press, Chaucer's *Works*, 1896, is generally considered to be one of the finest books printed since Gutenberg. A number of the Press's publications were enhanced by the illustrations of Morris's friend Edward Burne-Jones.

Sparling, H. Halliday, *The Kelmscott Press and William Morris Master-Craftsman*, 1924 (reprinted, 1975).
McLean, Ruari, *Modern Book Design from William Morris to the Present Day*, 1958.
Peterson, William S., *Bibliography of the Kelmscott Press*, Oxford, 1984.
────── *The Kelmscott Press*, Oxford, 1991.
William Morris: Ornamentation and Illustrations from the Kelmscott Chaucer, with an Introduction by Fridolf Johnson, Dover, New York, 1973.

The first page of the Kelmscott *Chaucer*, 1896.

L

Lackington, James (1746–1815)
James Lackington's significance in the history of bookselling in England lies firstly in his business methods and secondly in the unprecedently large shop that he built in Finsbury Square. He was an illiterate shoemaker scraping a living in the West Country when contact with John Wesley's new 'methodistical' creed, encouraged him to teach himself to read and write. He came to London and exchanged leather-bound shoes for leather-bound books, opening a small bookshop in Chiswell Street.

Lackington explains in his memoirs how he ran his business. He undercut his fellow-dealers, taking only a small profit, allowed no credit whatsoever, wrote his own catalogues (some 8,000 books twice a year) and bought up remainder stock to resell at full price. He seems to have had little aesthetic appreciation of fine books and was not too popular in the trade; he was first and last a businessman, working long hours, spending little on himself and ploughing back his profits into stock.

In 1795 Lackington opened 'The Temple of the Muses' in the newly built Finsbury Square. It was arranged on a circular plan below a central lantern; the better quality books were displayed on the ground floor, the cheaper stock in the galleries above. There was a 'lounging room', large light windows and an impressive circular counter. The shop was large enough for a coach and horses to be driven round the inside on the opening day, a feat which Lackington repeated later. The outside of the premises

Token produced by James Lackington with his own portrait, 1794

appears in an engraving in Elmes's *Metropolitan Improvements* of 1825.

Lackington retired early, leaving the business to his nephew George. It was bought later by Jones and Co., the publishers, and eventually burned to the ground in 1841. The shop was a feature of London life in the early nineteenth century and Lackington's account of contemporary bookselling practice holds much interest for his successors.

Lackington, James, *Memoirs of the First 45 Years of the Life of James Lackington*, 1791 (frequently reprinted up to 1815, and in 1974).

Laid down
Damaged or fragile leaves which have been backed with paper, or occasionally with

linen, are described as 'laid down'; the same term is sometimes used of the original spine or backstrip of a book that has been rebacked.

Large paper
During the eighteenth century it was a frequent practice for a small number of copies of a book to be printed on paper of a larger size, and often of a finer quality, than that used for the main print run. These copies (sometimes known as fine or imperial paper copies) were intended for presentation, for subscribers, or simply for sale at an increased price. The practice has continued in later times, though often as something of an affectation. Large paper copies are not necessarily of better appearance than their smaller fellows, as a typographically well-balanced page will often be marred by unduly wide margins; nor should they be assumed to be of either earlier or later date than the main edition, as simultaneous issue is more probable. Some reticence is also needed in the use of the term, as wide margins do not necessarily indicate a special copy. With these reservations, it may be said that large paper copies do in some instances represent a handsome and desirable variant, and that they have sometimes been associated with books that invite manuscript annotation.

Leaf book
An essay, generally produced in a limited edition, on a particular celebrated book, printer or period of bibliographical history, which has been enhanced by the inclusion of one or more leaves from a broken copy of the original book or books discussed. While leaf books may disconcert purists, their existence seems preferable to the destruction or abandonment of a severely incomplete copy of a rare and important book; they enable collectors of modest means to possess at least shards of the milestones of bibliographical history, and booksellers to make a little money. One of the most famous is Alfred E. Newton's *A Noble Fragment*, New York, 1921, which contains a leaf from the Gutenberg Bible.

Leather
Leather bindings are customarily identified in catalogue descriptions as morocco (or goatskin), calf (or vellum), sheep (or roan), or pigskin. Less common materials, now unfashionable, include deerskin, elephant or rhinoceros hide (once favoured for books on big game hunting and taxidermy) and sealskin, a handsome and hard-wearing leather resembling morocco.

Morocco This term had a specific meaning in the sixteenth century, when goatskin leathers of North African origin were imported into Western Europe from Turkey and the Levant; but it is now used to describe all goatskin materials, irrespective of their place of origin. The principal qualities of morocco are its ready receptivity to dye and its differing textures when tanned. Niger morocco, which comes from West Africa, is a particularly durable but fine-grained leather, much favoured for fine bindings; red and green, in many gradations, are the most common colours. Levant morocco, a looser-grained skin which is usually highly polished, was originally imported from the Near East, but more recently from North and South Africa; the South African skins are sometimes described as 'Cape Levant'. Oasis morocco also had its origin in South Africa, but the name is now used to describe a cheaper variety of Niger morocco, attractively grained but less durable.

The terms 'straight grain' and 'crushed'

morocco describe the appearance given to the surface of the leather by ridging or pressurizing processes during manufacture.

Calf In England, calf has always been strongly favoured as a staple binding material, comparatively inexpensive, quietly attractive in its natural colour but receptive to dye, and durable if properly tanned. These qualities made it a particularly suitable leather for trade, or bookseller's, bindings in the seventeenth and eighteenth centuries, and full or half calf predominates in many libraries formed in those times. Calf has no discernible grain, and its smooth surface has lent itself to a number of decorative processes. Tree calf, a once-popular staining technique which produced an effect similar to a wood grain, is still well regarded; but the process sometimes tended to harm the surface of the skin. Etruscan bindings, introduced by EDWARDS OF HALIFAX, involved the staining of the calf with acid, usually in terracotta and black, to achieve a classical style augmented with Greek and Roman motifs. A somewhat similar though more random effect is seen in Spanish calf, with the sides of the binding streaked or flecked by red and green acid dyes. These were chemical processes, as was that which produced the effect known as sprinkled calf, while the appearance of diced calf was achieved by stamping a pattern of diamond squares into the leather. Another variant, known as divinity calf, was much used in the nineteenth century for the binding of devotional books; a rather ungainly appearance was achieved by the use of soberly dyed calf, usually with bevelled boards, red edges and intersecting rules on the covers. Reversed (or rough) calf is a term used to describe calf skin used with the flesh side outwards. It is often found on large books bound in the sixteenth, seventeenth and eighteenth centuries, but in later years its use was largely confined to ledgers and similar volumes of records.

Russia, once widely used, is usually a variety of cowhide rather than of calf. Tanned by a special process developed in Russia late in the sixteenth century, it was given a smooth and distinguished appearance by the application of birch-bark oil; but it was inclined to deteriorate, especially at the joints, and is now little used.

Vellum Though usually made from calf skin, vellum had a quite different appearance as a binding material. The skin is untanned, de-greased by soaking in lime, and smoothed with pumice. The process produces a firm and durable surface, and though good-looking in its natural colour, the skin can be dyed. Its employment as a binding material can take the form of limp vellum, much used in the sixteenth and seventeenth centuries, or of a full or partial covering of boards, as with other leather bindings. Vellum has, however, a tendency to respond to variations of atmosphere by warping more or less irretrievably, and this can be especially disturbing when it is used over boards rather than in limp form. It has, on the credit side, the advantage of being more easily cleaned than many binding surfaces. Vellum has also been used since medieval times as a medium for writing or printing, and a few copies of private press books have often been printed on vellum.

Sheep Sheepskin is generally regarded as much inferior to morocco or calf as a binding material, as its surface is far less stable and it tends to split and tear more readily. It has little natural grain, but the roan variety, once popular as a cheap sub-

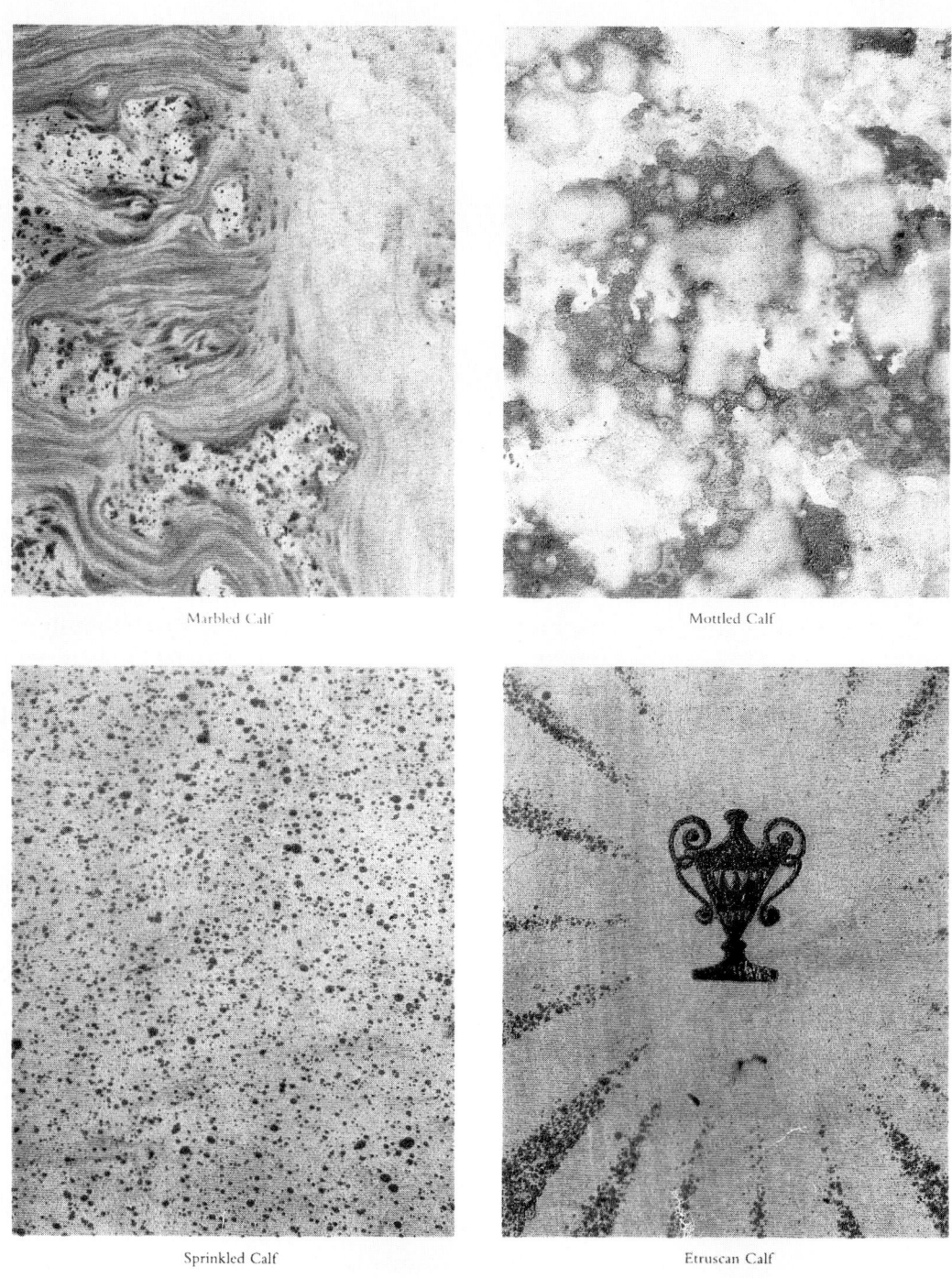

Some samples of leather. [Christie's]

stitute for morocco, was often given an imitation grain. Sheepskin has sometimes survived well on small books, where it is subjected to little stress; but skiver, the thinnest and cheapest variety, is notoriously unsatisfactory.

Pigskin Pigskin is a relatively little-used binding material, even though it wears well if suitably tanned. Its colour and texture are unsuited to conventional decoration, and its limited flexibility makes it awkward for the binding of small books. For larger volumes – the ASHENDENE PRESS's *Thucydides* is an example – it can look and feel appropriate, and has occasionally been cleverly simulated; but genuine pigskin can easily be recognized by penetrating, rather than superficial, hair-holes.

Description of bindings A word must be said about inconsistencies in the description of leather bindings. Full morocco (calf, etc.) is unequivocal. Half morocco (calf, etc.) is generally taken to indicate that spine and corners are leather bound, with cloth or paper sides; but this style is sometimes described as a three-quarter binding. The term 'quarter leather' usually describes a leather spine only, but is occasionally used for a narrowly bound spine with leather corners. 'Morocco-backed' boards, or 'vellum-backed' cloth is perhaps a better formula for 'quarter bindings'. However, these inconsistencies have no very serious consequences, and will no doubt be resolved in the fullness of time.

Left Book Club

The Club came into being in 1936 as a consequence of the social malaise and economic depression of the inter-war years. As the economy of the country lapsed from immediate post-war recovery into the poverty and unemployment of the early 1930s, workers, intellectuals and politicians were becoming increasingly aware of the menace of the dictatorships in Germany, Italy and Spain. The principal aim was to enlighten, and this prompted the formation of the Left Book Club. Victor Gollancz, together with Harold Laski and John Strachey, chose the books, issued monthly, 'at the lowest possible price'. The subjects covered included social and political issues, biography and international affairs. Membership of the Club grew rapidly, drawn largely from the cities, the universities and the industrial areas.

Pacifism and the prevention of war were among the principal objects of the Left Book Club, but so too was resistance to fascism; and by 1939 it was clear that the two aims were incompatible. The fortunes of the Club declined after the outbreak of war, and, though it continued throughout the war years, the last book, G. D. H. Cole's *The Meaning of Marxism*, was published in October, 1948.

Many prominent writers were published by the Club: Stephen Spender, George Orwell, Sidney and Beatrice Webb and Arthur Koestler among them. The books, in familiar red paper-covered boards, or limp orange linen covers, are little collected as a group today, but Orwell's *The Road to Wigan Pier*, Strachey's *The Theory and Practice of Socialism* and Koestler's *Spanish Testament* are among the important books which first appeared under the Club's imprint.

Lewis, John, *The Left Book Club, An Historical Record*, 1970.

Lettering-piece

A leather label on a book's spine is sometimes described more impressively as a lettering-piece. These labels are usually of thinly pared morocco, and for decorative effect are often of a different colour from that of the binding leather.

Levant
See LEATHER

Lewis, Charles (1786–1836)
Coming from a German family, as did so many of the best-known London binders of this period, Charles Lewis was apprenticed to his eminent fellow-countryman, HENRY WALTHER. Walther's refusal to allow his apprentice to move on from forwarding to finishing forced Lewis to work after hours practising the finer aspects of his craft and he eventually established his own bindery in Scotland Yard.

As his business prospered he moved to more fashionable premises in St James and worked for some time, together with KALTHOEBER, at William Beckford's library at Fonthill.

He followed a simple English classic style, paying much attention to basic craftsmanship; DIBDIN describes his books as opening 'on silken hinges'. Many of his tools were copies of those used by the great continental binders. Fine bindings bearing his stamp may well have been executed after his death.

Library of Congress
The Library of Congress, on Capitol Hill in Washington DC, holds a similar place in the life of America as does the BRITISH LIBRARY in this country, though it is not officially the national library. It is a deposit library for all material printed in the United States, is responsible for the NATIONAL UNION CATALOG and plays an important part in the development of bibliographical study and research.

Limited edition
It might be argued that all editions are limited, normally to the number of copies the publisher thinks he might possibly be able to sell; but in the world of rare books the term applies to an edition of a book, not necessarily the first, limited to a specified number of copies. Occasionally, a COLOPHON boasts the words 'Limited Edition' without giving a figure; but books are not always what they claim for themselves.

From a commercial point of view, the words can mean anything or nothing; limited editions exist in numbers varying from one to ten thousand, or more. The familiar law of supply and demand rules here as elsewhere. But, speaking broadly if not recklessly, any book printed in an edition of more than a couple of hundred can usually be tracked down, somewhere in the trade, without too much difficulty. Below that very approximate figure, public and private collections tend to absorb sufficient copies to reduce drastically the numbers available. However, particularly in recent years, artificial rarities abound, and even the most 'completist' collector may feel well able to live without some bizarre variant.

Many books issued without limitation statements were, of course, produced in smaller quantities than certain limited editions; indeed, other things being equal, a trade edition of, say, 500 copies is likely to be scarcer than a limited edition of the same number, presumably because it will have been less carefully kept.

Limited Editions Club
The Club was founded by George Macy in New York in 1929, with the aim of achieving in the United States the standard of book production – typography, presswork,

illustration and binding – that William Morris and his successors had been striving for in England in earlier decades. Macy's ideal, however, lay not in medievalism, but in the application of the best of contemporary illustration and design to the classics of world literature. He returned to earlier methods of bookselling by subscription: members of the club, limited to 1500, paid in advance for the 12 books a year that Macy published.

The first book, *Gulliver's Travels*, was followed by classical texts, the Bible, Shakespeare (in 38 volumes illustrated by 38 artists), French, German and Spanish texts, the Koran, and American novels. BRUCE ROGERS contributed many designs (including a reworking of early Florentine woodcuts for an edition of *Aesop's Fables*). Other illustrators and designers included Picasso, Matisse, Masereel, Mardersteig, Francis Meynell, Rockwell Kent and E. A. Dwiggins. The Club's logo, redesigned from time to time, is an outline, within a circle, of three seated figures reading.

When George Macy died in 1956 the Club faltered; but in 1979, it was taken over by Sidney Shiff and his family, who have continued to direct its fortunes. They pursue the original aim of combining subject matter and illustration in a harmonious whole for the benefit of the modern reader. Fewer books are produced than in Macy's day, but the quality remains high. Recent publications, often with illustrations by contemporary artists, have included works by Seamus Heaney, Kafka and Günter Grass. The Club's special contribution to modern book production has been the marriage of modern art with important world literature.

Petro, Pamela, The Limited Editions Club, *The Private Library*, Summer 1985 and Summer 1986.

Lithograph
See TECHNIQUES OF ILLUSTRATION

Livre d'artiste
A lavishly produced illustrated book whose distinguishing feature is that every aspect of its production was supervised by the artist whose original graphics it contains. As the term suggests, livres d'artiste originated in France, but important examples have been produced in Germany, the United States and (to a lesser extent) Britain. Almost all are valuable, some very much so; important names include Chagall, Miró and Picasso, among many others.

Loeb Classics
Dr James Loeb, a scholarly American banker, founded a classical library in 1910 to publish Latin and Greek texts in inexpensive editions. Heinemann published the series in England, where it proved highly successful. The original text and a scholarly translation appeared side by side and brought the enjoyment of classical literature to a wider readership.

The London Library
Founded in 1841 at the suggestion of Thomas Carlyle, the London Library is a private subscription library which offers a unique service to its members. Situated in St James's Square, it now houses about a million books in all European languages and on most subjects, though science, technology, and law are not widely represented.

Although a large reading room is available to members, with a comprehensive range of reference works shelved around the walls, the Library is particularly valuable to scholars, writers and readers because of the lending service it offers. Subscribers may borrow up to ten books at a time, more if they live outside London, and may retain them for a month or longer. A wide range of periodicals is also held and these, together with transactions of learned societies, can also be taken out of the Library.

The London Library catalogues for acquisitions up to 1950 are housed in the entrance hall in heavy red folios; accessions after that date are listed on index cards, but in 1990 the Library embarked on the installation of a computer system. Members fetch their own books and may browse freely along the shelves. An ambitious expansion scheme to extend the Library's facilities is due to be completed shortly.

The London Library provides possibly the greatest range of books for borrowing of any library in the world. Few works of significance published in England in the last few centuries are absent from its catalogues, and it is especially strong in the fields of literature, bibliography, history and topography. It is also one of the most curious and pleasant places to spend any part of a working day. David Cecil described it as 'a supreme example of what the voluntary spirit can achieve at its best . . . it is the spirit of a friend'.

Grindea, Miron (ed.), *The London Library*, 1978.
Wells, John, *Rude Words*, 1991.

Long S

The long S, resembling an f but without the cross-bar, follows the example set by manuscript lettering. It appeared at the beginning and in the middle of words (though not at the end) until about the end of the eighteenth century. It was discarded in favour of the ordinary S by John Bell in the first volume of his *British Theatre* in 1791 and is seldom seen after 1800, except as an affectation. McKerrow remarks that the Post Office London Directory was still using it until 1824 and adds haughtily: 'One would perhaps expect survivals in publications of this sort.' The presence or absence of the old-style letter can be useful for approximating a date for undated books.

Lowndes, William Thomas (1798–1843) The first edition of Lowndes's *Bibliographer's Manual of English Literature* was published by WILLIAM PICKERING in 1834. Lowndes felt that bibliography was a much neglected science in England; in his Preface he quotes Dr Johnson: 'By the means of Catalogues only can be known what has been written on every part of learning.' Starting with a list of some 20,000 entries he soon found the work expanding to some 50,000. It was reprinted by BOHN in four volumes in 1858, enlarged and corrected, and reprinted again – the last edition – in 1869.

Although much of the information provided by Lowndes has been corrected or amplified by subsequent study, his manual remains a useful general reference work for the bookseller. It includes concise notes on the merits of the books listed, as well as details of format, plates and other information. The numerous references to prices realized by books at important sales are now only of antiquarian interest, but there is much out-of-the-way information that cannot easily be found elsewhere.

M

Made-up copy
A book whose imperfections have been made good by the insertion of one or more pages, or plates, from another copy is known as 'made-up'. Such insertions are often difficult to detect, especially if the book has subsequently been rebound; but when evident they should always be mentioned in a catalogue description: 'pp 29–32 supplied from another copy' is the usual form of words. The avowed 'making-up' of a very scarce book may occasionally be defended; but generally the practice must be considered dubious. The term 'made-up' is not appropriate when missing leaves have been supplied in pen or type FACSIMILE, though this measure is no less in need of clear indication.

Marbled paper
Marbling, an ancient Japanese art taken up in the Middle Ages by Persians, is achieved by immersing paper (or its edges) in a solution of size on which float prepared water-colours swirled into patterns. The paper is soaked in the solution and the colour is then 'fixed'.

The use of marbled ENDPAPERS in England dates from about the middle of the seventeenth century, but the paper itself was usually imported, principally from Holland. Marbled paper was always a feature of quality craft binding rather than trade work. The patterns were consistent so that styles could be reordered; they bore such evocative names as Gold Vein, Stormont Antique Spot and French Shell.

When repairing an early book, a careful binder will try to find contemporary marbled paper to renew the endpapers.

Loring, Rosamond B., *Decorated Book Papers*, Cambridge, Massachusetts, 1952.
McKay, Barry (ed.), *Marbling Methods and Receipts from Four Centuries with Other Instructions Useful to Bookbinders*, Kidlington, 1990.
———, *Patterns and Pigments in English Marbled Papers*, Kidlington, 1988.
Woolnough, C. W., *The Whole Art of Marbling*, 1881 (reprinted Kidlington, 1985).

Mardersteig, Hans
See OFFICINA BODONI

Marginalia
Anything written in the margin of a book after it was published. (The term does not apply, for instance, to manuscript corrections put in before publication.) Although marginalia can be of considerable interest and importance – Boswell's annotations to the works of Johnson, for instance, would be vastly desirable – many, particularly in more recent books, are no more than defacements.

Mauchline ware
In 1825 the Smith brothers of Mauchline in Ayrshire began producing wooden snuff-boxes and other knick-knacks decorated with transfers of Scottish views and tartans. Mauchline ware, which by this time included bookbindings, enjoyed considerable success at the Great Exhibition of 1851. The wood used was usually sycamore and

the illustrations were clear and attractive. Queen Victoria's love of Scotland helped to boost sales but production slowed down after the First World War and finally ceased in the 1930s.

Mauchline ware bindings, though attractive in appearance, are impractical for readers; the spines are often fragile and the wooden boards too weighty for their contents.

Baker, John, *Mauchline Souvenirs*, Aylesbury, 1985.
Buist, J. S., *Mauchline Ware*, Burns Chronicle, 1977, Fourth Series, Volume II.

Mearne, Samuel (1624–83)
Mearne was appointed bookbinder to Charles II at his Restoration in 1660. His earlier career, after he had completed his apprenticeship as a binder, had been in selling books, but he came to prominence in his royal appointment, although he often had difficulty in obtaining payment. Mearne's earliest bindings were often blind tooled, the designs becoming more decorative and the spines more elaborate as time went on. Many of the books he bound incorporated the Royal cipher in the design and were of a religious nature. His tools were often flowers and animals mentioned in the Bible: roses, lilies, lions, etc., sometimes with cottage-roof borders or coloured onlays, and a painting on the fore-edge under the gilt. Samuel Mearne was succeeded by his son, Charles, but many of his unnamed contemporaries, producing work of equal quality, are known only by their style and their tools, e.g. The Queen's Binder, the Royal Heads Binder, the Naval Binder.

Nixon, Howard M., *English Restoration Bookbindings*, 1974.

Medical books
See SCIENCE AND MEDICINE

Middleton, Bernard (1924–)
Having trained at the British Museum, Middleton was manager of the ZAEHNSDORF bindery until he set up his own workshop in 1953. He was a founder member of Designer Bookbinders, and has written several important books on bookbinding. His designs are often geometric in conception and are usually signed with his monogram.

Military and Naval Books
Tony Gilbert

'No kind of history so fascinates mankind as the history of wars . . . Brilliant exploits, deeds of valour and of self-devotion . . . the surrounding incidents, the pomp and circumstance, the actual conflict, the all changing scenery, even the horror and devastation are so picturesque, that the gravest historian must feel how much of the interest of his work will be centred in those pages which glow with the lurid light of war.' Gen. Sir E. B. Hamley (1824–93).

MILITARY AND NAVAL BOOKS

The art of war

Of the classical authors whose works were printed in the fifteenth century, the best known and most likely to be encountered today is Vegetius, whose *De Re Militari* is important for its study of the Romans and their methods; first published in 1475, it was translated into English by John Sadler in 1572. One of the best editions is the Augsburg of 1476, which incorporated the superb woodcuts of Robertus Valturius from his *De Re Militari* of 1472; these depict both naval and military machines of war, including a fantastic missile-firing dragon. Another early authority used by Vegetius was S. Julius Frontinus: *The Stratagemes, Sleyghtes, and Policies of Warre*, translated by Richard Morysine, appeared in 1539. In his turn, Frontinus was recommended by Ælian, and in 1616 John Bingham issued *The Tactiks of Ælian or Art of Embattailing an Army after ye Grecian Manner*, with a second part in 1629. Much praised, and used extensively in the Thirty Years War, it was frequently bound with the works of Vegetius and Frontinus in the sixteenth and seventeenth centuries.

Roger Ascham dedicated his *Toxophilus* to Henry VIII in 1545. A skilled archer, he would have approved of the sentiments expressed in Peter Whitehorne's 1560 translation of Nicolò Machiavelli's *The Arte of Warre*, in which the Harquebus is described as a weapon suitable only for frightening the simple country folk. However, the firearm was triumphant, as is evident in Jacob de Gheyn's *The Exercise of Armes for Calivres, Muskettes and Pikes*, published in English in 1607 out of gratitude to the British who fought for the United Provinces under Prince Maurice of Nassau. The 117 magnificent plates, especially fine when found coloured, illustrate the development of arms and costumes of the period.

The first Englishman to write on gunnery, in 1587, was William Bourne in *The Art of Shooting Great Ordnaunce . . . Eyther by Sea or by Lande*, though perhaps the best edition is that of 1643 where it is combined with the equally renowned Robert Norton's *The Gunners Dialogue with the Art of Great Artillery*. In the study of pyrotechnics, the earliest English exponents were Francis Malthus with *A Treatise on Artificial Fireworks both for Warres and Recreation*, 1629, and John Babington in his *Pyrotechnica*, 1635. Two other excellent works, both published in 1639, are Robert Norwood's *Fortification or Architecture Military*, and *The Animadversions of Warre* by Robert Ward, the former the earliest English book devoted entirely to its subject, the latter a fine work on all aspects of the art of war.

Two French works of some significance are both by famous marshals, de Vauban and de Saxe: the very rare first English translation of de Vauban's *The New Method of Fortification*, 1691, and Count Maurice de Saxe's *Reveries, or Memoirs upon the Art of War*, 1757, containing 40 fine copper plates. De Saxe apparently wrote his *Reveries* while ill, over 13 nights, 'to kill time'. An important series of six works in English were those of the German-born John Muller, starting in 1747 with *The Attac* (sic) *and Defence of Fortified Places*; all of these ran to several editions. Karl von Clausewitz's outstanding contribution to military (and political) thought, *Vom Kriege*, was published posthumously by his widow in three volumes, 1832–4. The best English edition is that of Col. J. J. Graham. Two Crimean War veterans call for mention. Captain Lewis (or Louis) Edward Nolan, of Balaclava fame, wrote the scarce *The Training of Cavalry Remount Horses, a New System*, with 21 plates by Alken, in 1852, and the better known *Cavalry; Its History and Tactics* in

MILITARY AND NAVAL BOOKS

1853. Gen. Sir Edward Bruce Hamley, also a veteran of the 1882 Egyptian Campaign, published his oft-reprinted *The Operations of War Explained and Illustrated* in 1866.

To turn to an author of whom much more later: Capt. B. H. Liddell Hart's classic study, *The Strategy of Indirect Approach*, 1941, was much revised and expanded in subsequent editions. The fourth-century Chinese classic, *The Art of War*, by Sun Tzu, best known in its 1963 translation by Samuel B. Griffith, is a work much praised by Liddell Hart, who supplied the introduction.

Military campaigns and battles

An extremely scarce study of ancient Greek warfare is W. W. Tarn's *Alexander the Great*, two volumes, 1948. A slim companion work is G. W. Marsden's *The Campaign of Gaugamela* (Alexander's defeat of the Persian Darius), 1964. Two influential and eminently collectable authors, Maj.-Gen. J. F. C. Fuller, and the previously mentioned Capt. Liddell Hart, also wrote on ancient warfare, among many subjects. A list of Fuller's best works must include *British Light Infantry in the Eighteenth Century*, 1925, *The Generalship of Alexander the Great*, 1958 and *Julius Caesar – Man, Soldier and Tyrant*, 1965. Fuller's opus magnum is the two-volume *Decisive Battles: Their Influence Upon History and Civilisation*, 1939–40, expanded to three volumes in 1954–6, to incorporate World War Two. Liddell Hart's list is no less impressive: *A Greater than Napoleon, Scipio Africanus*, 1927, *Sherman, The Genius of the Civil War*, 1930, *The Ghost of Napoleon*, 1933 and *T. E. Lawrence – In Arabia and After*, 1934.

An American author who did not quite complete his series on the great captains is Lt.-Col. T. A. Dodge. Published in Boston, his studies of the life and times of Alexander and Gustavus Adolphus came out in 1890, Hannibal in 1891, Caesar in 1892 and finally the

Field Marshal Count Maurice de Saxe, *Reveries or Memoirs Upon the Art of War*, 1757.

four-volume *Napoleon*, 1904–7. A further four volumes on Frederick the Great were advertised as completing the series but were never issued.

A work originally envisaged as a four-volume set, but whose eventual 20 volumes take pride of place in many collections, is The Hon. (later Sir) John W. Fortescue's *A History of the British Army*, 1899–1930. With maps throughout the text and in the six separate map volumes, and with a text ranging from 1066 to 1870, it has no rival. However, Sir Charles Oman did match Fortescue's expertise with his own peerless work, albeit covering a shorter period: *A History of the Peninsular War*, seven volumes, 1902–30. Mention must also be made of Oman's two other classic works – *A History of the Art of War in the Middle Ages*, 1898, expanded into two volumes in 1924, and *A History of the Art of War in the Sixteenth Century*, 1937.

Two very different but equally scarce accounts of the Thirty Years War are Sir Lionel Cust's *Lives of the Warriors of the Thirty Years War*, 1865, curious for its passport-size photographic portrait illustrations, and Professor Michael Roberts's *Gustavus Adolphus, A History of Sweden, 1611–1632*, two volumes, 1953–8. For the English Civil War, a well-known contemporary account is Joshua Sprigge's *Anglia Rediviva . . . Being the History . . . of the Army . . . under Sir Thomas Fairfax*, 1647, with its folding view of the Battle of Naseby and (frequently missing) portrait frontispiece of Fairfax. Two later and sought-after titles are *Cromwell as a Soldier*, by Lt.-Col. T. S. Baldock, 1899, and *The Regimental History of Cromwell's Army* by Sir Charles Firth, two volumes, 1940.

The prolific William Coxe produced a fine work, as well as a superb specimen of printing, with his three-volume *Memoirs of John Duke of Marlborough*, 1818–19, with its splendid folding and coloured battle maps, portraits and facsimile documents. Sir Winston Churchill's tribute to his illustrious ancestor, *Marlborough, His Life and Times*, four volumes, 1933–38, is also well illustrated and nicely produced, even if the plum-coloured cloth is invariably faded on the spines – a problem avoided by those fortunate enough to track down one of the 155 signed copies in orange morocco.

Brief mention should be made of several key books covering the remainder of the eighteenth century, up to the Napoleonic Wars: *Fontenoy and Great Britain's Share in the War of the Austrian Succession, 1741–48*, 1906, by F. H. Skrine; *His Britannic Majesty's Army in Germany during the Seven Years' War*, 1966, by Lt.-Gen. Sir Reginald Savoury; and finally, the fine quarto by Captain John Drinkwater, *A History of the Siege of Gibraltar*, 1785, with its folding copper-engraved plates.

With the Napoleonic Wars, and more specifically the Peninsular War in Spain and Portugal, we come to the most popular area for military history. Oman's *Wellington's Army, 1809–14*, 1912, is an indispensable handbook, while a sound introductory work for the whole period is David G. Chandler's *The Campaigns of Napoleon*, 1967. For the early part of the Wars Col. R. W. Phipp's *The Armies of the First French Republic and the Rise of the Marshals of Napoleon I*, five volumes, 1926–39, is an uncommon set. For the Emperor himself, there is the elusive *Napoleon as a General*, by Count Yorck von Wartenburg, two volumes, 1902. Of the more contemporary accounts of Waterloo, the best is probably Capt. William Siborne's *History of the War in France and Belgium in 1815*, two volumes, 1844, with its fine atlas of maps and plans, engraved by a process that reveals the contours of the ground when a light is shone on the maps from a certain angle. The finest account

Capt. G. Trevelyan Williams, *The Historical Records of the 11th Hussars, Prince Albert's Own*, 1908.

MILITARY AND NAVAL BOOKS

is the exceedingly rare *Napoleon and Waterloo, the Emperor's Campaign with the Armée du Nord, 1815,* by Captain A. F. Becke, two volumes, 1914. A more contemporary counterpart to Oman's work is Maj.-Gen. Sir W. F. P. Napier's *History of the War in the Peninsula and the South of France,* six volumes, 1828–40. This is a handsome set, with 55 maps, but the text is somewhat flawed by the airing of personal grievances. More reliable, perhaps, is Lt.-Col. John Gurwood's editing of *The Dispatches of Field Marshal The Duke of Wellington . . . from 1799 to 1818,* 13 volumes, 1837–9, including the elusive index, though the best edition is that in eight volumes, 1844–7.

From other works on the Peninsular war, a short selection combining accuracy, rarity and popularity can be mentioned: Sir Robert Ker Porter's *Letters from Portugal and Spain . . . 1808–9,* 1809, with six aquatint plates; Col. W. Tomkinson's *The Diary of a Cavalry Officer . . . 1809–15,* 1894; Lt. William Grattan's *Adventures with the Connaught Rangers, 1804–14,* 1847 (and his sequel of 1853), Baron C. Ompteda's *Memoir and Letters of . . ., Col. in the King's German Legion,* 1894; James Anton's *Retrospect of a Military Life . . .,* 1841; *The Autobiography and Services of Sir Jas. McGrigor, Bart., late Dir. Gen. of the Medical Dept.,* 1861, Capt. Sir John Kincaid's *Adventures in the Rifle Brigade . . . 1810–1815,* 1830; Col. John Leach's *Rough Sketches of the Life of an Old Soldier . . .,* 1831; William Surtees' *Twenty-Five Years in the Rifle Brigade,* 1833; Brig.-Gen. F. C. Beatson's *With Wellington in the Pyrenees . . . 1813,* 1914; and his two later works. The hundred years between Waterloo and the outbreak of the Great War is covered by books relating to the Crimean War, the Indian Mutiny and the Franco–Prussian, Zulu, Boer and Russo–Japanese wars. William Kinglake's *The Invasion of the Crimea,* eight volumes, 1864–87, is still unsurpassed, as is J. W. Kaye and Col. G. B. Malleson's *A History of the Sepoy War in India, 1857–8,* three volumes, 1864–76, and *The History of the Indian Mutiny, 1857–9,* three volumes, 1878–80, which should be augmented by the Analytical Index compiled by F. Pincott, 1880. The best English work on the American Civil War, and quite possibly the finest military biography ever written, is Lt.-Col. G. F. R. Henderson's *Stonewall Jackson and the American Civil War,* exceedingly scarce in the two-volume 1898 first edition. Col. Henderson also wrote two fine works on the Franco–Prussian War, *The Battle of Spicheren . . . 1870,* 1891, and *The Battle of Worth,* 1899, whilst Michael Howard's *The Franco–Prussian War . . . 1870–71,* 1961, is a fine overall study. *The Narrative of the Field Operations Connected with the Zulu War of 1879,* 1881, compiled by J. S. Rothwell, is almost impossible to find, and the 1907 reprint is also rare. Other contemporary accounts of this campaign are *The South African Campaign, 1879,* by J. P. MacKinnon and Sydney Shadbolt, and F. E. Colenso and Lt.-Col. E. C. L. Durnford's *History of the Zulu War and Its Origins* – both published in 1880. Shadbolt also produced a two volume account of *The Afghan Campaigns of 1878–80,* 1881–2, with fine portrait photographs. Sir Winston Churchill's first two published works were both admirable campaign studies: *The Story of the Malakand Field Force,* 1898, and the finely illustrated *The River War, An Historical Account of the Reconquest of the Sudan,* two volumes, 1899. Churchill also wrote two well-regarded Boer War books, *London to Ladysmith via Pretoria,* 1900, and *Ian Hamilton's March,* 1901. The standard account is Maj.-Gen. J. F. Maurice and H. Grant's *History of the War in South Africa, 1899–1902,* four volumes of text and four of maps, 1906–10, though *The Times History of the War in South Africa,* seven volumes, 1900–09, edited by L. S. Amery, is perhaps more

15th Ludhiana Sikhs, from *The Armies of India*, by Maj. G. F. MacMunn, 1911.

accessible. There are several extensive official and semi-official accounts of the Russo–Japanese War, all of them quite scarce; of other works, the best are perhaps Gen. Sir Ian Hamilton's *A Staff Officer's Scrap Book . . .*, two volumes, 1905–7, and Charles A'Court Repington's *The War in the Far East*, 1906.

For the events leading to the start of the Great War, there is the elusive *The Origins of the War of 1914* by Luigi Albertini, three volumes, 1952. The various British official histories are invaluable, if a little dry. First and foremost is Brig.-Gen. Sir James E. Edmonds's massive *Military Operations in France and Belgium, 1914–1918*, 26 volumes of text, maps and appendices, 1922–47. The most popular of the other multi-volume sets is *Gallipoli*, four volumes, 1929–32 by Brig.-Gen. C. F. Aspinall-Oglander. Of the single-volume official histories, Lt.-Col. Charles Hordern's *East Africa, August 1914–September, 1916*, Volume I (all published), 1941, and Brig.-Gen. F. J. Moberly's *Operations in Persia, 1914–1919*, 1929, are the rarest.

Three sets worthy of mention are Winston Churchill's *The World Crisis*, five volumes in six, 1923–31 (including the elusive final volume); the 22 volumes of *The Times History of the War, 1914–20*, in red cloth or morocco; and Sir Arthur Conan Doyle's *The British Campaign in France and Flanders*, six volumes, 1916–20. A brief list of other titles should include Gen. Sir Ian Hamilton's *Gallipoli Diary*, two volumes, 1920, Col. T. E. Lawrence's *Revolt in the Desert*, 1927, John Buchan's *The History of the South African Forces in France*, 1920, Gen. P. E. Von Lettow-Vorbeck's *My Reminiscences of East Africa*, 1920, and the extraordinary Lt.-Col. A. G. Martin's *Mother Country Fatherland, The Story of a British Born German Soldier*, 1936. More recent studies include Alistair Horne's *The Price of Glory – Verdun, 1916*, 1962, Alexander McKee's *Vimy Ridge*, 1966, and Martin Middlebrook's *The First Day of the Somme, 1st July, 1916*, 1971.

Military aviation came of age in the Great War, and the British Official History, *The War in the Air*, seven volumes, 1922–37, by Walter Raleigh and H. A. Jones, is a worthy account. Fred. T. Jane's *All the World's Airships* (later renamed Aircraft) was started as an annual in 1909, and all the wartime issues are desirable. Claude Graham-White and Harry Harper co-authored several fine works, such as *Aircraft in the Great War: A Record and Study*, 1915. Other useful titles are E. C. Middleton's *The Great War in the Air*, four volumes, 1920, W. A. Bishop's *Winged Warfare; Hunting the Huns in the Air*, 1918; F. Gibbon's *The Red Knight of Germany; Baron von Richthofen*, 1930; Harold Rosher's *In the R.N.A.S.*, 1917; and Kenneth Poolman's *Zeppelins Over England*, 1960. Lastly, a fine technical study is J. M. Bruce's much sought-after *British Aeroplanes, 1914–18*, 1957.

The Official Histories are just as significant for the Second World War as for the First, from the multi-volume sets on *Grand Strategy*, *The War Against Japan*, and *The Mediterranean and the Middle East*, to the single-volume *The Campaign in Norway*, 1952, by T. K. Derry and the controversial *S.O.E. in France, 1940–44*, by M. R. D. Foot, 1966, of which the first printing was recalled by the publishers.

For a general account, Winston Churchill's *The Second World War*, six volumes, 1948–54 (which was actually first published in the USA) is still valid; a concise one-volume edition followed in 1959. From the Allied side, there is the scarce *Crisis in the Desert, May–June 1942*, 1952, by J. A. I. Agar-Hamilton and L. C. Turner, and the same authors' more common *The Sidi Rezeg Battles, 1941*, 1957, I. McD. G. Stewart's *The Struggle for*

Crete, A Story of Lost Opportunity, 1966, Field Marshal Sir William Slim's fine tribute to the Forgotten (XIV) Army in Burma, *Defeat Into Victory*, 1956, the heroic Violette Szabo's story by R. J. Minney, *Carve Her Name With Pride*, 1956, *The Memoirs of Marshal Zhukov*, 1971 and the much wanted *The Codebreakers, The Story of Secret Writing*, by David Kahn, 1966.

From the Axis side, there is the excellent insight given by Capt. Liddell Hart in his *The Other Side of the Hill*, 1948, the best edition being the second revision of 1951; Liddell Hart also edited *The Rommel Papers*, 1953. Other works include Field Marshal Erich von Manstein's *Lost Victories*, 1958, the strangely unfinished *Hitler's War on Russia*, two volumes, 1964–70, by Paul Carell (a pseudonym for the German journalist Paul Karl Schmidt), and Arthur Swinson's *Four Samurai, A Quartet of Japanese Army Commanders in the Second World War*, 1968.

Two of the best accounts of World War II aviation are Sir C. Webster's and Noble Frankland's *The Strategic Air Offensive Against Germany, 1939–45*, four volumes, 1961, and Denis Richard's and H. St. G. Saunder's *R.A.F., 1939–45*, three volumes, 1953–4. Also worthy of mention are Squadron Leader H. T. Sutton's *Raiders Approach, The Fighting Tradition of R.A.F. Hornchurch and Sutton's Farm*, 1956; Francis K. Mason's *Battle Over Britain*, 1969; Adolf Galland's *The First and the Last, the German Fighter Force in World War II*, 1955; and *Samurai*, by Saburo Sakai, 1959.

Among post-war studies, Gregory Blaxland's *The Regiments Depart, A History of the British Army, 1945–70*, 1971, is excellent, as is Julian Amery's elusive *Sons of the Eagle, A Study in Guerilla Warfare*, 1948, perhaps anticipating later Balkan problems.

Arms and Armour

The Duello, or Single Combat of John Selden, 1610, is thought to be the earliest authoritative work about duelling in English. However, the best known and best illustrated work on fencing is *L'Ecole des Armes* of Domenico Angelo, 1763, first translated as *The School of Fencing* by Rowlandson in 1787; the 47 copperplates are superb, and are reproduced to this day. Capt. Alfred Hutton was the pre-eminent Victorian authority, with his *Cold Steel: a Practical Treatise on the Sabre*, 1889, among his best books. *The Book of the Sword* by Capt. Sir Richard Burton in 1884, was the first of a projected series, but no further volumes were forthcoming. For a fine general illustrated study, there is nothing to match Francis Grose's *Military Antiquities Respecting a History of the English Army from the Conquest to the Present Time*, two quarto volumes, 1786–8, with 80 fine copper plates of arms, armour, firearms, artillery, etc. The best edition is that of 1812, which incorporates *A Treatise on Ancient Armour and Weapons, together with a Supplement . . . being Illustrations of Ancient and Asiatic Armour and Weapons*, adding a further engraved title and 61 copper plates. Sir Samuel Rush Meyrick's *A Critical Inquiry into Antient Armour . . .*, three volumes, folio, 1824, is finely illustrated with 80 plates, 70 of which are coloured aquatints, many heightened in gold and silver; an enlarged edition came out in 1844. Even more colourful is *Der Rittersaal, 1842*, by F. M. von Reibisch and Dr F. Kottenkamp, translated in 1857 by the Rev. A. Löwy as *The History of Chivalry and Ancient Armour . . . Knighthood, the Tournament and Trials by Single Combat*. This oblong quarto has 62 splendid coloured plates, 24 of which are folding, and those of mounted knights jousting in all their medieval finery are quite breathtaking. Later works of importance include Sir Guy Francis Laking's *A Record of European Armour and Arms through Seven Centuries*, five volumes, 1920–22. A rare supplement to this work is the 1925 *A Record of Armour Sales 1881–1924*, by F. H. Cripps-Day.

With regard to projectiles, both large and small, a classic work is the 1729 first English edition of *The Great Art of Artillery* by Casimir Simienowicz. Sir William Congreve first published his *Details of the Rocket System* in 1814, with a further work illustrated by coloured plates in 1827. William Greener, the Birmingham gunmaker, first issued *The Gun* in 1835; by 1910 it had reached a ninth edition. An enduring Victorian work was George Agar Hansard's *The Book of Archery*, 1840, while two interesting historical studies were Sir Ralph Payne-Gallwey's *The Crossbow, Medieval and Modern*, 1903, and *A Summary of the History, Construction and Effects in Warfare of the Projectile Throwing Engines of the Ancients*, 1907. Reverting to firearms, H. Ommundsen and E. H. Robinson's *Rifles and Ammunition and Rifle Shooting*, 1915, and Howard L. Blackmore's *British Military Firearms, 1650–1850*, 1961, are both significant, as is Lt.-Col. G. S. Hutchinson's *Machine Guns . . .*, 1938.

Unit histories

This sector of military literature is so extensive that those who wish to explore it are best advised to consult the bibliographies compiled by Roger Perkins and A. S. White (see final section); but mention should be made of the Historical Records series of Richard Cannon, of which about 70 were issued in the period 1835–53. Normally in blind stamped red cloth, there are also rarer full morocco-bound presentation copies, as well as two distinct issues of the coloured plates, lithographed or wood engraved; subjects range from The Life Guards to The Cape Mounted Rifles. Among the best known unit histories are Rudyard Kipling's two-volume work on *The Irish Guards in the Great War*, 1925, and Liddell Hart's ever-popular *The Tanks, The History of the Royal Tank Regiment*, two volumes, 1959. Lt.-Col. H. Moyse-Bartlett's *The King's African Rifles*, 1956, is representative of some excellent records of overseas units.

Colour plate books

The best-known naval and military colour plate books are those by J. Jenkins, *The Martial Achievements of Great Britain and Her Allies; from 1799 to 1815*, 1814–15, and the rarer and more desirable *The Naval Achievements . . . 1793–1817*, 1816–17, with 52 and 55 aquatint plates respectively. Infrequently, coloured portraits of the Duke of Wellington (in the former) and Lords Nelson and St Vincent (in the latter) may be found, whilst watermarks should be checked for pre-publication dates if better coloured copies are desired.

Some fine uniform books of the period are Frederick Baron d'Eben's *The Swedish Army*, 1808, with 25 aquatints, and C. H. Smith's *Costume of the Army of the British Empire, 1814*, 1815, with 61 plates. Some small but most unusual plates are a feature of J. Aspin's *The Naval and Military Exploits which have Distinguished the Reign of King George the Third*, 1820;

the frontispiece is normal, but the 33 (occasionally 34 or 35) plates are all circular, approximately 6.5 cms in diameter. Another excellent set from the same year is *The Naval Chronology of Great Britain . . . 1803–1816*, by J. Ralfe, in three volumes with 60 fine plates, though the colouring can be variable, and original coloured copies are scarce. The Crimean War is featured in E. T. Dolby's *Sketches in the Baltic*, 1854, with 17 coloured lithograph plates; one of these depicts the first act of heroism to be awarded the V.C., that of the future Rear Adm. C. D. Lucas throwing a live Russian shell overboard from HMS Hecla. This campaign is also the subject of the better known *The Seat of War in the East* by William Simpson, two volumes, 1855–6, with 81 coloured (or more commonly tinted) lithograph plates of the Charge of the Light Brigade and other scenes.

Some later uniform books include Walter Richards' two sets, *Her Majesty's Army*, three volumes, 1886–92, and *His Majesty's Territorial Army*, four volumes, 1910–11. For the Indian Army, W. Y. Carman's *Indian Army Uniforms*, two volumes, 1961–69, the earlier Cavalry volume being especially scarce.

Of the many books on honours and awards, one of the best illustrated is John Horley Mayo's *Medals and Decorations of the British Army*, two volumes, 1897, with 37 lavishly coloured plates. Sir O'Moore Creagh and E. M. Humphries's *The V.C. and D.S.O.*, three volumes, 1924, is a compendious work containing 1,748 portrait illustrations, while less weighty but no less rare is Sir John Smyth's *The Story of the V.C.*, 1963. A beautifully illustrated work on battle flags calls for mention: Samuel Milne's *The Standards and Colours of the Army*, 1893, in a limited edition.

Naval history

The cornerstone of any naval collection is Sir W. L. Clowes's monumental *The Royal Navy – A History*, seven volumes, 1897–1903, resplendent in its blue cloth gilt binding and admirably illustrated and indexed. History is even recorded on its title-pages, as one of the contributors, Theodore (Teddy) Roosevelt, progressed from Assistant Secretary, US Navy, through Colonel, US Army (the Roughriders), and Governor of New York State, to President of the USA during the time of the work's publication.

An earlier work of note is Samuel Pepys's *Memoirs Relating to the State of the Royal Navy of England*, 1690; Pepys was Secretary to the Admiralty, 1686–88. The first printed Signal Book was Jonathan Greenwood's *The Sailing and Fighting Instructions . . .*, 1714. The copper plates are hand coloured, and all copies seem to have a slight variance in illustration. Dr J. Campbell's *Lives of the British Admirals* was first published in four volumes, 1742–44; the best edition is that of 1779, with four engraved frontispieces and six fine folding engraved maps, though the most textually complete is the eight-volume 1812–17 edition of Henry Redhead Yorke. Thomas Riley Blanckley's *A Naval Expositor*, a fine work much enhanced by over 300 fine small copper engravings, ran to two editions in 1750 and 1755. However, the best known naval dictionary is William Falconer's *An Universal Dictionary of the Marine*, 1769, published as late as 1830 in a revised form with extra plates, by William Burney. Anglo-French feelings of the time are exemplified by this entry in the Dictionary: 'Retreat, the order or disposition in which a Fleet of French men of war decline engagement, or fly from a pursuing enemy'.

Of numerous fine technical works of the period, a rare one is Marmaduke Stalkartt's *Naval Architecture*, 1781, with text volume and 14 separate plans. The turn of the century saw the issue of the two best known works by the prolific David Steel: *The Elements and Practice of Rigging and Seamanship*, 1794, with its plates with movable volvelles, and *Naval Architecture*, two volumes, 1805, the atlas volume of 38 large draughts (39 in later editions) being quite scarce. In between these two works was published John Charnock's *A History of Marine Architecture*, three volumes, 1800–02, with 100 plates, several of which are often lacking, especially the draught of the *Flying Proa*.

1809 saw the publication of the first significant biography of Nelson, the Rev. J. S. Clarke and J. M'Arthur's *The Life of Admiral Lord Nelson*, two volumes, handsomely illustrated with copper engravings. The most famous, though, was Robert Southey's *The Life of Nelson*, two volumes, 1813, scarcer still in its 1814 second edition. Some time later, *The Dispatches and Letters of Vice-Admiral Lord Viscount Nelson*, seven volumes, 1844–46, were produced by Sir N. H. Nicolas. Of later biographies, Capt. A. T. Mahan's *The Life of Nelson . . .*, two volumes, 1897, is an excellent study (to rank alongside Mahan's many other fine works, especially *The Influence of Sea Power upon History, 1660–1783*, 1890); while in the twentieth century, there is still nothing to match Carola Oman's *Nelson*, 1947. Two fine accounts of Nelson's last battle are Julian S. Corbett's *The Campaign of Trafalgar*, 1910, and the extremely rare *The Naval Campaign of 1805 – Trafalgar*, two volumes, 1933, a translation by Constance Eastwick of Edouard Desbrière's equally elusive 1907 original. Yet another sought-after title is Arthur Bugler's *HMS Victory, Building, Restoration and Repair*, two volumes, 1966, the definitive work on Nelson's flagship with wonderfully detailed plans in the second volume.

A large set which gives contemporary accounts of people, places and events of Nelson's time and earlier is *The Naval Chronicle*, published by Bunney and Gold between 1799 and 1818 in forty volumes, containing over 500 plates, portraits and maps – though no two sets seem alike in their illustrations. Another fine set is *The Naval History of Great Britain*, by William James, five volumes, 1822–24, though the best edition is the third, 1837, in six volumes, with the continuation by Capt. F. Chamier; a seventh edition appeared as late as 1886.

The finest Victorian naval architecture work is the massive three folio volumes of *The Modern System of Naval Architecture*, by John Scott Russell, 1864–5, with 168 plates. The transition from sail to steam is well illustrated in C. R. Low's *Her Majesty's Navy*, three volumes, 1892, with its fine chromolithograph plates.

Lord Brassey founded in 1886 his *Naval Annual*, later to become the *Armed Forces Yearbook*, encompassing the armies and air forces of the world. Fred T. Jane started his remarkable annual, *All the World's Fighting Ships*, in 1898, refusing to use photo illustrations until the 1900 edition, as he considered them less accurate than his own drawings. All the early editions are rare, and others such as the 1947–8 Jubilee edition are also sought after. Another long running series, the publications of the Navy Records Society, was first issued in the familiar blue and white buckram in 1894, though now, some 130 volumes later, bound in plain blue cloth. The rarest of the series is volume 34, *Drawings of the Battle of Sole Bay*, 1907, consisting of ten large folding coloured plates and a pamphlet of text. Two timely studies of the Russo–Japanese War were Jane's *The Imperial*

Russian Navy, 1899, which he revised in 1904 to accompany *The Imperial Japanese Navy* of the same year.

For the 1914–18 War, *The Official History, Naval Operations*, by Julian S. Corbett and Henry Newbolt, five volumes in nine, 1920–31, is the standard work. A second edition of volume three, on the Battle of Jutland, was issued in 1940, making use of the German official history, but much of the stock of this volume was ironically burned during the Blitz. Perhaps a greater work is Arthur J. Marder's *From the Dreadnought to Scapa Flow – The Royal Navy in the Fisher Era, 1904–1919*, five volumes, 1961–70, with its good maps and illustrations and a fine critical bibliography. Marder also edited Lord Fisher's papers as *Fear God and Dread Nought*, three volumes, 1952–59. Other official histories of note are A. S. Hurd's *The Merchant Navy*, three volumes, 1921–29, and A. C. Bell's *A History of the Blockade of Germany . . .* 1937, both quite rare. A selection of other important works includes Admiral Sir Reginald Bacon's *The Dover Patrol, 1915–1917*, two volumes, 1919, and R. H. Gibson and Maurice Prendergast's *The German Submarine War 1914–18*, 1931. On the German side, there are *Admiral Hipper*, by Capt. Hugo von Waldeyer-Hartz, 1933, *Kiel and Jutland* by Cdr. Georg von Hase, 1921, and Cdr. Ernst Hashagen's *The Log of a U-Boat Commander*, 1931. Surely the most prolific author on the Great War at sea was Edward Keble Chatterton, with ten books ranging from *Q-ships and Their Story*, 1922, to *Beating the U-Boats*, 1943, all relying upon first-hand accounts.

In 1925 Hector C. Bywater published his remarkably prophetic *The Great Pacific War – A History of the American–Japanese Campaign of 1931–33*, predicting Pearl Harbor and the invasion of the Philippines. Also during the inter-war period several titles were published which are now virtually unobtainable, the most sought after being R. G. Albion's *Forests and Sea Power – The Timber Problem of the Royal Navy 1652–1862*, 1926, and Admiral Sir Herbert Richmond's *The Navy in the War of 1739–1748*, three volumes, 1920; another that is far from common is Cdr. J. H. Owen's *War at Sea Under Queen Anne, 1702–08*, 1938.

The Second World War Official History, Capt. S. W. Roskill's *The War at Sea, 1939–45*, three volumes in four, 1954–61, is both sought after and scarce, having been out of print for many years. Another fine official history is the South African, *War in the Southern Oceans, 1939–45*, by L. C. F. Turner, 1961. A selection of other good works includes Admiral Viscount A. B. Cunningham's *A Sailor's Odyssey*, the late Lt.-Cdr. Peter Scott's *The Battle of the Narrow Seas*, 1945, Sir Philip Vian's *Action This Day*, 1960, and Capt. Donald MacIntyre's *The Battle for the Pacific*, 1966; and the memoirs of Admiral Karl Doenitz, *Ten Years and Twenty Days*, 1958, and of Grand Admiral Erich Raeder, *My Life*, 1960.

A selection of significant books published since the Second World War would include Oscar Parkes' comprehensive *British Battleships, 1860–1950*, 1966, and its companion by Edgar J. March, *British Destroyers*, 1966. Alfred E. Weightman's *Heraldry in the Royal Navy Crests and Badges of H.M. Ships*, 1957, is yet to be superseded, as is *Medicine in the Navy 1200–1900*, four volumes, 1957–63, by J. J. Keevil, C. Lloyd and J. L. S. Coulter. Capt. Jack Broome's *Make a Signal*, 1955, is a detailed and amusing history of naval messages, while more serious scientific study is to be found in Lt.-Cdr. David W. Water's *The Art of Navigation*, 1958. Charles Hocking's *Dictionary of Disasters at Sea During the Age of Steam 1824–1962*, two volumes, 1969, is a fine work of reference, as is *Ships of the Royal Navy*, two volumes, 1969–70, by J. J. Colledge.

In closing, two long-established journals may be commended; as well as containing articles of historical importance, these are most useful for their reviews of books (especially the numerous reprints of classic works), their detailed reference sources and their general promotion of interest in naval and military studies: *The Mariner's Mirror*, the International Journal of the Society for Nautical Research, published since 1911; and *The Journal of the Society of Army Historical Research*, published since 1921. Both are issued quarterly.

Albion, Robert, *Naval and Maritime History, An annotated Bibliography*, Newton Abbot, 1951 (4th edn, with supplement by B. W. Larrabee, Mystic, Connecticut, 1972–88).

Cockle, Maurice J. D., *A Bibliography of Military Books up to 1642*, 1900 (reprinted 1978).

Cowie, Leonard W., *Lord Nelson, 1758–1805 – A Bibliography*, Westport, Connecticut, 1990.

Enser, A. G. S., *A Subject Bibliography of the First World War*, 1979.

—— *A Subject Bibliography of the Second World War*, 1977.

Falls, Cyril, *War Books, An Annotated Bibliography of Books About the Great War*, 1930 (reprinted 1989).

Higham, Robin, *A Guide to the Sources of British Military History*, 1972 (reprinted with supplement, New York, 1988).

Lake, Fred and Wright, Hal, *Bibliography of Archery*, Manchester, 1974.

National Maritime Museum, *Catalogue of the Library*, 5 parts in 7 volumes (all published), 1968–76.

Perkins, Roger, *Regiments of the Empire, A Bibliography*, Newton Abbot, 1989.

Riling, Ray, *Guns and Shooting – A Selected Chronological Bibliography*, New York, 1951.

Smith, Myron J., *World War I in the Air; a Bibliography and a Chronology*, three volumes, Metuchen, New Jersey, 1976–77.

Thimm, Carl A., *A Complete Bibliography of Fencing and Duelling*, 1891 (reprinted New York, 1968).

White, A. S., *A Bibliography of Regimental Histories of the British Army*, 1965 (revised, 1993).

Woods, Frederick, *A Bibliography of the Works of Sir Winston Churchill, KG, OM, CH*, 1963 (revised, Godalming, 1979).

Miniature books

Although some collectors of miniature books (and furnishers of dolls' houses) may limit themselves to the very smallest readable size of page, the generally accepted definitions require a height of no more than two to three inches. Craftsmen engaged in the production of such tiny books – printers, illustrators, typographers, binders – must be able to work to a scale necessitating the greatest precision, and many such volumes are of great charm.

Early miniature manuscripts and INCUNABULA provide evidence of a very ancient art. Printed books of the early period are usually of a religious nature: books of hours, breviaries, prayer books that can be held comfortably in a closed hand. Latin and Greek classics in miniature form were favoured in the seventeenth century, and by the eighteenth any printed work might well appear as a tiny reproduction. History, poetry and children's stories were printed as miniatures, frequently illustrated with woodcuts or copperplate engravings; some, published as a series, were housed in their own tiny bookcases.

The almanacs and calendars of the eighteenth and nineteenth centuries were conveniently portable, usually bound in decorative morocco with a matching SLIPCASE. Many charming little books were produced

Miniature book in filigree binding, 2½ × 1⅝ins. [H. M. Fletcher]

to encourage young people to read. Modern miniature books tend to be marvels of technical skill but have little in common with the craftsmanship of earlier examples.

Alderson, Brian, Miniature Libraries for the Young, *The Private Library*, Spring, 1983.
Bondy, Louis, *Miniature Books*, 1981.
Hodgson, J. E., Miniature Books for Collectors, *The Connoisseur*, August, 1936.
Houghton, Jr., Arthur, *The Collection of Miniature Books formed by Arthur A. Houghton, Jr.*, Sale Catalogue, 1979.
Spielmann, Percy, *Catalogue of the Library of Miniature Books Collected by Percy Edwin Spielmann . . . together with some Descriptive Summaries*, 1961.

Mint

A synonym for 'fine' which seems to have crept into the book world from that of coin collecting. Since books, unlike coins, are not minted, its use seems to many to strike an unhappy note. Cataloguers who use it tend to have a looser interpretation than others of the word 'fine', which they are liable to use in the sense of 'How are you? I'm fine, thanks' rather than 'A fine, crisp copy'.

Modern First Editions

Angus O'Neill

Most people know what an IQ is. But what does it measure? The consensus of opinion today is that what it measures is the capacity to perform in intelligence tests. Similarly, everyone reading this book will know that modern first editions are what modern first edition dealers deal in. But perhaps we can do a little better than this.

The word 'modern' seems out of place, now, when applied to Max Beerbohm or W. B. Yeats. But in John Carter's time 'modern first editions' went back as far as 1900, or even earlier, and they continue to do so today. Perhaps it is more helpful to think of the word not in the dictionary sense of 'pertaining to the present', but rather as pertaining to the Modern Movement in literature and art. The world of art has found a convenient way around the problem by designating more recent works as 'contemporary', thus defining 'modern' as being (very roughly) 1900–1950; but the phrase 'contemporary first editions' fails to appeal, largely because first edition collectors are after rarity, not availability, which the word 'contemporary' implies. So, to the disappointment of those who hesitate to be identified with purveyors of books that are in many cases still warm from the press, we seem to be stuck with the word.

Despite its faults, the word 'modern' does have the merit of recalling one of the very few really useful books on the subject, Cyril Connolly's *The Modern Movement*, 1965. Some might think that with Henry James he starts a little early, though not by far; and inevitably much has happened since the death of William Carlos Williams, his latest author. But his choice is as interesting and as responsible as one man's is ever likely to be, and his critical comments remain illuminating. Of course everyone has his reservations about Connolly; many feel, for instance, that he includes too many French writers at the expense of Germans or Italians. But he identifies the tradition with accuracy, and provides a basis for stimulating discussion; and there is no contemporary author collected today who does not owe much to several in Connolly's pantheon.

The other component of the phrase 'first edition' is dealt with under its own heading. But a word may usefully be said here about second and later editions. Collectors of the literature of earlier centuries often hold these in some esteem; sometimes, of course, this is because the 'first' is unavailable or prohibitively expensive, at other times because there are textual or historical changes; but second or third editions of Milton or Swift have a value. In general, second editions of Eliot or Woolf do not. As with all generalizations in the world of books, exceptions immediately leap to mind; the rule does not apply to Joyce, for instance, partly because there are so few 'A-items',[1] partly because the history of Joyce's problems with publishers, printers and censors is itself a fascinating theme for a collection. And the world has room for only a few collectors of the works of T. S. Eliot who disdain the London trade edition of *Poems Written in Early Youth*, 1967, preferring to wait for one of the 12 numbered copies of the 1950 Stockholm edition. But these are the exceptions, and the rule is that a miss is as good as a mile where modern firsts are concerned.

One debate that has rumbled on for decades, never acquiring enough energy to attain the status of a 'controversy', is what John Carter called 'following the flag'. Although this term has never really caught on, neither has any alternative, so it may as well remain. The question it poses is whether one should collect the first editions of a particular author by strict priority of issue, or whether one should concentrate on the first edition to be published in the author's own country. The problem usually concerns English first editions of American authors, or vice-versa; the solution is entirely a matter of taste. The general feeling today is that if, as with Hemingway's *Across the River and into the Trees*,

---

[1] Most author-bibliographies divide publications into at least three categories: the 'A' series (books wholly by the author concerned), the 'B' series (books with contributions by the author) and the 'C' series (periodicals with contributions by the author). Further categories often follow, but only the first three have passed into everyday usage.

Ernest Hemingway, *The Old Man and the Sea*, first edition, New York 1952. Acceptable copies in clean dust wrappers of this common title (75,000 copies were printed) normally sell for a few tens of pounds, but this exceptionally fine example would command a substantial premium.

1950, where the English edition appeared a few days before the American, the priority is slight and probably accidental, only a pedant would make many claims for the 'true first'; whereas if there were some deliberate and interesting explanation for an unexpected priority (as with Graham Greene's *Monsignor Quixote*, first published by a relation of the author's in Canada in 1982), the collector would rightly prefer the unusual. Less defensible is the tendency of many British collectors (and dealers) to satisfy themselves with first English editions, even of the most obviously American authors; they are easier to find, in Britain at least, but that was never the point of collecting.

Collectors of modern first editions are not only looking for books. Some seek literary periodicals in which their chosen authors appear; but the gradual decline of the institutional market has led to a situation where only the glamorous periodicals find ready buyers. Runs of *Blast* or *The Criterion* sell easily; odd numbers of *The Cornhill* don't. Almost all collectors, on the other hand, welcome the chance to add spice to their collections by including autograph material, usually in the form of letters or manuscripts, sometimes with presentation copies. Recordings of writers reading their own work are avidly collected; often, as with Joyce's reading of *Anna Livia Plurabelle* (an extract from *Finnegans Wake*), they provide easier access to a difficult work than any number of critical volumes. The desire to amass all kinds of related promotional and commemorative material (which scarcely existed until recent times) perhaps finds its zenith (or nadir) among collectors of Ian Fleming's Bond books, who gather up toy cars and posters with the enthusiasm of children. Paintings of, or by, writers often command prices rather higher than their intrinsic quality might lead one to expect; the daubs of D. H. Lawrence are an extreme example of that. Memorabilia in general are impossible to generalize about, except to urge some restraint; a gold-topped walking stick is one thing, an old pair of slippers another.

'COMPLETISM' might usefully be addressed here. This slangy but useful term identifies the practice of going for every last item in the bibliography, no matter how peripheral, trivial, dull, or unlikely. Completism is, as one might expect, not discouraged by booksellers who have an incomplete run of periodicals to shift, or a collection of translations into foreign languages. The extent to which individual authors are affected by it varies widely, but not unpredictably; collectors of Winston Churchill, for instance, tend to feel that the 'A' and 'B' items will use up enough of their space, time and resources, whereas T. E. Lawrence fanatics, given only a handful of primary targets, will happily accumulate anything which refers to him.

One constant problem which even now afflicts both dealers and collectors needs to be considered: the prevalence of hostility, on the part of surprisingly many fellow enthusiasts for the printed book, towards modern first editions. A number of possible explanations suggest themselves.

First is the perceived idea that the study of modern firsts requires less in the way of scholarship than other categories of book. This is easily refuted by even a casual glance at a bibliography by, say, Bloomfield or Gallup; the origins of this belief may lie in the fact that most twentieth-century books, being machine-made, do not always require the close physical analysis demanded by earlier books, but anyone with some experience will testify that modern firsts have quite enough bibliographical complications. This prejudice, though, is lamentably reinforced by the carelessness with which many first edition dealers catalogue their stock. Too many catalogues refer to 'J. R. R. Tolkein' and 'Louis MacNiece', for instance, and worse errors abound.

The second accusation levelled at modern first dealers is that of dust-wrapper fetishism. Traditionalist collectors have been heard to snort that they collect books, not dust-wrappers; and to an outsider it may seem strange that the presence of a wrapper can increase the price of a book tenfold or more. But all collectors value fine condition; and why not? Besides, those who disparage the importance of dust-wrappers are often quite happy to pay comparable premiums for nineteenth-century books in publisher's cloth or boards. And the undeniable attractiveness of many dust-wrappers, as well as their bibliographical importance, must excuse the collector's insistence on their presence. Whether one likes it or not, all but a handful of books published after 1939 are valueless (as first editions) without them.

The third line of attack centres on what is sometimes called 'flavour of the month' collecting. This criticism is somewhat harder to refute. The recent past is inevitably subject to more frequent reassessment than the established canon of 'classics', and even there changes occur more often than many realize. Other factors intrude: the death of Samuel Beckett, for instance, stimulated renewed interest in his work, and the Salman Rushdie affair has sustained prices for his earlier books which a few years ago seemed highly speculative. But many of the 'flavour of the month' accusations, while they could reasonably have been made during the boom years of the 1920s (to whose price levels, in real terms, we have never been in the slightest danger of returning), now turn out for the most part to be based on single, isolated instances, such as D. M. Thomas's novel *The White Hotel*, once catalogued at £350, which now languishes at a fraction of that price.

This 'climate of suspicion' has been dealt with at some length because it crops up so often. In fact, it all comes down to snobbery of a kind. Modern first editions do not generally look valuable, in the same way as most other collectable books; consequently they often turn up cheaply. Thus, many collectors (and dealers) cut their teeth on them; questions such as 'What does eightvo mean?' are more often heard in the arena of modern firsts than among incunabulists. Ultimately, though, the best way for dealers to refute criticism is by taking the trouble to be accurate.

There are various ways in which modern first editions are collected. Some collections are thematic; both World Wars, and the Spanish Civil War, are popular subjects, for instance. Many revolve around individual imprints, such as the Hogarth Press, or John Lehmann; others just concentrate on 'highlights' such as the most important post-war British novels. But the great majority of collections are those of the output of a single author, or a small group of writers.

Geoffrey Madan, in his *Notebooks*, Oxford, 1981, quotes Lord Cunliffe (giving evidence before a Royal Commission in happier days for the British economy) as saying that 'the Bank of England reserves were "very, very considerable". When pressed to give an even approximate figure, he replied that he would be "very, very reluctant to add to what he had said" '. The question so often asked by fellow dealers, 'Which authors are you looking for?', invites a similarly evasive response; suffice to say that all the important writers are collected by somebody, somewhere. Late first editions of Galsworthy or Masefield will not sell as easily as late first editions of Isherwood or Nabokov; but the scarcest early

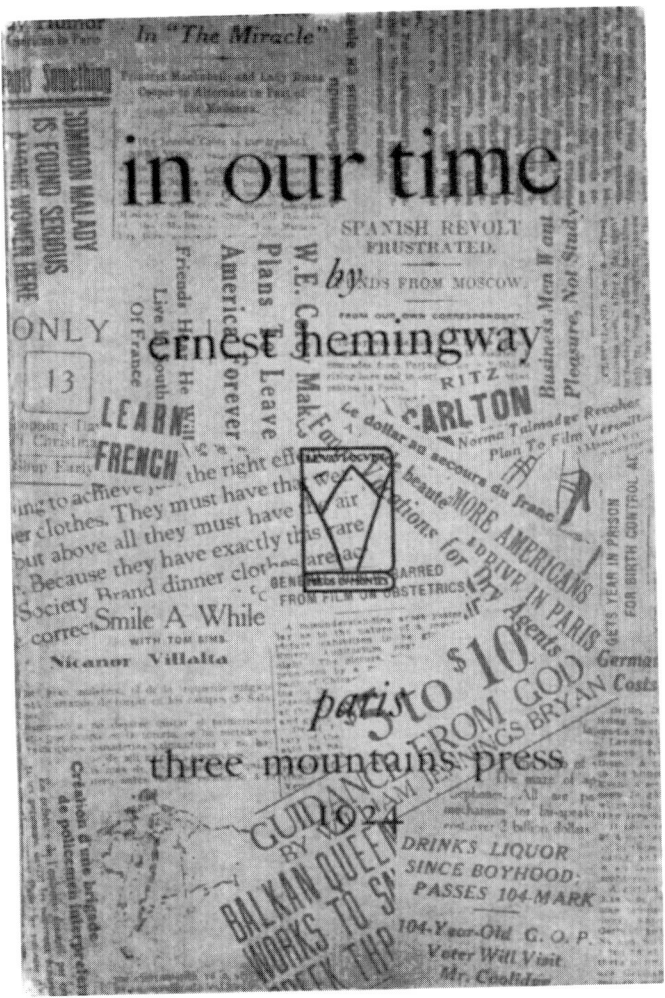

Hemingway's second book, published in an edition of 170 copies.

items are still in demand. Fashions are constantly changing, anyway; and perhaps the best advice on the subject of which authors are collectable and to what extent, is not to take too much notice of any of the published guide books, all of which contain errors varying from the minor to the horrifying. Experience is the only guide.

Outside the mainstream, however, some cautious advice might be given. Travel writers, from Robert Byron to Bruce Chatwin, are much collected; humorists, with a very few exceptions, such as Osbert Lancaster, are not. Children's books, dealt with elsewhere, overlap with modern firsts somewhere around Tolkien and C. S. Lewis, who sell readily. All but the most celebrated anthologies tend to stay on the shelves for a long time. Illustrators, especially wood-engravers, are popular; some fit closely into the 'private press' market, but others, such as Max Beerbohm and Rex Whistler, are collected in their own right. Detective fiction and science fiction are often in very great demand, but condition is even more important than in other fields. Subjects such as economics, politics and philosophy occasionally find their way into modern first edition sections, usually when a personality cult has arisen for one particular author (Keynes, Churchill, or Bertrand Russell). But these reflections are very general and are subject to constant revision.

Much of the advice given in the preceding paragraphs has been negative. More could be given; don't take your prices from other people's catalogues unless your books are in the same condition, and not always then; don't bother with books whose title-pages bear inscriptions by anyone other than the author, or with ex-library copies, or with rebound books. Don't 'improve' books by adding dust-wrappers from other copies; they never quite match and it looks like sharp practice. And so on. But, more positively, modern first editions remain one of the few areas where interesting collections can be formed at all levels, and where the chances of an interesting discovery remain high; one consequence of this is that customers tend to be enthusiastic, and many bookshop owners have found that first edition collectors gradually develop an interest in more recondite, and often more expensive, subjects. Dealing in first editions brings one into contact with a number of living writers, which can be disappointing but is more usually fascinating. Increased international travel during the twentieth century has made writers' lives, and hence their publishing histories, much more cosmopolitan than previously, with the result that foreign travel can often be rewarding, and not just to Paris. Finally, first editions have one great advantage over most other collectable books: if all else fails, you can always read them.

The Modern Movement

Cyril Connolly's influential book, published in 1965, was sub-titled *One Hundred Key Books from England, France and America, 1880–1950*. The modern movement, as he perceived it, 'began as a revolt against the bourgeois in France, the Victorians in England, the puritanism and materialism in America'. The authors chosen by Connolly range from Flaubert and Henry James (though James 'does not completely belong to the movement'), to Pound and Orwell. Connolly's tastes were unashamedly individual, but his book provides a challenging 'wants list' for many collectors of modern first editions. The appended 'Bibliography of English and French Editions' gives little more than titles, publishers and dates.

Monograph
A work dealing with a specific, usually limited, subject or branch of a subject in considerable detail. The word is sometimes used to describe an art book devoted to the work of a single artist; it is unlikely to be used of a CATALOGUE RAISONNÉ, as this latter term is more specific and carries considerably more weight.

Morison, Stanley (1889–1967)
In 1912 the young Stanley Morison purchased the Printing Supplement to *The Times*, a newspaper he was not in the habit of reading. Immediately he became aware of a new dimension in book production and indeed in his own life. The aesthetic pleasure which he derived from fine type design led him to obtain a post at the *Imprint*, a printing journal run by Gerald Meynell. He went on to work for the publishers Burns and Oates and then for the newly formed Cloister Press in Manchester. The Press remained in business for only a year but while he was there Morison and others formed the Fleuron Society. Unable to agree on the practical aims of a society concerned with printing and typography, the members established instead a journal, THE FLEURON.

In 1923, the Monotype Corporation appointed Morison as their typographical adviser; he introduced to their range typefaces based on those designed by BASKERVILLE and Caslon and also accepted a similar appointment with Cambridge University Press, contriving to combine the typographical needs of a commercial publishing house, the demands of the University and the occasional production of fine volumes in the tradition of the private press movement. In 1928 he became a director of the publishers Victor Gollancz and under his direction the familiar yellow DUST-WRAPPERS with bold black or purple type appeared. A year later he was asked by *The Times* to advise them on a change of typography and expressed his intention of making the paper 'the finest piece of printing, without exception, in the world'. The use of Times New Roman has since become indispensable to many printers, and is one of the most common typefaces in use today.

Stanley Morison made many friends and his wide interests – railways, pantomime, philately, among them – kept him always occupied. He wrote several books on printing and typography (perhaps the best-known being *Four Centuries of Fine Printing*, 1924, reprinted 1949), a five-volume *History of The Times*, and many contributions to journals.

Barker, Nicolas, *Stanley Morison*, 1972.
Carter, John, *A Handlist of the Writings of Stanley Morison to 1950*, Cambridge, 1950.
Moran, James, *Stanley Morison: his Typographic Achievement*, 1971.

Morocco
See LEATHER

Moxon, Edward (1801–1858)
Edward Moxon worked as a young man at Longman's, writing poetry while he learned the bookselling trade, and meeting influential members of the London literary world. He set up in business on his own with the help of the poet Samuel Rogers and married the adopted daughter of Charles Lamb. Moxon's business flourished and he published works by Tennyson (the 'Moxon Tennyson', usually so called),

Browning, Southey and Wordsworth. His editions of the Victorian poets are valued today principally for the illustrations by artists such as Millais, Maclise, the Brothers Dalziel and Rossetti.

Munby, Alan Noel Latimer (1913–1975) Munby's best-remembered contribution to antiquarian scholarship remains the work he did on the books and manuscripts of the manic collector, SIR THOMAS PHILLIPPS (five volumes of *Phillipps' Studies*). Munby graduated from King's College, Cambridge in 1934 and went to work first for Quaritch and then for Sotheby's. He spent most of the Second World War in prisoner-of-war camps and returned to become librarian of his old college.

Munby's comprehensive work on the Phillipps collection did not deter him from contributing many essays and short pieces to literary journals, his scholarship always lightened by a sharp but kindly wit: ghost stories, a short novel, real and imaginary adventures in the book-collecting world and many learned reviews and essays, were collected posthumously in *Essays and Papers*, 1977, edited by Nicolas Barker. He wrote on autographs and calligraphy, on the libraries and sale catalogues of distinguished collectors, indeed on bibliographical subjects of all kinds.

N

National Union Catalog

The American equivalent to the British Library catalogues was, until 1956, the Library of Congress Printed Card Catalog. This title was changed in 1956 to become the National Union Catalog; the listing was expanded to include holdings in other American libraries up to 1967 (125 volumes) and revised and reprinted in 1968–72 (104 volumes). It can often provide information not readily obtainable from the British Library, as it gives locations and indications of rarity.

Natural History Books

Gillian Stone

A Greene Forest: or a Naturall Historie, 1567, by Malet uses for the first time in English the term 'natural history'. 'Historie' is used without the dimension of time, in the classical sense of 'historia' meaning both enquiry and account. Pliny the Elder, who died of a heart attack getting too close to watch the eruption of Vesuvius which destroyed Pompeii, wrote *Historia Naturalis*, first printed in Venice in 1469. An English translation by Philemon Holland came out in 1601.

Natural history: what sort of sense can we make of a subject so vast it covers all the known world and even penetrates through literature and fancy into the world of the imagination? It overlaps with the sciences which grew out of it; with art in the portrayal of the beauties of the natural world; with the economics which is about the practical use of the raw materials of nature. The books about it fall into certain groups but there is also a chronology in their production. This short essay tries to represent both these aspects. The headings of the short sections indicate some fields of collecting.

Herbals and bestiaries

Plant and animal lore go back beyond recording and are associated with culinary and medical practice. Medieval herbals and bestiaries were based on classical writers, notably Aristotle and Dioscorides. Incunables and sixteenth-century printed herbals used woodcut illustrations, often crude, sometimes accurate, sometimes fantastical. These were traded between printers so the same ones recur in different works. Schoeffer, Brunfels, Bock, Fuchs, Bankes, and Dodoens all produced great herbals. Fuchs's *De Historia Stirpium*, Basle, 1542, was particularly well illustrated.

John Gerard's *Herball*, 1636. [Pickering & Chatto Ltd.]

Gerard, whose garden in Holborn grew 'over a thousand herbs', wrote a catalogue of them, *The Herball*, in 1597. Johnson's improvement of *Gerard's Herbal*, 1636, used Plantin plates. Parkinson, who punned his name in the title of his gardening book, *Paradisi in Sole*, 1629, also wrote a herbal, *Theatricum Botanicum*, 1640. Culpeper's herbal was printed in his *Physical Directory*, 1649 (later *The English Physician Enlarged*). John Hill, an apothecary, thought a 'quack' by some and 'maligned' by others, published in 1756 *The British Herbal: an History of Plants and Trees, Native of Britain, cultivated for Use or Beauty*. Both Culpeper's and Hill's herbals were much republished and abridged for the popular market and cheap Culpepers are available today. Then there is Elizabeth Blackwell, whose husband was in the debtor's prison. To get him out, she drew, engraved, coloured and published her lovely two-volume work *A Curious Herbal*, 1739.

Bestiaries were more fanciful than herbals and often emblematic, though some early works such as *Hortus Sanitatis*, 1491, contained animals as well as plants. There were incunable editions of Theobald's *Physiologus* but generally bestiaries are rare. Modern translations include the 1928 Roxburghe Club edition of *A Latin Bestiary*, edited by M. R. James, and T. H. White's *Book of Beasts*, 1954.

Plant hunters and travellers

Voyagers and explorers brought back descriptions and specimens of plants and animals and the numbers of known species developed steadily from a few hundreds to the hundreds of thousands known today. Drake and Raleigh collected plants; John Tradescant obtained American plants from the Virginia company and his son made several trips to the colony – *Museum Tradescantiarum*, 1656, includes their importations. John Banister wrote a *Catalogue of Plants observed by me in Virginia* which was included in John Ray's *Historia Plantarum*, 1688. Maria Merian and her daughter Dorothea went off to Surinam and painted insects (*Over der Voortteeling . . . Surinaemsche Insecten*, 1719). Sir Hans Sloane (*Voyage to the Islands of Madera, Barbados, . . . and Jamaica*, 1707–25), Mark Catesby (*Natural History of Carolina &c*, 1730–47), William Dampier, Labillardière, Humboldt, the botanists and zoologists on the major voyages from Captain Cook's to the *Beagle*, were a few of the many who travelled and reported. David Douglas hunted plants in North America and later expeditions such as that of the *Erebus* and *Terror*, the *Challenger*, the Yarkand Mission to Central Asia and those to the Antarctic in the twentieth century, all contributed. Complete sets of the reports are rare but individual sections do appear on the market.

More recently plant hunters like Kingdon Ward and Reginald Farrer, who travelled in China, wrote on the subject, and their books are now collected.

Scientific natural history

The growing interest in scientific observation and experiment both influenced and stimulated knowledge of the natural world, and the seventeenth century saw the establishment of scientific societies and the publication of important books. In England the Royal Society was founded in 1662 and many of its first publications were on natural history; they included works by Evelyn (*Sylva, or a Discourse of Forest Trees*, 1664), Hooke (*Micrographia*, 1665), Malpighi (*Anatome Plantarum*, 1675) and Nehemiah Grew (*Anatomy of Plants*, 1682). John Ray went 'botanizing' on the continent with Francis Willughby, who died soon after, and Ray helped complete his *Ornithologia*, 1676 and *De Historia Piscium*, 1686. Ray's own work on plants is very important: his *Catalogus Plantarum circa Cantabrigiam Nascentium*, 1660, a tiny notable book, was the first county flora. The first issue bears the Cambridge imprint, the second has a cancel title-page bearing a London 1660 imprint. Ray made a 'natural' classification of plants (in *Methodus Plantarum Nova*, 1682) which was used for a century until it was superseded by that of Linnaeus. He was also the inspiration for the formation in 1844 of the Ray Society, which published monographs on all aspects of scientific natural history.

Geology

The surface of the earth was long taken for granted as permanent, apart from the cataclysms of volcano and earthquake; Kercher studied these and wrote *Mundus Subterraneus*, 1665. There were nevertheless some puzzling features. How, thought Steno the Dane at about the same time, did marine fossils occur in high places? Canal cutting and mining threw up more evidence that they must have been laid down under ancient seas. De Luc, de Saussure, Werner, Buffon, Hutton and Cuvier all wrote on the dilemma. In 1815 William Smith, an engineer, published his geological map *Definition of the Strata of England and Wales*, following it with a pair of volumes in the following two years. Stratigraphy had arrived. Meanwhile William Buckland, professor of geology at Oxford, an eccentric as likely to serve crocodile at table as panther, believed in the Deluge and wrote *Reliquae Diluvianae*, 1823. He also wrote one of the Bridgewater Treatises, a series of works published to support Natural Theology in the face of Science. Charles Lyell's *Principles of Geology*, 1830–33 was the beginning of modern geology. Murchison's *Silurian System*, 1839, and De la Beche's reports for the newly formed Geological Survey were also important. Later in the century, Suess, Bertrand and Willis wrote on mountain building and collapse. Wegener, in 1912, proposed the theory of Continental Drift, taken up later by Holmes and Du Toit.

Botany

William Turner is known as the 'father of English botany' because he recorded and located for the first time about 300 British plants. His *Lybellus de Herbaria Novus* was printed by John Bydell in 1538. He wrote a 'Greke, Latin, Englishe, Duche and Frenche' dictionary of plant names that 'Herbaries and Apotecaries use' and also wrote on birds.

In the eighteenth century Ingen-Housz was outstanding in being the first to observe the process of photosynthesis, recounted in his *Experiments upon Vegetables*, 1779. The dominant botanist was Linnaeus or Count von Linné whose system of binomial classification revolutionized both botany and zoology. His numerous publications include *Systema Naturae Regnum Vegetabile*, Leyden, 1735. The tenth edition, Stockholm 1758–9, extended his method to animals. In England Linnaean ideas were disseminated by, among others, Benjamin Stillingfleet, *Tracts*, 1759, William Withering, *Botanical Arrangement*, 1776 and Richard Pulteney, *A General View of the Writings of Linnaeus*, 1781. A young man called J. E. Smith bought Linnaeus's collections from his widow and founded the Linnaean Society; he was the author of *English Botany*, 1790–1814, which James Sowerby illustrated; Smith was put out when people kept referring to it as 'Sowerby's Botany'. Sowerby also illustrated other works – notably William Curtis's *Flora Londiniensis*, 1775–98 and also, from 1787, Curtis's *Botanical Magazine*. This journal continues to the present day, though since 1984 it has been known as the *Kew Magazine*.

Much nineteenth-century English botany revolves round Kew and the Hooker family. Kew Gardens had been established from the interest and the collections of George III. Information and specimens were sent here from all over the country by eager and devoted amateur botanists and from all over the world by dedicated travellers. Sir William Jackson Hooker travelled on the continent and, with Captain Beechey, to the Pacific. He published among other works *Exotic Botany*, 1823–27 and the ten-volume *Icones Plantarum*, [1836] 1837–54; as Director of Kew he opened the gardens to the public. His son, Sir Joseph Dalton Hooker, succeeded him as Director and collaborated with the botanist Bentham on the classic *Handbook of British Flora*, 1863–65. He wrote *Himalayan Journals*, 1854 and the next year brought out his beautiful folio *Rhododendrons of Sikkim-Himalaya*, 1849–51, with plates after his own drawings by W. H. Finch. Kew's role was crucial in the theft of the wild rubber plant from Brazil and its introduction to Malaya whose plantations captured the world market.

Zoology

Aristotle had observed the animal world quite well, and Pliny's descriptions, while sometimes bizarre, for the most part portray recognizable creatures, but Gesner's four-volume *Historia Animalium*, 1555–58 'marks the beginnings of modern zoology'; a fifth volume, 1587, was about snakes. Aldrovandi wrote on birds, chickens, serpents, dragons, quadrupeds and monsters; these works were published between 1599 and 1657. Topsell wrote *Historie of Foure-Footed Beasts*, 1607, and . . . *of Serpents*, 1608. The interest in comparative anatomy led to more exact knowledge of the structure of animal life, and medical men from Harvey to John Hunter contributed, as did the artist, Stubbs, in his *Anatomy Of the Horse*, 1766. Leeuwenhoek looked through the microscope at his 'little animals' and he sent much of his work to the *Philosophical Transactions* of the Royal Society. Swammerdam wrote *Historia Insectorum*, 1669 and his posthumously published *Bybel der Naturae*, 1737–38, translated by Floyd as *The Book of Nature*, 1758. Edward Tyson wrote on the *Orang-utang*, 1699. Then, towards the end of the eighteenth century, the great compendious natural history works by Buffon, Pennant and Cuvier gave much more precise detail about the whole range of vertebrates and invertebrates.

Exotic creatures lived in menageries. These live animals and birds, and particularly their stuffed continuance in death, provided the examples used by the natural history artists of the period. Edward Lear stayed at Knowsley Hall and contributed the bird illustrations to Gray's *Gleanings from the Menagerie and Aviary at Knowsley Hall*, 1846; B. W. Hopkins depicted the hoofed quadrupeds.

NATURAL HISTORY BOOKS

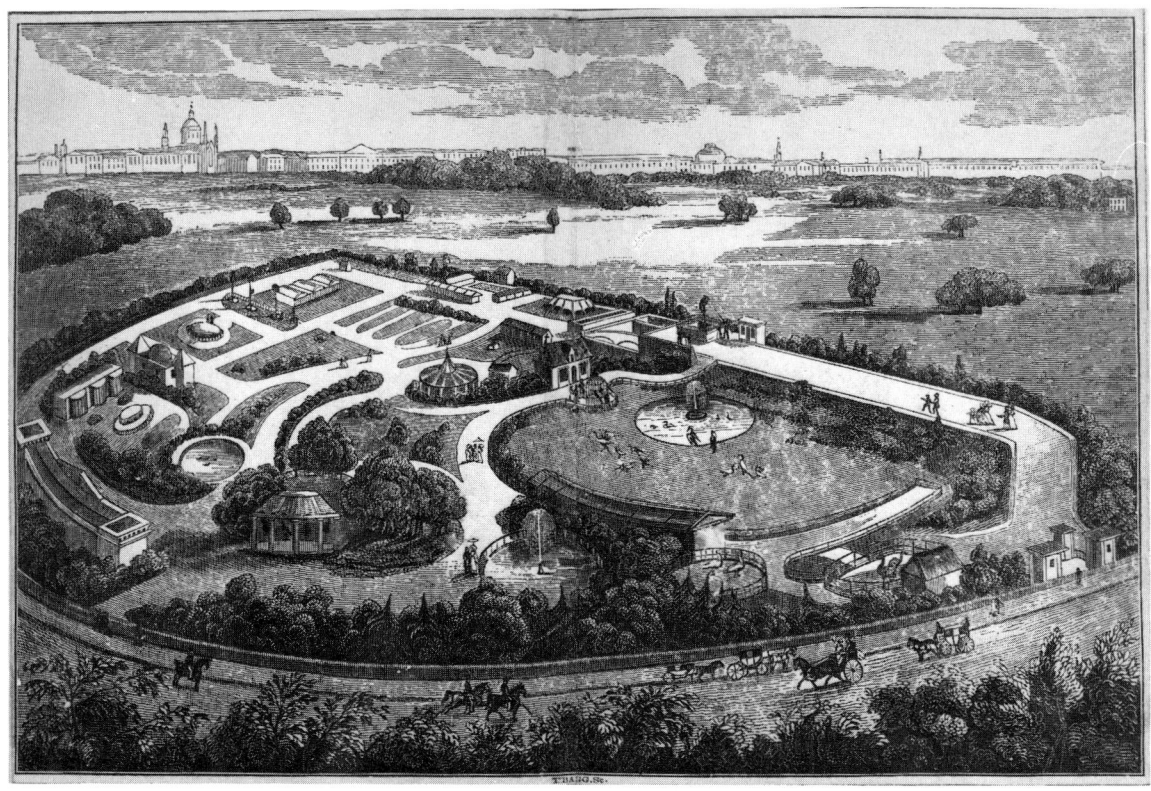

Frontispiece of *The Zoological Keepsake for the Year 1830*. [Titles of Oxford]

Darwin and natural selection

Nineteenth-century scientific natural history was dominated by Darwin and his controversial theories. In his youth he had read *Zoonomia*, 1794–96, by his grandfather Erasmus Darwin. He found in it seeds which, reinforced by his own findings on the voyage of the *Beagle*, and by the geological teaching of Charles Lyell, led to the publication in 1859 of *On the Origin of Species*. It was one of the most influential books of all time. Darwin, a shy man, was goaded into publication by the discovery that young Alfred Wallace in the Eastern Archipelago had stumbled on the same principles of natural selection. Wallace's *Contributions to the Theory of Natural Selection* did not come out until 1870, and his most important work is *The Geographical Distribution of Animals*, two volumes, 1876. The first edition of the *Origin* is one of the most desirable books for a collector; a fine copy of the first issue is of great value, and the market is so strong that many later editions are readily saleable. The complex details of the various editions and of Darwin's other writings are well covered in Freeman's bibliography of his works. Darwin was fiercely opposed on religious grounds, notably by Owen and Sedgwick, but supported by Thomas Huxley. There are collectors for the subsequent stream of books on evolution. The controversy continues today.

NATURAL HISTORY BOOKS

Natural history books with colour plates

Scientific natural history in printed form had often been presented in dull-looking treatises, perhaps illustrated with a few uncoloured engravings but in the eighteenth century came books adorned with hand-coloured plates. John Martyn's *Historia Plantarum Rariorum*, 1728–32, was the first botanical book to use colour printing, and Eleazar and Elizabeth Albin's *Natural History of Birds*, 1733–38, was the first hand-coloured bird book. On the continent *Le Grand Jardin de l'Univers*, 1785–91, had 200 hand-coloured plates. Pierre Bullard himself drew and printed in colour 602 plates for his 13-volume *Herbier de France*, 1780–1808. Earlier representations of birds and animals seem stiff and gawky, like the stuffed specimens from which they were drawn, but they have a charm of their own and likeness improved as the art of taxidermy developed. Later artists drew from life.

George Edwards, Moses Harris, Catesby, Levaillant, Donovan, Martyn, Nozeman, Houttuyn, Thornton, Redouté, Jaquin, Ehret, Wilson, Selby, Audubon, Agassiz, Gould, Lear, Reichenbach, Elliot, Wolf, Bowdler Sharpe, Sclater, Elwes – these are some of the names that over two centuries peal out a triumph of colour, observation, imagination, technique, art and money, in the most marvellous hand-coloured flowers and birds and butterflies, jewel-like insects, golden antelopes, iridescent fishes. Some of them painted, some engraved, some employed their wives, some engaged artists, but all one way or another played a part in the splendour of these natural history books. They were produced

The Night-Blowing Cereus from Dr. Thornton's *Temple of Flora*, 30th May 1800 [The Schuster Gallery]

Ducks, from John Gould's *The Birds of Great Britain*, 1862–73 [The Schuster Gallery]

for sale to wealthy collectors in the process of building fine libraries. Many came out in parts like Levaillant's *Histoire Naturelle des Oiseaux d'Afrique*, 1796–1812, or Selby's *Illustrations of British Ornithology*, 1818–1834.

Audubon, who came from America in search of engravers for his great *Birds of America*, 1827–38 was inspired by Selby to print life-size birds. The firm of Lizars in Edinburgh engraved the first ten plates, and the rest of the work was given to Havell's in London. The arrangement of the birds is often extraordinary. How else could you get a flamingo on to even a double elephant folio? The land and seascapes are wonderfully diminished yet clear and detailed. It is the most valuable of all natural history books.

In the 1830s John and Elizabeth Gould started their great series of bird books. After Elizabeth's death, Gould, who continued to make sketches and to do the administrative work, employed artists like Lear, Richter and Wolf. The Goulds went to Australia and painted hundreds of new species for what is now the most expensive of the series, *Birds of Australia*, 1840–69. *Mammals of Australia* came out in 1845–63.

Excursions, societies and popular natural history

As far back as the seventeenth century, 'herbarizing' was an activity for individuals and groups. The Society of Apothecaries ran trips for apprentices to learn in the field the 'simples' they would use. The botanists of the august Royal Society, finding too many of its members to be what later came to be known as 'closet' naturalists, started to meet informally at the Temple Coffee House and formed a Botanic Club, to get out into the country. Sir Hans Sloane, whose huge collections of books as well as natural history specimens eventually formed the basis of the British Museum, was a member. Local societies grew all over the country, collecting plants and fossils and small animals and insects, especially butterflies. Notes taken on or after these outings were often written up and became detailed contributions to the sum of knowledge. Societies also recorded their activities and findings in Proceedings and Transactions, particularly in the nineteenth century. Many of these are ephemeral, difficult to find and obscurely collected. The literature connected with these societies, though often scrappy and seemingly hotch-potch, mixed with antiquities and family history, has a cumulative importance out of proportion to some of the individual items. The writings often formed the basis of county floras and faunas.

By the nineteenth century, great numbers of amateurs were involved, women as well as men, from all walks of society. Many of the popular works of Victorian times were written by women: Anne Pratt, Agnes Catlow, Eliza Brightwen (*Wild Nature won by Kindness*, 1890), and Mrs Gatty, for instance. Usually closely observed and accurately recorded, the works were sometimes mixed with religious sentiment – the gist being that Nature existed to teach people about the Almighty. Men too followed this line. Hugh Miller (*Old Red Sandstone*, 1846), P. H. Gosse (*A Year at the Shore*, 1865) and Charles Kingsley wrote minutely observed and very religious natural history books. Books in profusion were written for children. A delightful example is *Country Walks of a Naturalist with his Children*, 1869, by Rev. William Houghton, who is better known for his two-volume *British Freshwater Fishes* with colour plates by Lydon. Most of these books tend to be octavo or duodecimo and are illustrated with wood-engravings or chromo-lithographs, or even hand-coloured plates. They were often bound in cloth stamped with imaginative vignettes.

Some sets and series

Lizars, the Edinburgh firm who engraved the early Audubon plates, was busy between 1833 and 1843 bringing out an ambitious popular series edited and in many cases written by Sir William Jardine who had written the text for Selby's *Birds*. The series was called *The Naturalist's Library* and is commonly known as 'Jardine'. The 40 volumes are subdivided into sets of one to four volumes, each complete in itself, on different species. Each small octavo volume has authoritative text and about 30 hand-coloured plates. Complete sets in fine condition are hard to find and are not easy to collate. Like the later series, Allen's *Natural History* and Lloyd's *Natural History* and Lydekker's six-volume set, *Royal Natural History*, 1893–96 (all with chromolithographic illustrations), these deal only with animals. This supports one meaning of 'natural history' given by the *OED* – that it is devoted exclusively to animal life. Not so the mid-century *Popular Natural History Series* published by Reeve and later Routledge. Squarish little books, each had 20 hand-coloured plates and catered soundly for all the 'crazes' of Victorian natural history – wild flowers, seaweeds, lichens, ferns, crustaceans, even *The Aquarium*, 1857. The twentieth-century equivalent is the *Wayside and Woodland Series*. Made to be used, in a tough format, these are concise, informative, well written and well illustrated.

An important series of separate regional works, Harvie-Brown's 11-volume *Fauna of Scotland*, 1887–1911, is almost never found complete and the parts are not listed together in Freeman's bibliography. Its ecological approach is a foretaste of the sort of work done by scientific natural historians decades later.

NATURAL HISTORY BOOKS

The New Naturalist

In the twentieth century the term 'naturalist' became respectable again after a long period of dismissal as amateur and sentimental. Country-lovers still wrote and read; some of their books were illustrated with the wood-engravings of the thirties, forties and fifties, by such artists as Dalglish, Agnes Miller Parker, and Robert Gibbings. *The Countryman* catered for this market, as did the Batsford books with their much collected Brian Cook dust-wrappers.

In his editorial to *The New Naturalist, a Journal of British Natural History*, 1948, James Fisher gives the object of the New Naturalist organization: 'to serve field workers with books . . . Its publications are ecological . . . deal with the ecology of communities . . . aspects of geology or weather . . . ecology of individual species.' This amounts to an important manifesto which set the tone for accessible scientific natural history books, both within the series and by publishers other than Collins. It foreshadowed the current importance of ecology, the environment, wild life and conservation.

The *New Naturalist Series* itself reached No. 80, *Caves*, by 1993. Some of the titles are scarce in relation to the demand by collectors and readers. Once Boyd's *A Country Parish*, 1951, was hardest to find; now later volumes compete for the peak of scarcity and price. Some of the most recent, *British Warblers*, 1985, for example, are now the most expensive, because the publishers catered for what they thought was a very limited market. The rush of collectors to buy left readers bereft and the reissue had a new inferior dust-wrapper. Clifford and Rosemary Ellis designed the wrappers for most of the series – most important for collectors. The monographs are separately numbered and slightly smaller in format.

The rest!

With limited space I have written more of English than continental books and would have liked to explore other facets of natural history: the field sports writers who deal in detail with the nature of the prey; collectable gardening and farming, forestry and entomology books; facsimiles; bird and flower books from the lower as well as the upper end of the market; the artists who have illustrated more nature books in this century than in all the years before.

One omission I will now put right. For many people the most famous natural history book of all is Gilbert White's *The Natural History of Selborne*, 1789. A fine first is sought by collectors. But it has gone into over two hundred editions and still people want it as a model of well-informed quiet attention to detail, plain language, and what Robert Graves calls 'the greatness, rareness, muchness, fewness of this precious only endless world in which you say you live'.

Arber, Agnes, *Herbals, Their Origin and Evolution: a Chapter in the History of Botany, 1470–1670*, Cambridge, 1912 (reprinted, 1938).

Bridson, G. and J. J. White, *Plant, Animal and Anatomical Illustrations in Art and Science: a Bibliographical Guide from the Sixteenth Century to the Present Day*, 1990.

British Museum (Natural History), *Catalogue of the Books Manuscripts &c*, 5 vols and supplement (3 vols), 1903–1940.
Curle, Richard, *The Ray Society: a Bibliographical History*, 1954.
Deacon, Margaret, *Scientists and the Sea, 1650–1900*, 1871.
Freeman, R. B., *British Natural History Books, 1495–1900*, Folkestone, 1980.
Gohau, Gabriel, *A History of Geology*, revised and translated by Albert V. and Margaret Carozzi, New Brunswick, 1990.
Harvard University, Museum of Comparative Zoology, *Catalogue of the Library*, 8 vols, Boston, 1967.
Henrey, Blanche, *British Botanical and Horticultural Literature before 1800*, 3 vols, 1975.
Lisney, Arthur Adrian, *A Bibliography of British Lepidoptera, 1608–1799*, 1960.
Lyte, C., *The Plant Hunters*, 1983.
Mullens, W. H. and Swann, H. K., *A Bibliography of British Ornithology from the Earliest Times to 1918*, [1919]–1920.
Nissen, Claus, *Die Botanische Buchillustration*, Stuttgart, 1966.
——— *Die Illustrierten Vogelbücher*, Stuttgart, 1953.
——— *Die Zoologische Buchillustration*, 2 vols, Stuttgart, 1966–78/79.
——— *Schöne Fischbücher*, Stuttgart, 1951.
Perkins Library, *Catalogue of the Walter Frank Perkins Agricultural Library*, Southampton, 1961.
Plesch, Arpad, *The Magnificent Botanical Library Of Stiftung Für Botanik*, 3 vols, 1975–76.
Quinby, Jane and Stevenson, Allan, Hunt Botanical Library, *Catalogue of Botanical Books*, 2 vols in 3, Pittsburgh, 1958–1961.
Rohde, E. S., *The Old English Herbals*, 1922.
Sitwell, Sacheverell and Handasyde Buchanan and James Fisher, *Fine Bird Books, 1700–1900*, 1953.
Sitwell, Sacheverell, Blunt, Wilfrid and Synge, P. M., *Great Flower Books*, 1956.
Zimmer, J. T., *Catalogue of the Edward E. Ayer Ornithological Library*, Chicago, 1926.

Nature printing

The practice of making impressions on paper of actual leaves, ferns and other similar objects has its origins in the earliest days of printing, but its successful use as a method of book illustration was first accomplished in Vienna in the early 1850s. Experiments were in progress concurrently in England, and these culminated in the books printed by William Bradbury (who had studied the process in Vienna) and Frederick Evans. Moore and Lindley's *The Ferns of Great Britain and Ireland*, 1855–1856, and Johnstone and Croall's *The Nature Printed British Seaweeds*, 1860, are among the best-known works illustrated in this way. The process employed electrotypes made from an impression of the plant on a plate of soft lead, and it was capable of giving a very detailed and accurate reproduction of such surface details as the veins of a leaf. However, nature printing could be used only for a limited range of subjects, and its last substantial achievement was the illustration, by means of some 50,000 transfers, of Denton's *Moths and Butterflies of the United States*, 1898–1900.

Cave, Roderick and Wakeman, Geoffrey, *Typographia Naturalis*, Wymondham, 1967.

New Cambridge Bibliography of English Literature

NCBEL follows a similar pattern to the original *Cambridge Bibliography of English Literature*, but with the important addition of a twentieth-century volume. It was published in 1969–77 under the editorship of George Watson and I. R. Willison, and comprises four volumes in chronological order (600–1660, 1660–1800, 1800–1900, 1900–1950) with an index volume. NCBEL aims to cover all literary authors native to or mainly resident in the British Isles, and lists both primary and secondary materials, 'works by' and 'works about'. Newspapers and magazines, annuals and year books, and other special areas are separately treated, and attention is given to some important non-literary categories, such as 'Philosophers, Theologians, Writers on Natural Science and Psychology'. NCBEL is readily obtainable, easy to consult and of considerable value as a work of initial reference. *A Shorter New Cambridge Bibliography of English Literature* was published in 1981.

Newbery, John (1713–1767)

John was the eldest and best-known member of a family that specialized in the publication of books for children. He came to London in 1744 and engaged in general publishing, including works by Johnson, Goldsmith and Christopher Smart. He must have been an agreeable, kindly man, for Johnson wrote to him asking 'if you could conveniently help me with two pounds'. Evidently the plea was successful for other requests followed!

Newbery was an astute businessman whose advertising methods might be admired today. He catered especially for young readers, though recent research has shown that he was not the first publisher to do so.

The most successful story carrying the Newbery imprint was undoubtedly *Goody Two-Shoes*; but he also published *The Little Pretty Pocket Book*, *The Lilliputian Magazine*, *A Little Lottery-Book for Children*, *Fables in Verse by Abraham Aesop* and many others offering both pleasurable and instructive reading.

After his death Newbery's business (he was also involved in selling patent medicines) was carried on by his son and his nephew (both named Francis) and nephew Francis's wife Elizabeth. John Newbery's importance is as the first major publisher of books that children might enjoy for their own sake rather than in order to be instructed.

Darton, F. J. Harvey, *Children's Books in England*, Cambridge, 1932 3rd edn., 1982.

Muir, Percy, *English Children's Books 1600–1900*, 1954 (reprinted, 1959).

Roscoe, Sydney, *John Newbery and his Successors, 1740–1814; a Bibliography*, 1973.

Welsh, Charles, *A Bookseller of the Last Century*, 1885 (reprinted, 1972).

Niger

See LEATHER

Nonesuch Press

The history of the Nonesuch Press is inseparable from that of its founder, Francis Meynell. His mother was the poet Alice Meynell, his father a publisher; the latter became managing director of Burns and Oates, where Francis Meynell acquired much of his early experience, and where he had the good fortune to meet STANLEY MORISON. An enthusiasm for left-wing politics led to some bizarre episodes, including the smuggling of jewels for the Bolsheviks, but Meynell's work, often with Morison, at the Pelican Press (founded 1916) shows seriousness of purpose. A particular feature of Meynell's style which developed during this period was 'allusive printing', or designing reprints in such a way as to pay graceful homage to the original printers without slavishly imitating their work.

Inspired more by WILLIAM PICKERING than by William Morris, Meynell, his second wife Vera Mendel and David Garnett founded the Nonesuch Press in 1923; their aim, as Sir Geoffrey Keynes has put it, was to produce beautiful books in a variety of styles at several different printing shops, using attractive papers and binding materials – all for the intelligent reader and at relatively low prices. Their first book, Donne's *Love Poems*, typifies their ability to spot a gap in the market, and fill it with both style and efficiency; the standard of editorship at the Nonesuch Press, moreover, was higher than at many other presses, as is shown by, for instance, Geoffrey Keynes's monumental three-volume edition of Blake (1925).

The Nonesuch Press was a remarkable commercial success. This was partly due to some inspired ideas such as *The Week-end Book*, 1924, reprinted many times, whose accessibility provoked Virginia Woolf's remark 'The Hogarth Press may not make money – but at least we did not publish The Week-end Book'; but it was also thanks to more solid projects such as the famous seven-volume Shakespeare (1929–33), which made a profit of eleven thousand pounds.

The boldness of design of many Nonesuch books, unfortunately, has left today's collectors and booksellers with some problems. Meynell's enthusiasm for vegetable parchment, while it led to some splendid books, was soon tempered by their tendency to warp; and many of the dyes used, such as the brilliant orange for the vellum of Dante's *La Divina Commedia*, 1928, have proved so fugitive that immaculate copies of some titles are almost impossible to find (and correspondingly prized when they appear). The decision to bind George Herbert's *The Temple*, 1927, in loose handwoven cloth was not particularly farsighted (although a number of fine copies have recently been in circulation); and the niger morocco used for many of the finest Nonesuch books – the Shakespeare, the *Iliad* and the *Odyssey*, Walton's *Works* – is sadly prone to discoloration. But this does not detract from Meynell's undoubted achievements; his decision to use a form of cigarette paper for the Coronation Shakespeare, 1953, for instance, was a stroke of brilliance.

In 1936 George Macy, founder of the LIMITED EDITIONS CLUB in New York, acquired a controlling interest in the Press. Some early projects were ambitious, most notably the Nonesuch Dickens. This splendid set (24 volumes in variously coloured buckram, 1937–38) received mixed critical acclaim, partly on account of the inclusion with each set of an engraver's plate for one of the original illustrations; David Garnett wrote in 1938 that 'the dispersal of a set of great historical interest and future usefulness is an act of vandalism which will give a permanent cachet of vulgarity to the edition'. However, the combined effects of depression and war curtailed the activities of the Press considerably, and for some years nothing appeared apart from the one-volume compendious editions of individual authors which had been successfully pioneered by Keynes's Blake in 1921.

In 1953 Francis Meynell regained control of the Press, in partnership with Max Reinhardt. The last major publication of the Press was the three-volume *Holy Bible*, 1963; after 1968 the Press lay dormant until the production of John Dreyfus's admirable *History* mentioned below.

Dreyfus, John, *A History of the Nonesuch Press*, with a descriptive catalogue, 1981.
Meynell, Francis, *My Lives*, 1971.

Numbered in the press
Many books published in limited editions are individually numbered. Usually the colophon is printed in the same way as the rest of the text, leaving a space for the variable part of the limitation statement – numbers, letters, a legend such as 'out of series', or occasionally the name of the recipient – to be inserted by hand. Sometimes, however, these variables are set up in type, and changed between successive impressions of the colophon; this process is, as may be imagined, laborious and expensive, and consequently is a more than averagely reliable indication of an important book.

Copies numbered in the press should not be confused with those whose producers have employed some sort of rotary stamp; the inelegance of this practice is usually reflected in other aspects of the book's design.

O

Obelisk Press

The Obelisk Press was founded in Paris in 1931 by Jack Kahane, a colourful expatriate from Manchester. Kahane had lived in France since the First World War, and married a Frenchwoman, Marcelle Eugénie Girodias; he enjoyed a decade of varying success as a novelist, during which censorship problems experienced with his most successful book *To Laugh and Grow Rich* gave him a lifelong interest in freedom of expression.

In 1928 he met the French publisher Henri Babou, and after prolonged discussions they produced, in 1930, a limited edition of Joyce's *Haveth Childers Everywhere*, a fragment of what was to become *Finnegans Wake*. Although initially slow to sell, this in time proved a commercial success, and the Obelisk Press was formally founded in 1931. Its first publication was an extensively revised reissue of *Storm*, a collection of short stories by Peter Neagoe, an American expatriate of Romanian origin. In 1933 the Press took over from Frank Harris the publication of his *My Life and Loves* which was banned in both England and the United States.

Perhaps the most important episode in the history of the Press began in 1932, when the American literary agent William Aspenwall Bradley sent Kahane the manuscript of Henry Miller's *Tropic of Cancer*. The content was such that even Kahane had some misgivings about publication, and the book did not appear until September, 1934; even then, Kahane arranged little publicity for the novel, and most of the marketing was done by Miller himself, with the help of Anaïs Nin, whose work was also published by the Obelisk Press.

Kahane's interest in publishing works banned in England, such as James Hanley's *Boy*, 1933, had attracted the attention of several young English writers having trouble with the censor, most notably Cyril Connolly, whose novel *The Rock Pool* was published by Obelisk in 1936, and Lawrence Durrell; his *The Black Book* appeared in 1938.

The Obelisk Press was an early casualty of the Second World War. The writers began to disappear: Miller left Paris in the summer of 1939, to visit Lawrence Durrell in Corfu. Then, two days after the outbreak of war, Kahane was found dead by his son Maurice Girodias; the latter, years later, was to continue the Obelisk tradition with his own OLYMPIA PRESS.

Many of the Obelisk Press titles were of negligible literary value, and are consequently of little interest now; but Kahane's achievements in pushing back the boundaries of censorship, and his encouragement of writers whose worth was proved by their subsequent careers, were valuable.

See also BLACK SUN PRESS

Octavo

Books of octavo (8vo) format have dominated publishing output since the early years of the seventeenth century. The term indicates sheets printed with 16 pages which have been folded three times to form eight leaves.

Officina Bodoni

Hans Mardersteig (1892–1977) printed his first books on the hand press that he set up in Montagnola, Switzerland, in 1922. He had obtained permission from the Museo Bodoniano at Parma to cast type from Giambattista Bodoni's eighteenth-century matrices, and he adopted the great Italian printer's name for his own press. When the Italian government commissioned the Officina Bodoni in 1927 to design and print a 49-volume edition of the works of D'Annunzio, the Press was removed to Verona, Mardersteig changing his name at that time to Giovanni. *Tutte Le Opere Di Gabriele D'Annunzio* was completed in 1936. During the early years in Switzerland, the Officina Bodoni's reputation for typographic design and presswork of the highest standards had already been assured by 22 notable volumes; these included Michelangelo's *Poesie*, 1923, Shelley's *Epipsychidion*, 1923 (the Press's first book in English), Goethe's *Marienbader Elegie*, 1923, *The Tempest*, 1924, and reprints of classic works on calligraphy. From the outset the Officina Bodoni followed the well-established private press formula of small, elegantly bound editions, often with a few copies printed on vellum; but Mardersteig's sureness of touch was such that even the most ambitious of his books remained unpretentious.

In Verona, as in Switzerland, the international breadth of Mardersteig's interests and friendships was reflected in the printing of books in Italian, French, German, Russian and English. Poetry had a large place in the Press's list, which included works by T. S. Eliot, C. Day Lewis, Hugh MacDiarmid, Ezra Pound and Dylan Thomas as well as earlier poets. During the 54 years of Mardersteig's work at the Press some 200 books were produced, many with illustrations printed on the Officina Bodoni's own lithographic and etching presses and often employing types, such as the well-known Dante, designed by Mardersteig. Charles Malin and Frederic Warde were among other type designers enlisted by Mardersteig, and Stanley Morison was also an ally. Several of the Press's books were enhanced by skilful modern recuttings of fifteenth- and sixteenth-century woodcuts; the 1973 two-volume *Aesop*, with 60 hand-coloured woodcuts, is judged by many to be one of the Officina Bodoni's most successful productions; but it is rivalled by Terence's *Andria*, 1971, for which Mardersteig made use of pearwood blocks, engraved after Dürer's drawings for a fifteenth-century edition which was never published. After World War Two, Mardersteig and his son Martino established the Stamperia Valdonega as a companion press. Its books were machine set and printed, and were thus within reach of a wider audience; but the same high standards of design prevailed.

Giovanni Mardersteig once described the printer's task as consisting of three duties: service to the author, in finding the form best suited to his work; service to the reader, in making reading pleasant and easy; and giving an attractive appearance to the whole book without imposing on it too much of his own personality. The Officina Bodoni's books admirably fulfil these aims, justifying Will Carter's description of his fellow printer as 'possibly the finest pressman the world has ever seen or is ever likely to see'.

Schmoller, Hans (ed.), *Giovanni Mardersteig, The Officina Bodoni, An Account of the Work of a Hand Press, 1923–1977*, Verona, 1980.

Offsetting

Offsetting is the accidental transference of printed matter from one page to the facing page. The offset matter may come from either text or plates, and may be caused by sheets having been folded or bound before the ink is dry, or by the book having become damp. Faint offsetting is not generally considered greatly objectionable, especially if text is offset on to text; but the prominent offsetting of plates on to text, or text on to plates, can be considered a more serious defect. Although it can often be considerably improved by the gentle use of a dry cleaning pad, a soft cloth bag filled with minute rubber particles, the direct use of a rubber is definitely not recommended.

Olympia Press

The Press was founded in Paris in 1953 by Maurice Girodias, son of the publisher Jack Kahane (see OBELISK PRESS). Girodias's publishing experience began in Paris in 1939; his 'Editions du Chène' achieved rapid success and were taken over by Hachette at the end of the 1940s. Disenchanted with the French literary scene, Girodias founded the Olympia Press to publish the work of English-language writers who were experiencing difficulties with censors elsewhere, such as Samuel Beckett, William S. Burroughs, Lawrence Durrell and Henry Miller; the green paperbacks in the 'Traveller's Companion' series soon became a familiar sight to British and American customs officers. In time, the Paris police began to show an unsympathetic interest; in 1956 the French authorities banned two of Girodias's publications, Nabokov's *Lolita* and J. P. Donleavy's *The Ginger Man*. Although the Press eventually won its case in February 1958, the return to power of General de Gaulle three months later marked the start of further problems.

First editions from the Olympia Press in fine condition are often of considerable interest to collectors, but only if the texts are of some literary merit; the Press was far from selective in this regard. Its output is, moreover, bibliographically complicated, and unfamiliar titles should not be described as first editions without consulting the relevant author-bibliography. In particular, the Press acquired the deplorable habit of issuing photographic reprints of certain titles without adjusting the colophon, or giving any other clear indication of posteriority. However, one useful rule of thumb exists. The Press's title-pages, set in plain text until late 1957, began (with minor exceptions) in early 1958 to appear with coloured borders composed of repeated ornaments; these colours were not preserved by the processes of photographic reproduction. Accordingly, black borders to title-pages are a bad sign.

Not all 'Olympia Press' books had anything to do with Maurice Girodias; the formula was often slavishly copied by unimaginative pornographers. Titles issued in association with the New English Library are of little interest. And 'Akbar del Piombo' was not, as many tyros maintain, the pseudonym of William S. Burroughs but of Norman Rubington.

Girodias, Maurice, *Between Books: A Manner of Press Release* (for the Frankfurt Book Fair), New York, (1973).

Kearney, Patrick J., *The Paris Olympia Press*, 1987.

Original graphics

The most desirable of twentieth-century illustrated books are those containing original graphics, i.e. illustrations printed from plates which were worked on directly by the artist, with or without help from a professional engraver, etcher or lithographer. Almost all such books are, necessarily, limited editions. Care should be taken to distinguish them from books illustrated with, for instance, 'wood engravings' which are no more than photographic reproductions of an original print.

Osborne collection

Edgar Osborne started his collection of children's books when he revisited his old home in Hampshire and came across some childhood treasures. His wife Mabel joined him in the search and together they built up one of the largest collections of children's books ever assembled. The library ranges over all forms of children's literature: fairy tales, religious manuals, moral tales, school stories and poetry. Edgar Osborne presented the collection to the Toronto Public Library in 1949 after his wife's death. Since then gifts and acquisitions have continued and the catalogue, an important bibliographic tool for the bookseller and collector, was published in 1958. At that time the earliest book was the 1566 Plantin edition of *Aesop's Fables*. By 1975, when the third edition of the catalogue appeared, the collection had acquired a copy of the *Historia di Lionbruno* of 1476, which includes the first known mention of the seven-league boots.

The two-volume catalogue, illustrated in colour and in black and white, is indispensable for research into early children's literature.

The original collection extends to the first years of the twentieth century, but a smaller library of later twentieth-century books was formed in honour of the first Osborne librarian, Lillian Smith.

St John, Judith (ed.), *The Osborne Collection of Early Children's Books, 1566–1910*; with an Introduction by Edward Osborne, 2 volumes, Toronto, 1958 (reprinted with corrections, 1966, 1973).

Out of series

The publishers of a limited edition generally consider that a small number of copies not destined for sale (e.g. author's copies, file copies, or review copies) may legitimately be produced in excess of the total specified in the colophon or prospectus. Accordingly, these do not use up letters or numbers reserved for the trade copies, and are instead designated 'out of series'.

Although this system, like that of 'artist's proofs', suggests possibilities for abuse, there are very few cases where a disproportionate number of 'out of series' copies seems to be in circulation; and, of course, many bear interesting presentation or association inscriptions. Other things being equal, the designation 'out of series' makes little or no difference to the book's value.

Overslip

An overslip is a hinged addition to a plate which, when lifted, shows a different detail below. The device is best known as the ingenious method used by Humphry Repton in his *Observations on the Theory and Practice of Landscape Gardening*, 1803, and in other works, to show how landscape features could be modified by such measures as the sinking of a fence or the alteration of a contour. Overslips easily become detached, and Repton's books (never inexpensive) are particularly highly valued when all are present and undamaged. A similar method is sometimes used in the illustration of scientific and technical works, as well as children's books.

P

Pagination
The sequence of a book's page numerals. Catalogue descriptions of modern books often indicate only the number of text pages ('229 pp'), but when full details are considered necessary, preliminary pages (including blank leaves) are designated by lower-case roman numerals; these numerals are enclosed in square brackets when (as in the case of title-pages) they do not actually appear in the book. In earlier books, especially those produced by more than one printer, page numbers, or folios, were sometimes incorrectly printed, and the terms *irregular* or *erratic pagination* are often used to indicate that the numerals do not follow a correct sequence; but specific details – 'page 214 misnumbered 204' – are preferable if the errors are few in number.

When a book brings together two or more previously published works, continuous pagination will always identify it as a collected edition, even though the individual title-pages may bear varying dates.

Paper
Francis Meynell used to boast that no paper-maker who dealt with the Nonesuch Press ever made money on the transaction. This adversarial stance between publishers and paper-makers is less unusual than one might imagine, and any attempt to understand the terminology of paper-making is liable to result in more rather than less sympathy for Meynell. Paper-makers have evolved a terminology of considerable complexity, in which patterns are no sooner discerned than disproved: adjectives vary substantially in meaning even within the narrowest subjects, while foreign words are recklessly imported, in the process undergoing changes of meaning which vary from the dramatic to the diametric. This terminology has been adopted with varying fidelity by publishers; by the time it reaches the antiquarian bookseller it may mean anything. Japon vellum is neither vellum nor Japanese; the French phrase 'papier de Chine' translates as 'rice paper' but has nothing to do with rice, being made from the pith of a small tree native to Formosa.

Laid paper, when it is held up to the light, exhibits a pattern of closely spaced parallel lines (known as 'laid' or 'wire' lines), crossed at right angles by much more widely spaced 'chain lines'. These lines were left by the chains at the bottom of the mould in which the paper was made.
Wove paper was developed in the early 1750s, perhaps by Baskerville; the use of a woven wire mesh created a remarkably even surface, which immediately became popular. Some machine-made wove paper deliberately imitates the lines in laid paper.

It is perhaps hardly surprising that the majority of booksellers, on the rare occasions when they feel obliged to specify details of the paper on which a book is printed, are content to quote from the colophon. This attitude, however, does the subject an injustice. As Tanselle writes in his essay *Bibliographical Description of Paper*, 'paper-making is a complex field with an

PAPIER-MÂCHÉ

immense technical literature'; WATERMARKS, in particular, are of increasing importance to both scholars and booksellers.

Clapperton, R. H., *Paper: An Historical Account*, Oxford, 1934.
Coleman, D. C., *The British Paper Industry*, Oxford, 1958.
Hunter, Dard, *Papermaking: the History and Technique of an Ancient Craft*, 2nd edn, New York, 1943 (reprinted, 1978).
Labarre, E. J., *Dictionary and Encyclopaedia of Paper and Paper-making*, 2nd edn, Amsterdam, 1952; supplement (by E. J. Loeber), Amsterdam, 1967.
Leif, Irving P., *An International Sourcebook of Paper History*, Folkestone, 1978.
Shorter, A. H., *Paper Mills and Paper-Makers in England, 1495–1800*, Hilversum, 1957.
——— *Papermaking in the British Isles*, Newton Abbot, 1971.
Tanselle, G. Thomas, *Selected Studies in Bibliography*, Charlottesville, Virginia, 1979.

Papier-mâché

Bernard Middleton describes papier-mâché as consisting of 'boiled and beaten paper cuttings with which is mixed a quantity of size which acts as a hardener'. Its use as a material for bookbinding is first recorded in about 1849 when it was moulded and stained to resemble medieval wooden boards, in deference to the prevailing fashion for things medieval. Works by Henry Noel Humphreys in particular were often bound fittingly in papier-mâché. The bindings tend to become brittle over the

Some books bound in papier-mâché.

years and are liable to crack or crumble; they are not easy to repair.

It should be noted that current research has questioned whether these bindings are in fact made of papier-mâché, although no alternative description has yet been established.

Parchment
The inner portion, or under-side of a split sheepskin, untanned but dried and dressed in much the same way as vellum. Parchment is essentially a writing surface, but is occasionally used for binding.

Parts
Although the publishing of books in parts, or instalments, is principally associated with the novels of Dickens and other Victorian novelists, the practice was first employed towards the end of the seventeenth century and was widely used in the eighteenth and early nineteenth centuries for the issuing of illustrated books, encyclopaedias and other substantial works of reference, as well as for works of literature. The main purpose of part publication (or 'issuing in numbers', as it was originally known) was to spread the cost of a work intended for a popular audience which would otherwise find it beyond their means. Many books were first issued in this way, and only later in book form; in some cases part issue was adopted for a reprint; and other books are known in part form only.

In the nineteenth century the rapid growth of the circulating libraries lessened the need for part publication, as Mudie's and others made reading matter quite cheaply available throughout the country; but when Chapman and Hall revived the practice in 1836 for Dickens's *Pickwick Papers*, it immediately assumed the important place in publishing history which it was to maintain for some 40 years. Dickens, Thackeray, Trollope and many other novelists of the period achieved a popularity which could best be exploited by part issue and, though the spreading of cost remained the main objective, the 'cliff-hanger' effect of instalment publication influenced both writer and reader.

As the Victorian part issues almost always preceded any other editions, they are keenly collected; but their fragility, and the many complicated 'points' that determine their status, make them both scarce and expensive in fine condition. The number of parts varies from 8 to 24, and occasionally more, with the final part usually containing the title-page and prelims, often with a frontispiece portrait to accompany the previously issued illustrations. The coloured outer wrappers were particularly vulnerable, and the inserted advertisements are often found to vary from one copy to another of the same part. A glance at such studies as Hatton and Cleaver's bibliography of Dickens's Novels issued in Parts is sufficient to indicate the many variants and complications which beset the cataloguer and the collector. Nevertheless the part issues of great nineteenth-century novelists, from Dickens to George Eliot, will always appeal to the collector sensitive to the reading habits of an author's time, and to the peculiar excitement of part issue.

Paste-down
That half of an ENDPAPER which is pasted on to the inside of the upper or lower cover of a book is known as the paste-down; the facing half is known as the (front or back) free endpaper.

Payne, Roger (1739–1797)

Roger Payne and his brother Thomas set up their first bindery near Leicester Square in about 1778, assisted by their namesake, the bookseller Thomas Payne. The brothers made a good team, Thomas being a skilled forwarder and Roger a gifted designer and finisher. When their partnership came to an end Roger took a new partner, Richard Weir, whose wife was a repairer and restorer of books. Unhappily both men were eccentric and both drank heavily; as a result their work gradually deteriorated and eventually their business failed.

Books bound by Roger Payne owed

Epictetus, *The Works*, 1758, bound by Payne, [Maggs Bros Ltd].

much in their conception and execution to his seventeenth-century predecessors, and in particular to SAMUEL MEARNE. Payne used the finest materials – russia leather, which was then fashionable, and straight-grained morocco – usually in dark blue, olive green or red. His designs were austerely elegant; often only the spines were decorated. Payne's favourite tools, which he designed himself, included classical motifs such as laurel wreaths, vine leaves, simple flowers and celestial symbols of the moon or stars.

Payne executed work for many of the great collectors of the time, such as the Rev. Cracherode, whose collection is now in the British Library, and at Eton, Earl Spencer, many of whose Payne bindings are in the John Rylands Library, and Sir Samuel Hoare, the banker. Payne's bills of account, when they have survived, add significantly to the value of his bindings. The GROLIER CLUB copy of Lilly's *Christian Astrology* contains such a bill: 'Bound in the very best manner . . . it is absolutely a very Extra Bound Book. I hope to be forgiven for saying so and unmatchable.' The cost, including cleaning 'it was very dirty and I am certain took full 2 days work', was £1.3.6d.

Pear Tree Press

When James Guthrie founded his press in 1899, his declared object was 'to provide an independent means of printing my own work in various fields'. Many of the 35 books issued by the press in the ensuing 40 years did indeed feature drawings, bookplates, poems and editorial contributions by James, Stuart and John Guthrie; other authors and illustrators of note included Edward Thomas, Laurence Housman, Eleanor Farjeon and Pickford Waller. Many would regard *To The Memory of Edward Thomas*, 1937, as the press's most successful book, but none of its publications is without distinction. The family involvement, as well as a certain delicacy of design, have something in common with the work of the DANIEL PRESS.

Penguin Books

In 1934 Allen Lane, aware of financial difficulties facing the publishing firm, The Bodley Head, of which he was a director, sought a solution in the production of a series of very cheap, well-produced reprints. Priced at 6d. each, the first Penguins were issued as a private enterprise by Lane and his brothers, with no financial backing by The Bodley Head. Booksellers were sceptical of the price, the durability and the status of the new cheap editions, but Woolworths ordered in bulk and the broad striped coloured covers soon became a familiar sight.

The Penguin logo was designed by the Bodley Head production department as a 'dignified but flippant' name for the new enterprise; in Charing Cross Road the books were dispensed from a 'Penguincubator' and railway bookstalls took them up eagerly. Gradually the range expanded to include Pelicans, Puffins, Penguin Specials, Penguin Classics and King Penguins. Illustrations began to appear on the covers and the subject matter included reference works, art history and science. Format changed to include larger sizes, and specialized markets such as children, universities and technical text-books were catered for. Designers for Penguin have included Alan Aldridge, Edward Ardizzone, David Gentleman, Gertrude Hermes and Lotte Reiniger. The widely admired typographic style owes much to the early influence of Jan Tschichold.

The first Penguin, André Maurois's *Ariel*, the life of Shelley, now commands a modest price as an important milestone in book history, though it must be in fine condition and complete with its DUST-WRAPPER. The next hundred or so titles attract some interest.

King Penguins have a considerable following. Inspired by the German Insel Bücher they first appeared in November 1939, their innovative colour illustrations a cheering venture in the early days of the war. Seventy-six appeared in all. Although most King Penguins are easy to find, condition can be a problem; a few, such as *Magic Books of Mexico*, *Egyptian Paintings* and *Birds of La Plata* are elusive.

[Williams, William Emrys], *The Penguin Story*, Harmondsworth, 1956.
Williams, Sir William E., *Allen Lane, A Personal Portrait*, 1973.
Fifty Penguin Years, foreword by Malcolm Bradbury, Harmondsworth, 1985.

Perfect binding

Perfect is a modern and somewhat flattering description of the type of binding in which adhesive techniques take the place of conventional sewing or stitching. The most effective of these adhesive methods, when used as an adjunct to other techniques, makes it possible for the book to be opened quite flat without risk of splitting; but in general this is hard to achieve. Bindings of this kind are largely confined to paperbacks, where the folds in the leaves, rather than being stitched, are trimmed away, so that the book consists of a collection of single sheets held together by glue.

Pforzheimer, Carl H. (1879–1957)

Carl Pforzheimer, an American banker, built up a collection of the works of Shelley matched only by those of the BRITISH LIBRARY and the BODLEIAN. The four-volume catalogue, *Shelley and His Circle*, is indispensable for the study of the English romantics; there are several other similar collections in the library. In 1987 the Shelley collection was transferred to the New York Public library where it is readily accessible to scholars and visitors.

Phillipps, Sir Thomas (1792–1872)

Thomas Phillipps was educated at Rugby and University College, Oxford. Even as a very young man he was constitutionally unable to throw away even the smallest piece of paper, asking his father to retain all his own letters. Soon after his marriage and the granting of his baronetcy, Phillipps's BIBLIOMANIA began to assume extraordinary proportions. He acquired books at auction sales and from booksellers all over Britain, and he set up the Middle Hill Press in about 1822 to print topographical manuscripts or works that he had written or transcribed, many of them unworthy of the labour. His debts increased and he fled to Switzerland for a while to avoid his creditors.

Post-Napoleonic Europe offered rich opportunities for the collector, and Phillipps purchased vast numbers of books and manuscripts from booksellers, monasteries and libraries in France, Belgium and Holland. The source of his finances at this stage is not entirely clear; certainly on his return his creditors were again waiting for him.

Throughout his life Phillipps's relationship with booksellers was difficult, even acrimonious. He was an ill-tempered customer, treating the trade with contempt, returning 'on approval' books after months of delay, refusing to pay for his purchases or insisting he had already done so, and resenting the trade's presence at sales he attended.

The obstinacy and ill humour that he showed towards most of his acquaintances led to setbacks for Phillipps in his personal career: Sir Robert Peel refused his application to head the new Records Commission, and his attempt to stand for Parliament was frustrated by his bankers' refusal to honour his candidacy bond. His unforgiving nature even led him to ruin his own son-in-law, James Halliwell, whose intellect and scholarship were superior to his own.

Phillipps's voracious search for books continued unabated throughout his life. He acquired a large number of manuscripts at the Heber sale, 1834–1836, outbidding the BODLEIAN LIBRARY, the BRITISH MUSEUM and continental buyers; and he bought too from Quaritch and Sotheran's, neither of whom stood any nonsense from him. When he moved house towards the end of his life he had to find room for 100,000 books, and after filling four rooms he still sought space for 200 tea-chests of manuscripts. He had been acquiring material continuously, even bartering where he could: 'You said you had some nice Larchpoles. Will you give me a good load and I in return will let you have all my copies of the Parliamentary Registers of this Borough . . .' wrote the Town Clerk of Evesham. Phillipps's aim, as he wrote to fellow-collector Robert Curzon, was to have 'one copy of every book in the world'.

Phillipps's temper worsened as he grew older. He ill-treated his long-suffering family and poor eyesight and attacks of gout did not help. He would not pay for assistance for his invalid wife, and allowed the house, inherited from his father, to fall into disrepair. When he died, at the age of 80, he left instructions that the library should remain as it was, with admission refused to booksellers, Roman Catholics or his estranged daughter and son-in-law.

Thomas Phillipps undoubtedly saved from destruction many tons of manuscripts, driving up their value at a time when the market was very weak. His expenditure is estimated at about a quarter of a million pounds and he made his collection available to scholars, cataloguing more than 23,000 items. After his death some duplicates were sold by Sotheby's in 1886 and several national libraries acquired further parts of the collection. Additional sales followed in the auction rooms, many books and manuscripts finding a place in the collections of J. PIERPONT MORGAN, Chester Beatty and HENRY E. HUNTINGTON. Finally in 1945 the London booksellers Lionel and Philip Robinson acquired the remaining part of the library, some items later reappearing when their own collections were sold in more recent years.

The story of the Robinsons' purchase and transfer to London of an unexamined and largely unknown treasure trove of vellum and paper, printed and handwritten, is set out by Philip Robinson in 'Recollections of Moving A Library', *The Book Collector*, Winter, 1986. Sir Thomas Phillipps collected books and manuscripts on an unprecedented scale. Such opportunities are unlikely to occur again.

Barker, Nicolas, *Portrait of an Obsession*, 1967, from Munby, *Phillipps Studies* (see below).
Munby, A. N. L., *Phillipps Studies*, 5 vols, Cambridge, 1951–60.

Photographic illustration

The use of photographic illustration in books effectively began with H. Fox Talbot's *The Pencil of Nature*, published in six parts between 1844 and 1846. Earlier contenders include Mrs Anna Atkins's *Photographs of British Algae*, 1843–53, which used Sir John Herschel's cyanotype, or blueprint, process, but many commentators feel that this is closer to nature printing than to photography.

When describing photographically illustrated books, a clear distinction should be made between those containing original prints and those with mere reproductions. Early examples of the former, as one might expect, can be extremely expensive; names such as Julia Margaret Cameron, Alvin Langdon Coburn, P. H. Emerson, Francis Frith, David Octavius Hill, Edward J. Steichen, and Alfred Stieglitz are much in demand, and the 1887 edition of Eadweard Muybridge's *Animal Locomotion*, a work of primary importance for representational artists ever since, is highly prized.

The market in later photographically illustrated books is a comparatively recent one, and reputations are constantly subject to revision, but fashionable names include Ansel Adams, Bill Brandt, Brassaï, Cartier-Bresson, Robert Doisneau, Robert Mapplethorpe, L. Moholy-Nagy and Leni Riefenstahl; as this list suggests, much of the impetus in this expanding field comes from America and the Continent. The work of British photographers such as Cecil Beaton or David Bailey can still be found quite cheaply.

Gernsheim, Helmut, *Incunabula of British Photographic Literature . . . 1839–75*, 1984.

Goldschmidt, Lucien, Naef, Weston J., *The Truthful Lens*, New York, 1980.

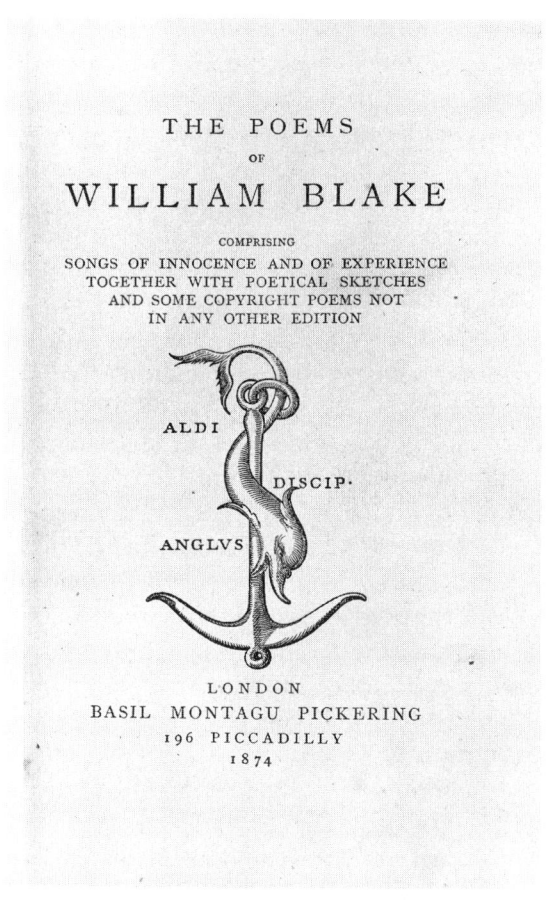

Pickering, William (1796–1854)

Publisher and bookseller, William Pickering was perhaps the illegitimate son of the second Earl Spencer; his Diamond Classics bore the Spencer arms on the title page, and were sometimes known as the 'Spencer Classics'. His early apprenticeship – one of his fellows was Thomas Sotheran – with John and Arthur Arch and later with Longmans, was followed by bookselling on his own account in Lincoln's Inn Fields.

Like many of his contemporaries Pickering combined the roles of bookseller and publisher, and the Diamond Classics were among his earliest publications. However, they were printed in small type which proved difficult to read; this led to his adoption of a more legible typeface for his 17-volume edition of the works of Bacon. STANLEY MORISON called him 'a printer who designed his books', and they are much appreciated by those who admire fine, unpretentious typography. Pickering used an adaptation of the ALDINE dolphin and anchor device on his title-pages, and his *Aldine Poets*, 53 titles in all, are highly regarded among collections of this kind; they were issued either in full morocco, bound by HAYDAY, or in blue cloth. Pickering is credited with the introduction of publisher's cloth, but the works most appreciated by modern collectors are the attractively printed poets in contemporary leather bindings.

Keynes, Geoffrey, *William Pickering Publisher – A Memoir and Checklist of his Publications*, The Fleuron, 1926 (reprinted, 1969).

Pictorial bindings

Pictorial decoration on cloth bindings has been largely superseded by DUST-WRAPPERS, though a few publishers – the Folio Society is a notable example – occasionally make striking use of this on their covers. In earlier periods vignettes on cloth spines were not uncommon, and pictorial boards flourished in the days of the 'yellow-back' novels of the nineteenth century. The de-

A pictorial binding, 1863.

Pierpont Morgan Library

J. Pierpont Morgan (1837–1913) was born into a family of wealth and distinction, whose ancestors settled in America in the eighteenth century. His grandfather, Joseph, acquired land and property in Connecticut, and his father established a mercantile and banking house in London which eventually became Morgan, Grenfell and Co. Pierpont inherited substantial wealth, and a cultivated interest in art and literature.

Young Morgan began collecting manuscript and autograph material as a schoolboy; after his father's death he set out earnestly to acquire illuminated manuscripts, incunabula, Shakespeare folios and autograph manuscripts by Dickens, Keats, Byron and others. Fine French and English bindings formed an important part of the collection, and as it expanded a special building was seen to be essential to house it properly. In 1906 Morgan completed the building of a splendid library and museum next to his own home in New York, where the whole collection could be suitably arranged.

After disposal of some of the art treasures to offset death duties, J. Pierpont Morgan's library and museum was transferred to a Board of Trustees and is incorporated as a Public Reference Library; the building has been enlarged to meet the growth of the collection. The founder's son controlled it, together with the Board until his death in 1943, and his grandson, Junius W. Morgan, formed an association of Fellows of the Library to ensure its financial well-being. The Fellows, some 500 in number, come from many countries, and contribute towards the cost and expansion of the collections.

Morgan purchased books from the leading dealers in the USA and Europe, and at the great auction sales of his time. The hoard of manuscripts amassed by SIR THOMAS PHILLIPPS led to many acquisitions, as did the discreet disposal of a number of private libraries. In addition to printed books (from CAXTON to William Morris) the collection includes drawings and paintings, sculpture, metalwork and porcelain.

The library is open to visitors and accredited scholars, and there are facilities for exhibitions and conferences. The library's exhibition catalogues often represent important contributions to their themes. Much attention is paid to conservation and research.

Pigskin
See LEATHER

Piracy

The unauthorized publication of another's intellectual property for one's own benefit.

As might be expected, the history of literary piracy is a long one, the more so as (surprisingly) an international system of copyright protection covering both the United Kingdom and the USA was not established until the 1950s.

There is no general rule about the desirability or otherwise of piracies in a collection, as there are so many circumstances to be taken into account in addition to the elusive enough question of personal taste; but, particularly where modern books are concerned, there seems to be a tendency to prefer authorized editions to piracies, especially when the latter are far removed in place or time from the author.

Plate book
This term may describe any book illustrated with separately printed plates, but it is in practice largely confined to books such as ACKERMANN's splendid nineteenth-century volumes, which are valued primarily for their fine coloured aquatints or lithographs. In more recent times, it has also been applied to the books whose topographical steel engravings have so comforted the print trade.

Pochoir
'A process used in book illustration, especially for limited editions, in which a monochrome print is coloured by hand, using a series of stencils; a print made by this process' – *OED*. Fine examples of this labour-intensive process, particularly popular in France during the second quarter of the twentieth century, are now highly valued.

Saudé, Jean, *Traité d'enluminure d'art au pochoir*, Paris, 1925.

Point
A point is understood by booksellers and collectors to be any feature of a book which serves to identify a first (or other significant) edition, issue or state. It may be as trivial a feature as a broken letter or as prominent as a differently coloured binding. It should command deference only if a competent bibliographer has established its significance beyond reasonable doubt.

Pollard, Alfred William (1859–1944)
A. W. Pollard joined the staff of the BRITISH MUSEUM in 1883 after a distinguished undergraduate career at Oxford. In 1892 the BIBLIOGRAPHICAL SOCIETY was founded by a group of scholars, headed by James MacAlister and Walter Copinger, to promote bibliography as a science and encourage research in the subject. Pollard was its first secretary, a post he held for more than 30 years. He was appointed Keeper of the Department of Printed Books at the Museum in 1919.

Pollard's special interest lay in Shakespearian scholarship and he published several works in that field. He also wrote on early illustrated books, contributed the volume on *Fine Books* to The Connoisseur's Library and, most importantly, compiled with G. R. Redgrave the *Short-Title Catalogue of English Books*.

Pollard, Henry Graham (1903–1976)
A FESTSCHRIFT published by the Oxford Bibliographical Society in 1975 in honour of Graham Pollard includes a brief memoir by JOHN CARTER. It tells the intriguing story of Pollard's Oxford career: his refusal to waste £5 on obtaining a master's degree, his acquaintance with Harold Acton, Cyril Connolly and Evelyn Waugh, his membership of the Young Communist League and his introduction of corduroy trousers 'to polite society'.

Pollard went straight into antiquarian bookselling from university, working for a time on a history of the trade. He became a close friend of STANLEY MORISON and his association with John Carter led to their investigation of 'certain nineteenth-century pamphlets' which resulted in the disclosure of the WISE forgeries.

Pollard's writings include accounts of the medieval book trade in Oxford, early English bindings, the history of newspapers, type design and contributions to the *Cambridge Bibliography of English Literature*. He was president of the Oxford Bibliographical Society from 1960 to 1961.

Posting and packing
The despatch of books by post plays a part

in virtually every bookselling operation, whether intermittently or (in the case of catalogue dealers) as a daily routine. In recent years many booksellers with large despatch requirements have tended to entrust the work to freight organizations, some of whom specialize in the handling of books and offer the advantages of such services as Accelerated Surface Post; but some thousands of books are packed and mailed by individual booksellers every day, and, as the great majority reach their destination safely and in good time, it may be said that all is well in this area of bookselling.

The advent of bubblewrap has simplified the essential task of protecting books against the impacts that every parcel must be expected to suffer, and the adhesive tapes which have almost entirely replaced string have rescued the edges of covers from a once common hazard. (Brown tape is much easier to use if warmed up, e.g. on a radiator.) Paper with a waterproof coating is nowadays readily available, and all in all modern materials and dispensers have both simplified and improved the packing of books. If any note of caution is needed, it concerns padded envelopes or jiffy bags; these serve well enough for single items of a sturdy kind, but are unsuitable for more vulnerable books, and should not be re-used. Some years ago, an ingenious corner protector was offered to booksellers – a triangular shield which looked promising but was in due course 'remaindered', perhaps because it tended to penetrate everything around it.

Postal services, both inland and overseas, are well described in the guides issued by the Post Office, but these do not always give all the information that may be useful to booksellers. The use of the Printed Matter Rate, for example – an economical surface rate for book parcels weighing up to 5 kg, needing no customs declaration – was at one time conditional on parcels remaining unsealed so that the contents could be easily examined. This involved awkward packing methods; but little prominence is given to the fact that normal packaging is permitted if a Sealing Permit is obtained from the Post Office.

Every bookseller will have his own policy in regard to registration, insurance and other aspects of mailing; but it should be mentioned that mailing books to a few overseas destinations – happily very few – has proved to be unwise in any circumstances. A word with an experienced dealer may be helpful.

Prelims
This accepted abbreviation of 'preliminary pages' applies to all those pages of a book, printed or blank, which precede the text. It is common practice for an author to write, and a printer to set, the prelims after the main text has been completed. The PAGINATION is separate, usually in Roman numerals, and the prelims may include any or all of the following: blanks, half-title, dedication, frontispiece, title-page, imprint, copyright notice, contents page, preface, introduction, list of plates or any other peripheral material. Bibliographers take particular note of prelims, which frequently give the only clues to priority of issue.

Presentation copy
Normally used only of books bearing presentation inscriptions from their author – or, occasionally, illustrator, designer or publisher.

In rare cases, an inscription may combine with external evidence to suggest strongly that, even though not inscribed by the author, a certain copy was indeed given away by him or her; for instance, an ownership signature and date may match up to an entry in the author's diary which reads 'Went round to see X. and gave her a copy of the A.B.C'. No matter how tempted one is to be categorical, though, one should never express more than moral certainty in such cases. More irritating, and more often met with, are 'presentation copies' which were clearly inscribed at the owner's request, sometimes even at bookshops' signing sessions; or, even worse, copies with inscribed bookplates, suggesting that the 'donor' never even handled the book, but instead replied to a request from an autograph hunter.

The words 'Presentation Copy' are sometimes found embossed on the PRELIMS, as with 'Review Copy'; these copies were almost invariably given away by the publisher for promotional purposes. This practice has declined, along with the embossing of REVIEW COPIES, probably for much the same reason.

Press books
See PRIVATE PRESS BOOKS

Presswork
It would be hard to improve on the definition given by G. A. Glaister, whose *Glossary of the Book*, 1960 (revised 1979), made such a notable contribution to the literature of book history: 'The printing off on paper of matter set up in type, and in modern usage, the care and attention devoted to this as revealed by the quality of the result'.

Prideaux, Sarah Treverbian (1853–1933)
A pupil of COBDEN-SANDERSON and ZAEHNSDORF in London, and then of Gruel in Paris. She remained an amateur but her bindings are much sought after for the quality of their design and execution. Working with only the finest materials, she used bold flower and scroll patterns with simple outline frames and borders and preferred to design for collectors who could appreciate true quality. Most of the books she bound related to writers and artists of the Arts and Crafts School such as William Morris and CHARLES RICKETTS. She taught KATHARINE ADAMS and wrote several books on bookbinding. Prideaux always signed and dated her work with her initials 'S. T. P.'.

Printing and the Mind of Man
During the planning of the 11th International Printing Machinery and Allied Trades Exhibition, which was to open in London in July 1963, the typographer Stanley Morison suggested that the industry should remind the world of the debt owed to the invention of printing. Something of the kind had been attempted at the Gutenberg Quincentenary Exhibition at Cambridge in 1940, but the IPEX exhibition was on a much grander scale, occupying both Earl's Court and Olympia. The Monotype Corporation sponsored both the bibliographical display and the catalogue, edited by John Carter and Percy Muir.

The exhibition catalogue, as had been intended, was later expanded by the same editors into a folio volume of some 300 pages, extensively illustrated, with an Introduction by Denys Hay. The full title is *Printing and the Mind of Man: a Descriptive Catalogue illustrating the Impact of Print on the Evolution of Western Civilisation during Five Centuries*. It is based on a selection of 424 works which over five centuries have had such an impact on the mind of man as literally to change the course of history. The first item is Gutenberg's *Bible*, printed in Mainz in c.1455; the last is the first edition, in *Parliamentary Debates*, of Churchill's 'Battle of Britain' speech delivered in the House of Commons in August, 1940.

Many of the works described in the book are of scientific interest, but art and architecture, religion and politics, travel and exploration, all have their place. So too do such themes as women's suffrage, scouting, broadcasting and children's literature.

Printing and the Mind of Man quickly achieved the status of a prestigious guide as well as inspiring collectors with a new theme, and the abbreviation PMM followed by the relevant item number lends weight to catalogue entries. The expanded work first appeared in 1967; a revised edition appeared in Munich in 1983.

Private Libraries Association

The Private Libraries Association has for many years played an important part in the encouragement of book collecting and in the provision of important amenities for the collector. The Association was founded in 1956 as an international society, 'to help readers in the organization, cataloguing and fuller enjoyment of their personal collections'. This aim has been vigorously pursued by means of the publication of an excellent quarterly journal, *The Private Library*; a quarterly newsletter and exchange list, with details of books members wish to obtain or to dispose of; a members' handbook giving addresses and collecting interests (found by many catalogue booksellers to be better as well as cheaper than any commercially available mailing list); and the issue of a series of highly regarded books, of which each member receives one free copy, on various aspects of printing, binding, illustration, collecting and related subjects. Contemporary private presses have always had a prominent place in the Association's interests, and its check-lists of Private Press books, published annually since 1960, provide a valuable record of work in this field.

Private Press Books

John Byrne

'And are there more books to look at upstairs?' asked an American dealer on a recent visit. 'Yes indeed. We keep our Private Press books there'. 'Oh . . . er . . . thanks', backing away towards the street, as if confronted by a notice warning intruders of large and bloodthirsty dogs. This was not an isolated reaction, and in the next few pages I shall consider the deterrent effect of the very term 'Private Press', why we are wrong to apply it to many of the books that we display upstairs, and why some people, at least, may be misguided simply to run away without so much as a backward glance.

A senior purist states that 'a private press must have a printing press and must choose the texts it prints'. There have been a great many in Britain, from Caxton's on, but it is outside the scope of this piece and of the writer's experience to discuss the religious or political pamphleteers of earlier centuries, or the lavish products of such wealthy men's ventures as Horace Walpole's Strawberry Hill and Colonel Thomas Johnes's Hafod Presses

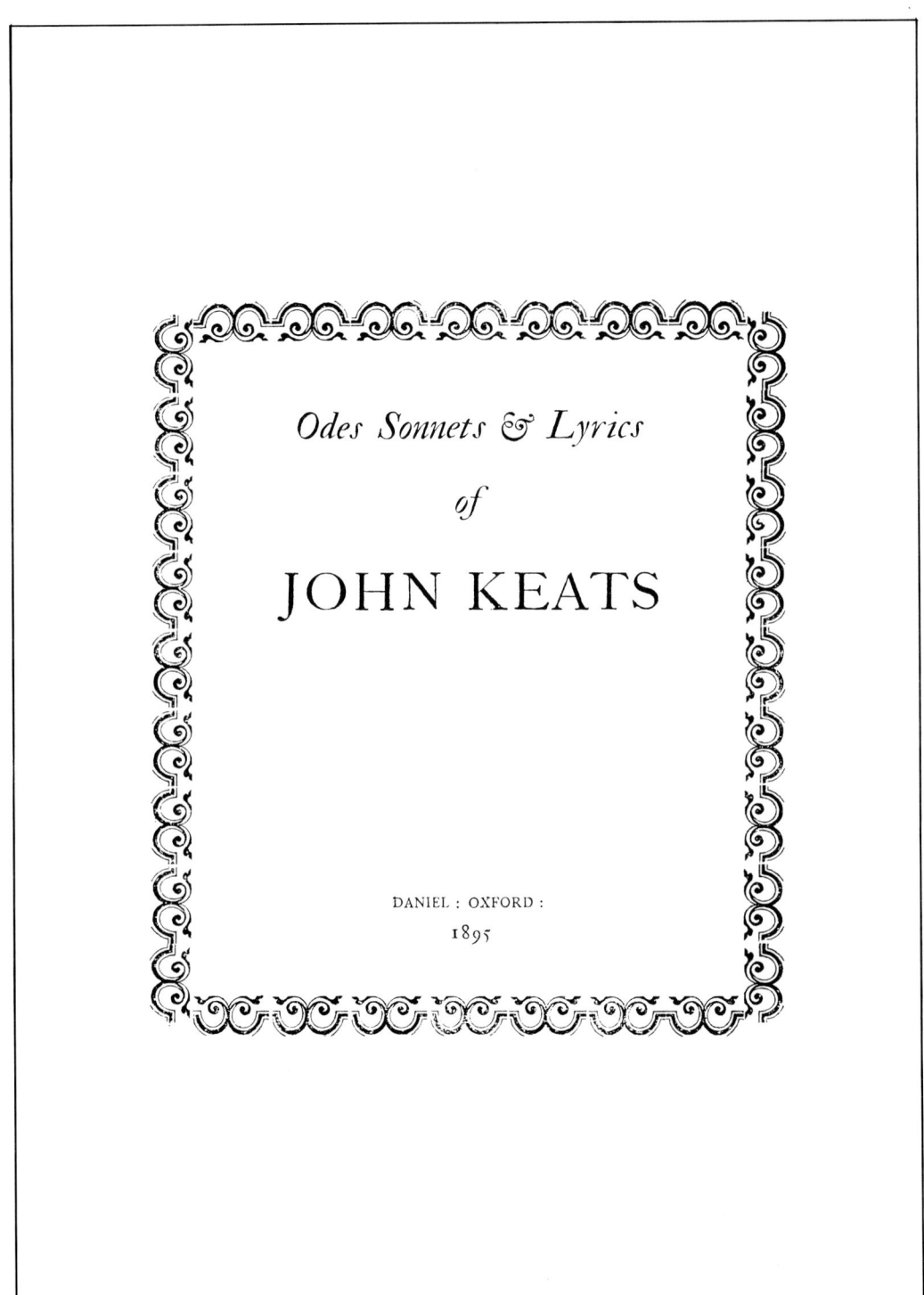

John Keats, *Odes, Sonnets & Lyrics*, Daniel Press, 1895. [Bertram Rota Ltd.]

(which is not to suggest – quite the reverse – that they are unworthy of attention). In any case it may be fair to suggest that it was with the birth of William Morris's Kelmscott Press, just over a hundred years ago, that the Private Presses acquired their apparently forbidding initial capital letters.

Morris too was a wealthy man, but he took his books more decisively into the commercial arena than his predecessors and, as successful poet, noisy socialist and influential designer, he was able to command attention for the late flowers of his long-harboured interest in printing. In next to no time a *movement* had sprung up, with just ten years seeing the foundation of the VALE (not for the purist, since Charles Ricketts did not own a press), Eragny, Ashendene, Essex House, Pear Tree and Doves Presses, most of them following the master's example in busily designing or commissioning their own proprietary types, printing small special issues of their books on vellum, and generally finding an eager market.

The work of all these has become thinner on the ground and more costly as yet more copies disappear into the permanent captivity of institutional collections. There may indeed be a mystique of élitism about them, and if they seem precious, that is precisely what they are. But only a fool would deny himself the pleasure even of looking at Lucien Pissarro's exquisite coloured wood-engravings in his Eragny books, of admiring the restrained beauty of the Doves (while debating if Cobden-Sanderson was not somewhat arrogant in putting all his chosen texts except the Bible into virtually identical format), of contrasting that arrogance with St John Hornby's care in his Ashendene work to select appropriate formats, from the delicate *Carmina* of Horace to the monumental Spenser, Boccaccio and Cervantes.

Every movement will attract its less talented adherents, and the books of Mr and Mrs H. G. Webb's Caradoc Press should surely have been strangled at birth, but I must confess to a fondness for the Essex House Press – 'printed in vile types on unsuitable paper' (Roderick Cave) – which, as a mouthpiece for the Guild of Handicraft, intermingled treatises on metalwork and proposals for architectural conservation with its 'great' poems, its Psalter and Prayer Book. In fact the presses of this period were responsible for issuing very few new texts, and Morris himself was treading a well-worn path in devoting much of his energies to the production of essentially definitive editions of the work of his own pen. But we should not overlook the Daniel Press, which preceded Morris and was entirely independent of his influence, yet lasted into the present century, having resurrected the famous Fell types and, among many books of modest charm, produced a number of first editions of Robert Bridges's poems.

By the outbreak of the First World War the immediately Morris-inspired revival of printing by hand had largely burnt itself out. At the Pear Tree Press, James Guthrie continued to plough his solitary furrow, experimenting delightfully with printing in colour from intaglio plates, most famously in the 1916 *Six Poems* by Edward Eastaway (Edward Thomas), and the Ashendene Press still had sporadic splendours up its sleeve, culminating in the great *Bibliography* of 1935. In the next few years, however, there came into being the presses with which anyone handling twentieth-century books must be rather more familiar. The collector of Eric Gill or David Jones needs a number of books printed, not very well, by H. D. C. Pepler's S. Dominic's Press (founded 1916). Leonard

Gordon Bottomley, *Midsummer Eve*, Pear Tree Press, with drawings by James Guthrie, 1905. [Bertram Rota Ltd.]

and Virginia Woolf's Hogarth Press (1917) was private in the purest sense to begin with, as they printed, again pretty poorly, texts by themselves and such friends as Eliot, Forster and Katherine Mansfield. No collection of Conrad, D. H. Lawrence, Aldington, de la Mare, Blunden, Wilde or Henry Williamson can be complete without one or more books from the Beaumont Press (1917), much of whose attractive work seems to me still undervalued. Among the earliest publications of the Golden Cockerel Press (1921) were the first books of A. E. Coppard, Richard Hughes and Peter Quennell. Later, too, Laura Riding and Robert Graves used their Seizin Press to promote their own work and that of their intimate circle. These are Private Press books, but seldom perceived or offered as such, the author or illustrator carrying the greater weight.

The inter-war period is most publicly dominated by the Golden Cockerel Press, which was responsible, once Robert Gibbings had assumed control in 1924, for a dramatically high proportion of the finest books illustrated with engravings by the proprietor himself, by Gill and Jones again, John and Paul Nash, John Farleigh, Blair Hughes-Stanton, Eric Ravilious. After Gibbings had relinquished the reins to Christopher Sandford and others in 1933 the Press ceased to print its own books, thus condemning itself to being labelled merely 'publisher' by pedants. But Sandford designed and supervised everything, just as Francis Meynell designed, while barely ever printing, everything issued under his prolific Nonesuch Press imprint. With bold and exuberant patrons and by importing from Europe both revived and new types, some commercial printers made books as fine as any 'private' presses could achieve with their hand-operated machines.

The 42 books produced between 1923 and 1940 by the Gregynog Press are rather more in the stately Ashendene tradition, and their appeal is more obviously limited to the collector of fine printing (who may admire several texts in Welsh while not understanding a word of them). Gregynog was specially privileged in being based upon generous private wealth and in having its own bindery, and if a rapid turnover of controllers makes the total output seem incoherent, there are plums to attract various tastes: first editions of Edward Thomas, W. H. Davies and even George Bernard Shaw; Hughes-Stanton's most extraordinary engravings and some of Reynolds Stone's earliest and most charming; superbly crafted special bindings.

Superb craftsmanship was not the hallmark of anything undertaken by the Seven Acres Press, started in Buckinghamshire by the American Loyd Haberly in 1925. In a later stint as Gregynog's controller Haberly oversaw at least two of its grandest books, while his *Medieval English Pavingtiles* (Shakespeare Head Press, 1937) is an undoubted success. In his independent efforts his gauche verses, inept woodcuts, printing and bindings command affection in a land famed for its fondness for gallant losers – and it should be noted that the sheer eccentricity of printing at home is a powerful draw for some collectors. Robert Gathorne-Hardy's and Kyrle Leng's Mill House Press has similar attractions though its amateurish printing cannot be deemed a failure, never aspiring to be more than an entertainment for its owners and their friends, among whom were Logan Pearsall Smith, Robert Bridges, Sassoon, Osbert Sitwell and Forster. Collectors of these authors treasure the rarity of very small editions rather than the accomplishment of the presentation.

Viscount Carlow's Corvinus Press, on the other hand, deserves greater attention and renown than it yet enjoys. The young Carlow was an enthusiastic collector of books,

SCULPTURE

An Essay on Stone-cutting, with a preface about God, by Eric Gill, T.O.S.D.

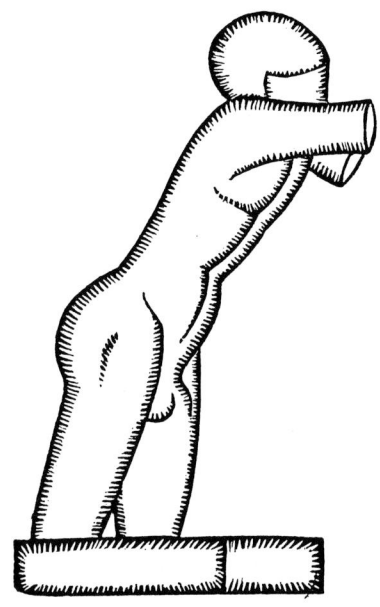

At Saint Dominic's Press, Ditchling, Sussex

Eric Gill, *Sculpture*, S. Dominic's Press, 1924. [Bertram Rota Ltd.]

manuscripts, fine bindings, literary friends, unusual types and even more unusual papers. His own attempts at printing were disastrous and so he employed a good pressman. Together they made some of the most distinctive books of the late 1930s, including several texts by T. E. Lawrence and new work by H. E. Bates, Edmund Blunden, Walter de la Mare, James Joyce and others. Two hundred copies were produced of Lawrence's *Diary* and 175 (25 of them signed) of Joyce's *Storiella as she is syung*, bound in brightest orange vellum, but many other editions were of 30 or fewer copies, destined for the Press's tiny list of subscribers or more often as gifts to Carlow's friends. They turn up most infrequently, as do the Carlows of this world, more's the pity.

While I have restricted my remarks to British presses, in deference to the insularity and monoglottism still prevalent here, no general view of this period can omit two continental ventures, each with strong British links. Harry Graf Kessler's Cranach Presse in Weimar produced a handful of the most justly admired books of the age, notably the 1930 *Hamlet*, with Gordon Craig's astonishing woodcuts. The 1931 *Duino Elegies* of Rilke finds a place in several different collections; it was co-translated and is signed by V. Sackville-West, has engraved initials by Eric Gill, and bears the imprint of the Hogarth Press.

First from Switzerland (1923–1927) and then from Verona for a further 50 years Hans (Giovanni) Mardersteig casts a giant shadow far beyond national boundaries. His presswork, his type-designs, his scholarship would have been remarkable independently of one another, and his reputation is so great that one hesitates as to whether to catalogue the 1960 *Four Quartets* (290 copies signed by the author) under Eliot or under Officina Bodoni.

Back in this country the Golden Cockerel Press continued to publish through and well after the Second World War, but with the death of the engraver John Buckland-Wright its later books dwindled into lavish poor taste. The two decades after the war contained only a few productions of real note. One was a wondrous flowering from the Stanbrook Abbey Press: in a few years from 1956 the Benedictine sisters in their print-shop, armed with elegant, newly acquired types by the eminent Dutch typographer Jan van Krimpen and with a devoted scriptorium, made several books – among them *Christmas Lyrics*, *Magi Venerunt* (1959) and Siegfried Sassoon's *The Path to Peace* (1960) celebrating his conversion – in which the love of the task well done seems to shine from the page. The short-lived Vine Press's most ambitious book, Herbert Read's *The Parliament of Women*, 1960, remains a delight, while in 1957 Morris Cox completed 14 of the 20 copies of *Yule Gammon*, the first of his Gogmagog Press's remarkable series of books, lately celebrated in a generously illustrated volume from the Private Libraries Association. Will Carter's Rampant Lions Press in Cambridge (in which his son Sebastian joined him in 1966) was meanwhile quietly consolidating a reputation for excellence in printing books, like Mardersteig, both for himself and on commission, as well as for the fine jobbing work which he has never disdained.

At this juncture it may be of interest to supply a fairly detailed case-history. In May 1970 Bertram Rota Ltd published its Catalogue 165, *Fine Printing*, the first devoted to this subject that the company had issued in several years. The catalogue contained 232 entries with a total face value of £7,615 11s. It included ten Kelmscotts, among them a Chaucer priced at £1,850 which did not find a buyer at the time, together with decent representations of the Ashendene, Doves, Essex House, Gregynog, Pear Tree and Seven Acres Presses. The title, however, expressed an honest recognition that, for instance, a number of the 34 Golden Cockerel books had been commercially printed, as had the 30 from the Nonesuch Press. I suspect that what we listed must have been some 90 per cent of our Fine Printing stock, 189 items were second-hand, and of these only 22 came from overseas – 17 from America, four from Holland and a single one from the Officina Bodoni. Of the 43 new books just six were American, five German and one (Officina Bodoni again) Italian. With the exceptions of five books for which it was sole distributor, the company owned everything, and everything was catalogued under imprint – nothing under printer or designer, where different.

Twenty-one years later Catalogue 257, *Fine Printing*, followed its similarly specialized predecessor by 18 months and offered 600 items selected from perhaps twice that number in stock. Only 269 books were second-hand, 178 of them British, 50 American, no fewer than 21 from the Officina Bodoni, and the remaining 20 from France, Germany, Italy, Holland and Australia. Of the 331 new books, 295 were owned by the company, 165 British, 85 American and 45 variously from Australia, Canada, Holland, Italy, France, Denmark and Poland. 36 items were held on consignment. The secondhand books included a good number printed at the Cambridge University and Curwen Presses, several printed by the Dutch house Enschedé and by the Stamperia Valdonega (the machine-printing offshoot of the Officina Bodoni), books designed by such American typographers as Bruce Rogers and Frederic Warde, or by the Dutchman A. A. M. Stols. From all these statistics it must be clear that fewer 'real' Private Press books come our way so that we have spread our net much more widely – quality, not manner of production, being the dominant criterion; also that we have made a considerable commitment to the handling of new work.

If earlier books have become harder to find, the bookseller enjoys advantages over the collector. William Ridler, indefatigable accumulator and lister, wrote in the introduction to his *Modern British Private Press Books*, 1971: '. . . it is most unlikely these days that a book from the Kelmscott Press will be discovered unregarded between one of the Waverley novels and a Swahili grammar'. Of course this is true as far as bookshops and fairs are concerned, but I have had my eye for years, in a friend's home, on a run of Doves Press books inscribed by Cobden-Sanderson to the present owner's grandparents. He knows that they are 'nice' and likes the association. Will his children care for them any more than for the tattered Dornford Yateses and the Ruth Rendell paperbacks with which they share a shelf?

Auctions have become another good source, especially since the major houses insist on minimum estimated values for lots. This means that, except for the obviously valuable things, two or 42 books will be lumped together, making viewing essential and effectively eliminating the private buyer. When an auction catalogue lists five Nonesuch books 'with 37 others from the same Press', as like as not the 37 others will include one or two that are really desirable, the cataloguer having apparently listed just the top five in the pile. Not long ago two of five 'others' lotted with three named items of scant significance proved to be the work of the Officina Bodoni.

Since the late 1960s many more individuals have acquired printing presses, as technological advances in the printing industry have led to them being dumped cheaply on the market. Some even have Monotype casters, greatly enlarging their capacities (and hand-set type is only as good as the hand and eye that set it). They also have an embarrassment of choice of texts, since *belles lettres* of all kinds are scorned by the giant publishing conglomerates. Indeed several of today's Fine Presses (their own term) are in fact small publishers who print their books, among them John and Rosalind Randle's Whittington, Simon Lawrence's Fleece and Michael Mitchell's Libanus Presses, of which the first and third also print extensively on commission for *soi-disant* Presses. The 'private' press is now largely the realm of the artist/printer. Ron King's Circle Press pioneered the introduction into fine books of such 'modern' techniques as screen-printing and continues to stretch the definition of 'book' in weird and inventive ways. Natalie d'Arbeloff, Ken Campbell, Shirley Jones and Susan Allix are making books of genuine and utterly individual distinction, their small and expensive editions necessarily aimed at the few. The many, alas, show little interest.

   I do not think it is possible for a bookseller to live on contemporary Fine Printing alone. The late Charlene Garry brought to her Basilisk Bookshop enormous enthusiasm and well-tried marketing skills. She scoured the globe for stock and committed multiple superlatives in her catalogues. But no amount of superlatives substitute for unfamiliar work being seen (and sometimes all too carelessly handled), requiring public premises. Small margins and volume were insufficient to offset overheads. The problems she encountered are still with us.

POEM

pen in hand
word
poem
paper
table
lamp
walls
room

suddenly   *looking up*
apprehensive

curtain sucked out
window wide open

did something   *creep out?*
creep in?

window wide open
curtain sucked out

slowly   *looking down*
trembling

room
walls
lamp
table
paper
poem
word
pen in hand

Morris Cox, *Poems 1970–1971*, Gogmagog Press, 1972. [Bertram Rota Ltd.]

Insularity is just one, but it is a sad truth that most of the American books we import (and there has been a veritable eruption of the 'book arts' in the USA) are bought by Americans when they have gone out of print or when a fluctuation in exchange rates causes the sterling price to be a bargain. Another dispiriting factor is that no sooner has one introduced a collector to the work of a Press that is new to him than he will introduce himself directly to the Press and they will walk hand in hand into the sunset, neatly if gratefully eliminating the bookseller. The printer prefers with good reason to sell at his full price rather than giving trade discount; the buyer may feel that he is in some sense a patron of the arts (and may sometimes negotiate his own favourable terms in any case).

Very rare, however, is the Press that has no need of the trade, and many are now offering more tempting discounts. I shall not be ordering from a brand new prospectus which gives no discount on single copies and only 20 per cent on multiples of a £30 book; and no confidence is inspired by another (announcing a £150 book) which includes the words 'handfull', 'humourous' and 'seperate'. It cannot be too strongly stressed that the prospectus must receive as much care as the book, or we are unlikely to want to see the book at all.

One problem that Charlene Garry did not have is that of immediate comparisons between older books and new; ours sit cheek by jowl. Many secondhand books can still be found at prices at which they could not be offered new (if indeed their quality could be matched), and I suspect that an ever higher proportion of new work goes straight into public collections. Libraries that have the interest will already have many of the older books and so are not obliged to make the same comparisons about value which confront the individual. Librarians, too, do not spend their own money, and for those printers who depend on selling their books for a modest livelihood – there are still blessedly many who print for fun, but none can afford to produce substantial work these days and they must remain unsung here – there must be a temptation to meet the requirements of Special Collections departments.

If people print what they like, of course they can come to like what sells, and I hear from some quarters that books without wood-engravings do not sell. I wonder whose fault this is and whether the printers may not have inadvertently narrowed the tastes of their customers. In any case my two best-sellers of recent years have been the totally unadorned editions of Shakespeare's *Sonnets* and *Hamlet* printed by the Tallone family in Northern Italy. These are beautifully done, not over-priced, and they make safe presents for christenings or twenty-first birthdays. This element of safety may be scoffed at; it is conventional to declare certain texts off-limits. Yet in 1908 Cobden-Sanderson declared: 'Great thoughts deserve and demand a great setting . . . and the great works of literature have *again and again* [my italics] to be set forth in forms suitable to their magnitude'. Succeeding generations may enjoy fresh printings of such warhorses as *The Song of Songs*, *The Rubaiyat* or *Sonnets from the Portuguese*, just as they undeniably need new translations of foreign classics, from Homer to Dostoievski and Proust. Fresh printings are to be deplored only when they are deplorably bad or deplorably dull, which too many have been. For myself, I do not want to see another compilation of disinterred engravings that were not much good when they were made and have certainly not been improved by the passage of time.

Admittedly the cult of wood-engraving has led to much improvement in the printing of blocks from the wood. Ian Mortimer (IM Imprimit) and Simon Lawrence are probably the present masters, while Graham Williams (Florin Press) achieved superb results, showing that there is no substitute for taking endless pains, until he recently forswore printing for sculpture. Engravings are most easily printed on certain smooth mouldmade papers, with a kiss-on-the-cheek rather than the solid smack of type or block against a more absorbent sheet, and these smooth papers are almost universally employed; the challenge and conquest of difficulty have become the preserve of the 'mad' artists. And typography seems to have become for many a secondary consideration, though I would warmly exonerate the Carters and others whose jobbing work has simply given them more practice in the art of making words look good on a page. Pure fine letterpress will not be treasured again if buyers do not have the chance to see it. Are today's printers inhibited still by Mardersteig's shadow, when they might be inspired by his example and by the continuing demand for his work?

Cave, Roderick, *The Private Press*, 1971.
Franklin, Colin, *The Private Presses*, 2nd edn, Aldershot, 1992.
Matrix (published annually since 1981 by Whittington Press).
Private Press Books (annual check-lists published by The Private Libraries Association).

Privately printed

This phrase seems to apply most readily to matter produced by a private individual rather than a publisher, and distributed other than through the usual trade channels; it does not imply that the item in question was given away. As the term was long ago found to quicken the pulse of collectors, its use was taken up by (among others) the publishers of potentially obscene material, where it implied a promise of salaciousness. Occasionally, both in this context and in that of possibly libellous material, the phrase was used with the intent of escaping the consequences of giving an imprint.

Among books printed privately with worthier motives, one category familiar to most booksellers is the memorial volume – especially the many tributes compiled by families bereaved in war.

Prize binding

Prize bindings are those that bear the crest of a school or other prize-giving institution, gilt or occasionally blind-stamped, on the upper cover; a BOOKPLATE usually records the name of the recipient and the nature of the prize. These bindings, typically in full or half calf with marbled edges and endpapers, are often of excellent quality. Fine eighteenth-century examples survive, as at Trinity College, Dublin. Such prizes were favoured by numerous schools during the nineteenth century and up to the First World War; they were often supplied by binders of distinction on a profitable 'production line' basis. Bernard Middleton, in *A History of English Craft Bookbinding Technique*, 1963 (second enlarged edition, 1978), recalls that one well-known bindery charged four shillings (20p!) in 1910 for a half calf 8vo prize binding. In later years prizes sometimes took the form of a book with the institution's crest stamped on the publisher's cloth binding.

Proctor, Robert George Collier (1868–1903)
Proctor catalogued 3,000 INCUNABULA at the BODLEIAN LIBRARY; while an assistant in the Department of Printed Books at the British Museum he compiled the *Index of Early Printed Books in the British Museum*, 1897–1903. These two works formed the basis of his most important contribution to the study of incunabula, the *Catalogue of Books Printed in the XVth Century* which was published after his mysterious death in Switzerland. He was particularly interested in early Greek printing and in Icelandic literature, but is best remembered for his system of bibliographical classification of incunabula – known as 'Proctor order'. This involved the listing of early books in chronological order by country, town and printer.

Johnson, Barry C., *Lost in the Alps. A Portrait of Robert Proctor*, 1985.

Proof copy
A copy of a book produced by the printer some time in advance of publication to enable the author and publishers to make final corrections not put right at previous stages of proofing. Proof copies are usually bound in wrappers, with or without a printed legend. Although they are often physically indistinguishable from ADVANCE COPIES, their bibliographical status is quite different.

One consequence of the increased popularity of first edition collecting since the mid-1970s has been the proliferation of proof and advance copies; instead of throwing them away, publishers' representatives and other staff now tend to guard them jealously, or take them directly to dealers in modern first editions. Consequently there are a good many recent ones about, and there are signs that the market has begun to allow for this.

Prospectus
A description of a forthcoming book, varying in format from a booklet to a single leaf, and usually circulated in order to obtain advance orders either from booksellers or from individual subscribers. Publishers of finely printed books, as might be expected, take considerable care with their prospectuses, which generally incorporate examples of anything innovative or exceptional in the typography or illustration of the book itself. Not only does the presence of a prospectus enhance a copy of the book it advertises, but the prospectus has become a worthwhile collector's item in its own right, offering as it does the opportunity to acquire splendid examples of the printer's art at a fraction of the price one would have to pay for a complete book.

Provenance
A book's previous ownership, or provenance, may be deduced from various evidence: a BOOKPLATE, label, or stamp, a SIGNATURE or INSCRIPTION, a recognizable shelf-mark, a crest or other identifiable feature on the binding. A bookseller's collation note may also be informative to those who can identify these pencillings.

Provenance is clearly of most interest to collectors when it reveals previous owners of special note or significance, and cataloguers can be relied upon to give full prominence to such information. Indeed, the use of the word provenance is generally confined to such cases; but in a broader sense, many collectors welcome evidence of previous ownership, even when it is of no special significance, simply as an indication of continuity in the enjoyment of a valued book.

Provincial Booksellers' Fairs Association

The PBFA, established in 1974, is the largest organization of antiquarian and secondhand booksellers in the UK, with over 600 members. It is run as a members' cooperative with committees at regional and national levels, with membership open to London dealers as well as to those outside the capital. Essentially a trade organization, the PBFA arranges nearly 200 book fairs each year throughout the country. The most important is held monthly in London, and in June this fair takes on an international dimension as visitors come from all over the world to the many book fairs and auction sales which take place around this time.

In addition to sponsoring and coordinating book fairs, the PBFA, which now owns its own headquarters, arranges lectures and seminars on various aspects of bookselling, provides support for members in difficulty and generally seeks to play a constructive part in the affairs of the antiquarian book trade. Its vigorous promotion of book fairs has been responsible for many changes in the scope and structure of the trade.

Pye, Sybil (1879–1958)

Sybil Pye taught herself to bind books, starting in 1906, with the help of DOUGLAS COCKERELL's *Bookbinding and the Care of Books*, 1901. She was much influenced and encouraged by CHARLES RICKETTS, who designed tools for her, and books from the VALE PRESS were among those she worked on. MAJOR J. R. ABBEY was one of those from whom she received commissions.

Her style was characterized by leather onlays in cubist and geometric designs, with much use of striking colours, together with black and white. Describing her own use of the colour and texture of leathers in her work, Sybil Pye wrote: 'When a pleasing combination of these has warmed the imagination, a design is worked out in very soft chalks and charcoal, the designs being constantly remodelled until they satisfy the eye.'

Pynson, Richard (d. 1530)

Pynson, a printer, came to London from his native Normandy and worked at first for WYNKYN DE WORDE. In about 1490 he took over the printing business of William de Machlinia in the parish of St Clements and, despite harassment because of his foreign origin, he soon became the leading printer of his day. He later moved to Fleet Street.

Pynson specialized in the printing of books on law and was appointed Printer to the King on the death of the first holder of that office, William Faques. He retained the

Logo designed by Edward Bawden

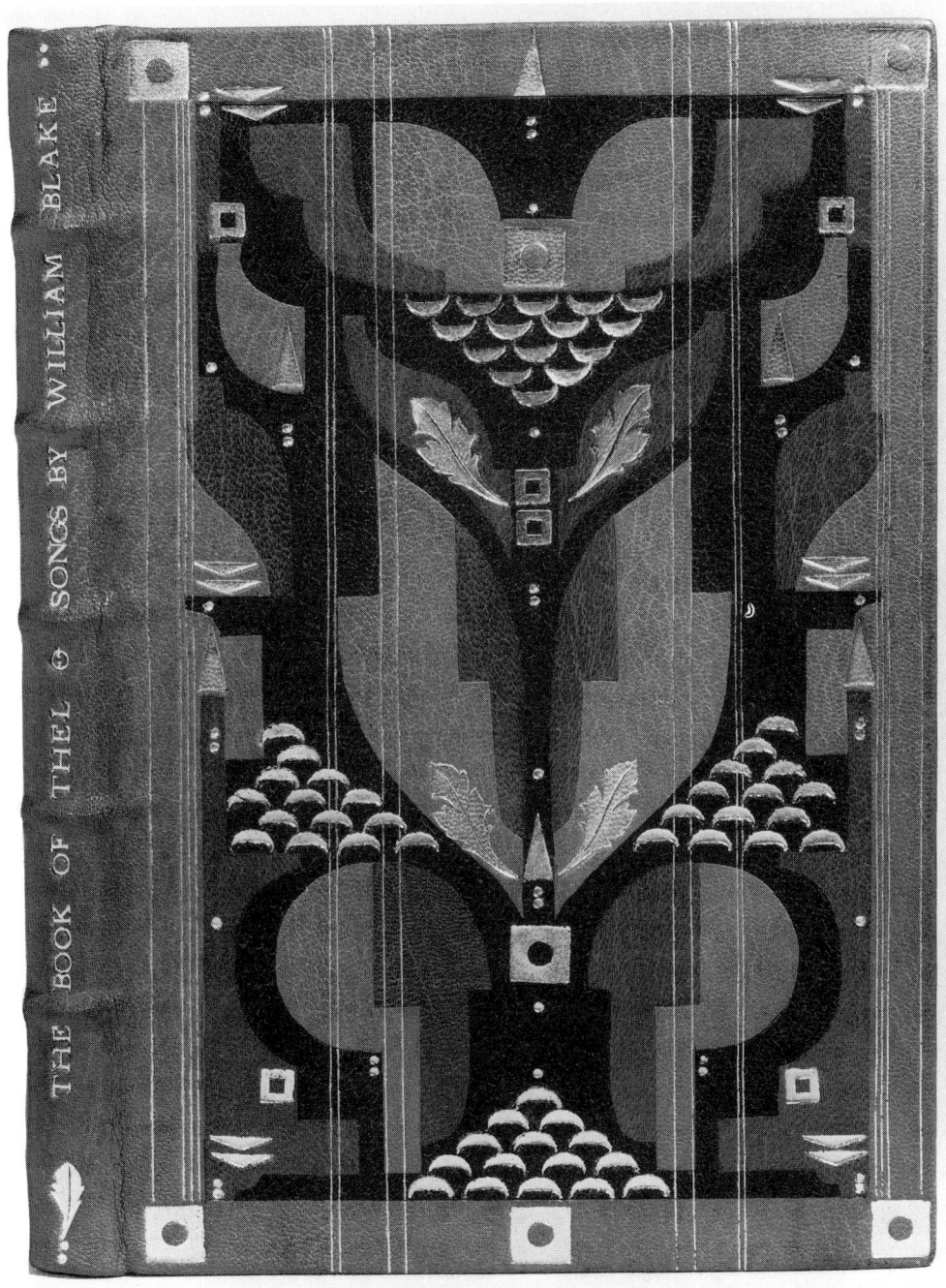

William Blake's *The Book of Thel*, bound by Sybil Pye, 1897 [Maggs Bros. Ltd.]

privilege when Henry VIII succeeded to the throne, printing the latter's *Assertio Septem Sacramentorum* which earned his master the title of Defender of the Faith.

Pynson is particularly remembered for introducing Roman type to British printing. He was also the first to use the term *cum privilegio* to indicate the right to publish.

Q

Quarto
Books of quarto (4to) format are those in which the printed sheet has been folded twice to produce leaves one quarter of the size of the sheet.

Queen's Quorum
Subtitled *A History of the Detective-Crime Short Story as Revealed by the 125 Most Important Books Published in this Field, 1845–1967*, this useful check-list was written by the detective story writer 'Ellery Queen' (a pseudonym for Frederic Dannay and Manfred B. Lee); it was first published in book form in 1951 and updated in 1969. Dannay formed a distinguished collection of books in various fields and this list of 'cornerstone' detective stories is often taken as a basis for forming collections, as with Connolly's THE MODERN MOVEMENT. As a result, a premium often attaches to the books he mentions.

R

Raised bands
Raised bands, in their genuine form, are the ridges which protrude from the spine of a leather-bound book where the gathered sections have been sewn on to horizontal cords. The ridges are absent only if the cords have been recessed to provide a flat spine. Some modern books cased in leather are embellished with false bands.

Ramage, John (1836–1900)
Ramage served his binding apprenticeship in London and then went on to work in Paris. He set up his own binderies first in Edinburgh and then in London. His work is held in high esteem; the designs are elegant, usually in the style of earlier binders, often making use of coloured onlays and silk doublures.

Rampant Lions Press
Will Carter founded the Press in Cambridge in 1949. One of the most consistently distinguished and delightful of contemporary printers, Carter was joined in 1966 by his son Sebastian; the Press has been used by a variety of publishers.

Sonnets from the Portuguese, by Elizabeth Barrett Browning, bound in specially made DOUGLAS COCKERELL marbled paper boards, and *Ecclesiastes* with chapter initials by Reynolds Stone, are typical of the works produced by the press.

[Carter, Sebastian], *The Rampant Lions Press: a Printing Workshop for Five Decades; Catalogue of an Exhibition at the Fitzwilliam Museum, Cambridge*, Cambridge, 1982.

Rarity
Any consideration of rarity in relation to books and book collecting must own its indebtedness to JOHN CARTER, who condensed his fuller study in *Taste and Technique in Book-Collecting* into three authoritative pages in *ABC For Book Collectors*. His analysis of absolute rarity, relative rarity, temporary rarity and localized rarity is hardly capable of amplification, let alone improvement; and fortunately these terms are broadly self-explanatory to those familiar with the buying and selling of antiquarian books. It is tempting to leave the field to Carter, only repeating after him Charles Lamb's shrewd observation that 'tenth editions are often scarcer than first editions'.

Nevertheless the words 'rare' and 'scarce' play such an important part in the evaluation and description of antiquarian books that a few further comments are needed. The 'localized rarity' category is perhaps less important than formerly, with the increase in international travel and the advent of the fax machine. John Carter touches only briefly on condition as a factor in the judgement of rarity, but it is one that has increased in significance as the collecting of modern FIRST EDITIONS has expanded. Many important modern books will never deserve to be customarily described as 'rare' or 'scarce', having been printed in relatively large numbers; but unmarked copies in DUST-WRAPPERS may well merit such a description, if only within Carter's 'relative rarity' category. A word may also be added about the increasing prevalence of 'artificial rarity', achieved by limiting an otherwise unremarkable book to a very small number of copies.

Booksellers and cataloguers should remember that the rarity of a book is of no importance unless it is in some way desirable.

Reading copy
This apparently otiose description is generally taken to mean that a book offered in a catalogue is little more than complete, and thus 'readable', though not in suitable condition for a collector. 'Working copies' are usually even worse. Some justification for the use of these terms lies in the tendency of fastidious collectors to acquire second copies of books they wish to retain in fine condition; or in the willingness of scholars/readers to tolerate any reasonable copy of a text which was suppressed or never reprinted, or is unaffordable in better condition.

Rebacked
A book is described as rebacked, rather than rebound, when the restorer has replaced only the spine or backstrip, retaining the original covers. Any kind of binding – leather, boards, wrappers, cloth – can be rebacked. Descriptions of rebacked books normally mention the material used in the repair if it differs from the original material, as when boards are rebacked with cloth or leather. The retention of the original spine, when this has been possible, is also mentioned ('original spine preserved' or 'laid down'), as is the retention of the original label.

Recto
The terms *recto* and *verso* are readily understood in bibliographical terminology as describing the upper and lower sides of a leaf, the recto thus being always the right-hand page of an open book designed to be read from left to right. Booksellers may find, however, that these terms, (sometimes abbreviated to 'r' and 'v') are not universally familiar, and plainer words such as 'front' and 'back' may occasionally be desirable.

Reissue
Either a reprint, or a new edition; but the term nowadays carries a strong implication that the book in question has been out of print for some time. Generally, modern reissues are only of interest to collectors either when the previous editions are textually corrupt or virtually unobtainable, or when a new introduction throws fresh light on the book or its author. However, this does not apply to early printed books where simultaneous issues and reissues are common, but may still be of interest.

Remainder
The remaining stock of a book, unsold by its publisher and disposed of to a bookseller or wholesaler to be offered at a reduced price. There is no longer a great stigma attached to this; in fact, many publishers now allow for a remainder sale in their costings.

Secondhand booksellers need to keep a watchful eye on the remainder shops, in order to avoid embarrassing pricing anomalies.

Remainder binding
The 'remainder' need not necessarily be in the form of bound books; in the nineteenth century it was usual, and in the twentieth not uncommon, for it to consist of unbound sheets, which were then bound up to the order of the new owner.

Reprint
A second, or subsequent, impression or edition.

Restoration and Repair

Rob Shepherd

All booksellers will be aware of the fragile nature of books. Rotting leather, discoloured and brittle paper, detached boards – these are just a few of the familiar ills that beset old books. The range of problems can be formidable. Books are, after all, the outcome of many processes, and this partly explains their vulnerability. Poorly manufactured materials, particularly paper and leather, are prone to decay, and bad binding techniques, such as paring leather too thinly, will cause inherent weaknesses. Atmospheric pollution is also a key factor. Sulphur dioxide, nitrogen dioxide and other pollutants can have disastrous effects. High levels of humidity and temperature can accelerate acid attack and form favourable conditions for the formation of mould. But sometimes the greatest threat to the preservation of old books comes from their custodians. Old bindings have been lost or ruined by clumsy or inappropriate repairs. Well-meaning collectors have frequently made repairs with unsuitable tapes and adhesives: sellotape is an excellent material for wrapping parcels, but was never designed for book repairs!

Conservation

Conservation, as applied to books, is a relatively new concept, but booksellers and collectors are increasingly aware of its importance, and there is now greater emphasis on the value of preservation rather than restoration.

Underlying this new emphasis on conservation, however, is a very real confusion. Everyone may agree that conservation is desirable but there is considerable uncertainty over the practicalities of the matter. Terms such as 'acid-free' and 'archival quality' may sound reassuring, but what do they really mean? Even the professional restorer or conservator can be confused by new theories and consequent conflict of opinion. The purpose of this article is to give some general advice on the basics of 'Book Conservation' and shed light on some of the major problems. Those who seek more detailed information, or wish to practise more advanced procedures should seek help from the text-books and professional organizations listed in **Notes I** and **II**. It is worth stressing that it is almost always wise to seek the help of a professional bookbinder or paper conservator.

Reference sources

It is important, in considering the conservation of any object, to understand something of its basic structure. Many bookbinding manuals have been published over the years, but

Rebacking a Book [Shepherd's Bookbinders]

little has been written on the history of bookbinding from a practical perspective, and studies tend, in most cases, to concentrate on aspects of cover design. Bernard Middleton's *A History of English Craft Bookbinding Technique* is a notable exception and gives a fascinating insight into how the book has evolved. A basic knowledge of bookbinding history can explain the reasons for many of the conservation problems of today. The literature of the subject is steadily expanding; bodies such as the Institute of Paper Conservation hold conferences, publish papers and produce newsletters. New information on the causes of, and remedies for, decaying paper and leather are constantly appearing.

The storage of books

Temperature and humidity play an important part in the preservation of paper and bindings. Relative humidity, that is, the percentage moisture saturation at a given temperature, is the critical factor. If the atmosphere is too damp, as it may be in basements, books will absorb moisture and this can cause mould-growth. Conversely, a low 'RH', often the result of central heating, causes embrittlement and cracking. Ideally, books should be kept at a relative humidity of between 40 and 50 per cent and at a temperature of 60° Fahrenheit or less. This is a little cool for most homes and bookshops, and a temperature of 70° Fahrenheit and an RH of 55 per cent to 65 per cent is acceptable. High temperatures, i.e. above 70°F, will increase the rate at which chemicals such as acids will attack books. Humidity can be measured with humidity indicator cards or a hygrometer. If the relative humidity is very high it can be controlled by the use of a dehumidifier. Alternatively, if the air is too dry, a humidifier can be used to replace moisture.

Location of shelving   This is largely a matter of common sense. Basements should, if possible, be avoided as should close proximity to radiators. Direct sunlight is also a hazard, raising the temperature, and causing spines to fade. Ventilation is important, with adequate space allowed behind the books for air to circulate; closed bookcases should be opened frequently.

Storage containers   There is now a large range of containers for books and paper which are marketed under the term 'archival-quality'. This term, when used to describe a storage box or similar item, implies that the materials used are free from harmful acids and chemicals. It is important, however, to seek advice when buying 'archival' products, as some items such as photographs require special protection.

Archival melinex is a clear plastic material which has been specifically developed for the safe storage of paper, and is proving a most useful product. Available in sheet form or as pockets, it is ideal for storing sheets of paper or slim pamphlets. It is also a very useful material for making a transparent dust-jacket.

Problems with paper

The most common complaint about paper is generally described by the term 'foxing'. This usually takes the form of brown spots and has many causes, including mould

Paper restoration: Janet Atkinson at Shepherd's Bookbinders

RESTORATION AND REPAIR

resulting from storage in damp conditions. It can also be a sign of acidity in the paper which in turn causes it to become brittle and weak. The introduction of woodpulp in the middle of the nineteenth century is responsible for the poor quality of much of the paper produced after that date, and often causes the whole surface to discolour and weaken.

The term 'acid-free' refers to paper that has a pH value of not less than seven (neutral). Generally speaking, paper produced before the introduction of woodpulp is often non-acidic and in relatively good condition, though problems may occur through acid migration from the binding materials or the atmosphere.

As to remedies: beware of any substances sold for the purpose of removing foxing; they will almost certainly contain bleaching agents which will harm the paper. Professional paper conservators can wash and de-acidify paper, reducing the effects of foxing with the careful use of chemicals. However, it is worth noting that, even in the hands of professionals, bleaching agents can weaken the paper and should be used cautiously. Pressure from dealers and collectors has undoubtedly encouraged the overuse of bleach, which as well as being harmful to the structure of the paper, causes it to assume a 'dead' white appearance.

Tears in the paper and loose pages are common problems. Professional advice and skills should be sought, but where these are not accessible, temporary repairs can be made if the correct materials and a little manual dexterity are employed. Pressure-sensitive and adhesive tapes will harm the paper and even tapes manufactured specifically for the purpose, such as 'Document Repair Tape', have their detractors among professional conservators. Adhesives should always be completely reversible (i.e. capable of being removed), and mending with Japanese tissue and rice or corn starch is generally regarded as the safest method. Jane Greenfield's *The Care of Fine Books*, pp. 87–91, gives further information.

Other problems, such as surface dirt and dust, can be alleviated by dry-cleaning. Dry-cleaning pads, containing granulated rubber, can be gently rubbed over the paper without abrading the surface and a stiff bristle brush can be used for brushing out accumulated dust from the gutter. An artist's half-inch paint brush with a round head is ideal for this purpose.

Corners that have become creased can be carefully folded back and pressed with the aid of a bonefolder. No one attempting even the most rudimentary repairs should be without a bonefolder: this humble object can be obtained from bookbinders' suppliers and should be about six inches long, with one end pointed.

Bindings

The primary purpose of a binding is to protect the book, and yet often the reverse occurs. Decaying bindings can cause great harm to their contents, and the decision as to whether to rebind a book, or conserve the original binding, must be a matter of individual judgement. Most booksellers instinctively wish to preserve original bindings where possible, and there are some basic procedures to be followed.

Before working on a binding, it is important to protect its contents. 'Clingfilm' is ideal for this purpose and should be generously wrapped around the bookblock before the application of leather dressing.

Cloth bindings   The introduction of cloth as a binding material in the 1820s enabled books to be bound quickly and economically, and in many ways cloth is a resilient material which responds well to repair. Frayed edges and knocked corners can be effectively conserved by the application of a little paste and gentle coaxing with a bonefolder. Loose threads and small tears can be pasted back into position, thus conserving and enhancing the book's appearance; but it is important to use a starch paste which, as well as being reversible, leaves little trace of adhesive when dry. The temptation to glue back detached spines should be resisted, as this will cause the spine to crack when the book is opened. Cleaning should be done with a proprietary book-cloth cleaner, and never with a water-based soap.

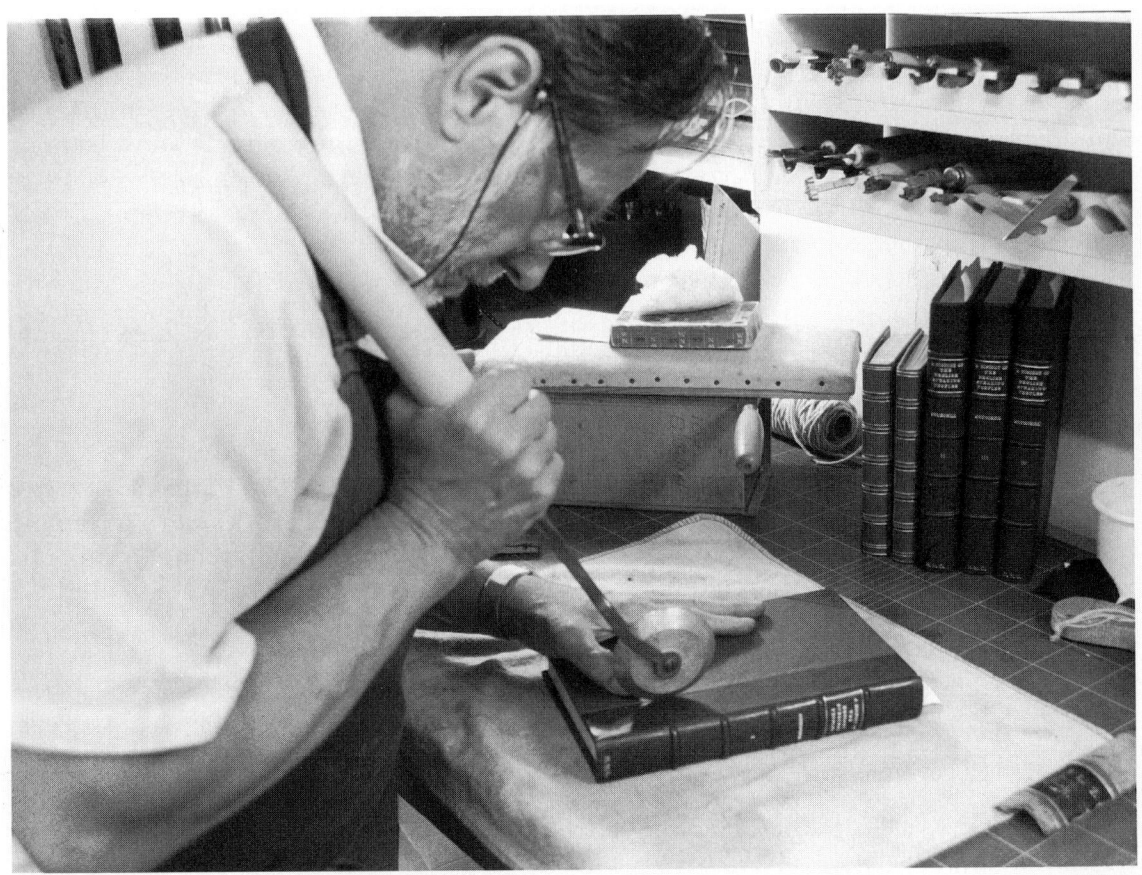

Gold tooling: Brian Hoy at Shepherd's Bookbinders

RESTORATION AND REPAIR

Leather bindings   The deterioration of bookbinding leather is the cause of much concern and research. The decline in tanning standards in the nineteenth century produced a great deal of inferior leather, a weakness exacerbated by a tendency in Victorian binderies to pare the leather very thinly. The results are all too obvious; books bound in earlier times are often of better quality leather, but the effects of atmospheric pollutants, such as those produced by gas lamps, have resulted in acidity and decay.

The worst manifestation of this decay is usually referred to as 'red rot'. This is something of a misnomer as the leather actually turns an orange colour, usually most obvious at the points of wear, such as along the joints and at the corners. Nothing can be done to reverse this process but the condition can at least be improved by the judicious use of leather dressing. Professional book restorers have a variety of formulae for consolidating leather that has severe 'red rot', but generally a standard leather dressing will help in all but the worst cases. The application of thin paste, particularly to broken corners and torn edges, will also consolidate the leather (see Note III).

The first point to note about leather dressing is that it will tend to darken old leather, particularly if it is very dry; scuffs and abrasions will also darken dramatically. A number of leather dressings are made specifically for books, the classic one being the 'British Museum Formula'. Caution should be observed in using this dressing, as it contains trichlorethane which, as well as being flammable, is also toxic. The trichlorethane helps the oils to penetrate the leather, but over-application is easy and can result in a sticky residue that is hard to shift. The original 'B.M. Leather Dressing' also contains beeswax in order to help polish the leather, but when used too freely the residue has caused books packed tightly on a shelf to become stuck together. A formula for a simple dressing without beeswax or trichlorethane, and which can be made at home, is given in Note III.

The three paramount rules to remember when applying leather dressing can be stated as follows:

1. Protect the pages of the book by inserting paper between the boards, or wrapping the bookblock in 'clingfilm'.
2. Use sparingly, and allow time for the dressing to penetrate.
3. Polish away any excess *before* returning the books to the shelves.

It is worth noting that in recent years there has been much research into the causes of leather decay and efforts have been made by some of the tanneries to adopt methods which will improve longevity. The latest advance in this field is the use of aluminium compounds in the tanning process. 'Aluminium tanned' leather is now available to bookbinders and its use should be encouraged.

For further information regarding the conservation of leather, and other subjects touched on in this article, see Notes I–IV.

Note I – Reference books

Baynes-Cope, A. D., *Caring for Books and Documents* [British Museum Publications, London], 1981 (2nd edn, 1989).

Cockerell, Douglas, *Bookbinding and the Care of Books*, 5th edn, 1971.

RESTORATION AND REPAIR

Cockerell, Sydney M., *The Repairing of Books*, 1958.
Diehl, Edith, *Bookbinding: Its Background and Technique*, 2 vols, New York, 1946 (reprinted New York, 1979).
Greenfield, Jane, *The Care of Fine Books*, 1988.
Horton, Carolyn, *Cleaning and Preserving Bindings and Related Materials*, 2nd edn, revised, Chicago, 1969.
Johnson, Arthur W., *Bookbinding*, 1986.
Middleton, Bernard C., *A History of English Craft Bookbinding Technique*, 1963 (2nd edn, 1978).
Plenderleith, H. J. and Werner A. E. A., *The Conservation of Antiquities and Works of Art; Treatment, Repair, and Restoration*, 1971, 2nd edn, (includes chapters on the causes of leather decay, and on paper conservation).
Plenderleith, H. J., *The Preservation of Leather Bookbindings*, British Museum Publications, 1947.

Note II – Colleges and professional organizations

In most large cities, there are a number of part-time courses available in bookbinding, and conservation (see below for London area). For people living outside a large city, it would be necessary to contact the local education authority.

Camberwell School of Arts and Crafts, Conservation Dept., Peckham Rd., London SE5 8UF (071–703 0987): For many years, Camberwell has been the foremost training ground for students of paper and book conservation.

Institute of Paper Conservation (IPC), Leigh Lodge, Leigh, Worcester WR6 5LB, England (0886 832323): The IPC exists to promote the preservation and restoration of books, documents, photographs, and works of art on paper. Members receive a quarterly newsletter and an annual journal. They also organize regular meetings and conferences.

National Preservation Office, The British Library, Great Russell Street, London WC1B 3DG (071–323 7612): The British Library acts as an enquiry point for advice and information on the preservation and conservation of books and documents.

London College of Printing (LCP), Bookbinding and Print Finishing, Elephant and Castle, London SE1 6SB (071–735 8484): The LCP runs full-time, part-time, and evening courses in bookbinding and conservation of library materials.

Leather Conservation Centre, 34 Guildhall Rd, Northhampton, NN1 1EW (0604 232723): Training is available in leather conservation and research into the deterioration of leather.

The Society of Archivists, c/o Hampshire Record Office, 20 Southgate Street, Winchester SO23 9EF (0962 63153): The professional society for archivists and archive conservators, furthering the interests of conservation by means of publications and conferences.

Note III – Formulae for paste and leather-dressing

1. Paste is easy to make, and is an ideal adhesive for general repairs to bindings and paper. It is completely reversible and free from harmful preservatives and acidic ingredients. Commercial pastes, such as wallpaper paste, should be avoided. The formula

given here is essentially the same as in Plenderleith, but with a slightly different method of preparation.

| White flour (not self-raising) | 100 grams |
| Water | 0.5 litre |

Mix the flour with a little water in an aluminium or enamel pan, taking care to smooth out any lumps. Add the rest of the water and stir. The solution at this stage should be of a milky consistency. Place the pan over heat and continue to stir. The paste will begin to thicken, and as soon as the first bubble appears, remove from the heat. Allow to cool with a lid on the pan to help prevent a crust. If stored in a cool environment, paste will keep for several days but should be discarded at the first sign of souring. It is, however, possible to add preservatives such as formalin (see Plenderleith).

Paste is incredibly versatile. It has high adhesive properties and is particularly suitable for repairs to cloth and leather bindings. For example, the moisture content in the paste will soften brittle leather and allow frayed edges and battered corners to be coaxed back into position. Thinned down it is also suitable for delicate paper repairs.

2. Leather dressing. There are many formulae for leather dressing, and opinions differ greatly on which is the best. Used carefully, the British Museum Formula is very effective, and is available from specialist suppliers. 'A simple dressing that can be made at home consists of 60% neat's-foot oil and 40% anhydrous lanolin (available from good chemists). If necessary, warm slightly to mix the oils together and keep in a screw-top jar.' (Carolyn Horton, *Cleaning and Preserving Bindings and Related Materials*).

Note IV – Refurbishment kit

The following list of basic tools and materials may be useful when undertaking minor repairs and refurbishment, and should be available from most craft shops or bookbinders' suppliers.

Archival polyester (Melinex) – available in sheet form for making dust-jackets.
Bonefolder (6" with one end pointed) – for creasing and coaxing material back into shape.
Bristle brush (½" diameter with a round head) – for brushing out inner margins.
Clingfilm – for protecting the bookblock during refurbishment.
Cloth – soft rag for polishing after leather-dressing.
Cotton wool (best quality [BPC]) – for applying leather dressing.
Cutting mat – self-healing cutting mats are widely available and facilitate accurate cutting, particularly of archival polyester.
Dry-cleaning pad – for surface cleaning of paper.
Rubber (eraser) – a good selection of hard and soft erasers should be kept to hand.
Scalpel knife, or craft knife.
Steel ruler (18" or 50 cm) – for using with the cutting mat.
Wheatstarch paste – See Note III.

Review copy
A complimentary copy of a book sent out by the publisher to any publication in which it might be given a review. For a time, the words 'review copy' were often embossed somewhere on the PRELIMS, but this practice has now ceased, perhaps because the increased difficulty the reviewer might have in selling the book would tend to diminish the goodwill its receipt was intended to generate. Such stamps, however, now make little difference to the value of a book. Review copies may occasionally provide helpful (though hardly conclusive) evidence in determining the priority of issue.

Ricketts, Charles (1866–1931)
Charles Ricketts was a designer with many talents: illustration, bookbinding, printing, typography and sculpture. Several of these skills found expression in the VALE PRESS, which Ricketts founded in 1896 together with his lifelong friend and partner, Charles Shannon. By 1903, when it came to an end, the press had produced 83 volumes in the best tradition of the English private press movement.

Ricketts' style of design changed considerably over the years. He was much influenced in his early work by Pre-Raphaelite ideas of medieval purity; Rossetti, in particular, won his deep admiration. His binding designs, some executed by SYBIL PYE, employed fine lines and intersecting rules in simple architectural patterns; but he also designed for Oscar Wilde's *A House of Pomegranates*, 1891, a typical art nouveau cover of lavish swirling movement, incorporating a peacock, a fountain and a pattern of pomegranates.

Ricketts and Shannon together founded, in 1889, *The Dial*, a magazine of literature and art whose contributors included Thomas Sturge Moore, Lucien Pissarro (whose ERAGNY PRESS had close links with Ricketts) and a young poet named John Gray who was the inspiration for Wilde's *Dorian Gray*. Ricketts' association with Wilde continued with the designs for *The Sphinx*, but much to his dismay its publication was eclipsed by the shock of Aubrey Beardsley's daring illustrations for *Salome*, 1894.

Other influences seen in Ricketts' work included his love of all things Japanese, the Italian masters of the High Renaissance, and both Greek and Celtic decoration. He painted in oils, engraved on wood, designed for the stage and created his own typefaces for the Press. When the Vale Press ended he destroyed the type, throwing it into the Thames. Every aspect of Ricketts' design for a book complemented the text: cover, TITLE-PAGE, illustration, printing, binding. He was a leading figure in the art nouveau movement and has a distinguished place in the history of British book design.

Delaney, J. G. P., *Charles Ricketts – A Biography*, Oxford, 1990.
Taylor, John Russell, *The Art Nouveau Book in Britain*, 1966.

Ring
The process of 'ringing' at an auction involves a system of conspiracy to defraud, and has been illegal since the passing of the Auctions (Bidding Agreements) Act, 1928. A group of bidders agrees before the sale on the prices they wish to pay. Its members then refrain from bidding against each other, and when the items are secured, inevitably at low prices, they meet after the sale for the 'knock-out', or settlement. This takes the form of a second 'auction' and each member of the ring receives a share of the difference between the sum paid to the auctioneer and the eventual

price reached. The loser is of course the vendor and, as a result, the auctioneer.

A fascinating account of such a conspiracy (not then illegal) is given in *Anatomy of an Auction: Rare Books at Ruxley Lodge, 1919*, by Arthur Freeman and Janet Ing Freeman (*The Book Collector*, Occasional Paper I, 1990); the same authors published *Post-Operational Notes* in *The Book Collector*, Autumn 1992. Members of the Antiquarian Booksellers' Association give an undertaking on election to membership that they will not participate in illegal auction practices; but despite the efforts of the Association, and of other bodies, ringing is known to persist, though it is perhaps more prevalent outside London. The large and varied attendances at major London sales make life more difficult for conspirators.

Rivière, Robert (1808–1882)
Robert Rivière, who came from a family of Huguenot artists, settled in Bath as a young binder-bookseller. Later he returned to London, where he had been educated, to set up his own bindery, encouraged particularly by an early client, the publisher WILLIAM PICKERING.

Rivière soon achieved considerable success with a wealthy and fashionable clientele who appreciated his somewhat flamboyant style. He popularized 'tree-marbled calf' as it was known then, and bound most of the COSWAY bindings designed for Sotheran's. He undertook several Royal commissions and exhibited at the Crystal Palace Exhibition of 1851, binding a special issue of the official catalogues in '2,000 skins of the best red morocco, and 1,500 yards of silk for the linings of the covers'.

The firm of Robert Riviere and Son (the 'son' was in fact Robert's grandson) closed down in 1939, but Bayntun's of Bath took over the business together with the bookbinding tools.

Roan
See LEATHER

Rogers, Bruce (1870–1957)
Bruce Rogers was brought up in Indiana, where he took a course in book illustration. He was already fascinated by letter-forms and, after working as a typographer in Boston, he became director of the Riverside Press, where D. B. Updike was also employed. His typography brought a new element of distinction to American book design. He reintroduced the Montaigne type and its successor, Centaur, and although he was a fine modern artist he appreciated and used freely the work of earlier craftsmen. Rogers came to England and worked for Cambridge University Press from 1917 to 1919; his damning report on the Press's machinery and equipment led to the appointment of STANLEY MORISON as director. Rogers worked, too, with Emery Walker, and for Oxford University Press, where in 1935 he designed the folio Oxford Lectern Bible. For this splendid volume – a commemoration of the First World War – he used his own Centaur type, recutting many of the letters to suit the generous scale of the book. Describing the work, Rogers tells how 'The words HOLY BIBLE were drawn and re-drawn six or eight times, in outline letters, in shaded letters, in red letters'.

Although best known as an outstanding typographer, Rogers was also a fine exponent of book design in its broadest sense. He interested himself in all aspects of book production and felt strongly that no part could be viewed in isolation. James M. Wells (in *Book Typography, 1815–1965*) describes Rogers' best work as 'distinguished for its clarity, its strong sense of style, its lack of pedantry, and its superb rightness in detail'. He designed several books for the LIMITED EDITIONS CLUB, and for the GROLIER CLUB.

Blumenthal, Joseph, *Bruce Rogers: A Life in Letters*, Austin, Texas, 1989.
—— *Typographic Years*, The Grolier Club, New York, 1982.
McKitterick, David, Bruce Rogers at Cambridge, 1917–19, *The Book Collector*, Summer, 1980.
Morison, Stanley, Day, Kenneth, *The Typographic Book, 1450–1935*, 1963.
Rogers, Bruce, *An Account of the Making of the Oxford Lectern Bible*, Oxford, 1936.

Rothschild Library

The 3rd Baron Rothschild started collecting eighteenth-century English literature as an undergraduate at Cambridge in 1932. The collection was eventually presented to Merton Hall and Lord Rothschild commissioned the catalogue which has proved such a valuable tool for the study of books of the period. The attention attracted by the formation of the collection had an important influence on book collecting trends during the years of Lord Rothschild's activity. Before the cataloguing got under way Lord Rothschild drew up *Proposals* for the system he intended to use. These he sent to leading bibliographical experts, including JOHN CARTER, SIR WALTER GREG, John Sparrow, Geoffrey Keynes and A. N. L. MUNBY. Their comments and suggestions were reflected in the scheme of the two-volume catalogue which was published by the Cambridge University Press in 1954.

The Rothschild Catalogue is arranged alphabetically by author, followed by a section on the BASKERVILLE, FOULIS and STRAWBERRY HILL presses and another on English, Scottish and Irish bindings, with further sections on pamphlets, plays and letters. The comprehensiveness of the collection gives the catalogue substantial importance in the assessment of eighteenth-century English literature, especially in the case of authors for whom no separate bibliographies exist.

The Rothschild Library: a Catalogue of the Collection of Eighteenth-century Printed Books formed by Lord Rothschild, Cambridge, 1954 (reprinted, London, 1969).

Roxburghe Club

THOMAS DIBDIN was the moving force behind the formation of the Roxburghe Club in 1812 after the sale of the third Duke of Roxburghe's splendid library had caused much excitement. The first meeting, with Earl Spencer in the chair, was attended by the Marquess of Blandford, Lords Gower and Morpeth and many other bibliophiles. After an excellent dinner toasts were drunk to the immortal memory of BIBLIOMANIA all over the world, to Valdarfer, printer of the Boccaccio of 1471, WILLIAM CAXTON, WYNKYN DE WORDE, RICHARD PYNSON, Julian Notary, William Faques, the ALDINE family, the Stephens (or Etiennes), and John, Duke of Roxburghe. Each member was required to sponsor a reprint of some early work appropriate to the Club's interests, and the scholarly tradition continued; Roxburghe Club publications, always handsomely printed and bound have been much collected. Among them are *A Thirteenth Century Bestiary in the library of Alnwick Castle*, 1958, John Donne's *Anatomy of the World*, (1611) 1951; *Aspects of French Eighteenth Century Typography* by John G. Dreyfus, 1982, and A. R. A. Hobson's *French and Italian Collec-*

tions and their Binding, illustrated by examples in the library of J. R. Abbey, 1953.

Barker, Nicolas, *The Publications of the Roxburghe Club, 1814–1962*, Cambridge, 1964.

Bigham, Clive, *The Roxburghe Club. Its History and its Members*, Oxford, 1928.

Rubrication

The printing in red of the first letter or word of a text otherwise printed in black. The term was first used in connection with medieval manuscripts, often of a liturgical nature, where the headings and directions were frequently left blank to be completed later in red. The tradition continued after the advent of printed books, with blue sometimes used as well as red. The word 'rubric', meaning an instruction or ordained course of action, originally meant the introductory direction for the conduct of divine service, printed or illuminated in red at the start of a prayer book. The term 'rubrication' also covers the use of red rules around the text.

Runner

A bookseller who buys and sells directly from shop to shop (or, nowadays, from shop to home-based specialist as well), thereby doing without private customers and premises, and (if successful) holding no stock. Runners are not popular with all booksellers; however, they have provided the trade with some of its most colourful characters. Many booksellers still remember with affection the not-so-young dealer who 'ran' the 24-volume Nonesuch Dickens, on foot, from Curzon Street to Berkeley Square; and it is rumoured that a younger contemporary travelled the London Underground systematically, meeting booksellers by arrangement on the platforms to offer his wares.

Snelling, O. F., *Rare Books and Rarer People*, 1982.

Russia
See LEATHER

S

Sabin, Joseph (1821–1881)
Bibliotheca Americana, A Bibliography of Books Relating to America from its Discovery to the Present Time, a 29-volume work, was not completed until many years after the death of its first compiler, Joseph Sabin, but is generally known by his name. In 1974 it was revised by L. S. Thompson and an author–title index was issued.

Sadleir, Michael (1888–1957)
A man of many talents – collector, author and publisher – Sadleir is today best remembered as a bibliographer. His interest in Victorian fiction began with his collecting of Trollope; it was always his aim that his collecting activity should lead to the publication of appropriate work and his first book, *Excursions in Victorian Bibliography*, 1922 (reissued, 1974), set him on this path. He aims to help his readers to 'a speedier knowledge of points and pitfalls in the collecting of their favourites than was easily accessible to myself'.

This first work deals with Trollope, Marryat, Disraeli, Wilkie Collins, Charles Reade, Whyte-Melville, Herman Melville and Mrs Gaskell; it was followed by two deeper studies of Trollope's life and work: *Trollope, A Commentary*, 1927, and *Trollope, A Bibliography*, 1928.

His collection of the works of the Victorian novelists continued to grow, influenced always by close attention to the bibliographical background, and he wrote a well-known novel himself, *Fanny By Gaslight*, which verged on the Gothic. His outstanding contribution to Victorian bibliography is *XIX Century Fiction*. This two-volume work, published in 1951 (reprinted, New York, 1969), is a catalogue of his own collection, and is essential to the understanding of the wealth of material of this period. The second volume describes Sadleir's remarkable special collections of YELLOW-BACK publications, and of some 45 series ranging from 'Breezy Library' to 'Vizetelly's Sensational Novels'.

A large part of Sadleir's library is now in America – his Trollope collection went to Princeton, the Gothic novels to Virginia. *The Evolution of Publishers' Binding Styles, 1870–1900*, 1930, and *New Paths in Book-Collecting*, 1934, remain, with his major work, to keep his achievements in the bibliophile's mind. JOHN CARTER once described Sadleir as 'the most accomplished book-collector of our time'.

Carter, John, *Books and Book-Collectors*, 1956.
Stokes, Roy, *Michael Sadleir 1888–1957*, 1980.

S. Dominic's Press
The private press of H. D. C. Pepler and Eric Gill, founded at Ditchling in Sussex in 1916. Pepler and Gill had worked together earlier in Hammersmith, using a hand press formerly owned by William Morris, where they produced Douglas Pepler's anti-capitalist satire *The Devil's Devices*, 1915, with woodcuts and engravings by Gill; this and various other publications under Pepler's own imprint may be considered alongside the output of S. (an

abbreviation for 'Saint') Dominic's Press itself.

The foundation of the Press coincided with Pepler's conversion to Roman Catholicism, and many of its publications are devotional in character; other titles testify to Pepler's and Gill's preoccupation with the craft movement. However, the charm of many S. Dominic's Press pieces is more delicate than these themes might suggest. Many titles present bibliographical problems; the tendency of the Press's workers to lighten the routine of hand-colouring, in particular, by varying their palettes during production exasperates the bibliographer as much as it delights the collector.

In 1937 the Press, which had been gaining ground commercially, installed a linotype machine; it changed hands in 1940, and was renamed The Ditchling Press. This Press continued to produce work of good quality, but has not captured the imagination of collectors to the same extent as its forerunner. A comprehensive bibliography of the Press is in course of preparation.

Gill, Evan, *Bibliography of Eric Gill*, 1953 (2nd edn., Winchester, 1991).

MacCarthy, Fiona, *Eric Gill*, 1989.

Sangorski and Sutcliffe

Francis Sangorski and George Sutcliffe, bookbinders, began their association in 1901 in Bloomsbury. They were known especially for their elaborate gilt and jewelled bindings, the first notable example being a copy of Spenser's *Epithalamion* bound in morocco and ornamented with pearls and a Tudor Rose. Their bindings for copies of the *Rubaiyat of Omar Khayyam* incorporated peacock feather designs inlaid with coloured leathers, gilt tooling and jewelled decoration. The most sumptuous of these, which went down with the *Titanic*, included (according to Bernard Middleton) sunken panels, vast quantities of gold leaf, thousands of precious stones and on the back cover 'a model of a Persian mandoline made of mahogany, inlaid with silver, satinwood and ebony'.

The firm still maintains one of the most distinguished binderies in the country and bound the Bible used at the coronation of Queen Elizabeth II. It employed at one time more than 100 staff, but its greatest days were perhaps before the First World War. It has now moved to premises in Bermondsey, where it is associated with ZAEHNSDORF Ltd.

Stonehouse, J. H. *The Story of the Great Omar*, 1933.

Scarce

See RARITY

Schwerdt, C. F. G. R.

The catalogue of Schwerdt's unrivalled collection of books on *Hunting, Hawking and Shooting*, privately printed in 1928–37 in a limited edition of 300 signed copies, has become an essential reference tool in this area. The books are alphabetically listed by author, with cross-references relating to artists, engravers, printers and publishers. It is fully illustrated, with useful bibliographical notes. The catalogue was reprinted in 1985.

Science and Medicine

Andrew Hunter

Books on science and medicine are usually grouped together, although, in an antiquarian book trade riven with specialities, the conjunction is tenuous. Most science dealers handle medicine, but medical specialists keep more strictly to their own field. More pronouncedly, collectors of either subject seldom overlap, and indeed most collectors have specialized interests within one subject or the other. There are of course exceptions to this rule: collectors of 'great books' who will be guided by *Printing and the Mind of Man*, Horblit, and the like, collectors of early printing or the illustrated books of the Renaissance, others whose various interests defy categorization. The best books, and even the majority of books, in both fields are international, and this is the underlying reason for the continuing strength of this section of the antiquarian book market. One of the pleasures of these subjects is precisely their cosmopolitanism. It is almost impossible to be nationalistic in science, though perhaps this is less true in medicine, where the biographical element is more prominent.

Most of the general rules of bookselling and collecting apply to science and medicine. It is the first editions of important works that are most in demand and most highly priced. Sometimes (perhaps more often than in other fields), later editions can outshine the first, or at least have an indisputable claim to being indispensable in a collection – for example, the second edition of Boyle's *New Experiments* (first 1660, second 1662) which contains 'Boyle's Law' for the first time; or again, if important parts of a mathematical paper are included in the supplements (e.g. Laplace's *Théorie Analytique des Probabilités*). Given the nature of scientific publishing after the foundation of the scientific periodical (the earliest surviving one is the *Philosophical Transactions of the Royal Society*, founded 1664), a great deal of what is important in the history of science and medicine has appeared in journals. These appearances (or even *offprints* from them) are not in general much sought after, however, and in any event, their garnering involves the dismemberment of otherwise useful runs. A few such appearances have been hallowed by PMM, and others which are genuinely famous will command significant sums of money, as might the crucial patents of revolutionary devices.

Importance and rarity determine price, but condition is of less moment than in other fields; clearly nobody wants poor copies, and there is a premium to be paid for the outstanding copy of a landmark of science, but ordinarily collectors of science and medicine are content with 'good' copies. Scientific and medical books are inherently scarcer than literary works, having had a circulation restricted to professionals – virtuosi rather than dilettanti – and there is less of a fetish about honest signs of wear. Science collectors are interested in facts and are not particularly moved by fine bindings or 'associations' – they will be pleased to have them, but not to pay for them.

Medical books have an ancient history, and for centuries a few texts enjoyed almost biblical status. Medicine is moreover a learned profession, and when physicians become wealthy the antiquarian instinct often emerges. Some of the great names in book-collecting

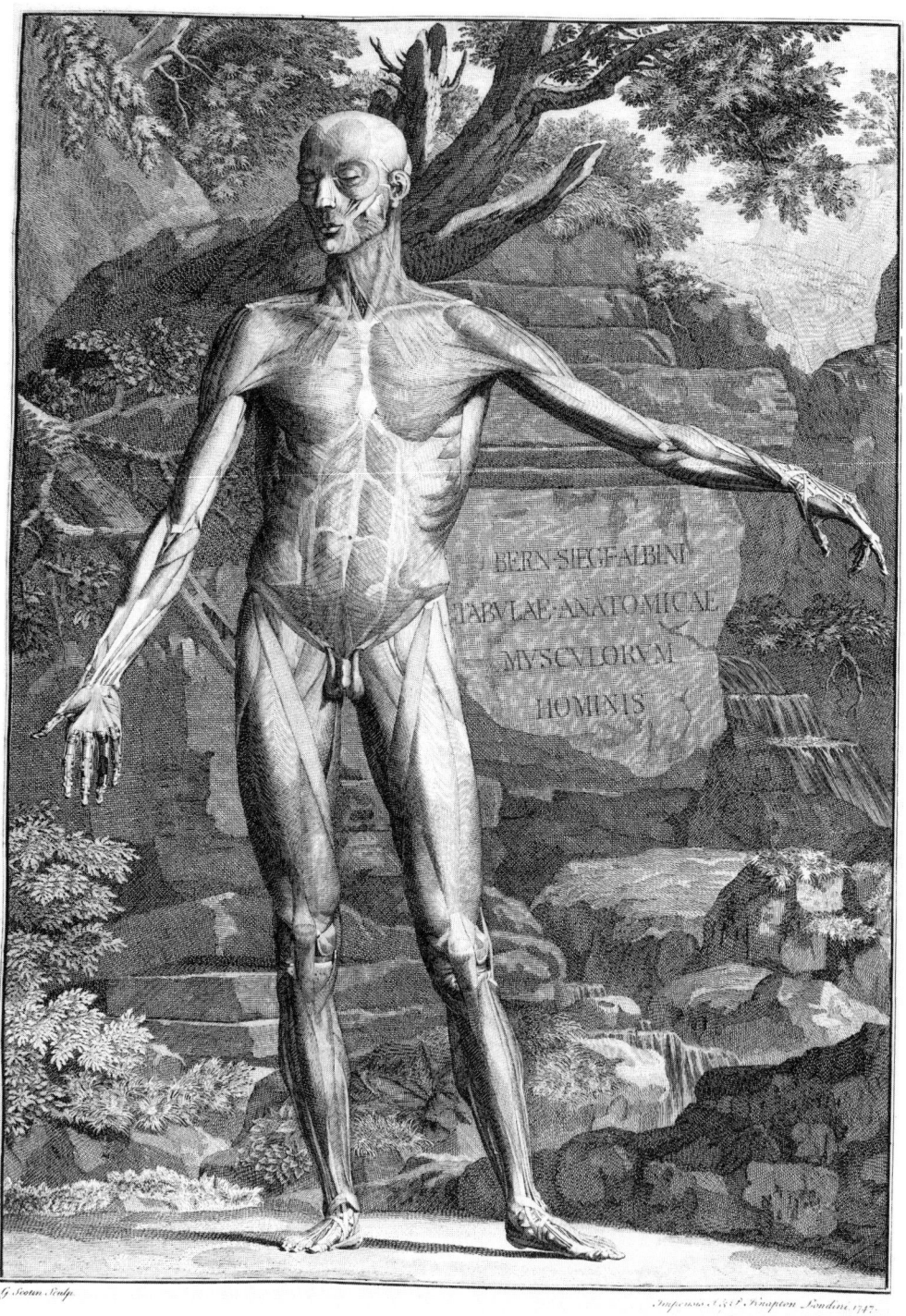

Bernard Siegfried Albinus, *Tables of the Skeleton and Muscles of the Human Body*, 1749. [Bernard Quaritch Ltd.]

history have been medical men, and to an extent the profession remains bibliophilic. Histories of medicine abound to guide the bookseller, from the most general to the most particular. Thornton's *Medical Books, Libraries and Collectors* (first published in 1949, 3rd edition, Aldershot, 1990) is a good introduction.

A single volume bibliographical guide to the history of medicine is provided by 'Garrison-Morton' which has recently gone into its fifth edition. It has some 8,000 entries from the beginning of printing until the present, with details of date, place of publication, printer, and a brief commentary. It is arranged according to the divisions of medical science, with general (anatomy and physiology) as well as particular (leprosy, spleen) headings, and is copiously indexed. There are plenty of medical books not in Garrison-Morton which are nevertheless collected, but the book is almost exhaustive in delineating the development of modern Western conventional medicine. It is perfunctory, however, on alternative medicine and only glances at areas which are of increasing interest, such as women practitioners – but here the specialist bookseller can give a lead. The next most widely used reference works are the catalogues of the National Library of Medicine in the United States; this is the largest medical library in the world, and anything not found in the catalogues has a fair claim to being scarce. Two American collection catalogues frequently culled for catalogue 'blurb' are *Heirs of Hippocrates* and *Notable Medical Books*. The latter, with 130 titles, is a guide to the 'high spots'; *Heirs of Hippocrates* (a new edition was recently published with more than 2,000 entries) gives a conspectus which only specialists need to augment. Garrison-Morton lists the histories and bibliographies for further reference.

Anatomy is the physician's and the bookseller's best friend. It is the fundamental study, and it has given rise to splendid and fascinating illustrations. Anatomical books are also of interest to the art historian and this tends to increase their price. The most famous book in the whole field of medicine is Vesalius' *De humani corporis fabrica*, Basle, 1543. Vesalius detected 108 errors in Galen, but the revolution which his book inaugurated was effected less by its text than by its illustrations, by Jan Stephan of Calcar and other followers of Titian. Hitherto, anatomical illustration had been uncritically traditional, whereas in Vesalius' book direct observation from dissection was used for the first time; this is what marks the book as the inauguration of the modern epoch. Even the most beautifully produced anatomical book, normally a folio of dignified proportions, was intended for practical use, usually in the anatomy theatre, so that surviving copies in fine condition are particularly rare. There are numerous histories of anatomical illustration; a recent book, *The Fabric of the Body*, by K. B. Roberts and J. D. W. Tomlinson, Oxford, 1992, is likely to become a widely used reference book.

Vying in importance, and exceeding the Vesalius in value, is the much rarer *Exercitatio anatomica de motu cordis et sanguinis in animalibus* (usually called simply *De motu cordis*) of William Harvey, printed in Frankfurt in 1628. German books of the Thirty Years' War period almost always suffer from browning, often quite disfiguring. Sometimes the paper is stable enough if ugly; sometimes it can be seen to disintegrate before the eyes; the latter case is a conundrum for lovers of original condition! Harvey's book is no exception, but in almost any state it is now worth some £100,000. Such is its revolutionary importance that the whole history of the circulation of the blood is a subject quite avidly collected,

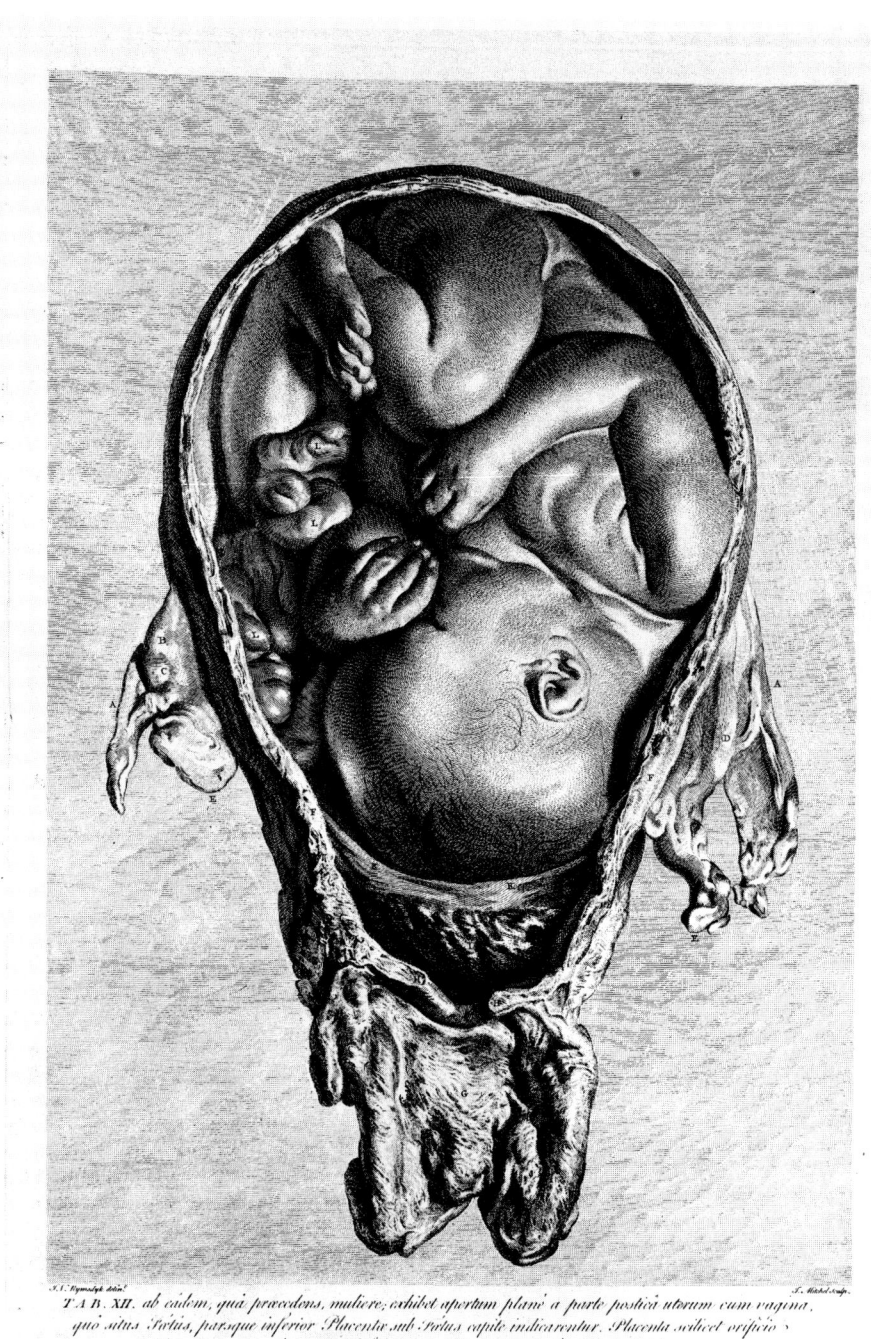

William Hunter, *Anatomia Uteri Humani Gravidi*, Baskerville, 1774. [Bernard Quaritch Ltd.]

SCIENCE AND MEDICINE

and Harvey's precursors, detractors and supporters share in his lustre. Cardiology as a subject on its own has numerous devotees, and by the same token, the physiological experimenters of the seventeenth century also have many followers.

The popular view of old medicine is of leeches and quacks, but these do not figure largely from the point of view of the collector. Broadly speaking, books in the following fields are most in demand: anatomy (starting with Vesalius), physiology (epitomised by Harvey), cardiology, neurology, dentistry (fuelled partly by Japanese demand in this area), gynaecology and obstetrics (some of the best known and most beautiful medical illustrations are obstetrical, e.g. William Hunter's *Anatomia uteri humani gravidi*, printed by Baskerville in 1774), ophthalmology and surgery. The great revolutionary, the original Bombast, Paracelsus, has many aficionados, attracted by his philosophy as much as by his medicine. Various other areas of medicine have a lesser following, among which may be mentioned the plague, tropical medicine, pharmacology, hospitals and nursing (Florence Nightingale is ever popular – beware the 'points' of *Notes on Nursing*[1]), and psychology.

Surgery, like anatomy, rejoices in well-illustrated books, and as surgeons tend to be well-to-do, these books are eagerly collected. Plastic surgery and brain surgery are important subdivisions of the subject, and wound management, antisepsis and anaesthesia are perennially sought after. Books on once popular operations such as lithotomy are common and do not command much attention. The monetary value of illustrations is demonstrated by the clear demarcation between illustrated and unillustrated surgeries (and anatomies) almost without regard to the importance of the text.

If we except engineers (whose province, technology, is only touched upon in this article), there is no ancient profession of scientist. Nevertheless the antiquarian instinct is latent among scientists, if only by virtue of the eponymous nature of much of the knowledge. The greatest stimulus to the trade in antiquarian science books is provided by the academic discipline of the history of science, which is a comparatively recent phenomenon, following the pioneering researches of George Sarton and Pierre Duhem. History of science societies are large and active, and institutions are still developing their history of science collections. There is as yet no science equivalent of the Wellcome Collection, or to the National Library of Science in America, but the British Science Museum Library approaches this status and is the most accessible library in which the bookseller can pursue research; the Wellcome Library is the equivalent for medical researches. One great collection was formed in the nineteenth century, by Guglielmo Libri, not all of whose books were acquired by honest means. The scientific portion of his enormous library was sold by Leigh Sotheby in 1861, and the two fat catalogues are still occasionally a useful bibliographical tool. The bench mark in the last quarter of the twentieth century is the Honeyman Collection, sold by Sotheby's in London in 1978–80 (amid some controversy, since Sotheby's had bought the collection, and the Buyer's Premium was still new). Some of the books in that sale have been on the market again quite recently, notably those which were purchased by the British Rail Pension Fund, and their 'track record' is a good indication of how far prices have advanced in the last decade. Although

---

[1] For the latest information on these points, see Victor Skretkowicz's article in *The Library*, March, 1993.

Galileo Galilei, *Dialogo . . . sopra i due massimi sistemi del mondo*, Florence, 1632. [Bernard Quaritch Ltd.]

the heroic age of science book collecting may have passed (the generation of Honeyman, Dibner, Horblit) the importance of the subject is increasingly seen in cultural terms. Thus to the purely historical interest of more traditional collectors, there are added political and social issues which broaden the appeal of seemingly merely technical books. The 1985 publication *Leviathan and the Air Pump; Hobbes, Boyle, and the Experimental Life*, by Stephen Shapin and Simon Schaffer, Princeton, 1985, is an example of this broadening of the subject.

The catalogue of one more 'heroic' collection has now just been published, that of Haskell F. Norman (father of the well-known medical dealer, Jeremy Norman of San Francisco), which has more than 2,500 entries described in just the sort of detail booksellers require. It will quickly join the list of bibliographies cited in booksellers' descriptions. Dr Norman is working on a 'top 100 medical books' selection, *à la* Horblit, which no doubt will quicken the demand for the works it numbers.

Few collectors aspire to comprehensiveness today, however, and most tend to collect a specific subject. This may be in a pioneering fashion, the subject not having previously been recognized and the result being perhaps a useful bibliography such as the recently published *Biblioteca Mechanica*, or again attention may be given to a subject which has been written about and indeed collected before, but not with bibliographical single-mindedness. An example is William Cole's *Chemical Literature, 1700–1860*; supplementing the two standard bibliographies of chemistry, Duveen and Ferguson, Cole's bibliography has, like Norman, at least one eye on the bookseller; it is dedicated to the late Jake Zeitlin, to whom much of the credit must go for cementing antiquarian science as a respectable branch of the trade. (Zeitlin, of course, should not be confused with Zeitlinger, whose series of catalogues for Sotheran are still occasionally used as a last resort when no other reference can be found.) Alternatively, a collector might pick a subject for which there already exists a model collection, such as the history of the microscope or mining. The single author collection so typical in the field of literature is less common, and unimportant works by great scientists will not have enough 'completists' pursuing them to make them expensive; Newton on the chronology of ancient kingdoms is a case in point. However, scraps of Galileiana or Kepleriana are snapped up, as are fleeting references to heliocentrism in the first half of the sixteenth century.

The most widely used and quoted source of reference is the *Dictionary of Scientific Biography*, published 1970–80, and available in reprint. Its basic biographical functions are admirably fulfilled, although some of its philosophy may now seem a little dated. The guides to bibliographies and to the secondary literature which follow each entry are especially useful. The one limitation of the work is that scientists who were alive at the time of writing are not included. Some medical biographies are included, but the work makes no pretension to being a scientific *DNB*.

The most strongly collected subject in science is astronomy, a theme which, like anatomy, permits of great beauty of illustration; it is moreover the subject which non-scientists can most easily identify with. However, the trade in celestial maps is on a small scale, and works of astronomy are not as systematically broken up as are those of geography. The two most celebrated books, however, are little illustrated. The most famous is Copernicus's *De revolutionibus orbium coelestium*, 1543, published the same year as Vesalius's great folio. Nobody can dispute the importance of this book, but hardly

Christoph Scheiner, *Oculus Hoc Est*, Innsbruck, 1619. [Bernard Quaritch Ltd.]

Johannes Hevelius, *Selenographia*, Danzig, 1647. [Bernard Quaritch Ltd.]

anyone can read it. The second most important book ('the greatest book in the history of science' – PMM) is Newton's *Philosophiae naturalis principia mathematica*, (always shortened to *Principia* – an abbreviation applied to other subjects, e.g. the *Principia* of non-Euclidean geometry, or the *Principia* of the chemical revolution). The price of the first edition of this work has increased in recent years, but the differential between a fine copy and a reasonably good one marks it as an icon rather than a scientific tool. Although the edition was quite small, it is not a rare book.

Although most of the highways and many of the byways of science have had their historians, astronomy so far lacks a large-scale account in English; this deficiency is in the course of being remedied with *The General History of Astronomy* in four volumes, published by Cambridge University Press, with the ubiquitous Professor Owen Gingerich at the head of the editorial board; at the time of writing only Volume 2A has appeared.

Books concerning scientific instruments are also popular. Some dealers combine books with instruments, but the collector of both is a rarer bird than might be expected. The books vary from splendid Renaissance folios to humble nineteenth-century trade catalogues, and books about television. The library of Harrison Horblit, part of which was sold by Sotheby's in 1974, was a collection of 'Early science, navigation, and travel', a description which indicates how wide is the scope given by an interest in instruments. The Horblit sale (only two parts were completed, ending at the letter G) included a copy of Copernicus' *De revolutionibus* inscribed by Joachim Rheticus, in effect a presentation copy. It sold for £44,000. The same copy made $430,000 in an important sale in 1991.

Mathematics is the queen of the sciences, and the high spots command handsome prices. There is a rapid falling off of interest, however, and mathematical books in general are relatively cheap. There are numerous histories, but no comprehensive bibliography. Other topics are covered by specialized bibliographies, or collection catalogues such as The Wheeler Gift, for electricity; Wheeler gives a useful summary of the contents of each book. Alchemy attracts a great deal of interest, either as a precursor of true science, or as a philosophical endeavour in its own right. Technology is almost a separate subject and its various aspects (engineering, say, or railways) are usually dealt with by specialists. Experimental and theoretical physics in all their myriad forms are collected at various points. The pace quickens as we approach the age of atomic physics, and there are probably as many collectors for Einstein as for Newton. The largest class of surviving scientific books is text books, but these rarely have anything of interest to collectors, and until their day comes they are little more than lumber.

In Great Britain the number of specialist dealers in science and medicine is quite small and even those who give secondary attention to these subjects are not numerous. Specialists are much more common in the United States; on the Continent and especially in France and Italy there are both specialists and dealers who have science and medicine among their specialities; the usual trade guides cover the field adequately. While some institutions will continue to build their collections, the great impetus from post-War America and latterly from Japan has faltered, and the health of the trade in the future depends on the cultivation of new private buyers primarily in Europe.

Besson, Alain, *Thornton's Medical Books, Libraries and Collectors*, 3rd edn, Aldershot, 1990.
Cole, William, A., *Chemical Literature 1700–1860*, 1988.

Dibner, Bern, *Heralds of Science as represented by two hundred epochal books and pamphlets selected from the Burndy Library*, Norwalk, Connecticut, 1955.
Dictionary of Scientific Biography, 18 vols, including index and supplements, New York, 1970–90.
Duveen, Denis L., *Bibliotheca alchemica et chemica*, 1949.
Eimas, Richard (ed.), *Heirs of Hippocrates*. The development of medicine in a catalogue of historic books in the Hardin Library for the Health Sciences, The University of Iowa. 3rd edition, Iowa, 1990.
Ferguson, John, *Biblotheca Chemica* (A catalogue of the alchemical, chemical and pharmaceutical books in the collection of the late James Young of Kelley and Durris), 2 vols, Glasgow, 1906 (reprinted 1954).
Garrison-Morton. See separate entry.
Honeyman Collection, The. See separate entry.
Hook, Diana H., Norman, Jeremy M., *The Haskell F. Norman Library of Science and Medicine*, 2 vols, San Francisco, 1991.
Horblit, Harrison D., *One Hundred Books Famous in Science*, The Grolier Club, New York, 1964.
Roberts, Verne L., Trent, Ivy, *Bibliotheca Mechanica*, New York, 1991.
Sarton, George, *Introduction to the History of Science*, 3 vols in 5, Baltimore, Maryland, 1927–48 (reprinted Huntington, New York, 1975).
Smith, David Eugene, *Rara arithmetica*. A catalogue of the arithmetics written before the year MDCI. 4th edn, New York, 1970.
Stillwell, Margaret Bingham, *The Awakening Interest in Science during the First Century of Printing*, New York, 1970.
Wallis, R. V., Wallis, P. J., *Biobibliography of British Mathematics and its Applications*, Part II (all so far published) 1701–1760, Newcastle-upon-Tyne, 1986.
Ward, Derek C., Carozzi, Albert V., *Geology Emerging. A Catalog illustrating the History of Geology (1500–1850)*, Illinois, 1984.
Wightman, W. P. D., *Science and the Renaissance*. An introduction to the study of the emergence of the sciences in the sixteenth century, 2 vols, 1962.
Williams, Trevor I. (ed.), *A Biographical Dictionary of Scientists*, 1969 (3rd edn, 1982).
Zeitlinger, Henry, *Bibliotheca Chemico-Mathematica*, 6 vols, including supplements, 1921–37.

Semé, Semis
A style of binding ornament characterized by repeated application of one small tool, such as a fleur-de-lys. A heraldic term, it derives from the French *semer*, to sow.

Sette of Odd Volumes
Bernard Quaritch founded this somewhat whimsical literary dining club in 1878. The number of members – 21, with 21 supplementary members – followed the number of volumes in the 1821 Variorum Edition of Shakespeare, and each member selected an alias, following something of a quasi-masonic ritual. His Oddship (the President) ruled over the brothers; members included at various times Brother Exaggeration (David Low), Brother Limner (John Hassall), Brother Blacksmith (Raymond Lister) and Brother Nutcracker (a brain surgeon).

The meetings of the Sette, which is still active, are not intended for serious debate. New members are introduced amid much hilarity and the rules includes such strictures as a fine for giving unasked-for advice.

Nevertheless, some of the addresses given at the Club's meetings and published as 'Privately Printed Opuscula' are of lasting interest; they include such varied titles as *Coloured Books for Children* by Charles Welsh, *Frederick, Baron Corvo* by A. J. A. Symons, *On Bores* by Vyvyan Holland, *The Heart of England* by S. P. B. Mais and *Test Flying Jet-propelled Aircraft* by Peter Cadbury. There are more than 100 of these booklets, attractively printed in small format and often combining humour with serious scholarship.

Lister, Raymond, The Sette of Odd Volumes, *The Private Library*, Summer 1980 (containing a check-list of titles) and Winter 1981.

Settlement
See RING

Shaved
See CROPPED

Sheep
See LEATHER

Short-Title Catalogue
The first edition of the *Short-Title Catalogue of Books Printed in England, Scotland, and Ireland, and of English books Printed Abroad, 1475–1640*, appeared in 1926. It was edited by A. W. POLLARD and G. R. Redgrave and published by the BIBLIOGRAPHICAL SOCIETY. The work covered all material printed in British languages wherever published, including ballads, pamphlets, proclamations and broadsheets of all kinds.

Inevitably the work soon needed revision; further material was uncovered, errors came to light and modern scholarship and extended research prompted the undertaking of a new edition of the STC. This commenced in 1948, under the editorship of W. A. Jackson and F. S. Ferguson; Volume II (I–Z) appeared first in 1976, to be followed by Volume I (A–H) in 1987 completed by Katharine F. Panzer. In effect it has turned out to be virtually a new work, offering a great deal of additional material and information on obscure works by prominent authors, additional locations of known publications, cross-references of undated TITLE-PAGES and answers to many other troublesome problems. As Arthur Freeman wrote in his review in the *Times Literary Supplement* of the second volume to appear (Volume I: A–H): 'Simple compassion towards the literary and historical scholar, presumed always (with justice) to be a little bewildered by the systems of analytical bibliography, informs many of the notes.'

The two-volume New Short-Title Catalogue is published by Oxford University Press. A third index volume came out in 1991.

Signatures
In the language of printing, signatures are the letters printed in the lower margin of the first page of each section, or GATHERING, of a book, as a guide to the binder in arranging the sheets in their correct order. Signatures normally consist of 23 letters, with J, U and W omitted from the alphabet; if more than 23 signatures are needed a second sequence will usually take the form AA (or Aa) followed by BB (or Bb) and further series as necessary. In bibliographical descriptions these subsequent alphabets are usually indicated as 2A, 2B etc. In some cases the printer will be found to have repeated the single-letter signatures, so that both the first and the twenty-fourth gathering will be signed A, the second and twenty-fifth B, etc.; this less satisfactory practice is indicated bibliographically as ^{2}A, ^{2}B, etc. It should be

mentioned that in some modern books signatures take the form of numerals rather than letters; but these books are unlikely to require collation.

Signatures generally provide reliable evidence of the completeness of a book, but it must be remembered that signing practices differ, especially in regard to preliminary leaves. These are sometimes signed with lower-case letters, or with symbols such as asterisks, and they are sometimes left unsigned; TITLE-PAGES are very rarely signed, but signatures are occasionally found on half-titles. In modern books preliminary leaves are often signed with roman numerals, and some American books are signed numerically throughout.

The incorporation of a register of signatures in a full bibliographical collation is part of a larger subject, to which PHILIP GASKELL's *Introduction to Bibliography* provides an excellent guide.

The term signature is often used, by extension, to describe the gathering itself; but as gathering, section or quire are variously appropriate, the extension of meaning is unnecessary and occasionally confusing.

Sayce, R. A., *Compositorial Practices and the Localization of Printed Books, 1530–1800*, Oxford Bibliographical Society, 1979.

Signed copy
A book signed by its author. Invariably at least as expensive as an unsigned copy, despite the old joke about the relative scarcity of the signed and unsigned copies of Edward Heath's *Sailing*; but often not much more expensive, especially when there is no demand for the book in any form.

Even the most off-hand presentation inscription makes a book more desirable than a mere signature.

Singleton
A single leaf, without a CONJUGATE; it may be either the surviving or the displaced half of a conjugate pair, or an extra leaf produced quite separately and bound in by a stub.

Sleeper
A book whose value has been (or appears to have been) overlooked by its cataloguer. 'Sleepers' which appear unnamed in auction lots should be collated with care, as auctioneers' conditions of sale almost always preclude the return of unnamed books for whatever reason. Despite protestations to the contrary by some senior members of the trade, sleepers still occur frequently at every level.

Slipcase
A box with one open edge designed to protect a book while leaving its spine open to view. A well-made slipcase allows the book to slide in and out comfortably without friction. Some slipcases are edged with leather to strengthen or decorate them, some have thumb-holes to allow easy withdrawal of the book (the book's covers may eventually show the position of the thumbhole through fading or wear) and some have a ribbon for the same purpose. The absence of a slipcase when one was provided on publication should be mentioned in the description of a book.

Solander case (or box)
Daniel Charles Solander (1736–1782), who invented this type of container, came to England from Sweden on the recommendation of Linnaeus. While Keeper of the Natural History Department of the British Museum, Solander devised a form of dropfront box for his botanical specimens. Resembling a book with a rounded spine and often in full or half leather, today's

solander case may have a catch to secure the lid and is used for loose prints or papers, or to protect a book.

Spanish calf
See LEATHER

Specialist libraries
Many libraries maintain special collections or concentrate on certain subjects. They may be difficult to locate, but most are noted in Moelwyn I. Williams' *A Directory of Rare Book and Special Collections in the United Kingdom and the Republic of Ireland*, 1985.

Spine
See BACKSTRIP

Sprinkled calf
See LEATHER

Stab-hole
Stabbing – the holding together of sheets of papyrus or other material by the use of thread drawn through holes in the left-hand margin – was used in the Far East before the invention of printing. Stabbing was outlawed in England by the Stationers' Company in 1586, books containing many leaves having become common, and it was succeeded by stitching in sections. Unlike stabbing, stitching penetrates the fold of the paper, not the margin of the page. Stabbing remained in use to hold together thin books, such as pamphlets, and the presence of 'stab-holes' can be taken to indicate a work bound up from the original parts.

Steel engraving
See TECHNIQUES OF ILLUSTRATION

Straight grain
See LEATHER

Strawberry Hill Press
Roderick Cave, in his excellent survey *The Private Press*, 1971, places his account of the Strawberry Hill Press in a chapter headed 'The Aristocratic Plaything', in company with the presses of Frederick the Great of Prussia, Madame de Pompadour, Benjamin Franklin and other grandees of the movement. The description is perhaps a fair one; Horace Walpole installed the press at his Twickenham villa in 1757 in order to print his own writings and those of his closest friends, and on occasion to produce instantly printed compliments for visiting ladies. ROBERT DODSLEY was allowed to sell a few of Strawberry Hill's publications, but most were either given away or sold for the benefit of the poor. The activities of the Press certainly reflected at every stage the aristocratic demeanour and ample wealth of its owner.

Nevertheless, Strawberry Hill's achievements well deserve the high regard in which they are now held. The handsome edition of Gray's *Odes* with which Walpole opened his list in 1757, his own *Catalogue of the Royal and Noble Authors of England*, 1758, and *Anecdotes of Painting in England*, 1785 – these and some 37 books and slighter pieces issued by the Press over a span of 40 years are much coveted by collectors of eighteenth-century English literature. The Press had its vicissitudes, not least in the variable skills of Walpole's printers, and some later critics, Stanley Morison and Updike among them, have spoken of its typographical standards with some reserve. However, many of the books have their own quiet elegance, and the Press gains greatly in importance from Horace Walpole's many points of contact with both fashionable and scholarly circles in England, France and Italy.

Hazen, A. T., Kirby, J. P., *A Bibliography of the Strawberry Hill Press* 1942 (reprinted, 1973).

Lewis, Wilmarth S., *Collector's Progress*, New York, 1951.

Stub

As books are made up of CONJUGATE leaves, the removal of one leaf will always leave a stub, however narrow, where it has been cut or torn away from its fellow. If the leaf was removed before the book was bound, the stub will necessarily have been left for stitching in; if it was removed, however skilfully, after binding, some vestige will be visible to careful scrutiny.

A clean-cut stub does not necessarily indicate the removal of a page; plates printed separately from text pages, or additional single leaves, require a stub if they are to be stitched rather than tipped-in. However, any stub which does not clearly serve such a purpose, and especially any stub that has been used for the insertion of a substitute leaf, should be very carefully investigated.

Subscription

Books published by subscription are those for whose publication guarantors, in the form of committed buyers, have been found in advance. The practice dates from the seventeenth century, but flourished in England in the eighteenth and nineteenth centuries; it was often used to finance the cost of producing large paper copies, which might be offered to subscribers for part payment in advance at a lower price than others would pay. Books published by subscription usually contain a list of subscribers; this will often include the names of a few booksellers, and may give an interesting glimpse of the upper reaches of the contemporary book-buying world. Subscribers to illustrated books were sometimes invited to 'sponsor' a plate, on which their name was then engraved. A subscriber's book-plate or inscription is well regarded by collectors, as is the presence of the original prospectus.

The practice is still in occasional use, generally to support the publication of books likely to interest only a relatively small readership.

T

Tail-piece
A VIGNETTE or ornamental device occupying the lower part of the last page of a chapter, or of some other section of a book, is known as a tail-piece. A head-piece is a similar (though slightly less common) illustration at the beginning of a chapter. THOMAS BEWICK is one of the best-known engravers of tail-pieces for which he occasionally provided delicately improper vignettes.

Tauchnitz, Bernard Christian (1816–1895)
In 1837 Tauchnitz published in Leipzig the first of his series of cheap editions of English classics. He continued to print works in English, with the permission of the authors, though owing to copyright restrictions the books were not available in England. More than 4,000 titles were issued, usually bound in WRAPPERS although various styles of 'house binding' appear; where the authors collaborated closely with Tauchnitz or altered their work at his instigation, these editions assume bibliographic importance in their own right. The cheap paper used by the firm was of reasonable quality but was unhappily persuasive in the spread of high acid-content products in the mass-publishing industry generally. Many titles were frequently reprinted, but first impressions may be identified by comparing the series number of the book in question with that of the latest title mentioned in advertisements or on the lower wrapper; the former should be greater.

The Leipzig premises were bombed in the Second World War and the business came to an end.

Todd, W. B. and Bowden, Ann, *Tauchnitz International Editions in English 1841–1955*, New York, 1988.

Techniques of illustration
Books with printed illustrations date back even to the days before movable type; techniques for the reproduction of images are many, but those most likely to be encountered by antiquarian booksellers are described below.

The processes fall into three main categories: the term 'intaglio printing' means that the image area is sunk into the level of the plate. Impressions are taken by inking the whole plate, wiping the surface clean, and pressing the paper hard enough against the plate to take up the ink left in the recesses. 'Relief printing' is the opposite process, where the surface (usually of a wooden block) is cut away, leaving the image standing out to be inked; thicker ink is used and the press glides lightly over the surface as in normal letterpress printing. Finally, surface processes are those, such as lithography, in which no cutting is involved.

Intaglio

Engraving This very general term usually indicates any print obtained by

TECHNIQUES OF ILLUSTRATION

incising a metal plate or wooden block. It may apply to illustrations, lettering or music, reproduced by the intaglio method, but should strictly be applied only to instances where the surface of the plate is worked upon with a graver or burin, forcing waste material upwards to be removed by a scraper.

The impression of the plate leaves a recessed margin around the image, known as the plate-mark. Artificial plate-marks are sometimes pretentiously applied to photographic reproductions.

Illustrations in books are often referred to as engravings when they are strictly speaking not engraved at all, but printed in relief or by a surface process such as lithography.

Copperplate Until about 1540 woodcuts had been the commonest, somewhat crude, medium of illustration. Copperplate engraving produced a much finer line and once the technique of reproduction on a printing press had been perfected, this form of illustration remained in common use for some three centuries; only in the 1820s was the copperplate largely superseded by the steel-engraving. Copperplate engraving was always a costly method of book illustration, involving several processes and the use of expensive material. Moreover, copper plates had a relatively short life and later impressions showed loss of clarity, but copper plates have remained in high regard for their aesthetically pleasing appearance.

Steel-engraving The use of steel plates for engraving illustrations originated in attempts, in the early years of the nineteenth century, to produce a clear, lasting and forgery-proof image for manufacturing banknotes. Steel is much harder than copper for such work and lasts considerably longer. The great numbers of topographical views produced in the 1830s and 1840s were ideal subjects for the new medium, where the finest of lines could be reproduced by the expert engraver. However, the engraving of a steel plate is a much more exacting task than working on copper, and a later process involved the electro-plating of an engraved copperplate with a fine coating of iron before printing; this could be renewed when it showed signs of wear.

Steel-engraving is the medium employed for many thousands of illustrations in Victorian literature, travel books and albums. Its precision has a certain chilliness, but most of the great artists of the period, Turner among them, had their work reproduced by means of steel plates.

Etching The earliest known form of etching was not intended to be printed at all; armourers waxed the metal they were working on and drew a design on it, with salt and vinegar providing the acidic action which allowed the design to appear.

Gradually, printing in relief from wooden blocks became more widespread and intaglio work more sophisticated. For reproduction purposes a metal plate is coated with an acid-resistant ground and the illustration drawn upon it with a fine needle. The immersion of the plate, usually of copper, in an acid solution burns out the finished design which holds the ink. Different effects can be obtained by varying the style of engraving, the strength of the acid and the length of immersion.

Aquatint A method which enables the etcher to achieve some of the effects of a watercolour painting. The etched plate is covered with resin, sand or a similar coating and immersed in acid, usually several times, to produce a textured background. Aquatinting is a monochrome process, though aquatints are frequently coloured later, the soft tones taking the colour with an almost three-dimensional effect.

Aquatinting is often used for landscape illustration where distance and perspective are important. The technique was much used in nineteenth-century colour plate books.

Relief processes

Woodcut The first printed illustrations in books were taken from the plank edges of wooden blocks. Such illustrations pre-date printing with movable type, and the two elements of image and text were used in tandem by the printers of block books. The crude effects of early woodcut soon gave way to more sophisticated treatment, as in the designs of Dürer. With the increased use of copper engraving for book illustration the use of wood declined, except on occasion for the small illustrations for chapbooks; but it was to be revived by wood engravers towards the end of the eighteenth century.

Wood-engraving The image of a wood-engraving does not occupy the plank edge of the block, as in woodcuts, but is instead incised into the highly polished surface of the end grain. Despite its name, it is not an intaglio process: the wood-engraver lightly inks the surface of the block, leaving the incised design blank, and the whiteness of the paper itself provides the image. The technique was perfected by THOMAS BEWICK, using boxwood. The tool used is a graver with which the finest lines can be produced; so, too, can softer effects of light and shade, as Bewick proved. As text and wood-engraving are printed together the illustration becomes an integral part of the book, and the printer's skills are essential to a 'happy marriage'.

After an interval, a fresh initiative in the use of wood-engraving for book illustration came with the work of the Dalziels and others in the 1860s; but now the artist did not always engrave his own design and this often led to an unsuccessful partnership. The Pre-Raphaelite school played a considerable part in the prominence of wood-engraving in Victorian England. However, towards the end of the century the fashion – and the talent – was beginning to wane (except in the case of books for children). It was sustained principally within the private press movement, which nurtured the distinguished work of such artists as Eric Ravilious, Gertrude Hermes, Eric Gill, Blair Hughes-Stanton, John Buckland-Wright and David Jones.

Wood-engraving should not be confused with scraper-board, a clay-surface paper board which produces similar effects with considerably less effort; many books have been illustrated with photographic reproduction of this technique, most notably by C. F. Tunnicliffe.

Surface processes

Lithography Aloysius Senefelder is credited with the invention in 1798 of the lithographic process, which involves drawing on stone with wax pencils, or some other greasy medium. The surface is wetted, leaving the illustrated area unaffected by the water. The ink used for the reproduction is also grease-based and will therefore adhere only to the area drawn upon, repelled by the water. The whole is then

Etching from Piranesi's *Il Carcere* (c.1778) [The Schuster Gallery]

printed on to the paper in a scraper press. The technique was at first called 'chemical printing' and is not unlike that involved in etching, except that the surface is not incised. Lithography has been widely used in book illustration from about 1820 and artists of the calibre of Daumier and Goya found that drawing directly on to the stone was particularly suitable for sketching and for caricature. The paper used in early lithographic illustration is now seen to be somewhat susceptible to FOXING and the quality of reproduction is often considered inferior to that achieved by steel or copper engraving; but the medium was much used throughout the twentieth century for the creation of *livres d'artiste*. Modern commercial lithographic processes are, by contrast, photographically based, and are successfully used in almost all areas of printing.

Bliss, D. P., *A History of Wood Engraving*, 1928.
Gascoigne, Bamber, *How To Identify Prints*, 1986.
Gray, Basil, *The English Print*, 1937.
Hayter, S. W., *About Prints*, Oxford, 1962 (reprinted, 1975).
Hind, A. M., *A History of the Woodcut in the XVth Century*, 2 vols, 1935.
Hunnisett, Basil, *Steel-Engraved Book Illustration in England*, 1980.
Leighton, Clare, *Wood Engraving of the 1930s*, 1936.
Lindley, Kenneth, *The Woodblock Engravers*, Newton Abbot, 1970.
Twyman, Michael, *Early Lithographed Books*, Pinner, 1990.

Three-decker

Although novels in three volumes were published before the nineteenth century, and have been published since, the term 'three-decker' is essentially a description of books of that period. Publication in three volumes is as characteristic a Victorian

publishing practice as publication in monthly parts.

Three Mountains Press

The private press of William Bird, an American journalist based in Paris. Although Bird originally envisaged producing limited editions of established classics, a meeting with Ernest Hemingway led to an introduction to Ezra Pound, who persuaded him to abandon this ambition in favour of contemporary experimental literature. The press operated between 1922 and 1926, and worked in close collaboration with Robert McAlmon's CONTACT EDITIONS. Its most celebrated publications include Hemingway's second book *In our time*, 170 copies, 1924, and Pound's *A Draft of XVI Cantos*, 90 copies, 1925. Bird later sold his Mathieu printing press for £300 to Nancy Cunard for her HOURS PRESS.

See also BLACK SUN PRESS

Ties

The practical, as distinct from decorative, purpose of ties is to hold together the covers of a book to prevent warping. As vellum is particularly liable to warp, ties were frequently attached to vellum-bound books, and sometimes to leather bindings, from the fifteenth to the eighteenth century. The narrow tapes, or ribbons, do not often survive, but the slots in which they were anchored, near the outer edges of the covers, are a common feature of early books. The later use of ties has been mainly decorative, though the original purpose is seen in their attachment to the vellum-bound LIMITED EDITIONS of recent times.

Timperley, Charles (1794–1873)
Timperley's *Dictionary of Printers and Printing*, 1839, has proved a useful tool for the student of the history of books and printing. It lists many hundreds of printers, booksellers and publishers, and gives much useful information about the trade. John Nichols' *Literary Anecdotes* provided Timperley with much of his material, but the fact that he was a working printer as well as a lively writer lent authority to the *Dictionary*. It was amended and enlarged in 1842 as the *Encyclopaedia of Typographical and Literary Anecdotes* and this version was reprinted in 1977.

Tipped-in
A page, plate, ERRATA SLIP or other item is described as tipped-in to a book if it has been inserted by means of gum or paste, usually at its inner edge. The term is most commonly used to describe the insertion of something extraneous, such as a letter or an annotation; but it may also describe a leaf that has become loose and has been re-inserted.

Plates mounted on a slightly larger leaf, as in many illustrated books of the 1920s and 1930s onwards, are sometimes incorrectly described as tipped-in.

Title-page
The earliest printed title-pages served simply to identify a book as it awaited binding, but by the end of the fifteenth century the author's name and the place and date of printing were usually included. Over the following few decades the title-page assumed a more elaborate form, often with a synopsis of the book's contents, an ornamental border or other decorative feature, and a list of booksellers' names and addresses to enhance its separate use as an advertisement. Subsequently, the amount of information contracted, and by the middle of the eighteenth century the title-page had taken on its now familiar form as a simple statement of essential facts.

Corbett, Margery, Lightbown, R., *The Comely Frontispiece: the Emblematic Title-Page in England, 1550–1660*, 1979.
McKerrow, R. B., Ferguson, F. S., *Title-Page Borders Used in England and Scotland, 1485–1640*, 1932.
Pollard, A. W., *Last Words on the History of the Title-Page*, 1891.

Trade edition
A book produced and destined for sale in the normal course of commerce, neither privately printed nor a limited edition; generally only used of a book which appeared previously, or simultaneously, in one or other of these forms.

Travel Books
Clive Farahar

It can truthfully be said that the whole world lies open to the collector and dealer in travel books. In the galaxy of subject headings under which to collect, from literature, colour-plate books, militaria, juvenilia, science and medicine, to botany, maps and incunabula, facets of all are embraced by travel. There is not an aspect of the human condition from birth to death, poverty to wealth, from rage, jealousy and greed to chivalry, bravery and endurance, that this splendid subject does not encompass.

In considering the collecting of travel literature, some awareness of the Minoan, Phoenician and Greek contributions to geography is desirable, but availability dictates that the bulk of the library will comprise books from the Great Age of exploration, from the late eighteenth century to the late nineteenth century, roughly from Cook to Livingstone and Stanley. It is a fact of commerce that rarity alone does create demand. While fifteenth- and sixteenth-century volumes of travel are excessively rare and expensive, the new collector cannot easily get the measure of his subject by acquiring such books. The more frequently he can purchase a book on a chosen subject and enlarge the collection, the happier the collector will be. Collectors have been known to sell their collections simply because there was nothing left to acquire and they were no longer enjoying the hunt; collectors and booksellers alike need the thrill of the chase and the savour of its rewards.

The earliest source work on English voyages is Richard Hakluyt's *The Principall Navigations, Voiages and Discoveries of the English Nation*, published in 1589. An enlarged edition in three volumes followed between 1598 and 1600. Joseph Sabin says in his *Dictionary of Books Relating to America*: 'It is difficult for the collector to overrate this remarkable collection of voyages.'

The accounts that Hakluyt printed were, for the most part, dramatic eyewitness reports by merchants, explorers, privateers and seamen. His editing of these original documents, together with some letters of state and some pilot or navigational guides to stretches of water, was sensitive and minimal. Richard David in his edition of Hakluyt (Boston, 1981), describes the narrators as 'almost as various as Chaucer's Canterbury Pilgrims . . .' One voice counterpoints another. An early employee of the Muscovy company writes a breezy account of life among the Samoyeds. Later his second-in-command hints, in a letter to his principals at home, that this breeziness goes too far and that their agent's fondness for the bottle is getting the Company a bad name. A year or two later, when the critic has succeeded to the headship of a trade mission to Persia, one of his juniors similarly hints that his boss is 'an old woman, too cautious and prim to succeed as an export sales manager.'

Later seventeenth-century editions of Hakluyt were revised and added to by Samuel Purchase. He was not as meticulous as Hakluyt, and as an editor and compiler he was from time to time injudicious and careless; but his collections are often the only sources of the early history of exploration.

The original editions of Hakluyt and Purchase are always expensive and difficult to find, but the MacLehose edition of Hakluyt in 12 volumes, Glasgow, 1903–1905, with its commentary and valuable index remains the most complete, and is within the financial reach of most collectors. The same may be claimed for the same publisher's edition of Purchase in 20 volumes, 1905–7. These editions were issued by the Hakluyt Society, founded in 1846 'to advance education by the publication of scholarly editions of voyages and travels', as part of their Extra Series. They issued a facsimile of the first edition in 1965 with a very useful index by Alison Quinn. The excellent publications of the Society are mostly reprints of old texts or publications of manuscripts not easily accessible, with scholarly commentaries and evaluations.

On the continent, Hakluyt gave the German engraver and publisher Theodore de Bry much help in the compilation of his great collection of voyages, *Indiam Orientalem*, known as the Petits Voyages, and *Indiam Occidentalem*, the Grands Voyages, issued in 25 parts between 1590 and 1634. The adjectives 'Grands' and 'Petits', describe the format of the volumes rather than the length or importance of the voyages. The collection represents a cosmopolitan view of the world and its explorers at that time, and the great glory of the collection is its splendid illustrations. Not since the *Nuremburg Chronicle* of 1493 had the European world been treated to such a topographical and anthropological spectacle.

Christopher Columbus was 41 years old when he set out on his voyage across the Atlantic, leaving Spain on 3 August 1492. He is credited with having discovered the New World, but the essential worth of his four voyages across the Atlantic to the West Indies was to show that it was possible to sail off to those 'mythical' parts of the globe and return safely; thus was the Age of Discovery initiated. Amerigo Vespucci on the other hand, the Spanish beef contractor whose four voyages in 1497–1503 did make mainland landfalls in Mexico and South America, probably discovered Brazil. Since 1490 Bristol merchants had regularly financed ships to search for the island of 'Brazil', and in 1496 John Cabot made landfall far to the north of Columbus and Vespucci, in either Newfoundland, Labrador or Nova Scotia – his description is not clear (see *The Journal of Christopher Columbus during his First Voyage 1492–93*, and *Documents relating to the Voyages of John Cabot and Gaspar Corte Real*, edited by Clements Markham, Hakluyt Society First Series lxxxvi, 1892). There followed during the first half of the sixteenth century a period of Spanish supremacy in discoveries in the New World. The original material relating to these discoveries is rare and expensive but once again the Hakluyt Society covers this period well for the scholar and collector. (For a list of Hakluyt Society publications see *Richard Hakluyt and His Successors*, Second Series xciii, 1946.)

In the late seventeenth and early eighteenth century, Europe saw a substantial increase in books on exploration of the Americas and also on the politics of their embryo colonies. The French were exploring from the St Lawrence Valley to the foot of the Rockies, and from the Hudson, down the Mississippi to the Gulf of Mexico. The English were active mainly on the western seaboard and in the far north, while the Spanish, with their South American predominance, were extending their knowledge of New Mexico and California.

Portugal, a pioneer of exploration since the days of Prince Henry the Navigator, Vasco da Gama and Albuquerque, had her discoveries and conquests celebrated in Faria Y Sousa's *Asia Portuguesa* and *Africa Portuguesa*, 1681 and 1695.

In Italy, it was Gian Battista Ramusio who chronicled the opening up of the world in

A Persian Breakfast, from *A Second Journey Through Persia . . .*, James Morier, 1818.

Navigationi e Viaggi, published in three volumes, 1563–1606. He corresponded with clerics and travellers from all over Europe, including Sebastian Cabot.

The sixteenth and seventeeth centuries saw the 'World Encompassed', its measure taken by the first circumnavigators, Drake and Cavendish. The next major voyages of discovery belong to William Dampier, the buccaneer. He reached Australia in 1686, and on his second voyage in 1699 in HMS *Roebuck* made one of the earliest surveys of that territory; but like the early Dutch explorers he encountered only the barren parts, so it is not surprising that his voyages did not immediately attract followers. Dampier's *Voyages* were not published until 1697–1703. In 1740–44 Lord Anson's voyage round the world, although not particularly distinguished geographically, touched the British sensibility. In a Europe beset with hostilities his voyage, and the spectacular capture of the *Acapulco* treasure galleon, brought him much fame and comparisons with Drake. The authorized narrative by Richard Walter, Anson's chaplain on the *Centurion*, appeared in 1748; within a year it had run into five editions, and 15 had appeared by 1776.

Captain James Cook has been called 'the greatest explorer of his age, the greatest maritime explorer of his country in any age'. His three circumnavigations of the globe from 1768 to 1779, when he was killed in Hawaii, are the great cornerstones of modern exploration. He was the first European to circumnavigate and map New Zealand, the first

Fort and Harbour of Aboukir, from Luigi Mayer's *Views in Egypt*, 1801.

to discover the eastern coast of Australia, the first to cross the Antarctic Circle, the first to chart the Pacific and the north-west coast of America. Quarto editions of his *Voyages*, in eight volumes with a large folio atlas, are not so uncommon. The demand for copies of the *Official Accounts* was so great that they were printed in large numbers and, in the case of the second voyage, in four editions. The condition of the bindings and of the plates has, however, taken on an excessive importance. It is not unusual to see a set in a sound contemporary binding priced at least at twice as much as another in an indifferent modern binding. A French edition, in fine contemporary mottled calf, however, would not be worth as much as a poor English set. It is generally the rule that English-speaking collectors, and therefore their booksellers, prefer an English text, or failing that one in the original language. The collector who sought 'the best editions of Cook' would want a second edition of the First Voyage, a first edition of the Second, and a third edition of the Third. This may seem perverse, but there is an addition to the text in the second edition of the First Voyage; the four editions of the Second Voyage are identical and the first edition is therefore more desirable; and the text of the Third Voyage was expanded in the third edition. The Hakluyt Society have published a definitive Cook, with the Life by Beaglehole, 1967–74. This is an invaluable set for the scholar, which has now reached the price that quarto editions were making 20 years ago.

Zulu Warriors from G. F. Angas's *The Kaffirs Illustrated*, 1849. [The Schuster Gallery]

All diaries kept on Cook's voyages were the property of the Admiralty and for use in the authorized edition, but some accounts did escape and appear before the official version. These pirated accounts, highly prized by collectors, are both rare and expensive. Some were poor productions adding little insight to the voyages, but others, notably Sidney Parkinson's account of Cook's First Voyage, add welcome colour to the otherwise rather dry Official Account.

After the success of Cook and of his European counterparts, notably La Perouse, the map of the globe was beginning to look quite modern in outline. The goals facing explorers seemed more limited, but this was in fact the beginning of the inland thrust which provides the dealer and collector with more literature on original travels and exploration than in any other period. In North America Mackenzie crossed the continent from the St Lawrence to the Pacific, in South America Humboldt was embarking on monumental travels into the interior, in Africa Bruce was exploring the Nile and Mungo Park the Niger. Niebuhr commenced at this time the detailed survey of Arabia, and Rennell was laying the foundations for the complete survey of the Indian subcontinent. The first settlers were arriving in Australia and inland exploration of that vast continent was beginning.

Australia, despite the inauspicious reports from the early Dutch voyagers and Dampier, left theorists and practical explorers alike wondering about the true nature and extent of Terra Australis, and asking whether it was part of the Great Southern Continent with which Ptolemy had so confidently balanced his world map. After Cook, the 'First Fleet' sailed to Botany Bay from England in 1788, establishing a convict settlement governed by Admiral Arthur Phillip, and named it after the first Viscount Sydney. As the colony grew the pressure to expand was great, but the barrier of the Blue Mountains made inland exploration arduous. The severe drought of 1813 made it vital for such exploration to succeed, and the account of the first inland expedition by Blaxland and Wentworth, *Tour of Discovery Across the Blue Mountains, New South Wales in 1813*, by Gregory Blaxland, is one of the rarest of all works of Australian exploration. From that point on, a new impetus was engendered for inland exploration. Sturt, Mitchell, Hovell and Hume discovered the Australian Alps; Oxley, Leichardt, and Burke and Wills were the first explorers to cross Australia from south to north in 1860; and many others made journeys of original discovery in the vast continent.

Before the bicentenary celebrations in 1988, prices in the field of Australiana had been erratic. Immediately afterwards it seemed that the massive price increases which had characterized the years leading up to the celebration had plummeted. In conjunction with a worldwide recession and severe internal pressure, Australian resources have not been supportive of the book market. In the summer of 1992, as a result of the recession, the important Longueville Collection was sold in London, with uneven results. The market remains unpredictable and it seems likely that other collections in this field may well be forced into the salerooms.

In the eighteenth century Jonathan Swift, himself author of the imaginary *Voyages of Gulliver*, wrote of Africa, 'So geographers in Afric Maps/with savage pictures fill the gaps/ and o'er inhabitable downs/Place elephants for want of towns'. He must surely have been referring to the celebrated map by Munster of 1570 with its Monoculi, Parrots and superb Elephant, decorating, apart from the Nile, a blank interior. Modern African exploration did not start until the formation of the British–African Association in 1788 to promote the discovery of Africa, but also to promote British trade and political interest. Mungo Park was commissioned by the directors to explore the great river Niger in West Africa, arriving there in 1795. His partially successful exploration established that the river did indeed flow eastward. He also picked up much useful information about the country through which he travelled, and his book *Travels in the Interior Districts of Africa*, 1799, gave valuable guides to the problems of health and economics of early African travel. In spite of its importance, his book is not a great rarity, and commands a price that is comparable with many mid nineteenth-century 'two decker' works of exploration. Once again the Hakluyt Society's four-volume *Missions to the Niger*, edited by Boville, second series, nos. 125, 128–30, 1964–66, gives a good account of the explorations of West Africa in the late eighteenth and early nineteenth centuries. By the middle of the nineteenth century only a very little of the eleven million square miles of this continent were known to Europeans and the vast heart was yet to be plumbed. It was Livingstone, who began explorations in Central Africa in 1849, and Barth, who set out for the Sahara and the Soudan in 1850, who marked the quickening of the pace in the illumination of the Dark Continent. The names of Speke, Burton, Baker, Grant, Stanley and many others in the next 40 years are notable for having given the centre of the map of Africa its essential features. Exploration literature, however, does not stop with Stanley in 1889; much of the finer detail was added by the work of surveyors, geologists, district commissioners and missionaries, continuing well into the twentieth century. It would be wrong to suggest that such a vast continent could ever fully yield up its secrets.

TRAVEL BOOKS

The Far East and China have always captured the imagination of collectors and travellers alike. With the magnificent description of his journeys and the account of his 17 years in China, Marco Polo is one of the earliest and best sources of information on this area. The Venetian trader, Nicolo Polo, took his son in 1271 on an extended business trip; travelling by sea to Acre, then on through Armenia, Persia and Asia, they followed the silk routes to Peking. During his long sojourn observing the lives and habits of the Chinese, Marco Polo also served for three years as the Governor of a Chinese city. There are many editions of Marco Polo's work, but the third revised edition of Yule and Cordier, with its scholarly concordance and commentary, two volumes, 1903, with the supplementary volume, 1926, remains the best.

With the surge of late eighteenth-century voyages, the subsequent advances in navigational, scientific and medical technique, gave nineteenth-century travel and exploration a degree of sophistication. Darwin joined the *Beagle* for the voyage on which he made the observations which led to the development of his theory of evolution (*On The Origin of Species*, 1859). The four-year voyage of the *Challenger*, 1872–76, provided 50 large volumes of most valuable scientific results. In the nineteenth century Americans, too, contributed to travel literature, with the voyage to the Antarctic and Pacific of Wilkes, and Commodore Perry's famous 1853 expedition to Japan with a gunboat to demand that the country open up for trade. The three-volume official report of the expedition, published in 1856, contains a famous plate of the interior of a Japanese bath house, known as the Bathing plate; although not called for in the list of plates, the work is incomplete without it.

A spirit of adventure is the prerequisite for the traveller and explorer but commerce, religion and politics are the strongest motives. Romantically, the lure of the spices and silks of the East, the furs of North America, the gold of California and Australia, and the ivory of Africa were powerful magnets; the proselytizing missionary, often working less conspicuously than the trader; the ruler needing to define his borders with a neighbour and to secure his country's own trade routes to the riches of the world, the desire to build powerful empires – all have been crucial in the acquisition of geographical knowledge.

Women travellers, however, fall into a category of their own. In her book *Wayward Women*, 1990, Jane Robinson explains succinctly: 'Men's travel accounts are traditionally concerned with What and Where, and women's with How and Why'. Their motive for travel and exploration is closer to the pure spirit of adventure unfettered by politics and commerce. Religion is the only territory in which women explore with the men. Lady Mary Wortley Montagu was the first woman to travel abroad purely for pleasure. Her letters, published after her death in 1763, gave the first glimpse to her readers of life in Turkey. Her open-mindedness and objectivity in reporting what she saw is quite astonishing. 'Gallantry and good-breeding are as different in different climates, as morality and religion'. She also allowed her son and baby daughter to be inoculated with smallpox, an idea she brought back with her to England 70 years before Jenner stumbled upon it.

Following Lady Mary Wortley Montagu there is a redoubtable cast of women travellers, many of whom were undoubtedly eccentric, like Lady Hester Stanhope who adopted Turkish male clothing and lived in a monastery near Mount Lebanon, and Nina

Mazuchelli whose grandly misjudged Himalayan Expedition has become a classic of mountaineering literature. Mary Kingsley, at the age of 30, having looked after her parents, finding on their death that she felt alone and unwanted, departed for West Africa. The photograph frontispiece to her *West African Studies*, 1899, suggests a character of great humour and spirit. Her comment to her readers after recounting a fall into a camouflaged pit barbed with sharpened ebony stakes was characteristic: 'It is at times like these moments you realize the blessings of a good thick skirt'. In the twentieth century Freya Stark was possibly the best-known lady traveller, combining a certain eccentricity with an exceptional style. Her books are keenly collected and her publishers have reissued all her travel writings. Gertrude Bell, Elspeth Huxley and others such as Dervla Murphy provide an important body of travel literature of the world through women's eyes. Dervla Murphy is certainly the most successful modern woman travel writer, following curiously in the Victorian maidenly tradition, with her accounts of bicycling in the Himalayan foothills and exploring Ethiopia on a donkey.

Polar explorers are perhaps the most extraordinary and complex of men. Women have played little part in this hostile area – with one great exception. Lady Franklin, who organized and financed many relief expeditions when her husband was lost looking for a North West Passage, was indirectly responsible for the gathering of much new information on the polar regions. The Franklin Search Expeditions revolutionized the map of the Arctic, and this was recognized by the award to Lady Franklin of the Royal Geographical Society's gold medal; she was the first woman to be so honoured. Mrs Peary went with her husband on his first polar expedition, but remained back at the base camp at Inglefield Gulf in Greenland. It was there that she gave birth to a daughter in 1892.

In the sixteenth and seventeenth centuries, attempts at penetration of the Arctic had met with failure. In the eighteenth century Daines Barrington, who was much struck by the possibility of reaching the North Pole, collected information from whalers and others who had voyaged in those regions and succeeded in interesting the British government and the Royal Society in the project. His *Paper on the Possibilities of Reaching the North Pole* was published in his *Miscellanies* in 1781 and aroused much interest. An enlarged edition, published in 1818, again gained much attention, but the search for a North West Passage obscured the Pole as an objective. Roald Amundsen was the first to successfully navigate the North West Passage in 1903–5 and determine the exact position of the North Magnetic Pole, and Robert Peary the first to claim the North Pole in 1909. There is now a considerable doubt about his claim, but there is no doubt that following his pioneering work it would only have been a matter of months before someone else would have claimed it.

The exploration of the Antarctic was much more difficult. The continent is further from Europe and surrounded by pack ice for much of the year. Captain Cook was the first to record his crossing of the Antarctic Circle on his second voyage, 17 January 1773, and the engraving which appears in the book, *The Ice Islands*, was the first authentic Antarctic view the world had seen. The Russian Expedition of 1819–21, commanded by Thaddeus von Bellinghausen, circumnavigated the Antarctic and continued Cook's survey of the South Sandwich Islands and South Georgia. His journal was translated from the Russian and issued by the Hakluyt Society in 1945. The circumnavigatory expedition of the French

TRAVEL BOOKS

under Dumont d'Urville, 1837–40, discovered Amélie Land and Côte Clarie, later to be claimed by the Wilkes expedition. The American Expedition of Charles Wilkes in 1838–42 charted Wilkes Land and the landfall they made during their Exploring Expedition. The British Expedition under James Clark Ross, 1839–43, was the first to break through the ice of the Ross Sea. During this century there have been many sealing and whaling expeditions which are not represented in travel literature. Towards the end of the century the first British Antarctic Expedition, 1898–1900, was the earliest expedition to spend the polar winter on the continent at Cape Adair. Scott's British National Expedition, 1901–4, was the first extensive exploration on land, examining the coast of Victoria Land and the Ross Ice Front, discovering King Edward VII Land and wintering at Hut Point on Ross Island. Finally, after great difficulties with their ship the *Discovery* being icebound from 1902 to 1904, they were eventually freed by *Morning* and by *Terra Nova*, the ship which Scott used for his last expedition. It was not until the Terra Nova Expedition of 1910–13 had already set out that Amundsen launched his bid for the Pole in Fritjof Nansen's ship the *Fram*. He reached the Pole just over a month before Scott and his companions.

Shackleton, who was on the first expedition, did not get on well with Scott and made two of his own expeditions to Antarctica. On the first, 1907–9, he set a record for going farthest south. On the second Trans-Antarctic Expedition his ship, the *Endurance*, was trapped and finally crushed by the ice, wrecking his plans to cross the continent by sledge. His open boat journey of 800 miles from Elephant Island to South Georgia is one of the great boat voyages of history, ranking with that of Captain Bligh to Timor, after he had been set adrift by the mutineers of the *Bounty*.

The twentieth century has seen the last blanks on the map of the globe filled in, and the prospect for exploratory travel has moved to outer space. However, this has not curtailed original travel literature. Wilfred Thesiger has been one of the last, if not the very last original traveller and explorer. His two books, *Arabian Sands*, 1959, and *The Marsh Arabs*, 1964, are classics in the field. Thesiger is in the mould of the great Arabian explorer, C. M. Doughty, whose *Travels in Arabia Deserta*, 1888, is considered a classic, a gripping and exciting story told with great sensitivity and style. T. E. Lawrence, who wrote a foreword to the 1921 reprint of *Arabia Deserta*, modelled his *Seven Pillars of Wisdom* on Doughty's style. This remarkable work was twice rewritten after the loss of the original manuscript. It was privately printed in 1926 and 100 copies were sold at 30 guineas each. Lawrence is reported to have lost £11,000 at that stage, but more than made up for the loss with the abridgement issued in the following year, *Revolt in the Desert*. The first trade edition of *Seven Pillars* did not come out until after his death, in 1935.

In time, as collectors and dealers alike become more and more familiar with their chosen field of collecting, the hunt is on for the obscure and rare. For example, every collector of Livingstone and of Africana will know about Stanley's book, *How I Found Livingstone*, 1872; but the Royal Geographical Society sent another expedition in search of Livingstone some years earlier which, although unsuccessful, was nevertheless a great feat of exploration which is quite overlooked. *The Search for Livingstone* by E. D. Young, 1868, is an exceptionally unprepossessing book, but for the collector it is rare and desirable. The bookseller and the collector have much to learn from each other as they progress through the bibliographic maze in search of their prizes. Stagnation dulls, and the key to good bookselling and collecting must surely be the striving for fresh opportunities, for exploration beyond the boundaries of one's own knowledge.

Baker, J. N. L., *A History of Geographical Discovery and Exploration*, 1931.
Beddie, M. K., *Bibliography of Captain James Cook*, 2nd edn, Sydney, 1970.
Catalogue of the Library of the National Maritime Museum, Volume One, Voyages and Travels, 1968.
Cordier, Henri, *Bibliotheca Indosinica*, 5 vols in 3, Paris 1912, (reprinted 1967).
——— *Bibliotheca Sinica*, 4 vols, 2nd edn, Paris, 1922–24.
Cumming, W. P., *The Exploration of North America, 1630–1776*, 1974.
Ferguson, John A., *Bibliography of Australia*, 5 vols, Sydney and Canberra, facsimile edition, 1951–75.
Hill, J. A., *Collection of Pacific Voyages*, 3 vols, San Diego, 1974, 1981, 1987.
Mendelssohn, S., *South African Bibliography*, 2 vols, 1910 (reprinted, 1968).
Pakenham, Thomas, *The Scramble for Africa*, 1992.
Palau y Dulcet, Antonio, *Manual del Librero Hispano-Americano*, 28 vols, 2nd edn, Barcelona, 1948–1977.
Ragatz, Lowell J., *Guide to the Study of British Caribbean History*, 1932.
Robinson, Jane, *Wayward Women, A Guide to Women Travellers*, Oxford, 1990.
Sabin. *See separate entry.*

Tree calf
See LEATHER

U

Uncut

The edges of almost all books printed before the days of publisher's bindings were intended to be cut smooth, irrespective of whether they were then to be gilded, marbled or stained. The description 'uncut' is only literally true of books which, for some reason, escaped the binder's trimming blade; but it is often used to indicate only that no further trimming has taken place after the initial preparation for binding. It is unnecessary to describe the edges of a modern cloth-bound book as uncut unless it has been rebound.

Unopened

A book is described as unopened if its leaves have been left untrimmed, so that the original folds remain intact at the top and at the fore-edges. Some unopened books will have been issued in this state; others may have remained untrimmed inadvertently. Most booksellers would probably agree that they present a delicate problem. The unopened state has an obvious appeal to the collector, as it virtually ensures fine internal condition; but it also obstructs the reasonable desire to look through the book, as an attempt to peer into the TITLE-PAGE or COLOPHON may cause ugly damage. To open or not to open? Each bookseller must judge the matter for himself; but if unopened leaves are to be separated, this should be done very patiently with a bone paper-knife, or failing this, with a none-too-sharp blade. The book trade is all too familiar with the distressing irregularities described by the words 'carelessly opened'.

V

Vale Press

Purists question the description of the Vale Press as a 'private press', for although its founder, CHARLES RICKETTS, originally planned to set up the Press at his home in The Vale, Chelsea, he was unable to obtain planning permission. As a result he arranged for a commercial printer, Ballantyne Press, to allocate plant and staff for the production of Vale Press books under his personal supervision. Although Ricketts' other interests included printmaking and painting, financial backing from W. L. Hacon, and the assistance of his publisher, John Lane, allowed him sufficient time to work at the design of his books.

Vale Press books are most frequently compared with those of the KELMSCOTT PRESS. Like those of William Morris, most of Ricketts' designs were Art Nouveau in inspiration; as with Kelmscott, most Vale title-pages were elaborate, with intricate patterns (often botanical) covering all the available space. But Ricketts' bindings were more varied and prettier in style, and the overall effect of his books is more relaxed than that of Morris's medievally inspired volumes. Both Kelmscott and Vale produced a very few copies on vellum of many titles.

The Press's most ambitious project was a 39-volume set of Shakespeare, published in an edition of 310 copies from 1900 to 1903; being unnumbered, volumes from the set are often now sold separately. The Vale Press maintained close links with Lucien Pissarro's ERAGNY PRESS until the former's closure in 1904.

Ricketts, Charles, *A Bibliography of the Books Issued by Hacon and Ricketts, 1896–1903*, 1904.

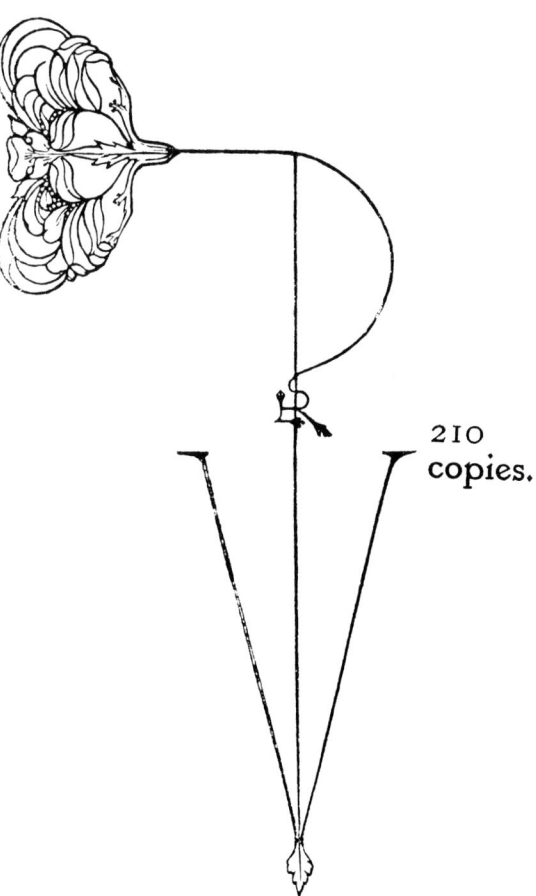

Colophon of *Lyrical Poems of Shelley*, Vale Press, 1898

Variant

The use of the term 'variant' in the description of a book indicates that the copy in question differs in some respect – binding, paper, text, advertisements – from other copies of the same edition. The term has a neutral connotation in that it does not imply any priority of issue; if (but only if) this is established will a more specific description be appropriate.

Variorum edition

The purpose of a Variorum edition is to bring together the variant readings, interpretations and notes of all the principal commentators who have studied an author's manuscripts or earlier editions. This is inevitably a laborious process, and is undertaken only when the literary importance of the texts justifies exhaustive study.

Vellucent
See CHIVERS

Vellum
See LEATHER

Verso
See RECTO

Victorian Books

Robin de Beaumont

Victorian books, and in particular Victorian illustrated books, have been the Cinderellas of collectors – and consequently of booksellers – until comparatively recently. Before 1950 virtually everything Victorian was deeply despised, although Britain retained much that was Victorian in its fabric, its outlook and its habits until well after the end of the last war. A younger post-war generation, without much money and with little in the shops, turned to junk shops and markets such as the Portobello Road to furnish their houses or flats from the contents of attics, usually nineteenth century. Victorian books, however, were another matter.

The 1951 Festival of Britain Exhibition, striving desperately to be 'modern' within the confines of post-war austerity, looked hard at Scandinavia with its clean lines, natural wood and spiky steel rods. Anything large, heavy or ornamental spoke of an affluence that was not in keeping with the times. Nevertheless, there were stirrings in high places. *The Architectural Review* was strong on Victorian type – Figgins or Playbill – and this was taken up by the brewers for their new pubs as they vandalized the Victorian originals. The Arts Council put on an exhibition in their offices in St James's Square, *Masterpieces of Victorian Photography 1840–1900 from the Gernsheim Collection*, in which even books illustrated by photographs were included. But this was pioneering. Even in the heady days of the photography boom in the 1970s only the big, important topographical books illustrated with photographs were in demand. The minor books, however attractive, like the 1861 *Sunshine in the Country*, are still unappreciated although they did appear in this exhibition. No institution took the slightest interest in Victorian books unless they were literary.

If there was little interest in books, there was a growing awareness that Victorian buildings were under threat, although it was 1958 before The Victorian Society was founded. John Betjeman, who was so involved in this, was one of the few who had collected Victorian illustrated books in the thirties, together with other kindred spirits like John Carter of Sotheby's, John Sparrow, the Warden of All Souls College, Oxford, and the wood engraver, Reynolds Stone. Michael Sadleir had been a collector of contemporary 'firsts' as an undergraduate, progressing via French Symbolistes, nineteenth-century Londoniana, books on coloured paper, obscure nineteenth-century private presses, Gothic novels and yellow-backs – to first and other editions of nineteenth-century literature in original cloth, in one to four volumes. This magnificent collection of 'XIX Century Fiction' and yellow-backs was given a suitable two-volume illustrated catalogue, printed in America in 1951, prior to its installation at UCLA in 1952. Here an attempt was made for the first time to identify and illustrate the various patterns of binding cloth used in the nineteenth century, and illustrations of 24 of these were given a wider audience in the Spring number of *The Book Collector*, 1953. As far as the 'High Victorian' illustrated books were concerned, by the end of the war those few who had collected in the thirties had lost interest and by 1960 had dispersed their collections, except perhaps for Reynolds Stone who seems to have collected quietly throughout his life.

It is generally the rule that new areas of collecting are discovered by a few, of whom one eventually writes a book on the subject that inspires a greater demand and consequent increase in prices; yet in the field of Victorian illustration two serious books on the subject

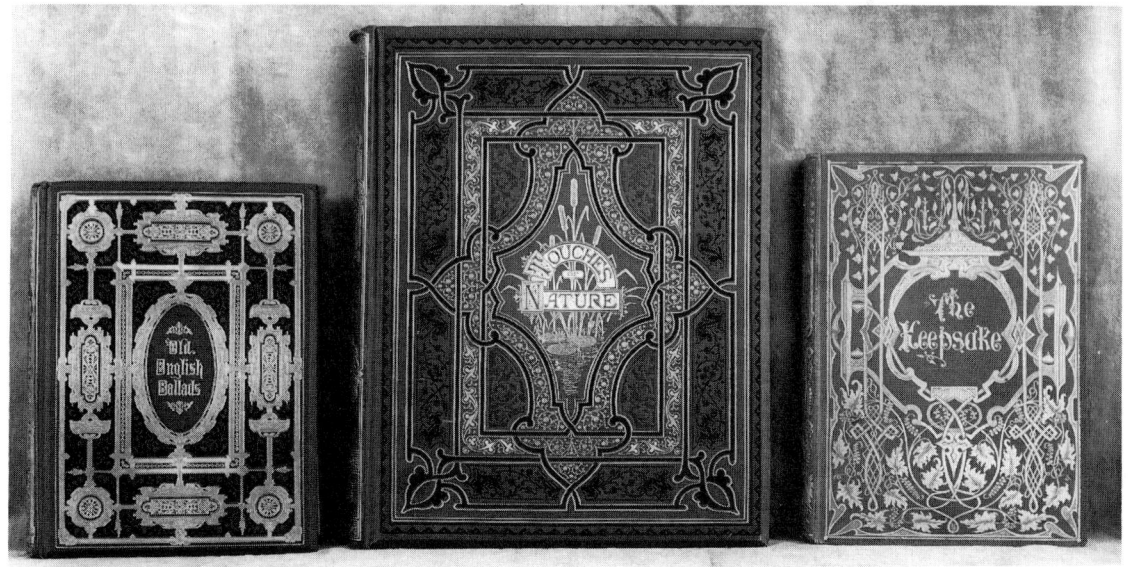

Examples of publishers' trade bindings; *Old English Ballads*, Ward, Lock and Tyler, n.d. (c.1868), designed by Albert Warren. *Touches of Nature*, Alexander Strahan, 1867, designed by Albert Warren. *The Keepsake*, David Bogue, 1855 (1854), designed by John Leighton.

The Preacher, Longman & Co., 1849. Publisher's profiled wooden boards with embossed leather spine designed throughout by Owen Jones. One of the most extraordinary publisher's bindings of the period.

were already available. The first such reference book was by Gleeson White, co-founder and editor with Charles Holme of *The Studio* in 1893 (although he soon gave that up, while continuing to contribute); it was published in 1897 as *English Illustration: 'The Sixties' 1857–70*. Here for the first time were recorded the books containing a peculiarly English series of illustrators. All the artists involved, and they included such figures as the Pre-Raphaelites Millais, Rossetti, Burne-Jones, Holman Hunt and Arthur Hughes from the Pre-Raphaelites; Fred Walker, Pinwell and North from the 'Idyllic School'; together with such strange fellows as Arthur Boyd Houghton and Simeon Solomon, treated their subjects seriously and were precisely unlike the caricaturists such as Cruikshank or 'Phiz' who have always retained such a strong following among English collectors. Much of their work first appeared in magazines, before being printed on better paper, either in collections of the work of an individual artist or included in new books, often with totally unsuitable text. Many of these books were either anthologies of poetry or unashamedly devotional.

It is little wonder, therefore, that so many of them were subsequently considered unsuitable collecting material. Nevertheless these books were prized when they appeared. For them, the artists drew the illustrations directly on to the wood block which was then cut by the professional firms of wood engravers; later, when it became technically

Holman Hunt's illustration to Tennyson's 'The Lady of Shalott', engraved by John Thompson for the Moxon *Tennyson's Poems*, 1857. (3¾ × 3¼ ins.)

possible, the designs were transferred photographically on to the wood block so that the original drawing could be saved. It is the staggering skill of these firms, the Dalziels or Swains, which should astound us today, but only if we understand what we are looking at. An illustration such as Holman Hunt's 'The Lady of Shalott' on page 67 of the 1857 Moxon Tennyson, is some 8 × 9.5 cm (3¼ × 3¾ in). In this, the magic web she weaves surrounds her and flows crazily through the whole design, changing as it does from black to white and back to black again. Wherever it is white the wood block is incised; where black the wood is cut away to allow the thread to stand in relief. Such a miracle of precision seems incredible; yet the design is remembered as Holman Hunt's and the tiny signature of the engraver, John Thompson, needs a magnifying glass to be seen clearly.

Gleeson White's book was successful enough to reach a third impression by 1906, but thereafter interest appears to have lapsed. It was not until after the First World War, in 1923, that the exceptionally comprehensive collection of Harold Hartley, combined with examples of the original wood blocks belonging to J. N. Hart, were given a major exhibition in, of all places, the National Gallery, Millbank or, as we know it, the Tate Gallery. Indeed this was possibly the only major exhibition comprising a selection of drawings, burnished proofs, and wood blocks for the 'Book Illustration of the Sixties'. Whether there was any connection between this and the issue of a major Victoria and Albert Museum Catalogue in 1919 of Modern Wood-Engravings, which included all the 'Sixties' artists, I have never been able to establish. For some reason that catalogue itself seems extraordinarily scarce and one wonders if it was ever widely published. Hartley himself wrote the introduction to the National Gallery catalogue and the exhibition then, astoundingly, went on tour, first to the Whitechapel Art Gallery and Birmingham in 1924, and then to Glasgow in 1925. Never again was the subject to have such exposure. The revival in interest that this generated led to the next major reference book, the Irish novelist Forrest Reid's *Illustrators of the Sixties*, which appeared in 1928. It was this book which was the stimulus for that new breed of collectors which included John Betjeman.

However, throughout the inter-war years institutions took very little notice. In 1933 H. H. Harrod gave his collection of 1860s illustrators to the V & A; about half of these either were, or came to be, in poor condition. In the 1950s, an eccentric dealer in St Martin's Court, off Charing Cross Road, managed to acquire a considerable archive from the descendants of the Dalziel Brothers, including family photographs, account books and their own copies of works they had produced at their Camden Press. This collection was offered to the V & A, who accepted a few items. The remainder were left in the dealer's chaotic upstairs room and were 'lost', or at any rate dispersed piecemeal. In 1955, Harold Hartley's son wanted to dispose of his father's outstanding collection. This comprised about a thousand proof wood-engravings, many burnished before numbers and with the artist's instructions to the engravers; 300 actual drawings; 80 wood blocks, including two for Allingham's *Music Master*, 1855; and nearly 500 of his Sixties books together with an almost complete collection of the periodicals in which the drawings first appeared: such as *Once a Week, The Cornhill,* and *Good Words*; not to mention a large collection of letters from the Dalziels to Hartley, Millais letters and a collection of books dealing with the artists' work. Quite rightly, he was anxious that the collection should not be broken up. For this whole collection he was asking £3,000 (about £35,000 at 1993 prices) but no one in Britain was interested. A far-sighted curator of the Boston Museum of Fine Arts, Mr Rossiter, arranged the purchase for his Museum – and there it languished in packing cases until comparatively recently. It is now at last being catalogued, but whether the catalogue will ever be published is doubtful.

Victorian colour printing had received some attention, though generally as part of wider studies. Martin Hardie, librarian at the V & A, wrote his *English Coloured Books* in 1906, ranging over the centuries from the fifteenth to the nineteenth, and on techniques from hand colouring via aquatints to full colour printing. R. M. Burch's *Colour Printing and Colour Printers*, 1910, though more specific in its technique, was even wider in range, including Europe, so that it is not until half way through the book that nineteenth-century England is dealt with. By far the most comprehensive study was C. T. Courtney Lewis's *The Story of Picture Printing in England during the XIXth Century*, [1928]. Lewis, who also wrote on Baxter, was the foremost authority and this book made a valuable contribution.

Nevertheless, there was still no reference work on Victorian books as such, even though all the factors which made the Victorian book, as an object, different from any that had appeared before, were evident by the time the Queen came to the throne in 1837. Until the arrival of cloth as a medium for binding in the early 1820s, books were issued in paper wrappers, or boards with paper labels, for subsequent binding, in vellum or in leather, to the owner's specification. By the early 1830s the application of gilt lettering directly on to the cloth had been perfected. Many of the innovations took time to become generally accepted, but they were there. For instance, *The Times* had been printed on a steam press since 1814 but it was some 40 years before this was commonly used for books. Until about 1870, all paper was normally dampened before printing, and the change from hand-made to machine-made was gradual. Nevertheless, by 1840 book cloth manufacture was a distinct trade, and different patterns, colours, stripes and spots were in vogue at different times in the 1840s and 1850s.

It was in this period that the greatest innovation and experiment took place, producing some of the most curious – and often impractical – trade bindings of the century. This was the period of Noel Humphreys and the heavily profiled so-called 'papier mâché'. (A proper analysis of the medium is still awaited: the one thing it is definitely *not* is papier mâché.) It was also the period of the chromolithographically illustrated books, associated with Owen Jones, with relievo leather 'Leake Patent' bindings, of the extraordinary book *The Preacher*, 1849, with its heat stamped wooden binding imitating hand carving, of glazed paper pictorially gilt and coloured bindings like Owen Jones' design on Leigh Hunt's *Jar of Honey on Mount Hybla* for the 1847 Christmas season; and much else of this kind. Other materials include the varnished paper-on-wood 'Mauchline' ware, tartan silk, and later, in the 1860s, the pretty, glazed paper simulating malachite with intricate incised gilding. Some of these processes must have been extraordinarily complicated to produce, especially in editions of 1000. All through the 1850s and 1860s gift books were produced with heavily bevelled boards on which both covers and spine were ornately gilt to intricate designs made possible by the invention of heavy arming and embossing presses. It seems to be invariably the case that the first edition of these books would have gilt to both covers, where subsequently the lower cover would show the same design in blind. Many of them have the monogram of the designer – John Leighton, Harry Rogers, Albert

Warren, etc. – somewhere in the design, though often this is hard to find. How a shop like Hatchards must have appeared at Christmas 1865!

None of this had been systematically recorded or given the status of serious study, though the books themselves were lying around, often on 'religious' or 'poetry' shelves. There had always been a few, a very few, dealers who had taken an interest, such as Heywood Hill, Ian Hodgkins – still a major source – and particularly Percy Muir and Laurie Deval at Elkin Mathews. Indeed, Percy Muir was later to write his *Victorian Illustrated Books* in 1971, having already published *English Children's Books* as early as 1954 in which he had naturally touched on the subject.

Then in 1963 the first comprehensive study was published, and it is really after this date that all other relevant books and exhibitions appear. This seminal work was Ruari McLean's *Victorian Book Design and Colour Printing*, based on the author's own extensive collection. Here, for the first time, the whole field was covered by a professional designer. Chapter headings included Whittingham and Pickering, Henry Shaw and Chiswick Press, early lithography and Owen Jones, Noel Humphreys, Joseph Cundall, styles in publishers' bindings and much, much more. This really was pioneering stuff and the first words in the book set the scene. 'More exciting things happened to book design between 1837 and 1890 than in any comparable period in the history of the world's printing; and most of it happened in London.' An enlarged and revised edition came out in 1972, a handsome quarto, with much colour printing and many more illustrations, which is still the best book on the subject. Two years later a companion volume dealt with *Victorian Publishers' Book-Bindings in Cloth and Leather* and once again McLean was breaking new ground. What was unashamedly a coffee-table book also combined a brief introduction with chapters on the techniques, designs and contemporary criticism, together with some 140 pages of illustrations of examples, many in colour. Finally the genre was on the map and institutions, particularly in America and Canada, began to show interest. McLean's own collection went to Massey College in Toronto; Tony Appleton in Brighton issued a catalogue in July 1971 of *XIX Century Colour Printing* which had, stuck on to the inside front cover, a note saying 'The contents of this catalogue have been sold as a collection. ISSUED FOR REFERENCE ONLY'. The 300 items were carefully catalogued and a complete section dealt with the various signed designer publishers' bindings, with the different binders' firms' labels noted. At last someone in the trade was showing an intelligent interest – and the collection was bought by the far-sighted College of Librarianship of Wales, in Aberystwyth. For the next eight years this collection was researched and catalogued by Douglas Ball, and in 1980 a very comprehensive, very limited loose-leaf folder was produced with each book occupying one page and heavily cross-referenced by author, title, publisher, printer, artist and binder. Out of this work grew Ball's doctoral thesis on *Victorian Publishers' Bindings* – which in turn became a book, published by the Library Association in 1985. Sadly Douglas Ball died the month before it came out, but his work is the most complete yet on the subject, invaluable as a reference work and very readable.

The last major collection of Victorian illustrated books, this time belonging to the other participant in the 1923 National Gallery Exhibition, and now 'The Property of the Executors of the late J. N. Hart Esq.' appeared at auction at Sotheby's in 1965. There were some 413 items, including many owned by Forrest Reid while researching his book, many association copies and many in splendid condition. Astoundingly, these 413 items were lumped into 17 lots, sandwiched between other properties belonging to Sir Osbert Sitwell and a collection of books on roses. Of these 17 lots, five were single items and one contained the two major books on the subject (Forrest Reid and Gleeson White), so that the remaining 11 lots contained stacks of these books. No institution was interested and the majority were bought by Pickering and Chatto acting for a wealthy American collector, Gordon N. Ray. These he gave to the Pierpont Morgan Library which, in 1976, issued a magnificent catalogue for an exhibition of Dr Ray's collection *The Illustrator and the Book in England from 1790 to 1914*, or rather what had started as a catalogue expanded into the first comprehensive study of 'a period during which England held its own in book illustration with any country in the world'. Although no such collection existed in Britain (except for the Harrod collection in the V & A, half of which was in vile condition) no British institution was interested enough to acquire these books; and even if one had been, no such finely produced scholarly work would have been forthcoming.

There now started to be general recognition that Victorian books were worthy of study and collection, and relative scarcity meant increasing prices. Booksellers' catalogues started to point out why some previously neglected books were of interest and institutions produced informative catalogues. Two of particular interest might be noted. In 1978, Joan Friedman at the Yale Center for British Art produced *Color Printing in England*, a fine catalogue for a section of the Paul Mellon collection. In 1987, Alice Beckwith of Providence College, Rhode Island, produced another fine catalogue for an exhibition at the Museum of Art, Rhode Island School of Design, entitled *Victorian Bibliomania, The Illuminated Book in 19th Century Britain*. At last, just at a time when the books themselves, in remotely acceptable condition, seemed to be disappearing from the booksellers' shelves, the demand was beginning to arise worldwide. Sadly, the finest collections have almost certainly left Britain already. One of the greatest has been put together privately by an American painter and architect within the last ten to 15 years and is now in California; but it is reasonable to expect that research will continue now that Victorian books have finally come in out of the cold.

Ball, Douglas, *Victorian Publishers' Bindings*, The Library Association, 1985.
Burch, R. M., *Colour Printing and Colour Printers*, 1910, reprinted, Edinburgh, 1983, with a foreword by Ruari McLean.
Faxon, W., *Literary Annuals and Gift Books 1823–1903*, Pinner, 1973.
Friedman, Joan M., *Color Printing in England 1486–1870*, New Haven, 1978.
Goldman, Paul, *Victorian Illustrated Books, 1855–70*, 1994.
Houfe, Simon, *The Dictionary of British Book Illustrators and Caricaturists 1800–1914*, Woodbridge, 1978.
——— *Fin de Siècle. The Illustration of the Nineties*, 1992.
Jamieson, Eleanore, *English Embossed Bindings 1825–1850*, Cambridge, 1972.
Lewis, C. T. Courtney, *The Story of Picture Printing in the XIXth Century*, [1928].
McLean, Ruari, *Victorian Book Design and Colour Printing*, 1963 (revised edn, 1972).
——— *Victorian Publishers' Book-Bindings in Paper*, 1983.
——— *Victorian Publishers' Book-Bindings in Cloth and Leather*, 1974.

Muir, Percy, *Victorian Illustrated Books*, 1971 (reprinted, 1985).
Ray, Gordon N., *The Illustrator and the Book in England from 1790 to 1914*, New York, 1976.
Reid, Forrest, *Illustrators of the Sixties*, 1928 (reprinted as *Illustrators of the Eighteen Sixties*, New York, 1975).
Wakeman, Geoffrey, *Victorian Book Illustration, The Technical Revolution*, Newton Abbot, 1973.
Wakeman, Geoffrey and Bridson, Gavin D. R., *A Guide to Nineteenth Century Colour Printers*, Loughborough, 1975.
White, Gleeson, *English Illustration: 'The Sixties' 1855–70*, 1906.

Vignette

In the context of book illustration, the term 'vignette' usually describes an ornamental design or drawing found on a TITLE-PAGE, or used as a head or TAIL-PIECE to a chapter. THOMAS BEWICK's small drawings are a celebrated example of this form of embellishment. More generally the term describes any illustration that is not confined by a border or by any other distinct outline.

W

Walther, Henry (fl.1790–1840)
A number of German bookbinders settled in London at the end of the eighteenth century. Henry Walther, working with JOHN BAUMGARTEN, produced extravagantly tooled morocco bindings for Earl Spencer and other wealthy collectors, but he could also turn out simple and elegant work, some of which is represented in the Storer collection at Eton College. He often signed books on the inner hinge.

Watermark
Papermakers first introduced an identifying mark into their manufacturing process some 700 years ago, by incorporating a symbol or monogram into the wire mesh of the mould in which the sheet of paper is formed; the sheet is slightly thinned where the wire device is located, and the watermark can thus be seen when the sheet is held up to the light. Almost all hand-made papers are watermarked, but the presence of such a mark does not necessarily signify hand-manufacture; contrived watermarks are often found in machine-made paper. During the seventeenth century smaller secondary, or countermarks, came into use; these appear in the other half of the sheet, opposite the watermark, and often identify the paper-maker by name or initials. Watermarks and countermarks have also been used to record dates of manufacture and sheet sizes.

Bibliographers have often found watermarks helpful, in much the same way as chain lines, in resolving uncertainties about the format and make-up of books, and in detecting the presence of cancels or inserted leaves. They are also occasionally useful, when their own history is well documented, in providing evidence of printing dates.

Beta-radiography, and new photographic techniques, have greatly assisted the reproduction of watermarks, and thus enlarged their role in bibliographical research.

Watermarks have, by their very nature, attracted not only bibliophiles but also conspiracy theorists. An extreme example of the latter was Harold Bayley, whose obsession with Albigensian and other heresies led Allan Stevenson to describe him as 'the most fantastic charlatan ever to write on watermarks'; his works were politely but repeatedly refuted by Briquet.

Briquet, C. M., *Les filigranes: dictionnaire historique de marques du papier, 1282–1600*, Paris, 1907 (reprinted, Amsterdam, 1968).
(Briquet's other works were collected in a single volume, *Opuscula*, Hilversum, 1955.)
Churchill, W. A., *Watermarks in Paper in Holland, England, France, etc., in the XVII and XVIII Centuries and their Interconnection*, Amsterdam, 1935 (reprinted, Rijswijk, 1965).
Heawood, Edward, *Watermarks Mainly of the 17th and 18th Centuries*, Hilversum, 1950.
Spector, Stephen, (ed.), *Essays in Paper Analysis*, 1987.

Wing

The abbreviation of the *Short-Title Catalogue of Books Printed in England, Scotland, Ireland and Wales and British America, and of English Books Printed in Other Countries, 1641–1700*. Donald Wing, of Yale University Library, compiled the three-volume work for The Index Society of America in 1945. It was a continuation of the SHORT-TITLE CATALOGUE, extending it to the year 1700. The basis for inclusion of a book in Wing is that the location of at least one surviving copy should be known. Entries are in alphabetical order of author, with place and date of publication noted, together with a maximum of ten known locations, five in Great Britain and five in the United States. Entry reference numbers are subdivided by alphabetical letters, e.g. F.912. Locations include over 200 libraries and collections.

The second edition of Wing was printed in New York, 1972–88. It was extensively revised as the result of nearly 40 years' work; an index volume of printers and publishers, with a chronological list, is in course of preparation.

The Wing revision team is based at Yale and the work is published by the Modern Language Association of America. A third edition of Volume I is in hand and will appear in book form, after which Wing will be revised and updated on-line; most is already in machine-readable form.

Wire-stitching

The use of wire staples as a binding method has been largely confined to pamphlets and periodicals. Towards the end of the nineteenth century, wire-stitching machines capable of stapling books were briefly in use, but the wire tended to rust and the method was abandoned.

Wise, Thomas J. (1859–1937)

Wise's love of literature, and particularly Romantic poetry, led him to form a fine collection of the first editions of the works of eighteenth- and nineteenth-century English authors, generally in fine condition and in original state. His admiration for such writers as Byron, Tennyson and the Brontës was informed by considerable scholarship, and he was instrumental in founding both the Shelley Society and the Browning Society. He compiled bibliographies of Byron, the Brontës, Tennyson, Swinburne, Robert and Elizabeth Barrett Browning and Wordsworth which, in spite of some inaccuracies and omissions, remain of considerable value. He was a member of the Roxburghe Club and was well regarded as a scholar and collector.

Wise's friendship with Harry Buxton Forman (1842–1917) began about 1882 when Wise expressed interest in Forman's edition of the works of Shelley (four volumes of poetry, 1876–77 and four of prose, 1880). A few years later the two cooperated in their first forgery, Shelley's *Poems and Sonnets*. These poems had appeared for the first time in Edward Dowden's biography of the poet of 1886. The following year they were printed separately by Richard Clay and Sons (who continued innocently to collaborate with the forgers) under the editorship of 'Charles Seymour' (who did not exist) and published by 'The Philadelphia Historical Society' (which also did not exist). The 'cooperation' between Thomas Wise and Harry Buxton Forman lasted until their deceptions were revealed in 1934 in JOHN CARTER and GRAHAM POLLARD's *An Enquiry into the Nature of Certain Nineteenth-Century Pamphlets*. In total the two had forged more than 100 pieces of work by well-known writers; some were hitherto unpublished pieces, some were apparently earlier editions of known works; some were separately printed pieces hitherto known only in collected editions, some had 'acquired' wrappers which had not previously been recorded. New 'caches' of printed material came on to the market unexpectedly.

Meanwhile Wise's reputation as a collector and bibliographer grew steadily. He acted for wealthy buyers in America and in Britain, continuing to write articles on literary subjects for learned journals. Forman died in 1917 and Wise retired from a successful career in the commodities market.

The unveiling of the fraud revealed a far greater range of forgery than had been suspected. Inconsistencies were found in types of paper, printing methods, publishers' imprints and textual accuracy. Wise died three years after the publication of *An Enquiry . . .*, having never seemed close to admitting his part in the conspiracy, dismissing the whole thing as a storm in a teacup and blaming the now already deceased Forman as the instigator. After his death his Library passed to the British Museum, including some books made-up with pages stolen from the Museum's own copies! Wise's name is still most closely associated with the dissemination of 'certain nineteenth-century pamphlets'.

The Ashley Library The Ashley Library – named after the road in London where Wise lived for many years – consisted of the collection of printed books, manuscripts and autograph letters assembled by Thomas Wise. The catalogue was published in 1922–36 by the Bibliographical Society to whom Wise had assigned the copyright. It was reprinted in 1971 with a new preface by Simon Nowell-Smith. Wise had published the first two volumes in 1905–8 in an edition said to consist of only 12 copies. The first complete edition, introduced by Richard Curle, was limited to 200 copies, privately printed. Wise's aim was to form 'a library of the first editions of the famous English poets and dramatists, in perfect state, from Elizabethan times to the present'. The catalogue lists and describes rare plays and masques, pamphlets, tracts and poetry, and includes many items which are not fully described elsewhere.

The collection is a strongly personal one and Wise was an aggressive and somewhat arrogant collector. The order of entries is at times difficult to follow, but there are indexes at the end of volumes 9 and 11. The later edition includes a bibliography of material relating to the Wise forgeries.

Barker, Nicolas, Collins, John, *A Sequel to 'An Enquiry . . .'*, 1982.
Carter, John, Pollard, Graham, *An Enquiry into the Nature of Certain Nineteenth-Century Pamphlets*, 1934 (reprinted, 1983).
Collins, John, *The Two Forgers*, Aldershot, 1992.
Foxon, David, *Thomas J. Wise and the pre-Restoration Drama*, 1959.
Partington, W. G., *Thomas J. Wise in the Original Cloth*, 1946.

With all faults

The terms *w.a.f.*, *with all faults*, and *sold not subject to return* are used (usually by auctioneers) to indicate that a book is offered for sale on the understanding that the seller will not enter into any discussion of its condition or completeness, either before or after sale. There are several circumstances in which this suspension of normal guarantees is considered to be a reasonable measure. An illustrated book, for example, may be known to vary in make-up from one copy to another, so that no 'correct' number of plates can be established. The advertisements 'called for' in a work issued in parts may not be authoritatively recorded. Collections of pamphlets and long runs of journals may be virtually impossible to collate, and in such cases the 'w.a.f.' warning may be explained as being 'due to the difficulty of collation'. Somewhat different (and perhaps less valid) reasons for a 'w.a.f.' disclaimer arise when the value of a book lies principally in its binding, or in its provenance, though the latter reason is now rarely given.

Although cataloguers may rightly bear in mind that no one expects a collection of several hundred volumes, offered at relatively low sums, to be rigorously checked, most experienced booksellers employ these terms very sparingly.

Woodcut
See TECHNIQUES OF ILLUSTRATION

Wood-engraving
See TECHNIQUES OF ILLUSTRATION

Worde, Wynkyn de
Born in Alsace, Wynkyn de Worde came to England in about 1473 as CAXTON's foreman. He may have learned printing in Cologne, for he was a proficient craftsman when he joined Caxton, and on the latter's death in 1491 he took over the press. In 1500 he moved to Fleet Street where he printed many works begun, or at least envisaged, by Caxton, using the same type and design. He retained many of Caxton's customers and continued to enjoy the patronage of the royal household. One of Caxton's works, *Vitas Patrum*, was, according to de Worde, 'translated out of French into English by William Caxton, late dead and finished it at the last day of his life'.

De Worde extended the subject matter of books produced by the early English printers to include secular themes, including law books and other textbooks; he was also the first to print musical notation. He was partly responsible for the increased importance of the TITLE PAGE, and adopted many different printers' marks. De Worde used italic type for the first time in England as well as gothic script, the Greek alphabet and other innovative expressions of the printer's craft.

Moran, James, *Wynkyn de Worde: Father of Fleet Street*, 2nd edn, revised 1976.
Plomer, H. R., *Wynkyn de Worde and his Contemporaries*, 1925.

Working copy
See READING COPY

World's Classics
The early years of the twentieth century saw a proliferation of inexpensive editions of classic works of literature. Publishers who issued their own 'libraries' included Nelson, Dent, Cassell, Methuen and several others who did not survive long enough to pursue this lucrative line in book production. One such was Grant Richards who, when his business collapsed in 1906, sold his World's Classics series to Oxford University Press. He had published by that time 66 titles, starting with *Jane Eyre*. Oxford continued the series with *The Tenant of Wildfell Hall*. The neat navy blue volumes, printed on INDIA PAPER, were immediately successful and OUP's reputation as general as well as academic publishers grew as a result.

The World's Classics were inexpensive – one shilling at the outset (the same as EVERYMAN), rising to two shillings in the 1920s – and they were both comfortable to handle and pleasant to read. Sir Humphrey Milford, who joined OUP in 1900, becoming Publisher to the University from 1913–1945, believed that the revival of interest in Trollope was in large part due to the publications of his novels in The World's Classics series.

Worming
The damage to the pages and binding of books described as 'worming' is caused by various species of paper-eating maggot. It has been well said that small wormholes have something of the character of 'honourable scars', and they are not generally considered greatly offensive; but extensive worming does occasionally cause something very close to disintegration. The worst effects are likely to be found in early books printed on rag paper; later machine-made papers seem to hold less attraction.

Wrap-around band
A strip of paper folded around the DUST-WRAPPER, bearing promotional material which either arrived too late for inclusion in the DUST-WRAPPER design or seemed too blatantly commercial to be included there. Generally the band proclaims that the book has won a prize, or been selected by a newspaper or book club for promotion; alternatively, it may carry an enthusiastic endorsement from some well-known figure.

Wrap-around bands tended to be discarded with even less hesitation than dust-wrappers, so (if they can be shown to belong to the book they encircle) they may add substantially to the price; although the dealer who holds a very condition-conscious customer to ransom over one may well lose some goodwill.

Many collectors (and not a few dealers) believe that wrap-around bands are a sign that condition mania has gone altogether too far. Moreover, their very nature suggests that the first copies on sale might have lacked them. On the other hand, they are often interesting, and cannot do any harm. And people used to throw away dust-wrappers . . .

Wrappers
Wrappers (as distinct from DUST-WRAPPERS) are paper covers used either as temporary protection for a book intended for binding, or as the permanent covers of the type of book now commonly known as a paperback. As a temporary covering, plain or marbled wrappers were used as an alternative to paper boards for books published before the advent of publisher's cloth; and they are similarly prized by collectors when they survive. Printed wrappers are generally of a later date; they lend a distinctive appearance to such series as the TAUCHNITZ editions.

X, Y & Z

Xylographica
See BLOCK BOOKS

Yapp edges
A form of binding, usually of limp leather, which overlaps the edges of the book. It was originally introduced for bibles and prayer books, enabling them to slip easily into a pocket; yapp edges are also found on small volumes of poetry, etc., especially those bound in suede.

Yellow-backs
This series of low-priced novels in distinctive covers was published to supply the first railway station bookstalls set up by W. H. Smith. The first book appeared in 1853; the bright yellow covers bore coloured illustrations of scenes from the books which sold usually at 1s 6d. They proved extremely popular. Forerunners of the later paperbacks, the novels were calculated to appeal to an increasingly literate Victorian England, ready to devour detective fiction, mystery stories, romance and, later, works on travel, history and biography. Yellow-backs have their collectors but the poor quality of paper and binding has taken its toll.

Carter, John (ed.), *New Paths in Book Collecting*, 1934.
Sadleir, Michael, *XIX Century Fiction*, 1951.

Zaehnsdorf
Joseph Zaehnsdorf came from Vienna to London where he started his own bindery in 1842. It remained a family firm until the end of the Second World War. The impressive premises near Cambridge Circus employed at one time more than 100 staff and held the Royal Warrant of Edward VII.

After the death of the last Zaehnsdorf in 1947 the control of the firm passed to another owner; however, the name was re-established in 1957. Zaehnsdorfs trained several distinguished binders including SARAH PRIDEAUX and Roger de Coverley, and the first Joseph's book about the craft remained a valuable aid to apprentices for many years.

Zaehnsdorf bindings have always been highly regarded for their restrained yet distinctive style; the firm was responsible for many of the inexpensive but well-executed prize bindings of the early part of the century.

Broomhead, Frank, *The Zaehnsdorfs (1842–1947), Craft Bookbinders*, Pinner, 1986.
Zaehnsdorf, Joseph W., *The Art of Bookbinding*, 2nd edn, 1890 (reprinted, Farnborough, 1967).

AUTHOR BIBLIOGRAPHIES

The following list is necessarily selective. It is confined to English-language authors, and a few illustrators. Only those bibliographies which contain precise information about primary publications are included: check-lists, and those 'bibliographies' which are no more than enumerative lists of criticism and other secondary material, are therefore omitted.

It is hoped that readers will usually find here the information they require; but they will sometimes need to turn to more extensive sources. HOWARD-HILL and BESTERMAN (who also list subject bibliographies) are among the most detailed works; THE NEW CAMBRIDGE BIBLIOGRAPHY OF ENGLISH LITERATURE also notes numerous bibliographies, and other important sources of information will be found at the end of many of the articles in this Companion.

A. E., pseudonym of George William Russell (1867–1935)
Denson, Alan, *Printed Writings of George William Russell (AE); A Bibliography, with Notes on his Pictures and Portraits*, London and Evanston, Illinois, 1961.

Ainsworth, William Harrison (1805–1882)
Locke, Harold, *A Bibliographical Catalogue of the Published Novels and Ballads of William Harrison Ainsworth*, 1925.

Allingham, William (1824–1889)
O'Hegarty, Patrick S., *A Bibliography of William Allingham*, Dublin, 1945.

Anstey, F., pseudonym of Thomas Anstey Guthrie (1856–1934)
Turner, Martin J., *A Bibliography of the Works of F. Anstey (Thomas Anstey Guthrie)*, 1931.

Arnold, Matthew (1822–1888)
Smart, Thomas Burnett, *The Bibliography of Matthew Arnold*, 1892, reprinted, New York, 1967; Norwood, Pennsylvania, 1974.

Ashbery, John (1927–   )
Kermani, David K., *John Ashbery: A Comprehensive Bibliography*, New York and London, 1976.

Auden, W. H. (1907–1973)
Bloomfield, B. C. and Mendelson, Edward, *W. H. Auden: A Bibliography 1924–1969*, 2nd edition, Charlottesville, Virginia, 1972.

Austen, Jane (1775–1817)
Gilson, David, *A Bibliography of Jane Austen*, Oxford, 1982.

Bacon, Francis, Baron Verulam and Viscount St Alban (1561–1626)
Gibson, Reginald W., *Francis Bacon: A Bibliography of his Works and of Baconiana to the year 1750*, Oxford, 1950;
———— supplement, Oxford, 1959.

Ballantyne, R. M. (1825–1894)
Quayle, Eric, *R. M. Ballantyne: A Bibliography of First Editions*, 1968.

Baring, Maurice (1874–1945)
Chaundy, Leslie, *A Bibliography of the First Editions of the Works of Maurice Baring*, 1925.

Barrie, Sir James M. (1860–1937)
Cutler, B. D., *Sir James M. Barrie: A Bibliography with Full Collations of the American Unauthorised Editions*, New York, 1931.

Bates, H. E. (1905–1974)
Eads, Peter, *H. E. Bates: A Bibliographical Study*, Winchester, 1990.

Beckett, Samuel (1906–1989)
Davis, R. J., *Essai de bibliographie des oeuvres de Samuel Beckett (1929–1966)*, in *Calepins de bibliographie* no. 2, Paris, 1971, revised 1972.

Beckford, William (1760–1844)
Chapman, Guy, *A Bibliography of William Beckford of Fonthill*, 1930.

Beerbohm, Max (1872–1956)
Gallatin, Albert E. and Oliver, L. M., *A Bibliography of the Works of Max Beerbohm*, Cambridge, Massachusetts, and London, 1952.

Behn, Aphra (1640–1689)
O'Donnell, Mary Ann, *An Annotated Bibliography of Primary and Secondary Sources*, New York and London, 1986.

Belloc, Hilaire (1870–1953)
Cahill, Patrick C., *The English First Editions of Hilaire Belloc: a Chronological Catalogue of 153 Works Attributed to that Author, including Transcripts of the Title-pages and a Collector's Description of the Pagination, Covers, Variants etc . . .*, 1953.

Bennett, Arnold (1867–1931)
Emery, Norman, *Arnold Bennett (1867–1931): A Bibliography*, Stoke on Trent, 1967.

Bentley, Richard (1662–1742)
Bartholomew, A. T., *Richard Bentley, D. D. A Bibliography of his Works and of all the Literature called forth by his Arts or his Writings*, Cambridge, 1908.

Berkeley, George (1685–1753)
Keynes, Sir Geoffrey L., *A Bibliography of George Berkeley, Bishop of Cloyne: his Works and his Critics in the Eighteenth Century*, Oxford, 1976.

Jessop, Thomas E., *A Bibliography of George Berkeley . . . with an Inventory of Berkeley's Manuscript Remains, by A. A. Luce*, 1934 (reprinted, New York, [1968]).

Bewick, Thomas (1753–1828)
Roscoe, Sydney, *Thomas Bewick: A Bibliography Raisonné of Editions of The General History of Quadrupeds, The History of British Birds and The Fables of Aesop issued in his Lifetime*, 1953 (reprinted, Folkestone, 1973).

Bishop, Elizabeth (1911–1979)
MacMahon, Candace W., *Elizabeth Bishop: A Bibliography 1927–1979*, Charlottesville, Virginia, 1980.

Blake, William (1757–1827)
Keynes, Sir Geoffrey L., *A Bibliography of William Blake*, New York, 1921.

Bentley, G. E., *Blake Books: Annotated Catalogues of William Blake's Writings in Illuminated Printing, in Conventional Typography and in Manuscripts and Reprints thereof . . .*, Oxford, 1977.

Blunden, Edmund (1896–1974)
Kirkpatrick, B. J., *A Bibliography of Edmund Blunden*, Oxford, 1979.

Borrow, George (1803–1881)
Collie, Michael and Fraser, Angus, *George Borrow: A Bibliographical Study*, Winchester, 1984.

Boswell, James (1740–1795)
Pottle, Frederick A., *The Literary Career of James Boswell, esq.: Being the Bibliographical Materials for a Life of Boswell*, Oxford, 1929.

Bowen, Elizabeth (1899–1973)
Sellery, J'nan M. and Harris, William O., *Elizabeth Bowen: A Bibliography*, Austin, Texas, 1981.

Bowles, Paul (1910–   )
Miller, Jeffrey, *Paul Bowles: A Descriptive Bibliography*, Santa Barbara, California, 1986.

Boyle, Robert (1627–1691)
Fulton, John F., *A Bibliography of the Honourable Robert Boyle*, 2nd edition, Oxford, 1961.

Bradbury, Ray (b. 1920)
Nolan, William F., *The Ray Bradbury Companion*, Detroit, Michigan, 1975.

Bridges, Robert (1844–1930)
McKay, George L., *A Bibliography of Robert Bridges*, New York and London, 1933 (reprinted, New York, 1966).

Brontë, The Family
Smith, Walter E., *The Brontë Sisters – A Bibliographical Catalogue*, Los Angeles, 1991.
Wise, Thomas J., *A Bibliography of the Writings in Prose and Verse of the Members of the Brontë Family*, 1917 (reprinted, 1965).

Brooke, Rupert (1887–1915)
Keynes, Sir Geoffrey L., *A Bibliography of Rupert Brooke*, 2nd edition, 1959.

Browne, Sir Thomas (1605–1682)
Keynes, Sir Geoffrey L., *A Bibliography of Sir Thomas Browne, Kt., MD*, 2nd edition, Oxford, 1968.

Browning, Elizabeth Barrett (1806–1861)
Barnes, Warner, *A Bibliography of Elizabeth Barrett Browning*, Austin, Texas, 1967.

Browning, Robert (1812–1889)
Broughton, Leslie N., Northup, Clark Sutherland and Pearsall, Robert, *Robert Browning: A Bibliography, 1830–1950* (Cornell Studies in English, vol. XXXIX), Ithaca, New York, 1953 (reprinted, New York, 1967).

Browning, Elizabeth and Robert
Wise, Thomas James, *A Browning Library*, 1929.

Buchan, John, Baron Tweedsmuir (1875–1940)
Blanchard, Robert G., *The First Editions of John Buchan: A Collector's Bibliography*, Hamden, Connecticut, 1981.

Hanna, Archibald, *John Buchan, 1875–1940: A Bibliography*, Hamden, Connecticut, 1953.

Bunyan, John (1628–1688)
Harrison, Frank M., *A Bibliography of the Works of John Bunyan* (Bibliographical Society Supplement No. 6), 1932.

Burke, Edmund (1729–1797)
Todd, William B., *A Bibliography of Edmund Burke*, revised edition, Godalming, Surrey, 1982.

Burns, Robert (1759–1796)
Egerer, Joel W., *A Bibliography of Robert Burns*, Edinburgh, 1964.

Burton, Sir Richard Francis (1821–1890)
Penzer, Norman M., *An Annotated Bibliography of Sir Richard Francis Burton*, 1923 (reprinted, New York, 1967, London, 1967).

Butler, Samuel (1835–1902)
Hoppé, Alfred J., *A Bibliography of the Writings of Samuel Butler, Author of Erewhon, and of Writings about Him*, [1925] (reprinted, New York, 1967).

Byron, George Gordon Noel, Baron (1788–1824)
Wise, Thomas J., *A Bibliography of the Writings in Verse and Prose of George Gordon Noel, Baron Byron*, 2 vols, 1932–3 (reprinted, 1964).

Campbell, Roy (1901–1957)
Parsons, D. S. J., *Roy Campbell: A Descriptive and Annotated Bibliography . . .*, New York and London, 1981.

Carlyle, Thomas (1795–1881)
Tarr, Rodger L., *Thomas Carlyle, A Descriptive Bibliography*, Oxford, 1989.

Carpenter, Edward (1844–1929)
[Carpenter, Edward], *A Bibliography of the Writings of Edward Carpenter; a Bibliographical Handbook for Collectors, Booksellers, Librarians and Others* [1916].

Carroll, Lewis, pseudonym of the Reverend C. L. Dodgson (1832–1898)
Williams, Sidney Herbert and Madan, Falconer, *The Lewis Carroll Handbook, revised and augmented by Roger Lancelyn Green, now further revised by Denis Crutch*, Folkestone, Kent, 1979.

Chandler, Raymond (1888–1959)
Bruccoli, Matthew J., *Raymond Chandler: A Descriptive Bibliography*, Pittsburgh, 1979.

Charles I (1600–1649)
Madan, Francis F., *A New Bibliography of the Eikon Basilike of King Charles the First, with a note on the authorship*, Oxford Bibliographical Society N.S. Vol. III, 1949.

Chatterton, Thomas (1752–1770)
Warren, Murray, *A Descriptive and Annotated Bibliography of Thomas Chatterton*, New York and London, 1977.

Chaucer, Geoffrey (d. 1400)
Skeat, Walter W., *The Chaucer Canon*, Oxford, 1900.

Chesterton, Gilbert Keith (1874–1936)
Sullivan, John, *G. K. Chesterton, A Bibliography*, 1958 (reprinted, Westport, Connecticut, 1974).
────── *Chesterton Continued, A Bibliographical Supplement*, [1968].

Churchill, Sir Winston Leonard Spencer (1874–1965)
Woods, Frederick W., *A Bibliography of the Works of Sir Winston Churchill*, 3rd edition, 1979.

Clare, John (1793–1864)
Esterman, Barbara, *John Clare, An Annotated Primary and Secondary Bibliography*, New York and London, 1985.

Cleveland, John (1613–1658)
Morris, Brian R., *John Cleveland, 1613–1658: A Bibliography of his Poems*, 1967.

Clough, Arthur Hugh (1819–1861)
Scott, Patrick Greig, *The Early Editions of Arthur Hugh Clough*, New York and London, 1977.

Cobbett, William (1763–1835)
Pearl, Morris L., *William Cobbett, A Bibliographical Account of his Life and Times*, 1953.

Coleridge, Samuel Taylor (1772–1834)
Wise, Thomas James, *A Bibliography of the Writings in Prose and Verse of Samuel Taylor Coleridge*, 1913.
────── *Coleridgeiana, being a supplement . . .*, 1919.
────── *Two Lake Poets, A Catalogue of Printed Books, Manuscripts and Autograph Letters by William Wordsworth and Samuel Taylor Coleridge*, 1927.

Collins, William Wilkie (1824–1889)
Parrish, Morris L. and Miller, E. V., *Wilkie Collins and Charles Reade: First Editions (with a Few Exceptions) in the Library at Dormy House . . .*, 1940 (reprinted, 1967).

Conrad, Joseph, pseudonym of Teodor Jozef Konrad Korzeniowski (1857–1924)
Wise, Thomas James, *A Bibliography of the Writings of Joseph Conrad, 1895–1920, 2nd edition, 1921 (reprinted, 1972)*.

────── *A Conrad Library: A Catalogue of Printed Books, Manuscripts, and Autograph Letters by Joseph Conrad . . . Collected by Thomas James Wise*, 1928.

Coppard, Alfred Edgar (1878–1957)
Schwartz, Jacob, *The Writings of Alfred Edgar Coppard: A Bibliography*, 1931.

Fabes, Gilbert H., *The First Editions of A. E. Coppard, A. P. Herbert and Charles Morgan, with Values and Bibliographical Points*, [1933] (reprinted, Philadelphia, 1972).

Corvo,
see Rolfe

Cowley, Abraham (1618–1667)
Perkin, Michael, *Abraham Cowley, A Bibliography*, Folkestone, Kent, 1977.

Cowper, William (1731–1800)
Russell, Norma H. H., *A Bibliography of William Cowper*, Oxford, 1963 (Oxford Bibliographical Society, New Series, Vol. XII).

Crabbe, George (1754–1832)
Bareham, T. and Gatrell, S., *A Bibliography of George Crabbe*, Folkestone, Kent and Hamden, Connecticut, 1978.

Craig, Edward Gordon (1872–1966)
Fletcher, Ifan K. and Rood, A., *Edward Gordon Craig, A Bibliography*, 1967.

Crane, Hart (1899–1932)
Schwartz, Joseph and Schweik, Robert C., *Hart Crane: A Descriptive Bibliography*, Pittsburgh, Pennsylvania, 1972.

Crane, Walter (1845–1915)
Massé, Gertrude C. E., *A Bibliography of First Editions of Books Illustrated by Walter Crane*, 1923.

Crashaw, Richard (1613?–1649)
Allison, Anthony F., *Four Metaphysical Poets . . . A Bibliographical Catalogue of the Early Editions of their Poetry and Prose (George Herbert; Richard Crashaw; Henry Vaughan; Andrew Marvell)*, Folkestone and London, 1973.

Cromwell, Oliver (1599–1658)
Abbott, Wilbur C., *A Bibliography of Oliver Cromwell: A List of Printed Materials Relating to Oliver Cromwell*, Cambridge, Massachusetts, 1929.

Cruikshank, George (1792–1878)
Cohn, Albert M., *George Cruikshank: A Catalogue Raisonné of the Work executed during the years 1806–1877, with Collations, Notes, Approximate Values, Facsimiles and Illustrations*, 2nd edition, 1924.

Cummings, E. E. (1894–1962)
Firmage, George J., *E. E. Cummings: A Bibliography*, Middletown, Connecticut, [1960].

Dalton, John (1766–1844)
Smyth, Albert L., *John Dalton, 1766–1844: A Bibliography of Works by and about Him*, Manchester, 1966.

Darwin, Charles (1809–1882)
Freeman, Richard B., *The Works of Charles Darwin: An Annotated Bibliographical Handlist*, 2nd edition, 1977.

Davenant, Sir William (1606–1668)
Blaydes, Sophia B. and Bordinat, Philip, *Sir William Davenant, An Annotated Bibliography 1629–1985*, New York and London, 1986.

Davy, Sir Humphry (1778–1829)
Fullmer, June Z., *Sir Humphry Davy's Published Works*, Cambridge, Massachusetts and London, 1969.

Defoe, Daniel (1660?–1731)
Moore, John Robert, *A Checklist of the Writings of Daniel Defoe*, 2nd edition, Hamden, Connecticut, 1971.

Hutchins, Henry C., *Robinson Crusoe and Its Printing, 1719–1731: A Bibliographical Study*, New York, 1925 (reprinted, New York, 1967).

Dekker, Thomas (c. 1572–1632)
Allison, Anthony F., *Thomas Dekker c. 1572–1632, A Bibliographical Catalogue of the Early Editions*, Folkestone and London, 1972.

De Quincey, Thomas (1785–1859)
Green, J. A., *Thomas De Quincey: A Bibliography based upon the De Quincey Collection in the Moss Side Library*, Manchester, 1909 (reprinted, New York, 1967).

Dibdin, Thomas Frognall (1776–1847)
Jackson, William A., *An Annotated List of the Publications of the Reverend Thomas Frognall Dibdin, D. D., based mainly on those in the Harvard College Library, with Notes of Others*, Cambridge, Massachusetts, 1965.

Dickens, Charles (1812–1870)
Eckel, John C., *The First Editions of the Writings of Charles Dickens and their Values: A Bibliography*, 2nd edition, 1932 (reprinted, New York, 1972).
Hatton, Thomas and Cleaver, Arthur H., *A Bibliography of the Periodical Works of Charles Dickens*, 1933 (reprinted, New York, 1973).
Miller, William, and Strange, E. H., *A Centenary Bibliography of the Pickwick Papers*, [1936].

Dickinson, Emily (1830–1886)
Myerson, Joel, *Emily Dickinson: A Descriptive Bibliography*, Pittsburgh, Pennsylvania, 1984.

Dobson, Henry Austin (1840–1921)
Dobson, Alban T. A., *A Bibliography of the First Editions of Published and Privately Printed Books and Pamphlets by Austin Dobson*, 1925.

Donne, John (1572–1631)
Keynes, Sir Geoffrey L., *A Bibliography of Dr John Donne*, 4th edition, Oxford, 1973.

Douglas, Norman (1868–1952)
Woolf, Cecil, *A Bibliography of the Works of Norman Douglas*, 1954.

Doyle, Sir Arthur Conan (1859–1930)
Green, Richard Lancelyn, and Gibson, John Michael, *A Bibliography of A. Conan Doyle*, Oxford, 1983.

Drayton, Michael (1563–1631)
Elton, Oliver, *Michael Drayton: A Critical Study, with a bibliography*, 1905.

Dryden, John (1631–1700)
Macdonald, Hugh, *John Dryden, A Bibliography of Early Editions and of Drydeniana*, Oxford, 1939 (reprinted, London, 1966).
Wise, Thomas James, *A Dryden Library*, 1930.

Duncan, Robert (1919–)
Bertholf, Robert J., *Robert Duncan: A Descriptive Bibliography*, Santa Rosa, California, 1986.

Eberhart, Richard (1904–)
Wright, Stuart, *Richard Eberhart: A Descriptive Bibliography, 1921–1987*, Westport, Connecticut and London, 1989.

Eliot, T. S. (1888–1965)
Gallup, Donald, *T. S. Eliot: A Bibliography*, 1952, 2nd edn, 1969.

Emerson, Ralph Waldo (1803–1882)
Myerson, Joel, *Ralph Waldo Emerson: A Descriptive Bibliography*, Pittsburgh, 1982.

Evelyn, John (1620–1706)
Keynes, Sir Geoffrey L., *John Evelyn, A Study in Bibliophily with a Bibliography of his Writings*, 2nd edition, Oxford, 1968.

Faulkner, William (1897–1962)
Meriwether, James B., *The Literary Career of William Faulkner: a Bibliographical Study*, Columbia, South Carolina, 1971.

Firbank, Arthur Annesley Ronald (1886–1926)
Benkovitz, Miriam J., *A Bibliography of Ronald Firbank*, 2nd edition, Oxford, 1982.

Fitzgerald, Edward (1809–1883)
Prideaux, William F., *Notes for a Bibliography of Edward Fitzgerald*, 1901 (reprinted, New York, 1967).

Fitzgerald, F. Scott (1896–1940)
Bruccoli, Matthew J., *F. Scott Fitzgerald: A Descriptive Bibliography*, Pittsburgh, 1972.
—— supplement, 1980.

Ford, Ford Madox (1873–1939)
Harvey, David Dow, *Ford Madox Ford 1873–1939: A Bibliography of Works and Criticism*, Princeton, New Jersey, 1962.

Forster, Edward Morgan (1879–1970)
Kirkpatrick, B. J., *A Bibliography of E. M. Forster*, 2nd edition, Oxford, 1985.

Frazer, Sir James George (1854–1941)
Besterman, Theodore D. N., *A Bibliography of Sir James Frazer*, 1934 (reprinted, 1968).

Frost, Robert (1874–1963)
Crane, Joan St C., *Robert Frost: A Descriptive Catalogue . . .*, 1974.

Fuller, Thomas (1608–1661)
Gibson, Strickland, *A Bibliography of the Works of Thomas Fuller, D. D.*, Oxford, 1936, Oxford Bibliographical Society.

Fuseli, Henry (1741–1825)
Weinglass, David H., *Prints and Engraved Illustrations by and after Henry Fuseli – A Catalogue Raisonné*, Aldershot, 1994.

Galsworthy, John (1867–1933)
Marrot, Harold V., *A Bibliography of Works of John Galsworthy*, New York, 1928 (reprinted, New York, 1967).

Gibbings, Robert (1889–1958)
Kirkus, Agnes M., *Robert Gibbings, A Bibliography; edited by Patience Empson and John Harris*, [1962].

Gibbon, Edward (1737–1794)
Norton, J. E., *A Bibliography of the Works of Edward Gibbon*, 2nd edition, 1970.

Gill, Eric (1882–1940)
Gill, Evan, *Eric Gill: A Bibliography*, 2nd edition, revised by D. Steven Corey and Julia Mackenzie, Winchester, 1991.

Gissing, George (1857–1903)
Collie, Michael, *George Gissing: A Bibliographical Study*, Winchester, 1985.

Goldsmith, Oliver (1728–1774)
Scott, Temple (pseud.), *Oliver Goldsmith Bibliographically and Biographically Considered: Based on the Collection of Material in the Library of W. M. Elkins*, New York, 1928 (reprinted, Philadelphia, 1977).

Gosse, Philip Henry (1810–1888)
Stageman, Peter F., *A Bibliography of the First Editions of Philip Henry Gosse F.R.S.*, Cambridge, 1955.

Graham, Robert Bontine Cunninghame (1852–1936)
Chaundy, Leslie, *A Bibliography of the First Editions of the Works of Robert Bontine Cunninghame Graham*, 1924.

Graunt, John (1620–1674)
see Petty

Graves, Robert (1895–1985)
Higginson, Fred H., *A Bibliography of the Writings of Robert Graves*, 2nd edition, revised by William Proctor Williams, Winchester, 1987.

Gray, Thomas (1716–1771)
Northup, Clark Sutherland, *A Bibliography of Thomas Gray*, New Haven, Connecticut and London, 1917.

Greene, Graham (1904–1991)
Wobbe, R. A., *Graham Greene: A Bibliography and Guide to Research*, New York and London, 1979.

Gunn, Thom (1929–)
Hagstrom, Jack W. C. and Bixby, George, *Thom Gunn: A Bibliography, 1940–1978*, 1979.

Haggard, Sir Henry Rider (1856–1925)
Scott, James E., *A Bibliography of the Works of Sir Henry Rider Haggard, 1856–1925*, Takeley, 1947.

Halley, Edmond (1656–1742)
McPike, Eugene F., *Dr. Edmond Halley, 1656–1742: A Bibliographical Guide to his Life and Work, Arranged Chronologically . . .*, 1939.

Hammett, Dashiell (1894–1961)
Layman, Richard, *Dashiell Hammett: A Descriptive Bibliography*, Pittsburgh, 1979.

Hardy, Thomas (1840–1928)
Purdy, Richard Little, *Thomas Hardy: A Bibliographical Study*, Oxford, 1954.

Harvey, Dr William (1578–1657)
Keynes, Sir Geoffrey L., *A Bibliography of the Writings of Dr William Harvey 1578–1659* (revised by Gweneth Whitteridge and Christine English), 3rd edition, Winchester, 1988.

Hawthorne, Nathaniel (1804–1864)
Clark, C. E. Frazer, Jr., *Nathaniel Hawthorne: A Descriptive Bibliography*, Pittsburgh, 1978.

Hazlitt, William (1778–1830)
Keynes, Sir Geoffrey L., *Bibliography of William Hazlitt*, 2nd edition, revised, Godalming, Surrey, 1981.

Hemingway, Ernest (1898–1961)
Hanneman, Audre, *Ernest Hemingway: A Comprehensive Bibliography*, Princeton, New Jersey, 1967.
—— supplement, 1975.

Henty, G. A. (1832–1902)
Arnold, Guy, *Hold Fast for England: G. A. Henty, Imperialist Boys' Writer*, 1980.
Dartt, Capt. R. L., *G. A. Henty: A Bibliography*, 1971.

Herbert, Sir Alan Patrick (1890–1971)
see Coppard

Herbert, George (1593–1633)
see Crashaw

Herrick, Robert (1591–1674)
Gertzman, Jay A., *Fantasy, Fashion and Affection: editions of Robert Herrick's Poetry for the Common Reader, 1810–1968*, Bowling Green, Ohio, 1986.

Hobbes, Thomas (1588–1679)
MacDonald, Hugh and Hargreaves, Joan M., *Thomas Hobbes, A Bibliography*, 1952.

Hogg, James (1770–1835)
Hughes, Gilliam, *Hogg's Prose – An Annotated Listing*, Stirling, 1985.
Mack, Douglas S., *Hogg's Verse and Drama – A Chronological Listing*, Stirling, 1990.

Holcroft, Thomas (1745–1809)
Colby, Elbridge, *A Bibliography of Thomas Holcroft*, New York, 1922.

Holland, Philemon (1552–1637)
[Silvette, Herbert], Catalogue of the Works of Philemon Holland of Coventry, Doctor of Physicke, 1600–1940, Charlottesville, VA, 1940.

Holmes, Oliver Wendell (1809–1894)
Currier, Thomas Franklin, *A Bibliography of Oliver Wendell Holmes*, New York, 1953.

Holtby, Winifred (1898–1935)
Taylor, Geoffrey Handley, *Winifred Holtby, A Concise and Selected Bibliography*, 1955.

Hooke, Robert (1635–1703)
Keynes, Sir Geoffrey L., *A Bibliography of Dr. Robert Hooke*, Oxford, 1960.

Hopkins, Gerard Manley (1844–1889)
Dunne, Tom, *Gerard Manley Hopkins: A Comprehensive Bibliography*, Oxford, 1976.

Housman, A. E. (1859–1936)
Carter, John and Sparrow, John, *A. E. Housman: A Bibliography*, 2nd edition, revised by William White, Godalming, Surrey, 1982.

Howard, John (1726–1790)
Baumgartner, Leona, *John Howard, 1726–1790, Hospital and Prison Reformer, A Bibliography*, Baltimore, Maryland, 1939.

Howell, James (1594?–1666)
Vann, William Harvey, *Notes on the Writings of James Howell*, Waco, Texas, 1924.

Hudson, William Henry (1841–1922)
Payne, John R., *W. H. Hudson: A Bibliography*, Folkestone, 1977.
Wolson, George F., *A Bibliography of the Writings of W. H. Hudson*, London and New York, 1922 (reprinted, New York, 1972).

Hughes, Ted (1930–)
Sagar, Keith and Tabor, Stephen, *Ted Hughes: A Bibliography, 1946–1980*, 1983.

Hughes, Thomas (1822–1896)
Parrish, Morris L. and Mann, B. K., *Charles Kingsley and Thomas Hughes: First Editions (with a few exceptions) in the Library at Dormy House*, 1936.

Hume, David (1711–1776)
Jessop, Thomas E., *A Bibliography of David Hume and of Scottish Philosophy from Francis Hutcheson to Lord Balfour*, 1938 (reprinted, New York, 1967).

Hunt, James Henry Leigh (1784–1859)
Mitchell, Alexander, *A Bibliography of the Writings of Leigh Hunt, with Critical Notes*, [1931].
Brewer, Luther A., *My Leigh Hunt Library*, Cedar Rapids, Iowa, 1932 (reprinted, New York, [1967]).

Huxley, Aldous Leonard (1894–1963)
Muir, Percival H. and Van Thal, Bert, *Bibliographies of the First Editions of books by Aldous Huxley and T. F. Powys*, 1927.
Eschelbach, Claire J. and Shober, J. L., *Aldous Huxley, A Bibliography, 1916–1959*, Berkeley, California, 1961.

Irving, Washington (1783–1859)
Williams, Stanley T. and Edge, Mary Allen, *A Bibliography of the Writings of Washington Irving: A Check List*, New York, 1936.

Isherwood, Christopher William Bradshaw (1904–1986)
Westby, Selmes and Brown C. M., *Christopher Isherwood: A Bibliography, 1923–1967*, Los Angeles, California, 1968.

James, Henry (1843–1916)
Edel, Leon and Laurence, Dan H., *A Bibliography of Henry James*, 3rd edition, revised with the assistance of James Rambeau, Oxford, 1982.

Jarrell, Randall (1914–1965)
Adams, Charles M., *Randall Jarrell: A Bibliography*, Chapel Hill, North Carolina, 1958.

Jefferies, Richard (1848–1887)
Miller, George and Matthews, Hugoe, *Richard Jefferies: A Bibliographical Study*, Aldershot, 1993.

Jeffers, Robinson (1887–1962)
Alberts, S. S., *A Bibliography of the Works of Robinson Jeffers*, Rye, New York, 1966.

Jenner, Edward (1749–1823)
LeFanu, William R., *A Bio-bibliography of Edward Jenner, 1749–1823*, revised edition, 1983.

Johnson, Charles (fl. 1724–1736)
Gosse, Philip H. G., *A Bibliography of the Works of Captain Charles Johnson*, 1927 (reprinted, New York, 1967).

Johnson, Samuel (1709–1784)
Courtney, William Prideaux and Smith, David Nichol, *A Bibliography of Samuel Johnson*, Oxford, 1925 (reprinted, 1968).

Joyce, James (1882–1941)
Slocum, John J. and Cahoon, Herbert, *A Bibliography of James Joyce, 1882–1941*, 1953.

Junius
Bowyer, T. H., *A Bibliographical Examination of the Earliest Editions of the Letters of Junius*, Charlottesville, Virginia, 1957.
Cordasco, Francesco, *A Junius Bibliography, with a Preliminary Essay on the Political Background, Text and Identity*, New York, 1949.

Keats, John (1795–1821)
MacGillivray, J. R., *Keats: A Bibliography and Reference Guide with an Essay on Keats' Reputation*, Toronto, 1949.

Kerouac, Jack (1922–1969)
Charters, Ann, *A Bibliography of Works by Jack Kerouac . . .*, 2nd edition, New York, 1975.

King, Henry (1592–1669)
Keynes, Sir Geoffrey L., *A Bibliography of Henry King D. D., Bishop of Chichester*, 1977.

Kingsley, Charles (1819–1875)
see Hughes, Thomas.

Kipling, Rudyard (1865–1936)
Stewart, James McG., *Rudyard Kipling: A Bibliographical Catalogue*, edited by A. W. Yeats, Toronto, 1959.

Livingston, Flora V., *Bibliography of the Works of Rudyard Kipling*, New York, 1927.
———— supplement, Cambridge, Massachusetts, 1938 (reprinted, New York, 1970).

Lamb, Charles (1775–1834) and Mary (1764–1847)
Thomson, J. C., *Bibliography of the Writings of Charles and Mary Lamb*, Hull, 1908.

Landor, Walter Savage (1775–1864)
Wise, Thomas James and Wheeler, Stephen, *A Bibliography of the Writings in Prose and Verse of Walter Savage Landor*, 1919 (reprinted, Folkestone and London, 1971).
———— *A Landor Library*, 1928.

Larkin, Philip (1922–1985)
Bloomfield, B. C., *Philip Larkin: A Bibliography, 1933–1976*, 1979.

Lawrence, David Herbert (1885–1930)
Roberts, Warren E., *A Bibliography of D. H. Lawrence*, 2nd edition, Oxford, 1982.

Lawrence, T. E. (1888–1935)
O'Brien, Philip M., *T. E. Lawrence: A Bibliography*, 1988.

Lear, Edward (1812–1888)
[Field, William B. O.], *Edward Lear on my Shelves*, [Munich], 1933.

Leech, John (1817–1864)
[Field, William B. O.], *John Leech on My Shelves*, [Munich], 1930 (reprinted, New York, 1970).

Le Gallienne, Richard (1866–1947)
Lingel, Robert J., *A Bibliographical Checklist of the Writings of Richard Le Gallienne*, Metuchen, New Jersey, 1926.

Lewis, Cecil Day (1904–1972)
Taylor, Geoffrey Handley, and Smith, Timothy d'Arch, *Cecil Day Lewis, The Poet Laureate: A Bibliography*, Chicago, 1968.

Lewis, Percy Wyndham (1882–1957)
Morrow, Bradford, and Lafourcade, Bernard, *A Bibliography of the Writings of Wyndham Lewis*, Santa Barbara, California, 1978.

Locke, John (1632–1704)
Attig, John C., *The Works of John Locke*, Westwood, Connecticut, 1985.

Lodge, Thomas (1558–1625)
Allison, Anthony F., *Thomas Lodge, 1558–1625: A Bibliographical Catalogue of the Early Editions*, Folkestone and London, 1973.

Lowry, Malcolm (1909–1957)
Woolmer, J. Howard, *Malcolm Lowry: A Bibliography*, Revere, Pennsylvania, 1983.

McCullers, Carson (1917–1967)
Shapiro, Adrian M., *et al.*, *Carson McCullers: A Descriptive Listing . . .*, New York and London, 1980.

MacDonald, George (1824–1905)
Shaberman, Raphael B., *George MacDonald: A Bibliographical Study*, Winchester, 1990.

Machen, Arthur Llewellyn Jones (1863–1947)
Goldstone, Adrian H. and Sweetser, W., *A Bibliography of Arthur Machen*, Austin, Texas, [1965] (reprinted, New York, 1973).

MacNeice, Louis (1907–1963)
Armitage, C. M. and Clark, Neil, *A Bibliography of the Works of Louis MacNeice*, 2nd edition, 1974.

MacPherson, James (1736–1796)
Black, George F., *MacPherson's Ossian and the Ossianic Controversy: A Contribution towards a Bibliography*, New York, 1926.

Mansfield, Katherine (1888–1923)
Kirkpatrick, B. J., *A Bibliography of Katherine Mansfield*, Oxford, 1989.

Markham, Gervase (1568–1637)
Poynter, F. N. L., *A Bibliography of Gervase Markham, 1568?–1637*, Oxford Bibliographical Society n.s. volume XI, Oxford, 1962.

Marlowe, Christopher (1564–1593)
Tannenbaum, Samuel A., *Christopher Marlowe – a Concise Bibliography*, New York, 1937.

Martineau, Harriet (1802–1876)
Rivlin, Joseph R., *Harriet Martineau: A Bibliography of her Separately Printed Books*, New York, 1947.

Marvell, Andrew (1621–1678)
see Crashaw.

Mary Stuart, Queen of Scots (1542–1587)
Scott, John, *A Bibliography of Works relating to Mary, Queen of Scots, 1544–1700*, Edinburgh, 1896.

Masefield, John (1878–1967)

Handley-Taylor, Geoffrey, *John Masefield, O. M.: A Bibliography and Eighty-first Birthday Tribute*, 1960.

Simmons, Charles H., *A Bibliography of John Masefield*, New York, 1930.

Mason, William (1724–1797)

Gaskell, J. Philip W., *The First Editions of William Mason*, Cambridge, 1951.

Maugham, William Somerset (1874–1965)

Stott, Raymond T., *A Bibliography of the Works of W. Somerset Maugham*, revised edition, 1973.

Melville, Herman (1819–1891)

Higgins, Brian, *Herman Melville – An Annotated Bibliography*, Boston, 1979.

Meredith, George (1828–1909)

Collie, Michael, *George Meredith: A Bibliography*, 1974.

Buxton Forman, Maurice, *A Bibliography of the Writings in Prose and Verse of George Meredith*, 1922.

—— *Meredithiana: Being a Supplement to the Bibliography of Meredith*, 1924.

Mill, John Stuart (1806–1873)

MacMinn, Ney L., ed., *Bibliography of the Published Writings of John Stuart Mill*, Evanston, Illinois, 1945.

Milton, John (1608–1674)

Shawcross, John T., *Milton: A Bibliography for the Years 1624–1700* (Medieval and Renaissance Texts and Studies, volume 30), Binghamton, New York, 1984.

Moore, George (1852–1933)

Gilcher, Edwin, *A Bibliography of George Moore*, Dekalb, Illinois, 1970.

—— supplement, Westport, Connecticut, and Gerrards Cross, Buckinghamshire, 1988.

Moore, Marianne (1887–1972)

Abbott, Craig S., *Marianne Moore: A Descriptive Bibliography*, Pittsburgh, 1977.

More, Thomas (1478–1535)

Gibson, Reginald W., *St. Thomas More: A Preliminary Bibliography of his Works and of Moreana to the year 1750, with a Bibliography of Utopiana compiled by R. W. Gibson and J. Max Patrick*, New Haven, Connecticut and London, 1961.

Morgan, Charles Longbridge (1894–1958)

see Coppard, A. E.

Morison, Stanley Arthur (1889–1967)
Appleton, Tony, *The Writings of Stanley Morison: A Handlist*, 1976.

Morris, William (1834–1896)
Scott, Temple (pseud.), *A Bibliography of the Works of William Morris*, 1897.

Mottram, Ralph Hale (1883–1971)
Fabes, Gilbert H., *The First Editions of Ralph Hale Mottram*, 1934 (reprinted, Folcroft, Pennsylvania, 1979).

Muir, Edwin (1887–1959)
Mellown, Elgin W., *Bibliography of the Writings of Edwin Muir*, University, Alabama and London, revised edition, 1970.

Nabokov, Vladimir (1899–1977)
Juliar, Michael, *Vladimir Nabokov: A Descriptive Bibliography*, New York and London, 1986.

Newman, John Henry (1801–1890)
Blehl, Vincent F., *John Henry Newman; a Bibliographical Catalogue of his Writings*, Charlottesville, Virginia, 1978.

Newton, Sir Isaac (1642–1727)
Gray, George J., *A Bibliography of the Works of Sir Isaac Newton, together with a List of Books illustrating his Life and Works*, 2nd edition, Cambridge, 1907 (reprinted, 1966).

Nightingale, Florence (1820–1910)
Bishop, William J. and Goldie, S., *A Bio-bibliography of Florence Nightingale*, 1962.

O'Casey, Sean (1880–1964)
Ayling, Ronald and Durkan, Michael J., *Sean O'Casey: A Bibliography*, 1978.

O'Hara, Frank (1926–1966)
Smith, Alexander, Jr., *Frank O'Hara: A Comprehensive Bibliography*, New York and London, 1979.

O'Neill, Eugene (1888–1953)
Atkinson, Jennifer McCabe, *Eugene O'Neill: A Descriptive Bibliography*, Pittsburgh, 1974.

Owen, Robert (1771–1858)
Williams, William, ed., *A Bibliography of Robert Owen, the Socialist, 1771–1858* (National Library of Wales), 2nd edition, Aberystwyth, 1925.

Paine, Thomas (1737–1809)
Gimbel, Richard, *A Bibliographical Check-list of* Common Sense *with an Account of its Publication*, New Haven, Connecticut and London, 1956.

Pater, Walter H. (1839–1894)
Wright, Samuel, *A Bibliography of the Writings of Walter H. Pater*, Folkestone, 1975.

Pepys, Samuel (1633–1703)
Chappell, Edwin, *Bibliographia Pepysiana*, Blackheath, 1933.

Petty, Sir William (1623–1687)
Keynes, Sir Geoffrey L., *A Bibliography of Sir William Petty, F.R.S., and of Observations on the Bills of Mortality by John Graunt, F.R.S.*, Oxford, 1971.

Plath, Sylvia (1932–1963)
Tabor, Stephen, *Sylvia Plath: An Analytical Bibliography*, 1987.

Poe, Edgar Allan (1809–1849)
Robertson, John W., *Bibliography of the Writings of Edgar A. Poe*, San Francisco, 1934 (reprinted, New York, 1969).

Pope, Alexander (1688–1744)
Griffith, Reginald Harvey, *Alexander Pope: A Bibliography, Volume 1, Pts I & II: Pope's own Writings, 1709–1734; 1734–1751*, Austin, Texas, 1922 and 1927 (reprinted, New York, 1975).
Guerinot, J. V., *Pamphlet Attacks on Alexander Pope, 1711–1744: A Descriptive Bibliography*, 1969.
Wise, Thomas James, *A Pope Library*, 1931.

Potter, Helen Beatrix (1866–1943)
Quinby, Jane, *Beatrix Potter, A Bibliographical Checklist*, New York, 1954.

Pound, Ezra (1885–1972)
Gallup, Donald, *Ezra Pound: A Bibliography*, Charlottesville, Virginia, and Godalming, Surrey, 1983.

Powys, John Cowper (1872–1963)
Siberell, Lloyd E., *A Bibliography of the First Editions of John Cowper Powys*, Cincinnati, Ohio, 1934 (reprinted, Norwood, Pennsylvania, 1976).

Powys, Theodore Francis (1875–1953)
see Huxley, Aldous Leonard.
Riley, Peter, *A Bibliography of T. F. Powys*, Hastings, 1967.

Powys, The family
Marlow, Louis, (pseudonym of Louis W. Wilkinson) *Welsh Ambassadors*, 2nd edition, 1971.

Priestley, Joseph (1733–1804)
Crook, Ronald E., *A Bibliography of Joseph Priestley, 1733–1804*, [1966].

Prior, Matthew (1664–1721)
Wright, H. Bunker and Spears, M. K., *The Literary Works of Matthew Prior*, Oxford, 1959.

Quarles, Francis (1592–1644)
Horden, John *Francis Quarles (1592–1644), A Bibliography of his Works to the Year 1800* (Oxford Bibliographical Society n.s. vol. II, 1948), Oxford, 1953.

Rackham, Arthur (1867–1939)
Latimore, Sarah B. and Haskell, G. C., *Arthur Rackham, A Bibliography*, Los Angeles, 1936 (reprinted, New York, 1967).

Ralegh, Sir Walter (1552?–1618)
Brushfield, T. N., *A Bibliography of Sir Walter Ralegh knt.*, 2nd edition, Exeter, 1908 (reprinted, New York, 1967, Hildesheim, 1969).

Ramsay, Allan (1686–1758)
Martin, Burns, *Bibliography of Allan Ramsay*, Glasgow, 1931.

Ray, John (1627–1705)
Keynes, Sir Geoffrey L., *John Ray, 1627–1705: A Bibliography 1660–1970*, 1951 (reprinted, Amsterdam, 1976).

Reade, Charles (1814–1884)
see Collins

Ricardo, David (1772–1823)
Franklin, Burt and Legman, G., *David Ricardo and Ricardian Theory: A Bibliographical Checklist*, New York, 1950.

Richardson, Samuel (1689–1761)
Sale, William Meritt, Jr, *Samuel Richardson, A Bibliographical Record of his Literary Career with Historical Notes*, New Haven, Connecticut and London, 1936 (reprinted, Hamden, Connecticut, 1969; Westport, Connecticut, 1977).

Riding, Laura (1901–1991)
Wexler, Joyce Piell, *Laura Riding: A Bibliography*, New York and London, 1981.

Rochester, John Wilmot, 2nd Earl of (1647–1680)
Prinz, Johannes, *Bibliography of the Works of the Earl of Rochester*, Leipzig, 1927.

Rolfe, Frederick ('Baron Corvo') (1860–1913)
Woolf, Cecil, *A Bibliography of Frederick Rolfe, Baron Corvo*, 2nd edition, 1972.

Ross, Martin
see Somerville.

Rossetti, Dante Gabriel (1828–1882)
Rossetti, William Michael, *Bibliography of the Works of Dante Gabriel Rossetti*, 1905.

Ruskin, John (1819–1900)
Cook, E. T. and Wedderburn, Alexander, *The Works of John Ruskin, vol. XXXVIII: Bibliography; Catalogue of Ruskin's drawings; Addenda and Corrigenda*, 1912.
Wise, Thomas James, *A Complete Bibliography of the Writings in Prose and Verse of John Ruskin*, 2 vols, 1893 (reprinted, 1964).

Sassoon, Siegfried (1886–1967)
Keynes, Geoffrey, *A Bibliography of Siegfried Sassoon*, 1962.

Sayers, Dorothy L. (1893–1957)
Gilbert, Colleen B., *A Bibliography of the Works of Dorothy L. Sayers*, 1979.

Scott, Sir Walter (1771–1832)
Worthington, Greville, *A Bibliography of the Waverley Novels*, 1931 (reprinted, Norwood, Pennsylvania, 1976).

Shakespeare, William (1564–1616)
A Shakespeare Bibliography: Catalogue of the Birmingham Shakespeare Library, 1900–1903 (reprinted, 1971).
Folger Shakespeare Library, Washington DC, *Catalog of the Shakespeare Collection*, Boston, Massachusetts, 1972.
Howard-Hill, T. H., *Shakespeare Bibliography and Textual Criticism: A Bibliography*, Oxford, 1971.
Jaggard, William, *Shakespeare Bibliography*, 1911 (reprinted, 1971).

Shaw, George Bernard (1856–1950)
Laurence, Dan H., *Bernard Shaw: A Bibliography*, 2 vols, Oxford, 1983.

Shelley, Percy Bysshe (1792–1822)
Graniss, Ruth S., *A Descriptive Catalogue of the First Editions in Book Form of the Writings of Percy Bysshe Shelley*, New York, 1923 (reprinted, Norwood, Pennsylvania, 1976).

Wise, Thomas James, *A Shelley Library: A Catalogue of Printed Books, Manuscripts, and Autograph Letters by Percy Bysshe Shelley, Harriet Shelley and Mary Wollstonecraft Shelley*, 1924 (reprinted, New York, 1971).

Sitwell, Edith, Osbert and Sacheverell
Fifoot, Richard, *A Bibliography of Edith, Osbert and Sacheverell Sitwell*, 2nd edition, revised, 1971.

Smart, Christopher (1722–1771)
Mahony, Robert and Rizzo, Betty W., *Christopher Smart: an Annotated Bibliography 1743–1983*, New York and London, 1984.

Smith, Adam (1723–1790)
Franklin, Burt, and Cordasco, Francesco, *Adam Smith, A Bibliographical Checklist*, New York, 1950.

Smollett, Tobias (1721–1771)
Wagoner, Mary, *Tobias Smollett: A Checklist of Editions of his Works and an Annotated Secondary Bibliography*, New York and London, 1984.

Somerville, Edith (1858–1949) and Ross, Martin (1862–1915)
Hudson, Elizabeth, *A Bibliography of the First Editions of the Works of E. Œ. Somerville and Martin Ross*, New York, 1942.

Southwell, Robert (1561–1595)
MacDonald, James H., *The Poems and Prose Writings of Robert Southwell, S. J.: A Bibliographical Study*, Oxford, 1937.

Spender, Stephen (1900–)
Kulkarni, H. B., *Stephen Spender, Works and Criticism: An Annotated Bibliography*, New York and London, 1976.

Spenser, Edmund (1552?–1599)
Johnson, Francis R., *A Critical Bibliography of the Works of Edmund Spenser printed before 1700*, Baltimore, Maryland, 1933 (reprinted, 1966).

Steinbeck, John (1902–1968)
Goldstone, Adrian H. and Payne, John R., *John Steinbeck: A Bibliographical Catalogue of the Adrian H. Goldstone Collection*, Austin, Texas, 1974.

Stephen, Leslie (1832–1904)
Fenwick, Gillian, *Leslie Stephen's Life in Letters, A Bibliographical Study*, Aldershot, 1993.

Sterne, Laurence (1713–1768)
Birley, Pauline, *The Early Printed Editions of Laurence Sterne, A Select Bibliography*, 1939.

Stevens, Wallace (1879–1955)

Edelstein, J. M., *Wallace Stevens: A Descriptive Bibliography*, Pittsburgh, PA, 1973.

Stevenson, Robert Louis (1850–1894)

McKay, George L., *A Stevenson Library: Vols 1 & 2: Printed Books, Pamphlets, Broadsides etc.*, New Haven, Connecticut, 1951–2 (Yale University, Beinecke Library).

Prideaux, W. F., *A Bibliography of the Works of Robert Louis Stevenson, A New and Revised Edition* (by Mrs Luther S. Livingston), 1917.

Rosenbach, A. S. W., *A Catalogue of the Books and Manuscripts of Robert Louis Stevenson in the Library of the late Harry Elkins Widener*, Philadelphia, Pa, 1913 (Harvard University Library) (reprinted, New York, 1968).

Strachey, (Giles) Lytton (1880–1932)

Edmonds, Michael, *Lytton Strachey: A Bibliography*, New York and London, 1981.

Summers, Montague (1880–1948)

Smith, Timothy d'A, *A Bibliography of the Works of Montague Summers*, 2nd revised edition, 1983.

Swift, Jonathan (1667–1745)

Teerink, Herman, *A Bibliography of the Writings of Jonathan Swift*, (edited by Arthur H. Scouten), 2nd edition revised and corrected, Philadelphia, PA, 1963.

Swinburne, Algernon Charles (1837–1909)

Wise, Thomas James, *A Bibliography of the Writings in Prose and Verse of Algernon Charles Swinburne* (Complete Works of A. C. Swinburne, vol XX), London and New York, 1927.

—— *A Swinburne Library*, 1925, revised, 1975.

Symonds, John Addington (1840–1893)

Babington, Percy L., *Bibliography of the Writings of John Addington Symonds*, 1925 (reprinted, New York, 1976).

Taylor, Jeremy (1613–1667)

Gathorne-Hardy, Robert and Williams, William Proctor, *A Bibliography of the Writings of Jeremy Taylor to 1700*, Dekalb, Illinois, 1971.

Taylor, The Family

Harris, G. Edward, *Contributions towards a Bibliography of the Taylors of Ongar and Stanford Rivers*, 1965.

Tennyson, Alfred, Lord (1809–1892)

Wise, Thomas James, *A Bibliography of the Writings of Alfred, Lord Tennyson*, 2 vols, 1908 (reprinted, 1967).

AUTHOR BIBLIOGRAPHIES

Thackeray, William Makepeace (1811–1863)
Van Duzer, Henry Sayre, *A Thackeray Library*, 1919 (reprinted, Port Washington, New York, 1965; New York 1967).

Thomas, Dylan (1914–1953)
Rolph, J. Alexander, *Dylan Thomas: A Bibliography*, London and New York, 1956.

Thomas, Edward (1878–1917)
Eckert, Robert P., *Edward Thomas, a Biography and a Bibliography*, 1937.

Thomson, James (1700–1748)
Campbell, Hilbert H., *James Thomson, 1700–1748: an Annotated Bibliography of Selected Editions and the Important Criticism*, New York, 1976.

Thoreau, Henry David (1817–1862)
Borst, Raymond R., *Henry David Thoreau: A Descriptive Bibliography*, Pittsburgh, 1982.

Thurber, James (1894–1961)
Bowden, Edwin T., *James Thurber: A Bibliography*, Columbus, Ohio, 1968.

Trollope, Anthony (1815–1882)
Sadleir, Michael, *Trollope: A Bibliography, An Analysis of the History and Structure of the Works of Anthony Trollope and a General Survey of the Effect of Original Publishing Conditions on a Book's Subsequent Rarity*, 1928 (reprinted, 1964).

Twain, Mark, pseudonym of Samuel Langhorne Clemens (1835–1910)
Johnson, Merle, *A Bibliography of the Works of Mark Twain . . .*, revised edition, New York and London, 1935.

Vaughan, Henry (1622–1695)
see Crashaw

Vonnegut, Kurt (1922–)
Pieratt, Asa B., Jr., et al., *Kurt Vonnegut: A Comprehensive Bibliography*, Hamden, Connecticut, 1987.

Walcott, Derek (1930–)
Goldstraw, Irma E., *Derek Walcott: An Annotated Bibliography of His Works*, New York and London, 1984.

Waley, Arthur David (1889–1966)
Johns, Francis A., *A Bibliography of Arthur Waley*, New Brunswick, New Jersey, and London, 1968.

Wallace, Richard Horatio Edgar (1875–1932)
Lofts, William O. G. and Adley, D. L., *The British Bibliography of Edgar Wallace*, 1969.

Walpole, Horace (1717–1797)
Hazen, A. T., *A Bibliography of Horace Walpole*, New Haven, Connecticut, 1948 (reprinted, New York and London, 1973).

Walton, Izaak (1593–1683)
Horne, Bernard S., *The Compleat Angler, 1653–1967: A New Bibliography*, Pittsburgh, Pennsylvania, 1970.

Warton, Joseph (1722–1800) and Thomas (1728–1790)
Vance, John A., *Joseph and Thomas Warton: an Annotated Bibliography*, New York and London, 1983.

Watts, Isaac (1674–1748)
Stone, Wilbur M., *The Divine and Moral Songs of Isaac Watts: an Essay and a Tentative List of Editions*, New York, 1918.

Wells, Herbert George (1866–1946)
Hammond, J. R., *Herbert George Wells: an Annotated Bibliography of his Works*, New York and London, 1977.

Wesley, John (1703–1791) and Charles (1707–1788)
Baker, Frank, *A Union Catalogue of the Publications of John and Charles Wesley*, Durham, North Carolina, 1966.

West, Dame Rebecca, pseudonym of Cicely Isabel Andrews (1892–1983)
Hutchinson, George E., *A Preliminary List of the Writings of Rebecca West, 1912–1951*, New Haven, Connecticut, 1957.

Wharton, Edith (1862–1937)
Garrison, Stephen, *Edith Wharton: A Descriptive Bibliography*, Pittsburgh, 1990.

White, Gilbert (1720–1793)
Martin, Edward A., *A Bibliography of Gilbert White, the Naturalist Antiquarian of Selborne*, 1934 (reprinted, 1970).

Whitman, Walt (1819–1892)
Frey, Ellen T., Wells, Carolyn and Goldsmith, Alfred F., *A Bibliography of Walt Whitman*, (one volume edition), Port Washington, New York, 1965.

Wilde, Oscar (1854–1900)
Mason, Stuart, pseudonym of Christopher Millard, *Bibliography of Oscar Wilde*, new edition, 1967.

Williams, William Carlos (1883–1963)
Wallace, Emily Mitchell, *A Bibliography of William Carlos Williams*, Middleton, Connecticut, 1968.

Williamson, Henry (1895–1977)
Girvan, I. Waveney, *A Bibliography and Critical Survey of the Works of Henry Williamson*, Chipping Campden, 1932.

Wodehouse, P. G. (1881–1975)
McIlvaine, Eileen, Heineman, James H. and Sheaby, Louise S., *P. G. Wodehouse: a Comprehensive Bibliography and Checklist*, New York, 1990.
Usborne, Richard, *Wodehouse at Work, a Study of the Books and Characters*, 1961.

Wollstonecraft, Mary (1759–1797)
Todd, Janet, *Mary Wollstonecraft: An Annotated Bibliography*, New York and London, 1976.
Windle, J. R., *Mary Wollstonecraft (Godwin): a Bibliography of her Writings, 1787–1982*, Los Angeles, 1988.

Woolf, Virginia (1882–1941)
Kirkpatrick, B. J., *A Bibliography of Virginia Woolf*, 3rd edition, Oxford, 1980.

Woolf, Leonard (1880–1969)
Luedeking, Leila and Edmonds, Michael, *Leonard Woolf – A Bibliography*, 1992.

Wordsworth, William (1770–1850)
Healey, George Harris, *The Cornell Wordsworth Collection*, Ithaca, New York, 1957.
Wise, Thomas James, *A Bibliography of the Writings in Prose and Verse of William Wordsworth*, 1916 (reprinted, 1971).
Two Lakes Poets, a Catalogue of Printed Books, Manuscripts and Autograph Letters by William Wordsworth and Samuel Taylor Coleridge, 1927 (reprinted, 1965).

Wright, John Buckland (1897–1954)
Reid, Anthony, *A Checklist of the Book Illustrations of John Buckland Wright, together with a Personal Memoir*, Pinner, 1968.
Wright, Christopher Buckland (ed.), *The Engravings of John Buckland Wright – a Catalogue Raisonné*, Aldershot, 1990.

Yeats, W. B. (1865–1939)
Wade, Allen, *A Bibliography of the Writings of W. B. Yeats*, 3rd edition revised and enlarged by Russell K. Alspach, 1968.

Young, Edward (1683–1765)
Pettit, Henry, *A Bibliography of Young's* Night Thoughts (University of Colorado studies, series in language and literature, 5), Boulder, Colorado, 1954.

APPENDIX I
Latin and other foreign place-names

Abbatisvilla = Abbeville
Abbendonia = Abingdon
Aberdonia, Abredonia = Aberdeen
Åbo = Turku
Agram, Agramum = Zagreb
Aix-la-Chapelle = Aachen
Aken = Aachen
Albani villa = St Albans
Albiburgum = Wittenberg
Alexandria = Alessandria
Ambianum = Amiens
Amstelodamum, Amstelredamum = Amsterdam
Andegavum = Angers
Andreopolis = St Andrews
Aneda = Edinburgh
Antuerpia, Antwerpia = Antwerp
Anvers = Antwerp
Aquae Sextiae = Aix-en-Provence
Aquisgranum = Aachen
Arctopolis = Bern
Areconium = Hereford
Arenacum = Arnhem
Aretinum, Aretium = Arezzo
Argentina, Argentoratum = Strasbourg
Asculum = Ascoli
Athenae Rauracae = Basle
Augusta Ausciorum = Auch
— Emerida = Merida
— Perusia = Perugia
— Taurinorum = Turin
— Tiberii = Regensburg
— Trevirorum = Trier
— Trinobantum = London
— Vindelicorum = Augsburg
Aurelia, Aureliacum, Aurelianum = Orléans
Aurelia Allobrogum = Geneva
Aureliae Aquensis = Baden-Baden
Avaricum = Bourges
Avenio = Avignon
Babenberga = Bamberg
Baile Átha Cliath = Dublin
Barcino, Barchino = Barcelona
Basilea = Basle
Bergen = Mons
Berolinum = Berlin
Bisuntia = Besançon
Bitturis, Bituriga = Bourges
Bituricum = Béziers
Bois-le-Duc = 's-Hertogenbosch
Bolonia = Boulogne
Bononia = Bologna
Bononia Gessoriacum = Boulogne
Bratislavia = Breslau (Wrocław)
Brixiae = Brescia
Brugge = Bruges
Brunswick = Braunschweig
Cadurcum = Cahors
Caesaraugusta = Saragossa
Cale = Porto
Caletum = Calais
Camberiacum = Chambéry
Camboricum, Cantabrigia = Cambridge
Cantuaria = Canterbury
Carnutum = Chartres

APPENDIX I

Ciudad de los Reyes = Lima
Colonia Agrippina = Cologne
— Allobrogum = Geneva
— Brandeburgica = Berlin
— Claudia = Cologne
— Munatiana = Basle
— Ubiorum = Cologne
Compluti = Alcala
Conimbrica = Coimbra
Constantinopolis = Istanbul
Dantiscum, Danzig = Gdańsk
Daventria = Deventer
Delphi = Delft
Deva = Chester
Divio, Diviodunum = Dijon
Divodurum = Metz
Doornik = Tournai
Dunelmia = Durham
Durobrivae = Rochester
Durovernum = Canterbury
Ebora = Evora
Eboracum = York
Elvetiorum Argentina = Strasbourg
Erfordia, Erphordia = Erfurt
Eridanium = Milan
Excestria, Exonia = Exeter
Felsina = Bologna
Fiorenza, Firenze = Florence
Francofurtum = Frankfurt
Fulgentium, Fulginia = Foligno
Gadavum, Gand, Gadavum, Gent = Ghent
Gebenna = Geneva
Gedanum = Gdańsk
Gena = Jena
Genabum = Orléans
Gênes, Genova, Genua = Genoa
— Ursorum = Osuna
Gippeswicum = Ipswich
Girona = Gerona
Glasgua = Glasgow
Gotorum = Lund
Graecium = Graz
Gratianopolis = Grenoble
Guelpherbytum = Wolfenbüttel
Gypeswicus = Ipswich
Haag, Den = The Hague

Hafnia = Copenhagen
Haga Comitum (Comitis) = The Hague
Hanovia = Hanau
Havnia = Copenhagen
Helenopolis = Frankfurt am Main
Herbipolis = Würzburg
Hispalis = Seville
Holma = Stockholm
Ianua = Genoa
Insula = Lille, Lindau
Insulis = Lille
Isca = Exeter
Janua = Genoa
Köln = Cologne
Königsberg = Kaliningrad
Kortrijk = Courtrai
Laibach = Ljubljana
Leida = Leiden/Leyden
Lemberg = L'vov
Lemovicense Castrum, Lemovicum = Limoges
Lemovicis = Aurillac
Leodicum, Leodium = Liège
Leopolis = L'vov
Leuven = Louvain
Liburnum = Leghorn (Livorno)
Limonum = Poitiers
Lingonae = Langres
Lipsia = Leipzig
Londinium = London
Londinium Scanorum = Lund
Lovania, Lovanium = Louvain
Lubicensis = Lübeck
Lublanum = Ljubljana
Lugdunum = Lyon
Lugdunum Batavorum = Leyden
Luik = Liège
Lutetia = Paris
Lüttich = Liège
Maguntia = Mainz
Mailand = Milan
Malines = Mechelen
Mantua Carpetanorum = Madrid
Medioburgum = Middelburg
Mediolanum = Milan
Moguntia = Mainz

441

Monachium, Monachum, Monacum = Munich
Montes = Mons
Moskovia = Moscow
Mülhausen = Mulhouse
Mutina = Modena
Myrtiletum = Heidelberg
Namnetes, Namnetus, Nannetes = Nantes
Nannetum = Nancy
Neapolis = Naples
Neapolis in Palatinata = Neustadt
— Nemetum = Neustadt
Neuenburg = Neuchâtel
Nicaea = Nice
Nizza = Nice
Nordovicum = Norwich
Norica, Norimberga = Nuremberg
Olisipo, Olyssipo = Lisbon
Oporto = Porto
Orvinum = Urbino
Oxonia = Oxford
Padova = Padua
Panhormum, Panormum = Palermo
Papia = Pavia
Parthenopae, Parthenope = Naples
Patavia = Padua, Passau
Patavium = Padua
Petriburgum = Peterborough
Petricordium = Périgueux
Placentia = Piacenza
Posonium = Bratislava
Prag, Praha = Prague
Pressburg = Bratislava
Ratisbona = Regensburg
Regnum = Chichester
Rijssel = Lille
Rothomagus, Rotomagus = Rouen
's-Gravenhage = The Hague
Saena, Saena Julia = Siena
Salisburgum, Salisburia = Salzburg
Salmantica = Salamanca
Sangallum = St Gallen

Sarum = Salisbury
Senae = Siena
Sublacense Monasterium = Subiaco
Suolla = Zwolle
Taurinum = Turin
Thermis Antoninis = Baden-Baden
Tholosa = Toulouse
Ticinum = Pavia
Tigurum = Zurich
Tolosa = Toulouse
Torino = Turin
Tornacum = Tournai
Trajectum = Utrecht, Maastricht
— ad Mosam = Maastricht
— ad Rhenum = Utrecht
— ad Viadrum = Frankfurt an der Oder
— Inferius = Utrecht
Trèves, Treviri = Trier
Turigum = Zurich
Turonis, Turonum = Tours
Ubii = Cologne
Ultraiectum, Ultrajectum = Utrecht
Ulyssipo = Lisbon
Urbs Vetus = Orvieto
Valentia = Valence, Valencia
Varcino = Barcelona
Varsavia, Varsovia = Warsaw
Venetia, Venezia = Venice
Venta, Venta Belgarum = Winchester
Verona = Berne
Vesuntium = Besançon
Vicentia = Vicenza
Villa Sancta Albani = St Albans
Vindobona = Vienna
Vinegia = Venice
Vintonia = Winchester
Virceburgum = Würzburg
Vormatia = Worms
Vratislavia = Breslau (Wrocław)
Wien = Vienna
Wigornia, Wigornum = Worcester
Wurtemberga = Württemberg

For a more comprehensive list, see Johann Graesse, Benedict and Plechl, *Orbis Latinus: Lexikon Lateinischer Geographischer Namen*, 3 vols, Braunschweig, 1972.

APPENDIX II

Roman numerals

The following is intended solely as a brief guide to the dating of printed books, and does not attempt to cover the whole subject. The Roman numerals generally encountered are:

    M (or CIƆ) = 1000
    D (or IƆ) = 500
    C   = 100
    L   = 50
    X   = 10
    V   = 5
    I   = 1

Numbers are formed by addition and subtraction. When symbols appear in descending order of value, they are simply added together, so that MDCCLXXVI = 1776. If one symbol precedes another of higher value, the former is subtracted from the latter: IV = 4, IX = 9, XL = 40, XC = 90, CM = 900. Low-value symbols do not precede very much higher ones, so that 1999 is expressed not as MIM but as MCMXCIX.

Sometimes numerals may be printed in lower case, and j may be substituted for the final i, so that mdciij = 1603.

APPENDIX III

The spread of printing – an illustrative table

This table illustrates the spread of printing since 1455 by listing the date and imprint of the earliest surviving printed books from a selection of countries. In many cases, printing in some form was carried out slightly earlier: these are only mentioned in footnotes where their priority is considerable. Some countries did not exist in their present form when printing began on what is now their territory; instances of this have not been noted except where they lead to anomalies. Where controversy exists, attempts have been made to indicate alternative opinions.

The history of printing in China and Japan is outside the scope of such a simplified presentation.

Country	City	Date
Argentina	La Plata	1700[1]
Australia	Sydney	1802[2]
Austria	Vienna	1482
Azores	Angra	1583
Belgium	Alost (Aalst)	1473
Brazil	Rio de Janeiro	1706[3]
Burma	Rangoon	1817
Canada	Québec	1765[4]
Chile	Santiago	1776
Colombia	Bogotá	1738/9
Cuba	Havana	1723/4[5]
Czech Republic	Plzeň (Pilsen)	c.1473/4[6]
Denmark	Ødense	1482
Ecuador	Quito	1754
England	Westminster	1476[7]
Finland	Åbo (Turku)	1642
France	Paris	1470[8]
Germany	Mainz	c.1455[9]
Greece	Salonica (Thessaloniki)	c.1512[10]
Greenland	Godthaab	1793[11]
Guatemala	Guatemala City	1660

APPENDIX III

Hungary	Buda	1473
Iceland	Hólar	1534[12]
India	Goa	1556
Indonesia	Batavia	1668
Iran	Tabrīs	1816[13]
Ireland	Dublin	1551
Italy	Subiaco	1464/5
Jamaica	Kingston	1734
Luxembourg		1578
Malta	Valletta	1643
Mauritius	Port-Louis	1768
Mexico	Mexico City	1540[14]
Netherlands	Utrecht	1473[15]
New Zealand	Paihia	1835[16]
Norway	Christiania (Oslo)	1643[17]
Paraguay	'Impresso en las Doctrinas'	1705[18]
Peru	Lima	1584
Philippines	Manila	1593[19]
Poland	Cracow	1475[20]
Portugal	Faro	1487
Romania	Tîrgovişte	1508
Russia	Moscow	1564[21]
Scotland	Edinburgh	1508
Slovakia	Presov	1573[22]
South Africa	Cape Town	1799[23]
Spain	Barcelona	1473[24]
Sri Lanka (Ceylon)	Colombo	1787
Sweden	Stockholm	1483
Switzerland	Basle	c.1470[25]
Tasmania	Hobart	1818
Thailand	Bangkok	1839
Turkey	Constantinople (Istanbul)	1503[26]
USA	Cambridge, Mass.	1640[27]
Uruguay	Montevideo	1807
Venezuela	Caracas	1808
Wales	Tref-Hedyn	1718

Notes

1. Or perhaps Córdoba de Tucumán, 1766.
2. The earliest surviving specimen of Australian printing dates from 1796.
3. Or perhaps 1747.

ANTIQUARIAN BOOKS

4. Broadsides, government acts and journals were printed in English in Halifax, Nova Scotia, as early as 1752; a French journal was published in Québec in 1764.
5. Or, possibly, 1707.
6. Some authorities date this book to 1468, but this date was probably copied from a manuscript by the printer. It may be even later, in which case the first printed book would date from 1475/6.
7. See CAXTON, who also printed the first book in the English language in Bruges in 1474.
8. Johann Mentelin was producing books in Strasbourg, now in France, at least a decade earlier.
9. See GUTENBERG.
10. In Hebrew. The first modern Greek press was founded on Chios in 1821.
11. A unique survivor, printed in the nearby settlement of Neu Herrnhut. No further printing was carried out in Greenland until 1855.
12. The Hólar in the Hjaltad valley. The press was established in 1530.
13. Or Tehran in the same year.
14. Printing began a year earlier but nothing from 1539 has survived.
15. Probably earlier; many books were not dated. (Claims for Laurens Janszoon Coster of Haarlem are no longer taken seriously.)
16. Preceded by a poorly printed Catechism, 1830.
17. Norway had been politically and linguistically dominated by Denmark since well before 1455.
18. Probably Loreto. The first book may well have been printed in 1700, but no copy has survived.
19. Or 1602.
20. Preceded by a calendar for 1474 (1473).
21. Although books were printed in Moscow a decade earlier, this was the first to be dated. Books were printed in Königsberg (Kaliningrad), in Russia at the time of writing, as early as 1524.
22. A small group of books from 1477–80 may conceivably have been printed in Pressburg (Bratislava), but the absence of any further printing in that city until 1594 seems to militate against it.
23. Preceded by an almanac for 1796 (1795), of which only a fragment survives.
24. The origins of printing in Spain are obscure; Saragossa, Segovia and Valencia are rival candidates. Books may have been produced in any of these cities (or indeed Barcelona) a year or two earlier.
25. Perhaps as early as 1468.
26. In Hebrew. The first Turkish press was established in Constantinople in 1726.
27. See BAY PSALM BOOK.

APPENDIX IV
Book trade directories

International League of Antiquarian Booksellers
 List of members of constituent associations; obtainable from the ABA, and from many of its members.

Antiquarian Booksellers' Association
 Directory of Members; issued annually (free).

Provincial Booksellers' Fairs Association
 List of members; issued annually.

Cole's Register of British Antiquarian and Secondhand Booksellers
 Published annually by The Clique Ltd.

Drif's Guide
 Geographical guide to bookshops in the British Isles, with brief descriptions and the compiler's own pungent shorthand comments.

Sheppard's Bookdealers in the British Isles
 Published by Richard Joseph Publishers Ltd. Includes useful additional information about book trade services, book sizes, etc. Published every two years.

Sheppard's European Bookdealers

Sheppard's Bookdealers in North America and Canada

Sheppard's Bookdealers in Australia, New Zealand and parts of the Pacific

Index

A computer-generated index to this Companion, consisting only of proper names, would of course be useless; but a fully comprehensive glossarial index would rival the book itself in length. Accordingly, this Index has been compiled selectively. It is weighted in favour of facts and topics on which the Companion would appear a likely source of information; a number of names have been omitted when they appear only in the obvious specialist articles, such articles being thematically indexed instead.

Page numbers in **bold** indicate principal entries, those in *italics* illustrations relating to their headings. Books are in general indexed under author rather than title, except where this would have been unhelpful.

A.B.A. *see* Antiquarian Booksellers' Association
Abbey, Major J.R., **7**, 137–9, 143, 344
ABCs, 13, 124
Ackermann, Rudolph, **8–9**, 138, *138*, *139*, 140–1, 142, 328–9
Acton, Eliza, 156
Acton, Harold, 329
Adam, Robert, 222
Adams, Ansel, 326
Adams, Katharine, 7, **9**, 29, 166, 331
Advance copies, **9**, 343
Advertisements, **10**
Aelian, 279
Aesop, 122, 214
Africa, books on, 391, 394
Ahlberg, Janet and Allen, 126, 130
Ainsworth, William Harrison, 48
Alastair (Hans Henning Voight), 256
Alberti, Leon Battista, 18, 25
Alchemy, books on, 374
Aldine Press, 7, **10–11**
Aldridge, Alan, 323
Aldus Manutius, 10–11, 259
Alken, Henry, 140
Allen, H. Warner, 162
Allibone, 11–12
Allingham, Helen, 58
Allix, Susan, 340
Almanacs, **12–13**
Alphabet books, **13**
Alston, Robin, 172, 182
Althorp, Viscount, 64–5
Ameliaranne series, 126
American Book Prices Current, **30**
Americas, discovery of, books on, 387–8
Amerine, Dr Maynard, 162
Ames, Joseph, **15**
Anatomy, books on, 367, 368

Anderson, Anne, 256
Anderson, Florence Mary, 256
Annuals, **15–16**
Answering machines, 113
Antarctic, books on, 392–3
Antiquarian Booksellers' Association, **16–17**, 73, 360
Apicius, 151, 161
Appel's Anastatic Press, 247
Appleton, Honor C., 256
Appleton, Tony, 404
approval, ordering on, 113
aquatint, 141–2, **381–2**
Arabian Nights, 127–8
Aragon, Louis, 244
Arch, J. & A., 326
archery, books on, 279, 287
Arctic, books on, 392
Ardizzone, Edward, 323
Ariel Press, 32
Armorial bindings, **17**
Arms and armour, books on, 286–7
Artillery, books on, 279, 287
Artists' autographs, 37
Art of war, books on the, 279–80
Ascham, Roger, 279
Ashbee, C. R., 211
Ashburnham Library, 136
Ashendene Press, 7, **29–30**, 136, 178, 273, 334, 338
Ashley Library, 106, **409**
Astronomy, books on, 371–4
Atkins, Mrs Anna, 325
Attwell, Mabel Lucie, 125, 256
Auctions, 4, **62–7**: buying and selling at, 66–7
Audubon, John James, **32**, **308**
Austen, John, 256
Austin, Richard T., 78
Australia, books on, 390–1

INDEX

Autographs, **32–44**: conservation, 44: provenance, 43: terminology, 39: values, 39
Autopens, 43
Ave Maria Lane, 91
Aviation, books on, 285, 286
Ayton, Richard, 140, 143

Babou, Henri, 315
Bachman, Rev. John, 32
Bacon, *Sir* Nicholas, 76, 80, 84
Baedeker, Karl, 45
Bailey, David, 326
Baker, Samuel, 63, 65–6
Balfour, Ronald, 256
Ball, Douglas, 404
Ballantyne Press, 397
Ballard, Thomas, 63
Balley, Richard, 220
Balston, papermakers, 131
Banks, *Sir* Joseph, 106
Bannerman, Helen, 126
Baret, John, 169
Barker, Mrs Anne, 155
Barker, Cecily Mary, 256
Barker, Christopher, 92
Barker, Nicolas, 231, 300
Barlow, Francis, 214
Barnard, Edward, 162
Barry, *Sir* Edward, 161
Bartlett, Roger, **46**, 220, 223
Barton, Rose, 58
Basilisk Bookshop, 340
Baskerville, John, **46**, 214, 299, 319, 361
Batchelors, paper-makers, 267
Batsford, publishers, 310
Battan, Anne, 155
battles, books on, 280–286
Bauer, John, 256
Baumgarten, John Ernst, **46**, 222, 267, 407
Bawden, Edward, 165
Baxter, George, **47**
Bay Psalm Book, **47**
Bayley, Harold, 407
Bayntun's, 360
Beardsley, Aubrey, 84, 249, 251, 359
Beaton, Cecil, 104, 326
Beaumont Press, 336
Beauvilliers, 157, *158*, 159
Beckett, Samuel, 243, 244, 296, 317
Beckford, William, 274
Beckwith, Alice, 405
Bedford, Francis, **47**
Bedford, Francis D., 125, 256
Beerbohm, Max, 292, 298
Beeton, Isabella, 156–7
Beeton, Sam, 156–7
Behn, Aphra, 214

Beilby, Ralph, 49
Bell, Andrew, 185
Bell, John, 276
Bell, Robert Anning, *250*
Bell, Vanessa, 243
Belloc, Hilaire, 162
Bennett, Arnold, 3
Bennett, Charles, 214
Bentley, Richard, **48**
Berkeley, Busby, 255
Bertall, 161
Bestall, Alfred, 126
Beste, Henry Digby, 170
Besterman, Theodore, **48**, 263
Bestiaries, **48–9**
Betjeman, John, 399, 402
Bewick, Thomas, **49–50**, 123, 214, 243, 380, 382, 406; bookplates, 78
Bibles, **50–51**
Bibliographical Society, **51**, 55, 329, 376, 409
Biggles, 126
Bijou, The, 15
Binders' tickets, **57–8**
Bird, William, 150, 244, 384
Black, A. & C., **58**, 96, 185
Black Sun Press, **60**
Blackwell, Elizabeth, 303
Blades, William, **60**
Blake, William, 214, 247, 249, 313
Bland, David, 140
Blandford, Marquis of, 64–5, 361
Bloomfield, B.C., 295
Bloomsbury group, 243
Blount, Edward, 92
Blueprints, 325
Blunt, Wilfrid Scawen, 136
BMC see *British Library Catalogue*
Bodley, *Sir* Thomas, 61
Bodoni, Giambattista, **62**, 316
Boer War, books on the, 283–4
Bohn, Henry George, 62
Bolleter's bookshop, *98*
Bologna, Francesco da, 11
Bond, Michael, 'Paddington' books, 126
Book Auction Records, **30**
Book Collector, The, 16, 55, **72**, 111
Book fairs, 3, 17, **72–3**
Book Handbook, The, 72
Bookpile, 78
Boreman, Thomas, 129–30
Bosse, Abraham, 18
botany, books on, 304–5
Botanic societies, 308–9
Boulenger, 157
Boulestin, Marcel, 162
Boutell, Henry S., 13
Bowers, Fredson T., 56, **103**, 232, 236

449

INDEX

Boyd Houghton, Arthur, 247, 400
Boyle, Eleanor V., 247–9
Boyle, Robert, 18, 365
Boyse, Daniel, *219*
Bradbury, William, 311
Bradley, W. A., 315
Bradshaw, Henry, 55
Brandstetter, Oscar, 165
Brandt, Bill, 326
Brassai, 326
Brazil, Angela, 126
Bremer Presse, **104**
Brent-Dyer, Elinor, 126
Bridgeman, Charles, 27
Bridges, Robert, 166, 334
Brillat-Savarin, Anthelme, 159
Briquet, C. M., 407
British Library, **104–8**: *Catalogue*, 107, 149, 262, 263, 264
British Museum Library *see* British Library
British Science Museum Library, 369
Brock, C.E., 246, 249
Brock, H.M., 246, 249
Brook type, 209
Brooks, Catherine, 155
Browne, Alexander, 21
Browne, Hablot K., 'Phiz', 205
Browne, *Sir* Thomas, 92, 165
Browning, Robert, letter from, *35*
Browning Society, 408
Broxbourne Library, 106, **108–9**
Brunet, Gustave, 133
Brunet, J.-C., **109**
Brussel, I. R., 15
Buchanan, William, 21
Buckland-Wright, John, 338
Bull, René, 253
Bumpus, J. & E., 78
Bunter, Billy, 126
Bunyan, John, 184, *192*
Burch, R. M., 403
Burger, Konrad, 240, 263
Burne-Jones, Edward, 24, 136, 247, 267, *268*, 400
Burns and Oates, 299, 312
Burroughs, William S., 317
Burton, Capt. Sir Richard, 286
Burton, Robert, *Anatomy of Melancholy*, 56
Byron, Lord, 40, 41
Byron, Robert, 298

Cabinet de Crozat, 23
Caldecott, Randolph, 214, 249
calf, 271
Cambridge Bibliography of English Literature, The, 55–6, 312, 329
Cambridge University Press, 131–2, 185, 299, 360
Camden Press, 402
Cameron, Julia Margaret, 326

Campaigns, military, books on, 280–286
Campbell, Ian, 162
Campbell, Ken, 340
Campion, Edmund, 133
cancelland, 110
cancellandum *see* cancelland
cancellans, 110
Cape Levant, 270
Caradoc Press, 334
Cardiology, books on, 369
Carême, Marie-Antoine (Antonin), 157, 159
Carlow, *Viscount*, 163, 178, 336–7
Carlyle, Thomas, 275
Carroll, Lewis, 106, 126–7, 130, 166, 247
Carter, John, vii, **110–11**, 112, 117, 133, 134, 164, 203, 216, 231, 232, 234, 292, 293, 329, 331, 348–9, 361, 363, 399, 408–9
Carter, Sebastian, 338, 342, 348
Carter, Will, 316, 338, 342, 348
Cartier-Bresson, Henri, 326
Caslon type, 211
Caslon, William, 46, 299
catalogue raisonné, **111**, 299
Catalogues, publishers', 10
Cato, 161
Cave, Roderick, 334, 378
Caxton, William, 10, 60, 90, 91, **120–21**, 261, 410
CBEL see New Cambridge Bibliography . . .
Cecil Court, 96
Cecil, *Lord* David, 104, 276
Celsus, 151
Centaur type, 360
'Centre-Rectangle Binder', The, 220
Chagall, Marc, 275
chain lines, 319
Chapbooks, **123**, *124*
Chapman, Christopher, 222
Chaptal, *Comte*, 161
Charing Cross Road, 5, 96
Chatwin, Bruce, 298
Chevreul, Michel-Eugene, 18–19
China, exploration of, books on, 392
'Chippendale' bookplates, 80, 82
Chiswick Press, 404
Chivers, Cedric, **131**, 181–2
Chromolithography, 142
Churchill, *Sir* Winston, 34, 35, 281, 283, 285, 295, 298, 332
Circle Press, 339–40
circumnavigation of the globe, books on, 388–9
Clarke, Harry, 256
Claude *see* Lorrain
Clausewitz, Karl von, 279
Clay, Richard, and sons, 408
Cleeve, Alexander, 220
Cleland, Elizabeth, 155
Cleverdon, Douglas, 72
Cloister Press, 299

Clowes, Sir W. L., 288
Cobden-Sanderson, T. J., 7, 9, 106, **134–6**, 164, 176–8, 226, 331, 334, 339, 341
Coburn, Alvin Langdon, 326
Cock, Christopher, 63
Cocker, Edward, 170
Cockerell, Douglas, 7, 9, 29–30, **136**, 174, 344
Cockerell, Sydney, 7, 29, **136–7**
Codewords, telegraphic, 114
Cole, G. D. H., 273
Cole, William, 371
Coles, Elisha, 170
colophon, **137**, 212
Colour plate books, **137–144**: on natural history, 307–8: military, 287–8
Columella, 161
Combe, William, *95*, 140, 141
Comenius, 127
Connolly, Cyril, 162, 292, 298–9, 315, 329, 347
Conservation, 350–8
Constable, Archibald, 185
Contact Editions, 384
Cook, Brian, 310
Cook, Captain James, 303, 388–90, 393
Cooper, Mary, 130
Copernicus, Nicolas, 371–4
Copinger, W. A., 51, 240, 262, 263, 329
copperplate, **381**
Copyright, 87, **163**: copyright deposit, 106
corrigenda, 211
Corvinus Press, **163**, 178, 336–7
Coster, Laurens Janszoon, 259
Cosway bindings, **163**, 360
Cosway, Richard, 163
Cotton, *Sir* Robert, 105, 106
Countermarks, 407
Courtney Lewis, C. T., 403
cowhide, 271
Cowley, John Lodge, 18
Cox, David, 21
Cox, Morris, 338, *340*
Cracherode, Rev. C. M., 106, 323
Craig, Edward Gordon, 164, 338
Cranach Presse, 137, **164**, 338
Crane, Walter, 13, 249
Crests, identification of, 17
Crimean War, books on the, 283
Croft, John, 161
Croft, P. J., 63
Croker, Samuel, 128
Crompton, Richmal, 126
Crosby, Caresse, 60
Crosby, Harry, 60
Crowder, Henry, 244
Croxall, Samuel, 214
crushed (morocco), 270–71
Culpeper, Nicholas, 303

cum privilegio, 346
Cunard, Nancy, 244, 384
Cundall, Joseph, 404
Curle, Richard, 409
Curll, Edmund, 94
Currie, Miss C. B., 163, 230
Curwen, Harold, 165, 174, 227
Curwen, Rev. John, 165
Curwen Press, 7–8, 24, 165, 226, 339
Curzon, Robert, 325
Cyanotype process, 325

Dahl, Roald, 124, 130
Dalziel Bros., 300, 382, 402
Daniel, Henry (C.H.O.), 166
Daniel Press, 29, 71, **166**, 323, 334
Daniell, William, 138, 140, 143
D'Annunzio, Gabriele, 316
d'Arbeloff, Natalie, 340
Darton, William, 130
Darwin, Charles, 306, 392
d'Aulnoy, Madame, 128
David, Elizabeth, 162
Davies, H. W., 263
Davies, Gwendoline, 236–7
Davies, Margaret, 236–7
De Bry, Theodore, 387
De Bury, Richard, 90
Decorations, military, books on, 288
De Coverley, Roger, 7, 134, 412
deerskin, 270
Defoe, Daniel, 128, 130, 173–4
De Gaulle, General, 317
Dejean, 161
De la Mare, Walter, 174
Del Piombo, Akbar, 317
De Machlinia, William, 344
dentistry, books on, 369
Department of Trade & Industry, 212
Derôme family, binders, **167**, 222
De Sorbière, Samuel, 92–4
Detmold, E. J., 214, 256
Deval, Laurie, 404
Devonshire, Duke of, 64
De Worde, *see* Worde
Dezallier d'Argenville, A. J., 27
Dial, The, 359
Dibdin, Thomas Frognall, 56, 57, 64–5, 66, 70, 95, **168**, 274, 361
Dibner, Bern, 371
diced (calf), 271
Dickens, Charles, 48, *205*
Dictionary of National Biography, 40, 118, 149, **173**
Dictionary of Scientific Biography, 371
Digby, *Sir* Kenelme, 153
Diringer, David, 13
Disney, Walt, 256

451

INDEX

Ditchling Press, 364
Divinity calf, 271
DNB see *Dictionary of National Biography*
Dodgson, *Rev.* C. L., *see* Carroll, Lewis
Dodsley, Robert, 94, **173–4**, *198*, *201*, 214, 378
Doheny, Estelle, 230
Doisneau, Robert, 133, 326
Donleavy, J. P., 317
Double Crown Club, 165, **174–6**
Douglas, Norman, 244
Doves Press, 134, 136, 164, **176–8**, 334, 338, 339, Doves Bindery, 7, 134, 136, 176–8
Dowden, Edward, 408
Doyle, Richard, 247, 249
Draft clean pad *see* Dry cleaning pad
Dreyfus, John, 313–4
Dropmore Press, 163, **178**
dry cleaning pad, 317, 354
Dubois, Urbain, 157, 159
Du Cane, Ella, 58
Du Four, Philippe Sylvestre, 155
Dulac, Edmond, 246, 251, 253
Dun Emer Press, 164
Dunton, John, 94
Duppa, Richard, 24
Dürer, Albrecht, 18, 316
Durrell, Lawrence, 315, 317
Dust-wrappers **178**, 296
Dwiggins, W. A., 227, 275
Dyson-Perrins, C. W., 9

Eastaway, Edward, 334
Edwards family, of Halifax, 131, **181–2**, *221*, 222, 230, 271
Edwards, Francis, 96
Edwards, Miss, binder, *225*
Ehrman, Albert, 108
Eighteenth-Century Short-Title Catalogue, 56, **182–3**, **200**
Einstein, Albert, 374
Eisenstein, Elizabeth L., 56
elephant hide, 270
Eliot, *Sir* Thomas, 169
Eliot, T. S., 108, 243, 293
Ellerman, *Sir* John, 150
Ellerman, Winifred, 150
Elliot, Thomas, 222
Ellis, Clifford, 310
Ellis, Rosemary, 310
Emerson, P. H., 326
Encyclopaedia Britannica, 118, **185–6**
Endeavour type, 211
endpapers, marbled, 277
Englemann, Godefrey, 132, 142
English Catalogue of Books, **186**
engraving, **380–1**
Enschedé, 339
Ephemera Society, **209**
Eragny Press, **209**, 334, 397

Erpenius, 183
Escoffier, Auguste, 159
Essex House Press, **211**, 334, 338
ESTC see *Eighteenth-Century Short-Title Catalogue*
etching, **381**
Eton College, 8, 323, 407
Etruscan bindings, 182, 222, 271, *272*
Evans, Edmund, 124, 249
Evans, Frederick, 311
Evans, Robert Harding, 64–5
Evelyn, John, 92, 106
Exchange rates, 1–2
Exploration: autographs, 38

Facsimiles: of autograph material, 41–2
Fairbairn, James, Book of Crests, 17
Fairfax, Arabella, 155
Fairlie-Bruce, Dorita, 126
Fairy books, 126
Faques, William, 344
Far East, books on, 392
Farleigh, John, 336
Fashionable Remembrancer, 13
Favre, Joseph, 159
Fell types, 29, 166, 334
Fenn, *Lady* Eleanor, 130
Ferrar, Nicholas, 184
Fétu, Emile, 159
Fireworks, books on, 279
First World War, books on, 285, 290
Fisher, Margery, 125
Fisher, Mrs, 155
Fleece Press, 339
Fleming, Ian, 295
Fletcher, H. M., 96
Fletcher, Robert, *98*
Fleuron Society, 227, 299
Fleuron, The, 165, **227–8**, 299
Florin Press, 342
Flowers, Desmond, 131
Folger, Henry Clay, 186, 187, 228
Folio Society, **229**, 327
Folkard, Charles J., 256
'Following the flag', 293
Fonthill, 274
Fore-edge painting, 182, **230**
Forgery, **230**, 408–9: of autograph material, 41
Forman, Harry Buxton, 408–9
Forrester, Joseph James, 161
Forster, E. M., 243
Fortescue, *Sir* John W., 281
Fortification, books on, 279
Foss, Hubert, 174
Foulis, Andrew, 233
Foulis, Robert, 233
Foulis, T. & N., 233
Foulis Press, **233**, 361

INDEX

Fowler Architectural Collection, 25
Fox Talbot, H., 325
Foxe, John, 92
foxing, **233**, 352–4, 384
Foxon, David, 200
Franco-Prussian War, books on the, 283
Franklin, Colin, 176
Freart, Roland, 25
Freeman's Oath forgery, 231
Friedman, Joan, 405
Friendship's Offering, 15
Frink, Elizabeth, 214
Frith, Francis, 326
Froissant, Jean, *188*, 191
Fry, Roger, 174
full (leather), 273
Fulleylove, John, 58
Furze, Roger, 229
Fust, Johann, 167, 238–9, 258–9

Gage–Cole, H., 164
Galen, 151, 367
Galignani, A. & W., 40, 41
Galileo, *370*, 371
Gallup, Donald, 295
Galsworthy, John, 296–8
Gardiner, Grace, 157
Garnett, David, 313
'Garrison-Morton', **234**, 367
Garry, Charlene, 340, 341
Gaskell, Philip, 55, 112, 137, 142, 232, 234, 236
Gathorne-Hardy, Robert, 336
Gay, John, 214
Gelée, or Gelléé, Claude (le Lorrain), *see* Lorrain
Gem, The, 15
Gentleman, David, 131, 323
geology, books on, 304
'Geometrical Compartment' binder, The, 222
George II, *King*, 105, 106
George III, *King*, 106
George IV, *King*, 105
Gerard, John, *302*, 303
Gibbings, Robert, 174, 235, 310, 336
Gibbs, James, 27
Gilbert, Philéas, 159
Gill, Eric, 24, 76, 164, 174, 236, 334, 336, 363–4
Gingerich, Owen, 374
Girodias, M. E., 315
Girodias, Maurice, 315, 317
Girtin, Thomas, 142
GKW, **235**, 262, 263, 264
Glaister, Geoffrey Ashall, 331
Glasse, Mrs Hannah, 155
Gleeson, Evelyn, 164
goatskin, 270
Goble, Warwick, 58, 256
Goethe, J. W. von, 18

Goff, Frederick, **235**, 262, 263, 264
Gogmagog Press, 338, *340*
Golden Cockerel Press, 24, **235–6**, 336, 338
Golden type, 267
Goldschmidt, E. P., 263
Goldsmith, Oliver, 128, 312
Gollancz, Victor, 273, 299
Gooden, Stephen, 84, 214
Goody Two-Shoes, 128, 130, 312
Gosden, Thomas, 230, **236**
Gouffé, Jules, 157
Gould, Elizabeth, 308
Gould, John, 308
Grandville, Jean, 214
Granger, James, 213
Grant, Duncan, 131
Grass, Günter, 275
Graves, Robert, 217, 243, 310, 336
Gray, Thomas, 174, *201*
'Great Omar', The, 364
Great War *see* First World War
Greenaway, Kate, 13, 249
Greene, Graham, 104, 295
Greg, W. W., 55, 103, **236**, 361
Gregynog Press, 7, **236–7**, 336, 338
Grenville, Thomas, 106
Gribelin, Simon, 80–82
Griffo, Francesco, 11
Grimm brothers, 128
Grimod de la Reynière, A.-B.-L., 159
Grolier, Jean, 7, 47, 220, 237
Grolier Club, The, **237**, 323, 360
Gruel, binder, 331
Guild of Handicraft, 211, 334
Guild of Women Binders, 7, *225*, 226, **237**
Gutenberg, Johannes, 121, **238–9**, 258–9, 267: *Bible*, 270, 331–2
Guthrie, James, 323, 334, 335
Gwinnett, Button, 40
Gynaecology, books on, 369

Haberly, Loyd, 336
Hacon, W. L., 397
Hafod Press, **240**, 332–4
Hague, Michael, 126
Hain, Ludwig, **240**, 262, 263, 264
Hakluyt, Richard the yr., 240, 386–7
Hakluyt Society, **240**, 387, 389, 391
half, leather, 273
Halkett, Samuel, 241
Halliwell, James, 325
Hamley, Gen. Sir E. B., 278, 280
Hanley, James, 315
Hanway, Jonas, 222
Hardie, Martin, 84, 132, 403
Hare, Augustus, 76
Harley, Edward, *Earl of Oxford*, 63

453

INDEX

Harley, Robert, *Earl of Oxford*, 105
Harmsworth, *Sir* Leicester, 228
Harris, Frank, 315
Harris, John, lexicographer, 171
Harris, John, publisher, 130
Harrison, Mrs Sarah, 155
Harrod, H. H., 402, 405
Hart, J. N., 402, 404–5
Hart-Davis, Rupert, 55
Hartley, Harold, 402
Harvey, Christopher, 184
Harvey, William, 367–9
Haskell, Francis, 23
Hassall, Joan, 78, 84
Hatchards, 96
Havell, Robert, 32, 140
Hay, Denys, 331
Hayday, James, **241**, 326–7
Heaney, Seamus, 3, 275
Heath, Ambrose, 162
Heath, Edward, 377
Heirs of Hippocrates, 367
heliocentrism, 371
Hemingway, Ernest, 150, 293–5, *294*, 384
Henry VIII, *King*, 344–6
Hentschel, Carl, 58, 251
Herbals, 301–3
Hering, Charles, 46, 222, **242**
Hermes, Gertrude, 237, 323
Herodotus, 151
Herrmann, Frank, 65
Herschel, *Sir* John, 325
Heseltine, Philip, 217
Hevelius, Johannes, *373*
Hewitt, Graily, 176
Heywood Hill, G., 404
Hill, David O., 326
Hill, Octavia, 136
Hind, Arthur M., 263
Hinman, Charlton, 56
Hippocrates, 161
Hissey, Jane, 126
Hoare, *Sir* Samuel, 323
Hobbes, Thomas, 92
Hobson, G. D., 7, 8
Hodgkins, Ian, 404
Hoe, Robert, 237, 245
Hoffmann, Heinrich, 127
Hofmann, Mark, 231
Hogarth Press, **242–3**, 296, 338
Hogarth, William, 78
Holland, Philemon, 301
Hollis, Thomas, 222
Holman Hunt, William, 400, *401*, 402
Homer, 151
Honeyman collection, **243**, 369, 371
Hooper, Horace, 185

Hoppus, Edward, 27
Horace, 151
Horblit, Harrison D., 365, 371, 374
Hordern, John, 241
Hornby, C. H. St. John, 7, 9, 29, 136, 334
Houlden, John, 220
Hours Press, **244**, 384
Housman, Laurence, 249
Hughes, Arthur, 400
Hughes-Stanton, Blair, 7, 237, 336
Hullmandel, Charles, 142
Humphrey, Duke, 61
humidity, 352
Hunter, William, *368*, 369
Huntington, Henry Edwards, 186, 244
Hutchins family, auctioneers, 95
Huth Library, 106

IGI, 262, 263, 264
I.L.A.B. *see* International League of Antiquarian Booksellers
IM Imprimit, 342
impression, 179–181
Imprint, The, 299
Incunabula Short-Title Catalogue, 56
Index Librorum Prohibitorum, 133
Indian Mutiny, books on the, 283
Ingpen, Roger, 227
ink, 43, 54
Inselbücher, 323–4
intaglio printing, 380–2
International League of Antiquarian Booksellers, 3, 16, **265**
Isherwood, Christopher, 243, 296
issue, 179–181
ISTC *see Incunabula Short-Title Catalogue*
Italic type, 11
Ivins, William, 23

Jackson, Holbrook, 56, 71, 174, 227
Jackson, John Baptist, 18
Jackson, William, 80, 82
Jaggard, William, 92
Jahrbuch der Auktionspreise, **30**
James, Henry, 293
James, M. R., 136, 303
Jane, Fred. T., 285, 289–90
Jardine, *Sir* William, 309
Jarring, G. A., 157
Jenson, Nicolaus, 11, 176, 259, 261, 267
Johnes, Thomas, 240, 332–4
Johns, W. E., 126
Johnson, Mary, 155
Johnson, Samuel, 63, 94, 128, 168–9, 170, 173–4, 276, 312
Johnston, Edward, 104, 164, 176, 177
Johnstone and Croall, 311
Jones, David, 237, 334, 336
Jones, Inigo, 25–7

INDEX

Jones, Owen, 132, 139, *400*, 403, 404
Jones, Shirley, 340
Joyce, James, 293, 295, 315, 337: *Ulysses*, 243
Judge, Max, 226
Jullien, A., 161

Kafka, Franz, 275
Kahane, Jack, 315, 317
Kalthoeber, Christian Samuel, 46, 222, **267**, 274
Kauffer, E. McKnight, 165
Keepsake, The, 15
Kelmscott Press, 7, 8, 134, 136, 176, 178, 211, 249, **267**, *268*, 334, 338, 339, 397: bookplates, 76n.: Chaucer, 7, 24, 134, 267, *268*, 338
Kemsley, *Lord*, 163, 178
Kennedy, Arthur, 171–2
Kennedy, Rev. James, 241
Kenny Herbert, *Col.* A. H., 157
Kent, Rockwell, 275
Kent, William, 27
Kepler, Johannes, 371
Ker, J. B., 171
Kessler, Harry *Graf*, 164, 338
Keynes, *Sir* Geoffrey, 55, 72, 174, 313, 361
Keynes, J. M., 243, 298
Kilner, Dorothy and Mary, 130
King, Jessie M., 84, 233, 249, 251
King, Ron, 339–40
Kipling, Rudyard, 214
Kirtley, John T., 217
Kitaj, R. B., 108
Kitchener, William, 157
'Knock-out', The, 359
Koch, Rudolf, 226
Koelhoff, Johann, 262
Koestler, Arthur, 273
Krause, Jakob, 7

Labbe, Philippe, 257, 261
Lacam, P., 159
Lackington, James, 58, *93*, 94–5, **269**
La Fontaine, Jean de, 214, *215*
laid paper, 319
Laing, John, 241
Lamb, Charles, 348
Lamb, Lynton, 131
Lancaster, Osbert, 298
Lane, Allen, 131, 323
Lang, Andrew, 126, 247
Langley, Batty, 27
Laplace, Pierre-Simon de, 365
Laporte, John, 21
Laski, Harold, 273
Laurel, Stan, letter from, *36*
La Varenne, F. P. de, 152–3
Laver, James, 162
Lawrence, D. H., 181, 295

Lawrence, Simon, 339, 342
Lawrence, T. E., 163, 285, 295, 337, 394
Leake Patent bindings, 403
Lear, Edward, 130, 140, 305, 308
leather dressing, 356; formulas, 358
Lee Priory Press, 71
Lee, *Sir* Sidney, 173
Lefler, Heinrich, 256
Lehmann, John, 243, 296
Leigh, George, 63, 95
Leigh Sotheby, auctioneers, 369
Leighton, Archibald, 133
Leighton, John, *399*, 403
Leng, Kyrle, 336
Le Prince, Jean Baptiste, 142
L'Estrange, Roger, 214
levant, 270
Lewis, Charles, 46, 242, **274**
Lewis, C. S., 298: 'Narnia' books, 130
Lewis, Stephen, 220
Lewis, Thomas, 220
Lewis, Walter, 131
Libanus Press, 339
Library, The, 55
Library of Congress, **274**, 301
Libri, Guglielmo, 369
Liddell Hart, Capt. B. H., 280, 286
Limited Editions Club, **274–5**, 313, 360
Linde, Andreas, 222
Lindsay, Jack, 217
Lindsay, Norman, 217
Lindsay, Philip, 217
Linnaeus, 377
Lintot, Bernard, 94
Literary autographs, 35
Literary Souvenir, The, 15
lithography, 9, 141–2, **382–4**: colouring, 142–3
Little Gidding, 184
Little Pretty Pocket Book, A, 129, 312
Livres d'artiste, 24, **275**
Lizars, W. H., engraver, 32, 308, 309
Locke, John, 127, 129, 163
Loeb, Dr James, **275**
London Almanack, The, 12
Lorrain, Claude, 27
Loudon, J. C., 27
Lovelace, Richard, *189*
Low, David, 84
Lowndes, William, 62, **276**

MacAlister, James, 329
McAlmon, Robert, 150, 384
MacDonald, George, 126, 128
McKenzie, D. F., 56
McKerrow, R. B., 55, 112, 150, 232, 234, 236, 276
McLean, Ruari, 176, 404
Maclise, Daniel, 300

455

INDEX

Macy, George, 274–5, 313
Madan, Geoffrey, 296
Maggs Bros., 96
Maggs, Ben, 16
Mahieu, Thomas, 220
mailing lists, 116
Maillol, Aristide, 164
Mailmerge, 145
Maittaire, Michel, 261
Malin, Charles, 316
Malraux, André, 23
Malton, James, 140
Mansfield, Katherine, 243
Mapplethorpe, Robert, 326
marbled calf, *372*
Mardersteig, Hans (Giovanni), 62, 275, **316**, 338, 342
Mardersteig, Martino, 316
Markham, Gervase, 153
Marks, Ben, 96
Marshall, John, 130
Masefield, John, 296–8
Masereel, Frans, 275
Mason, J. H., 164
Massey, Dudley, 203
Massialot, 153
Masters, Thomas, 157
Mathematics, books on, 374
Matisse, Henri, 275
Mauchline ware, **277–8**, 403
Maurois, André, 323
May, Robert, 153, *154*
Mayer, Luigi, *389*
Mearne, Charles, 220, 278
Mearne, Samuel, 106, 164, *182*, 220, 230, **278**, 322
Medals, books on, 288
Medici, Cosimo de, 46
Medicine: autographs, 37–8
Medicine, books on, **365–9**
Mellon, Paul, 8
Mendel, Vera (Meynell), 313
Menon, 153
Menpes, Dorothy, 58
Menpes, Mortimer, 58
Mercurius Rusticus, 57
Merian family, 303
Messel, Oliver, 29
Messisbugo, Christoforo, 153
Meynell, Alice, 312
Meynell, *Sir* Francis, 174, 176, 227, 275, 312–4, 319, 336
Meynell, Gerald, 299, 312
Michel, Marius, 226
Microcosm of London, 9
Middle Hill Press, 71, 324
Middleton, Bernard, 278, 320, 342
Military books: autographs, 37
Mill House Press, 336
Millais, J. E., 300, 400, 402

Miller, Henry, 315, 317
Milne, A. A., 'Pooh' books, 126
Milton, John, 92, 110, 293
Miniature Almanack, 13
Minsheu, John, 171
Mirandola family, 11
Miró, Joan, 275
Mitchell, Michael, 339
Moholy-Nagy, L., 326
Monnier family, binders, 222
Monotype Corporation, 299, 331
Montagné, P., 159
Montaigne type, 360
Moore, Francis 'Old', 12
Moore, George, 244
Moore and Lindley, 311
Morewood, Samuel, 161
Morgan, J. Pierpont, 186, 328
Morier, James, *388*
Morison, Stanley, 131, 165, 183, 227, **299**, 312–3, 316, 326, 329, 331, 360
morocco, 270–71
Morris, William, 7, 9, 134, 136, 176, 211, 251, 267, 331, 334, 363, 397
Mortimer, Ian, 342
Morton's Medical Bibliography, 234
mottled calf, 272
Moxon, Edward, **299–300**: 'Moxon Tennyson', *401*, 402
Moxon, Elizabeth, 155
Mudie's Library, 321
Muir, Percy, 110, 199–200, 203, 243, 331, 404
Munby, A.N.L., 7, 63, 72, 361, 202
Murray, Fairfax, 263
Murray, James, 169, 170
Murray's Guides, 45
Murrell, John, 153
musical autographs, 36–7
Muybridge, Eadweard, 326

Nabokov, Vladimir, 296, 317
Napoleon, 40
Napoleonic Wars, books on, 281–3
Nash, John, 336
Nash, Paul, 165, 174, 336
National Library of Science in America, 369
National Union Catalog, 274, **301**
Naturalist's Library, The, 309
Nature Printing, **311**
Naval architecture, books on, 289
'Naval Binder', The, 220
Naval books: autographs, 37
Naval history, books on, 288–291
NCBEL see *New Cambridge Bibliography* . . .
Neagoe, Peter, 315
Negro (anthology), 244
Nelson, Horatio *Viscount*, 289
Nesbit, E., 130

INDEX

Neurology, books on, 369
New Cambridge Bibliography of English Literature, The, 55–6, **312**
New, E. H., 78
New Naturalist, The, 310
Newbery, John, 124, 128–30, **312**
Newbery family, 312
Newdigate, Bernard, 227
Newton, A. Edward, 51, 270
Newton, *Sir* Isaac, 18, 371, 374
Nichols, John, 385
Nicholson, William, 13
Nielsen, Kay, 246, 252–3, 256
niger (morocco), 270
Nightingale, Florence, 157, 369
Nignon, Edouard, 159
Nin, Anaïs, 315
Nikirk, Robert, 187
Noel Humphreys, Henry, 132, 320, 403, 404
Nollekens, Joseph, 176
Nonesuch Press, 165, **312–4**, 319, 336, 338, 339
Norman, Haskell F., 371
North, John William, 400
Nowell-Smith, Simon, 409
Nuremberg Chronicle, 387
Nutt, Frederic, 157

oasis morocco, 270
Obelisk Press, **315**
Obstetrics, books on, 369
OED see Oxford English Dictionary
Officina Bodoni, 62, 257, **316**, 338, 339
Ogilby, John, 94, 214
Oliver, Michael, 7–8
Olschki, Leo, 259
Olympia Press, 315, **317**
Ophthalmology, books on, 369
Opie, Peter, 200
original boards, *204*
Orwell, George, 104, 110, 273
Osborne, Edgar, 318
Osborne, Mabel, 318
Osborne, Thomas, 63
Oxenham, Elsie J., 126
Oxford, Earls of, *see* Harley
Oxford English Dictionary, 149, 170
packing, 329–30
'Paddington' books, 126
Padeloup family, binders, 222
Palladio, Andrea, 25
Palmer, Sutton, 58
Panizzi, *Sir* Anthony, 105, 106, 107
Papé, Frank C., 256
paper, **319–20**: and autograph material, 42–3
Papier de Chine, 319
papier-mâché, 222, **320–21**
Papworth, John, *140*, 141

Paracelsus, 369
Parker, Agnes Miller, 214
Parker, George, 170
Parrish, Maxfield, 256
Partridge, Eric, 170, 174
paste, 355; formula, 357–8
Pasteur, Louis, 161
Paternoster Row, 91
Paterson, Samuel, 95
Payne, Roger, 222, **322**
Payne, Thomas, binder, 321–2
Payne, Thomas, bookseller, 322
PBFA *see* Provincial Booksellers' Fairs Association
Peacham, Henry, 184
Pear Tree Press, **323**, 334, *335*, 338
Pearse, Philippa, 125
Pearse, Susan B., 126
Peel, *Sir* Robert, 324–5
Peignot, Gabriel, 32
Pelican Press, 312–3
Pellechet, M., 262, 263, 264
Penguin Books, **323–4**
Peninsular War, books on the, 281
Pepler, H.D.C., 334, 363–4
Pepys, Samuel, 21, 78, 84, 288
'perfect' bindings, 239
Performing arts: autographs, 37
Perrault, Charles, 128
Perrault, Claude, 25
Petyt, Thomas, 13
Pevner, *Sir* Nikolaus, 25
Phaidon Press, 24
'Philadelphia Historical Society, The', 408
Phillipps, *Sir* Thomas, 63, 71, **324–5**
'Phiz' (Hablot K. Browne), *205*
Picasso, Pablo, 275
Pickering, William, 276, 313, **326–7**, 360, 404
Pickering and Chatto, 405
pictorial bindings, *207*, 327–8, *327*
pigskin, 273
Pilkington, Matthew, 24
Pinwell, George, 400
Pissarro, Camille, 209
Pissarro, Esther, 84, 209
Pissarro, Lucien, 84, 209, 334, 397
planographic *see* surface processes
Plant hunters, books by, 303
Plat, *Sir* Hugh, 153
plate-mark, 381
Platina, J. B., 151, 161
Pliny, the elder, 301
PMM see Printing and the Mind of Man
Pochoir, 165
Pogany, Willy, 253, 255, 256
Polain, M.-L., 262, 263, 264
Polar exploration, books on, 392–3
Pollard, A. W., 55, 236, **329**, 376

457

INDEX

Pollard, H. Graham, 108, 110, 231, **329**, 408–9
Pope, Alexander, 173–4, *196*
Portland, *Duke of*, 47
postage and packing, 117–8
Post Office boxes, 117
Potter, Beatrix, 126, 247
Pound, Ezra, 244, 384
Poussin, Nicolas, 27
Powell, Roger, 7
Pozzo, Andrea, 18
Prayer Book type, 211
Price, Francis, 27
Prideaux, Sarah, 9, *224*, 226, **331**, 414
Prime Ministers, autographs of, 34
Printing and the Mind of Man, 110, **331–2**, 365, 374
Private Libraries Association, **332**, 338
Private Library, The, 332
Proctor, Robert, 55, **343**
Proctor order, 343
Prokosch, Frederic, 231–2
Prout, Samuel, 9, 140
Provincial Booksellers' Fairs Association, 73, 111, **344**
Pugin, Augustus, 8
Purchase, Samuel, 386–7
Pye, Sybil, 7, 226, **344**, *345*, 359
Pyle, Howard, 256
Pyne, W. H., 140, *141*
Pynson, Richard, 90, **344–6**
Pyrotechnics, *see* fireworks

Quaritch, Bernard, 62, 96, 136, 325, 375
Quarles, Francis, 184
quarter (leather), 273
Queen, Ellery, 347
'Queen's binders', The, 220

Rabelais, François, 152
Rackham, Arthur, 125, 214, 246, 247, 251–3, *252*, 256
Raffald, Elizabeth, 155
Rainbird, George, 162
Rampant Lions Press, 338, **348**
Randle, John and Rosalind, 339
Raverat, Gwen, 29
Ravilious, Eric, 24, 165, 236, 336
Rawlinson, Richard, 63
Ray, Gordon, 140, 405
red rot, 356
Redgrave, G. R., 376
Rees-Mogg, William *Lord*, 1
Regimental histories, books on, 287
Rehberg, Freidrich, 24
Reichling, Dietrich, 240, 263, 264
Reid, Forrest, 402, 405
Reinhardt, Max, 313
Reiniger, Lotte, 323
Reitlinger, Gerald, *The Economics of Taste*, 25
relief printing, 380, 382

Rennie, John, 57
Repository of Arts, The, 8, 9
Repository of the Arts, The, 8
Repton, Humphrey, 318
reversed calf, 271
Rheticus, Joachim, 374
rhinoceros hide, 270
Rhys, Ernest, 212
Rhys, Jean, 181
Richards, Frank, 126
Ricketts, Charles, 209, 249, 331, 334, 344, **359**, 397
Rider, William, 168
Riding, Laura, 336
Ridler, William, 339
Riefenstahl, Leni, 326
Riverside Press, 360
Rivière, Robert, 163, 167, **360**
roan, 271–3
Roberts, David, 140, 143
Robinson, Charles, 214, 249–50, 255
Robinson, Lionel and Philip, 325
Robinson, W. Heath, 251, 255
Rogers, Bruce, 275, 339, **360–1**
Rogers, Harry, 403
Rosenbach, Dr. A.S.W., 47, 186
Rosenthal, Jacques, 259
Rosenwald, Lessing, 263, 264
Rossetti, Christina, 249
Rossetti, Dante Gabriel, 247, 300, 359, 400
Rota, Bertrain, Ltd., 338–9
Rothenstein, *Sir* William, 174
Rothschild, *Lord*, 361
rough calf, 271
Rountree, Harry, 256
Routledge, George, 249
Rowlandson, Thomas, 9, *95*, 140, 141
Roxburghe Club, 7, 136, 303, **361–2**, 408
Roxburghe, John, *Duke of*, 64, 361
Royal autographs, 34
Royal Heads binder, 278
Royal Miniature Almanack, 13
Rubeus, Jacobus, 267
Rubington, Norman, 317
Rundle, Maria Elizabeth, 155, *156*
Rupert Bear, 126
Rushdie, Salman, 14, 296
Ruskin, John, 136
Russell, Bertrand, 298
Russia (leather), 271, 322
Russo-Japanese Wars, books on the, 283–4, 289–90
Rutherston, Albert, 165

Sadleir, Michael, 133, 203–6, **363**, 399
S. Dominic's Press, 334, **363–4**
St Paul's Churchyard, 91
Salerno, School of, 152
Salles, P., 159

Sandford, Christopher, 236, 336
Sandys, Frederick, 247
Sangorski and Sutcliffe, 163, **364**
Sangorski, Francis, 136, 364
Santiagoe, Daniel, 157
Saubertus, J., 261
Sawyer, Charles, 96
Scamozzi, Vincent, 25
Scappi, Bartolomeo, 152
Scheiner, Christoph, *372*
Schinkel, Carl F., 27
Schloss's Bijou Almanacs, 12–13
Schoeffer, Peter, 167, 216, 238–9, 258–9, 267
Science: autographs, 37–8
Science, books on, **369–75**
Scientific instruments, books on, 374
Scientific natural history, books on, 303–4
Scott of Edinburgh, binder, 222
scraper-board, 382
Scriblerian, The, 195–7
sealskin, 270
Searle, Ronald, 131
Second World War, books on, 285–6, 290
Sedgley, Richard, 220
Seizin Press, 336
Selden, John, 286
Sell Cotman, John, 142
Sellers, Charles, 161
Sendak, Maurice, 126
Senefelder, J. A., 9, 142, 382
Senn, C. H., 157
Serlio, Sebastiano, 25
Settle, Elkanah, 222
Seven Acres Press, 336, 338
'Seymour, Charles', 408
Shaaber, M. A., 190
Shakespeare Head Press, 9, 336
Shandean, The, 200
Shannon, Charles, 209, 359
Shaw, Henry, 132, 404
sheep, sheepskin, 271–3
Shelley, Mary, 95
Shelley, Percy Bysshe, 95, 324
Shelley Society, 408
Sherborn, C. W., 82
Sheridan, R. B., 82
Shoberl, Frederick, 9
Short-Title Catalogue, 15, 55, 190, **376**, 408
Shotter Boys, T., 140
Sidgwick, Frank, 227
Simon, André, 162
Simon, Oliver, 7–8, 165, 174, 227
Simons, Anna, 104
Simpson, John, 157
Sinclair, Catherine, 130
Sitwell, Osbert, 174
skiver, 273

Sloane, *Sir* Hans, 105, 106, 303
Smart, Christopher, 312
Smellie, William, 185
Smirke, *Sir* Robert, 105
Smith, Adam, *The Wealth of Nations*, 1
Smith, E., 155
Smith, Elder & Co., 173
Smith, George, 173
Smith, James, 27
Smith, W. H., 412: bindery, 29–30, 136
Société de la Reliure Originale, 7
Soho Bibliographies, 55
Solander, Daniel, 377–8
Solomon, Simeon, 400
Solon, Leon, 45–6
Sotheby, John, 63
Sotheran, 96, *97*, 163, 325, 326, 360
Sowerby, James, 18
Soyer, Alexis, 157
Spanish calf, 271
Sparrow, John, 361, 399
Speechly, William, 162
Spencer, Earl, 64–5, 168, 323, 326, 361, 407
Spender, Stephen, 273
Sprinkled calf, 271, *272*
Staggemeier and Welcher, 222
Stamperia Valdonega, 316, 339
Stanbrook Abbey Press, 338
Stanley, *Sir* John, Bt., 63
staples, 408
Stark, Freya, 137
state, 179–181
Stationers' Company, The, 12, 61, 90, 92, 94, 378
Steel, Flora Annie, 157
Steel, Robert, 220
steel-engraving, **381**
Steichen, Edward J., 326
Stephen, *Sir* Leslie, 173
Sterne, Laurence, 174
Stevengraphs, 74
Stevens, Henry, 16
Stevenson, Allan, 407
Stevenson, Robert Louis, 249–50
Stieglitz, Alfred, 326
Stillwell, Margaret, 235, 263
Stirling-Maxwell, William, 24
Stols, A.A.M., 339
Stone, Reynolds, 76, 131, 336, 399
Stonyhurst Gospel MS, 218
Storage of books, 352
Storey, Harold, 96
Strachey, John, 273
straight grain (morocco), 270–71, 322–23
Stratton, Helen, *254*
Strawberry Hill Press, 71, 332–4, 361, **378–9**
Struwwelpeter, 127
Stuart, James and Revett, N. 27

INDEX

Stuart, James 'Athenian', 222
Subiaco type, 29
surface processes, of printing, 380, **382–4**
Surgery, books on, 369
Surtees, R. S., 140
Sutcliffe, George, 136, 364
Sutherland, *Duchess of*, 46
Swains, engravers, 402
Sweynheim & Pannartz, 29, 57
Swift, Jonathan, 128, 293, 391
Switzer, Stephen, 27
Symons, A.J.A., 226
Symons, Arthur, 244

Taillevent, Guillaume, 151
Tallone family, printers, 341
Tanselle, Thomas, 319–20
Tarrant, Margaret, 256
Tauchnitz, 60, **380**
Technology, books on, 374
Telegraphic addresses, 119
'Temple of the Muses, The', *93*, 94–5, **269**
Ten Little Niggers, 126
Tenggren, Gustaf, 256
Terry, Richard, 157
Thomas, Alan, 11, 50–51, 140, 258, 238–9
Thomas, D. M., 296
Thomas, Edward, 323, 334
Thompson, H. Y., 136
Thompson, John, *401*, 402
Thomson, Hugh, *248*, 249, 251, 256
Thorpe, Thomas, 92
Three Mountains Press, 150, 244
three-quarter (leather), 273
Times, The, 185, 299: Times New Roman type, 299
Timlin, William, 256
Tolkien, J.R.R., 298
Tonson, Jacob, 94
Tooley, R. V., 138–9
Tourtel, Mary, 126
trade discount, 101, 119
Tradescant, John, 303
Travel: autographs, 38
Traveller's Companion Series, 317
tree calf, 271, 360
Troy type, 267
Tunnicliffe, C. F., 382
Turner, J.M.W., 142
Turner, William, 161
Tusser, Thomas, 152

Uniform, books on, 287–8
Unit histories, books on, 287
Universities, American, 2
Updike, D. B., 227, 360
Upton, Florence and Bertha, 126
Urban, Joseph, 256

Valdarfer, 64, 361
Vale Press, 209, 334, 344, 359, **397**
Vale type, 209
Van Allsburg, Chris, 126
Van Krimpen, Jan, 338
variant, 179–181, **398**
Vasari, Giorgio, 23
Vegetius, Rinatus, 279
vellum, 271
Vesalius, Andreas, 367
Viala & Vermorel, 161
Vicaire, Georges, 151
Vignola, J., 25
Vine Press, 338
Vitruvius, 25
Vizetelly, 161

Waagen, Gustave, 21–2, 25
w.a.f., 409–10
Wain, Louis, 126: sketch, *38*
Walker, Emery, 29, 134, 136, 176, 360
Walker, Fred, 400
Walpole, Horace, 21, 24, 105, 174, 332–4, 378–9
Walpole, *Sir* Robert, 21, 34
Walther, Henry, 46, 222, 274, 407
Walton, Izaak, 92, 236
Warburg Institute, 24
Ward, Samuel, 161
Warde, Frederic, 316, 339
Wark, Ralph, 230
Warlock, Peter *see* Heseltine, Philip
Warne, Frederick, 249
Warre, James, 161
Warren, Albert, *399*, 403–4
watermarks, 320
Watson, George, 312
Watts, Isaac, 127
Waugh, Evelyn, 329
Webb, Beatrice, 273
Webb, Mr & Mrs H. G., 334
Webb, Sidney, 273
Webster, Noah, 169
Week-end Book, The, 313
Weinreb, Ben, 4, 25
Weir, Harrison, 13
Weir, Richard, 322
Wellcome collection, 369
Wellcome library, 369
Werkman, H. N., 133
Wesley, John, 169, 269
Whatman paper, 46, 131
Whistler, Rex, 78, 84, 298
Whitaker's Almanac, 12
Whitaker's Cumulative Book List, 186
Whitaker, Thomas, 161
White, Gilbert, 310
White, Gleeson, 40, 402

INDEX

Whitney, Geoffrey, 184
Whittingham, Charles, 404
Whittington Press, 339
Wiegand, Willy, 104
Wilberforce family, 80
Wilde, Oscar, 359
Willcox Smith, Jessie, 256
Willebeek le Mair, Henriette, 256
William and Mary, College of, 230
'William' books, 126
Williams, Graham, 342
Williams, William Carlos, 293
Willison, I. R., 312
Wine, books on, 161–2
Wing, Donald G., 55, 190, **408**
Wise, Thomas J., 231, **408–9**
Wither, George, 92, 184
Wolff, Robert L., 203, 206
Wolley, Hannah, 153
women travellers, books by, 392–3
Wood, Robert, 27
woodcut, 381, **382**
wood-engraving, **382**
Woodward, Alice B., 125, 256

Woolf, Leonard, 242–3, 334–6
Woolf, Virginia, 242–3, 293, 313, 334–6
Worde, Wynkyn de, 121, 122, 127, 344, **410**
World in Miniature, The, 9
World War I *see* First World War
World War II *see* Second World War
wove paper, 319
Wyatt, M. Digby, 140
Wyatt, Leo, 76
Wyeth, N. C., 256

Yale University, 8
Yeats, Elizabeth, 164
Yeats, Jack B., 164
Yeats, Lily, 164
Yeats, W. B., 164, 257, 292
Yellow-backs, 363, 399
Young, Edward, 198

Zaehnsdorf, 134, 278, 331, **412**
Zeitlin, Jake, 371
Zoology, books on, 305
Zulu War, books on the, 283–4
Zwemmer, Anton, 24–5